www.wadsworth.com

www.wadsworth.com is the World Wide Web site for Wadsworth and is your direct source to dozens of online resources.

At *www.wadsworth.com* you can find out about supplements, demonstration software, and student resources. You can also send e-mail to many of our authors and preview new publications and exciting new technologies.

www.wadsworth.com
Changing the way the world learns®

Nations and Governments

Comparative Politics in Regional Perspective

ABOUT THE AUTHOR

Thomas Magstadt earned his doctorate at the Johns Hopkins School of Advanced International Studies (SAIS). He is the author of *Understanding Politics: Ideas, Institutions, and Issues* (Thomson/Wadsworth, 2003), now in its sixth edition; and *An Empire If You Can Keep It: Power and Principle in American Foreign Policy* (Congressional Quarterly Press, 2004). He has also published many scholarly papers and articles and is a frequent op-ed contributor to newspapers. He has taught in and chaired the political science departments at the University of Nebraska at Kearney and Augustana College in Sioux Falls in the 1970s and 1980s. He served as an intelligence analyst (1983–1986), a Visiting Professor at the Air War College (1990–1992), and a Fulbright Scholar in the Czech Republic (1994–1996), before turning to full-time writing. He lives in Westwood Hills, Kansas — close to the heart of Kansas City.

Nations and Governments

Comparative Politics in Regional Perspective

FIFTH EDITION

Thomas M. Magstadt

THOMSON
WADSWORTH

Australia • Canada • Mexico • Singapore • Spain • United Kingdom • United States

THOMSON
WADSWORTH

Publisher: Clark Baxter
Executive Editor: David Tatom
Development Editor: Scott Spoolman
Assistant Editor: Rebecca Green
Editorial Assistant: Reena Thomas
Technology Project Manager: Michelle Vardeman
Marketing Manager: Janise Fry
Marketing Assistant: Tara Pierson
Advertising Project Manager: Stacey Purviance
Project Manager, Editorial Production: Ray Crawford/ Matt Ballantyne
Art Director: Maria Epes
Print/Media Buyer: Judy Inouye
Permissions Editor: Kiely Sexton
Production Service: Stratford Publishing Services
Copy Editor: Leslie Connor
Cover Designer: Jeanette Barber, Silver Valley Graphic Design
Cover Image: Copyright © Getty Images
Compositor: Stratford Publishing Services
Printer: Webcom

Printed in Canada

1 2 3 4 5 6 7 08 07 06 05 04

For more information about our products, contact us at:

Thomson Learning Academic Resource Center
1-800-423-0563

For permission to use material from this text, contact us by:
Phone: 1-800-730-2214
Fax: 1-800-730-2215

Web: http://www.thomsonrights.com

Library of Congress Control Number: 2004103285

Wadsworth/Thomson Learning
10 Davis Drive
Belmont, CA 94002-3098
USA

Asia
Thomson Learning
5 Shenton Way #01-01
UIC Building
Singapore 068808

Australia/New Zealand
Thomson Learning
102 Dodd Street
Southbank, Victoria 3006
Australia

Canada
Nelson
1120 Birchmount Road
Toronto, Ontario M1K 5G4
Canada

Europe/Middle East/Africa
Thomson Learning
High Holborn House
50/51 Bedford Row
London WC1R 4LR
United Kingdom

Latin America
Thomson Learning
Seneca, 53
Colonia Polanco
11560 Mexico D.F.
Mexico

Spain/Portugal
Paraninfo
Calle Magallanes, 25
28015 Madrid, Spain

BRIEF CONTENTS

CONTENTS

Part V Latin America

FEATURES AND MAPS

Features

Democracy in America

What If?

Contrast and Comparison

Maps

PREFACE

This edition of *Nations and Governments: Comparative Politics in Regional Perspective* updates the fourth edition, which appeared in 2001. The architecture and approach of the book remains as it was in that edition.

There is no standard way of teaching comparative politics to beginning students. Basic questions such as what conceptual model or approach to use and what countries to feature depend heavily on individual preferences. The approach taken in this book is compatible with most contemporary theoretical perspectives in the discipline, and the regional framework guarantees that both instructors and students will have an opportunity to explore in greater depth the parts of the world that interest them most. At the same time, whoever would enter upon the study of comparative politics must be prepared to venture beyond his or her own comfort zone.

Plan of the Book and the Revision

The study of comparative politics can be overwhelming, especially for students who have not lived or traveled extensively abroad. Indeed, the fact that most students (and Americans in general) are not very familiar with the outside world is one good reason to study comparative politics region by region.

To help bring the world into focus, the text organizes it into six familiar regions: Western Europe, Eastern (or Slavic) Europe, Asia, Latin America, the Middle East, and sub-Saharan Africa. The importance of historical and contextual differences among regions continues to be reflected in the structure of this book. Each region is covered in a two-chapter sequence. The first chapter focuses on geography, history, culture, and other factors that combine to create the political setting for politics in a given region or country; the second chapter examines contemporary political institutions and processes and looks at the problems and prospects of key countries in each region. The first chapter in each sequence deals with the past and with factors that change slowly, if at all. The second chapter deals with the present, which is often fast-changing in today's world, and the trends that give us a glimpse of the future. Patterns common to the region as a whole, as well as tendencies toward greater regionalism, are stressed wherever the facts warrant. In each section, two or three countries receive special emphasis as case studies and are tracked through both chapters. Other countries in each region are examined in the text, tables, and boxes when deemed appropriate. Looking at comparative politics from a regional as well as a national perspective helps students do what this book is meant to do—compare and contrast politics in different places.

Special Features of This Edition

I have updated and revised the text to reflect recent changes in the regions and countries covered in this book. To enhance the text, I have added figures, tables, and charts and updated the existing ones to reflect the latest available statistics. In addition, readers will find three types of feature boxes in each chapter:

- **Democracy in America** These boxes compare historical experiences, political institutions, and public policies of other countries with those of the United States and help students gain deeper insights into politics and society both at home and abroad.
- **What If?** These offer hypothetical situations and encourage students to think critically about concepts as well as current and historical events. They also invite students to imagine themselves in similar situations and to decide what they would do. These boxes often spark classroom discussion and can provide ideas for research papers.
- **Contrast and Comparison** These boxes look at distinctive features of countries that are not treated as case studies in the chapters but which provide illuminating contrasts or points of comparison with countries that are.

In the current edition, a list of useful Web sites follows the Suggested Readings section at the end of each chapter.

This edition, like the previous one, includes an extensive end-of-book glossary. Boldface terms in the text signal glossary entries, making them easy to locate for review.

Summary of Chapters

Part I: Introduction

Chapter 1 introduces the study of comparative politics and explores why the comparative method is such a valuable aid to understanding the world. *Chapter 2* gives students a close look at various kinds of political systems and introduces some theoretical approaches to economic and political development, with an emphasis on regional patterns and trends. Taken together, these two chapters lay the foundation for the rest of the book.

Part II: Western Europe

Chapters 3 and 4 focus on Western Europe and the European Community. The results of recent national elections in the United Kingdom, France, and Germany and the problems facing all three postindustrial democracies are discussed at length, as is the movement toward greater economic integration within a European Union poised to expand into Eastern Europe. Not only will the EU admit ten new member states in 2004, but it also appeared close to adopting a formal constitution aimed at creating a framework for future steps toward greater political as well as economic integration.

Part III: Russia and Slavic Europe

Chapters 5 and 6 present a fresh look at Russia and Slavic (Eastern) Europe, a region that will, for the foreseeable future, continue to experience exhilarating changes and wrenching adjustments. This region encompasses many Slavic-speaking nations, but not all the former Soviet-bloc states are inhabited by Slavs (two of the most notable exceptions being Hungary and Romania). Three countries—Russia, the Czech Republic (formerly Czechoslovakia), and Yugoslavia (now a rump state encompassing only Serbia and Montenegro)—are featured as case studies. The themes in this section include the breakup of several former states (the USSR, Czechoslovakia, and Yugoslavia), the transition from centrally planned to market economies, the attempt to institute liberal democratic governments, and the political instability that has accompanied this remarkable and unprecedented transformation. The fifth edition covers the end of the Yeltsin era and the first years of the Putin era, yet another orderly change of government in the Czech Republic (and the retirement of President Vaclav Havel), and a new beginning in Serbia (formerly Yugoslavia) following the downfall of the dictator Slobodan Milosevic.

Part IV: Asia

Chapters 7 and 8 present politics in Asia, with a spotlight on China, Japan, and India. The challenge of a resurgent China continues to be one of the major topics in this section. Another continuing theme examines the recent tumult in Japan's economy and political system, which for four decades was dominated by a single party. The fact that Japan's sparkling success as a trading nation has not immunized Japan against financial turmoil and recession is another important issue. Finally, we explore India's remarkable success in sustaining democratic institutions in the face of huge obstacles and discuss signs of new economic stirrings in the world's largest democracy.

Part V: Latin America

Chapters 9 and 10 look at Latin America. The process of liberalization that brought popularly elected governments to nearly all the countries of South America in the 1980s has not been reversed, but democracy in many of these societies is still beset by various crosscurrents. The challenges to democratic governments continue to come in many forms: insurgencies, drug-related political violence, corrupt leaders, chronic budget deficits, dangerously high inflation and unemployment, and heavy foreign debts. But there are also new issues in this edition: signs of economic recovery and democracy taking hold in a region only recently dominated by dictators.The announcement in October 2003 that the United States and Chile had agreed to form a free-trade zone was viewed by some experts as a significant step toward creating a "Free Trade Area of the

Americas" that would eventually encompass virtually all of Latin America. The fact that it followed implementation of the North American Free Trade Agreement (NAFTA) in the early 1990s hinted at the possibility that regional structures similar to those now existing in Europe might in time evolve in the Western Hemisphere. These topics are explored in depth in this section, which features Mexico and Brazil as case studies.

Part VI: The Middle East

Chapters 11 and 12 treat the Middle East and North Africa, including discussions of the roles of nationalism and tradition in Arab politics, the strong sense of cultural identity imparted by ancient Arab civilizations and traditions, the tendency toward religious and political extremes, and the sharp contrasts between the rich Arab states and the poorer ones. The countries chosen as case studies are Israel and Egypt. Israel is a logical choice, despite its diminutive size, because it is the most militarily powerful and economically prosperous state in the Middle East, and because it has figured prominently in so much of the conflict that has plagued the region for so long. Egypt was selected because it illustrates so many of the elements found in different parts of the Arab world, including an authoritarian but nominally democratic state; a relatively stagnant economy dependent on Western trade and aid; a growing population with two few opportunities for personal advancement; tensions between Islamic militants and moderate supporters of the government; a mass-based popular organization, the Muslim Brotherhood, posing a potential challenge to the secular state; and finally a government torn between Western presures to crack down on terrorism and undertake political and economic reforms on the one hand, and domestic pressures to oppose the West and resist Westernization on the other. This edition includes timely material on the escalation of Israeli-Palestinian violence following the September 11, 2001, terrorist attacks against the United States; the subsequent tensions between the West and Arab world; and the invasion of Iraq in the spring of 2003.

Part VII: Sub-Saharan Africa

Chapters 13 and 14 cover sub-Saharan Africa, with Nigeria and South Africa receiving special attention. New pressures for democratic reforms have not led to hoped-for results in many countries in this part of the world, but at the end of the 1990s the military stepped aside in Nigeria. South Africa's abandonment of apartheid and its tumultuous transition toward some form of majority-rule democracy is one of the continuing topics in this section. The economic and political prospects for Nigeria and South Africa—and for the whole region—is another major theme in this section. A discussion focuses on the volatile and tragic situation in war-torn West Africa and the Congo.

Acknowledgments

I wish to acknowledge those who offered helpful suggestions during this and previous revisions of *Nations and Governments:* Seth Asumah, State University of New York at Cortland; Philip Kelly, Emporia State University; Jean Poulard, Indiana University Northwest; Cynthia Boaz, University of San Francisco; Michael Alvarez, De Paul University; Ronald Hrebenar, University of Utah; Waltraud Morales, University of Central Florida; Robert Charles Angel, University of South Carolina; Louis Hayes, University of Montana; Carolyn Warner, Arizona State University; Forest Grieves, University of Montana; Trevor Morris, Methodist College; David Titus, Wesleyan University; Freeman Wright, California State University–Fresno; Craig Arceneaux, California Polytechnic State University–San Luis Obispo; Lyman H. Heine, California State University–Fresno; Matthias Kaelberer, Iowa State University; Jonathan Olsen, University of Wisconsin–Parkside; and James W. Warhola, University of Maine.

Scott Spoolman did the lion's share of the editing and a good deal more to bring the fifth edition of *Nations and Governments* to fruition. He fixed all the things that needed fixing and went out of his way to make my job easier.

A project of this magnitude always comes at a high cost to immediate family members, as my sons, David and Michael, will attest. How often they both asked when they wanted my attention, "Daddy, when will you be finished with THAT BOOK!"

PART I
Introduction

NORWAY
SWEDEN
ESTONIA
LATVIA
RUSSIA
DENMARK
LITHUANIA
(Russia)
GREAT BRITAIN
IRELAND
NETH.
BELARUS
GERMANY
POLAND
BELGIUM
CZECH REP.
LUX.
LIECH.
SLOVAKIA
MOLDOVA
UKRAINE
FRANCE
SWITZ.
AUSTRIA
HUNGARY
ROMANIA
SLOVENIA
CROATIA
ANDORRA
MONACO
SAN MARINO
BOSNIA & HERZ.
YUGO.
BULGARIA
GEORGIA
PORTUGAL
ALBANIA
MACEDONIA
ARMENIA
SPAIN
ITALY
TURKEY
GREECE
AZERBAIJAN
Gibraltar
MALTA
CYPRUS
SYRIA
IRAN
TUNISIA
LEBANON
MOROCCO
ISRAEL
IRAQ
West Bank
ALGERIA
Gaza Strip
KUWAIT
LIBYA
EGYPT
JORDAN
ICELAND
NORWAY
SWEDEN
FINLAND
R U S S I A
KAZAKHSTAN
MONGOLIA
UZBEKISTAN
KYRGYZSTAN
TURKMEN.
TAJIKISTAN
N. KOREA
JAPAN
S. KOREA
C H I N A
PACIFIC OCEAN
IRAN
AFGHAN.
NEPAL
BHUTAN
BAHRAIN
PAKISTAN
W. Sahara (Mor.)
ALGERIA
LIBYA
EGYPT
QATAR
SAUDI ARABIA
UNITED ARAB EMIRATES
INDIA
MYANMAR (BURMA)
TAIWAN
BANGL.
LAOS
Hong Kong (China)
OMAN
ERITREA
SUDAN
YEMEN
THAILAND
VIETNAM
PHILIPPINES
DJIBOUTI
CAMB.
ETHIOPIA
FED. STATES of MICRONESIA
MARSHALL IS.
CEN. AFR. REP.
SRI LANKA
BRUNEI
PALAU
RWANDA
SOMALIA
UGANDA
MALDIVES
MALAYSIA
ZAIRE (Dem. Rep. Congo)
KENYA
SINGAPORE
NAURU
K I R I B A T I
BURUNDI
TANZANIA
SEYCHELLES
I N D O N E S I A
PAPUA NEW GUINEA
SOLOMON IS.
TUVALU
MALAWI
COMOROS
ANGOLA
ZAMBIA
INDIAN OCEAN
W. SAMOA
ATLANTIC OCEAN
MOZAMBIQUE
VANUATU
FIJI
NAMIBIA
ZIMB.
MAURITIUS
BOTS.
MADAGASCAR
TONGA
AUSTRALIA
SWAZILAND
SOUTH AFRICA
LESOTHO
NEW ZEALAND
MAURITANIA
NIGER
MALI
CHAD
SENEGAL
GAMBIA
BURKINA FASO
GUINEA
GUINEA BISSAU
NIGERIA
CÔTE D'IVOIRE
SIERRA LEONE
GHANA
BENIN
LIBERIA
TOGO
CAMEROON
EQUATORIAL GUINEA
ATLANTIC OCEAN
SAO TOME & PRINCIPE
GABON
REP. CONGO
Cabinda (Angola)

Part I Outline: Introduction

CHAPTER 1

Comparative Politics and the Regional Perspective

Aim at an exact Knowledge of the Nature, End, and Means of Government. Compare the different forms of it with each other and each of them with their Effects on the public and private Happiness.

— John Adams

Why study politics? For better or worse, politics affects our lives in countless ways. Virtually no one in today's world lives beyond the pale of government, and governing is essentially a political process. In other words, no one lives outside the political and legal confines of the state because there is no piece of territory anywhere in the world that is not claimed by at least one state.

The state itself is a human invention — it does not simply occur like the four seasons whether or not there are people around to experience it. States have existed in one form or another for several millennia, but the modern state, organized around the concept of the nation, has only existed since about the seventeenth century. It is too seldom noticed that the so-called nation-state was at first a strictly *regional* phenomenon, not a global one. Today, nation-states are found in every region of the world, but this remarkable fact is a testament to the success of one region, Europe, in gaining temporary mastery over all the others. The point here is not that one region is better than another, but rather that *it is impossible to make sense of the modern world without giving due consideration to the role of regions as well as nation-states.*

This book, as its title clearly indicates, takes a close look at both regions and national governments and seeks to demonstrate the key role each plays in the formation and evolution of the other. Implicit is the view that the popular fascination with globalism is somewhat misplaced, that the age of nationalism is far from over, and that if a new age is dawning (a big "if") it is likely to be an age of regionalism.

Source: John Adams, *Diary and Autobiography,* Hyman H. Butterfield, ed., 4 vols. (Cambridge, Massachusetts, 1961, I, 72–73), and cited in Fawn M. Brodie, *Thomas Jefferson: An Intimate History* (New York: W.W. Norton and Company, Inc., 1974), p. 98.

Why Compare?

"Know thyself," admonished the oracle of Apollo at Delphi in the seventh century. These two words, probably the most famous words of wisdom to come out of Greek philosophy, suggest the value of making comparisons. "An age-old idea of philosophers is that knowledge of the self is gained through knowledge of others."[1] What is true of individuals is also true of societies.

Comparison is an excellent antidote to **ethnocentrism** (a narrow view of the world based on one's own culture, religion, nationality, and so on). Indeed, there is perhaps no better way to gain perspective on one's own society than to view it from afar, through the eyes of others.

Foreigners have made some of the most penetrating analyses of American political and social institutions. Few scholars would dispute that *Democracy in America,* an incisive two-volume study written by Alexis de Tocqueville, a Frenchman who visited the United States in the 1830s, retains much of its relevance and validity in the twenty-first century. Similarly, in the early 1900s an Englishman named James Bryce showed in *The American Commonwealth* how the U.S. system of candidate selection tends to eliminate many of the best-qualified individuals. (No wonder voters often grumble about having to choose between Tweedledum and Tweedledee!)

By the same token, American observers have provided penetrating insights into other societies. In the 1970s, Hedrick Smith's daring best seller, *The Russians* (1976), provided brilliant insights into Soviet society at a time when the Soviet Union was largely off-limits to most foreigners. Soviet censors banned Smith's book and Smith himself was declared persona non grata (a diplomatic-legal device for banishing foreigners considered undesirable). In those days, the Soviet rulers discouraged unauthorized contacts between outsiders and Soviet writers, intellectuals, dissidents, or, indeed, even ordinary citizens. Soviet citizens who heard about the book naturally wanted to see it. A guide from the state travel agency for foreign visitors (Intourist) pleaded with me to slip her a copy that one of my students had (accidentally) "smuggled" across the border. She obviously knew about "the book" but had apparently never seen it, even though English-speaking Intourist guides often had access to Western publications denied to the general public. In the privacy of his modest, sparsely furnished Moscow flat, a distinguished Soviet scholar, who had read bootlegged excerpts from the book, expressed anger and dismay at the hypocrisy of the party "bosses." This gray-haired intellectual recounted a personal experience that corroborated Smith's account of a privileged political, managerial, and artistic elite flourishing in the very shadow of the Kremlin. "I have lived here all my life," he added with a note of bitterness, "and yet I found out things about this country I never knew."

Examples such as these are not as difficult to find as we might think. Why can outsiders so often see things that insiders cannot? It is precisely because these things are so obvious. What seems ordinary or natural to native dwellers may in fact be unique.

Most of us are not very objective about ourselves. Indeed, perhaps nothing is more deadly to objectivity than love of one's own (children, country, self, and so on). We regularly err in evaluating our own strengths and weaknesses. Hence, "Americans" are often (rightly or wrongly) accused of moral arrogance, of treating our own values, beliefs, ideas, and institutions as the embodiment of universal truth. To some extent, these criticisms are the price the United States pays for its success — good fortune often causes more envy than admiration. Nonetheless, it is noteworthy that America's tendency to intervene in the internal politics of other countries after World War II on grounds that we had a moral duty to fight against Marxist tyranny — from Guatemala (1953) to Vietnam (1961–1975) to the tiny island of Grenada (1983) — was widely viewed abroad, *even among our closest allies,* as naive and hypocritical. Our belief in the superiority of our institutions coexists paradoxically with widespread cynicism about politics and politicians. In reality, our institutions are not so perfect nor our politicians so imperfect as we commonly suppose. The best (and perhaps only) way to adjust our thinking is by means of comparison.

Almost everyone has a political viewpoint, but few people have the time or inclination to pursue politics intensively. Therefore, many people's understanding of politics is clouded by myths and misconceptions. The same can of course be said about other fields of knowledge, but there is a crucial difference: In the behavioral sciences, from psychology to politics, the way people think about the field actually affects the things (behaviors) being observed, classified, and analyzed.

For example, public opinion polls are designed to show voters what they (the voters) are thinking, how they are leaning, and what the outcome of a given election might be at that moment in time. But polls themselves can become important factors in elections, boosting the standing of some candidates and deflating the hopes of others. Because a good part of this sorting out process takes place early on in a campaign season, polls can help to make or break candidates. Similarly, when Western political scientists, economists, sociologists, and historians write about the shortcomings of governments in different parts of the world they may do it as an academic or theoretical exercise, but the books and articles written by professors may be read and used as ammunition by dissidents in the countries whose governments are being criticized. The fact that totalitarian states (see Chapter 2) routinely censor the press, tightly control the importation and distribution of foreign publications, and severely punish possession of forbidden literature is strong circumstantial evidence that political science affects politics (and vice versa). On the other hand, astronomy does not affect the workings of the solar system.

Why do we compare? Here are some reasons.

- Comparison is a useful way to evaluate what we see and hear about the world beyond our shores, as well as about our own society.
- What the public believes can have a significant impact on what government does, especially in democratic countries.
- Political myths, to the detriment of the nation (and possibly the world), may be used to prop up policies that have outlived their usefulness.
- An attempt to identify and explain the fundamental patterns of political behavior across different societies and cultures may help us arrive at useful theoretical generalizations.
- Finally, by comparing our own political institutions, processes, ideas, and traditions with those of others, we can learn more about ourselves.

Having looked at why comparison is useful in political science, we turn to a consideration of how **comparative politics** is done. Is it an art or a science? Any such

What If? BOX 1.1

Founding a New Republic: What Would You Do?

In the West, the story of the attempt to teach or learn about politics by comparative means and methods begins with the ancient Greeks, but we will begin at a less distant time and place — with the American Revolution and the subsequent founding of the modern world's first representative democracy (or "republic"). The American Founders claimed to have constructed a "new science of politics." The theoretical underpinnings of the U.S. Constitution can be found in *The Federalist,* written by Alexander Hamilton, James Madison, and John Jay during the campaign for the Constitution's ratification.*

Try this mental exercise: imagine yourself to be Alexander Hamilton, James Madison, or John Jay. What sort of a political system would you create? How would you go about designing it? What purposes would you want it to serve? What dangers would you want it to guard against? Ask yourself this question as well: is there one form of government that is best, everywhere and always, or is the best form of government relative to the particular time and place?

Answering these questions should help you develop a sense of what you think good government is all about and how it might best be achieved under different sets of circumstances. Discuss your answers with a classmate. The best (and most enjoyable) way to learn is to engage in lively discussions with one's peers. Educated citizens in ancient Greece and colonial America did this, with results that left an indelible imprint on world history.

*Alexander Hamilton, John Jay, and James Madison, *The Federalist* (New York: Modern Library, 1964), no. 9, pp. 48–49.

discussion must touch on philosophy, as well as methods and measurement in the study of politics. Some political questions do lend themselves to measurement, but many do not. Where measurement is impossible, other less "scientific" methods must be found. The alternative — not asking important questions — is neither desirable nor scientific.

The Logic of Comparative Politics

Comparative politics is as old as political science itself. The Greek philosopher Aristotle (384–322 BCE), a pioneer in the science of politics, set standards for the discipline that have survived to the present. Aristotle compared existing political systems in order to theorize about the best possible regime. (See Box 1.1.) Yet Aristotle's ultimate concerns were ethical in nature — he was interested in questions of justice. His empirical investigations were driven by such questions as: What is the **good life**? What form of government is best? What is the relationship between the type of political regime in a given place and the moral character of the people who live under it? As we embark on this exploration of the contemporary world's major political systems, we should remind ourselves that others, following Aristotle, have been doing the same through the ages. Whatever the purpose (whether to create a new political order, to understand what makes a particular form of government tick, or simply to "know thy enemy") the comparative study of politics is an essential part of the undergraduate political science curriculum.

Aristotle appreciated the importance of both theory and method. The term *theory* refers to concepts, ideas, or bodies of thought that purport to explain, predict, or prescribe political systems, patterns, processes, and trends. Political forms are sets of institutions (such as legislatures, executives, bureaucracies, and judiciaries) that together constitute systems or regimes (for example, the British parliamentary system or the monarchy of Saudi Arabia); political processes include interest articulation and opinion formation, elections, coalition building, and bargaining.

References to methods (or methodology) can be confusing or even intimidating, but they need not be. The **scientific method** has two aspects — induction and deduction. *Deduction* involves abstract thought and logical reasoning. For example, the idea that constitutional democracy is the best form of government is a premise that few Americans doubt. Most people would also agree that India is a democracy. Logically, if democracy is the best form of government and India is a democracy, then India ought to be stable and prosperous.

Although the logic of this proposition is unassailable, its truth is not. India is neither stable nor prosperous by American standards. This suggests that either the premise equating democracy with good government is false or that India is not a democracy or that there is something wrong with American standards. How do we solve this riddle?

To know whether India does or does not have good government, we must seek empirical (factual) evidence. We can begin with some sort of hypothesis (a proposition to be proved or disproved), define our variables (standards for measuring the success of democracy), and proceed to test the hypothesis by gathering all relevant data, classifying these data, comparing them with similar data from other countries, and drawing conclusions from concrete facts (rather than abstract reasoning). This form of analysis is called *induction.*

The **deductive approach** is most often associated with **normative political theory,** which can be defined as the study of goodness and justice in public life. The **inductive approach,** which focuses on what is rather than what ought to be, is favored by modern proponents of **behavioralism.** Is one approach better or more fruitful than the other?

Significantly, Aristotle did not choose between normative and empirical methods but instead blended the two, with results that are still studied some 2,300 years later. As a groundbreaking theorist, Aristotle formed hypotheses about political life that he then tested for historical, factual, and logical validity. History provided empirical data for his comparative analyses. A collection of all the constitutions that were available at that time — 158 — was kept at the Lyceum, where Aristotle taught. In Aristotle's political thought, "The man of science appears again and again behind the student of politics."[2]

This is perhaps as good a place as any to raise one of the most perplexing questions of political science: is it possible to measure the performance of political systems objectively or do certain obstacles (such as ethnocentrism, governmental secrecy, and imperfect data) foredoom all such efforts to failure? Think about it and be prepared to step out of your comfort zone and into the world beyond America's shores — the world of comparative politics.

Politics in Regional Perspective

Domestic political patterns and political development do not necessarily stay within a single country's borders. They often reflect **transnational** or regional traits and circumstances. (The term *transnational* means "transcending national boundaries.") The world may be divided into an array of small regions or just a few large ones. A common cultural core, geographic proximity, economic interdependence, similarity in political traditions, or some combination of these factors may define regions. For example, Latin America can be treated either as a single region or as two regions, Central America and South America; in turn, South America can be divided into three regions — Amazonia (mostly Brazil), the Andean countries (Venezuela, Colombia, Ecuador, Peru, and Bolivia), and the Southern Cone (Chile and Argentina plus Uruguay and Paraguay). Similarly, Asia can be subdivided into Central Asia (Afghanistan, Kyrgystan, Kazakhstan, Tajikistan, Uzbekistan, and Turkmenistan), South Asia (India, Pakistan, and Sri Lanka), Southeast Asia (Vietnam, Cambodia, Thailand, Malaysia, and Indonesia, among others), East Asia (China mainly), and Northeast Asia (China, Russia, the two Koreas, and Japan).* No matter how broadly regions are defined, large and powerful states will likely be major players (have a strong presence) in more than one regional system (as Russia is in both Europe and Asia, for example, and the United States is in both North and South America).

Moreover, there is no general agreement on how or where to draw the boundary lines for different regions. Should Mexico be included in Central or North America? Should Japan be included in East Asia or the Western Pacific? Should Turkey be considered part of the Middle East or Europe? This book divides the world into six major regions:

1. Western Europe (Part II)
2. Russia and Slavic Europe (Part III)
3. Asia (East Asia — China, Central South Asia, Southeast Asia, and Northeast Asia) (Part IV)
4. Latin America (Mexico, Central America, and South America — Amazonia-Brazil, the Andean countries, and the Southern Cone) (Part V)
5. The Middle East (including North Africa and the Persian Gulf) (Part VI)
6. Sub-Saharan Africa (East Africa, West Africa, and Southern Africa)

These regions do not correspond precisely to continents, although continental boundaries provide a partial basis for the sixfold division. Geographic location and proximity are important factors, but so are other commonalities, including history, culture, language, religion, population characteristics, climate, natural resources, economic structure, and quality of life (infant mortality rate, per capita income, life expectancy, and the like).

Regions can also be viewed as subsystems, or **subordinate systems,** in which regional powers regularly interact with one another. A subordinate system consists of

*I have deliberately excluded the Persian Gulf states, which are actually Southwestern Asia, because we commonly consider this area as the core of the Middle East.

"two or more proximate and interacting states that have some common ethnic, linguistic, cultural, social, and historic bonds, and whose sense of identity is sometimes increased by the actions and attitudes of states external to the system."[3] Another characteristic of a subordinate system is that regional issues are often at the root of local conflicts (for example, Palestine in the Middle East) and of attempts at collaboration (such as the European Union in Western Europe). Finally, regional subsystems are the largest arena in which nation-states have succeeded in establishing hegemony (political control).[4] Subordinate systems, according to one useful model: (1) are delimited (having clearly defined boundaries), with a primary stress on a geographic region; (2) have at least three actors (states); (3) are objectively recognized as constituting a distinctive community, region, or segment of the global system; and (4) are conscious of a common regional identity.[5] This checklist emphasizes the importance of both geography and cultural identity in comparative politics. It suggests that the countries of a given region are in general more closely related to each other than to countries outside the region (which does not, however, mean that they are always on friendly terms). If it is true that regional subsystems are politically and economically significant, we can expect to find some clues as to why patterns and trends occur the way they do in a given country by looking at what is happening (or has happened) in the surrounding "neighborhood" (region).

Globalization and the Regional Approach

Globalization refers to the process by which various values, institutions, technologies, and products, as well as a certain lifestyle associated with advanced postindustrial societies, are spreading to all parts of the world (though not everyone agrees on the pace, extent, or significance of this process). Proponents of this theory view globalization as ineluctable, all pervasive, and transforming. They emphasize the expanding role of the "information superhighway" (the Internet, cellular phone service, and the satellite-based mass media), giant multinational corporations (MNCs), and international organizations as proof of the irreversibility of globalization. Skeptics recognize the existence of powerful globalizing tendencies, but stress the continued role of local loyalties (tribalism and nationalism), religion, resource scarcity, ethnic conflict, tradition, and other forces that create resistance to social change. They argue that the widening chasm between the most advanced and least developed countries (encompassing most of Africa, as well as large parts of Eastern Europe, Asia, and Latin America) proves that globalization is a work in progress, not an accomplished fact.[6] (See Figures 1.1 and 1.2.)

The current popularity of the term *globalization* makes it impossible for students of comparative politics to ignore it *as a concept* even if *as a process* it is controversial. On its face, the theory of globalization is at odds with preexisting worldviews that have long emphasized the key role of nationalism, geography, and culture in explaining politics on the world stage. It is not, however, at odds with the regional approach used in this book — in fact, regionalism is in some measure one of the consequences of globalization because the same forces that facilitate greater cooperation and fuel intensified competition on the world stage also create incentive for greater coordination on the regional level.

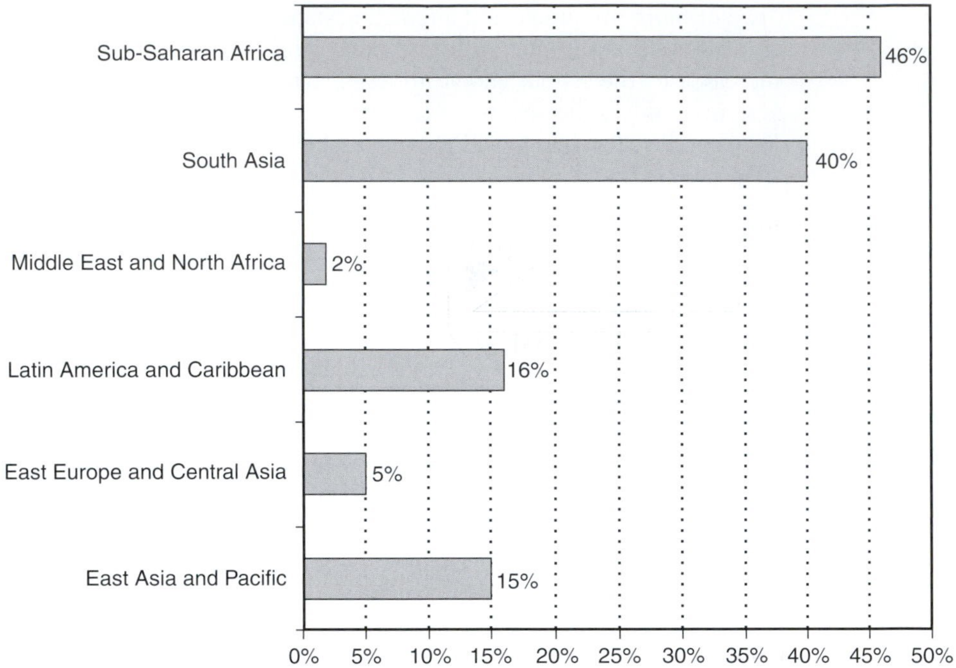

Figure 1.1 A Regional Comparison of World Poverty (people living on less than the local purchasing power parity [PPP] equivalent of $1 a day)

Source: World Bank Atlas (Washington, D.C.: International Bank for Reconstruction and Development, 2000). Copyright 2000 by World Bank. Reprinted with permission of World Bank.

The world that globalists see emerging is one in which many of the "old" boundaries and barriers that have divided the world into warring camps (whether clans, tribes, or nations) for so long are being eroded by powerful modernizing (and, some argue, democratizing) forces that transcend lines of demarcation drawn on maps. There is at least a kernel of truth in this notion: no recess of the earth, no matter how remote, can escape the intrusions of the modern world. However, there is no real contradiction between the old and the new views: both processes — change and inertia — are present in all societies, always have been and always will be. Thus, regionalism and globalism are best seen as different expressions of the same dominant political forces and economic processes at work in the world today.

Regional Influences on Politics

Many region-linked factors have a bearing on governmental structures and policies. For the sake of brevity we will group these factors first by resources and demographic characteristics and then by history and culture. After that we will consider the effects of the processes of modernization and development.

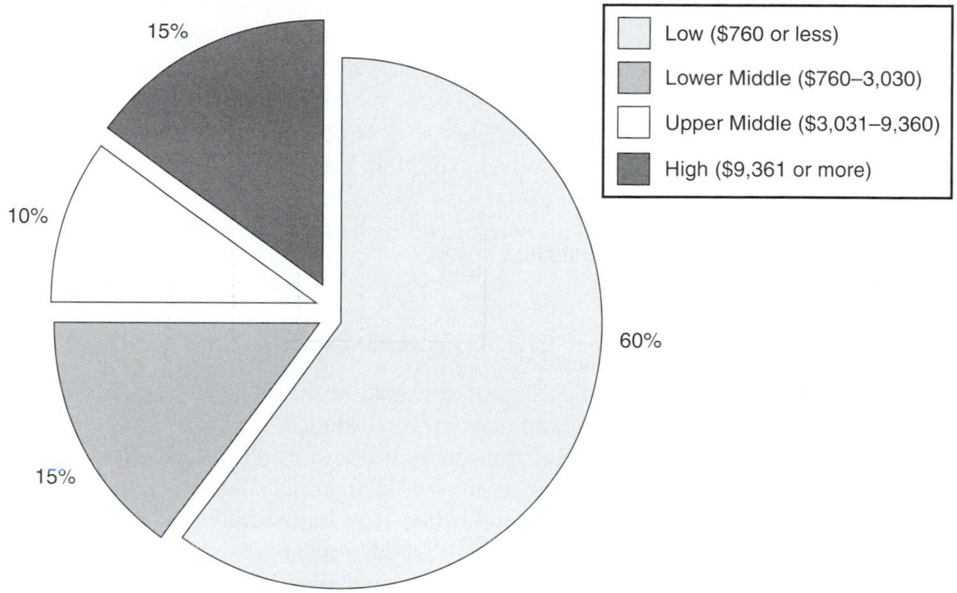

Figure 1.2 It's a Small World After All . . . and Poor (distribution of world population among economies grouped by GNP per capita)

Source: World Bank Atlas (Washington, D.C.: International Bank for Reconstruction and Development, 2000). Copyright 2000 by World Bank. Reprinted with permission of World Bank.

Why Are Regions Different? The Role of Biodiversity New research and scholarship in the field of evolutionary biology point strongly to the conclusion that such elemental factors as native flora and fauna (plants and animals) together with climate, soil, and water resources account for contrasting rates and forms of social and political development in different regions of the world. In this vein, Jared Diamond, a professor of physiology at the UCLA School of Medicine, argues compellingly in his book *Guns, Germs, and Steel: The Fate of Human Societies* (1997) that environmental factors are responsible for picking history's "winners" and "losers."[7] (Thus, Diamond demolishes theories of development based on racial or cultural superiority.)

According to Diamond, modern science has found mounting evidence for the biblical notion of a Garden of Eden — actually several such "gardens." Agriculture is the key. The story begins in the Stone Age when, as luck would have it, certain regions had a comparative advantage over other regions — namely a far greater natural abundance of plant and animal wildlife suitable for domestication. This disparity, Diamond argues, largely explains the differing fates of different peoples in different regions. Thus, the earliest conversion of societies from the hunter-gatherer stage to the farmer-herder stage reflects ecological factors, not differences in racial or ethnic qualities. The greatly varying rates at which food production spread from centers of origin — mainly, the Middle East ("Fertile Crescent"), China, Central America ("Mesoamerica") — had a lot to do with features of climate and geography — such as differing sizes, locations, and even shapes of continents. Finally, Diamond shows how subsequent economic development and military conquest turned on agriculture and the domestication of animals (notably pigs, cows, sheep, and horses). Societies able to produce reliable food surpluses and harness animal power were more likely to develop writing, technology, and government, as well as create weapons of war. In addition, Europeans inadvertently transported "weapons" of mass destruction to the New World and other colonial areas, namely communicable diseases (germs). Far more natives died of epidemics than by the sword.

Climate, Geography, and Natural Resources

Oddly, some of the simplest explanations of social and political differences are seldom explored. Climate and ecology, for instance, distinguish nations of the northern latitudes from nations of the southern ones in politically significant ways. Differences in soil and latitude (temperate versus tropical climates) influence dietary preferences, nutritional standards, and what economists call "comparative advantage" in agriculture. Hence, not only food, feed, and fiber for domestic markets but also export crops reflect the underlying structural realities established by nature and sometimes modified — for better or worse — by human engineering (for example, the construction of dams for hydroelectric power generation and irrigation, the building of transportation systems, the draining of swamps, and the like). Historically, these differences have played a crucial role in determining the pace, timing, type, and level of economic development found in a given region or state.

Western Europe In Western Europe, it is impossible to talk about soil and climate in the singular. It makes sense only to speak of soils and climates because there is so much diversity within that relatively compact geographic area. The diversity includes the marine west coast climate associated with the Atlantic Ocean and the dry summer climate of the Mediterranean. It also includes various mountain ranges (most notably the mighty Alps of the interior) and semirugged terrain, as well as flat and relatively featureless plains. The soils also vary but are generally favorable to horticulture or agriculture. Finally, Western Europe is relatively rich in the natural resources that powered the Industrial Revolution, especially coal and steel. Thanks to the discovery of large oil deposits in the North Sea, Western Europe also has an abundant source of petroleum.

An interesting example of how geography and politics are linked can be found in Immanuel Wallerstein's impressive study on the "modern world system" (part of the book's title).[8] Wallerstein traces the origins of the Eurocentric "world economy" to the little country of Portugal, which began looking outward in the sixteenth century, opting for seafaring exploration, rather than war and conquest on the Continent, as the path to national wealth and glory. Nothing made that choice inevitable, but Portugal's location (its capital, Lisbon, is sited on a natural harbor) and favorable ocean currents made it possible. (See Box 1.2.)

Contrast and Comparison

BOX 1.2

American Imperialism: Geography and Destiny

The story of American imperialism — how the United States grew from a small band of former colonies huddled along the Atlantic Coast into a continental empire of federated states — is very different from the history of European imperialism. America's early history illustrates the importance of geography in shaping the political destiny of nations. In fact, the doctrine of Manifest Destiny, which was used to justify the westward expansion of the United States in the nineteenth century, was focused on geography. The doctrine asserted that it was imperative for the United States to expand to its natural geographical limits — first to the Mississippi River, then to the Rocky Mountains, and eventually to the Pacific Ocean. Imperative or not, there was without question a strong geographic influence at work. As the saying goes, power abhors a vacuum: the vast western wilderness of North America was sparsely populated and the great powers of Europe, an ocean away, did not pose a challenge.

The fact that the United States is flanked by two oceans and has nonthreatening neighbors to the north (Canada) and south (Mexico) has also played a role in forming American traditions, institutions, and policies. The oceans insulated the country without isolating it, at once serving as a bulwark against invasion and as a gateway to the markets of Asia and Europe. The absence of external threats gave a young nation time to mature and develop, allowing it to grow strong economically without having to divert large sums into military expenditures.

The famous historian Frederick Jackson Turner argued eloquently that the frontier played a seminal role in shaping America's self-image, values, and ideals. Whether Jackson was right or wrong, it is true that even today certain values such as individualism and self-reliance, which were strongly associated with the frontier experience, remain key elements in the political culture of the United States.

Europe's conquest of "new worlds" went well beyond geography: it extended to science and technology as well, setting the stage for the Industrial Revolution. Why did Europe race ahead of the rest of the world at a certain point in history? The existence of a temperate climate in Western Europe and a rich variety of native plant and animal life suitable for domestication (for example, grains and horses) were key factors. The development of agriculture (as opposed to a nomadic hunting and gathering existence) made permanent settlements and food surpluses possible, which in turn made the "luxury" of learning (manifested in the development of written language and mathematics) possible, if not inevitable.

However, agriculture was not invented in Europe, nor was writing (crucial for keeping records and building a knowledge base). We leave that part of the story for our discussion of the Middle East. For now, suffice it to say that Europe was ideally situated, both geographically and ecologically, to benefit from the knowledge developed by civilizations in another time and place.

Eastern Europe Eastern Europe also displays considerable variety in topography, but in soil and climate it is far less fortunate than Western Europe. Russia, the giant in the region, is characterized by flat rolling plains and cold temperatures west of the Urals (the European part); the same is true of the area east of the Urals only more so — the vast plains of central Siberia are covered in forests; northern Siberia is tundra (buried under a thick layer of snow and ice in winter, the ground never thaws). Siberia is rich in natural resources, but brutally cold most of the year, and sparsely populated, except for major industrial cities such as Krasnoyarsk, Novosibirsk, and Irkutsk built during the communist era.

Unlike Western Europe, Russia has never solved the riddle of agriculture — how to produce enough food for its sizeable population; the problem is not a lack of fertile soil so much as the short (and unreliable) growing season. During the Khrushchev era (1957–1964), the government attempted to bring "virgin lands" in Central Asia under the plow; the ill-conceived experiment failed miserably from an agricultural standpoint and had ecologically disastrous consequences.

On the other, Russia is extremely well endowed with natural resources, including hydrocarbons (coal, oil, and natural gas), precious metals (including gold), and timber. Russia's economic development reflects its natural advantages — electric power generation, metallurgy, oil refining, chemicals, and textiles are among Russia's most important categories of industrial output.

Many knowledgeable observers have commented on the relationship between the harsh and unforgiving climate on the one hand, and Russia's authoritarian political culture, on the other. The general picture is one of adversity and a threatening environment. Add the element of a vast territory with few natural barriers to invasion, and it is small wonder that Russia's rulers historically used harsh, no-nonsense methods to maintain control of the population.

Slavic Central Europe and the Balkans differ significantly from Russia, but differ also in geographic position from Western Europe. The countries of Central Europe have been called the "lands in between" — between empires and powerful states. Poland is a classical example of a country threatened by Russia from the east and Germany from the west. Similarly, the Czechs historically have been ruled or dominated by the Austrians (the Hapsburg Empire), the Germans (Nazi occupation), and the Russians (Soviet era). These countries also are dependent on external sources for oil and natural gas, a critical resource in combustion engine–powered modern economies. In sum, Eastern Europe's historical fate appears to have been strongly conditioned (if not determined) by factors beyond human control — factors that nudge the non-Russian nations of the region (against their will, of course) toward subjugation and dependency. The chain reaction that brought down one communist regime after another in 1989 gave many nations in the region a rare taste of freedom from foreign domination.

Asia Like Europe, Asia exhibits a variety of soils and climates. If anything, the contrasts are even greater in Asia. In the far north (Russia) is Siberia; in northeastern China is the fertile Manchurian plain and cool forest (the latter feature is similar to Eastern Europe). A major producer of grains and soybeans, Manchuria is also rich in mineral resources, including China's largest oilfield as well as large coal and iron ore reserves. The largest part of China (and much of Indochina) is moist and subtropical. Central China is the country's main breadbasket. Sichuan contains some 10 percent of the country's population (a number roughly equivalent to the entire population of Japan). The capital, Beijing, and its port city of Tianjing, together with the eastern coastal provinces form the industrial base of China. The hub of China's heavy industry and commerce is Shanghai, China's largest city, and its satellites. The southeastern coast (Guangdong province) is also a fast-growing urban-industrial area. The deep western interior of China and the eastern part of Central Asia is a vast cool desert. The Himalayas of Tibet (a disputed part of China at present) are the world's highest mountain range.

China has several major river systems. China's great rivers played a major role in the development of the country's ancient system of "permanent agriculture" based on dams and dikes for flood control and irrigation. These water-management systems helped to support a large population that, in turn, provided ample labor for massive public-works projects (symbolized by the Great Wall). Such large-scale projects would have been impossible without a centralized bureaucratic state.

Indochina is largely subtropical with dense canopies of vegetation blanketing large areas. Further south, in Malaysia, Indonesia, and the Philippines, the monsoons (heavy seasonal rains) are predominant and tropical rain forests (jungles) cover much of the landmass.

South Asia also has a variety of climates from monsoons (Bangladesh, Myanman, and the west coast of India) and moist subtropical (northern India) to warm desert (much of Pakistan). Much of southern India is savanna (similar in topography to large parts of sub-Saharan Africa).

Across the length and breadth of Asia, most natural resources can be found in abundance. China, for example, has commercial deposits of most minerals and the world's largest reserves of a dozen or more. China is the world's largest producer of coal and also has large oil reserves. Indonesia produces oil, natural gas, bauxite, nickel, and rubber; India exports iron ore and cut diamonds, and so on.

Most of Asia is much closer to the equator than Western Europe or North America. It is therefore warmer and either much wetter or much dryer. What direct effects climatic differences have had on politics in Asia is difficult to say, but there are some striking facts with important political implications that deserve mention. First, population sizes are so much greater in Asia than in Europe or North America (or any other region, for that matter). Together, India and China alone account for more than one-third of the world's total population. Pakistan, Bangladesh, and Indonesia are also among the populous states in the world. Precisely how climate influences population dynamics is a mystery, but clearly it is an important factor. Second, the political traditions of Asia are autocratic. As we shall see, great empires existed in China, Cambodia, India, and Persia (present-day Iran). Positing a two-step connection between climate and population and between population and politics does not require a great leap of imagination. (Of course, proving it is quite another matter.)

The French political philosopher Baron de Montesquieu, for example, in his classic *L'esprit des lois* ("the spirit of the laws"), decried "the vices of climate." Montesquieu believed that climate is detrimental to progress when it causes indolence, as it does (or appears to do) in extremely hot regions. He applied this logic to India, for example, where the predominant religion, Hinduism, encourages passivity. Although we can argue with Montesquieu on specific points, it is hard to deny that climatic factors affect food production and that natural events such as droughts and floods can imperil human life.

It is easy to see how geography influences politics and the flow of history, but Montesquieu even posited a connection between climate and form of government. He argued that despotism was more natural to hot climates and that liberty was more natural to inhabitants of temperate and cold areas. He pointed out that Asia, with its political tradition of oriental despotism, has no temperate zone, in contrast to Europe (or North America), which has an extensive one.[9]

Latin America Latin America's geography differs from North America's in one obvious way: proximity to the equator. The climates of Central America and most of South America are thus much warmer than most of North America and the soils are not conducive to grain production (with the exception of Argentina, which exports wheat). Central America and the vast Amazon region of South America are tropical rain forest, whereas the central region of South America (east of the Andes) is an immense savanna. The majestic Andean mountain range stretches down the western side of the continent all the way from Colombia in the north to Chile in the south.

Latin America has a variety of precious minerals including copper, gold, diamonds, and emeralds, as well as oil and natural gas (mainly in Venezuela, Colombia, and Ecuador). In terms of natural resources, therefore, Latin America is not poor.

Nonetheless, there is no denying that North America and Latin America until recently have been worlds apart politically, socially, and economically, even though they both exist in the same hemisphere. There are no doubt many reasons (including the aftereffects of the Spanish Conquest, but climate and geography have certainly played some role in shaping the region's political traditions. First, there were great empires in South America but none in North America; in other words, the south was more advanced than the north. Why? Proving exactly how climate and geography influenced the evolution (or absence) of civilizations is, to repeat, impossible; but denying that these factors played a role is equally impossible. Second, the civilizations of South America lagged behind Europe in technology and industry — how else to explain the relative ease with which the Spanish (and Portuguese) conquered the peoples and empires of the "New World"? As we noted earlier, recent studies in evolutionary biology argue cogently that geography and climate — and therefore the vegetation and wildlife native to different regions — are important keys to understanding why agriculture, industry, and the implements of war developed earlier and faster in Europe than other regions.

Third, natural barriers to military expansion — deserts, jungles, mountains, and savannas — help to explain why Latin America's independent states have been permanent fixtures of political geography for nearly two centuries. The opposite was true in North America, where natural boundaries became excuses for (rather than barriers to) expansion. No Latin American state has emerged as a modern-day empire builder; conversely, even small states have survived basically intact. Costa Rica does not even have a standing army.

The Middle East and North Africa As every college student who has taken World History 101 knows, the Middle East is often considered the "cradle of civilization." The ancient Egyptians, for example, developed both agriculture and architecture on a grand scale, as well as written language, astronomy, and the arts. The story actually begins even earlier, in Mesopotamia, with the Sumerians who developed a system of writing on clay tablets using pictographs to keep records after 4000 BCE. By 3000 BCE, the Sumerians had developed a cuneiform (wedge-shaped) script as a complete syllabic alphabet; this idea was soon adapted by neighboring peoples.

Writing and learning go hand in hand, as do learning and abstract thinking. Small wonder, then, that several of the world's great monotheistic religions — most notably Judaism, Christianity, and Islam — originated in this region. Sumerian civilization was based on large cities and organized around temples and priestly bureaucracies with the surrounding plains watered by vast irrigation works and farmed by traction plows. The Sumerians developed a good deal of "modern" technology, including sailboats, wheeled vehicles, and even metallurgy.

Why did this flowering of human creativity and ingenuity occur first in the Middle East? Was it entirely accidental? There was evidently more at work than mere accident. Agriculture appears to be the key — the possibility of shifting from a nomadic to a settled existence. But why did agriculture develop when and where it did? Evolutionary biology has unearthed a wealth of clues, making it possible to glimpse the biodiversity of different regions of the earth at the dawn of recorded history. What is especially clear is that the amount of diversity was not at all uniform, that some regions had a far greater variety of native plants and animals than others did, and, of critical importance, that the Middle East was richly endowed with the right *kind* of plant and animal life — that is, the kind that could be adapted to human use. Grains, fruits, and vegetables of all kinds can be found on this list, as well as grazing animals (sheep and cows) and draft animals (horses and camels).

Again, the logic of the earliest examples of human development is that a particular "package" of biodiversity set the stage for exploitation of nature (agriculture). Farming and shepherding (a settled way of life) gradually replaced hunting and gathering (a nomadic existence). The economic and social development that accompanied the emergence of human communities made a division of labor possible for the first time ever — those who did physical work (farmers, soldiers) and those who did mental work (scribes, priests).

What might have caused the decline and fall of these early civilizations is beyond the scope of this book. From a comparative political standpoint, what is intriguing is the way another region (Europe) was able to piggyback on the accomplishments of the Sumerians, Egyptians, and others; the fact that civilizations evolved in Greece and Rome, moving from the Middle East to Western Europe in stages (we will discuss Asia); and that intercourse between Europe and the Middle East was facilitated by geography — a land bridge and the relatively tame Mediterranean Sea.

Sub-Saharan Africa Africa is a paradox. We know that Africa is the birthplace of the human species, and that people migrated out of Africa to other parts of the earth. We know, too, that Africans developed impressive cultures (but apparently not written languages), and even empires. But Africa virtually stopped "developing" at some point, which left its peoples at a great disadvantage when first the Arabs, and later the Europeans, arrived. Why?

The story of Africa is the same as that of the Middle East — only turned on its head. It is a story of biodiversity, but a different kind of biodiversity. The climate and soils of Africa are not so conducive to agriculture as the temperate zones of Europe and North America. Moreover, the exotic plants and animals native to Africa are by and large not easily adapted to agriculture or husbandry. For example, many of Africa's large animals are migratory or aggressive (or both). Except for the stripes, zebras look like horses or mules but they have a very different nature and are ill suited to domestication. Nor, paradoxically, is there an abundance of edible native plants, even in the region's lush equatorial jungles.

Sub-Saharan Africa has mineral wealth but the climate and soils of the region are for the most part not as conducive to diversified agriculture as the temperate zones. Lacking a strong farming tradition, the peoples of the region faced severe obstacles to economic development. Capital formation (based on surplus production, profits, and savings) is a necessary ingredient in any recipe for industrialization.

If Africa did not "take off" as other regions of the world have at different times, it is probably not due primarily to human failure, therefore, but rather to "natural causes." Later, a political-historical cause — namely colonialism — would also contribute to the tragedy of today's Africa. In many African countries today, a vicious cycle is at work, one that is extremely difficult to break. Poverty and malnutrition are pressing problems because of the absence of economic development and jobs for sub-Saharan Africa's youthful population (over half the population is under age fifteen). The political implications, which are profound, will be discussed in the last chapter of this book.

If the natural environment provides layers of rich data for comparative politics, the same can be said of the human environment. Both environments vary significantly from region to region and, indeed, can best be studied on a regional scale. Next, we turn to the human variables in politics, mindful of the fact that we human beings are, to a greater extent than we often recognize, creatures of nature.

Language, Culture, Religion, and History

There are four important elements of the political setting in every country that were created not by nature but by human beings who are the ancestors of people living there now. It is this very fact — the ancestral origins of history, language, culture, and religion — that helps to explain the passionate attachment people so often have to ideas, habits, and opinions that may seem strange to "foreigners." If tourists make no attempt to speak a word of the language of the country they are visiting, for example, it is not simply a slight to the current inhabitants; rather, it can be seen as an insult to past generations who suffered and sacrificed for the sake of the homeland. (Indeed, ancestor worship is still practiced in some countries, and even in the West it is common for people to visit and decorate the graves of deceased parents and grandparents, as well as monuments to national heroes of the past.)

The reasons why history, language, culture, and religion evoke strong passions go beyond the issue of ancestry, however. Think about it — is your own identity not closely linked to your location? How do you know who you are and where or how you fit into the scheme of things? Answers to these questions would be unthinkable (literally) if we (1) were not part of a larger whole (community, society, nation) with a history all its own; (2) did not have a common language (otherwise how could we communicate?); and (3) lacked the "knowledge" of life's profoundest mysteries that comes from transmitted (or inherited) values, both cultural and spiritual.

In the following section, the four facets mentioned above will be woven together rather than put into separate compartments for two reasons that are worth noting. First, in real life we do not compartmentalize our values according to source or category. Most of the time, we are not, in fact, even conscious of where our values come from — they are simply a part of who we are and we would not know ourselves without them. Second, it is impossible to treat each region in exactly the same way because, for example, the weight of religion is felt more heavily in the Middle East and North Africa than in Sub-Saharan Africa; or, to take another example, the role of language in politics is quite different in Latin America than in Eastern Europe.

In the modern world of nation-states, we seldom think in terms of whole civilizations. Yet there have been great civilizations in every region of the world at different times in history. In most cases, these civilizations were closely identified with vast and powerful empires. The empires have disappeared, but the imprint of civilizations on regions where they once held sway has certainly not. We start with the most familiar: Europe. But, as we will soon see, civilization did not start (or end) in Europe.

(Western) European Civilization Language is an important part of Europe's common cultural heritage. Whether in Greek, Latin, French, or English, Europeans have been able to talk to each other, exchange ideas, and share a common body of knowledge for over two millennia.

Political Scientist Jurg Steiner points to the importance of region-linked factors when he writes, "Europe is not only a geographical region, but a cultural concept." European nations "are bound together by a common culture based on centuries of close interaction."[10] This common culture is rooted in part in a common religious heritage. Before the twentieth century, historians frequently referred to Europe as "Christendom" because Christianity was officially enshrined and popularly embraced as the one true faith throughout the Continent. Indeed, monarchs even ruled by "divine right," meaning that the church was used to legitimize the state.

In addition to language, culture, and religion, the nations of Western Europe share many common historical experiences. The Renaissance and Reformation, the Enlightenment, and the Industrial Revolution all left a strong cultural imprint on European art, architecture, music, philosophy, and literature. Europe's wars and concerted efforts to develop traditions, procedures, and structures of diplomacy also contributed to this process. These experiences had a cumulative effect, promoting the evolution of certain common "European" political values and norms — a kind of moral consensus grounded in humanistic values. Manifestations of this consensus include attempts at conflict management through treaties, the "balance of power" mechanism, and international organizations such as the Concert of Europe and the congress system of the nineteenth century.[11] In contemporary times, the success of the European Union (EU; see Chapter 4) is testimony to the notion that the various national cultures of Europe contain elements of a common European culture (not to mention the widespread use of English).

Slavic (Eastern) Europe The word *Slavic* is emphasized here for two reasons. First, the predominant ethnicity of East Europeans is Slavic: most of the peoples of the region (Russians, Poles, Ukrainians, Czechs, Slovaks, Bulgarians, Serbs, Croats, Slovenes, and others) speak a Slavic (Slavonic) language. In Russia and Bulgaria, for example, the alphabet in use is Cyrillic (invented by a Greek missionary named Cyril), rather than Roman. Immediately, the traveler from Western Europe encounters a language that not only sounds but also looks distinctly "foreign."

It is difficult to exaggerate the importance of language in the development of a national consciousness or, to put a finer point on it, the relationship between language and culture. Czechs, for example, use the Roman alphabet and resist speaking foreign languages. Few foreigners (including other Slavs) speak a word of Czech. This situation reinforces a sense of cultural isolation that most Czechs appear to prefer. The nineteenth-century Czech "national revival" was closely associated with a revitalized interest in the Czech language, as well as Czech literature and music. Czechs enjoy foreign books, films, and music, but the "high culture" that they most treasure encompasses works by Czech composers, writers, and filmmakers. What is true of Czechs is also true in varying degrees of Russians, Poles, Serbs, and other Slavic nationalities.

Religion also separates Eastern and Western Europe. Whereas Roman Catholicism and the Reformation (Protestantism) had a major impact on West European culture, Eastern Europe embraced the Eastern (Greek) Orthodox variant of Christianity, Poland being the most obvious (but not the only) exception. As a result, from Russia to the Balkans, the Vatican had neither spiritual authority nor political influence. In Russia, the absence of an external source of religious authority meant that the "state" (czarist monarchy) was free to work out its own relationship with the church (patriarchate), which it did with a vengeance. The result was a leviathan based on a mutual-interest alliance between church and state — the state gave Russian Orthodoxy a religious monopoly and the church legitimized the czar's political monopoly (by recognizing his "divine right" to rule).

Finally, the history of Eastern Europe diverges from that of Western Europe in countless ways (we can only scratch the surface here). First, Russia and other Slavic parts of Europe were ravaged as a result of the Mongol invasion and occupation beginning in the twelfth century. That experience is still part of the living history of the region — Russian schoolchildren still learn about it and Russian adults still talk about it. Second, most of Slavic Europe (including Russia) did not participate in the Renaissance and Reformation. Third, Eastern Europe generally sat on the sidelines during the Industrial Revolution of the nineteenth century; at the beginning of the twentieth century these countries were still essentially agrarian (societies based on agricultural economies). Fourth, East European nations were often losers or pawns (or both) in Europe's modern wars. Between 1850 and 1917, Great Britain, Japan, and Germany each defeated Russia. (After World War I, the Western powers, including the United States, invaded Russia and tried — but failed — to overthrow a revolutionary "Soviet" government they did not like.) Poland was actually partitioned — divided up into several parts at the end of the eighteenth century. Czechs, Slovaks, and other nations were ruled by German-speaking Hapsburgs, invaded and occupied by Nazi Germany, and later subjugated by the Soviet Union.

These examples will suffice for the moment to suggest the role of language, culture, religion, and history in Eastern Europe. They also provide a glimpse of the invisible divide that exists between these two "halves" of the same continent.

Asia In Asia, the imprint of Chinese on the languages of Japan, Korea, and Vietnam is unmistakable. Buddhism (which originated in India but migrated to flourish elsewhere) and patron-client relations are two other distinct traditions that have exerted powerful influences on the historical development of most nations of the region.

Asia is home to several full-blown civilizations. The first known Chinese civilization dates back to the Shang dynasty (1523 BCE); already during this early period a writing system based on pictographs was in use. Much earlier, circa 3000–1500 BCE, an urban civilization with a writing system still undeciphered stretched across the Indus Valley and along the Arabian Sea. These two examples point to the early origins of modern China and India, respectively. It is always difficult to trace the ancient linguistic, cultural, and religious roots of modern societies, but the farther back in time these roots go, the deeper they tend to run.

Unlike the West, where the Judeo-Christian tradition casts a wide net and has no strong rivals, in Asia there are many religions, including several with mass followings in different countries. Hinduism is the religion of most Indians, but India also has a huge Muslim population, and Pakistan is a Muslim country. Islam is also very strong throughout Southeast Asia, where it competes with Buddhism, as well as Christianity (and even Hinduism). Buddhism also has deep traditional roots in Tibet and China, as well as Korea and Japan. In addition, China is the birthplace of Confucianism and Taoism. Confucianism is arguably a system of ethics more than a religion, but Taoism qualifies as a religion (it stresses humility and piety). In Japan, Buddhism (an imported religion) competes with Shintoism (a homegrown religion).

Although China (the "Middle Kingdom") was geographically well positioned to influence the cultural development of Korea, Japan, and Indochina, India as a civilization preceded and rivaled China (though not in a military sense). These two great civilizations and the empires they spawned were divided by geography (the Himalayas), but even more by language, religion, and culture. These differences may be seen to weigh against considering Asia a single region. But as we noted in the previous section, other factors — particularly climate and population dynamics — weigh on the other side.

If language, culture, and religion separated India and China from each other, they also separated both from the West. When the British colonized India they imposed the English language (civil service, schools, and the like). Today, English and Hindi share the center stage as the languages of India's political and social elites. Not so in China, where Europeans intruded later, competed with each other, and never penetrated very deeply into the interior of China (geographically or culturally).

China has proven to be more resistant to outside influence; India has been more receptive (willingly or not) to Westernization. However, one of the recent changes in Asia is a subtle reversal of roles between India and China. After the death of Mao Zedong, China began to open to the West, luring foreign investment and seeking markets around the world. India, by contrast, resisted making changes in its protectionist economic policies. If history is any guide, however, China will stop well short of Westernization and India will open up to globalization. In fact, both of these predictions appear to be coming true.

Latin America In Latin America, the Spanish and Portuguese languages and Roman Catholic religion provide elements of a common "Latin" tradition. The Spanish conquest and, later, the hemispheric dominance of the United States have also aided in the accretion of a common regional political culture. The cruelty, extravagance, and plundering ways of the Spanish in the New World set the tone for politics in the region long before its peoples gained their independence (in the 1820s). One of the salient features of Latin societies today is extreme social inequality — the rich are very rich (and often flaunt it), the poor are very poor. Another traditional feature was corrupt military rule backed by owners of huge estates (called *latifundia*) and aided and abetted by a compliant Roman Catholic establishment (also a large property owner).

At the same time, language and culture, no less than geographic distance, separated Spanish-speaking Latin America from English-speaking North America. Mexico and Canada share a border with the United States but the historic relationship between Washington, D.C., and Ottawa has been consistently more cordial than that between the United States and Mexico. Indeed, the latter have been aptly called "distant neighbors."

Perhaps nothing is more central to the history of Latin America than the role of the colossus to the north — the United States. Beginning with the Monroe Doctrine in 1821, the United States began to assert its "right" to a special sphere of influence in the Western Hemisphere. (See Box 1.3.) Texas and the Southwest (including Nevada, Arizona, and California) were the spoils of war (the Mexican-American War, to be precise). A half century later (in 1898), the United States fought (and won) a war against Spain for control of Cuba (as well as the Philippines). The list goes on, but the bottom line is that the United States is seen throughout much of Latin America as a bully. President Theodore ("Teddy") Roosevelt's advice to "walk softly but carry a big stick" in Latin America was followed by other American presidents, except that after World War II they did not bother to "walk softly." Instead, the United States intervened militarily in several countries to prevent what it viewed as a "threat to peace and stability" (a euphemism for communist subversion during the Cold War).

Even if this interventionist policy was justified, many Latin Americans resented it (and remember it). This lingering ill will is not as evident today as it was in decades past, but it smolders beneath the surface of politics; it is the sort of thing that tends to appear at times of national crisis when demagogues (unprincipled politicians) are looking for an emotional issue to stir up the public and gain a fast popular following.

The authoritarian tradition competes with a revolutionary-democratic tradition personified by Bolivia's Simón Bolívar ("the liberator"), Mexico's Emiliano Zapata, and Venezuela's Romulo Betancourt in the 1950s. Beginning in the 1980s, the liberal tradition has prevailed for the first time ever as civilian democratic rule is now found throughout the region.

The Middle East and North Africa In the Middle East, Islam and the Arabic language impart a cultural unity that sets the nations of this region apart from other nations. As we noted earlier, the culture of the Arab world has roots in ancient civiliza-

Democracy in America

BOX 1.3

The Monroe Doctrine

Not long after the War of 1812, which pitted the United States against Great Britain, Americans began to worry about threats from other European states. The defeat of Napoléon Bonaparte and subsequent restoration of the French monarchy, the creation of the Concert of Europe (a loose alliance of conservative monarchies, including Austria, France, Great Britain, Prussia, Russia, and Spain), and the crumbling of the Spanish Empire in Central and South America set the stage for possible European intervention against revolution in the Western Hemisphere. The United States was the world's leading (and only surviving) example of successful revolution (after Napoléon's downfall). President James Monroe (1817–1825) saw in the anti-Spanish revolts to the south both a danger and an opportunity. Monroe at first hesitated to establish formal diplomatic relations with five new governments — La Plata (now Argentina), Chile, Peru, Colombia, and Mexico — unless Great Britain would do so too, but when the British refused he went ahead on his own. In 1823, when Europe's "concert" of monarchies authorized France to intevene in Spain (where a revolution had just overthrown Bourbon rule), Monroe feared that they might next support an effort by France to retake Spain's lost colonies in the New World. He also worried that the British might try to take Cuba. On the theory that the best defense is a good offense, Monroe took a bold step by enunciating a policy that would eventually gain fame as the Monroe Doctrine. "The American continents," he declared, ". . . are henceforth not to be considered as subjects for future colonization by any European powers." Any attempt by such a power to challenge the sovereignty of existing governments in the Western Hemisphere would be considered "the manifestation of an unfriendly disposition toward the United States." In addition, the United States would return the favor: "Our policy in regard to Europe . . . is not to interfere in the internal concerns of any of its powers."* The Monroe Doctrine nicely illustrates how history, geography, and politics are linked.

*Henry Steele Commager and Milton Cantor, *Documents of American History,* 10th ed., Volume I to 1898 (Englewood Cliffs, N.J.: Prentice-Hall, 1988), pp. 235–237.

tions — the oldest anywhere on earth. The Islamic religion is embraced throughout the region and well beyond, stretching eastward across the face of south and Southeast Asia.

Islam was a latecomer, however. Judaism arrived first on the scene; then came its offshoot, Christianity. Both religions migrated to Europe (indeed, Christianity found a new home there). In the seventh century CE, a charismatic Arab named Muhammad founded a new religion based on elements of Judaism and Christianity. Islam prospered and spread, eventually eclipsing both Judaism and Christianity in the region. Judaism never disappeared but there was no Jewish kingdom or state in the Middle East until after World War II, when Israel was created. Politics in the Middle East have been dominated by the "Arab-Israeli conflict" ever since. The issues in this conflict are more geopolitical (involving disputed territory) than strictly religious or ethnic, but there is no doubt that religion, language, and culture reinforce the animosities that have fueled the wars and terrorism in the region for half a century. Nothing symbolizes the divisive role of religion more than the city of Jerusalem, which is sacred to Jews, Muslims, and Christians alike.

Sub-Saharan Africa Finally, even Black Africa, with its rich cultural diversity, exhibits some common historical and sociopolitical patterns. These include animism (a belief in spirits and demons) and tribalism (political and social organization based on ethnic ties or kinship). In addition, the nations of Black Africa — like those of the Middle East and Asia — remained European colonies until well into the twentieth century.

However, the chief pattern in contemporary Africa south of the Sahara is fragmentation, poverty, and disease. Poverty and epidemics stalk the land. Even in countries rich in oil and other natural resources (for example, Nigeria, the Congo, and Angola) the people are poor and often malnourished. Meanwhile, governments in this region are among the most corrupt in the world. The picture is not pretty, no matter how one looks at it. Why?

To be sure, nature has not always been kind, but the history of colonialism in Africa, the slave trade, the stigma of color imposed by pale-skinned conquerors, the abruptness of the European departure after World War II, and the dislocations and degradation these experiences caused are also important factors. Africa was carved up into unnatural pieces by Europeans over the course of several centuries and then hastily put back together into a patchwork of new states (again by Europeans) after 1945. The plethora of cultures, languages, and tribal-ethnic groups has made the task of nation building difficult nearly everywhere and impossible in many places. The very concept of a nation-state does not fit into the sub-Saharan frame very well at all. In many ways, it is at odds with the ethnic-linguistic-cultural traditions of the region. Seen in this perspective, it is not surprising that Black Africa is in such bad shape.

Economic Disparities

Although concepts like development and modernization are usually associated with the developing nations of Africa, Asia, and Latin America, they have universal validity. Nation-states are the building blocks of the modern international order. Levels of economic and political development vary from one nation or region to the next, but problems such as national integration (or disintegration) are not confined to any one nation or region.

Regional patterns and trends are often multidimensional. Economic patterns quite commonly correlate with population trends and even with environmental changes. The region-by-region sketches that follow illustrate this point.

Western Europe and North America The wealthiest countries, with per capita gross national product (GNP) averaging above $25,000, are nearly all in Western Europe and North America; the most notable exceptions are Japan, South Korea, and Australia. (GNP is the total value of all goods and services produced by the economy of a given country in a single year; **per capita GNP** is the total value divided by the number of people living in that country.) These countries also have the lowest population growth rates, the highest life expectancies, the lowest infant mortality rates, the highest daily calorie supply per capita, and zero illiteracy rates. Statistical indicators of this kind, which can be used as a basis for comparison, allow us to draw inferences about relative standards of living in different countries and regions. (See Figure 1.3.)

Eastern Europe The former socialist countries of Eastern Europe include Russia, the Ukraine, Belarus, Latvia, Lithuania, Estonia, Poland, Hungary, the Czech Republic,

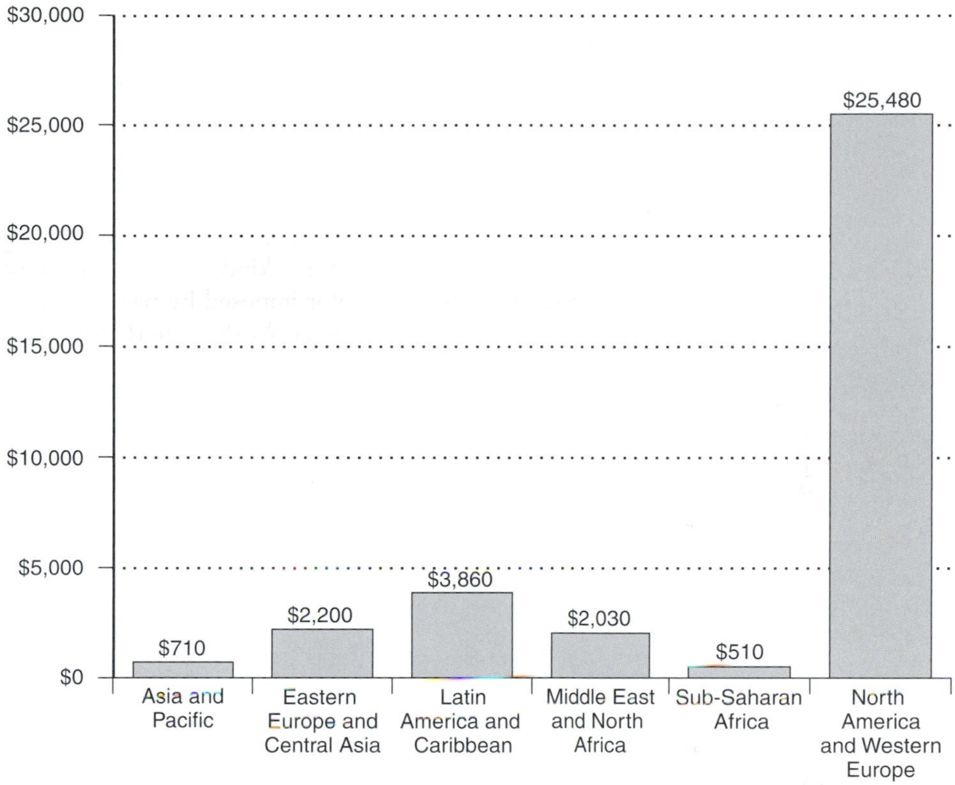

Figure 1.3 How the West Towers over the Rest (GNP per capita in U.S. dollars, 1998)

Source: World Bank Atlas (Washington, D.C.: International Bank for Reconstruction and Development, 2000). Copyright 2000 by World Bank. Reprinted with permission of World Bank.

Slovakia, Bulgaria, Romania, Yugoslavia (Serbia and Montenegro), Croatia, Slovenia, and Bosnia. All of these countries (with the exception of Slovenia) have per capita annual incomes that are far below those of Western Europe and North America. (Slovenia, the richest of the Slavic countries, is about equal to Portugal and Spain, the poorest of the EU countries.) On the other hand, population growth rates are generally low, life expectancy is high (over age seventy), and illiteracy rates are less than 5 percent. Agriculture continues to play a significantly larger role in the national economy than in the postindustrial West. Per capita GNP in the former communist states actually fell during the 1990s, reflecting painful adjustments of shifting from centrally planned to market-based economies. The key point here is that the figures — as well as the patterns and trends they trace — reflect certain striking similarities in the experience of most every nation in the region.

Asia Asia is characterized by glaring disparities between the richest and poorest countries. Japan ranks second in the world as an economic power, trailing only the United States. Its per capita GNP in the late 1990s was among the highest in the world (higher in real terms, for example, than in Great Britain, France, or Germany). By contrast, Bangladesh, with a population nearly the size of Japan's, had one of the smallest per capital GNPs in the world. Asia also has the two most populous countries on the planet, China (1.3 billion) and India (1.1 billion), plus four other countries — Indonesia (214 million), Japan (127 million), Pakistan (150 million), and Bangladesh (135 million) — that rank in the top ten. These six countries account for over half the world's current population. But population growth rates have fallen in Asia due in part to tough population control policies in India and China and in part to rapid economic development in certain countries — in stark contrast to the continuing high birthrates in the Arab world and sub-Saharan Africa.

Although Asia is still the setting for some of the world's worst poverty, it is also the scene of many of the most dynamic economies. Joining Japan, the countries of South Korea, Taiwan, Hong Kong, and Singapore have become high-tech trading nations. Communist China has had one of the fastest-growing economies since the early 1990s, and the economies of Thailand, Malaysia, and Indonesia grew not only in absolute terms but also in per capita terms between 1980 and 1991. Indeed, the phenomenal economic growth in Asia can be viewed as a regional trend. If it continues unabated, it will propel Asia to a dominant position in the world economy within a decade or two.

Latin America Latin America's richest countries (Mexico, Costa Rica, Panama, Venezuela, Brazil, Argentina, and Chile) have about the same per capita income levels as the most prosperous former socialist countries (Poland, Hungary, the Czech Republic, Slovenia, and Estonia). On most other social and economic measures, Latin America falls somewhere between North America and Western Europe, on the one hand, and the Arab world or sub-Saharan Africa on the other.

Economically, the region can be subdivided into Central and South America, with most of the relatively prosperous states located south of the Isthmus of Panama and most of the poorest states situated north of it. The richer states include Colombia, Venezuela, Brazil, Argentina, Uruguay, and Chile. Of these, Chile was the most impressive performer in the 1990s. The poorest states are Guatemala, Honduras, El Salvador, and Nicaragua in Central America, and Bolivia, Peru, Paraguay, Ecuador, Suriname, and Guyana in South America. Based on estimates of purchasing power parity (PPP) done by the World Bank every year, the average person living in Poland, for example, was considerably better off than his or her counterpart living in Peru or Paraguay (not to mention impoverished Nicaragua or Honduras), but not as well off as the average person living in Chile or Argentina. If you were an "average" citizen living in Brazil or Mexico, Venezuela or Colombia (or even Panama, surprisingly) your income expectations would have been more or less on a par with the average wage earner in Poland.

The Middle East and North Africa The gap between the richest countries and the poorest in the "Arab world" (as this region is often called) is actually a gulf. Per capita GNP in the United Arab Emirates is thought to be among the highest in the world (although the government there chooses not to make this information public). In

Sudan, by contrast, it is among the lowest. This region is the only one in the world that depends so singularly for its wealth on one resource, oil. Because of this lopsided oil dependence, the region as a whole is vulnerable to disruptions in the world market. The oil glut of the early 1980s hit the oil-exporting Arab states so hard that most of them actually registered negative per capita growth rates between 1980 and 1991.

High population growth rates in the Middle East match those of sub-Saharan Africa. The Middle Eastern Arab states grew at a rate of more than 3 percent a year in the 1980s (compared to less than 0.5 percent in most of Western Europe, for example). The average Arab woman, like her African counterpart, bears five or more children. Life expectancy is significantly higher in the Arab world than in sub-Saharan Africa but lower than in Europe, North America, China, Australia, and most of Latin America. The infant mortality rate is similar to Latin America's but much higher than in the other regions.

A striking trait common to all Arab countries — a trait related to Arab culture — is that women constitute less than one-fourth of the labor force (the lowest of any region in the world). The only exceptions in the Middle East or North Africa are two non-Arab countries: Israel and Turkey.

Sub-Saharan Africa The countries of sub-Saharan Africa have annual per capita incomes of $500 or less. (See Box 1.4.) The share of agriculture in GNP is generally among the highest in the world; the share of investment in GNP is among the lowest. Many countries in sub-Saharan Africa still have an average annual population growth rate of more than 3 percent. Life expectancy at birth, with few exceptions, is fifty years or less (compared with Western Europe and North America, where it is seventy-three years or more). If you are born in Sierra Leone (West Africa), you can expect to die by age thirty-seven. The **fertility rate** (number of live births per woman of childbearing age) is the highest in the world, as is the **infant mortality rate.** (The latter measures the number of infant deaths relative to the number of live births in a given year; see Figure 1.4.) Unsurprisingly, the daily calorie supply per capita is the lowest in the world, as is annual water use per capita.

A popular misconception about sub-Saharan Africa is that it is overpopulated. In fact, Africa has the lowest population density of any region covered in this book. The population problem Africa faces is in the future, given its dangerously high growth rate. It is also a ratio problem: the ratio of population to resources, schools, jobs, arable land, and so on. (See Figure 1.5.)

Of course, any broad overview of regional differences is bound to neglect many subtle physical and cultural characteristics that distinguish one region from another. Such an overview does, however, illustrate the fact that major geographic, cultural, social, and economic differences do exist and suggests that a regional approach to comparative politics is likely to yield valuable insights into the reasons why nations are not all governed in the same way and why certain patterns of politics are either unique to a particular region or more prevalent in some regions than in others. That said, the regional differences painted here in broad brushstrokes are examined in greater depth and detail in subsequent chapters.

A Rich Nation, A Poor Continent BOX 1.4

by Jeffrey Sachs
New York Times, July 9, 2003

At a time when President Bush has lavished billions of dollars in tax cuts on the richest Americans, his trip to Africa presents him with the perfect opportunity to call on them to take some responsibility for the dire state of the world's poorest citizens. According to a recent report from the Internal Revenue Service, some 400 super-rich Americans had an average income of nearly $174 million each, or a combined income of $69 billion, in 2000. Incredibly, that's more than the combined incomes of the 166 million people living in four of the countries that the president is visiting this week: Nigeria, Senegal, Uganda and Botswana. America's richest individuals could actually change the course of Africa's history . . .

. . . poverty throughout the continent is a matter of life and death — indeed, mainly death. While the average life expectancy in the United States is now 77 years, it is less than 50 years in most of Africa, and less than 40 years in some of the AIDS-ravaged countries. Until the pandemics of AIDS, tuberculosis, malaria and other killer diseases are brought under control in Africa, economic development and political stability will remain crippled. A breakthrough on disease control, conversely, would help to unleash a virtuous circle of rising productivity, better education, lower fertility rates — and then lead to further increases in health and prosperity.

Yet Africa's poverty makes this an unbeatable problem without more help from the United States and other wealthy countries. In the United States, annual

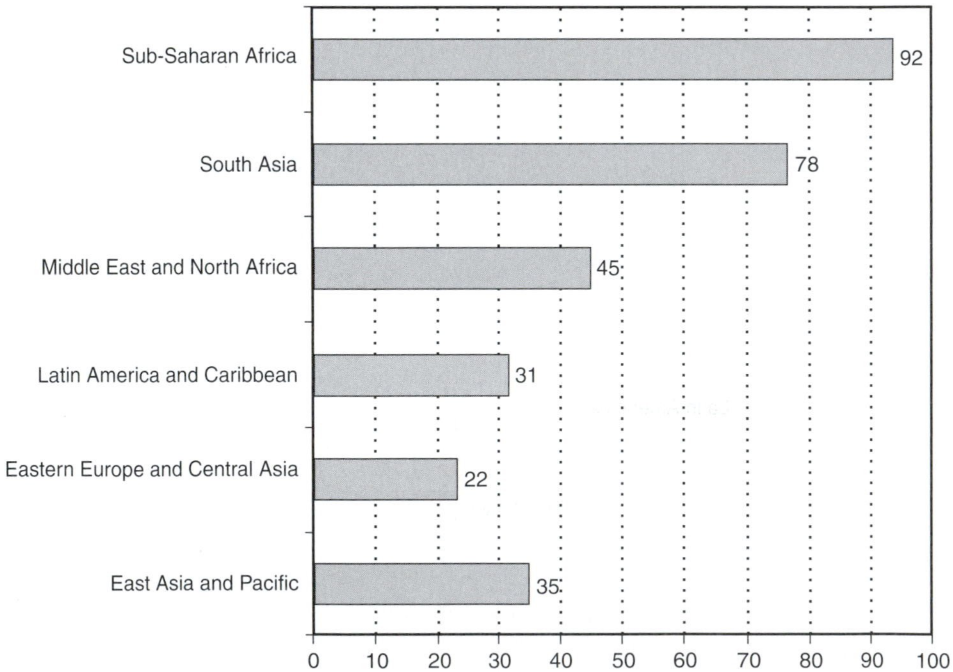

Figure 1.4 Deadly Differences: Infant Mortality Rates by Region (deaths per 1,000 live births)

Source: World Bank Atlas (Washington, D.C.: International Bank for Reconstruction and Development, 2000). Copyright 2000 by World Bank. Reprinted with permission of World Bank.

public spending on health care averages about $2,000 per person, according to the World Health Organization. In Africa, public health spending is around $10 per person per year — not enough to keep the population alive.

[According to the World Health Organization, if] rich countries contributed a total of around $25 billion per year, the increased investments in disease prevention and treatment could prevent around eight million deaths each year in poor countries throughout the world. The United States' share would be around $8 billion, given the size of its economy in relation to other donors. Most of this money is needed in Africa, where the countries are among the poorest and the disease burden is the highest.

Here's where America's richest 400 could change history. In 1995, the top 400 income earners paid almost 30 percent of their incomes in taxes. After the Bush tax cuts and other factors, the proportion will be less than 18 percent. Suppose the super-rich applied their tax savings toward Africa's survival. That extra 10 percent of income — which translates to nearly $7 billion based on the incomes in 2000 — would provide a huge chunk of the $8 billion that the United States should contribute to the global health care effort . . . could there be a better way to give meaning to vast wealth?

Of course, it's strange to rely on only the goodwill of a few hundred super-rich people to save the lives of millions of the poor. All Americans need to share responsibility for such an effort, not only for humanitarian reasons, but also for practical public health reasons. Yet given the huge tax cuts that have gone to the wealthiest Americans, the moral and practical obligations facing them are greater than ever.

Our world is dangerously out of kilter when a few hundred people in the United States command more income than 166 million people in Africa — with millions of the poor dying each year as a result of their impoverishment. Perhaps most remarkable of all is that such bald facts are rarely noticed in this country. . . .

Jeffrey D. Sachs is director of the Earth Institute at Columbia University. The full article is available on the World Wide Web at www.nytimes.com/2003/07/09/opinion.

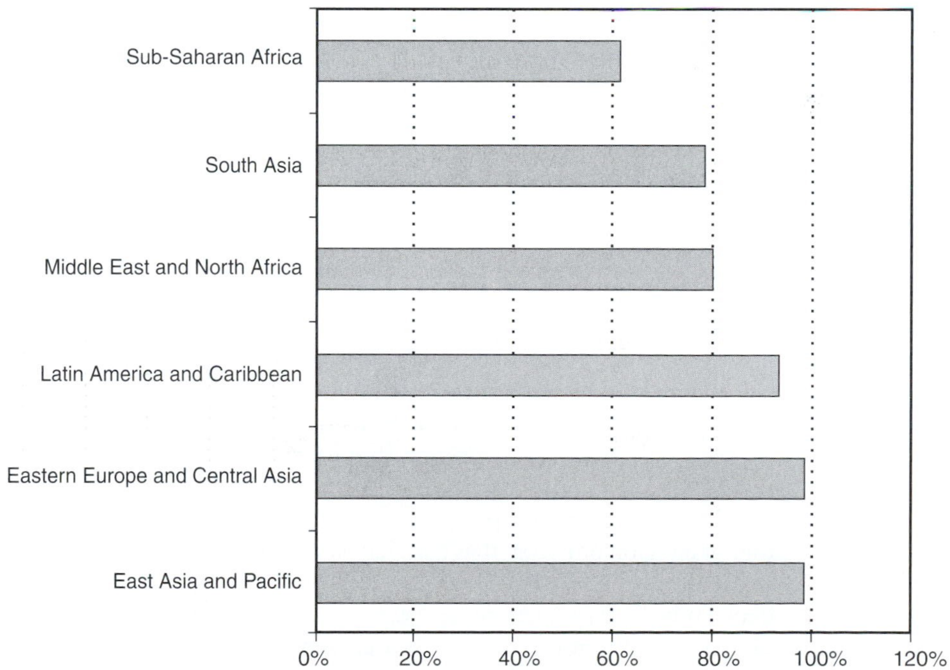

Figure 1.5 Right or Privilege? Basic Education (net primary enrollment ratio)

Source: UNESCO estimates, 1999.

A Conceptual Framework: Three Questions

This book combines the ancient Greek penchant for asking fruitful questions with an appreciation of the insights offered by modern-day students of human behavior — in particular, behavior relevant to the problems of governing complex modern societies. Three questions serve as a conceptual framework for this book. The first question deals with political setting, the second with patterns of rule, and the third with problems and prospects. To understand why governments of a certain type appear in a given time and place it is necessary to consider the background and context of politics (political setting). The distribution of political power and authority (patterns of rule) in a society has a direct bearing on who gets what, when, and how. It answers the all-important question: Who decides? Finally, to evaluate the performance of a government it is necessary to consider what problems the society is facing and how effective (or ineffective) the government is at devising solutions. Solving problems in politics is the task of public policy. Examining a country's prospects in the light of its problems — and its government's attempts to find solutions — requires the observer to look at current policies and trends for clues as to what the future might hold.

Political Setting: How Do Unique Factors Such as Environment, Culture, and History Influence Politics in Different Countries and Regions?

We will answer this question by asking and exploring a series of related questions. First, how do environmental factors such as geography, climate, and natural resources affect political values, perceptions, traditions, and institutions in a given region or nation? This question involves *political ecology* — the relationship between political institutions and the physical or natural environment to which the societies of a given region have had to adapt.

Second, do cultural factors — religious, ethnic, and linguistic differences — complicate the problems of governing? Do they stress the political system in ways that threaten stability? Do they disrupt the economy? Do these factors preclude or necessitate any particular forms of government? The focus here is on the *political culture* (civic values including attitudes, beliefs, myths, and collective memories that motivate people) and *political socialization* (the ways in which political culture is transmitted from one generation to the next).

Third, are there any particularly traumatic, triumphant, or tragic events in the history of a region or nation that have left an indelible mark on the character of its people? Every society has a collective memory in which it stores "data" about episodes and incidents in its history. Victories and defeats in war, revolutions, plagues and other natural disasters, and times of trouble or a golden age act as a kind of lens or filter through which people perceive the world and interpret current events. As a consequence, political perception — a close relative of attitude, opinion, and orientation — rarely, if ever, corresponds perfectly to reality. Just as we need to know something about a person's history to understand that person's personality, so we need to know something about a people's history to understand how *social psychology* impinges on politics.

One well-known example of how environmental and ethnic factors can influence political institutions and cultures can be found in Africa and Asia. When the European **imperialist powers** (countries such as Great Britain, France, Belgium, Portugal, and the Netherlands) pulled back from colonial territories in Africa and Asia after World War II, little thought was given to whether the new nation-states created by the retreating colonizers would be viable. As a consequence, they often were (and are) a collection of many different ethnolinguistic groups, frequently lacking natural resources and arable land and having few if any common folkways, religious traditions, or shared experiences to hold the society together. Ethnic conflict has often occurred in the context of poverty, lack of formal education, unemployment, epidemics, and overpopulation in the former colonies; given this volatile mixture, it is perhaps not too surprising that bureaucratic-authoritarian regimes, often awash in corruption, have been common in the former colonial regions until recently. Moreover, the rejection of Western institutions (including democracy) was a natural concomitant of the anti-imperialism that swept across the so-called Third World in the second half of the twentieth century.

Patterns of Rule: How and Why Do Political Institutions, Patterns, and Trends Vary from One Region of the World to Another and What Forces Drive Change?

The forms of government existing in a given region vary according to time and place. Democracies have existed in North America and Western Europe for a long time, but until recently authoritarian rule was common nearly everywhere else. Democracies and authoritarian governments differ in important ways that deserve our attention. Not all authoritarian governments are equally repressive, however. By the same token, not all democracies are equally liberal. What kinds of democracies exist and how do they differ? What about authoritarian governments? What are the salient characteristics of totalitarianism (the most extreme form of authoritarian rule)?

If the patterns of rule vary, so do the trends. At different times, political waves roll across whole regions. Democratization has been the most recent such wave. Democracies are functioning in places where they did not exist until recently. In some places, authoritarian rule is changing, but it is premature to say that democracy has triumphed. In other places, dictators have trampled on fledgling democratic institutions.

What causes a given form of government to appear when and where it does? Similarly, what starts a trend (or swing) in one direction or the other (democracy versus authoritarianism)? Some answers — or parts of an answer — can be found outside of a given region. Other answers can only be found within individual countries. And some answers are common to whole regions. It is often said that "imitation is the sincerest form of flattery" and that "nothing succeeds like success." When one country's economy takes off (for example, Japan's or Germany's) other countries in the region take notice. When a country wins a war other countries take notice. Hence, when the United

States won the Cold War against the Soviet Union, democracy and free enterprise (keeping the role of the state in the economy at a minimum) received a big boost all around the world. We can only begin to answer this question here; other answers will be found in the chapters to follow.

The desire for prosperity is universal — every nation wants a healthy and growing economy. The onset of globalization has meant that countries are more or less forced to choose the ways of the West. The healthiest economies in the world today are market economies (based on the laws of supply and demand rather than state planning) located in North America and Western Europe. The richest countries are home to the biggest banks and stock markets. The governments of these rich countries (led by the United States) have the biggest voice in key international organizations, including the World Bank, which makes hard currency loans to governments in need of financial help. The United States and its European allies also have the largest influence in the World Trade Organization (WTO), which sets the rules for international trade and decides who will be allowed to participate on equal terms and who will not. (For example, the United States blocked admission of the People's Republic of China until very recently.)

By viewing societies and governments from a regional perspective, we can easily observe certain patterns that may be less than obvious if we merely focus on individual countries. For example, many people know that Great Britain, France, and Germany are democracies (governments in which political power is vested in popularly elected legislature). Fewer people know that most Western European countries did not have full-fledged legislatures elected by universal male suffrage (all adult males allowed to vote) at the turn of the twentieth century or that since the mid-1970s all the countries of Western Europe have been democratically governed — a truly extraordinary development that is generally taken for granted now. Moreover, following the collapse of communism in Eastern Europe (1989), it is probable that democracy and market economies will become the norm for the entire continent in the twenty-first century.

Not every region displays the uniformity found in Europe; nonetheless, distinct patterns and trends do exist. Rarely do democracies and authoritarian systems coexist easily in the same region. Democracies are most comfortable with other democracies; dictatorships are distinctly uncomfortable with democracies, if for no other reason than this: people desire the same liberty their neighbors have. We will, however, note where different types of governments do coexist within the same region and shed as much light as possible on why this is the case.

Although our main concern is to look at the fundamental forms of government found in a given region, we will not ignore important differences between and among practitioners of a particular form. For example, Great Britain, France, and Germany are all democracies, but they show major differences in the way they conduct elections, organize the government, apportion political power, and choose their chief executives. By contrast, the Middle East displays a variety of authoritarian regimes: the theocratic (religion-based) Iranian state; the feudal monarchies of the Arabian Peninsula; the modern monarchies of Jordan and Morocco; the personal dictatorships of Syria, Iraq, and Libya; and the mixed regime of Egypt.

All the political systems touched on here will be defined and examined in Chapter 2. Describing the patterns and trends of different regions of the globe is relatively simple; explaining them is not. Later chapters will suggest explanations, but let the reader be warned: clear-cut answers are not always possible in the study of politics.

Problems and Prospects: How Effectively Do the Political Systems under Examination Actually Perform the Functions of Governance?

This question raises many other questions. How do we measure or even define success (effectiveness) in the governance of a given society? Is there one set of criteria with universal validity or is success culturally (that is, locally rather than globally) determined? Can a political system be effective if the economy is going nowhere and the people are poor by Western standards? Are Western standards the same as global standards? If so, why? Because Western standards embody some universal ideals or because the West is economically and militarily dominant?

Aristotle argued that the proper aim of politics is not simply to sustain life but to seek the good life. Philosophers since Aristotle who have contemplated this concept have differed greatly about its meaning. What exactly is the good life?

Our study of comparative politics will take into account both the tangible and intangible "goods" implicit in the notion of the good life. Liberty is small consolation for people who are starving or destitute — hence we look at economic policy and performance in each region and country being studied. By the same token, many people who have adequate food and shelter find life empty and monotonous if they lack freedom of speech or freedom of religion. Thus, we also look at recent elections, the political opposition, the role of the mass media, and the party (or parties in power), as well as who leads the government and how.

The difficulty in making comparisons is not one of knowing where people are well off and where they are oppressed or wanting. Rather it is connecting their condition with a particular political order that gets complicated. To what extent is poverty in a given context a function of environment (for example, frequent famines), and to what extent is it a function of politics? For example, where poverty and conflict are both present they are most likely related — if the governments involved are not seeking ways, and taking all possible steps, to stop a prolonged war (either by defeating the enemy or negotiating a settlement), they are at least partially to blame for the suffering that results. Where freedoms are denied or curtailed, are popular sacrifices compensated by a steadily increasing standard of living or greater security? For example, Singapore (a city-state at the southern tip of Malaysia in Southeast Asia) is very prosperous, but it is not very democratic by Western standards. If the people of Singapore are happy with the trade-off between prosperity and liberty, it is, arguably, nobody else's business.

Questions of this kind defy simple answers. But as Socrates showed long ago, it is worthwhile to grapple with puzzling questions even if clear answers are sometimes beyond our reach.

In this book we take a regional approach for the most practical of all reasons: It works. Looking at the world through the prism of regions provides both a simple organizing principle and a more fruitful basis than globalism for explaining the various patterns of politics, mass opinion, and public policy that we will encounter on our academic "excursion" around the globe this semester. Its beauty lies not only in its simplicity, but also in its economy — it explains the most with the least.

We begin with the most familiar region (Western Europe) and countries (the United Kingdom, France, and Germany) and then move on to Eastern Europe (less familiar), Asia, Latin America, the Middle East, and finally sub-Saharan Africa. All of these latter regions are quite unfamiliar to most Americans, so you are not alone if you know little or nothing about Nigeria or the Czech Republic right now. But take heart: by the end of the term you will be on top of the world.

SUMMARY

Comparative politics is the original "form" of political science going all the way back to the ancient Greeks. Although the regions of the world are difficult to define precisely, a regional approach to comparative politics has advantages over other approaches. First, it highlights social, cultural, historical, economic, and political features common to all or most of the states within a given geographic area. Second, it provides a basis for comparison not only between and among states but also across regional boundaries. To the extent that generalizations can be made about politics within regions, a regional approach is more efficient than more traditional state-centered approaches. At the same time, choosing key countries as case studies within each major region — Western Europe, Slavic (Eastern) Europe, the Middle East, Asia, sub-Saharan Africa, and Latin America — gives concrete form to abstract generalizations.

KEY TERMS

ethnocentrism
comparative politics
good life
scientific method
deductive approach
normative political theory
inductive approach
behavioralism
transnational
subordinate systems
globalization
per capita GNP
fertility rate
infant mortality rate
imperialist powers

STUDY QUESTIONS

1. What is a "region"? How important is geography in defining a region? What other factors are important, and why?
2. What are the major regions of the world? Can most "super-regions" be divided into subregions? If so, what are some examples of such a subdivision?

3. Is North America a region? If so, what are its boundaries? Are Mexico and Canada natural parts of this region? Why, or why not? Is the North American Free Trade Agreement (NAFTA) logical when viewed in a regional perspective?
4. How do history and culture shape political traditions and practices from region to region? Give some examples of regional patterns that you have read about or perhaps witnessed firsthand. (Suggestion: Ask a foreign student on your campus to answer this question; not only will you learn a lot but also you will probably make a new friend.)
5. To what degree do such variables as climate, resources, food, and population play a role in shaping political institutions? Do you think that such variables might also influence national character? If so, can you think of any examples?

SUGGESTED READINGS

Aristotle. *Politics.* Ernest Baker, ed. and trans. New York: Oxford University Press, 1958.

Cantori, Louis T., and Stephen L. Spiegel. *The International Politics of Regions: A Comparative Approach.* Englewood Cliffs, N.J.: Prentice-Hall, 1970.

Diamond, Jared. *Guns, Germs, and Steel: The Fate of Human Societies.* New York: Norton, 1997.

Friedman, Thomas. *The Lexus and the Olive Tree: Understanding Globalization.* Garden City, N.Y.: Anchor, 2000.

Lane, Ruth. *The Art of Comparative Politics.* Boston: Allyn & Bacon, 1997.

Sealey, Raphael. *A History of the Greek City-States ca. 700–338 B.C.* Berkeley: University of California, 1976.

SUGGESTED WEB SITES

http://www.cia.gov/cia/publications/factbook/
http://www.worldbank.org/
http://www.agora.stm.it
http://www.gd.net.org/
http://www.state.gov/
http://world.localgov.org/

NOTES

1. Mattei Dogan and Dominique Pelassy, *How to Compare Nations: Strategies in Comparative Politics* (Chatham, N.J.: Chatham House, 1984), p. 5.
2. Aristotle, *Politics,* Ernest Baker, ed. and trans. (New York: Oxford University Press, 1958); see especially the Introduction, pp. xxviii–xxix.

3. Louis T. Cantori and Stephen L. Spiegel, *The International Politics of Regions: A Comparative Approach* (Englewood Cliffs, N.J.: Prentice-Hall, 1970), p. 6.
4. See John Mearsheimer, *The Tragedy of the Great Powers* (New York: Norton, 2001), pp. 40–42.
5. Michael Brecher, "The Subordinate System of Southern Asia," *Asian Survey,* vol. 15, no. 2 (January 1963), p. 220. Brecher adds two additional criteria: The principal units of power (nation-states) are relatively inferior to the dominant units in the global system; and changes in the global system have a greater effect on the subordinate system than vice versa. These two criteria, however, raise serious questions; for example, they would appear to rule out Eastern Europe as a subsystem when the Soviet Union was one of the two "dominant units" in the world or the Western Hemisphere today because the United States is both a global and regional power.
6. See, for example, Jeffrey Sachs, "A New Map of the World," *The Economist,* July 24, 2000, pp. 99–101. Sachs points out that "15% of the earth's population provides nearly all of the world's technology innovations." About half of the world's population "adopt[s] these technologies in production and consumption." The rest — roughly a third of the global community — is "technologically disconnected." Sachs calls for a wholesale rethinking of development and concludes that "the shortcomings of the current strategy of globalization [are] painfully evident."
7. Jared Diamond, *Guns, Germs, and Steel: The Fate of Human Societies* (New York: Norton, 1997).
8. Immanuel Wallerstein, *The Modern World System I: Capitalist Agriculture and the Origins of the European World Economy in the 16th Century* (New York: Academic Press, 1979), pp. 38–57.
9. See Henry J. Merry, *Montesquieu's System of Natural Government* (West Lafayette, Ind.: Purdue University Press, 1970), especially pp. 51–53.
10. Jurg Steiner, *European Democracies* (White Plains, N.Y.: Longman, 1986), p. 1.
11. See Hans Morganthau and Ken Thompson, *Politics among Nations: The Struggle for Power and Peace* (New York: Knopf, 1985), pp. 233–240.

CHAPTER 2

Models, Regimes, and Regions

This chapter looks at political models and regimes found in the contemporary world. We will focus on the **state,** defined as a society with a government operating within recognized territorial boundaries. A sovereign state is one that is politically independent, makes its own laws, and takes precautions against attack or encroachment by other states. Sovereignty exists as a *political* fact when a government controls or rules a country, and as a *legal* fact when other states formally recognize its existence.

The Idea of the State

For a time, the state nearly disappeared from the radar screen of political science in the United States. Caught up in the rush to escape the constraints of the "old" political science (which focused on government and treated it as a single, unified entity), some political scientists argued that the concept of a unified state characterized by a harmony of interests (rather than constant conflict) did not fit reality. These behavioralists (as they are called) shifted the emphasis from the formal institutions and written rules of government to the actual *behavior* of the individuals involved in the processes of government. The American political scene, they argued, presented a messy picture in the face of constant wrangling between Congress and the White House, the Supreme Court and Congress, the federal government and state governments, and the like. Indeed, it often seems as though nothing ever gets settled in American politics (witness the abortion issue or school prayer) — a "fact" that reinforces the argument for a pluralistic view of society and a downgrading of the state's role in the political system.

Not everybody jumped on the bandwagon to abandon the state, however. For example, Samuel Huntington, a famous Harvard political science professor, maintained that government in the United States is like government nowhere else in the world and therefore the American experience is not necessarily the best guide to understanding politics in other places. Focusing on the key role of the state as the stabilizer and source of law and order in society, Huntington demonstrated the value of this approach in a pioneering book on political development. The logic of Huntington's thesis is compelling: the first order of priority in newly independent states, he argued, is to keep order (or prevent disorder), which means, among other things, that the role of the military in internal politics is often a key factor (by contrast, note that the military plays almost no role in politics in the United States).[1]

One thing is certain: the state is central to an understanding of political systems and processes in the modern world. We turn now to a consideration of the different types of states (also called "regimes") in existence today.

Democracy or Dictatorship: Procrustean Models

In Greek mythology, Procrustes was a giant who forced hapless travelers to fit into one of two beds of unequal length by stretching them or cutting off their legs. Likewise, political observers have a tendency to fit all political regimes into one of two models: democracy or dictatorship.

Within the discipline there is no general agreement among comparativists (specialists in comparative politics) as to how best to classify political systems. At least since Aristotle first attempted to do so, the temptation has been irresistible. Indeed, classification of species and specimens is one hallmark of science.

The most common classification schemes stress concentration (or diffusion) of power or levels of economic development (often termed *modernization*). Classifications based on power distribution tend to draw a sharp distinction between democratic and authoritarian regimes. **Democratic regimes** (described later) are typically based on formal constitutions that protect citizens' rights and call for free elections at regular intervals. **Authoritarian regimes** concentrate power in the hands of one ruler or a ruling few (often high-ranking military officers) and rely on ideology, religion, or personal charisma (rather than constitutions and elections) as a source of moral authority. During the heyday of the **Cold War,** a third form called **totalitarian** was often added to the analysis as a separate and distinct regime type. Totalitarianism, as we will see, is an extreme form of authoritarian rule that is so named because this type of regime seeks a total concentration of political power and obliterates individual rights.

Other classifications appear at first glance to deviate from this simple breakdown, but on closer examination are really quite similar. Thus, one scholar identifies the following four types: folk systems, bureaucratic-authoritarian systems, reconciliation systems, and mobilization systems.[2] Except for folk systems (found in premodern societies), the "new" models in this scheme closely resemble the old ones — only the names have been changed. The bureaucratic-authoritarian model is obviously nothing new; reconciliation systems are in fact democracies (found primarily in Western Europe and North America until recently); and mobilization systems fit squarely into the totalitarian model (long exemplified by the former Soviet Union and its satellites, North Korea, Cuba, and the People's Republic of China).

For a long time, classifications based on levels of development featured two basic stereotypes: developed and **developing countries.** The latter are also known as **less developed countries (LDCs)** or **underdeveloped countries (UDCs)**. This simplistic dichotomy has recently given way to more complex models better able to accommodate the diversity found in all regions of the globe today, as we will see later in this and subsequent chapters.

Thanks to the Cold War, two sharply contrasting political systems — **constitutional democracy** and **totalitarian dictatorship** — made an indelible mark on world politics in the twentieth century. The Cold War was not only about the rivalry between the United States and the Soviet Union, but also between two diametrically opposed political systems. It is still possible that in some places where totalitarian structures toppled at the end of the Cold War (including Russia, Ukraine, Belarus, Georgia, Armenia, Azerbaijan, and the Central Asian "republics"), they will be supplanted by more traditional forms of top-down **authoritarian rule** rather than by pluralistic political systems. Is liberal democracy really on the advance worldwide, as optimists in the West believe?[3] Can totalitarianism now be relegated to the dustbin of history? We cannot answer these questions with certainty — no one can. What we can (and will) do is to look at patterns and trends around the world and try to imagine what the future holds. In political matters, the best forecasts are often based on well-informed intuition.

A common obstacle to clear thinking in any field of study is the tendency to confuse models of reality with reality itself. This observation is especially pertinent to political science, partly because the stuff of politics is largely intangible. Thus, a note of caution is in order at the outset. The political systems (or models) sketched here are theoretical constructs — they do not exist in pure form anywhere. Nonetheless, it is useful to discuss different forms of government in the abstract before moving on to describe and analyze concrete forms. Hence, this chapter will rely more heavily on deductive reasoning than will subsequent chapters.

Constitutional Democracy: Presidential versus Parliamentary

World War I dealt a deathblow to the monarchies of Europe and cleared the way for a new era. Whereas there were many monarchies and few republics at the start of the twentieth century, the situation was reversed at its end. By 2000, democracies were well entrenched in Western Europe and North America and had emerged in Eastern Europe and Latin America, as well. In Asia, Japan and India had been constitutional democracies since 1947. Several other Asian countries had also taken steps toward democratization, and the dawning of democracy in sub-Saharan Africa in the nineties heightened the sense that political liberty was finally coming of age. But despite the adoption of democratic forms in many developing countries real political power remained corrupted, concentrated, and controlled by a ruling elite.[4]

In the era of decolonization after World War II, various national governments and international organizations instituted programs of economic and technical assistance to the developing areas in the belief that durable, modern political institutions require economic development and social progress. Often, the hidden agenda was to establish democratic governments that would serve as bulwarks against revolution and would align themselves with the West. The Cold War formed the background for much of the economic and military assistance to the **Third World**.*

If democracy is making inroads in many regions of the globe today it is in part because it has been promoted by the United States at a time when America is the pre-eminent power in the world. But the other part of the story is domestic rather than international, local rather than global: It is the story of people with hopes and dreams who are drawn to a given "model" not because of ideology or abstract ideals because one political-economic system works and another does not. As Winston Churchill, the illustrious British prime minister during World War II, once remarked, "Democracy is the worst form of government ever invented — except for all the others."

To say that one system works better than another, however, begs the question, what do people want or expect from government? Although there is always room for argument, the answer is surprisingly simple. At a minimum, people everywhere want security (food, shelter, police protection, health care, and so on). Most people also want prosperity (at least a job and enough income to live decently) and liberty (although precisely what kind and how much varies). People typically do not demand complete equality but reject glaring inequality. Finally, people want "justice," which is an elusive concept but almost always entails some combination of the other four "core values" (security, prosperity, liberty, and equality). Justice in a narrower sense requires an independent legal system based on fair laws and an impartial bench.

What type of system is most likely (a) to pursue these ends and (b) to do so successfully? The reader is probably thinking that the answer is easy: democracy. Fine, but what *kind* of democracy? (There's more than one kind, of course.) There are two basic forms of democracy in the contemporary world: presidential and parliamentary. The United States exemplifies the former, Great Britain the latter.

Presidential Democracy: The American Model

The system we are calling **presidential democracy** features a popularly elected chief executive (president) with a wide array of constitutional powers. It is a system that is grounded in the political theory of the American Founders (most notably James Madison, Alexander Hamilton, and Thomas Jefferson), as well as the early American colonists' experience in local self-government. A key concept in this "new science of politics," as Madison called it, is the **separation of powers,** which sets up the legislative, executive, and judicial branches of the national government as distinct structures, each responsible to different constituencies for the exercise of their respective powers and

*The term *Third World* is shorthand for the developing countries. It has fallen into disuse due to disparities that now exist in Asia and elsewhere, the diversity of economic systems, and the end of the Cold War.

Democracy in America

BOX 2.1

A Presidential System? Yes, but No "Blank Check"

"But the great security against a gradual concentration of the several powers in the same department, consists in giving to those who administer each department, the necessary constitutional means, and personal motives, to resist encroachments of the others. . . . Ambition must be made to counteract ambition."

Thus wrote James Madison in *The Federalist* No. 51. The Constitution of the United States represents the American Founders' attempt to institutionalize a system of checks and balances. The Congress makes the laws, not the president. The president can veto legislation, but the Congress can override a veto with a two-thirds majority in both houses. These are but two familiar examples of how these branches counter-balance each other.

So why call it a "presidential" system? First, the president is the only national leader with a broad popular mandate, the only figure who has a legitimate claim to speak for, and to act on behalf of, the majority. Second, in the twentieth century, the president's role as commander in chief during two world wars and the Cold War underscored the importance of strong executive leadership.

But as the forced resignation of Richard Nixon (1973) and the impeachment (but not conviction) of Bill Clinton (1999) prove, Congress can still check presidential power. And as the dashed reelection hopes of both Jimmy Carter (1980) and George Bush (1992) prove, the electorate can also check presidents.

---

functions. (The branches are separate in the sense that no member of the government can serve in more than one branch at any given time.)

The Founders' basic idea was a simple one. What governments do, above all, is make and enforce society's rules. Given that governments must formulate, enforce, and interpret laws (rules), it was logical and rational to create a legislature to perform the first of these functions (rule making), an executive to carry out the second function (rule implementation), and a judiciary to oversee the third function (rule interpretation). This is one reason why American (rather than, say, British or French) political scientists developed the theory of structural-functionalism nearly a century and a half later — a theory, which, although it purported to be universal just happened to fit the specific American experience like a glove.* (Remember that the American Revolution occurred during the Enlightenment in the second half of the eighteenth century, which is also known as the Age of Reason; contemporary political thought in the United States is rooted in the rationalism and pragmatism of that earlier period.)

Because the Founders believed that the concentration of power inevitably leads to **tyranny,** they created an ingenious and intricate system of checks and balances — a system made possible only by the very separation of powers mentioned earlier. (See Box 2.1.) Hence, the U.S. Congress is given the "power of the purse," meaning the power to levy taxes and to decide how and where to spend the revenues flowing into the

---

*Structural-functionalism posits that political systems are similar to machines that have certain functions. They can only perform these functions efficiently if they have the right sort of structures (institutions) for doing so. Hence, governments not only must be able to make rules, but also to enforce and interpret the rules. Simplified, these "functions" of government require corresponding structures (legislature, executive, and judiciary). These "structures" in turn correspond to the branches of government found in the U.S. Constitution.

national treasury each year. The president may (and does) propose an annual budget and members of the cabinet, consisting of the heads of the various departments and agencies, may try to influence congressional appropriations (spending bills), but Congress has the final say in money matters. The U.S. Congress also has the power to regulate interstate and foreign commerce — a vital function in a federal system with fifty states (not counting the District of Columbia) and a relatively freewheeling **market economy.** In addition, Congress alone has the power to declare war. Although this brief sketch is far from complete, it suffices to indicate the breadth of congressional powers under the U.S. Constitution. Also, because the Founders wanted to emphasize the importance of "we, the people," they placed the legislative functions in Article I of the Constitution, reasoning (logically) that Congress is the most representative (or democratic) branch of government.

The powers and duties of the chief executive (president) are defined in Article II of the Constitution. In the U.S. system, the president is both head of state (similar to the role of a king or queen in constitutional monarchies) and head of government (the counterpart to prime ministers in parliamentary systems). In addition, the president is the commander in chief of the armed forces and has the power to appoint high officials such as cabinet officers and federal judges (including Supreme Court justices). Also, the president can issue executive orders, which are rules the government (federal bureaucracy) must follow (and thus similar in effect to laws) but which do not require congressional approval.

In the United States, the president is the only national leader who enjoys a mandate from the entire national electorate. (See Box 2.2.) The president alone speaks for the nation and personifies "America" in the eyes of the world. Presidential elections are held every four years and presidents have been limited to two terms of office since ratification of the Twenty-Second Amendment in 1951.

By contrast, members of the House of Representatives serve particular districts (subdivisions of states) and are elected for brief two-year terms. Districts are apportioned on the basis of population. Hence, California had fifty-two seats in the House after the 1990 Census, whereas sparsely populated states such as South Dakota and Montana had only one each. Every state gets two senators, however, regardless of population or geographic size. Senators are elected for six-year terms on a statewide basis. Senators thus have a broader mandate and a good deal more job security than House members. All money bills originate in the House of Representatives (lower house) but must be approved by both houses, while the Senate alone ratifies treaties. In this manner, legislative powers are divided up between the two houses.

In a few areas, power and authority are shared — for example, the government's war powers. Congress has the power to raise and support armies, to provide and maintain a navy, to make the rules regulating the armed forces, and to declare war. However, as already mentioned, the president is the commander in chief, meaning that he outranks all military officers, including four-star generals and rear admirals. It is the president, above all, who decides whether to negotiate, when and where to fight wars, and when and how to withdraw from a conflict. Clearly, any major military action requires the cooperation of both branches.

Similarly, the presidential powers of appointment are not absolute. The president "appoints" federal judges (including Supreme Court justices) as well as cabinet mem-

Contrast and Comparison

BOX 2.2

The Electoral College Does What?! The View from Abroad

Elections in America are extremely democratic, right? If you happened to be living abroad on November 7, 2000, when the most inconclusive presidential election in American history occurred it did not look very democratic at all. Why not? Think about it.

First, the popular election was "won" by Al Gore, the Democrat. Second, early in the evening as the election returns were coming in, the major television networks (including CNN) declared George Bush, the Republican, the winner, after he had apparently taken the state of Florida. If that confused (or confuses) you, imagine how it looked to people in foreign countries who had never heard of the Electoral College.

What exactly is the Electoral College? It is a group of men and women who meet in Washington, D.C., once every four years (on December 18) to elect the president of the United States. *Nothing like it exists anywhere else in the world.*

"Hold on, one minute" you might be saying, "the people elect the president, don't they?" Not exactly. What "the people" actually do is to vote for the electors who prefer the same candidate they prefer.

Got it? OK, one more time. For each presidential candidate there is a list of electors in each state. In effect, there are really fifty elections (fifty states) — the elections decide who the electors will be. The candidate who wins a simple majority of the votes in a given state wins all of that state's electoral votes (the exact number is based on population and mirrors the state's congressional representation). It is called a winner-takes-all system. In order to win the presidency, therefore, a candidate must win in the big states (including California, New York, Ohio, Illinois, Michigan, Pennsylvania, Texas, and, of course, Florida) that have the largest number of electoral votes.

So if you want to become president remember that it is not enough to win a majority of the popular votes or even a majority of the states — you have to win in certain key states and then keep your fingers crossed that "your" electors will not have a change of heart between November 7 and December 18.

To people watching from afar, this system does not make much sense and it certainly does not look very democratic. Nor did the fact that a raft of lawyers and judges (plus several weeks' time) were needed to sort out the 2000 election inspire confidence in the "world's greatest democracy" among America's friends and allies abroad.

bers and other high-ranking civilian officials and military officers with the "advice and consent" of the Senate. In other words, the upper house of the legislature in the American system can (and sometimes does) refuse to endorse the president's first choice. (Technically, the president merely nominates individuals for top jobs in the government; a given nominee is not actually appointed until confirmed by the Senate.) Note the critical importance of precision in the use of language here: such is often the case in a system that places the highest value on the **rule of law** — which is, on the Constitution, statutes, and contracts.

Under the U.S. Constitution, power is deliberately diffused (giving each citizen a vote and a voice), separated into three sets of functions (denying any one branch the capacity to dominate the other two or rule autonomously) and divided (giving states certain powers not exercised by the federal government). In practice, the ambiguities created by this system mean that the power to govern is to some extent up for grabs.

Exercising the power of judicial review, the Supreme Court decides constitutional questions arising from disputes between the executive and legislative branches. In addition, the Supreme Court often gets deeply immersed in the actual making of public policy by interpreting laws in landmark cases brought to it on appeal from lower federal courts.

As a result, American national politics is often characterized by policy disputes and struggles for ascendancy, especially between the president and Congress. In sum, the separation of powers sets up a permanent tug-of-war among the three branches of the federal government each seeking to prevail on controversial policy issues (gun control, abortion, or trade with Communist China, to cite but a few examples). At the same time, a wide array of constitutional checks and balances helps ensure against two hypothetical threats to liberty: the potential despotism of a rogue president and the danger that Congress might become the willing instrument of a tyrannical majority.

Perhaps the closest parallels to the American system are found in Argentina. The parliamentary brand of democracy has had little appeal in Latin America, where elected civilian presidents have replaced military dictators and juntas. Not so in the Arab world and much of Black Africa, where authoritarianism is still the norm. Asia is a more ambiguous case: despite the region's recent flirtation with democracy, far-reaching political reform has lagged far behind economic liberalization.

Parliamentary Democracy: The British Model

In **parliamentary systems,** the chief executive is typically a prime minister rather than a president. The British **Westminster model** is widely renowned as the first of its kind. The majority party in Parliament chooses the prime minister. To become prime minister, one must first win a seat in Parliament — the elective lower house, known as the **House of Commons** — by standing for election in a local constituency and then be chosen by one's peers in the legislature. Note that rather than a separation of powers, there is a **fusion of powers.** The prime minister (PM) and cabinet members (collectively called "the government") are chosen from the leadership of the majority party in Parliament and as members of the government the PM and cabinet continue to hold seats in the powerful lower house of Parliament.

The British legislative system is bicameral, meaning there are two chambers. The upper house, known as the **House of Lords,** is not an elective body. It members are either hereditary members (aristocratic "Peers") or appointed by the Queen ("Life Peers"). This body plays an important advisory and review role in the legislative process, but it can only delay, not prevent, passage of legislative action by the lower house (see Chapter 4).

A British-style parliamentary system has several distinct advantages. First, the government encounters few obstacles to getting its policies, programs, and budgets approved by the legislative assembly because it almost always has a majority (although it often depends on a coalition in multiparty systems where no single party has an absolute majority of seats in the parliament). Second, if the government falters for whatever reason, it can be forced out at any time by a "no confidence" vote in the parliament. Third, the government can dissolve the parliament at any time and call for new elections. This power helps the leadership maintain party discipline and gives the party in power the opportunity to choose an auspicious time for new elections. (In the British system, a government must call new elections at least once every five years.)

Although the British parliamentary system has not been exported wholesale to other countries, its basic design has been widely emulated. (Canada, Australia, and New Zealand, all former British colonies, are among the few that have copied the United Kingdom in detail.) Most countries do not require that cabinet ministers be members of Parliament; the Netherlands actually forbids them to be. Most parliaments serve for fixed terms, and some cannot be prematurely dissolved. Ideally, parliamentary governments have the backing of majority parties or coalitions, but in some cases (for example, in the Scandinavian countries) minority governments are more common. The ceremonial chief of state is sometimes an indirectly elected president rather than a hereditary monarch (Germany, for example). In France and Russia, the president is more powerful than the prime minister. In the Czech Republic, the president plays no role in running the government but performs important diplomatic and ceremonial functions. Nonetheless, it is fair to say that the British Parliament, as the first and oldest, is the model the world knows best and the one to which other parliamentary systems are most often compared.

Some countries combine features of both the American and British models. France, for example, has a popularly elected president and a prime minister chosen by the majority party in parliament (called the National Assembly). French presidents are directly elected for five-year terms, can run for reelection, and have the power to appoint and dismiss prime ministers and dissolve parliament. Whether nations choose one model or the other (or some combination of the two), the goal is always essentially the same: limited government. The idea of democracy is nicely summed up in the phrase, "a government of laws, not of men." The contrast with authoritarian regimes, which we will discuss next, is stark indeed.

Authoritarian Systems

Authoritarianism remains a prevalent form of government in Africa, the Middle East, and much of Asia. Until the 1980s, it was also the norm in Latin America. Even in Western Europe, it was present on the Iberian Peninsula (Spain and Portugal) until the mid-1970s.

There are many forms of authoritarian government, but most share certain characteristics. First, no radical transformation, restructuring, or penetration of society is attempted; the ruling elite aims, above all, to maintain the status quo. Second, there is usually a wealthy, elite class often closely linked to the ruler or rulers by ties of family, friendship, and mutual benefit. Third, the security forces (especially the army) often play a key role in government, even where they do not rule directly. Fourth, popular participation in politics ("mass mobilization") is typically discouraged (in contrast to Marxist-Leninist regimes). Fifth, political and sometimes civil liberties are curbed or denied. The ruling elite assumes a defensive posture: tolerate no challenges from opposition parties or groups, but otherwise let sleeping dogs lie. Hold elections for the sake of appearances, but rig the outcome.

Authoritarian systems come in many forms. In the contemporary world, three generic types can be identified:

1. Personal dictatorships (tyrannies)
2. Military oligarchies (juntas)
3. Dynastic regimes (monarchies)

Personal Dictatorships

In one form or another, dictatorships — systems based on the supreme power of a single ruler — have long dominated the pages of history. Indeed, they were prevalent in Aristotle's day (as noted earlier, he called them tyrannies — rule by a tyrant), but the twentieth century had its share, too. Totalitarian tyrants like Hitler and Stalin certainly imitated the behavior Aristotle ascribes to the tyrants of ancient times, who were famous (or infamous) for "the 'lopping off' of outstanding men and men of spirit."[5] Some other methods of personal rule, according to Aristotle, included the following:

> the forbidding of common meals, clubs, and anything of a like character — or, in other words, a defensive attitude against everything likely to produce the two qualities of mutual confidence and a high spirit . . . the adoption of every means for making every subject as much of a stranger as is possible to every other . . . [requiring] every resident to be constantly appearing in public . . . endeavouring to get information about every man's sayings and doings. This entails a secret police. . . . (Men are not so likely to speak their minds if they go in fear of a secret police; and if they do speak out, they are less likely to go undetected.)[6]

In sum, Aristotle teaches that tyrants have three basic aims. First, to break the spirit of the people. Second, to sow mutual mistrust: "Tyranny is never overthrown until men can begin to trust one another." Third, to make the people incapable of action: "Nobody attempts the impossible."

Ironically, personalistic rule cannot be permanently institutionalized for one simple reason: No ruler, however cunning or cruel, can succeed himself. Even the most absolute dictator is mortal. But choosing an **heir apparent** is risky because the anointed one may become an impatient rival.

Today, Aristotle's penetrating insights into the dynamics of tyranny — and the strategy and tactics of tyrants — prefigure the later musings of the fifteenth-century thinker Niccolò Machiavelli. Machiavelli's famous book, *The Prince,* reads like a how-to handbook for aspiring autocrats.[7] In the language of politics, the word *Machiavellian* is often used to describe someone who is calculating, cunning, and cruel. Fortunately, not all personal dictators are brutal and bloodthirsty. Nonetheless, personal dictatorships are too often associated with extreme political repression and arbitrary rule. Witness Saddam Hussein (the so-called Butcher of Baghdad) in Iraq until his ouster in 2003 or the equally brutal former dictator of Uganda Idi Amin, to cite but two examples among many in the decades after World War II. A short list of the worst of this lot is mute testimony to the inherent dangers of dictatorship.[8]

Personal dictators come in many guises. They usually gain power through force or fraud, often by means of a **coup d'etat** (sudden power seizure) or a rigged election. They may start out as military officers, charismatic liberators, or even religious gurus.[9] Regardless of background, tyrants must rely on loyal security forces to keep them in power. As Robert Jackson and Carl Rosberg observed in *Personal Rule in Black Africa* (1982), the key to dictatorship is the link "between the tyrant and his mercenaries, without whom tyranny is impossible."[10] Not surprisingly, military officers often run modern tyrannies.

Military Regimes

Only where military rule has been institutionalized can a military regime be said to exist. In this type of authoritarian government, there is typically a general who is "first among equals," because someone must personify (or put a face on) the regime as well as perform the ceremonial and symbolic functions of a chief executive. Nonetheless, military rule of this kind is collegial — meaning rule by committee, council, or cabal — rather than personal.

Where military rule is institutionalized there is seldom a charismatic or popular leader. The powers of the chief executive are apportioned among several high-ranking military officers who form a **junta** or ruling **oligarchy.** Military juntas have a long history, particularly (though by no means exclusively) in Latin America, where military intervention in domestic politics is a tradition.

Countries in which the army is dominant or frequently intervenes in politics are sometimes called **praetorian states.**[11] Military regimes typically come to power via a coup d'etat (power seizure). In some parts of the world, coups have occurred with astonishing frequency. One scholar counted eighty-eight military coups in fifty-two countries between 1958 and 1969.[12] In the 1970s, the military intervened in every Latin American country except Mexico and Costa Rica, according to Eric Nordlinger, who goes on to point out that military intervention became a fixture of Third World politics after World War II:

> Between 1945 and 1976, soldiers carried out successful coups in half of the eighteen Asian states. By 1976 the soldiers had made at least one successful or unsuccessful attempt to seize power in two-thirds of the Middle Eastern and North African states. They established military regimes in Egypt, Syria, Iraq, the Sudan, Libya, and Algeria. . . . By 1976 coups had occurred in more than half of the African countries, and in that year the military occupied the seat of government in half of them.[13]

According to Nordlinger, the study of military regimes "is the study of one of the most common, and thus characteristic, aspects of non-Western politics."

Why military rule was so common (and still is not uncommon) is a complicated question, but the short answer is that in developing countries there are often few if any well-established institutions and many sources of civil strife (for example, ethnic or religious differences). In these circumstances, the army is often the only cohesive institution with the capacity to maintain (or restore) order. And generals, no less than civilian politicians, become addicted to power. As Lord Acton, a wise observer of politics and history, once said: "Power corrupts, absolute power corrupts absolutely."

In Latin America (and to a lesser degree in Asia and sub-Saharan Africa), the picture has changed. Until the 1980s, Latin America was the most coup-prone region in the world. Military juntas were the rule, representative democracies the exception. Only in Mexico, Costa Rica, Venezuela, and Colombia were democratic institutions a part of the political tradition. One by one South America's military rulers relinquished power to popularly elected civilian politicians . . . in Ecuador (1979), Peru (1980), Bolivia (1982), Argentina (1983), Uruguay (1985), and Brazil (1985). Despite regional tensions arising from civil wars in El Salvador and Nicaragua, several Central American states that were previously under military sway also moved toward civilian rule in the 1990s.

Military rule by committee (junta) appeared to be on the decline at the end of the twentieth century. However, another form of authoritarianism that was far more anachronistic in the modern world displayed a surprising resilience in one region. Dynastic regimes collapsed in Europe after World War I and nearly everywhere else after World War II. However, in the Arab Middle East a number of ruling dynasties have been able to hang on.

Dynastic Regimes

Dynastic rule, or **monarchy,** was the most common form of authoritarianism (and government) nearly everywhere in the world until the twentieth century. Monarchs have gone by different names in different places — king, emperor, caliph, sultan, emir, mogul, and czar, to name a few. Whatever the title, **absolute monarchs** rule as a birthright — they inherit power. In Europe and elsewhere, kings and emperors often reinforced this dynastic claim by asserting a god-ordained **divine right** to rule. Only in the Middle East and North Africa has this form of authoritarianism continued to thrive (with a few obscure exceptions), due perhaps to the relatively homogenous populations of most of these states, the social conservativism inculcated by the Islamic religion, and the concentration of enormous wealth (generated by oil profits) in the hands of the ruling family. Of course, where Europe's monarchs have not been dethroned (as in Great Britain, Spain, Scandinavia, and the Benelux countries, for example) they reign, but do not rule.

Monarchs continue to rule as well as reign in Jordan (King Abdullah), Saudi Arabia (King Fahd), and Morocco (King Hassan II). Autocratic rulers called sultans or emirs also govern the oil-rich "ministates" of Kuwait, Bahrain, Oman, Qatar, and the United Arab Emirates. It is probably no accident that oil and dynastic rule go hand in hand in this part of the world — monarchs need money to stay in power and they get it by fair means or foul (for example, through heavy taxes and various forms of human bondage). But the abundance of "black gold" (oil) gives modern Arab monarchs an alternative to unpopular taxes and slave labor.

Beyond the Middle East, monarchies are few and far between. Only in such obscure places as Swaziland, Nepal, Bahrain, Bhutan, and Tonga can they still be found.

Is monarchy a vanishing species of authoritarianism? Since the nineteenth century this form of rule has undergone a precipitous decline, one that accelerated after World War II. Countries in which monarchies have fallen or been displaced in recent decades include Afghanistan (1973), Burundi (1966), Cambodia (1955), Egypt (1952), Ethiopia (1974), Iran (1979), Iraq (1958), Libya (1969), and Tunisia (1957). And unlike military regimes, which come and go, monarchs once deposed are seldom if ever restored to power. Spain is a partial exception: there the monarchy was restored in the 1970s after dictator Francisco Franco's death, but Spain's popular new monarch King Juan Carlos, having played a role in the transition to democracy, gracefully stepped out of the political limelight and settled into a life of royal splendor as a beloved figurehead.

Monarchs are generally more enlightened than the kings and emperors of the past. They no longer rule as cruel and sadistic dictators, as the worst of them once did. But in the twentieth century there arose a new form of oppressive government in place of the absolute monarchy (or absolutism) of old — a form more terrifying in its pursuit of total power than anything the tyrants of antiquity could have imagined.

Totalitarian and Post-Totalitarian Regimes

Totalitarianism is a concept of relatively recent vintage. It was first applied to the system established in the Soviet Union during the long and bloody reign of Joseph Stalin and to the Nazi regime in Germany under Adolf Hitler, in which millions of European Jews and other people were put to death in extermination camps. The term is appropriate because the political systems set up by Stalin and Hitler were characterized by a *total* concentration of power at the center (in Stalin's case, in the hands of a single individual).

A pivotal feature of the totalitarian model is the presence of an all-encompassing and monolithic party organization that functions like a state within a state. This party is controlled by an omnipotent dictator or by a committee comprising leading members of the oligarchic elite (the term *oligarchic* here refers to a privileged political class who monopolize power). Members of the elite make decisions in secret and rely heavily on secret police to intimidate and mobilize the society. In the Stalinist variant, the party apparatus and the state bureaucracy were inextricably intertwined; the bureaucracy implemented policies, while the party acted as the dictator's whip hand and watchdog.

Carl Friedrich and Zbigniew Brzezinski list the following six characteristics of all totalitarian regimes:

1. An official ideology covering all aspects of human existence to which every member of the society must adhere, not only by outer forms but also by inner convictions
2. A single mass party led by one person and consisting of relatively small proportions of the total population, which acts as the official ideology's priesthood
3. A system of terrorist police controls making full use of modern technology for spying and surveillance

4. Centralized state control of the mass media
5. Confiscation of all arms and explosives previously in private hands
6. Centralized state control of the economy through bureaucratic coordination of all productive enterprises[14]

In the full-blown totalitarian state, political liberties and other human rights are nonexistent. Dissidence and nonconformity are not tolerated; citizens who do not submit often vanish in the night, dispatched to labor camps or the firing squad. The press is state-controlled, and the performing arts are tightly regulated. Newspapers, books, movies, and radio and television programming are censored. No independent group or association of any kind is permitted. The educational system is geared to the regime's political objectives, and the curriculum is infused with ideological content.

Totalitarian rulers, by definition, aim at a radical restructuring of society. To achieve such ambitious goals as rapid industrialization, social transformation, and territorial expansion, they must resort to **mass mobilization.** As a consequence, passive obedience on the part of the masses is not enough; active participation is required. Ardor is an order. Truth is treason. To maximize state control, society must be infiltrated right down to the family structure so that no one can hide anything from the state, including subversive thoughts or feelings. Today's computerized systems of air transportation, mass communications, information management, electronic surveillance, and increasingly sophisticated internal security place formidable new means and methods of control at the disposal of the modern state. At the same time, the proliferation of personal computers, along with wide access to the Internet, has made the isolation of individuals from the outside world (a hallmark of totalitarian states) more difficult.

The *potential* for totalitarian rule would appear to be inherent in the technology associated with economic development (cameras, telephones, eavesdropping devices, television, computers, and so on), but the twentieth century provides several striking examples (Russia, China, and Cambodia) of totalitarianism arising in societies with large peasant populations and economies still based primarily on agriculture. At the same time, the Nazi example shows that advanced industrial societies are not immune.

Before its collapse in 1989–1991, the Soviet Union was the prototype for the Marxist-Leninist form of totalitarian rule. Lenin readily acknowledged his intellectual debt to Karl Marx, but he took Marxism and recast it into an ideology suitable for use as a kind of state religion. Ever since the triumph of Lenin's *Bolsheviki* in the October Revolution of 1917, the propagation of a state-sponsored ideology, **Marxism-Leninism,** imposed on society by means of intimidation and censorship, has been a trademark of Soviet-type regimes. (Note that the words *propagation* and *propaganda* have the same root — in this case, to spread or disseminate or reproduce the official version of reality to the exclusion of all other versions.)

The history of Soviet Russian rule suggests that when totalitarian regimes mellow the result can be a **post-totalitarian state.** In this phase, power remains concentrated in a single, all-encompassing party organization that continues to rule through a subservient state bureaucracy. Elections are held regularly, but in the absence of a competitive party system, they are still little more than window dressing. Civil liberties (free speech, freedom of the press, freedom of association and assembly, freedom of movement, and so on) may not be entirely repressed but are severely restricted. Periods of relative leniency toward dissenters alternate with crackdowns on dissent.

In the case of Soviet Russia, the concept of a post-totalitarian phase is useful, but difficult to pinpoint. Did the post-totalitarian phase start with the death of Stalin in 1953 or with the elevation of Mikhail Gorbachev to the pinnacle of Soviet power in 1985? In the 1980s, under the influence of Gorbachev's *perestroika* (restructuring) campaign, several communist states implemented market-oriented economic reforms and relaxed internal police-state controls (press censorship, foreign travel restrictions). In 1991, tumultuous events in the Soviet Union brought the edifice of Communist Party–state rule there crashing down. Two years earlier, popular uprisings had culminated in the downfall of communist governments in Eastern Europe and the dissolution of the Soviet-created military alliance known as the Warsaw Pact.

Communist dictatorships also sprouted in Asia, sub-Saharan Africa, the Middle East, and Latin America in the decades after World War II. At century's end, only a few of these regimes were still in power — the collapse of the Soviet Union dealt a severe blow to both the communist ideology and the system it had inspired. It also deprived the surviving communist states of an important source of political and economic support. Finally, and perhaps most importantly, it undercut the idea of central planning (associated with Soviet-style communism) and pointed to the superiority of market-based economic systems. We turn now to a discussion of economic models.

Economic Models and Political Systems

Two rival models dominated economic debates during the Cold War. The West (led by the United States) promoted the idea that prosperity and democracy were the fruits of a market economy (defined and discussed in the next section). The "Eastern Bloc" (led by the Soviet Union) countered that **capitalism** was inherently unfair because it benefited the rich at the expense of the poor. The Soviet Union therefore set out to prove that an antimarket model — the so-called command economy — was not only more efficient but also far better suited to provide for the basic human needs of the working class (the vast majority of society as defined by the proponents of this view). Great Britain and the Scandinavian countries pursued a third way, the welfare state, which sought to combine the best, and escape the worst, of both systems.

Market Economies

Democracies are typically associated with a market economy. The marketplace is the only path to economic success in this model, which features minimal state interference in business or the **private sector.** The forces of supply and demand are allowed to operate without extensive state regulation. This minimalist, hands-off approach is known as a **laissez-faire** policy. The profit motive provides the incentive for individuals to work hard, compete vigorously, improve the quality of the services or products they deliver, and strive for excellence. In theory, coercion and exhortation are unnecessary because individuals in such a **free-enterprise system** are self-motivated.

The whole concept of laissez-faire as originally expounded by the Scottish economist Adam Smith in the late eighteenth century posited a natural harmony of interests in society. Individuals behaving rationally (trying to get rich) in a free-enterprise system would unwittingly serve the needs of society as a whole. By earning as much money as possible, spending some and saving the rest, investing soundly, and playing by the rules so as not to jeopardize the legal order on which contractual obligations ultimately depend, individuals engaged in the pursuit of selfish ends create the means to social wealth. Moreover, since innovation and invention are richly rewarded, there is a built-in guarantee that efficiencies in the economy, which benefit everyone, will be continually improved.

In reality, no pure market economies exist. All market economies are mixed enterprise systems, meaning that the operation of market forces is regulated in varying degrees by government. For example, the money supply is generally controlled by a central bank (in the United States, the Federal Reserve Board performs this function).

Governments also use fiscal policy (taxes and spending programs) to regulate the economy. They raise taxes and cut spending to cool down an "overheated" economy, that is, one experiencing rapid price inflation often due largely to the push and pull of consumer demand and escalating wages; or they lower taxes and increase spending to resuscitate the economy. They subsidize farmers and offer tax incentives to encourage selective expansion of business and industry (for example, in real estate and export-oriented manufacturing). In the **emerging democracies** of Eastern Europe, as well as many developing countries, the state heavily subsidizes the general populace by providing food, fuel, and other necessities at prices below actual cost. Subsidies and low tax revenues are two major causes of chronic budget deficits in Eastern Europe, the Middle East, Africa, and Latin America, but ruling elites in these regions are often reluctant to discontinue them because of the hardships that would result and the danger of provoking riots and regime-threatening unrest.

Command Economies

In a **command economy,** public goods (and state interests) take priority over private interests, industry and commerce are owned and operated by the state, and central planning, rather than the marketplace, regulates production of goods and services. The state heavily subsidizes consumption: people live in subsidized public housing, depend on subsidized public transportation, and receive free education, medical care, and many other social services. Nearly everyone works in the public sector (for state-run enterprises). The same government that provides the subsidies pays low salaries that make the subsidies necessary.

Command economies are so named because businesses respond to instructions from above rather than to consumer preferences (demand) from below. An overall plan is developed each year for every sector of the economy, setting production targets that are broken down into monthly quotas. Every factory, farm, and enterprise is expected to fulfill its monthly quota. Rewards, in the form of bonuses, are given for overfulfillment; underfulfillment can derail the career of the plant manager, who is ultimately held responsible.

This system maximizes state (or party) control, which is the chief reason why Stalin created it in the first place. It enables the ruler to shape the economy, extract and allocate resources (including land, labor, and investment capital), and concentrate on a particular objective, such as military-industrial development. Stalinist political economy stressed the primacy of heavy industry, which meant everything from coal and steel production to hydroelectric power and machine tools for heavy construction and infrastructure (roads, bridges, dams, and the like). "Heavy industry" was also a euphemism for a major Soviet arms buildup, the genesis of a permanent wartime economy that eventually created a superpower arsenal rivaled only by that of the United States.

Stalin proved that the command economy can induce rapid economic development in the early stages of industrialization if enough slave labor is available. Even apart from the obvious moral issues it raises, the Stalinist system also has major liabilities as a model for sustained economic growth. For example, it becomes increasingly cumbersome to administer as the economy modernizes and diversifies. Although Stalin proved that the initial stages of industrialization can be forced by *quantitative inputs* — massive amounts of conscript labor, capital squeezed from agriculture, and the export (for hard currency) of raw materials extracted without regard to human costs or future needs — it is now clear that sustained economic growth in an age of rapidly advancing technology requires *qualitative inputs* (applied research, managerial skills, innovative ideas and attitudes, entrepreneurship, vision, investment strategies, risk taking). In the 1970s and 1980s, command economies lagged way behind the most dynamic market economies. This relative decline was the major reason why Mikhail Gorbachev launched the Soviet reform movement in the mid-1980s; it is also the reason for the collapse of Europe's communist states a few years later.

The command economies of the Soviet Union and Eastern Europe were closely associated with the communist ideal of extreme equality and universal, comprehensive state-provided social insurance (health care, disability, retirement, and the like). The ideal is admirable, but to pay for such a system requires a productive labor force and a vibrant, growing economy. Communism did provide more or less equally for the basic needs of all members of society, keeping wages relatively uniform — hence physicians and engineers were not paid much more than factory workers (and sometimes less). However, in general, incentives were lacking, hard work was the exception, and labor productivity lagged way behind the West. But is it necessary to choose between security (socialism or communism) and prosperity (capitalism)? Cannot both be achieved? We will consider this question next.

Welfare-State Systems

The welfare state first appeared in Western Europe after World War II as an attempt to blend capitalism and **socialism.** For Europeans, at once repelled by the excesses of Stalinism and appalled by the Great Depression (which brought social upheaval and a devastating war to the Continent), the search for a middle way was a moral and political imperative. In these circumstances, the overarching question was, Can two seemingly incompatible models of political economy be harmonized? A half century later, the results of this experiment were (and still are) hotly debated on both sides of the Atlantic Ocean.

In this model, the state plays a major role in redistributing wealth without completely taking over its production. Some key parts of the economy (the so-called strategic heights) — for example, railroads, airlines, harbors, and public utilities — are nationalized (state-owned and -operated). The rest of the economy remains in the private sector, where the market operates without undue interference in an invigorating climate of competition and low tariffs. The government, however, uses **fiscal** and **monetary policies** to regulate the economy. High tax revenues and "targeted" budget expenditures place powerful tools in the hands of a benevolent state, which oversees a vast system of "cradle to the grave" social programs. Education and health care are free (or heavily subsidized); employees are protected against loss of income due to sickness, injury, or layoffs; the elderly and disabled receive pensions; and the like.

This balancing act between a strong state and a market economy, in theory, produces the best of both worlds — an efficient economy and a just society. Finally, there is a political payoff as well, order and stability, which feeds back into the economy.

Today, the welfare state is institutionalized throughout Europe but, as we will see, its theoretical and practical foundations were deeply shaken by the disappointing economic performance of Great Britain in particular in the 1960s and 1970s. Nonetheless, the welfare state model is firmly entrenched in most of Europe; the positive results possible in well-run welfare states are showcased in a number of Scandinavian countries, as well as in Belgium and the Netherlands. The Netherlands, for example, has an impressive social safety net and has also enjoyed steady economic growth, combined with low inflation and unemployment, despite high tax rates. By contrast, the emerging democracies of Eastern Europe, with a legacy of extreme "welfare state" dependency, are struggling to redefine the relationship between state and society in a period of difficult and economically painful transition.

Does economic transition have to be difficult and painful? Judging from dozens of examples in different regions of the world, the answer is yes — especially if it is done in a hurry. Does it always have to be done in a hurry? Again, the answer in today's world is yes. In the world of the eighteenth and nineteenth centuries, when the Industrial Revolution occurred in the West, the dimensions of time and space were more abundant. As everybody knows, the pace of change accelerated tremendously in the twentieth century and continues to accelerate as technology changes the way we live. The same is obviously true of "inner space": modern air travel, satellite communications, and the computer-based worldwide Web have caused the world we live in to shrink dramatically, creating a kind of "global community." In these conditions, the many adjustments individuals and whole societies must make to catch up with the West or compete in the new "world economy" have to be made very abruptly. As we are about to see, these adjustments are never easy. We turn now to the perplexing topic of political and economic development on which turns the fate of the vast majority of the world's population.

Is Keynes Dead? The Rise of Monetarism

The political economy embodied in the welfare state is most often associated with the ideas of John Maynard Keynes (1883–1946), a British economist who emphasized the "pump priming" role of government. Keynes advocated deficit spending by government to counteract recessions (slowdowns) in the economy. The real problem at such times is unemployment, not inflation, Keynes argued. The economy cannot recover as long as lots of people have no jobs and no money to spend. When consumers cannot spend, the government must do it. He further theorized that government spending, by boosting the economy, would eventually pay for itself in the form of enhanced tax revenues.

The idea that public debt is not necessarily bad was (and still is) controversial because it goes against the everyday experience of individuals (taxpayers) and, generally speaking, the "rules of the road" in the private sector. However, the necessity for public works and relief programs in the Great Depression of the 1930s made "believers" out of many skeptics. Similarly, after World War II, stimulating the rapid recovery of devastated economies in Western Europe also required active governmental involvement — including foreign aid (the Marshall Plan) and deficit spending on a large scale.

During the Cold War era (1945–1989), Western democracies followed Keynesian tax and spend policies, creating a mosaic of welfare states that imitated the British system and stretched from Scandinavia to the Mediterranean. As Western Europe prospered, welfare state programs expanded and became a fundamental part of the "social contract" on the Continent — any attempt to dismantle these programs became politically unthinkable. Government expenditures for such programs climbed from 10 to 20 percent of GNP in the 1950s to one-quarter or even one-third of GNP in the 1970s.[15]

Thus, there is a wide consensus in favor of welfare state policies in Europe (in contrast to the United States and Japan). However, there are still significant differences within Europe, despite recent efforts by the European Union to harmonize national economics among its member states. (See Table 2.1.) The United States has never officially embraced the welfare state, but statistics tell a somewhat different story. Japan has been the most resistant to welfare-state policies of all the advanced postindustrial countries.

Of course, a big, wide social safety net that catches everybody is costly. The most generous welfare states also, not surprisingly, take the biggest tax bite. Note in Table 2.2 that the top tax rate varies considerably among the world's richest countries. All tax personal incomes at higher rates than they tax businesses but the spread is much larger in countries such as Belgium, Denmark, and Germany than in Sweden, the United Kingdom, or the United States. Even more significant is where the top tax rate kicks in — for example, the nominal rate is the same in both the United Kingdom and the United States (and much lower in Sweden), but it kicks in at a much higher level in the United States than in either the United Kingdom or Sweden (where everyone who makes over about $27,000 surrenders roughly one-third of it to the state).

The high cost of the welfare state became a major political issue in the United Kingdom in the late 1970s when the Conservative Party, then led by Margaret Thatcher, came to power on a platform calling for change. (Thatcher's reforms are detailed in Chapter 4.) At about the same time, Ronald Reagan, a conservative Republican, was elected president in the United States. Reagan embraced "supply side" economics, the

Table 2.1 "Welfare" Spending in Developed Countries (% share of GDP)

Country	1980	1990	1995
Belgium	24.6	25.6	27.1
Canada	13.2	17.6	18.2
Denmark	27.5	28.1	32.0
France	23.5	26.7	30.0
Germany	23.7	23.2	28.0
Italy	18.4	23.0	23.7
Japan	9.9	11.2	13.8
Sweden	29.8	32.2	33.0
United Kingdom	18.3	19.5	22.5
United States	13.4	13.5	15.8

Note: The word *welfare* is put in quotes because it is often used in a pejorative sense in the United States and because it does not necessarily denote a "giveaway" program. Social spending in developed countries refers to pensions, health care, unemployment compensation, education, family allowances, and the like. These programs may or may not significantly redistribute wealth, depending on who pays, how, and when, and who benefits, how, and when.
Source: Organization for Economic Cooperation and Development, *Social Expenditure Data Base 1980–1996.*

very antithesis of Keynesian fiscal policies that stress deficit spending. Both Thatcher and Reagan favored cutting taxes (especially on business) and lowering interest rates to stimulate output (supply) and investment. Higher output, according to the theory, creates more jobs; more jobs means more purchasing power and higher consumption (demand). Thus, the steady expansion of goods and services keeps prices down even as demand rises. Prosperity, in this model, is driven by the private sector, not the state.

It is worth noting, however, that even the redoubtable Margaret Thatcher did little more than tinker with the British welfare system — serious tampering would have been political suicide. By the same token, the conservative Reagan administration accounted for the largest budget deficits (largely defense-related) in American history at that time.* It was this huge deficit and the flagging economy that gave Bill Clinton his "issue" in 1992. He promised to "reinvent" government by downsizing the federal bureaucracy and farming out various services to the private sector. This new economic policy would bring down the deficit and stimulate business activity. Thus, Clinton rejected both "Reaganomics" and Keynesian economics, opting for a "neoliberal" policy: combining an emphasis on the private sector and the free market with welfare reform and a balanced budget.

The Clinton model appeared to work: the U.S. economy grew steadily, the federal deficit declined sharply, and the stock market surged. In the United Kingdom, the new Labour Prime Minister Tony Blair followed the Clinton prescription (without, however, moving against the national health system and other hallowed welfare programs).

*The George W. Bush administration, however, set a new record with a budget deficit estimated at around $400 billion in 2003.

Table 2.2 Comparative Marginal Tax Rates, 1998

Country	Top Tax Rate	On Individual Income Over ($)	Corporate Top Tax Rate (%)
Belgium	55	65,547	39
Canada	29	41,370	38
Denmark	58	—	34
France	—	—	33
Germany	53	66,988	30
Italy	46	181,801	37
Japan	50	230,592	38
Netherlands	60	51,373	35
Sweden	31	27,198	28
United Kingdom	40	44,580	31
United States	40	278,450	35

Source: World Bank, *World Development Report 1999/2000.*

In retrospect, the Clinton approach to political economy was part of a larger transition in public-policy thinking. The White House can influence economic policy in other countries, both directly (through aid and trade policies) and indirectly (through its leading role in the International Monetary Fund and World Bank). Thus, the United States was often accused of trying to impose its own preferences (stability over growth) on developing countries in return for IMF special drawing rights (SDRs) and World Bank loans. Stability calls for tight money policies (high interest rates) and balanced budgets (high taxes and curbs on spending). Economic growth, say the critics, calls for the opposite approach — "easy money" policies, tax cuts, and deficit spending.

In sum, Keynesian economics, for now at least, has gone into partial eclipse; neoliberal policies emphasizing market principles have taken its place. But there are two caveats: first, the welfare state in Europe is probably here to stay; second, in the United States, the George W. Bush administration has adopted a "neoconservative" approach to economic policy that emphasizes tax cuts for corporations and the wealthy and low interest rates (expansion of the money supply) to stimulate business and investment combined with deficit spending (a Keynesian measure). The result has been a skyrocketing federal deficit engineered by "America's most profligate president since the Vietnam war" in the words of the *Economist,* a well-known British weekly newspaper.[16]

Economic theories are necessary and useful but economies rarely if ever conform to abstract models. Similarly, economic policies are rarely if ever purely of one kind or another. As we have seen, the business-oriented policies of Margaret Thatcher coexisted with welfare-state programs of previous British postwar governments, much as George W. Bush's "easy money" policies (called monetarist) have not stood in the way of deficit spending (Keynesian). Both Keynesians and monetarists agree that spending is the key to economic expansion. The point of dispute between the two is who should control spending: those who favor fiscal policy want the public sector to take the lead and those who favor monetary policy want the private sector to do it. But, to repeat, when it comes to policy (as opposed to partisan political rhetoric) both sides recognize that the public and private sectors each play an important role.

Transitional Systems

There are basically two ways for political regimes and economic systems to change — they can change abruptly (revolution) or gradually (evolution). In Asia and Latin America, many countries experienced a peaceful transition from authoritarian to democratic government in the 1980s. These countries did not all stop at exactly the same place on the "road to democracy" (the People's Republic of China, for example, made market reforms while keeping tight political control of the society), but democratization brought significant change from South Korea to Southeast Asia and all across Latin America. After 1989, when the communist regimes of Eastern Europe toppled like falling dominoes, a new and different transition process occurred in many of these countries. This process involved nothing short of the wholesale conversion of political and economic systems from centrally planned, one-party dictatorships to market-based democracies (see Chapter 6).

Politics and Development

No comparative study of political systems is complete without some mention of **development.** The Western concept of development is sometimes used as a synonym for **modernization.** Thus, development theory can be seen as an intellectual outgrowth of the idea of progress. Anyone who believes in progress must also believe that human beings are capable of building a better world. This belief is often associated with optimism, idealism, rationalism, and faith in the future — essentially Western notions.

Development theorists have usually assumed that sovereign states are here to stay. Therefore, the modern state provides the framework for most models of development. But progress is no longer automatically set in the context of the modern state — regional structures can also play an important role, as the European Union (EU), which will be discussed in Chapters 3 and 4, demonstrates.

What Is Development?

Development can be defined as "the increasing capacity to make rational use of natural and human resources for social ends."[17] It is a key concept in all the natural and social sciences because it stresses the role of human ingenuity and intelligence and holds out the hope that scientific research will be richly rewarded.

Anthropologists and sociologists stress sociocultural aspects of development such as values, beliefs, taboos, attitudes, and orientations. They also focus on interpersonal and group relations (families, clans, and tribes or ethnic, religious, and other distinct groups in society). Economists stress changes in patterns of production and distribution, consumption, and investment. Political scientists focus mainly on changes in patterns of power and authority. As societies develop, how do power relationships change? What is gained and what is lost? Are certain kinds of government more suitable for developing societies than others? Political economists try to answer these kinds of questions by combining the disciplines and analytical tools of economics and political science. The study of political economy is logical because global and national markets are never free of state intervention and regulation — in other words, totally free markets (economies operating in a political void) do not exist. By the same token, governments are always effected in countless ways by economic trends and cycles — both internal (which they regulate) and external (which they do not).

Closing the Circle: Development and Regime Type

Are some types of regimes more adept than others at implementing policies aimed at rapid economic development? Common sense and experience both suggest that regimes in which power and authority are centralized or concentrated are more effective at mobilizing society and dealing with conflict (most often by crushing opposition). Such regimes are sometimes called **mobilization systems.** They may be authoritarian or totalitarian in form. If the leadership fastens onto economic development as its supreme goal, a mobilization regime, by definition, is well equipped to do the job. By the same token, if the leaders set some other goal, such as military conquest or international prestige, they can also divert resources and postpone purely economic priorities indefinitely (as Germany and Japan did between the two world wars).

Democratic governments place social harmony, personal liberty, and political compromise above rapid economic development. They typically try to accommodate rather than repress competing interest groups, which means that public policy is the result of compromises more than coherent plans predicated on clearly articulated goals. The pace and direction of economic growth depends heavily on consumer choice. Regimes of this type are sometimes called **reconciliation systems.**

In the early stages of economic development, mobilization regimes can accomplish rapid growth. But beyond a certain point, reconciliation regimes now appear to be the more successful and more sustainable of the two — that is perhaps the most important lesson learned from the collapse of communist regimes in the Soviet Union and Eastern Europe (circa 1990). As we shall see later, the Soviet Union and its allies (mobilization systems) could not keep up with the pace of economic growth in the United States, the EU, Japan, and other market-based democracies; on the other hand, China has been able to do so, but only by **privatization** — in effect, by decoupling the economy from the centralized political system.

In many developing nations, national pride and political goals have often taken precedence over economic rationality or bargaining and trade-offs among competing interests. Building a large steel mill or a sports stadium, starting a national airline, or acquiring sophisticated jet fighters can have more to do with politics than with economics or defense. Above all, most developing nations want to escape the external dependency they associate with colonialism. In practical terms, this desire has often translated into policies aimed at economic self-reliance.

These policies have proven to be self-defeating, which means the sooner they are discarded the better. But discarding old policies often necessitates discarding old policy makers — and that is seldom easy. In sum, significant regime change usually precedes or parallels economic reforms (as it clearly did in Eastern Europe after 1989). Economic reforms, in turn, often lead to more stable political systems.

From Nation-States to Region-States?

In this chapter we have shown that regime patterns vary from nation to nation and from region to region. The nation-building tasks and problems confronting most of sub-Saharan Africa are not identical to those facing the former communist states of Eastern Europe, and the development issues that are most pressing in Latin America are different from those facing Western Europe.

Europe has traveled well down the road toward economic unification. The nations of South America and Southeast Asia have taken steps in this direction as well. Many of these efforts gained new momentum in the 1990s. In 1992, Mexico joined the United States and Canada in a plan to establish a free-trade association (or common market) in North America. Finally, there has been talk of a new economic trade bloc emerging in Asia, which would include the Association of South East Asian Nations (ASEAN) plus Japan, China, and South Korea.[18] Will supranational political regimes evolve out of the processes of regional economic integration now taking place in Europe, Asia, and the Americas?

Patterns and trends around the globe hint at the possibility that the twenty-first century will be the age of regionalism much as the nineteenth and twentieth centuries were the age of nationalism. (See Box 2.3.) Regionalism is not likely to replace ethnic particularism or nationalism any time soon, but the success of the EU and the challenge posed by the North American Free Trade Association (NAFTA) are stimulating similar efforts in other regions of the globe. In matters of political economy, as in fashion, the rich and powerful often set the trends, competition drives behavior, and imitation is the sincerest form of flattery.

A Travel Advisory . . .

As we embark on our journey of discovery to the various regions of the world keep in mind the models and regimes you have read about in this chapter. And remember: models are not to be confused with reality; regimes, on the other hand, are real enough, but they rarely fit any model to perfection. If and when they do, we have to suspect that the "model" is actually a particular regime in disguise.

What If?

BOX 2.3

Regional Institution Building

What if our current allegiance to the nation-state were superseded by a new allegiance to a supranational or international organization? In the twentieth century, two world wars caused leaders to cast about for alternatives to the nation-state. The League of Nations was a direct outgrowth of the horrifying devastation World War I left in its wake. Similarly, the establishment of the United Nations (UN) after World War II issued from a recognition that the historical structure of international relations (or lack thereof) urgently required a rethinking and overhaul.

The most enthusiastic early UN supporters believed that a new world order was about to dawn. The UN, they posited, heralded the beginning of the end of the nation-state. These one-world advocates were well meaning but sadly mistaken, as the turbulent history of the last half of the twentieth century amply testifies. What no one could foresee in 1945 was the existence of a third way, an alternative between nation-states and world government.

The existence of such an alternative (or third way) is now clear, even if the future is not. The emergence of regional organizations all over the globe is potentially one of the most far-reaching political changes to occur in three or four centuries. The European Union is presently history's most successful example of regional institution building. Will Belgians, Germans, and Italians eventually feel more European than Belgian, German, or Italian? Today, that seems doubtful. Certainly, people everywhere still tend to be nationalistic, patriotic, and sometimes even xenophobic (fearing and hating foreigners).

We can be properly skeptical of extravagant claims regarding the historical meaning of the regionalization trends now afoot in the world, but there is no doubt that these trends have already begun to change the face of politics on both the national and the international levels. Regions will not replace nation-states as the major vessels of government in the near future. The consequences, should they ever do so, are impossible to predict. Would the world be a safer or a more dangerous place? Would it be more economically vibrant or less so? Would it be easier or harder for people to invest, travel, and trade on a global scale? What do you think?

SUMMARY

Aristotle's ancient classification scheme accommodates nearly all forms of modern government. It works for a full range of political systems from highly pluralistic democracies to highly autocratic dictatorships. Totalitarian regimes represent the one notable exception. Classical political philosophy is relevant to the problems of political development. Modern empirical approaches have also shed light on the processes of development. Theories of political development try to answer the following question: how do societies create the political cultures and the political structures without which a modern nation-state cannot exist?

Postindustrial societies in Europe, North America, Asia, and elsewhere are the products of a long process of political development. In Europe and North America, this process was largely the result of internal forces. Societies in the former colonial areas (the so-called Third World) underwent rapid political and economic development in the second half of the twentieth century. The pace of change has been much faster than it was in Europe and North America, and the forces of change were (initially, at least) largely external rather than internal. Similarly, the models urged on Third World states by First and Second World powers were alien models that often did not fit easily into indigenous cultures. These developmental differences are among the factors that have led to the emergence of regional institutions and a growing emphasis on regional economic trade, aid, and development. The success of the European Union is another factor. If this trend continues, it will profoundly affect politics as we know it on both the national and the international level.

KEY TERMS

state
democratic regimes
authoritarian regimes
Cold War
totalitarian
developing countries
less developed countries (LDCs)
underdeveloped countries (UDCs)
constitutional democracy
totalitarian dictatorship
authoritarian rule
Third World
presidential democracy
separation of powers
tyranny
market economy
rule of law
parliamentary systems
Westminster model
House of Commons
fusion of powers
House of Lords
heir apparent
coup d'etat
junta
oligarchy
praetorian states
dynastic rule
monarchy
absolute monarchs
divine right
mass mobilization
Marxism-Leninism
post-totalitarian state
capitalism
private sector
laissez-faire
free-enterprise system
emerging democracies
command economy
socialism
fiscal policy
monetary policy
development
modernization
mobilization systems
reconciliation systems
privatization

STUDY QUESTIONS

1. What are some major differences between presidential and parliamentary democracies? What are the advantages and disadvantages of each? In your opinion, which system is better?
2. What is authoritarianism? What modern forms has it assumed? Where is it most relevant, and why?

3. How does totalitarianism differ from authoritarianism? What principal forms has totalitarianism assumed, and where has it prevailed? In your opinion, is totalitarianism a thing of the past? Why, or why not?
4. Define *development* as it relates to states and societies.
5. What are the various theories and approaches to development? Which, if any, are especially illuminating?
6. From a developmental perspective, what is the relationship between politics and economics? Between politics and culture? Between politics and society?
7. What is the nature of the debate about the proper role of the state in economic development?
8. Define the term *welfare state* and give some examples. Taking into account the models of political economy discussed in Chapter 2, would you prefer to live in a country more like Sweden or more like Japan? Explain.
9. Explain monetarism and how it differs from the economic theories of John Maynard Keynes.

SUGGESTED READINGS

Arendt, Hannah. *Totalitarianism.* Orlando, Fla.: Harcourt Brace, 1968.

Aristotle. *Politics.* Ernest Barker, ed. and trans. New York: Oxford University Press, 1962.

Bailey, Sydney. *British Parliamentary Democracy,* 3rd ed. Westport, Conn.: Greenwood, 1978.

Crick, Bernard. *Basic Forms of Government: A Sketch and a Model.* London: Macmillan, 1980.

Diamond, Martin. *The Founding of the Democratic Republic.* Itasca, Ill.: Peacock, 1981.

Dicey, A. V. *Introduction to the Study of the Law of the Constitution.* New York: St. Martin's, 1982.

Friedrich, Carl. *Limited Government: A Comparison.* Englewood Cliffs, N.J.: Prentice-Hall, 1974.

Friedrich, Carl, and Zbigniew Brzezinski. *Totalitarian Dictatorship and Autocracy.* New York: Praeger, 1965.

Hamilton, Alexander, John Jay, and James Madison. *The Federalist.* New York: McGraw-Hill, 1964.

Latey, Maurice. *Patterns of Tyranny.* New York: Atheneum, 1969.

Machiavelli, Niccolò. "The Prince." In *The Prince and Other Discourses.* New York: McGraw-Hill, 1950.

Menze, Ernest, ed. *Totalitarianism Reconsidered.* Port Washington, N.Y.: Kennikat, 1981.

Moore, Barrington. *Social Origins of Dictatorship and Democracy.* Boston: Beacon Press, 1966.

Orwell, George. *Nineteen Eighty-four.* New York: New American Library, 1983.

Ottaway, Marina. *Democracy Challenged: The Rise of Semi-Authoritarianism.* Washington, D.C.: Carnegie Endowment of International Peace, 2003.

Ponchaud, François. *Cambodia: Year Zero.* New York: Holt, 1978.

Rubin, Barry. *Modern Dictators.* New York: New American Library, 1988.

SUGGESTED WEB SITES

http://electionresources.org
http://www.worldpolicy.org/globalrights/
http://www.psr.keele.ac.uk/election.htm
http://dodgson.ucsd.edu/lij/
http://www.odci.gov/cia/publications/index.html
http://zimmer.csufresno.edu/~johnsh/econ_EDL.htm
http://www.economist.com/

NOTES

1. Samuel Huntington, *Political Order in Changing Societies* (New Haven, Conn.: Yale University Press, 1968).
2. Charles F. Andrain, *Comparative Political Systems: Policy Performance and Social Change* (Armonk, N.Y.: Sharpe, 1994), pp. 13–90.
3. See, for example, Francis Fukuyama's much-talked-about book *The End of History and the Last Man* (New York: Maxwell Macmillan International, 1992).
4. See, for example, "Phoney Democracies," *The Economist,* June 24, 2000, pp.17–18.
5. Aristotle, *Politics.* Ernest Barker, ed. and trans. (New York: Oxford University Press, 1958), p. 244.
6. Ibid., pp. 244–245.
7. Niccolò Machiavelli, *The Prince,* Harvey C. Mansfield, Jr., trans. (Chicago: University of Chicago Press, 1985).
8. One of the first military officers to seize power and then establish a highly personalistic dictatorship was Egypt's Gamal Abdel Nasser. Military officers who have become personal dictators include Saddam Hussein (Iraq), Muammar al-Qaddafi (Libya), Mengistu Haile Miriam (Ethiopia), Samuel Doe (Liberia), Jerry Rawlings (Ghana), Hafez al-Assad (Syria), Muhammad Zia ul-Haq (Pakistan), Muhammad Ershad (Bangladesh), Manuel Noriega (Panama), and Alfredo Stroessner (Paraguay). Uganda under Idi Amin and the Central African Republic under Jean-Bedel Bokassa, both ousted in 1979, are two particularly gruesome examples of tyranny at the hands of personal dictators who began as obscure military officers. General Rafael Trujillo of the Dominican Republic ruled with an iron hand for thirty years

until his assassination in 1961. General Anastasio Somoza of Nicaragua, overthrown by the Sandinistas in 1979, is yet another example of a modern-day tyrant.

9. There have been some notorious civilian tyrants in the postwar period, too. They are often demagogues — visionaries with a gift of eloquence and a lust for power. Several of the charismatic Third World figures who led their nations to independence after World War II were able to translate their popularity into a formula for personal rule. They are gone now. Several of the most notable were Sukarno in Indonesia (1945–1966), Kwame Nkrumah in Ghana (1957–1966), and Ahmed Sekou Toure in Guinea (1958–1984). Sukarno and Nkrumah were ousted by military coups. Several civilian dictators have fallen more recently. The Shah of Iran was ousted in 1979; several years later, Ferdinand Marcos in the Philippines and the notorious Jean-Claude ("Baby Doc") Duvalier in Haiti met a similar fate.
10. Robert Jackson and Carl Rosberg, *Personal Rule in Black Africa: Princes, Autocrats, Prophets, Tyrants* (Berkeley: University of California Press, 1982), p. 235.
11. See, Huntington, *Political Order in Changing Societies;* see also, Amos Perlmutter, ed., *The Military and Politics in Modern Times* (New Haven, Conn.: Yale University Press, 1977), p. 4.
12. Samuel H. Finer, *Comparative Politics* (London: Penguin, 1970).
13. Eric Nordlinger, *Soldiers and Politics: Military Coups and Governments* (Englewood Cliffs, N.J.: Prentice-Hall, 1977), p. 6.
14. Carl J. Friedrich and Zbigniew Brzezinski, *Totalitarian Dictatorship and Autocracy* (Cambridge, Mass.: Harvard University Press, 1956), p. 9.
15. Christopher Pierson, *Beyond the Welfare State?* (University Park: Pennsylvania State University Press, 1991), p. 128.
16. Lexington, "Red George," *The Economist,* July 5, 2003, p. 30.
17. James H. Mittleman, *Out from Underdevelopment: Prospects for the Third World* (New York: St. Martin's, 1988), p. 22. Among the most highly respected developmental theorists in political science are David Easton, *The Political System* (New York: Knopf, 1977), and "An Approach to the Analysis of a Political System," *World Politics,* April 1957; Gabriel Almond and James Coleman, *The Politics of the Developing Areas* (Princeton, N.J.: Princeton University Press, 1960); Gabriel Almond and G. Bingham Powell, *Comparative Politics: A Developmental Approach* (Boston: Little, Brown, 1966); Huntington, *Political Order in Changing Societies;* and Lucian Pye, *Aspects of Political Development* (Boston: Little, Brown, 1966).
18. See, for example, Bernard K. Gordon, "A High-Risk Trade Policy," *Foreign Affairs,* July/August 2003, p. 107.

PART II:

Western Europe

United Kingdom

Area: 94, 399 square miles

Population: 60.3 million

Density per square mile: 620

Language(s): English, Gaelic, Welsh

Literacy rate: 99%

Major religion(s): Anglican, Roman Catholic

Monetary unit: pound sterling

GNP: 1998 = $1.26 trillion; 2003 = $1.77 trillion (est.)

GNP per capita: 1998 = $21,410 (PPP adjusted = $20,314); 2003 = $29,360

GNP growth rate: 1998 = 2.0%; 2003 (2Q) = 1.8%

Average yearly inflation rate (1990–1999): 3.0%

Recent inflation rate: 3.1% (July 2003)

Unemployment rate: 5.1% (July 2003)

France

Area: 210,038 square miles

Population: 60.2 million

Density per square mile: 277

Language(s): French

Literacy rate: 99%

Major religion(s): Roman Catholic

Monetary unit: franc (euro)

GNP: $1.465 trillion (1998)

GNP per capita: 1998 = $24,210 (PPP adjusted: $21,214); 2003 = $27,890 (est.)

GNP growth rate: 2003 (3Q) = –0.3%

Average yearly inflation rate (1990–1999): 1.7%

Current inflation rate: 1.9% (July 2003)

Unemployment rate: 9.3% (July 2003)

Germany

Area: 137,753 square miles

Population: 81.8 million

Density per square mile: 594

Language(s): German

Literacy rate: 99%

Monetary unit: Deutsch mark (euro)

GNP: 1998 = $2.179 trillion; 2003 = $2.392 trillion (est.)

GNP per capita: 1998 = $26,570 (PPP adjusted: $22,026); 2003 = $29,210 (est.)

GNP growth rate: 1998 = 0.9%; 2003 (2Q) = –0.2%

Average yearly inflation rate (1990–1998): 2.2%

Recent inflation rate: 0.9% (July 2003)

Unemployment rate: 10.7% (July 2003)

Reykjavik
ICELAND
Atlantic Ocean
North Sea
IRELAND
Dublin
UNITED KINGDOM
London
NORWAY
Oslo
SWEDEN
Stockholm
FINLAND
Helsinki
Tallinn
ESTONIA
RUSSIA
Moscow
Riga
LATVIA
Baltic Sea
Copenhagen
DENMARK
LITHUANIA
Vilnius
Minsk
BELARUS
Amsterdam
NETH.
Berlin
Warsaw
POLAND
Kiev
UKRAINE
Brussels
BELG.
GERMANY
Prague
CZECH REP.
SLOVAKIA
Bratislava
MOLDOVA
Paris
LUX.
LIECH.
Vienna
Budapest
Chisinau
SWITZ.
Bern
AUSTRIA
HUNGARY
FRANCE
ROMANIA
Ljubljana
SLOVENIA
Zagreb
BOSNIA & HERZ.
Belgrade
Bucharest
Black Sea
SAN MARINO
CROATIA
Sarajevo
SERBIA & MONT.
BULGARIA
ANDORRA
MONACO
ITALY
Sofia
Skopje
MAC.
PORTUGAL
Madrid
Rome
Tirana
Ankara
VATICAN CITY
Lisbon
SPAIN
GREECE
TURKEY
ALBANIA
Athens
Nicosia
Algiers
Tunis
Rabat
CYPRUS
MALTA
Valletta
MOROCCO
Mediterranean Sea
ALGERIA
TUNISIA
Tripoli
LIBYA
Cairo
EGYPT

Part II Outline: Western Europe

Chapter 3: The Western Political Heritage

Regional Overview

Environmental Influences

Historical and Cultural Factors

The New Ideological Marketplace

Imperialism and the European System

The Totalitarian Interlude

War and Revolution: An Ambiguous Legacy

Case Studies: The United Kingdom, France, and Germany

- The United Kingdom
- France
- Germany

Chapter 4: The Triumph of Parliaments and Pluralism

Western Europe's Economic Miracle

The Problems of Postindustrial Society

Case Studies: The United Kingdom, France, and Germany

- The United Kingdom: Mother of Parliaments
- France's Fifth Republic
- Germany's Unified Federal Democracy

The European Union: An Embryonic State?

CHAPTER 3

The Western Political Heritage

During the heyday of the Cold War, it was common to divide Europe into two parts: Western Europe, rooted in classical Greek and Roman civilizations, and Slavic (or Eastern) Europe, a commingling of Slavic, Scandinavian, Mongolian, and Byzantine cultures. The division resulted from a specific set of historical circumstances, above all, the ideological rivalry between the capitalist United States and the communist Soviet Union.

East-West tensions ran high until 1989, a year of momentous events in Europe, when the Cold War finally came undone. Several milestones marked this sudden end to the dominant and defining conflict of the postwar era, including the overthrow of communist regimes throughout Eastern Europe, the demolition of the Berlin Wall, the reunification of Germany, Soviet troop withdrawals from the territory of former Warsaw Pact allies, and bilateral cuts (reductions on both sides) in conventional military forces. At the same time, however, the north-south split within the European Union (caused by the fact that the northern countries are richer than the southern); the reemergence of the Balkan states as independent actors; the presence of historic, geographic, and economic antecedents for distinct Mediterranean, Germanic, and Scandinavian subregions; and the decision of several EU members to remain outside of the single currency (euro) area all point to the conclusion that, despite the movement toward greater economic integration in the 1990s, new obstacles to a truly unified Europe are likely to appear in the twenty-first century.

Regional Overview

Although every society has its unique features, there are many similarities among contemporary Western European states, similarities so striking that they can only be attributed to a certain cross-fertilization and overlapping of linguistic, cultural, religious, literary, and intellectual experiences. Democratic government is one striking feature common to all — until quite recently, no other region of the world, with the exception of North America (which, of course, is closely tied to Western Europe, historically and culturally), had embraced liberalism and pluralism so unequivocally. By the same token, all the Western European countries embrace market-oriented capitalism, as opposed to the state-centered economic planning long associated with Soviet-style command economies. Moreover, all these societies boast a large, well-educated, relatively affluent urban middle class that is employed increasingly in the service sector (law, medicine, education, banking, insurance, and the like), rather than in agriculture or manufacturing.

The south, however, lags behind the north economically; Spain, Portugal, Greece, and the southern regions of France and Italy have been the least prosperous parts of Western Europe in modern times. The reasons for this north-south disparity are not entirely clear, but probably have something to do with natural resources (the south has few); climate and culture — the pace of life in the Mediterranean is generally slower than in northern Europe, and Spaniards, Italians, and Greeks often exhibit a less intense work ethic than, say, Germans or Norwegians; and politics — Greece and Italy have both experienced recurring governmental instability, while Spain and Portugal were fascist dictatorships until the 1970s.

Urbanization and economic diversification throughout Western Europe have been accompanied by the growth of materialism and secularism. Religion is still important to many individuals and families, but in most of the region secularization of society has weakened the moral authority of church and synagogue alike. Belief in the potential of science and technology to solve all human problems is now the norm nearly everywhere. This reliance on reason and science as opposed to divine providence is a distinctive feature of Western civilization since the early days of the Renaissance (beginning in the late fifteenth century).

Western Europe also has a distinctive intellectual tradition. The effects of the Renaissance, the Reformation, and the Enlightenment were confined almost exclusively to the West. Profoundly influential in modern European history, these formative cultural and spiritual movements merely rippled the surface of Russian society, culture, and politics. The overthrow of czarist rule in 1917 brought to power a band of revolutionaries who espoused a Western ideology (Marxism), but the institutions that replaced czarism had little in common with the ideals of humanism and liberalism inspired by the Enlightenment.

The broad patterns just noted are familiar to anyone who has grown up in a Western country. What is not familiar is how these patterns evolved and why they are unique to the West. In Part II we will trace the outlines of this evolution. By the end of the book, we will have done so for every region of the world in the interest of gaining a clearer understanding of the context of politics in each. In the following section, we look at how the natural environment influences politics in Western Europe.

Environmental Influences

The great peninsula of Western Europe is not separated from the deep interior continent by mountains, jungles, or seas; the topographic grain of the region runs east and west rather than north and south. A low mountain range, the Carpathians, separates the

Balkans to the south from a vast plain that extends to the Baltic Sea. "In this belt lies a huge morass, the Pripet Marsh, a barrier equal to or surpassing the mountains." However, "wide-open gateways" of firm ground flank it.[1]

This flat, expansive east-west geography for European history creates something of a paradox. On the one hand, there has been interaction between the two parts of Europe — peninsular and interior — for many centuries; on the other hand, the two parts developed along largely separate lines. There is no solid line that divides Europe, but rather "several kinds of transitions: the break between Roman-German culture and Greek-Slavic culture; the broad span where hill-bordered lowland on or near salt water gives way to featureless inland plains; the coarse versus fine mesh of transport routes; the dominance of continental over marine climate; the political boundary of Russia."[2]

The political significance of this geography is profound. In brief, it has encouraged the development of two Europes. Even today, when physical distance is no longer a hindrance to communication, an invisible curtain separates the two. We explore the nature and origins of that curtain next.

The European Nursery

For most of the modern era, Western Europe has been the seedbed of innovative ideas in science, technology, and politics. Not surprisingly, no part of the globe was left untouched by the power of these ideas and the institutions they spawned:

> Beginning with very small areas, uniform in climate and resources and isolated from neighbors, the Western tradition has moved into larger spaces, adapted itself to varied climates and landforms, and learned to use a multiplicity of resources. In the process, isolation has given way to a worldwide net of communication. Possessing a unique combination of favorable natural conditions, Europeans maintained political dominance and economic leadership in the successive worlds of which they have been a part.[3]

Although the metaphor of Europe as a nursery may overstate European influence and understate indigenous developments in many other regions of the world, the concept holds more than a grain of truth. From the beginning of the great European explorations during the fifteenth-century Renaissance to the Age of Imperialism and the Industrial Revolution four hundred years later, Europe made a deep imprint on every region of the world. Indeed, as Table 3.1 shows, Europe accounted for over three-fifths of the world's total manufacturing output by 1900; moreover, this dramatic shift had resulted in the economic eclipse of the Third World, including China and India.[4] Why did Western Europe display such enormous vigor during this protracted period? Could physical, geographic, or climatic factors have contributed to this burst of creative energy?

Nature's Benevolence

Western Europe does enjoy certain natural advantages over most other regions of the world. Its climate displays a wide variety without extremes. "No area of equal size on earth is so favored in climate — both in its variety and in its suitability for human life."[5] Its soils and climates are generally conducive to agriculture, yet minerals are also abundant:

Table 3.1 Relative Shares of World Manufacturing Output, 1750–1900 (percent)

	1750	1800	1830	1860	1880	1900
Europe	23.2	28.1	34.2	53.2	61.3	62.0
United Kingdom	1.9	4.3	9.5	19.9	22.9	18.5
Hapsburg Empire	2.9	3.2	3.2	4.2	4.4	4.7
France	4.0	4.2	5.2	7.9	7.8	6.8
German States/Germany	2.9	3.5	3.5	4.9	8.5	13.2
Italian States/Italy	2.4	2.5	2.3	2.5	2.5	2.5
Russia	5.0	5.6	5.6	7.0	7.6	8.8
United States	0.1	0.8	2.4	7.2	14.7	23.6
Japan	3.8	3.5	2.8	2.6	2.4	2.4
Third World	73.0	67.7	60.5	36.6	20.9	11.0
China	32.8	33.3	29.8	19.7	12.5	6.2
India/Pakistan	24.5	19.7	17.6	8.6	2.8	1.7

Source: Paul Kennedy, *The Rise and Fall of the Great Powers* (New York: Random House, 1987), p. 149.

> Two of the three most critical soil fertilizers are present in large quantities, and the third can be manufactured from local resources. Rich coal fields occur from Scotland to Poland, and ample iron ores for steel making lie not far from coal. The Western economic order since the Industrial Revolution has been based on these two minerals.[6]

Northwestern Europe thus became the center of the Industrial Revolution. Coal deposits and rivers were crucial. According to a scholar of the 1920s:

> Modern industry is based upon the use of coal and to a [lesser] degree on "white coal," or waterpower. Coal is necessary in the making of iron and steel and for the operation of the machines in factories. Since coal is bulky and expensive to transport, it is usually easier to bring raw materials that are to be converted into manufactured articles to the vicinity of the mines than vice versa. As a consequence, many of the great manufacturing centers, particularly those of Germany, England, and Belgium, cluster near the coalfields. . . .
>
> It is a very important fact that there is almost no coal at all in the Alpine-Mediterranean Region. This circumstance, perhaps no less than the reorientation of the world's trade routes to the Atlantic which followed the discovery of America and the sea route to the Indies, helps explain why the Mediterranean countries have not experienced the tremendous industrial development and the growth of huge cities so characteristic of Northwestern Europe.[7]

It was no accident, for example, that in the 1920s twenty-seven of Great Britain's forty largest cities were situated near coal deposits and that eleven of Germany's forty-seven cities of 100,000 people or more were on coal beds.[8]

Rivers were important as a source of hydroelectric power and, like the sea, as a means of commerce, communication, and transport. The main waterway of modern Europe has run along the Atlantic Coast of the Continent rather than the Mediterranean. With only a few exceptions, the principal seaports are located on or near the mouths of rivers.

The large number of rivers and seaports facilitated trade, transport, and travel, as well as the spread of ideas and institutions within Europe. In addition, they afforded Western Europe ease of access to the outside world and served as a powerful stimulus to transoceanic exploration, conquest, colonization, and commerce. These developments preceded and helped set the stage for the Industrial Revolution.[9]

Historical and Cultural Factors

Why did Western Europe develop differently from other regions? One reason often given is that Europe was able to develop at its own pace. This "modernization from within" contrasts sharply with the externally induced social change that occurred in the Middle East, Africa, Asia, and Latin America. Europe in the Middle Ages was very much like today's developing countries were a century ago. But unlike the Third World, Europe was not conquered and colonized by more technologically advanced invaders. It is true that the Chinese and Ottoman empires were both ahead of medieval Europe in state organization and technology. Indeed, the Ottoman Empire pressed the periphery of Western Europe, reaching the outskirts of Vienna in the sixteenth century. But by this time the Ottoman state was overextended and past its zenith.

Thus, Western Europe could evolve slowly, with less urgency and along lines that were natural to its indigenous peoples and cultures. It is noteworthy that the European countries most immune to outside invasion (Britain and Scandinavia) evolved quite differently from Germany and Italy, which in turn have followed paths different from Eastern Europe and the Balkans.

The fact that Western Europe has a feudal Roman Catholic legacy and the United States does not also deserves brief mention here. Because the caste-like relationships of feudalism never existed in the New World, Americans often fail to understand the political implications of class structure. The feudal heritage and the pervasiveness of Roman Catholicism eventually led to struggles over class and religion in Europe and to the rise of church-based political parties. By contrast, there is no feudal or aristocratic tradition in the United States, and the constitutional separation of church and state has limited the role of organized religion in American politics.

Also striking is the absence in the United States of the socialist labor parties so commonplace in Western Europe. The lack of such parties in the United States results in part from the early establishment of universal white male suffrage. In Europe, with the major exception of France, the working class had to fight for the franchise, and to this end it supported political movements that persisted for decades afterward.

Religion: Renaissance and Reformation

The Italian **Renaissance** was revolutionary in its focus on the earthly notion of human beings as the center of all things. Whereas Christianity stressed that divine providence sets the shape and course of history, the giants of the Renaissance believed in the surpassing powers of the human will and intellect.

Until the Protestant **Reformation** in the sixteenth century, Roman Catholicism was the universal religion of Europe dating back to the early days of the Holy Roman Empire (800–1806). The Reformation started in 1517–1520 when Martin Luther led a revolt, later joined by John Calvin and other dissidents within the church, to liberate the faith from a corrupt papacy. The protest — hence the term *Protestant* — was against Rome, not against Christianity. The Reformation was a time of tumult and change, but in the end it revitalized Christianity and reaffirmed its dominance of the West's moral and spiritual life. Moreover, the movement Luther launched turned into a social upheaval with political ramifications that surprised and alarmed Luther himself. (Luther bitterly denounced the violent excesses of rampaging antipapists.)

Was the Reformation a cause or an effect of secularization in the modern world? Probably both. By successfully challenging Rome's spiritual authority (for example, by denying the pope's infallibility), it undermined religion in general — in this sense it was a cause. But the Renaissance with its spirit of adventure, inquiry, iconoclasm, and intellectual ferment no doubt incited church reformers like Luther and Calvin — in this sense the Reformation was an effect.

The Renaissance and the Reformation together fed into powerful new intellectual, economic, and political undercurrents that emerged in the form of the Scientific Revolution, the Age of Enlightenment, the Industrial Revolution, and the Age of Imperialism — but first came mercantilism, which we look at next.

Mercantilism: The Western Origins of the World Economy

The system of **mercantilism** refers to the means devised by England and France to deal with the economic challenge posed by Holland in the seventeenth century. As formulated in France under Louis XIV (1643–1715), mercantilism was a policy aimed at impeding or preventing the importation of Dutch products by imposing high tariffs, banning the use of third-country ships in foreign trade and commerce, and subsidizing domestic shippers and manufacturers. Mercantilism equated wealth with money and judged nations by the size of their **balance of trade** surplus or decifit.[10] Mercantilism also reflected the desire to promote national producers and manufacturers (an early version of the **infant industries** development strategy).

In Holland, England, and France, mercantilism provided the impetus for the acquisition of colonial empires. The instruments of this early empire-building rivalry were the great merchant companies, notably the Dutch East India Company and the English East India Company. (A French Company of the Indies was also established later.) Thanks to broad charter authority granted by home governments, these great companies not only "conducted the business" of shipping and trading but also "exercised rights of sovereignty" in the colonies.[11] The key role of mercantilism in the rise and fall of the great powers in Europe during this period has been well documented by historians.[12]

The Scientific Revolution

The urge to conquer new worlds in the sixteenth and seventeenth centuries was no less evident in domestic than in international affairs. The **Scientific Revolution,** as this period has come to be known, was a time of tremendous intellectual vitality. Pioneers of modern science like Copernicus, Galileo, Descartes, Francis Bacon, and Isaac Newton gave new meaning to the humanistic impulses associated with the Renaissance. In little more than a century and a half, they revolutionized our understanding of the physical world and laid the foundations of the natural sciences, including physics, chemistry, biology, and astronomy. In so doing, they also laid the foundations of modernity, with all its implications for good or evil. They gave future generations the tools to conquer nature and paved the way for the **secular humanism** of today, a philosophy that stresses the potential of humankind, using scientific as well as political means, to solve social and economic problems.

It is impossible to understand the idealistic roots of democracy or socialism (or democratic socialism) in the modern world without appreciating the tremendous impact of science on the way people think, live, and die. In eighteenth-century Europe, a spectacular presentiment of the power of science to change how we think and live occurred in the decades prior to the great revolutions that rocked both the old and the new worlds. This sequence of events — a revolution in ideas about the world followed by bold attempts to change it — was no mere coincidence.

The Enlightenment: From Science to Secularism

The eighteenth-century **Enlightenment** was a significantly new way of looking at humanity and the world, emphasizing human reason over blind faith. (This period is also known as the Age of Reason.) The morality linked to Enlightenment ideas and ideals was readily identifiable in the Judeo-Christian tradition and the ethical systems of Greek and Roman antiquity: the Golden Rule of the New Testament, the Golden Mean of the Greek philosophers, and the emphasis on honesty and other conventional virtues. Two elements of Roman Catholic dogma, however, were rejected. One was the key role of the holy sacraments (such as the ritual breaking of bread and drinking of wine known as Holy Communion, and the giving of last rites at the time of death) as the path to salvation; the other was the central importance of asceticism, self-deprivation, and resistance to temptation (broadly defined as worldly pleasures).

In place of the notion that suffering and self-sacrifice were divinely ordained tests of faith, Enlightenment thinkers (principally the French **philosophes**) developed the doctrine of **ethical hedonism,** which held that ordinary human desires were natural and good, not things to be denied or ashamed of. The orthodox Christian teaching on the inherent evil in human beings (the doctrine of original sin) was replaced by a belief in humanity's innate goodness. Enlightenment thinkers dreamed of "a world without conflict, without harshness, with men of intelligence and goodwill working independently, each for his own welfare, yet all together for common interests as well."[13]

The French philosophes did for the social sciences what the giants of the Scientific Revolution did for the natural sciences. They focused on the workings of the empirical world (fact and experience) and sought the truth about human nature and social behavior through introspection. By this method the philosophes developed trenchant critiques of established social values and political institutions. The overriding aim, however, was not to disparage existing customs and beliefs but rather to make the world a better place for the majority of human beings, rich and poor alike.

Politically, the philosophes seem surprisingly moderate (and modern) by today's standards. In general, they did not advocate anything so radical as the dismantling of the nation-state system or even the overthrow of Europe's absolute monarchs. Instead they envisioned a new social order in which the rule of law bound rulers and ruled alike and all citizens were guaranteed equal rights. They did not seek economic equality or common ownership of property — indeed they seldom called for the abolition of noble titles and ranks — but they did favor eliminating aristocratic powers and privileges.

The transformation envisioned by the rational thinkers of the eighteenth century was by no means bloody, nor did the possibility of violent mass revolution greatly concern them. In retrospect it clearly should have, for the kind of radical change they embraced would come only after a protracted period of civil strife. The first upheaval occurred in France.

The French Revolution

The **French Revolution** of 1789 was not the inevitable result of the intellectual dissent associated with the Enlightenment but rather the product of complex social, economic, and political difficulties. It began as a rebellion of the nobility against what this class regarded as unfair and onerous taxation imposed by King Louis XVI. The execution of Louis XVI in 1793 was a turning point in French (and European) history. Radicals called **Jacobins** gained control and set about creating a "republic of virtue" — a thinly veiled tyranny run by zealots in search of utopia.

The "fever" stage of the French Revolution did not last long: it soon gave way to the so-called Thermidorean reaction. The Thermidoreans rejected both popular government, which they saw as synonymous with mob rule, and absolute monarchy rooted in heredity and privilege. Under the guise of republicanism, they set up a kind of ruling committee known as the Directory. This regime lasted about five years before giving way to the dictatorship of Napoléon Bonaparte.

The French Revolution makes for a fascinating study. For our purposes, the essential point is that this revolution, despite its ultimate failure in France, was a presentiment of things to come. Popular demands for democracy and social justice would accompany another kind of revolution, namely, the Industrial Revolution. This revolution would change the way work and workers were organized, what they produced, and where, when, and how they produced it. In the process, this revolution would shake Europe to its very foundations.

The Industrial Revolution and Its Consequences

The rise of liberalism in nineteenth-century Europe was facilitated by the application of science to production. The new economic frontiers opening up made constitutional democracy attractive to the rising commercial middle class, which would now have the political means to protect and expand its economic interests. At the same time, the factory system fostered by expanding markets and new technologies, created a new class of wage laborers, which transformed the structure of previously rural, agriculturally based, aristocratic societies, with consequences that could hardly have been imagined at the time.

The use of mechanical energy to increase labor productivity was a key feature of the **Industrial Revolution.** Textile manufacturing and mining were the first industrial sectors to be mechanized; virtually all others followed. One of the early social consequences was the exploitation of workers — including children — for profit; another, as Karl Marx noted, was the concentration of labor, which in time gave rise to new social forces that changed Western European politics forever.

The coming of age of coal-fueled, steam-powered machines provided the impetus for the construction of railroads and canals. It revolutionized modes of transportation and communication, making farming far more efficient and less labor-intensive in the process. Industrialization led to the rise of modern urban centers — a process that occurred in a relatively short time span, especially in the United States, Germany, Russia, and Japan. Of course, these four rising powers were to play the major roles in the unfolding drama of world politics in the twentieth century. (See Table 3.2.)

Table 3.2 Urban Population of the Powers (in millions) and as a Percentage of Total Population, 1890–1938

Country	1890	1900	1910	1913	1920	1928	1938
1. Great Britain (1)	11.2 (29.9%)	13.5 (32.8%)	15.3 (34.9%)	15.8 (34.6%)	16.6 (37.3%)	17.5 (38.2%)	18.7 (39.2%)
2. United States (2)	9.6 (15.3%)	14.6 (18.7%)	20.3 (22.0%)	22.5 (23.1%)	27.4 (25.9%)	34.3 (28.7%)	45.1 (32.8%)
3. Germany (4)	5.6 (11.3%)	8.7 (15.5%)	12.9 (20.0%)	14.1 (21.0%)	15.3 (35.7%)	19.1 (34.4%)	20.7 (30.2%)
4. France (3)	4.5 (11.7%)	5.2 (13.3%)	5.7 (14.4%)	5.9 (14.8%)	5.9 (15.1%)	6.3 (15.3%)	6.3 (15.0%)
5. Russia (8)	4.3 (3.6%)	6.6 (4.8%)	10.2 (6.4%)	12.3 (7.0%)	4.0 (3.1%)	10.7 (7.1%)	36.5 (20.2%)
6. Italy (5)	2.7 (9.0%)	3.1 (9.6%)	3.8 (11.0%)	4.1 (11.6%)	5.0 (13.2%)	6.5 (16.1%)	8.0 (18.2%)
7. Japan (6)	2.5 (6.3%)	3.8 (8.6%)	5.8 (10.3%)	6.6 (12.8%)	6.4 (11.6%)	9.7 (15.6%)	20.7 (28.6%)
8. Austria-Hungary (7)	2.4 (5.6%)	3.1 (6.6%)	4.2 (8.2%)	4.6 (8.8%)	—	—	—

Source: Paul Kennedy, *The Rise and Fall of the Great Powers* (New York: Random House, 1987), p. 200.

Today we can see the results of the Industrial Revolution all around us, especially urbanization and its accompanying ills. Big cities, elaborate highway systems, mammoth shopping malls, a depopulated countryside, chronic agricultural surpluses, air and water pollution, urban sprawl, traffic congestion, and high crime rates — these are just a few of the economic and social consequences of the Industrial Revolution.

The New Ideological Marketplace

Along with socioeconomic changes came changes in political thinking. Three competing public philosophies — or ideologies — competed for the hearts and minds of the people in the nineteenth century (and, for that matter, still do): liberalism, socialism, and conservatism.

Liberalism

At the time of its inception in revolutionary France, **liberalism** represented a middle way between the extreme egalitarianism of the Jacobins and the inherited wealth, power, and privilege of the old aristocratic order. It was ideally suited to the interests of the emerging middle class, for whom liberty ranked above equality in the hierarchy of political values. Politically, liberalism decried arbitrary and repressive rule, press censorship, laws conferring special privilege on hereditary aristocracies, and discrimination against individuals on the basis of race or religion. Economically, it stressed property rights and other middle-class interests.

Influenced by Adam Smith and others, nineteenth-century liberals embraced the view that free competition among nations and individuals, unrestrained by tariffs and monopolies, would inevitably produce the greatest prosperity for the largest number; that unemployment, hunger, and deprivation were nature's way of regulating population growth; and that wages are determined not by capitalists seeking to maximize profits and minimize costs but by the "iron law" of supply and demand.

Because liberalism represented rather narrow economic interests (by contemporary standards, nineteenth-century liberalism was stiffly conservative), advocates of democracy and republicanism stepped forward — in England they were called radicals. And as the Industrial Revolution came of age, the working class also came of age. For the champions of this underclass, "bourgeois" democracy was too cautious and too compatible with capitalism. Instead, they turned to socialism. In so doing, they founded a movement that continues to have millions of followers in Europe right down to the present.

Socialism

There are many varieties of **socialism** but they share a common distaste for private ownership of the means of production (that is, free enterprise). Money (the object of capitalist enterprise) is viewed as the root of all evil in society. Socialism disdains the profit motive and advocates basic equality in the distribution of material goods. It takes an optimistic view of human nature, and it blames greed, envy, corruption, and crime on injustices built into the nature of capitalistic society. Remove the social causes of antisocial behavior, in this view, and domestic tranquility will surely follow.

In the United States, socialism is often erroneously equated with one of its offshoots, namely communism. Communism, however, is simply an extreme brand of socialism often associated with the advocacy of violent revolution. To be exact, not all communists even embrace violent revolution as a means of overthrowing capitalism — some communists, for example, believe that capitalism can be defeated via free elections in which informed voters choose socialism. Indeed, something resembling that process has occurred at various times in various countries, including many in Western Europe, although the result in virtually every case has been to place more moderate socialist parties in power rather than communist parties per se. During the Cold War, Communism (with a capital *C*) came to refer to a specific brand of socialism associated with the October Revolution in Russia and with the ideas of Lenin and Stalin (discussed in Chapters 5 and 6). Perhaps because of the emotional and political intensity of the Cold War rivalry, it is still difficult for many observers to separate the theory of socialism from its troubled and often turbulent history.

Conservatism

While liberalism, republicanism, and socialism were vying for the allegiance of newly emerging social forces in Great Britain and on the Continent, the advocates of **conservatism** were trying to preserve traditional values and protect the old order. The most important conservative thinker was Edmund Burke (1729–1797). In his book *Reflections on the French Revolution,* written in 1790, Burke warned that nations which discard customs, beliefs, and institutions rooted in the past in their endeavor to build a perfect society risk chaos and political catastrophe. No doubt the victims of the Jacobin terror would have agreed.

Against the background of the advancing Industrial Revolution, these crosscurrents — liberalism, socialism, and conservatism — competed for primacy in Western Europe during the nineteenth century and most of the twentieth.

Social Class and Politics

As the previous discussion suggests, the political spectrum in Europe is much broader and more diversified than in the United States. The conventional American understanding of "class" can be misleading when applied in the European setting. There social class has played a major role in defining ideological positions and creating political parties. To a much greater extent than in the United States, class consciousness has long been a motive force in European politics, and ideological divisions are often as important in election campaigns and outcomes as policy differences (although the political cultures of Europe appear to be changing and perhaps even converging, as we will discover later).

Historically, political parties in Europe have reflected the evolving class structure of European society. Center-right parties — the Christian Democrats in Germany, the Gaullists and neo-Gaullists in France, the Conservatives (Tories) in Great Britain — have historically represented conservative, middle-class farming and business interests. Center-left parties (Social Democrats and Socialists) have sought to appeal to the commercial and professional classes. And the far-left Communist Party has represented the working class and intellectuals. Center-right parties often support welfare-state policies of the kind most conservative Republicans in the United States detest. Parties of the far right were very popular in many European countries during the tumultuous period between World War I and World War II. Far-right parties (discussed in the following chapter) were discredited and even outlawed after World War II, but showed signs of staging a comeback in some places during the 1990s — especially among youths and blue-collar workers. Center-left parties are ideologically similar to the most liberal elements of the U.S. Democratic Party. Far-left parties have never had much appeal in North America.

Why would some Europeans identify with the Communist Party? First, throughout Europe, the communists have historically fought for the rights of workers, as have the Socialists and the Social Democrats. Second, in World War II, the communists generally put up the strongest resistance to the Nazis and Fascists, and many voters in France and Italy showed their appreciation by voting for Communist Party candidates in the elections held after the war. Third, the communist parties of Western Europe are not subversive or revolutionary organizations. In most cases, they disavow violence and participate in elections like other responsible political parties.

Nonetheless, communist parties have fallen on hard times in Europe, both East and West. In the West, the reasons are not difficult to discern: the industrial workforce — the communists' main constituency — has dwindled in proportion to service-sector jobholders in recent decades; measures protecting workers from exploitation or abuse at the hands of profit-minded capitalists are in force; and the communist parties have failed to broaden their base or build lasting coalitions with other parties. But the severest blow to left-wing parties was the toppling of communist governments in Eastern Europe and the disintegration of the Soviet Union in the span of only three years (1989–1991).

Some examples will help to clarify the class character of European political parties. In Great Britain, the Labour Party emerged as the champion of the working class around a century ago. The party has always been closely linked to the British trade union movement. The absence of a significant Marxist party in Great Britain can be explained partly by the rise of the Labour Party and partly by the fact that the British ruling elite pursued relatively progressive policies, making economic and political concessions to the workers. On the Continent, socialist, communist, and social democratic parties all competed for the allegiance of the workers.

The Christian Democratic Party in Germany exemplifies another ideological strand in European politics. Throughout Europe, religion has long been a politically potent force. In Germany, both Roman Catholics and Protestants have viewed Marxism with alarm, in part because of its atheistic bent. Christian Democrats are strong advocates of democracy and free enterprise. Hence they represented a coalition of middle-class elements (farming, business, banking, the professions) and working-class people for whom religion was as important as bread-and-butter issues. Today, with the fading of the "communist threat," the religious dimension of politics in Germany is no longer of great significance. Instead, both the Christian Democrats and the Social Democrats are essentially centrist parties, the former stressing free enterprise and the latter advocating state intervention to share the nation's considerable wealth more equitably. But it is important to recognize that many "conservative" parties in Western Europe, including the Christian Democrats, support welfare-state policies, in sharp contrast to the political right in the United States.

New problems and changing conditions have produced new parties, one example being the Greens. Green parties sprang up throughout Western Europe in the 1960s and 1970s in response to growing fear of a nuclear catastrophe. In the 1970s and 1980s, the Greens became increasingly concerned with other environmental concerns. In the Federal Republic of Germany, where they have had some electoral success in recent times, they continued to oppose nuclear weapons and nuclear power plants but began to focus more and more on air and water pollution. Their support is drawn largely from the universities — both professors and students — and white-collar workers. Their main opponents are farmers (who use large quantities of pesticides and chemical fertilizers), industrialists, and developers (who tend to place economic growth ahead of environmental protection).

Imperialism and the European System

The second half of the nineteenth century is often called the **Age of Imperialism,** at which time began a new wave of European colonial expansion. Expansionism was the order of the day in North America too, although the United States was engaged in carving out a continental rather than an overseas empire and the territories it annexed became states rather than colonies. (See Box 3.1.) Earlier in the same century, people had become disillusioned with empires and colonies, partly because of successful revolutions in the Americas against England, Spain, and Portugal. Industrialization diverted attention from external expansion in favor of internal development, and the new emphasis on free trade removed much of the rationale for global empire building. British Prime Minister Benjamin Disraeli expressed the tenor of the times in 1852. "These wretched colonies," he said, "will all be independent too in a few years and are a millstone around our necks."

Theories of Colonial Rule

As industry grew, Europe's economic and political leaders began to seek new sources of raw materials and new markets for their products. After 1870, free trade gave way to protectionist policies, and soon a race for new colonies began. A plethora of theories defending colonial expansion were expounded. Alfred T. Mahan's geopolitical concepts were used to "prove" that great powers could not survive without overseas possessions. Charles Darwin's concept of the survival of the fittest was used to "prove" that colonialism was in accordance with the inexorable laws of nature. Rudyard Kipling wrote about the "white man's burden" (to spread civilization to a benighted world).

Democracy in America

BOX 3.1

The United States: Made in Europe?

The first waves of immigrants to America came primarily from Europe. The colonies were established by a European power (the United Kingdom). The official language of the United States (English) is a Europan language, as is the major unofficial language spoken (Spanish) by a growing segment of the population. The dominant Judeo-Christian religious traditions of the United States also were brought by Europeans. Finally, the ideas of the Enlightenment — specifically the works of political philosophers from Plato to Locke, Rousseau, and Montesquieu — inspired the American Revolution and the Framers of the U.S. Constitution. By the same token, the British "common law" tradition formed the basis for the American legal system.

Even today, many Americans look upon Europe with a mixture of admiration and curiosity. Every summer, American tourists pour into Europe (infusing lots of U.S. dollars into the local economy wherever they go). Europe is the playground of America's rich and famous. Even for middle-class Americans, visiting the great cities of Europe — London, Paris, Rome, Prague, and others — is considered essential. And at home, Americans are the non-European world's most avid consumers of European products: Swedish and German cars, Italian cuisine, French wine, Dutch beer, Swiss watches, and the like.

The relationship between the United States and Europe is complex and contradictory. The influence of American pop music, films, youth fashions, and multinational corporations is obvious everywhere in Europe. Many Europeans have a love-hate relationship with the United States as a result. The same individuals who resent the way in which a creeping "Americanization" has eroded national customs and lifestyles since World War II also favor a continued American military presence in Europe, for example.

Why is there such ambivalence? Europeans had to adjust to a changed world after World War II, a world in which Europe was no longer at center stage. The second half of the twentieth century (until the early 1990s) was dominated by two superpowers: the United States and the Soviet Union. Western Europeans feared Soviet military power and felt threatened by Moscow. Most Europeans recognized the value of American arms and money (and welcomed both), but many felt humiliated by the need for either. Many also were frustrated at the popularity of American culture (which Europeans sometimes see as an oxymoron).

Even U.S. President McKinley claimed that God had spoken to him on the eve of the Spanish-American War (1898), commissioning the United States to take the Philippines and Christianize "our brown brothers."

By the end of the nineteenth century, all of Asia and Africa had been colonized. Even China had lost its sovereign status: it was subjugated through a series of treaties that gave various European powers special rights and prerogatives. Africa in 1914 was under the colonial sway of no fewer than seven European nations — Belgium, France, Germany, Great Britain, Italy, Portugal, and Spain. In fact, only two independent nations remained — Ethiopia and Liberia.

The Classical Balance of Power

Paradoxically, as Europe approached the zenith of its power, it was also reaching the end of its preeminence in world affairs. For centuries the international system had been synonymous with the European system. Since the Treaty of Westphalia (1648), the rulers and statesmen of Europe had recognized the existence of a **balance of power,** a system that preserved order and prevented the hegemony of any one state over the others.

This uniquely European system grew out of shared values forged over the centuries. In 1871, Edward Gibbon, author of *The Decline and Fall of the Roman Empire,* proposed, "to consider Europe as one great republic, whose various inhabitants have attained almost the same level of politeness and cultivation."

> The balance of power will then continue to fluctuate, and the prosperity of our own or the neighboring kingdoms may be alternately exalted or depressed; but these events cannot essentially injure our general state of happiness, the system of arts, and law, and the manners which so advantageously distinguish, above the rest of mankind, the Europeans and their colonies.[14]

During the heyday of the European balance-of-power era, many of the great thinkers made implicit reference to the intellectual and moral foundations that undergirded a de facto political unity. For example, a French thinker named Fenelon, noted, "Christendom forms a kind of general republic which has its common interests, fears, and precautions." Rousseau asserted, "The nations of Europe form among themselves an invisible nation"; and the great Enlightenment philosopher of international law Vattel wrote, "Europe forms a political system, a body where the whole is connected by the relations and different interests of nations inhabiting this part of the world."[15] In sum, the fuel that kept "the motor of the balance of power moving," according to this thesis, "is the intellectual and moral foundation of Western civilization, the intellectual and moral climate within which the protagonists of eighteenth-century society moved and which permeated all their thought and action."[16]

Beyond a common worldview, the main features of the European balance-of-power model can be summarized as follows:

- Numerous sovereign powers — five to ten significant state actors are present at any given time.
- Flexible alliances — state actors are pragmatic and unencumbered by ideological baggage.
- Limited objectives — state actors do not pursue goals that threaten the existence of other states.
- Limited means — strategies, tactics, and armaments employed in pursuit of national interests are circumscribed by both the state of technology and moral constraints.
- A keeper of the balance — as an island power aloof from the affairs of the Continent, Great Britain was ideally situated to play the role of "honest broker" by intervening on the Continent to prevent France or any other great power from establishing an empire that would pose a threat to the British Isles.

The Demise of the Eurocentric System

Ironically, the globalization brought about by imperialism hastened the demise of this Eurocentric international system. In the years leading up to World War I, the European system showed signs of decrepitude: alliances turned rigid, an unrestrained arms race occurred, ideological divisions sharpened, and nationalism spread.[17]

U.S. President Woodrow Wilson conceived of the League of Nations as an alternative to nationalism and the European balance-of-power system. Although it never worked, it prefigured the emergence of a new global system with the United States and Japan (later the United States and the Soviet Union) as the major non-European powers.

The Totalitarian Interlude

A dark shadow fell across the political landscape of Europe after World War I. An extreme left-wing ideology, the Marxist-Leninist form of **communism,** triumphed in Russia in 1917, and an extreme right-wing ideology, **fascism,** gained ascendancy in Italy a few years later. But it was in Germany between the two world wars that the battle lines between the extremist ideologies of the left and right were drawn most sharply and fatefully.

The German defeat in World War I was humiliating, and harsh peace terms were imposed. Following an unconditional surrender, Germany was forced by the Treaty of Versailles to accept a "war guilt" clause, in effect an admission of responsibility and liability for the death and destruction caused by the war. The treaty imposed a parliamentary democracy on Germany (the ill-fated Weimar Republic), assessed heavy reparations and indemnities against Germany, and called for permanent unilateral German disarmament.

Understandably, this treaty was never popular in Germany. Nor was the Weimar Republic, which carried the stigma of Versailles. But it was the draconian economic burdens imposed by the treaty that proved to be the undoing of the Weimar government and the making of Adolf Hitler's Nazi Party.

In the early 1920s, hyperinflation (skyrocketing prices) left the German middle class impoverished. The worldwide stock market collapse of 1929 delivered the coup de grâce. Foreign banks called in their loans to Germany, and a wave of protectionism brought international trade to a near standstill. Repression spread across the industrialized world, and unemployment grew to epidemic proportions. In the chaos and despair that ensued, extremism found fertile soil. Germany became a hothouse for radical ideologies, especially National Socialism.

National Socialism (Nazism) had much in common with other extreme right-wing (fascist) ideologies. It was ultranationalistic, glorifying the German *Volk* as a chosen people and enshrining a mythical *Volksgeist* (popular spirit) as the force that defined, united, and guided the German nation. Among its highest values were loyalty to the leader, obedience to authority, and courage in the face of danger. The Nazis glorified power; for true believers, violence was a virtue, and war would bring triumph rather than tragedy.

Hitler came to power legally. His Nazi Party had a larger following in the early 1930s than any of its competitors. The Nazi leader was popular in part because he told the German people what they wanted to hear. For example, he attributed Germany's defeat in World War I not to German failings but to a stab in the back by communists and Jews (he tended to equate the two). He also pandered to German prejudices, particularly anti-Semitism. Jews became a convenient scapegoat for nearly everything that was wrong with German society. In sum, National Socialism was a doctrine of hatred, prejudice, violence, and revenge.

Such dark sentiments were not confined to Germany. The roots of European fascism were in Italy, and the branches reached far and wide. Fascism triumphed in a relatively mild form in Spain in the 1930s. It also took hold in Eastern Europe; fascist regimes in Hungary, Romania, and Bulgaria collaborated with Hitler in the early stages of World War II. Moreover, even where fascism failed to gain the upper hand, its sympathizers occasionally made their presence felt. In southern France, for instance, the so-called Vichy regime collaborated with Hitler during the war. On the other side of the globe, a militaristic, expansionist, and fanatically nationalistic regime closely resembling the fascist model came to power in Japan in the 1930s.

Why did fascism arise so suddenly and virulently in both Europe and Asia between the two world wars? First, the Great Depression of the 1930s shattered national economies and caused societies to turn inward (for example, adopting high "protectionist" tariffs). Second, the results of World War I, as we have seen, set the stage for Germany's attempt to redeem itself for the humiliating defeat it suffered; in Asia, China's ongoing political turmoil was an open invitation to Japanese aggression. Third, governments placed too much faith in the capability of an untested international organization (the League of Nations) to maintain the peace.

We turn now to a brief consideration of the recurrent problems of war and revolution in European history. These violent episodes form a bloodstained backdrop to the study of Europe's political experience prior to 1945.

War and Revolution: An Ambiguous Legacy

One thing is certain: war has played a major role in shaping the modern history of Western Europe. As we have seen, revolution — the domestic equivalent of war — has also been an integral part of European history during the past two centuries. (More recently, terrorism has intruded on the political scene as well.) The conclusion cannot be escaped that collective violence is a European tradition, despite its civilization. (See Box 3.2.)

The implications of this dark side of Europe's heritage are not obvious. Perhaps a violent history predisposes individuals or societies to violence. But this is not necessarily the case. In fact, the cataclysmic events that tore Europe asunder in the twentieth century could just as well have the opposite effect in the twenty-first century: to make succeeding generations determined not to repeat the same mistakes.

Similarly, the nations of Western Europe have firsthand experience with the burdens of imperialism and with the pitfalls of unrestrained nationalism. It may be that these lessons will be forgotten or that they were never properly learned. But from the vantage point of the present, it appears as though most Europeans, chastened by

Contrast and Comparison

BOX 3.2

Europe's War System: A Balance of Power?

When the late Middle Ages gave way to the early modern era (beginning in the fifteenth century), the political landscape changed fundamentally: nation-states ruled by absolute monarchs redrew the map of Europe. Nations (communities based on a common language and culture) became the basis for states — independent and competing political units. The object of competition often involved dynastic succession (who would inherit a vacated throne) or disputed territory, and the form of competition involved war.

The new order based on nation-states was self-contradictory: monarchs were powerful but perpetually insecure because there was no guarantee (and there were no rules) against armed aggression. This state of affairs gave rise to a unique system of international relations based on a concept called the *balance of power* — monarchs would make treaties and alliances with other monarchs (often secretly) to counterbalance the power of one monarch whom they all feared. An attack on a state was often viewed as an attack on the "system" or the "balance."

Critics of the balance-of-power system call it the "war system." If its purpose was to prevent war and bloodshed, they argue, it failed miserably. Wars have been a recurring phenomenon in Europe since the nation-state system emerged from the morass of the Middle Ages.

Defenders of the European system argue that, in the absence of a balancing mechanism, war would likely have been more frequent and less restrained. They point out that before the twentieth century, when the classical balance-of-power system broke down, wars were generally limited in scope, if not always in duration. By contrast, several all-out wars have been fought since that time, suggesting that once the old European order collapsed, there was nothing equally effective to take its place.

Today, the European system is a "no-war system" and the old balance-of-power model has been replaced by a two-tier model in which members of the EU are enmeshed in close economic and political ties of mutual benefit, while the EU and North Atlantic Treaty Organization (NATO), led by an external power, the United States, counterbalance Russia, the only plausible outside threat to the new European international order.

Europe's violent past, are eager to find a different pathway to the future. (It is a different story in the Balkans, as bitter ethnic conflicts in Yugoslavia recently demonstrated.)

World War II sealed the fate of the European system and, for a time at least, relegated the former great powers (and colonial overlords) of Europe to second-rate status. As a result of two devastating wars on the Continent, France, Germany, and Great Britain — the core countries of Western Europe — were forced to turn to the United States for succor and security. The Marshall Plan and the North Atlantic Treaty Organization (NATO), two American postwar initiatives, symbolized the decline and fall of Western Europe.

As we will see in the following chapter, obituaries for Western Europe were premature. The recovery of the Continent, highlighted by economic miracles in Germany and Italy, the resurgence of democratic rule, and the integration of national economies into a single trading bloc now called the **European Union** (popularly known as the **Common Market**), has brought into being a new economic superpower.

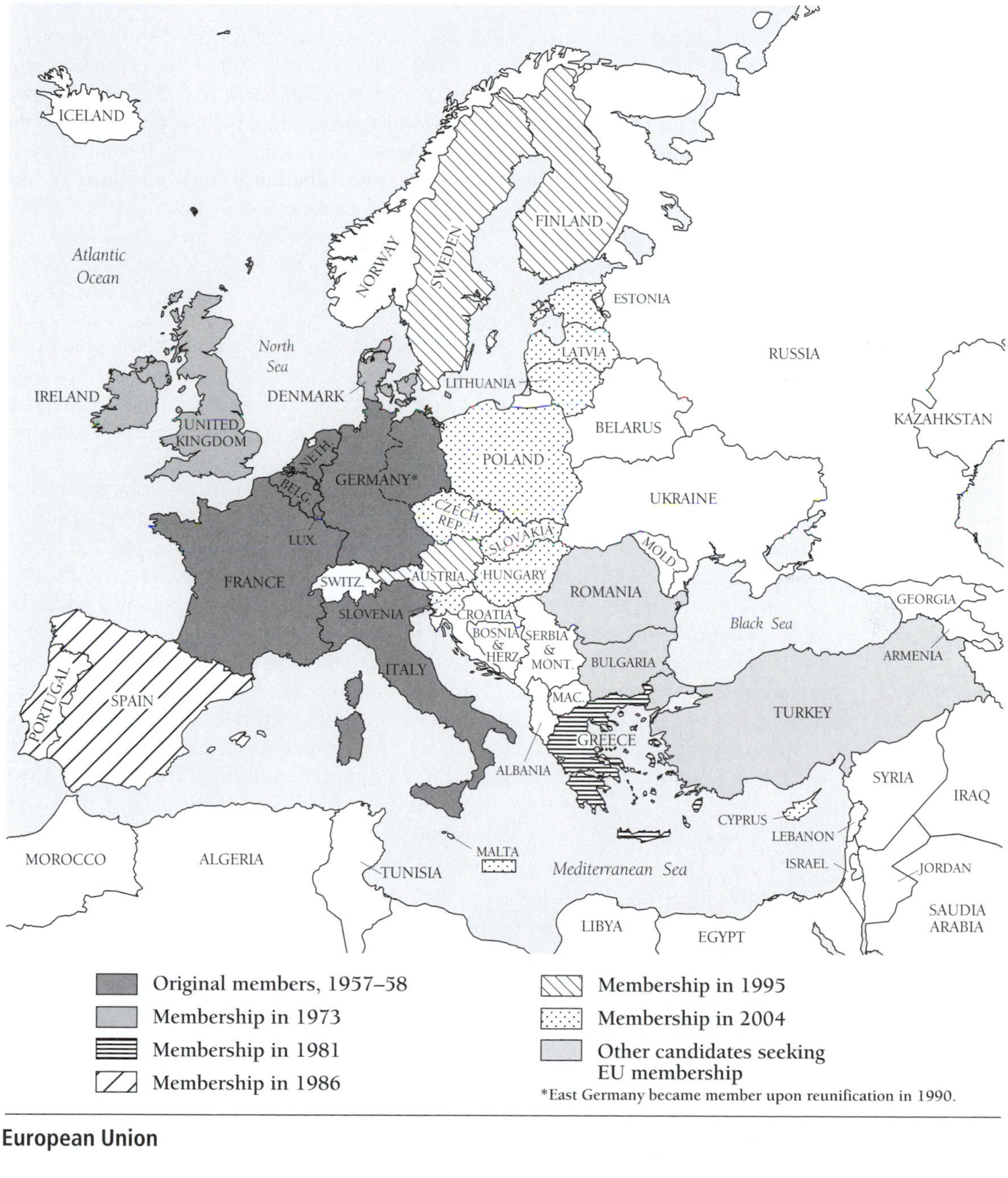

European Union

Case Studies: The United Kingdom, France, and Germany

In 2004, the United Kingdom, France, and Germany had a combined population of roughly 203 million (compared to about 280 million in the United States) and a combined GDP second only to that of the United States. Together with Italy, they form the inner core of the European Union, the world's largest trading bloc. Along with Russia, they are the major European military powers — France and Great Britain possess nuclear weapons, and Germany has the third largest economy in the world (Japan ranks second behind the United States).

The United Kingdom

Roughly the size of Oregon, the United Kingdom is a relatively small island nation that has played a disproportionately large role in modern European history. The distance from the northern tip of Scotland to the southern coast of England is slightly less than six hundred miles. Because it is long and narrow, the ocean is never very far away — even in the so-called Midlands, the coast is less than a two-hour drive away.

The United Kingdom comprises four distinct regions, the ancestral homelands of the country's four major ethnic groups: England in the south, Scotland in the north, Wales in the west, and Northern Ireland, a few miles west of Scotland across the North Channel of the Irish Sea. The island on which England, Scotland, and Wales are located is known as Great Britain. More than four-fifths of the population lives in England. The United Kingdom is one of the most densely populated countries in the world; its population density is greater than India's and ten times that of the United States. In England, there are more than nine hundred people per square mile, more than in Japan. Overcrowding is now a fact of life that has serious implications for politics and public policy.

The political, financial, and cultural center of the nation is London: in this respect, few nations are more highly centralized. With a population in excess of 7 million, London, the capital, is one of the largest cities in the world. Most of the major banks, corporations, newspapers, and television networks are also located there. So, too, are the British equivalents of Wall Street, Broadway, and Hollywood. Finally, many of Britain's most famous historical and cultural landmarks and tourist attractions — Buckingham Palace, the Tower of London, Westminster Abbey, Big Ben, the British Parliament, St. Paul's Cathedral — are in London.

England First The historical domination of Great Britain by England and England by London would presumably have created strong pressures toward homogenization and can easily give rise to the false impression that the British people are, in fact, all alike; that there is an extremely high degree of social harmony; and that whatever political problems the nation might have, disunity is not one of them. As noted earlier, the United Kingdom has four distinct nationality groups: the English, the Scots, the Welsh, and the Irish. Although English is spoken throughout the country and the political system is a unitary one, each region has its own separate identity, including language, history, customs, and folkways. There is no large nonwhite minority in Great Britain, but the influx of immigrants from former British colonies has led to racial tensions and tighter restrictions on immigration in recent times.

Island of Stability Of great importance, historically, is that England became a unified kingdom under a strong centralized government much earlier than most of the continental states. England was already a single kingdom before the Norman Conquest in 1066. One effect of this early unification was to give the English a more secure sense of nationality (expressed in a less fervent form of nationalism) than either the French or the Germans. Another effect is that British statesmen in modern times have been able to concentrate on taming the power of the central government rather than trying to build a state. By contrast, France was not consolidated as a nation-state under a king until the fifteenth century, and then only after great and prolonged struggles. Until recently, the French had to work long and hard at creating a state that could overcome the great nobles, assimilate a variety of provincial peoples, languages, and cultures, and eventually impose republicanism on conservative sections of the country that preferred the papacy and the monarchy to bourgeois politicians. Germany was unified for the first time only in 1870, and then, of course, reunified only in 1991.

Great Britain's political stability derives in part from its geography. Separated from the Continent by the English Channel, its internal boundaries have changed very little over the centuries. Wales has belonged to England since the thirteenth century and was formally united with England in 1535. Nonetheless, Wales has its own capital, Cardiff, and its own distinct national language, Welsh, still spoken by perhaps one-fourth of the population. Scotland was joined to England in 1707 but has its own legal, educational, and local government systems. Ireland accepted union with England in 1800, but religious differences (Ireland is Roman Catholic; England, Anglican) and economic disparities made the marriage unworkable. In 1922, following years of bloody civil war, Ireland became independent, but the six northeastern counties of Ulster (Northern Ireland) remained in the United Kingdom and were granted home rule.

Historically speaking, the lack of boundary disputes and incursions by external enemies has meant that Britain has avoided the destabilizing effects of having to digest new chunks of territory, assimilate new populations, or adjust to foreign rule. Problems arising from the presence of disaffected or displaced minorities have likewise been relatively few (except for Northern Ireland). These circumstances created an environment conducive to the comparatively peaceful evolution of the British political system from a monarchy to a parliamentary democracy.

England's Channel Externally, the English Channel, a mere twenty miles wide at its narrowest point, has played a major role in shaping British political history. For centuries it was a geographic barrier to invasion (the last successful invasion was the Norman Conquest). It also enabled England to remain aloof from many of the conflicts on the Continent. England's advantageous geopolitical position meant that the British crown could act as the keeper of the balance, choosing when and when not to get involved in the game of power politics on the Continent.

Because the threat of invasion was minimal, the British never had to maintain a large standing army, and the military was never a serious threat to civilian rule. Instead, the nation concentrated on building a powerful naval force that enabled it to dominate the seaways in the eighteenth and nineteenth centuries. One consequence of the small-army, large-navy system was that the absolute power of the monarchy was never so absolute in England as on the Continent. Unlike armies, navies are not useful as instruments of repression or coercion at home.

A Maritime Tradition Great Britain's geography goes far toward explaining its historic rise to economic prowess. A strong maritime tradition and an auspicious location at Europe's gateway to the North Atlantic placed the British in an ideal position to establish a foothold in the New World. The opening of new Atlantic trade routes made Britain a major international financial and commercial center. The need to protect these routes in both war and peace in turn provided the incentive to build a strong navy. Sea power made possible the growth of a colonial empire, which counteracted any temptation to lapse into the isolationism of an island fortress.

Even so, the United Kingdom did not seek to become an integral part of Europe. Instead, the British have traditionally been self-reliant and independent in both domestic and foreign affairs, viewing entanglements on the Continent with a mixture of disinterest and disdain. This tradition of aloofness helps explain why the United Kingdom did not join the Common Market in 1958, when it was formed.[18] Many British subjects continue to be wary of the European Union and question whether the benefits of membership outweigh the burdens. Thus, the opening of a railway tunnel under the English Channel (the "Chunnel") in 1994 has historic importance for symbolic as well as economic reasons.

Another legacy of Britain's strong maritime tradition is an attachment to the doctrine of free trade. Tariffs were steadily reduced, and by the middle of the nineteenth century, British agriculture was largely unprotected. The existence of overseas colonies, British naval supremacy, and the cost effectiveness of oceanic transport encouraged the importation of food, and this in turn freed up domestic resources for industrialization. Today the United Kingdom is highly dependent on agricultural imports.

Not surprisingly, the British have long paid close attention to the **balance of payments.** Food imports must be offset by the export of manufactured goods; fluctuations in exchange rates, domestic inflation, foreign competition, and changes in consumer habits at home and abroad can all have serious political and economic ramifications in a country so deeply enmeshed in the international economy.

The Origins of Parliament British history has clearly been influenced by geography, but geography also exerts a force of its own on contemporary British politics and government. The British are not the island's original inhabitants but instead are descendants of Angles, Saxons, and Jutes from Germany. The Celts (Welsh, Scots, and Irish) were there first.

Until the eleventh century, Britain was invaded repeatedly. The Danes ruled the country from 1016 to 1042. In 1066, William the Conqueror invaded from Normandy (in what is known as the Norman Conquest), established a monarchy, and introduced the **feudal system.** Under this system, the nobility were granted certain rights and privileges (land entitlements, access to the royal court, and others) in exchange for loyalty to the king and the acceptance of various duties and obligations (paying taxes, defending the realm, keeping the peace). Disputes over these rights and duties were settled in a council of lords convened by the king.

In 1212 and 1213, King John summoned various clergymen, barons, knights, and other dignitaries "to speak" about the affairs of the realm. (The word *parliament* derives from the French verb *parler,* meaning "to speak.") From these humble origins evolved the concepts of constitutionalism and parliamentary government.

In the beginning **Parliament** was a kind of royal sounding board and advisory council rather than a check on the monarch's power and authority. In time, the right of barons to approve taxes became the right of Parliament to originate all revenue and spending bills. Along the way there were occasional battles between Parliament and the king — none more fateful than the one begun in 1629, when Charles I dissolved Parliament and proceeded to rule as a tyrant. In 1650, Oliver Cromwell led a revolution that overthrew the monarchy (Charles I was beheaded) and established a short-lived republic.

The Puritan Revolution The issue of religion was also a factor in the revolution. As a result of a doctrinal dispute with the pope, the Anglican church had replaced the Roman Catholic church as the established religion in England more than a century earlier, but controversy over the break with Rome still raged. When James II, a Roman Catholic, tried to reopen the religious question, forcing a showdown between Parliament and the monarchy, he was deposed in a bloodless coup. Rather than abolish the monarchy, Parliament invited the king's Protestant daughter, Mary, and her husband, William, to share the crown. By accepting, they implicitly recognized the supremacy of Parliament. Since 1689, no British monarch has challenged this constitutional principle.

The Emergence of Parliamentary Rule In the seventeenth century, Whigs (liberals) and Tories (conservatives) evolved from factions into full-fledged political parties. Finally, the idea of **cabinet rule** — in which the leaders of the majority party in Parliament act as a board of directors (called the Government) to set policy, make key decisions in crisis situations, and manage the bureaucracy — emerged as an integral part of the British constitutional system. In the nineteenth century, the government gradually extended the franchise, but males over the age of twenty-one were excluded until 1918 unless they owned property. Women finally won the right to vote in 1918, as well, but even then only women over the age of thirty were enfranchised (lowered to twenty-one in 1928).

Until quite recently, British democracy was entirely indirect — that is, the voters elected representatives (members of Parliament or MPs) who made the laws. Even the chief executive (or prime minister) is chosen indirectly (by the majority party in Parliament). But in 1975, two years after joining the European Union, a new Labour government headed by Harold Wilson, kept a campaign promise by putting the question of EU membership to a popular vote — a referendum. The public approved British membership by more than a two-thirds margin. Perhaps equally important, British voters were given an opportunity at direct democracy on the national level for the first time in British history. (See Box 3.3.)

What If?

BOX 3.3

National Referendums: Anything Is Possible

What if the British prime minister, Tony Blair, keeps his promise to hold referendums on many of the important issues facing the country? In 1975 the first referendum ever in British history occurred over the question of whether to join the Common Market. (The proposal passed, but the controversy did not.) Now the voters have decided they like the idea of a national referendum. Who needs those blowhards in Parliament, anyway? If Tony Blair meant what he said during the campaign, a vote for Labour was, at a minimum, a vote for referendums on the European single currency, on Scottish and Welsh devolution (or autonomy), and on electoral reform. (Referendums on Ulster, on London's government, and on English devolution were also under consideration.) In short, questions that could fundamentally alter the shape and character of the United Kingdom forever might be put to a direct vote.

Stalin's foreign minister, V. M. Molotov, once quipped, "The disadvantage of free elections is that you can never be sure who is going to win them." The same can be said of referendums. As California voters learned in the 1970s, a single referendum can turn a tax system topsy-turvy, and in a democracy, legislators are not at liberty to then reverse the course. The United States, however, has never held a national referendum. What if it did? Or, more likely, what if the British should hold five or six referendums in the next few years? Imagine what could happen. The United Kingdom might cease to be united or might break into smaller parts like the former Yugoslavia. It might opt out of Europe or lead the way toward a European federation. It might even decide to abolish the monarchy. In theory, anything is possible.

France's path to democracy is very different from Britain's — more tortuous and turbulent by far. The form of France's democracy is also quite different from Britain's, although, as we will see, it borrows heavily from the British experience.

France

About the size of Texas, France is located in a pivotal position on the Continent. Although it shares a border with six other countries (Spain, Italy, Switzerland, Germany, Luxembourg, and Belgium), France is demarcated by natural boundaries, with one fateful exception. To the north is the English Channel; to the west, the Bay of Biscay; to the southwest, the Pyrenees Mountains; to the south, the Mediterranean Sea; and to the southeast, the Alps. In the northeast, however, France and Germany have historically engaged in confrontation and conflict over disputed territories along the southern Rhine River (particularly in a resource-rich region known as the Saar) and in Alsace-Lorraine. There are no insurmountable barriers to invasion in this region: even Belgium, which poses no direct military threat, was a geostrategic liability for France before World War II because it could (and did) serve as a springboard for German armed aggression.

Internally, France has an extensive network of navigable rivers, canals, and railways, combined with a compact geography. This fact, along with natural boundaries, has contributed to a strong sense of national identity and a high degree of political and economic integration. French is now the first language and Roman Catholicism the religion of the great majority of the population.

Even so, the French people are far from homogenous; indeed, customs, attitudes, and opinions vary significantly from region to region. Historically, Roman civilization strongly influenced the south of France while Germanic culture influenced the north. Economically, too, there is an important division: the south and west are rural, conservative, and relatively poor, whereas the north and east are industrially developed, growth-oriented, and relatively prosperous.

France remained a nation of shopkeepers, artisans, and small farmers longer than most other Western industrial democracies. Although the actual numbers of self-employed producers and proprietors in traditional sectors of the economy have declined sharply since the 1950s, family owned shops are still fairly common and French individualism is as vibrant as ever.

Paris versus the Provinces Paris is to France as London is to Great Britain. Nearly one-fifth of France's total population — some 10 million people — lives in Paris or its suburbs. Paris dominates the political, economic, cultural, and intellectual life of the country. It is the banking center and industrial hub. More than one-third of all commercial and financial profits are earned in Paris, which also accounts for over half of France's domestic wholesale and retail trade. Paris is one of Europe's most popular tourist attractions, with its rich historical heritage, magnificent architecture, world-famous art museums, beautiful parks, and fine restaurants. The Louvre, the Cathedral of Nôtre-Dame, the Eiffel Tower, Montmartre, and the Champs-Élysées are only a few of the landmarks that give Paris its distinctive character.

The division between Paris and the provinces is etched deeply into French culture, society, and politics. The contrast between the high culture and hustle and bustle of Paris and the rustic and relatively relaxed pace of life in the provinces is made all the more significant because France remains less urban than other industrialized countries. France has only six cities with populations over 500,000, in which only about one-third of the French people live (by comparison, fully one-half of the British population lives in big cities).

Subsidies and Stagnation Although France kept pace with industrialization elsewhere on the Continent during the nineteenth century, the French economy (and society) stagnated in the first half of the twentieth century. One reason is that, unlike Great Britain, which stressed free trade and welcomed competition, France instituted protectionist policies to prevent competition, both foreign and domestic. Tariffs, quotas, cartels, and subsidies were the chosen instruments of France's economic strategy. Roughly one-third of the French national budget was still allocated to direct or indirect subsidies in the 1950s.

French business practices also impeded growth and change. The family firm (along with the family farm) was the foundation of the French economy. Turning a bigger profit, capturing a larger market share, opening up new product lines, modifying consumer habits, expanding, diversifying, modernizing — these were not primary considerations.

In fact, competition was regarded as unethical. A business was viewed as a family tradition, a way of life. Many businesses were owned and operated by the same family for generations, even centuries.

Despite a diversified manufacturing industry and state-initiated efforts at technological modernization, French farmers — numbering 2.5 million, or about 8 percent of the labor force — remain a powerful force in domestic politics. France has an abundance of arable land and a variety of climates conducive to farming. As a consequence, France is not only agriculturally self-sufficient but also a major food exporter, accounting for a quarter of the European Union's total agricultural output. As we shall see, France's desire to protect its farm producers and buttress its position as the Continent's paramount food exporter has long been a source of tension within the EU.

Indicative Planning after World War II After World War II, the French government took the lead in directing the reconstruction effort and revitalizing the economy. Through so-called indicative planning and modernization commissions, the state set targets for growth in specific industries, using a combination of arm-twisting and incentives to persuade the private sector to comply.

Industrial production doubled between 1952 and 1963, and then grew by another 70 percent in the next decade. By the early 1980s, the French economy had surpassed Great Britain's and was gaining on that of West Germany. France's per capita GNP was higher than Japan's, and it was increasing faster than that of any other major Western democracy. A relatively high rate of inflation was a chronic problem (often running in double digits between 1975 and 1984), but that was gradually brought under control as well, falling to a mere 1 percent or so by the end of the 1990s. France's "economic miracle" has lost some of its luster but the French economy nonetheless remains the fifth largest in the world — only slightly smaller than the United Kingdom's.

Population Blues France experienced zero population growth long before it was fashionable. Between 1860 and 1940, France's population held steady while that of surrounding countries, especially Germany, was taking off. For France this situation was particularly alarming because both its population and its per capita income had fallen far below that of Great Britain and France on the eve of World War I. (See Table 3.3.) France was the only Roman Catholic nation in the world in which population was not increasing. Between the wars, the population actually started shrinking (in part reflecting the loss of 1.5 million Frenchmen in World War I).

Most of France's population growth in recent years is the result of immigration from former French colonies in North Africa. Some 5 million immigrants sought refuge in France by 1990, at a time when unemployment in the nation was nearing 10 percent (it rose to around 12 percent in 1996 and remains in double digits). The destabilizing effects of this volatile mix will be discussed in subsequent chapters.

Religion and Society The fact that France is a predominantly Roman Catholic society today speaks volumes about French history but says little about the role of religion in France. Religion has long been at or near the center of civil strife. In the sixteenth century, French Protestants (called Huguenots), who wanted to bring the Reformation

Table 3.3 France and the Other Great Powers in 1914: A Three-Dimensional Comparison

Country	National Income (billions of U.S. dollars)	Population (millions)	Per Capita Income (U.S. dollars)
United States	37	90	377
Great Britain	11	45	244
Germany	12	65	184
France	6	39	153
Italy	4	37	108
Japan	2	55	36

Source: Paul Kennedy, *The Rise and Fall of the Great Powers* (New York, Random House, 1987), p. 243.

to France, fought church loyalists, who wanted to preserve Catholicism as the one true faith. The Edict of Nantes (1598) brought religious toleration and peace, but the struggle resumed in the next century, culminating in the decree of King Louis XIV that all of France would be Roman Catholic. Religion was a factor in the French Revolution (1789), but this time it was Catholics against anticlericals (opponents of the church) rather than Catholics against Protestants. Historically, the church has been a conservative force in French society, opposed to republicanism and allied with the monarch, its protector. Religious controversy in general and anticlericalism in particular thus have deep roots in French political history. This fact helps explain why both the Communist and the Socialist Parties have, at different times, enjoyed a large popular following in postwar France, despite the incompatibility of Marxist and Christian doctrines.

Hence the appearance of religious unity in present-day France is deceptive. The great majority of the French people are Roman Catholic (over 70 percent are baptized in the church), but most are nonpracticing.

Even so, the church plays a significant role in French society through its extensive primary and secondary private school system. Since the early 1950s, church and state have cooperated closely in the area of education, with the state providing considerable financial support for parochial schools and the church accepting state-defined regulations and curricular standards. But in the 1980s, when the ruling Socialist Party proposed further steps to integrate (and possibly absorb) the Catholic schools into the public school system, a mass protest in Paris persuaded the government to drop the idea.

France's Turbulent History Absolute monarchs ruled France for some eight hundred years prior to the French Revolution. This long stretch of centralized rule, which reached its zenith during the reign of Louis XIV (1643–1715), is no doubt one reason why France developed a strong sense of national identity.

But the political system degenerated under the despotic Louis XVI, and French society became increasingly polarized. A kind of representative assembly, the Estates

General, had been in existence since the fourteenth century, and judicial bodies called *parlements* occasionally served as royal sounding boards or advisory councils. Thus the mechanisms for political accommodation were available but were little used. Unlike the British monarchy, French kings were loath to compromise with the aristocracy or the rising middle class.

Louis XVI's decision to suspend the *parlements* helped to precipitate the French Revolution, which was a watershed in European history. Its impact went far beyond France. It was the prelude to a century of turmoil, division, and disunity. The short-lived First Republic soon gave way to the First Empire under Napoléon Bonaparte. Napoléon continued to pay lip service to the republican ideal and held occasional plebiscites (special issue-based elections, sometimes also called referendums) to underscore his popular mandate, but in reality he established a personal dictatorship not much different from an absolute monarchy.

Louis XVIII and the House of Bourbon regained the throne in 1814, after Napoléon abdicated and went into exile. (He attempted a military comeback in 1816, but was defeated at Waterloo and taken as a prisoner of war to the island of St. Helena, where he died in 1821.) The Bourbons were said to have learned nothing and forgotten nothing. In 1848, a revolt again toppled the monarchy and led to the Second Republic, which like the First, was short-lived. Louis Napoleon, the nephew of Napoléon Bonaparte, emerged as the new popular leader; following in his uncle's footsteps, he crowned himself emperor in 1852.

The Second Empire lasted until 1870, when France was defeated by Germany in the Franco-Prussian War. This defeat and the election of a large number of reactionary monarchists to the National Assembly alarmed progressive elements of all persuasions. Radicals violently opposed to the monarchy and the church, perhaps influenced by Marxism, set up a rival government in the capital, the so-called Paris Commune. A bloody civil war ensued in which 20,000 people died during the last week of fighting alone.

The Third Republic came into being in 1876 and lasted until World War II — the longest-surviving political system since the French Revolution. However, divisive party politics and a weak executive impaired the workings of government and tarnished democracy's image in the eyes of many French voters.

A Contradictory Legacy World War I caused great damage in France, but the Third Republic somehow survived. World War II, however, sounded its death knell. France has tried a dozen different political systems since 1789, including five republics. (We will look at France's two post–World War II republics in Chapter 4.) The contradictions of French politics over the last two centuries can be summarized as follows:

- A belief in republicanism combined with a mistrust of government expressed in the insistence on a weak executive under the Third and Fourth republics
- A susceptibility to Bonapartism expressed in the occasional emergence of a "white knight on horseback" (Napoléon Bonaparte, Louis Napoleon, Georges Boulanger, and Charles de Gaulle), as well as the occasional resort to plebiscites to renew the leader's popular mandate

- A tendency toward polarization expressed in the historic dichotomies of reactionary versus revolutionary, royalist versus socialist and communist, papist versus the anticlericalist, and republican versus authoritarian
- A high level of patriotism and national pride combined with a marked tendency toward popular revolt against the symbols and substance of national authority

Compared with Great Britain, France has historically been less stable and cohesive. France has lacked the continuity that is the hallmark of British parliamentary rule. And France's economic policies have until recently been autarkic and protectionist, in contrast to the British stress on free trade and competition.

We turn now to Germany, the country that nearly conquered all of Europe twice in the first half of the twentieth century. Although utterly devastated in 1945 (at the end of World War II), Germany is again a powerhouse in Europe, but it is a different Germany from the one that twice ravaged Europe. Also, unlike France and Britain, Germany was a late arrival in the "family" of European nation-states. We look at the origins and development of the German nation-state next.

Germany

A century ago, Germany was the preeminent military power on the Continent. For forty-five years following World War II, it was divided into two distinct parts — the Federal Republic of Germany (West Germany) and the German Democratic Republic (East Germany). After a popular uprising against communist rule in East Germany and the subsequent opening of the intra-German border in 1989, the movement toward German unification proceeded rapidly and was completed in October 1990.

Germany's Precarious Geography Germany's geographic position on the Continent places it at the crossroads of Europe. Unlike Great Britain or France, Germany does not have natural boundaries, and this fact shaped the nation's fate in several ways. For centuries, whenever wars were fought in Europe, German territory was apt to be a battleground. There are at least three reasons for this: Germany is centrally located; until late in the nineteenth century it was divided into many principalities (feudal territories ruled by princes), most of them small; and the absence of geographic barriers made German lands accessible to the armies of neighboring states.

Having no natural boundaries, however, also meant that industrious Germans (many of whom were successful entrepreneurs) could spread out and settle in adjacent territories without being cut off from their homeland. As a result, German culture became disseminated well beyond Germany proper. When Hitler seized the Sudetenland from Czechoslovakia, he did so on the grounds that most of the people there were Germans. He justified Nazi aggression in general on Germany's ostensible need for lebensraum (living space). This argument was false, but it made sense to a nation long accustomed to migrating into neighboring areas.

Germany's geographic vulnerability influenced its history in other ways as well. If, as is often said, the best defense is a good offense, then one logical response to the danger of invasion is to go on the offensive. For hundreds of years, the fragmented Germany was unable to follow such a strategy. In the eighteenth century, however, the German state of Prussia emerged as a major power under Frederick the Great, who ruled from 1740 to 1786. Frederick enlarged Prussia considerably (he took Silesia from Austria and acquired another large chunk of territory from Poland). From this time forward, the ideal of the military state was a prominent part of the German weltanschauung (worldview).

The Concept of Germany Largely because of the struggle against the empire-hungry Napoléon, the concept of a German nation began to emerge. The German Confederation created at the Congress of Vienna in 1815 was a modest precursor of the modern German state, but rivalry between Austria and Prussia, distaste for reform, and the claims of German princes combined to block an early move toward German unification. The loose confederation, which awarded Vienna the permanent presidency, encompassed thirty-nine sovereign entities running the gamut from the formidable Austrian Empire and Prussia to four free cities. For example, the Diet (assembly) that was supposed to meet at Frankfurt was more a council of ambassadors than an elective assembly, and a unanimous vote was required on important matters. Also, the confederation's legislative powers were severely restricted. In practice the league was important in German politics only on the rare occasions when Prince Metternich, the great Austrian statesman, found it convenient.

Metternich used the confederation, for example, to suppress student protests inspired by pan-German nationalism and liberalism, both despised by the ruling elites. After the assassination of a reactionary writer, the confederation was used as the vehicle to launch the draconian Carlsbad Decrees of 1819.[19] Although there was considerable ferment in intellectual circles, German society as a whole — still largely rural but with a growing urban-industrial labor force — remained rather more tranquil than elsewhere in Europe.

From Prussia to Germany In Prussia, the landowning Junkers were allied with the crown. The noble Junker class supplied most of the officers for the royal army and for the top posts in the state administration:

> Sons of burghers filled state posts in the lower echelons and shared in decision making on municipal affairs. The skillful and efficient bureaucracy of Prussia set standards that other German states sought to imitate. The peasant masses in overwhelmingly rural "Germany" seemed content to allow public business to be conducted by their social betters.[20]

Prussia was an efficient monarchy. Under the enlightened rule of Frederick William III, the state continued to support education and promote economic growth. A common tariff, established in 1818 in all its territories, lowered duties (discouraging smugglers as well as opening up the economy to competition) and allowed free entry of raw materials (a spur to industrial development). These progressive measures worked remarkably well — so well that nearly all the German states except Austria soon joined Prussia's customs union, the Zollverein. "By 1834 over twenty-three million Germans, living in an area larger than New York, Pennsylvania, and New England combined, were exchanging goods freely."[21] In retrospect, the Prussian experiment in economic integration can be seen as an early forerunner of the European Union.

The Zollverein was a tonic to commerce. By mid-century, manufacturing and trade were facilitated by an intricate railroad network built and subsidized mainly by Prussia. Economic integration, in turn, facilitated political unification. It is possible that the new Europe of the twenty-first century, under the impetus of the EU, which also began as a customs union, will imitate the German experience. At the very least, there may be a parallel between the role Prussia played in the formation of the modern German state and the key role Germany is now playing in Europe.

Economic development brought social dislocations as modern factories, both foreign and domestic, displaced the old trades. Signs of popular discontent and political disturbances began to appear, rooted in a newly emerging commercial-industrial class structure as dissidents and agitators demanded what were then radical reforms, including a graduated income tax and guarantees of the right to work. In some parts of the confederation, kings and princes made limited concessions to liberalism. In Prussia, Frederick William IV, the most liberal of the Prussian monarchs, convened a united Landtag (a representative assembly) in 1847, but soon had second thoughts. The revolutionary turmoil that erupted throughout Europe in 1848 brought class conflict to the surface in German society. Landed gentry were pitted against the middle class (factory owners, bankers, lawyers, professors), the middle class against the workers, and peasants against liberals of all stripes. The revolts in the German states (and Austria) failed to depose the rulers, who were supported by loyal armies.

The clamor for constitutional change in Prussia and elsewhere mingled with nationalistic fervor. Talk of German unification in time became commonplace to the point where even the Prussian Hohenzollern and Austrian Hapsburg rulers paid it lip service. Ironically, dreams of a powerful and united German state continued to be associated with a desire for liberal democratic government.

From Bismarck to Hitler Otto von Bismarck unified Germany in 1871, having gained wide popular support at home following impressive military victories over Austria (in 1866) and France (in 1870). The German Empire (called the Second Reich) was the product of triumph and the prelude to tragedy for the German people.[22] Germany under Bismarck became the most powerful state in Europe. Over the next seventy-five years, Germany would fight and lose two world wars, undergo a tumultuous revolution, and embrace the totalitarian designs of a raving tyrant, Adolf Hitler.

Whether or not German aggression was the real cause of World War I, the allied powers placed this stigma on Germany when they insisted on a "war guilt" clause as a pivotal feature of the Versailles treaty ending that war. U.S. President Woodrow Wilson spoke for many of his contemporaries when he blamed the war on two prominent features of prewar German politics: nationalism and autocracy. He believed that one way to prevent future wars in Europe was to remake Germany (and other autocratic regimes) in the image of a parliamentary democracy. Where there are popular controls on government, Wilson theorized, war is likely to be a last resort because, if people are given a choice, they will choose not to fight and die except in self-defense.

The Weimar Republic, Germany's first constitutional system, was born in these inauspicious circumstances. The new German government had several marks against it from the start. First, it was a symbol of Germany's humiliating defeat in World War I. Second, it was imposed by the victorious powers — the German people were never consulted. Third, it was un-German: Germany had no prior experience with republican government, and there was little in German history or culture to underpin any kind of democracy. Fourth, it was associated with a draconian peace that extracted onerous and punitive war reparations and indemnities from Germany. Fifth, it was powerless to protect legitimate German interests against continuing foreign encroachments (for example, Germany was required to finance an allied army of occupation in the Rhineland for fifteen years). Not surprisingly, when the economy went into a tailspin (as it did at least twice in the 1920s), popular disenchantment with the form of government opened the door to demagoguery and dictatorship.

Hitler's Third Reich was an aberration made possible by the impact of a worldwide depression on an already beleaguered German economy and society. Although Hitler came to power legally, he had no respect for laws and constitutions. As chancellor, he quickly obtained an enabling act from the German Reichstag (parliament). Thus armed with the power to rule by decree, Hitler instituted one of the most repressive and brutal tyrannies in history.

At a conference in Munich in September 1938, Hitler demanded that the Sudetenland be ceded to Germany. The following year Hitler and Stalin made an infamous deal, known as the Molotov-Ribbentrop Pact. Ostensibly a nonaggression pact, it was the device by which the two dictators divided up Poland, and Hitler "conceded" the Baltic states and Bessarabia (now called Moldavia, at the time part of Romania) to the Soviet Union. The Holocaust — the genocidal murder of nearly 6 million Jews and a like number of others (including Poles, Gypsies, Magyars, and homosexuals) — stands as the most heinous symbol of Nazi totalitarian rule.

A lively academic debate about Germany's role in the outbreak of World War I continues, but there is little question that Germany was the aggressor in World War II. Nonetheless, the Allies (except for the Soviet Union) did not seek a punitive peace after Germany's defeat in 1945; in fact, the United States and Great Britain, viewing a viable Germany as a valuable future ally against Soviet military expansion, actually shielded West Germany from Soviet and French demands for huge reparations payments.

In sum, Germany's political history is much shorter than that of France and Britain, much more authoritarian, more militaristic, and more aggressive (with the notable exception of Napoleonic France, which preceded the birth of modern Germany by more than half a century). Germany's geography (in the heart of Central Europe), relatively large population, and abundant natural resources needed for industrialization (especially coal and iron ore) made a policy of military expansionism possible. At the same time, Germany's geography, in contrast to Britain's, made a policy of aloofness from the affairs of the Continent infeasible. After 1945, Germany changed dramatically, embracing democratic institutions (imposed for a second time by the victorious powers, especially the United States and Great Britain). However, unlike France and Britain, where democracy has deep internal roots and developed gradually over time, Germany's democracy is still young, has external roots, and was created on the spot, so to speak. As we will see in the next chapter, the German people have nonetheless demonstrated a strong commitment to democracy and to the ideal of "Greater Europe" as opposed to the expansionist idea of "Greater Germany."

SUMMARY

Europe is a mix of many cultures and nations with distinct languages, cultures, histories, and political traditions. Nonetheless, Western Europe has a common core of values and beliefs reflecting the pervasive and enduring influence of Christianity, the Renaissance and Reformation, the Scientific Revolution, the Enlightenment, the Industrial Revolution, and the Age of Imperialism. The salubrious climate and compact geography of the Continent and the accessibility of maritime highways to the world outside have also contributed to the development of a distinctly Western outlook among the peoples of this region. In Chapter 4 we explore contemporary patterns of politics and government, which are the fruits of this heritage.

KEY TERMS

Renaissance
Reformation
mercantilism
balance of trade
infant industries
Scientific Revolution
secular humanism
Enlightenment
philosophes
ethical hedonism
French Revolution
Jacobins
Industrial Revolution
liberalism
socialism
conservatism
Age of Imperialism
balance of power
communism
fascism
National Socialism (Nazism)
European Union (Common Market)
balance of payments
feudal system
Parliament
cabinet rule

STUDY QUESTIONS

1. What are the seminal features of European civilization relative to the shaping of the political cultures of the Continent?
2. In what sense has totalitarianism shaped both the history and the political landscape of Europe in the twentieth century?

3. Why was Europe so prone to war in the first half of the twentieth century? Why was it immune from war during most of the second half?
4. Identify specific features of European geography and climate that have helped to shape its history and explain the relationships you choose to highlight.
5. Why did you think the concept of the nation-state originated in Europe rather than somewhere else? What is the relationship between the emergence of the nation-state, on the one hand, and familiar concepts like the balance of power, sovereignty, and diplomatic immunity on the other?
6. Briefly compare and contrast the United Kingdom, France, and Germany in terms of geography and history. In your view, how important is geography in explaining the differences? Give two or three examples of ways you think these differences are reflected in the respective political cultures and institutions of these three countries.

SUGGESTED READINGS

Bernstein, Richard. *Fragile Glory: A Portrait of France and the French.* Regina, Saskatchewan: Plume, 1991.

Elias, Norbert. *The Germans.* New York: Columbia University Press, 1996.

Horne, John N. *De Gaulle and Modern France.* New York: St. Martin's, 1995.

Kennedy, Paul. *The Rise and Fall of the Great Powers: Economic Change and Military Conflict from 1500 to 2000.* New York: Random House, 1987.

Kissinger, Henry. *A World Restored: The Politics of Conservatism in a Revolutionary Age.* New York: Grosset & Dunlap, 1964.

Ladurie, Emmanuel L. *The Ancien Régime: A History of France 1610–1770.* Cambridge, Mass.: Blackwell, 1996.

Potter, David. *A History of France, 1460–1560: The Emergence of a Nation-State.* New York: St. Martin's, 1995.

Stewart, John. *The British Empire: An Encyclopedia of the Crown's Holdings, 1493 through 1995.* Jefferson, N.C.: McFarland, 1996.

Tindall, Gillian. *Celestine: Voices from a French Village.* New York: Holt, 1996.

SUGGESTED WEB SITES

http://www.gksoft.com/govt/en/europa.html
http://www.politicalresources.net/europe.htm
http://www.benne.luna.nl/pp/eur/index.htm
http://www.democ.uci.edu/resource.htm

NOTES

1. Derwent Whittlesey, *Environmental Foundations of European History* (Norwalk, Conn.: Appleton & Lang, 1949), p. 140.
2. Ibid., p. 141.
3. Ibid., p. 132.
4. See Paul Kennedy, *The Rise and Fall of the Great Powers: Economic Change and Military Conflict from 1500 to 2000* (New York: Random House, 1987), pp. 148–150.
5. Whittlesey, *Environmental Foundations,* p. 138.
6. Ibid.
7. John Kirtland Wright, *The Geographical Basis of European History* (New York: Holt, 1928), pp. 78–79.
8. Ibid.
9. Ibid.
10. Bryce Lyon, Herbert H. Rowen, and Theodore S. Hamerow, *A History of the Western World* (Skokie, Ill.: Rand McNally, 1969), p. 443.
11. Ibid., p. 444.
12. See Kennedy, *Rise and Fall of the Great Powers.*
13. Lyon et al., *History of the Western World,* p. 509.
14. Edward Gibbon, *The Decline and Fall of the Roman Empire,* vol. 3 (1781) (London: Allen Lane/Penguin, 1994), p. 511.
15. Hans Morganthau and Kenneth Thompson, *Politics among Nations: The Struggle for Power and Peace,* 6th ed. (New York: Knopf, 1985), p. 235.
16. Ibid., p. 238.
17. See Ludwig Dehio, *The Precarious Balance: Four Centuries of the European Power Struggle* (New York: Vintage Books, 1962).
18. The British rejected membership in the Common Market in 1958; several years later they tried to join but were thwarted by President de Gaulle of France. Only after de Gaulle's departure from government (and subsequent death) was the United Kingdom admitted to the European Community, later renamed the European Union.
19. The Carlsbad Decrees intensified censorship, banned radical professors and students (including Karl Marx), and outlawed political clubs. They also required each member state to appoint commissioners to monitor and certify the universities for ideological reliability.
20. Arthur J. May, *The Age of Metternich* (New York: Holt, 1963), p. 40.
21. Ibid., p. 44.
22. The Holy Roman Empire was First Reich in German history.

CHAPTER 4

The Triumph of Parliaments and Pluralism

The political systems of Western Europe are not identical, but the similarities far outweigh the differences. Since the mid-1970s, when dictatorships in Spain and Portugal and military rule in Greece ended, every country in Western Europe has been governed by civilian rulers who came to power through free elections. Hence the governments of the region display a remarkably consistent pattern too uniform to be mere coincidence. The countries of Eastern Europe joined the ranks of democratic states in the 1990s, of course. We explore Europe's other half in Chapters 5 and 6.

European democracies vary in specifics, but they have several salient features in common. They are based on clearly defined principles and governments are elected by universal suffrage. With the exception of Great Britain, all the states of Western Europe have written constitutions. Many also continue to have monarchs who now serve as symbols (frequently called *figureheads*), performing many of the ceremonial and formal functions of government, having long ago lost the substance of sovereign power. For this reason, some of these governments are described as **constitutional monarchies** — a term that is somewhat misleading because in actuality they are representative democracies resembling the British model. Spain, Belgium, Luxembourg, the Netherlands, Denmark, Norway, Sweden are in this category. In these countries, the monarch reigns but does not rule — the king or queen is the ceremonial head of state, but an elected parliament makes the laws and chooses the government, consisting of the prime minister and the cabinet, who make policy and oversee the day-to-day operations of the bureaucracy. A constitutional monarch could theoretically intercede in the political process, but to do so might place the institution of the monarchy at risk.

Another striking similarity among the countries of Western Europe is a high standard of living based on strong, liberal (market) economies. Most of these national economies are now integrated into the supranational economy of the European Union (EU). Some countries are, of course, more prosperous than others, but the least prosperous EU countries (Greece and Portugal) are on roughly the same level as Slovenia, the most prosperous country in Eastern Europe. In the next section, we will take a brief look at Western Europe's remarkable economic success.

Western Europe's Economic Miracle

Immediately after World War II, U.S. President Harry Truman made several key decisions regarding the future of Europe. First, Washington abandoned isolationist policies and assumed primary responsibility for stimulating economic recovery on the Continent. This decision took the form of the European Recovery Program, better known as the **Marshall Plan,** approved by Congress in 1948. Second, it embarked on a course of reconciliation rather than retribution toward Germany. Third, it made a long-term commitment to Western European security by creating the **North Atlantic Treaty Organization (NATO).** This initiative removed any lingering doubts in Europe about whether the United States would risk war to defend democracy and freedom on the other side of the Atlantic.

Fourth, and perhaps least appreciated at the time, the United States encouraged economic cooperation among the Western European democracies. The first manifestation of this policy was the **Organization for European Economic Cooperation (OEEC),** set up to administer Marshall Plan aid. (In 1961, the Organization for Economic Cooperation and Development, or OECD, replaced the OEEC; the twenty-four nation OECD included member-states of both the European Economic Community and the European Free Trade Association, popularly known as the EFTA, plus the United States, Canada, and Japan.) The OEEC countries pledged to develop intra-European trade by reducing tariffs and other barriers to its expansion.[1] As things turned out, this lofty rhetoric foretold developments that would transform Western Europe from a blighted region into the world's most dynamic trading bloc.

Postwar Europe's first step toward economic integration was to create the European Coal and Steel Community (ECSC) in 1952. The ECSC, which established a framework for sharing strategic resources, set the stage for formation of the European Economic Community (EEC), or Common Market, in 1958. The result was a customs union, meaning that the six charter members (France, West Germany, Italy, Belgium, the Netherlands, and Luxembourg) agreed to remove tariffs on trade among themselves and set common tariffs on trade with others. This became the nucleus of the present-day **European Union (EU),** which now includes Austria, Denmark, Finland, Great Britain, Greece, Ireland, Portugal, Spain, and Sweden. Beginning in 2004, ten new members will join in the largest EU expansion ever.

France, West Germany, and Italy were all undergoing an "economic miracle" during the 1950s. The miracle was not that they recovered but that they recovered so rapidly. Within a decade of the war's end, industry was up and running again, granaries were bulging, and roads, railways, and bridges were rebuilt. This rising tide lifted all boats — the resurgence of the bigger nations boosted economic growth in the smaller ones.

But along with prosperity came new problems. As industry became increasingly automated and the workforce shifted from manufacturing to the service sector, the challenges facing the governments of the region changed rapidly, and the very pace of change itself became a major challenge. At the same time, the Common Market — today's European Union — came of age, creating new opportunities for the member nations but also bringing new tensions and necessitating sometimes painful adjustments. Moreover, just as Europe appeared to be regaining its historical role as the world's foremost economic

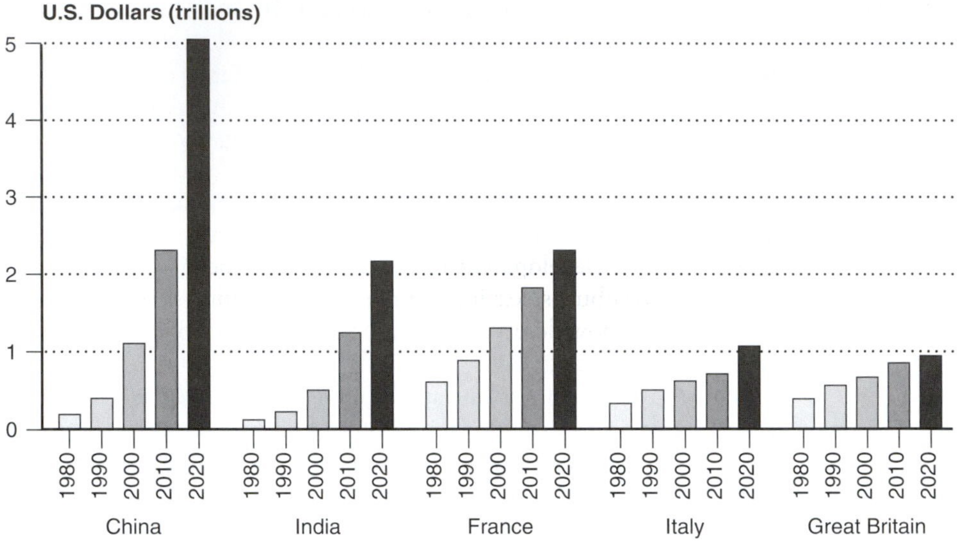

Figure 4.1 Projected Gross Domestic Product for China, India, and Certain Western European Nations, 1980–2020 (1980 constant U.S. dollars)

Note: Projection for China assumes a 7 percent growth rate 1980–1985 and 8 percent thereafter, for India, 5.5 percent 1980–1985 and 7 percent thereafter; other countries, average annual rates as in 1970–1982.

Sources: The Economist; International Monetary Fund.

engine, new challenges were arising in Asia. (See Figure 4.1.) Japan was second only to the United States as an economic power, and a dynamic and potentially hegemonic China served notice that Europe and North America would face a formidable new trade rival in the coming decades.

We will return to the EU later in this chapter when we assess the prospects for Western Europe, but first we will discuss some problems associated with the postindustrial stage of development in Great Britain, France, and Germany. In many respects, the problems these countries are encountering typify the whole region.

The Problems of Postindustrial Society

The Industrial Revolution brought a major shift in the economic foundations of both American and European society. The transition from farming to manufacturing entailed a massive demographic shift from rural to urban settings — a shift accompanied by secularization, the breakup of the extended family, and a sharp rise in the need for governmental regulation and intervention (particularly in such areas as public utilities and social services). Major advances in living standards, political gains by organized labor (such as the right to strike), and consumer-related technological innovation offset the problems associated with this "revolution."

Economically, postindustrial society is characterized by a whole series of shifts: from the manufacturing to the service sector (banking, insurance, advertising, marketing, management, and so on), from domestic to international markets, from a cash-and-carry economy to one based on credit and installment buying, from one-income to two-income families, and from a saving culture to a consuming culture. Postindustrialism also brings **overdevelopment** or **reverse development** (characterized by outmigration from cities to suburbs, leaving slums and deteriorating schools, services, and tax bases); these concepts now deserve a place alongside underdevelopment in economics texts.

Overdevelopment is exemplified by the megalopolis: concentrations of people and urban sprawl. Such cities as London, Paris, Rome, Milan, Madrid, and Athens can be considered contemporary Western European megalopolises. The dynamics of economic growth in postindustrial nations lure people to big cities in search of high-paying jobs, professional opportunities, social status, and cultural activities. But as cities become more and more overcrowded, population growth typically outruns the capacity of local government to maintain adequate police and fire protection, sanitation, schools, hospitals, streets, parks, and other amenities.

With overcrowding comes a host of social problems, including traffic congestion, air pollution, crime, juvenile delinquency, drug abuse, high divorce rates, domestic violence, homelessness, and increased stress, which can exacerbate all the other problems. A related issue is surge immigration, which has generated fears of an unbridled flow of newcomers from the east (the Slavic countries) and the south (North Africa). Legal immigration to Western Europe was only a small fraction of the total, which included millions of illegal immigrants living there in the early 1990s. This influx is costly for host governments (many immigrants need health care, housing, education, and other social services), disruptive for communities, and potentially destabilizing. It stands to reason that people are more likely to resent foreigners when they already feel cramped for space or squeezed for jobs.

One reason for the job crunch is that postindustrial societies have failed to solve the economic problems associated with the capitalist business cycle. Since 1970, unemployment rates have varied from a low of less than 1.0 percent of the total labor force (West Germany, 1970) to a high of more than 21 percent (Spain, 1985). In the mid-1980s, the United Kingdom, the Netherlands, and France (plus Belgium and Spain) all hit double-digit unemployment. (See Table 4.1.) Inflation rates have also fluctuated widely in Western Europe. Germany and the Netherlands have long enjoyed relatively stable inflation rates, but the United Kingdom, France, and Italy were on inflation roller coasters until the 1990s. (See Table 4.2.) These ups and downs tend to erode consumers' confidence in the economy and voters' confidence in the government. A dilemma that has plagued postindustrial democracies is the teeter-totter effect of disinflation versus full-employment policies: falling unemployment tends to be accompanied by rising inflation, whereas price stabilization (low inflation) is usually associated with rising unemployment.

Table 4.1 Unemployment Rates, 1970–1996: Leading Industrial Democracies (percentage of total labor force)

Country	1970	1975	1980	1985	1990	1996*	2000	2003†
France	2.5	4.0	6.3	10.2	8.9	12.5	9.6	9.3
Germany	0.8	3.6	2.9	7.2	4.9	10.2‡	9.4	10.6
Italy	5.3	5.8	7.5	9.6	10.3	12.1	10.5	8.8
Japan	1.1	1.9	2.0	2.6	2.1	3.4	4.6	5.4
Netherlands	1.0	5.2	6.0	10.6	7.5	6.5	2.5	5.3
Sweden	1.5	1.6	2.0	2.8	1.5	8.8	5.1	3.4
United Kingdom	3.0	4.3	6.4	11.2	6.8	7.6	5.3	5.2
United States	4.8	8.3	7.0	7.1	5.4	5.4	3.9	5.8

*Midyear; *The Economist,* September 7, 1996, p. 98.
†Midyear; *The Economist,* July 16, 2003, p. 88.
‡Unemployment in Germany rose to 10.3 percent in the fall of 1996.
Sources: OECD, *Economic Outlook* 48, no. 12 (December 1990) and 51, no. 6 (June 1992).

Politically, postindustrial nations face problems paradoxically arising from past economic and technological successes. As society changes, new circumstances give rise to new political forces. For example, the increase in life expectancy (combined with an early retirement option for many employees) has created a powerful new interest group consisting of senior citizens and retirees who are demanding more and better social services. The fact that most households now have two breadwinners means that even an expanding economy is no guarantee against unemployment (and underemployment). Minorities and first-time workers tend to be hit hardest by joblessness. University-educated people may be forced to take low-paying menial jobs for which they are overqualified. Moreover, immigrants are willing — even eager — to take dirty jobs and work for low wages (which they do, of course, out of sheer necessity). The consequences of all these factors are disillusionment and resentment.

Threats to the environment also give rise to new policy problems: air and water pollution, noise abatement, chemical and nuclear waste disposal, deforestation, and wildlife conservation are but a few examples. Air pollution is largely an urban scourge — it is caused by emissions from automobiles, mass-transit vehicles, and smokestack industries. But the cost of cleaning the air (and of most other environmental ameliorations) must ultimately be borne by all taxpayers and consumers, no matter where they happen to live.

A fundamental political question in every society is who gets what, when, and how; an equally fundamental question is who *pays* what, when, and how. Eastern Europe is too poor to pay so Western Europe will have to do it or it will not get done any time soon.

A fundamental issue facing postindustrial states is defining the role of the state in the economy, the environment, and society. The West's romance with the free market was rekindled by British Prime Minister Margaret Thatcher in 1979 and was reinforced by the administrations of U.S. President Ronald Reagan and West German Chancellor

Table 4.2 Inflation Rates, 1970–2003: Leading Industrial Democracies (percentages)

Country	1970	1975	1980	1985	1990	1995–1996*	2003†
France	5.9	11.8	13.3	5.8	3.4	2.2	1.8
Germany	3.4	5.9	5.4	2.2	2.7	1.6	1.0
Italy	5.0	17.1	21.3	9.2	6.5	3.6	2.6
Japan	7.7	11.8	7.7	2.0	3.1	—	–0.2
Netherlands	3.7	10.2	6.5	2.2	2.5	1.8	2.2
Sweden	10.6	11.7	13.7	7.4	10.5	0.8	1.9
United Kingdom	6.4	24.2	18.0	6.1	9.5	2.2	3.0
United States	5.9	9.1	13.5	3.6	5.4	3.0	2.1

*Data in this column are for mid-1995 to mid-1996; see *The Economist,* August 17, 1996, p. 80.
†Data in this column are for mid-2003; see *The Economist,* July 12, 2003, p. 88.
Sources: International Monetary Fund, *Government Finance Statistics Yearbook 1991,* vol. 54 (Washington, D.C.: IMP, 1991), p. 116–119; OECD, *Economic Outlook* 50 (December 1991): 56.

Helmut Kohl. France (under a Socialist president) tried to buck the conservative trend in the early 1980s, but failed when the economy faltered badly. In 1986, a center-right coalition won control of the National Assembly from the Socialists, ushering in center-right government. The Socialists were left with little choice but to move to the right or lose the presidency.

The taming of the French Socialists points to one other feature of postindustrial politics: a narrowing of the differences between parties of the right and parties of the left. Extremist parties at both ends of the political spectrum fell by the wayside — at least temporarily. Ideology was downplayed. Government and opposition alike advocated pragmatic solutions to economic and social problems. These trends reflected a middle-of-the-road popular consensus.

The decade of 1990s began with a disturbing tendency toward right-wing extremism in several Western European countries, including France, Germany, and Italy. However, the rising tide of intolerance receded as the decade drew to a close.

Case Studies: The United Kingdom, France, and Germany

We turn now to a closer examination of three key countries in Western Europe: the United Kingdom (Great Britain and Northern Ireland), France, and Germany. These three countries, with a combined population of over 200 million people at present, form a triangle of enormous economic wealth, but lack commensurate military power for reasons (and with consequences) that will be explored later in this chapter. France and Germany have been at the core of an experiment in supranational integration since the 1950s. The United Kingdom joined this undertaking belatedly in the 1970s, but to this date remains somewhat aloof from it economically and politically. All three countries

The United Kingdom

have dynamic market economies, generous social welfare programs, and stable democracies. But these similarities conceal important differences — differences that make all the talk of creating a "United States of Europe" premature, if not altogether preposterous.

The United Kingdom: Mother of Parliaments

In contrast to the United States, whose founders developed elaborate theoretical underpinnings for its political system, in Great Britain the political tradition is an outgrowth of centuries of history, experiment, and legal precedent. A theory of British constitutionalism can be found in the writings and speeches of Edmund Burke, who in the late eighteenth century celebrated the role of continuity and stability in the development of Britain's evolving political system. Burke stressed the importance of Great Britain's long, unbroken chain of political development, during which economic equality and political liberty evolved side by side.

The Unwritten Constitution

The United Kingdom — both a **parliamentary democracy** and a constitutional monarchy — has never adopted a written constitution. Rather it is the product of four elements: statutory law, common law, custom and convention, and works of authority. In truth, the British constitution is so deeply embedded in the political culture that trying to write it down would probably undermine its authority by reopening political debates long settled.

Today the normal method of amending and augmenting the British constitution is **statutory law,** which originates from acts of Parliament. The Parliament Act of 1911 that reduced the legislative role of the House of Lords is a prime example. Elected **members of Parliament** (MPs) in the **House of Commons** (lower house) make statutory law. (The role of the **House of Lords,** or upper house, in the legislative process will be discussed shortly.

Common law is judge-made law. It is based on legal rulings and decisions passed down through generations that are generally upheld in the courts. At one time common law played a crucial role in the evolution of the British system. For example, it is the basis of the principle of parliamentary sovereignty. A. V. Dicey, a great nineteenth-century British political thinker, considered this principle one of the two main pillars of the British constitution (the other being the rule of law). Common law now plays a secondary role.

Custom and convention are long-standing practices not based on statutory or common law. Rather they are rooted in nothing but the perceived logic of the system itself. They must be observed in order for the government to run smoothly and efficiently. For example, it is important for symbolic reasons for the Crown (Queen Elizabeth II at present) to give acts of Parliament its royal assent. A law that did not have the royal stamp of approval would seem somehow not legitimate. The last time a British monarch refused to give assent to an act of Parliament was in the 1700s. Another custom is the monarch's dissolving Parliament and calling for new elections, at the prime minister's request, if the government receives a vote of no confidence.

Tracts known as **works of authority,** esteemed for the quality of reasoning they exhibit and the reputation of the scholars who produced them, constitute a final source of constitutional law. In addition to Dicey, prominent British constitutional authorities include John Austin and Walter Bagehot, among others.

There is no power of judicial review in Great Britain. Government ministers, judges, and administrative officials can interpret the constitution in specific instances, but in general, acts of Parliament are supreme. And there are no extraordinary procedures for amending the British constitution; statutes and common law are changed by ordinary legislation (that is, they require a simple majority in the House of Commons).

Two seminal ideas underpin British politics: parliamentary sovereignty and the rule of law. Dicey defined **parliamentary sovereignty** as "the right to make or unmake any law whatever; and, further, that no person or body is recognized by the law of England as having a right to override or set aside the legislation of Parliament." The **rule of law,** according to Dicey, means two things. First, "no man is punishable . . . except for a distinct breach of law established . . . before ordinary courts of the land." Second, "no man is above the law . . . whatever his rank." Dicey also observed that "the constitution is pervaded by the rule of law" in the sense that the general principles of the constitution are themselves "the result of judicial decision determining the rights of private persons in particular cases brought before the courts."[2]

The British parliamentary system has four salient characteristics. First, it is a centralized or **unitary system,** in contrast to the federal system found in the United States or Germany. The central government possesses all the powers of government and delegates to local governments only as much authority as it deems necessary and proper. Consequently, London has complete power over the local authorities; thus, the concept of reserved powers — in other words, powers residing in the individual states — has no relevance in the British system.

Second, a **fusion of powers** exists at the national level in place of the separation of powers found in the United States. The U.S. presidential system bars members of Congress from concurrently holding a cabinet office. In contrast, the British cabinet consists of the leaders of the majority party in the House of Commons. Normally, election to Parliament is a prerequisite to becoming a cabinet member. After an election, the head of the victorious party in Parliament (the prime minister) names the other members (ministers) of the new cabinet; following a pro forma vote of approval by the party's majority in the House of Commons, a government is formed. (In a multiparty system, the government will often be formed by a coalition of two or more parties.) The cabinet, headed by the prime minister, is responsible for formulating and initiating legislation. Although all members of Parliament, including the opposition, are free to question and criticize the government, the majority party is virtually assured that its legislative proposals will pass.

A third key feature is **collective ministerial responsibility.** The prime minister and cabinet (the government) are members of Parliament and exercise executive power only so long as they continue to enjoy the backing of a parliamentary majority. The government must be prepared to answer the questions about its policies before both houses of Parliament. The collective aspect of ministerial responsibility relates to the fact that cabinet members are expected to support all policies, actions, and decisions of the government in public; they may dissent only behind closed doors.

Fourth, the British model features a **two-party system.** This does not mean that there are only two political parties in existence but rather that two major parties tend to alternate in power. (In contrast to the situation elsewhere in Europe, the victorious party in British elections has no need to enter into coalitions with smaller parties.) Furthermore, British political parties present relatively clear policy alternatives to the electorate, to a far greater extent than do the two major parties in the United States. British political parties are more disciplined than the two major parties in the United States. Consequently, when a party wins an election and forms a government, it can almost always put its program into effect without legislative obstruction.

Westminster: Where the Lower House Has the Upper Hand

In Parliament the British have fused the political symbols, ceremonies, and conventions of the past with the changing realities of the present. They have retained an element of aristocracy in the House of Lords, but since 1911 have lodged primary legislative power in the House of Commons. Westminster, where Parliament sits, is virtually synonymous with the British government.

The House of Lords consists of approximately 1,100 members, of whom about four-fifths are hereditary peers. The remaining members include the bishops of the Church of England, Lords of Appeal in Ordinary (without the power of judicial review but otherwise similar in function to the U.S. Supreme Court), and other life peers (distinguished British subjects appointed by the monarch). Typically, only about two hundred to three hundred members of the Lords attend sessions regularly. The upper chamber has not had power to veto money bills since 1911 and since 1949 can only delay passage of other bills for one year.

The precarious position of the Lords is suggested by the fact that they rarely go against the House of Commons. Indeed, they have done so only four times in more than eighty years and only once in recent times.[3] The Lords fear that if they become too assertive in obstructing or delaying legislation, the upper house will be abolished.

The House of Commons consists of approximately 650 members elected by plurality vote in single-member districts for five-year terms, subject to dissolution by the Crown on the advice of the prime minister. The seats are apportioned according to population, so England's share is slightly more than 80 percent of the total, followed by Scotland, Wales, and Northern Ireland. (A tenacious Scottish nationalist movement seeks full independence for Scotland.) The House of Commons approves or rejects legislation and provides an "oratorical battleground" where the opposition can and often does go on the offensive, forcing the prime minister and cabinet to defend the government's actions and policies.

Parliament is the sole source of legislative power in the British system. It alone can make new laws and repeal or revise old ones. This power gives the majority party enormous leverage; theoretically, it could reshape the entire political system by one simple parliamentary act. But the political obstacles to drastic structural change are formidable. The existing system has broad national support. Any attempt to reorder the system would risk a tumultuous outpouring of public indignation. In Great Britain, when the government loses public support, it is expected to resign.

Moreover, the opposition party would join the public in protesting any fundamental change in the system. The role of the opposition is, quite simply, to oppose — if it does not do so, it is acting irresponsibly. Thus, the majority party and the opposition both have a vital role to play. No major party is ever irrelevant, win or lose. This point is underscored by the traditional name given to the party out of power: Her (or His) Majesty's Loyal Opposition.

The government controls the legislative process. After a bill is formally introduced in the House of Commons, the government decides when it will be debated. Except for the nineteen "opposition days" during each session of Parliament, the government has control of the legislative agenda. Bills go through three readings — one when they are introduced, another when they are debated, and a third when they are voted on. Floor debate occurs after the second reading. This is a crucial point in the process: bills approved at this stage usually enjoy clear sailing the rest of the way. Following debate, bills go to standing committees.

In contrast to the committee system in the U.S. Congress, British committees are often very large (up to fifty members) and are not specialized. However, because the personnel of a committee changes with each bill and members can volunteer for each bill, members with expertise or special concerns do get to consider bills of particular interest to them. In this way the party leaders are able to satisfy membership demands for participation without actually conceding any power of great importance. Committees' powers are narrowly circumscribed: they refine the language of legislation, but they may not redefine the legislation itself. They rarely pass an amendment unless the minister of the relevant department proposes it. The majority party always controls the committees by the same margin that it enjoys in the full House of Commons.

Next comes the report stage, during which amendments can be approved or rejected. The government's amendments are almost always passed; any private member's amendment at this stage is generally rejected unless it has the blessing of the government. Bills dealing with constitutional issues are handled differently: they go to a "committee of the whole" — the entire House of Commons is the committee. If a bill of this nature is passed without amendments, it does not have to go through the report stage.

The third reading in the House of Commons occurs when a bill is voted on in final form. If it passes, it goes to the House of Lords, which can amend it, but only if the House of Commons approves. The final step is the granting of royal assent by the Crown — a mere formality but one that preserves the symbolism so important to the legitimization of government in Great Britain.

It may sound as though the legislative process is cut and dried, with the government holding all the trump cards. In point of fact, the opposition has ample opportunity to criticize, embarrass, and call the government to account. The most important opposition device is question time. Every day, Monday through Thursday, government ministers must answer questions on the floor of the House of Commons; twice a week, the prime minister must answer questions as well. Question time makes politics something of a spectacle in Great Britain. It puts a premium on debate skills and forces policy makers to justify their actions and decisions continuously — not only to Parliament but to the British people as well.

If the government loses its popular support, it may either resign or risk a vote of no confidence in Parliament. If Parliament passes such a motion or defeats a government bill with a vote of confidence attached, the government must, by convention, resign and either permit another party leader to form a government or ask the monarch to dissolve Parliament and call new elections. This procedure was last invoked in 1979, when the Labour Party lost on a vote of confidence, resigned, and opened the door to the Conservative Party, which subsequently won the elections and held power until May of 1997. The threat of a no-confidence vote can also play a role in making or breaking governments, as it did in the last days of Margaret Thatcher's tenure as prime minister.

Under normal circumstances, the government need not worry about losing important votes in Parliament. The majority party members are led by the government's chief whip, who holds a salaried position. The chief whip helps the government set the schedule in Parliament and keeps the cabinet briefed on developments there. Above all, the chief whip is responsible for party discipline, which in the British context means ensuring that majority-party MPs support government policy and vote to pass government bills. (The opposition and minor parties also have whips, who perform the same disciplinary functions.)

The House of Lords passes on legislation and can offer amendments, but its lawmaking powers are quite limited. It can delay money bills for no more than one month, and all other legislation for no more than one year. Generally, the Lords confine themselves to scrutinizing legislation, refining the language, and occasionally offering an amendment to reinforce rather than weaken the bill's original intent.

The British system features a fusion of powers. This fusion is strikingly evident in the judicial functions of the House of Lords, which serves as the highest court of appeals in Great Britain. In that, it is similar to the U.S. Supreme Court, except that the House of Lords does not have the power to declare legislative acts unconstitutional.

Some critics argue that the House of Lords is an anachronism and should either be abolished altogether or replaced by a democratically elected upper house. But the British remain steeped in tradition, and there is little popular support for far-reaching political reform.

10 Downing Street: Prime Minister and Cabinet

The prime minister holds the most powerful position in the British system of "cabinet government," acting simultaneously as chief executive, majority party leader, and principal adviser to the Crown. The prime minister appoints and dismisses cabinet members, sets the legislative agenda, decides major policy issues, directs the bureaucracy, and manages the nation's diplomatic affairs. Being both head of government and leader of the parliamentary majority, the prime minister has enormous authority. Some critics have asserted that the British prime minister is a virtual dictator, but this charge is greatly

What If? BOX 4.1

Parliamentary Sovereignty Is No Blank Check

What if British Prime Minister Tony Blair decided to make fundamental changes in the way democracy in Britain functions? After all, the Labour Party had been shut out of power for nearly two decades under the existing system. What if Labour not only pushed through a Labour-friendly reform of the electoral system but also abolished the monarchy, all aristocratic titles, and the House of Lords? The principle of parliamentary sovereignty means that the party in power can theoretically do anything, as there is no written constitution or judicial review in Great Britain. So why wouldn't Blair and party make some radical changes?

In fact, however, there are good reasons for the party in power to refrain from taking undue advantage of the electorate's fleeting favor. The British people cherish their nation's traditions (much as Americans venerate the U.S. Constitution). Unlike an American president, a British prime minister can be brought down at any time by a simple vote of no confidence. If the government causes a furor by its action (or inaction) on an issue that the voters care about, it can be forced out of office almost instantly. In the past, British governments have on occasion departed in disgrace because of sex or spy scandals. In the future, a government might fall because one party or the other steps over the blurred line between making policy and breaking with tradition. For this reason, both parties are likely to be more fierce when serving as the opposition party rather than the party in power.

---

exaggerated. (See Box 4.1.) Besides the ever-present possibility of a no-confidence vote, there are systemic liabilities that tend to offset a prime minister's powers. For instance, a prime minister cannot blame Parliament for failed government policies the way U.S. presidents can blame Congress. As British prime ministers have discovered, the more power chief executives wield, the more responsibility they must bear for the outcome.

British voters do not vote for the prime minister in national elections the way American voters vote for the president; rather, the majority party in Parliament chooses a prime minister. The choice is always a foregone conclusion, however, because each party selects a leader at its convention before a general election. This part of the process is similar to the nominating conventions in the United States, except that future prime ministers do not have to face grueling primaries.

The formation and functioning of the cabinet illustrate the fusion of legislative and executive powers in the British system. The prime minister chooses leading MPs to serve in the cabinet. There is no limit on the size of the cabinet; each prime minister decides which departments will have cabinet representation, although certain ministers — among them chancellor of the exchequer (treasury), foreign secretary, and home secretary — are always included. The cabinet's functions include final determination of proposals to be submitted to Parliament, supreme control of the national executive, and continuous coordination of the administrative departments.

The cabinet operates under the principle of collective responsibility. Publicly, all cabinet members must support the government's policies without reservation, even if they disagree among themselves in private. A cabinet member who cannot support a decision is expected to resign.

The cabinet generally convenes once a week in the Cabinet Room at the prime minister's residence, 10 Downing Street. The chief whip normally attends cabinet meetings, which are chaired by the prime minister. Votes are rarely taken, the prime minister instead preferring to seek consensus or to listen to the discussion and then declare a decision. The precise nature of cabinet meetings is shrouded in mystery: tradition, self-restraint, and the Official Secrets Act keep leaks to a minimum.

There are two schools of thought regarding the extent of the prime minister's powers. One school views the prime minister as omnipotent, having the final authority to decide all matters and to appoint or dismiss cabinet members at will. The other school stresses that any politician who gets a cabinet post is powerful in his or her own right. Creating a cabinet is a political act: the prime minister must placate other powerful cabinet members and protect party unity. The widely reported policy differences between Prime Minister Tony Blair and Treasury Chancellor Gordon Brown in 2002 illustrated this point.[4]

Coordination and communication between the cabinet and the subordinate levels of the government are done through cabinet committees and the Cabinet Office. Originally, the committees were created to deal with particular issues; today there are about twenty-five permanent cabinet committees responsible for interdepartmental coordination and oversight in various issue areas. There are also over one hundred ad hoc committees to handle specific issues and facilitate two-way communication between the cabinet and the appropriate government departments.

The Cabinet Office also houses a secretariat that handles the cabinet's administrative affairs. It assists in coordinating the operations of government, keeps noncabinet ministers informed of cabinet decisions, prepares and circulates the agenda for cabinet meetings (and cabinet committee meetings), and the like. With the growth of the powers, functions, and responsibilities of the executive, the secretariat has become an indispensable part of the government's administrative apparatus.

Whitehall: Administrative Nerve Center

The cabinet is the pinnacle of the central government, but the departments are the building blocks. Headquartered in Whitehall, the departments run the day-to-day business of the government. They are supervised by a minister or by a secretary of state. (Recall that not all departments enjoy cabinet status.) Each departmental minister is assisted by at least one junior minister called a parliamentary secretary. The largest departments may also have parliamentary undersecretaries. All these officials (about a hundred in all, plus the cabinet posts) are members of the majority party whom the prime minister appoints.

Department ministers are in charge of main administrative units of the government and must perform a variety of managerial functions, including motivating and monitoring the large number of civil servants who staff the department. The minister's chief aide is the permanent secretary, a senior civil servant who has the broad administrative experience and substantive expertise that a politically appointed minister may lack. Nevertheless, ultimate responsibility for departmental performance rests squarely on the minister's shoulders. A minister's most important and difficult task can be to persuade, bully, cajole, and otherwise induce the civil servants at the working levels of government to implement policy according to the government's wishes.

Parties and Elections

Traditionally, Great Britain has had a two-party system, but throughout most of the twentieth century there have been three major national political parties: the Conservative (or Tory) Party, the Labour Party, and the Liberal Party. For a century, control of the government has alternated between the Conservatives and Labour, but there have been various attempts to revitalize the Liberal Party, and in the 1980s even to fashion a whole new party movement from like-minded elements of Labour and Liberals. Irish, Scottish, and Welsh nationalism are also notable factors in British elections. Irish nationalism led to the creation of an independent state of Ireland after World War I and continues to bedevil the British in Ulster (Northern Ireland); a nettlesome Scottish nationalism also continues to be a burr under the saddle of Westminster politicians for whom English domination is a given.

The Conservatives ruled without interruption during the 1980s. In 1987, Margaret Thatcher became the first (and only) British prime minister in the twentieth century to lead a party to three consecutive election victories. Thatcher stepped down near the end of 1990 in the face of flagging popular support for her brand of conservativism. Her mild-mannered successor, John Major, was a sharp contrast in style and also proved to be surprisingly original in substance. Two years later, Major survived a major test when the Conservative Party won a narrow majority in Parliament — one which nevertheless enabled the Tories to rule for another five years.

In terms of doctrine, the British Conservative Party can be loosely compared with the U.S. Republican Party under President Ronald Reagan; although in contrast to conservatives in the United States, British politicians of the center-right accept a welfare state, which even after the Thatcher reforms is still relatively generous in redistributing society's wealth from the top down. Mrs. Thatcher's imprint on British society was perhaps deeper and more lasting than President Reagan's because the United States, unlike Great Britain, has never had a comprehensive cradle-to-the-grave system of social insurance (including, for example, national health care).

Thatcher sought to reduce the size of government, curb spending, denationalize (or reprivatize) industry, cut taxes, maintain a strong independent nuclear strike force, and remain in the European Union. She also encouraged private home ownership and self-reliance, advocated partial privatization of the National Health System (NHS), and opposed modernizing Britain's state-owned railway system. In addition, she tried to break the grip of the trade unions on the nation's domestic economic policy. In pushing this ambitious program of governmental retrenchment and economic revitalization, Thatcher was aided by the fact that the Conservative Party is relatively cohesive, without deep ideological divisions or warring factions.

By contrast, the Labour Party is a coalition of disparate interests. Originally an outgrowth of the British trade union movement, it was founded as the party of the working class. It became the main opposition party in the 1920s. From the outset, it distanced itself from the once-powerful Liberal Party by embracing a moderate form of socialism. For example, policies advocated in the 1980s and 1990s included renationalization of industry, unilateral nuclear disarmament, withdrawal from the EU, closing of U.S. military bases, expansion of the social welfare system, higher taxes for the wealthy, and concessions to organized labor.

After World War I, the Labour Party became the major (and only) alternative to Tory government. But the rise of Labour in the first two decades of the twentieth century was matched by its near-demise in the last two decades of the century. Following its electoral defeat in 1979, the party was split by struggle between the left wing and moderate factions. The moderates opposed both the party's stance favoring British withdrawal from the EU and a change in the party's method of selecting its leader. The new Social Democratic Party, founded by disaffected Labourites, was the bitter fruit of this struggle. The defection weakened the Labour Party but did not give rise to a viable alternative.

In the late 1980s, following its third straight election defeat, the party began to shift toward the center in an effort to get back into the political mainstream, which had moved to the right under the influence of Prime Minister Thatcher's theories and policies. Due in part to continued internal divisions over ideology and policy, however, it would be another decade before this process would finally bring Labour back to power.[5] By then Britain's main party of the "left" would have a whole new look — that of its youthful, moderate, and market-friendly leader, Tony Blair.

Today Labour is no longer simply a working-class party. It is an umbrella organization appealing not only to workers but also to middle-class civil servants, teachers, housewives, peace activists, welfare recipients, students, pensioners, the jobless, the homeless, and the otherwise poor and downtrodden. Under Prime Minister Blair's leadership, Labour has also reached out to the business community and the professions. As indicated earlier, Mr. Blair's "new" Labour Party has discarded "old" Labour's ideologically inspired policy objectives, and downplayed ideology, full stop.

British voters and parties have shown little enthusiasm for fundamental realignments or even temporary coalitions. In the 1983 elections, for example, the Social Democrats and the Liberals formed such a coalition, which they called the Alliance. The two parties kept their campaign finances separate but issued a joint manifesto urging government action to relieve unemployment, cuts in military spending, redoubled arms control efforts, expanded welfare programs, continued membership in the EU, and incentives for private enterprise. The Alliance was designed to offer the British voters a middle-of-the-road alternative to the right-leaning Conservatives and left-leaning Labourites, however it met with little success at the polls.

In addition to the Liberals, minor parties in Great Britain include the Greens, the Scottish Nationalist Party, the Unionist Party, the Nationalist Front Party, and the Communist Party. All third parties face two fundamental obstacles — tradition and the **first past the post** electoral system. On tradition, Sydney Bailey's observation is apposite:

> There is nothing sacred in the number two, but the fact is that for by far the greater part of the three centuries during which parties in the modern sense have existed in Britain there have been two major parties, a Government party and an Opposition party.[6]

British voters, like voters in most countries with a history of stable government, are reluctant to vote for parties they consider untested. This rational-traditional voting behavior is reinforced by an electoral system based on single-member districts and selection by plurality vote (whoever gets the most votes wins) — a system imitated in the United States, but rarely found elsewhere in the world. (See Box 4.2.)

Democracy in America

BOX 4.2

The U.S. Electoral System: Borrowed, but Not Copied

The method used to elect members of both houses of the U.S. Congress places third parties at a huge disadvantage. The basic idea is borrowed from the British first past the post system. Here is how it works. Only one seat in the House or Senate is alloted to each voting district. There is no limit as to the number of candidates that can, in theory, be placed on the ballot, but only candidates from well-established parties with structures, funds, and a base of die-hard supporters can expect to have a chance of winning. The reason lies in the riddle and arithmetic of plurality voting: whoever gets the largest number of votes (not necessarily an absolute majority) is the winner. Normally, a candidate who is not endorsed by one of the two major parties cannot get more votes than both of the candidates who are endorsed. The more candidates there are on the ballot, the less likely it is for a "third-party" candidate to win. Say there are five candidates for a congressional seat in upstate New York. Candidates A and B are endorsed by the Republican and Democratic Parties, respectively. Candidate C is an Independent (no party), D is endorsed by the Greens, and E is a Libertarian. It is unlikely that the Republican and Democratic candidates will together poll less than 70 to 80 percent of the vote, but suppose the split in this hypothetical race is 32 percent for the Republican candidate and 28 percent for the Democrat, thus leaving a hefty 40 percent of the vote "available" to the other three candidates. That would mean that Candidates C, D, or E would have to win more than 80 percent of the remaining votes to finish ahead of the Republican candidate — an impossible assignment. Note that in this example, Candidate A (the Republican) wins with less than one-third of the vote. In fact, such an outcome is highly unlikely because most third parties gave up trying to win elections in the United States long ago. Occasional attempts by third-party candidates, most recently Ralph Nader of the Green Party, have all failed to make a serious challenge to the system, although they have arguably had an impact on a particular campaign, such as moving the candidate of a major party to the left or right, depending on the specific circumstances.

Defenders of the single-member-district, plurality vote (SMDPV) system stress that having just two major parties produces more stable government and forces both parties toward the moderate center. They also argue that in a two-party system, the political parties act as agents of compromise among competing interest groups, or, in the language of political science, as *interest aggregators,* taking disparate interests and melding them into *satisficing** party platforms. Critics say that this system is undemocratic; keeps new voices, faces, and ideas out of politics; and deprives voters of a meaningful choice. Moreover, they say, it is self-perpetuating because the two major parties have a mutual interest in blocking political reform (witness the failure thus far of efforts to enact campaign finance reform).

The alternative is proportional representation (PR). Some version of PR is in use in most countries today, although there has been a swing toward a limited use of SMDPV in recent times. Historically, the SMDPV system has not been widely copied — it remains an Anglo-American oddity.

**Satisficing* refers to a solution that somewhat satisfies all parties, giving each just enough to suffice.

The Electoral System In the British system, parliamentary elections must be held at least every five years, but the prime minister has the prerogative of calling elections sooner. Negative circumstances, such as a vote of no confidence or a scandal, can force early elections. More often, the prime minister will try to capitalize on a momentary surge in public approval to win another five-year term. For example, in 1983, when the British defeated Argentina in a war over the Falkland Islands, Prime Minister Thatcher called early elections to take advantage of the resulting surge in her personal popularity.

By contrast, John Major did not call early elections in 1991 because public displeasure with the Tory government at that time was high (as evidenced by the large loss of town hall seats in local elections). By waiting to hold parliamentary elections until the spring of 1992, Major was able to ride out the storm, and the Conservatives won a fourth consecutive term in office — the first British party to do so in 150 years.

British elections are short and simple compared with those in the United States. In the United States, president, senators, and representatives are elected to terms of different lengths, and national elections are staggered, taking place every two years. As a result, campaigns are frequent, and it seems as though one election barely ends before the next begins. In Great Britain there is normally one national election every four or five years.

Elections take place when the prime minister formally asks the monarch to dissolve Parliament, a procedure that usually takes about ten days. Balloting occurs no more than three weeks after a royal proclamation summons a new Parliament. As a rule, the prime minister dissolves Parliament before the five-year term is up. Because the government can decide precisely when the next election is to be held, however, the party in power has an advantage over the opposition.

All British subjects eighteen years of age or older are eligible to vote, provided that they have registered. Because voting registers are produced only once a year now, it can take up to sixteen months for a voter to qualify. However, in Great Britain, local officials have an obligation to get everybody registered, which is not the case in the United States. The result is that virtually every adult is registered in the United Kingdom, in sharp contrast to the United States, where only half the eligible voters may be registered at any given time.

The British invented the first past the post system. Each party in a voting district (called a *constituency*) fields a single candidate, and whoever gets a plurality of the votes wins. It is theoretically possible to win this type of election with a small fraction of the popular vote (the more candidates, the less likely it is that anyone will receive an absolute majority). This system — which is also used in the United States, of course — has been widely criticized on the grounds that it distorts the actual voting results. In 1979, for example, the Conservative Party won 339 seats in Parliament, a clear majority; if the seats had been distributed in proportion to the votes, however, the Conservatives would have won only 279, well short of a majority. Only in 1900, 1906, 1931, and 1935 would the government have won a working majority in Parliament if the seats were distributed in direct proportion to the votes.[7] On the other hand, the British have not been plagued by weak minority governments, which are quite common in many other parliamentary democracies.

The Ebb of Electoral Reform There has been considerable debate in Great Britain over changing the way MPs are elected. The advocates of change want a proportional representation system of one kind or another. Tradition is a formidable obstacle to such a change. Another is the logic of the British two-party system, which ensures that one party or the other will have a working majority in Parliament. As we have seen, the electoral system sometimes greatly magnifies the winning party's parliamentary majority.[8] Changing the system would reduce the odds that any single party would win a working majority. Parties would be forced to enter into coalitions in order to form a government. The tides of political reform ebb and flow in every democracy; in the United Kingdom there was no high tide in sight at the century's turning.

In sum, British elections are like those in the United States in regard to the method of election (plurality vote in single-member districts), but that is where the similarity ends. British national elections are more party-oriented than those in the United States, where the personality, reputation, and charisma of the individual candidate are often paramount. Also, British elections are much shorter and less costly. Because the government can put its programs into effect in the British system, the party in power is held strictly accountable for the condition of the country. That is why in 1979, when the British economy was in the doldrums, the voters ousted the Labour Party and put the Conservatives (Tories) in power. That is also why in 1997 the voters ousted the Tories.

Public Opinion and Pressure Groups

We have already alluded to the role of public opinion in the British system. Prime ministers often decide when to call new elections on the basis of opinion polls. Conversely, when a government's popular approval rating falls, it may be forced to resign. Thus, public opinion is likely to have a more direct impact on government in Great Britain, where the prime minister and cabinet have an indefinite term of office, than in the United States, where the president and administration have a fixed term.

Public opinion polling can be critical in any democratic society, but it is especially important in the British system, where success or failure in elections is often a question of timing. It is also important because a steady or sudden drop in the government's popularity can induce it to resign or prompt a confidence vote in Parliament. Consequently, the accuracy of polls is more than a matter of theoretical interest. The 1992 elections demonstrated that polls and pollsters are no more infallible in the United Kingdom than elsewhere. All the polls on the eve of the elections predicted that the outcome would be very close and that Labour would have the edge. They also predicted that the outcome might be a "hung Parliament," with neither major party attaining a clear majority in the House of Commons.[9] These predictions all turned out to be wrong.

Pressure groups began gaining influence in the United Kingdom after World War II. In fact, prior to the Tories' victory in 1979, the trade unions and big business had become so powerful that some experts began to describe the system as "corporatist." The heralds of the **corporatist model** argued that a new triple alliance of government, big business, and organized labor was becoming more powerful than Parliament. However, there is little reason to believe that the parliamentary system itself is in jeopardy. Indeed, Prime Minister Thatcher greatly reduced organized labor's clout in economic policy formulation, and union membership declined by more than 20 percent between 1979 and 1986 in the United Kingdom.[10] Critics note that organized labor's loss has been big business's gain — a lament also heard in the United States dating back to the early 1980s.

In the British system, pressure groups are most effective when they can establish lines of communication with the civil service. For the most part, it is the executive branch (the cabinet and the various ministries and departments) that formulates public policy in the British system, in contrast to the United States where lobbying Congress is as important as establishing contacts within the bureaucracy. British pressure groups therefore generally bypass Parliament altogether.

We turn now from institutional patterns to the challenges facing British government in recent years. We also will assess the performance of the government and consider Britain's prospects for the future in the light of current problems and available policy choices (solutions).

Problems and Prospects

The most persistent policy problem in the United Kingdom for much of the postwar period was the disappointing performance of the economy. After World War II, the British people were asked to sacrifice for the future: those with more should sacrifice more. A welfare state would be created with the available resources — that would be society's reward. Marshall Plan funds would be used for capital investment, not for current consumption. These policies were widely hailed by outside observers as a shining example of the regenerative powers of democracy. Yet the long-run result was not an economic miracle as occurred in West Germany and Italy but rather economic decay.

The Economy: A British Disease, a British Cure The United Kingdom stagnated as Germany, Italy, and France made a rapid economic recovery in the 1950s and 1960s. When OPEC oil prices skyrocketed in the early 1970s, inflation soared in Western Europe. In the United Kingdom, the annual inflation rate exceeded 20 percent at one point. Voters wondered whether any government, Conservative or Labour, could revive the British economy. The discovery of oil and gas in the North Sea brought the prospect of energy self-sufficiency — one of the only bright spots in a gloomy picture. A new economic phenomenon called **stagflation** — stagnating growth accompanied by high inflation — appeared. According to **Keynesian economic theory,** market economies can be expected to go through business cycles of "boom" and "bust." In periods of rapid growth, inflation is a problem (prescribed cure: budget cuts, higher taxes and interest rates); in periods of recession, unemployment is a problem (prescribed cure: deficit spending, lower taxes and interest rates). But in the 1970s the British economy was hit by inflation and recession at the same time.

Full employment became a permanent priority of British public policy after the worldwide Depression of the 1930s. Indeed, the jobless rate is a key measure of governmental performance in the United Kingdom. Starting in the 1970s, however, unemployment inched steadily upward, and by the mid-1980s hit record levels. Public opinion polls reinforced the impression that the state of the economy was a potential time bomb for the government.

Yet the British economy bounced back in the 1980s under the free-market policies of Prime Minister Margaret Thatcher's Conservative government. The official index of leading economic indicators (stock prices, interest rates, housing starts) rose faster during the six months leading up to the 1987 election than at any time since the early 1970s, and propelled the Conservatives to a third straight victory at the polls.

Thatcherism Reappraised In 1979, Prime Minister Thatcher had focused on one fundamental question: What is the proper balance between government intervention and free enterprise? She blamed Great Britain's sagging economy on the excesses of a cradle-to-the-grave welfare state in which an ever-expanding public sector encroached on and undercut the private sector. Elect a Conservative government, she vowed, and things will be different.

Thatcher kept her promise: she denationalized industry, gave big business new investment incentives, cut taxes, and curtailed welfare spending. The British economy did revive, but there was little cause for celebration. "Amid a revivified economy, Britain's decaying inner cities are the worst blot on eight years of Tory government," proclaimed *The Economist* — a conservative British newsweekly.[11] In the 1987 campaign, Thatcher promised to rehabilitate the inner cities, correct chronic housing problems, liberate schools from heavy-handed local controls, and reform local taxes. But some of these problems proved intractable, and at least one of her solutions, a new poll tax, drew jeers from the public. Her image as a tough, no-nonsense problem solver was now badly tarnished although she managed to remain in power for a few more years.

Making a "Major" Change When John Major replaced Margaret Thatcher as prime minister in November 1990 he seemed uncertain whether to stay the course Thatcher had charted, or chart a new one. He chose the latter in June 1991 when he told members of his ruling Conservative Party that he would attend the European Union summit at Maastricht and play a constructive role in negotiating a treaty aimed at establishing a common currency. Declaring, "Britain must not be sidelined," Major threw in his lot with the pro-Europe faction against Thatcher's antifederalists. Although he did not commit the United Kingdom to a Europe-wide currency immediately, his acceptance in principle of a monetary union cleared the way for the next giant step toward a unified Europe. This strategy was designed, in Major's words, to prevent Britain from remaining Europe's "odd man out."

Recession returned in the early 1990s, with inflation approaching double digits, unemployment on the rise, and burgeoning budget deficits. These disturbing trends forced John Major's Tory government to introduce tough austerity measures. Major's tight fiscal and monetary policies brought down inflation and unemployment levels significantly, but the sacrifices implicit in these measures — for example, reduced public spending — led to public dissatisfaction and mounting criticism even within the Conservative Party. Major hung on by a thread until the 1997 elections when Labour galloped back into power with one of the largest landside majorities in modern British history.

The Problem of Northern Ireland Violence and civil strife in Northern Ireland continue to divert attention, energy, and resources from domestic ills. Militant Irish nationalists, claiming to represent the Roman Catholic minority, have waged a guerilla war against Protestant-backed British rule since the late 1960s. The **Provisional Irish Republican Army (IRA)** uses terrorist tactics to achieve its objective of separation from the United Kingdom and union with the Republic of Ireland. Such a union would transform the Protestant majority in **Ulster** (Northern Ireland) into a minority in Roman Catholic Ireland. Militant Ulster Protestants have also used terrorism against Catholics in Northern Ireland. An end to the bloody deadlock, which had cost nearly 3,000 lives by 1990, is still elsewhere.

Nor is the IRA likely to abandon the struggle. In February 1991, IRA terrorists carried out a mortar attack on 10 Downing Street, the prime minister's official residence, while the cabinet was in session there. Although nobody was hurt, the terrorists had tried to decapitate the British government. Heroic efforts by Peter Brooke, Great Britain's secretary for Northern Ireland, led to a new round of talks in April and May 1991 among all parties except Sinn Fein, the political wing of the outlawed IRA, but the talks broke down the following July.

In the ensuing years, Northern Ireland remained a combat zone. Peace talks bore fruit in 1994 when the IRA and Protestant military groups agreed to a cease-fire, but a permanent settlement eluded the parties. The hopes raised by U.S. President Bill Clinton's visit in late 1995 quickly evaporated. The leadership of Sinn Fein continued to demand "inclusive" dialogue without preconditions. For its part, London was loath to pressure union loyalists into negotiating with Sinn Fein unless or until the IRA promised to stop killing people. In early 1997, bombing attacks against Ulster Catholics, apparently the work of loyalist guerillas, resumed. Both sides were once again sinking into the murderous morass of terrorism.

In the late 1990s, Protestants and Catholics, weary of the violence, finally came to terms. Some 3,200 people had been killed in three decades of civil strife. Following lengthy negotiations led by U.S. Ambassador George J. Mitchell, the parties agreed to a settlement — the so-called Good Friday agreement. In the referenda that followed, huge majorities in both Northern Ireland and Ireland endorsed the proposed settlement. After a false start and a new round of negotiations, a twelve-member cabinet responsible to an elected assembly replaced direct British rule at the end of 1999. Northern Ireland would remain in the United Kingdom but assume responsibility for schools, public transportation, finance, and the like. London would continue to set policy in the areas of taxation, foreign affairs, defense, and external trade. Two major questions remained unanswered: First, when and how would a surrender of weapons by Protestant and Catholic paramilitary groups take place? Second, would Northern Ireland stay in the United Kingdom or merge with the Republic of Ireland? The fate of Northern Ireland's 1.6 million people turned on whether these two volatile issues could be addressed without triggering a new round of violence.

A Republic of Scotland? Demands for greater local autonomy (independence from London) dating back to the 1960s led Prime Minister Tony Blair to present new proposals for devolution to Scotland and Wales in 1997. Although some leaders of the Scottish National Party favored outright independence, most Scottish voters were leery of such a drastic measure. In September 1997, the Scottish electorate overwhelmingly approved the Blair government's plan calling for a Scottish legislature and a chief executive to be known as the first minister. In the first separate Scottish elections (held in 1999) the Labour Party won the most seats, but not enough seats to form government outright. The Scottish National Party finished second, enough to serve notice that the political idea of an independent Scotland was alive and well. Devolution also occurred in Wales in the late 1990s, but Welsh voters are wary of big changes in this direction and are content with limited local self-rule.

Foreign and Defense Policy Long before the 2003 war in Iraq caused a political furor in the United Kingdom, British foreign and defense policies have fueled a good deal of controversy. When the United Kingdom joined the United States in a face-off with France and Germany over how to handle the Iraqi problem, it was a case of déjà vu for Europeans with a memory. In the 1960s, France under de Gaulle loudly denounced Britain's **special relationship** with the United States (based on America's origins as a British colony, a common language, common legal traditions, and, finally, the close Anglo-American alliance during World War II). The fact that London at first chose not to join the Common Market underscored the British desire to remain aloof from the Continent. When the United Kingdom belatedly applied for membership, French President Charles de Gaulle vetoed it. Not until de Gaulle was gone from the scene was the United Kingdom finally admitted, along with Ireland and Denmark, in 1973. But lingering doubts about British loyalties and London's own ambivalence toward the Common Market, reinforced by Margaret Thatcher's personal anti-European stance, continued to obstruct efforts to build bridges (figuratively speaking) across the English Channel. Only under John Major was the United Kingdom re-oriented toward Europe. But London's hesitant embrace of the EU was called into question in 1996 when controversy arose over the European response to "Mad Cow" disease (a mysterious and deadly illness traced to cattle and transmitted to humans through the consumption of beef from infected animals). It would fall to a new government unencumbered by all the baggage of the recent past to redefine the United Kingdom's relationship to Europe.

"New Labour": Blair in the Chair The Conservatives paid dearly in the 1997 general election for equivocating and fighting among themselves on the question of Europe and whether to support the **European Monetary Union (EMU).** The British electorate, weary of the Tories after eighteen years of Conservative rule, gave Tony Blair's Labour Party a landslide victory. With 45 percent of the popular vote, Labour won almost two-thirds of the seats in Parliament, burying the Conservatives. The vote swing in the 1997 election was extraordinary: Labour gained 10 percentage points over the previous (1992) election, while the Conservatives lost 11 percentage points. At age forty-three, Blair became the youngest British prime minister in nearly two hundred years and headed the largest Labour majority ever.

In power, Blair quickly established a distinctive leadership style, pursuing market-friendly economic policies designed to stimulate growth, create jobs, boost productivity, and fight inflation. His social policies aimed at reducing crime and improving education. In foreign policy he adopted an activist stance that included a major British role in the Balkans plus a commitment to sort out Britain's ongoing problems within the European Union — above all, whether and when to join the **euro.** (The word *euro* here refers to the single currency in which 12 EU members, including Germany, France, and Italy, currently participate.) In the fall of 2000, Blair boldly ordered British commandos into Sierra Leone, where rebels had brutalized the civilian population, and threatened the stability of neighboring states.

When U.S. President George W. Bush declared a "war on terrorism" following the September 11, 2001, attacks on the World Trade Center and the Pentagon, Blair pledged the British government's full support. At a special ceremony commemorating those who died in the attacks (including British citizens), the royal band played "The Star Spangled Banner" in a show of sympathy and solidarity that is rare in the annals of international relations. Blair followed up by committing British troops to the American-led invasion of Afghanistan later in 2001. At times, he seemed to be a step ahead of President Bush in the rush to retaliate against the perpetrators of the 9/11 terrorist acts. Despite antiwar demonstrations in the United Kingdom and strong opposition from France and Germany, Blair never wavered in his support for the U.S. position as President Bush called for a preemptive war against Iraq. The war came in March 2003, and British troops again joined the invading American military forces. The occupation of Iraq turned out to be a messy affair. Questions about the truthfulness of the Blair government in presenting evidence of Saddam Hussein's alleged efforts to obtain uranium from Niger in West Africa embarrassed Blair in the summer of 2003, but the prime minister did not blink. Instead, he vigorously defended the decision to go to war and stood by secret information (officially known as foreign intelligence) that, he said, proved it was the right decision.

On the home front, Blair did not undertake bold new initiatives or set about systematically undoing Margaret Thatcher's handiwork, but rather sought to tackle high-priority problems by setting specific targets in various policy areas. In advancing his **New Labour** agenda, Blair displayed charm, wit, and a Clinton-like penchant for public relations, demonstrating a reference for accommodation over confrontation and often appearing to defer difficult decisions. This combination of style and strategy worked fairly well for a time but by the summer of 2000 things started falling apart. Most damaging were leaks to the press that included a candid political strategy memo written by Mr. Blair himself and another written by the prime minister's pollster. In his memo, Blair admitted to "a sense that the government — and this even applies to me — are somehow out of touch with gut British instincts," while his pollster characterized the government as "drifting, growing almost monthly weaker and more diffuse."[12] Even more damaging than the contents of these (and other) leaked memos was the impression they conveyed of a prime minister dithering and a government spinning out of control.

The Blair government stood firm in 2000 when lorry (truck) drivers, angry at having to pay over $4.30 a gallon for diesel fuel, staged a blockade of refineries and oil depots and traffic slowdowns throughout the country, briefly crippling the economy and causing a great deal of inconvenience all around. Blair refused to lower the stiff British tax at the pump (the highest in Europe) that the public blamed for the problem.

The question of Europe, however, increasingly dominated the domestic agenda. Blair apparently intended to take the United Kingdom the rest of the way into the European Union by joining the European Monetary Union (EMU), but the events of 9/11 had sidetracked British politics, and renewed tensions between the United Kingdom and France (as well as Germany) over the war in Iraq rekindled distrust on both sides of the English Channel. Within his own party he faced a challenge from skeptics (including Treasury Chancellor Gordon Brown) who questioned the wisdom of surrendering control over monetary policy to the European Union — at least until the euro system proved itself capable of maintaining price stability and stimulating growth in a dozen national economies.

In Sum . . . Tony Blair brought a fresh, new look to British politics, but the old problems did not go away. Many of these problems were similar to those found in other high-income, postindustrial societies and none appeared likely to precipitate any kind of domestic crisis in the near future. The near-term prospects for the United Kingdom appear to be very good, but just how good depends in no small part on how the British ultimately balance nationalism and supranationalism. Given the potential for *four different brands* of nationalism in Britain — Irish, Scottish, and Welsh, as well as English — any tilt toward nationalism is fraught with political dangers. The other course — fully joining Europe — is a better bet to pay big dividends.

France's Fifth Republic

France has hosted five different republics in two centuries, during which time the United States, home of the other pioneering democracy, has had but one. The French have tried no fewer than fifteen constitutions since the French Revolution in 1789. The current republic is now over four decades old — a noteworthy achievement, considering that its predecessor, adopted in the wake of World War II, endured a scant twelve years. During that time, French governments lasted an average of only six months. So it is small wonder that political instability was both the cause of the Fourth Republic's early demise and the principal malady the Fifth Republic's Constitution was designed to cure.

A Hybrid System

The Constitution of the **Fifth Republic** is a composite of France's earlier constitutions. It incorporates presidential, plebiscitarian, parliamentary, and republican features, along with certain innovations insisted on by the Fifth Republic's founder and first president, General Charles de Gaulle.

The hallmark of the current Constitution is the pivotal role of the president, which contrasts sharply with its predecessors. Under the Third and Fourth Republics, the president was little more than a figurehead who rubber-stamped measures passed by the parliament. Chosen by the legislature acting as an electoral college, presidents were captives of that body. French parliaments were notoriously fragmented and ineffectual, which meant that the French government was often adrift. Presidents had the power to appoint prime ministers (with legislative approval) and to dissolve the parliament, but that was all. Real power, to the extent that it existed at all, was lodged in the prime minister and cabinet, who were often paralyzed by a perpetually divided parliament.

To remedy this situation, General de Gaulle stressed the need for a strong and dignified president who would be aloof from fractious party politics and could guide the nation, mediate among the parties, and discipline (or circumvent) the parliament in the

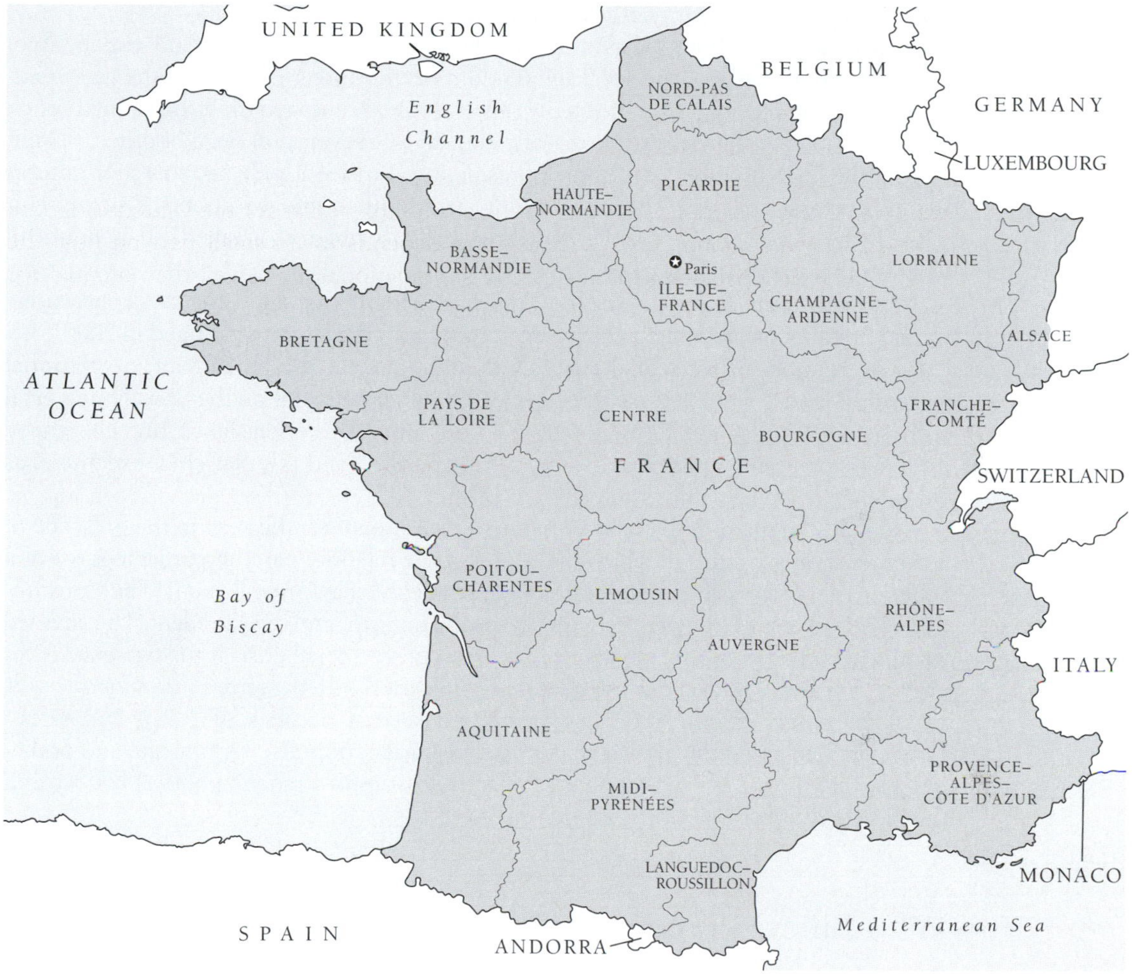

France

interests of unity, stability, and efficiency. As a champion of French nationalism who despised the narrow particularism of petty politicians, the controversial de Gaulle was both admired by many for his leadership abilities and reviled by others for his allegedly Bonapartist tendencies.

The plebiscitarian aspect of the present Constitution has its historical roots in the populist nature of Napoléon Bonaparte's rule and, more specifically, in the French Constitution of 1852. A **plebiscite** is a direct vote of the people about some issue or policy of political importance to the nation. The idea of taking issues directly to the people sounds democratic, but in the hands of a demagogic leader, it can be an instrument of dictatorship. Hence a popular president can use plebiscites to get around the parliament, in effect establishing a personalistic (and deliberately antirepublican) form of rule. A modern-day Bonaparte also has the potential to bully the legislature in other ways discussed at greater length later in this chapter.

An example of how Charles de Gaulle used these expansive (and expandable) presidential powers was the 1962 referendum on the direct election of the president. De Gaulle decided somewhat belatedly that it would strengthen the hand of the French president (namely, himself) to be directly elected to a seven-year term of office. (Originally in the Fifth Republic, the French president was indirectly elected to a shorter term by an electoral college.) The referendum was popular, and to nobody's surprise, it passed (the imperious de Gaulle had threatened to resign if it failed). It is doubtful whether this amendment was ever constitutional.

As in the American system, the French president can stand for two consecutive terms. France's presidents now serve five-year terms (the law was changed in 2000).

The republican facet of the system is embodied in the parliament, or **National Assembly,** whose members are directly elected by secret ballot on the basis of universal suffrage. But under the Fifth Republic's Constitution, the legislative branch can be bullied — or even circumvented — by a strong-willed and popular chief executive, as President de Gaulle demonstrated.

Finally, the quasi-parliamentary nature of the system can be seen in the presence of a cabinet-style executive in which the leader of the majority party in parliament (or of a coalition) chooses a cabinet and forms a government (as in Great Britain). The Constitution divides executive powers between the prime minister and the president. This divided (dual) executive arrangement can give rise to a constitutional crisis if the two executives are not on parallel tracks (discussed later in connection with the term *cohabitation*).

The present Constitution has weathered several decades of storm and stress. Longevity begets legitimacy. The mix of authoritarian, populist, republican, and parliamentary characteristics mirrors both the complexities of France's political history and the ideological diversity of the French electorate.

Who Rules? President and Prime Minister

France has a unique **divided,** or **dual, executive:** a president with ample constitutional prerogatives to act and a prime minister who is the head of the government. This arrangement may seem impracticable, but it has worked reasonably well in the French context.

Almost all Western European governments are of the parliamentary variety in which the executive is chosen by the parliament and cabinet members are also party leaders in the legislature. Parliamentary rule can lead to governmental instability, especially where a multiparty system and an ideologically fragmented or polarized electorate prevent any single party from gaining a clear majority. Coalition governments are often vulnerable to votes of no confidence about controversial issues. Under some conditions, coalitions can even produce the expectation of instability, which may in time become a self-fulfilling prophecy.

In a presidential system, the chief executive is chosen by the people for a fixed term. Except in extraordinary circumstances using cumbersome procedures, the legislative branch does not have the power to oust the president. Thus, in one sense the presidential system has greater stability than the parliamentary system. By contrast, presidential government lacks the flexibility of the parliamentary system. In the former, if a scandal occurs or public support wanes, the government cannot simply resign and call for new elections; it can do so in the latter.

The French system aims for the best of both worlds, combining a strong president with a parliamentary form of government. Both fusion of powers and separation of powers are present: the prime minister and cabinet are linked by party ties and constitutional logic to the National Assembly, but the president is elected separately and is not directly affected by the vicissitudes of parliamentary politics. The government can be censured and forced to resign; the president can dissolve the parliament as often as once every twelve months. (This power has been used very sparingly.)

In general, the Constitution positions the president as an arbitrator charged with settling differences among conflicting interests. Elected for a five-year term and eligible for reelection, a popular president can dominate the political system for a decade and remain aloof from the more demeaning aspects of everyday politics. To win, a presidential candidate must gain an absolute majority of the votes cast. If no candidate wins such a majority, a runoff election is held. This **two-ballot system** ensures that whoever is elected will be the first or second choice of the majority of voters and thus that the president will have a national mandate. Having a president endorsed by only a minority of the electorate would not be an auspicious start for a new government, especially in a country like France with a tradition of divisive politics.

Today, thanks to de Gaulle, the French president possesses in practice the powers that the British monarch has in theory. These include the power to appoint the prime minister (although the president must carefully weigh the balance of power among the parties in the parliament before making this choice). The president has the power to dissolve the National Assembly and can even exercise dictatorial powers simply by declaring a state of emergency (after consultation with the Constitutional Council). The power to call a national referendum in certain key areas also places the president in a strategic position to manage political conflict and manipulate the system to produce the desired outcome.

In dealing with the National Assembly, the executive branch (when united) has several constitutional weapons at its disposal. For example, the prime minister (most likely in close consultation with the president) can ask for broad "decree" powers and can combine such a request with a vote of confidence. In other words, the National Assembly must either grant the request, which means that the government can make laws by fiat (without parliamentary approval), or face dissolution. The government can put a controversial bill into a bundle with other legislation expected to win easy approval and can demand a **package vote.** This tactic forces the National Assembly either to approve a single measure that many members may oppose or to vote down legislation that the majority favors.

During most of the Fifth Republic, prime ministers have played a subordinate role. Even so, powers they possess are far greater than was the case under the Third and Fourth Republics. President and prime minister can cooperate to push legislation through the National Assembly or can block measures they oppose.

Although prime ministers are often overshadowed by presidents, they have important political and administrative functions. The prime minister typically supervises and coordinates the work of the cabinet ministers, acts as the principal liaison between the executive and legislative branches, and, in the absence of a parliamentary majority, mediates among the parties in the governing coalition. This was one of the main responsibilities of Michel Rocard, who became prime minister in 1988 after the Socialists won in parliamentary elections but fell short of a clear majority. Another normal function of the prime minister is to direct and lead the election campaign in the National Assembly; it is politically risky (and perhaps undignified) for the president to get personally involved in legislative elections.

The policy role of the prime minister in the French system depends on a number of variables. If the president and prime minister are from the same party much depends on the personality of the president. Under a commanding figure like de Gaulle or Mitterrand, the prime minister can be reduced to a largely advisory role in policy. If the two chief executives are from different parties and embrace different ideologies, the prime minister will have the lead in policy matters because his or her party has a popular mandate and controls a majority of the votes (if not seats) in the parliament.

Unlike presidents, prime ministers have no job security. Rocard's term in office was plagued by economic problems; he resigned in May 1991 and was replaced by Édith Cresson, France's first female prime minister. Cresson was controversial from the start; having failed to halt a downslide in Socialist popularity, she resigned ten months later, after the Socialist Party made its worst showing since World War II in local and regional elections. Similarly, Conservative Prime Minister Alain Joppé had no choice but to relinquish power to a Socialist rival, Lionel Jospin in June 1997 after a center-right defeat in early elections called by President Chirac.

The power of the French cabinet, along with that of the prime minister, was reduced by the de Gaulle Constitution. As a rule, cabinet members owe their positions and the scope of their power to the president. The cabinet grew in both size and importance after de Gaulle's departure in 1969. Cabinet members are drawn from diverse walks of life; many come from the elite ranks of the civil service (see below). Unlike their British counterparts, members of the National Assembly must formally resign from the legislature to take a cabinet position. In practice, however, cabinet ministers only temporarily relinquish their parliamentary seats to a surrogate; as soon as they leave the government, they typically go back to the National Assembly. Another French wrinkle is that ministers are often simultaneously mayors of major cities as well. Thus, when Jacques Chaban-Delmas was prime minister (1969–1972), he continued as mayor of Bordeaux; and when Jacques Chirac became prime minister for the second time (1986–1988), he stayed on as mayor of Paris.

French Technocracy: The Civil Service

The basic components of the French civil service are known as ***les grands corps,*** which include the Council of State, the Court of Accounts, the Finance Inspectorate, two corps of engineers, and the diplomatic service. The civil servants in these organizations are graduates of prestigious public policy and engineering schools known as ***les grandes écoles,*** of which the most famous is the ***École Nationale d'Administration*** **(ENA).** They dominate virtually all segments of the French administration. In many cases, top officials in the government (and chief executive officers of major French corporations as well) are recruited from the elite ranks of the civil service (about one-third of France's ambassadors are graduates of ENA, for example). Indeed, it is not fanciful for these French **technocrats** (professional public administrators with strong science backgrounds) to imagine themselves becoming president or prime minister someday — alumni of ENA have risen to both of these pinnacles of power in the past. (The term *technocrat* was invented by the French — it combines *bureaucrat* with *technologist* and derives from the emphasis in French public administration on mathematics and engineering.)

Until recently, France's highly centralized unitary system precluded any large role for local government. In the classical French system, most decisions were made in Paris, and **prefects** (officials appointed by the government) supervised the mayors of municipalities in the various *départements* (intermediate administrative districts). In this traditional **tutelage system,** prefects were powerful links between Paris and the provinces, but this role has been undermined by decentralization, with more power given both to the cities and to regional governments. Today the big-city mayors are important figures in French government.

France's civil service is a reassuring institutional presence in a country where party politics has historically often been chaotic. Since the advent of the Fifth Republic, however, the French parliament (National Assembly and Senate) has operated under constitutional rules that give it an important role in governing but minimize its potential for mischief.

The Taming of the Parliament

The French parliament wielded most of the power under the Third (1871–1940) and Fourth (1946–1958) Republics. The instability and paralysis of parliamentary government during that often-turbulent era led directly to the curbing of the powers of the parliament by the present Constitution. The fulcrum of French government moved to the presidency under the Fifth Republic.

The legislature comprises an upper and a lower house — the National Assembly and the **Senate,** respectively. With two exceptions, the National Assembly and the Senate share power equally. The former has the right to examine the budget first, and the cabinet is responsible to the National Assembly rather than to the Senate.

The French use a unique double-ballot method of election. Deputies run for office in single-member districts; if no candidate wins an absolute majority (a likely outcome), the two highest vote getters on the first ballot then compete in a runoff election to determine the winner in each district. This system has an interesting twist: parties can form alliances for the second vote, in effect dividing up voting districts according to which party's candidate has the best chance of winning in each district. In the 1997 elections, for example, between-election alliances enabled the communists to win thirty-eight seats in the National Assembly with a share of the popular vote only about half as large as Jean Le Pen's extreme right National Front, which won only one seat.

In a sense, the French parliament is more interesting for the powers it does not have than for the powers it has. First, it cannot meet for more than six months each year. Second, almost all legislation originates in the executive branch. The National Assembly has absolutely no power to introduce budget measures. If it fails to approve the government's budget by a certain deadline, the budget can be enacted by executive decree. (It is typical in parliamentary systems for members to be forbidden to propose spending money or reduce taxes.) Moreover, as noted earlier, the parliament can be compelled by the executive to cast a package vote on several pieces of legislation at once. Also, the government can make any particular vote a vote of confidence. In a confidence vote, a measure is considered approved unless the National Assembly passes a censure resolution by an absolute majority of the members. This means that only the votes in favor of censure are counted; abstentions have the effect of opposing censure. The deck is stacked, so to speak, in favor of the government.

At times, President de Gaulle creatively combined provisions of the Constitution to maximize presidential leverage over the parties in the parliament. Thus, for example, he was not above calling for a package vote on some part of his overall program and then making the vote itself a matter of confidence.

The committee system in the Fifth Republic is a cross between the U.S. Congress and the British House of Commons. As in the British system, there are only six standing committees. But as in the United States, they are specialized. Most committees have more than one hundred members. Membership on committees is apportioned according to party strength in the parliament. Unlike their American counterparts, committees in the French parliament cannot change the substance of government bills. There are other differences as well. Investigative committees can be created to probe government actions, but they have limited powers. The length of time they may investigate is set, they cannot investigate matters that are being handled by the judiciary, their findings must be reported to a standing committee for approval or rejection, and, to minimize leaks, they may meet only in closed sessions. Committee assignments are used as a means to distribute power among the parties and to give the opposition a formal role in the political process.

An electoral college consisting of members of the National Assembly and representatives of local governments indirectly elects the Senate. Its 300-plus members serve nine-year terms, and Senate elections are staggered at three-year intervals. The Senate is autonomous and cannot be dissolved by the president.

The French Senate gives disproportionate representation to rural areas and thus acts as a counterweight to the urban-oriented National Assembly. Although it is weaker than the Assembly, the Senate may reject government bills. (The Assembly can override a Senate veto, however.) The Senate's chief role is to keep the government honest by using question time to challenge policy makers and decision makers.

Unlike Great Britain or the United States, France has frequently had a problem with governmental instability instigated by quarrelsome and uncompromising political parties. The French parliament typically has at least five or six political parties represented at any given time and no one party has a clear majority. We look at the contemporary spectrum of political parties in France in the next section.

A Multiparty System

France continues to have an array of political parties ranging across the spectrum from extreme right to extreme left. Traditionally, the Socialists and Communists have been the two main parties on the left. From the end of World War II until the late 1970s, the Communist Party generally garnered around 20 percent of the popular vote. The 1980s saw a steady erosion of Communist Party strength and a corresponding rise in the relative strength of the Socialists.

It was in the 1980s that the center-left (led by the Socialist Party) finally tipped the scales against the center-right. In 1981, the Socialists not only won the presidency but also gained a clear majority in the National Assembly. Although support for the Socialist Party dropped in the 1986 elections, France's Socialist president, François Mitterrand, easily won reelection to a second term in 1988. By 1990, rising unemployment and budgetary constraints that hit traditionally left-leaning lower-income groups hardest sent the Socialists' popularity into a nosedive.

On the political right (which stresses French independence and a competitive economy), **Gaullist parties** under various names predominated in the decades after the Fifth Republic's inception. De Gaulle himself never founded a party; indeed, he was contemptuous of political parties in general. Nonetheless, his followers kept the Gaullist legacy alive for a time under the banner of the Gaullist Union of Democrats for the Republic (UDR) and later under a neo-Gaullist party, the Rally for the Republic (RPR), headed by Jacques Chirac.

In 1978, President Valéry Giscard d'Estaing created a new political formation, the Union for French Democracy (UDF), a coalition of several center-right parties and some smaller groups. An RPR-UDF alliance produced a center-right victory in the 1978 national elections, despite a determined effort by the Socialists and Communists to close ranks and enforce "republican discipline" in the second round of balloting. The RPR and UDF shared many elements of a common political philosophy, both favoring strong presidential government, a centralized administrative system, and free-market economic policies; but personal ambitions and myopic leadership prevented them from cooperating fully and helped the Socialists gain power in the 1980s. As we shall see, the Gaullist parties made a strong comeback in the 1990s.

In addition, splinter parties on both the left and the right have arisen from time to time. One such party, the **National Front,** has become firmly rooted in a disenchanted segment of the French electorate. The leader of this movement, Jean-Marie Le Pen, did surprisingly well in his first presidential bid in 1988. In the subsequent legislative elections, the extreme-right National Front — which espouses nationalistic, racist, anti-immigrant policies — made a poor showing, but in the 1992 balloting it bounced back, finishing only a little behind the governing Socialist Party. At the same time, the two environmental parties together garnered slightly more votes than the National Front, prompting at least one commentator to suggest (prematurely, in retrospect) that France's party system was being transformed.[13]

From de Gaulle to Chirac: Testing the System

In 1964, Prime Minister Georges Pompidou described the delicate institutional balance of the Fifth Republic:

> France has now chosen a system midway between the American presidential regime and the British parliamentary regime, where the chief of state, who formulates general policy, has the basis of authority in universal suffrage but can only exercise his function with a government that he may have chosen and named, but which in order to survive, must maintain the confidence of the Assembly.[14]

The Fifth Republic has provided France with unprecedented political stability. The personality of de Gaulle was certainly a factor in the early years. De Gaulle's influence extended well beyond his presidency. His opposition to domestic communism, his emphasis on France's sovereign independence (symbolized by the French nuclear strike force), his concern with enhancing French prestige in Europe and beyond, and his desire for economic growth without extensive nationalization of industry were all continued by his two presidential successors, Georges Pompidou (1969–1974) and Valéry Giscard d'Estaing (1974–1981). The National Assembly and the French voters have also broadly supported these policies.

But in 1981 this national consensus fell away when, for the first time ever, the Socialist Party won a clear majority in the National Assembly and a Socialist, François Mitterrand, was elected president. The Socialist victories portended a turn to the left in the form of expanded welfare programs, deficit spending on a grand scale, greater nationalization of French industry, worker participation in management, administrative decentralization, and abolition of capital punishment. The realization of this agenda, however, was hampered by deepening domestic difficulties — in particular, high unemployment and economic stagnation — which adversely affected the Socialists' popularity.

The Short-Lived "Rupture with Capitalism" In February 1982, the Socialist government nationalized the "commanding heights" of the economy — that is to say, it took over key industries as well as banks and lending institutions. The newly nationalized industries employed hundreds of thousands of workers and represented a significant slice of France's total gross national product (GNP) and exports. After the new nationalizations, the public sector accounted for nearly one-third of industrial sales and nearly a quarter of the French workforce. In addition, the state gained near-total control of France's banking and credit systems. This "rupture with capitalism" cost French taxpayers well over 40 billion francs, as the state bought its way back into key sectors of the economy. (A dollar was worth between seven and eight francs in the 1990s, but exchange rates vary over time.)

The idea behind the nationalization program was to enhance the state's power to bring about rapid capital formation, economic modernization, and state-managed growth. The plan foundered when the government allowed state-owned enterprises to pursue their own strategies rather than conforming to a central plan. At the same time, the Mitterrand government, anxious to avoid embarrassment, poured money into the newly nationalized industries through budget allocations and loans from state-owned banks. These transfusions depleted the treasury but did not revive the "patients," as one industry after another sank into the rising sea of red ink.

But the consequences of Mitterrand's false start in 1981 could not easily be swept under the rug. The budget deficit rose sharply, inflation remained high when it was falling elsewhere in the EU, and the trade deficit suddenly mushroomed. In the face of these rapidly deteriorating conditions, Mitterrand bit the bullet: in 1983, the government reversed engines and adopted a tough austerity program (called "rigor" by crow-eating Socialist politicians).

The austerity measures involved holding wages down, curbing budget increases, and strictly controlling the money supply. But the response was sluggish. France's growth rate fell below that of most other Western European nations, while inflation stayed high. At the same time, France endured several consecutive "double deficits" (simultaneous budget and trade shortfalls). The chronic trade deficit was particularly troubling because it suggested a loss of French competitiveness in the world market.

To make matters worse, unemployment climbed steadily under Socialist rule. Even a state-mandated job creation program had little effect. If the Socialist Party, with its strong commitment to the working class, could not even guarantee jobs for people who wanted to work, the voters were almost certain to punish its candidates at the polls.

Soon the president and then the political system itself came under fire. The president was criticized for being too aloof from political pressures and public opinion, and the system was criticized for being overly politicized. Because presidential elections at the time were held every seven years and parliamentary elections at least every five years, elections — and preparations for them — came to dominate French politics. Legislative or presidential elections were held twelve times between 1962 and 1988. One authority asserted that "long-range programs gave place to expediency, and party alignments obeyed the logic of electoral tactics rather than policy making."[15]

A severe test of the system came in the 1986 national elections, when the center-right parties won a narrow majority. Compelled by that outcome a conservative prime minister, Socialist President Mitterrand asked the leader of a neo-Gaullist party, Jacques Chirac, to form a new government. The Fifth Republic had been created with a built-in time bomb that seemed about to detonate: a divided executive was in power. The president and the prime minister belonged to opposing parties, had different agendas, and looked to different constituencies.

Cohabitation: The Taming of the Left With the economy still in a slump, the Socialists lost the 1986 election to a center-right coalition headed by Jacques Chirac. The French Constitution, with its unique dual executive, was now put to one of its most severe tests: Could two leaders with radically different philosophies share power without bringing the country to a constitutional crisis? Prime Minister Chirac sought to denationalize firms and banks that the Socialists had earlier brought under state control. His more general aim was to deregulate the economy and return the initiative to the private sector.

To no one's surprise, this **cohabitation** amounted to little more than treading water until the 1988 presidential election. President Mitterrand campaigned for reelection on a pragmatic, market-oriented platform that closely resembled that of his principal center-right opponent, Prime Minister Chirac. Mitterrand promised voters that there would be no repeat of the failed Socialist experiment of 1981 — no nationalizations, no new corporate taxes, and no quixotic measures like his earlier attempt at shortening the workweek.

Voters believed him, and Mitterrand won a second term by a comfortable margin. Pollsters predicted that the Socialists would win a clear majority (289 seats) in National Assembly elections the following month, but they were wrong. Contrary to expectations, the center-right parties captured enough seats to leave Mitterrand's party thirteen seats short of a majority. The message of the electorate was fairly clear: Give us a middle-of-the-road government and cut the ideological rhetoric.

President Mitterrand got the message. His moderation in domestic policy was matched by prudence in foreign policy, including firm support for NATO (in contrast to the Gaullist tradition, which stressed strategic self-reliance and a special role vis-à-vis the two superpowers). At the same time, he pursued defense policies long popular in France, bolstering the nation's independent nuclear strike force (the third largest in the world) while promoting strategic and conventional arms reduction in Europe and beyond. Under Mitterrand, France played a leadership role in the European Union as well.

The Rise of the Extreme Right Despite the resounding vote for moderate parties and policies, the surprising popularity of right-wing extremist Jean-Marie Le Pen in the 1988 presidential race struck a discordant note. Le Pen campaigned on a nationalistic and racist platform that critics denounced as a new form of fascism. The target of his wrath was the influx of immigrants from France's former colonies in Africa and Asia. His neofascist message struck a responsive chord with hundreds of thousands of French voters.

Why? The rise of the National Front was a reflection of social and economic troubles facing France in the late 1980s and early 1990s. Unemployment and underemployment aggravated racial and ethnic tensions in French society, as did urban overcrowding, rising crime rates, drug abuse, and traffic congestion.

The National Front did not fade out of the picture in the 1990s, as has often happened with upstart political parties in France. When he again ran for president in 1995, Le Pen did slightly better than he had done seven years earlier. In response, both Mitterrand's Socialists and later Chirac's Gaullists tried to preempt the extreme right and satisfy a spreading xenophobia within French society by adopting tough measures aimed at curbing illegal immigration.

Cohabitation: Acts II and III History repeated itself in 1993 when the center-right again won a majority (roughly 80 percent) of the seats in parliamentary elections and Mitterrand was again forced to name a leader of the archrival neo-Gaullist RPR, Édouard Balladur, to head a new government. The Mitterand era came to an end in 1995. Chirac was elected president in a close race, defeating the Socialist candidate,

Lionel Jospin. At the time of Chirac's victory, the center-right not only claimed four-fifths of the National Assembly seats and two-thirds of the Senate, but also controlled twenty of twenty-two regional councils, most departmental councils, and many of the larger municipal councils. In 1997, President Chirac called surprise parliamentary elections in the expectation of receiving a mandate for his conservative economic policies. The French electorate once again surprised the politicians and pundits by handing the parties of the left, led by the Socialists a resounding victory. The result was to force Chirac to accept a Socialist government, headed by his political rival, Lionel Jospin, the man he had narrowly defeated in his quest for the presidency two years earlier. Cohabitation between Chirac and Jospin was uneasy. France's government was perhaps not adrift but it was going nowhere.

The Elections of 2002 The presidential election of 2002 was bizarre. In the first round of balloting, the French electorate expressed its extreme displeasure by saying to Chirac and Jospin, in effect, "A plague on both your houses." Chirac out-polled the others but received only one in every five votes cast — a dismal result for the incumbent president. For Prime Minister Jospin, however, the outcome was humiliating: he finished behind the extreme right-wing candidate Jean-Marie Le Pen. Most incredibly, Le Pen came within three percentage points of beating Chirac. The results stunned France (and Europe). In the second round of balloting, Chirac received four out of five votes cast (82 percent), the largest margin of any president in the history of the Fifth Republic.[16]

The parliamentary elections in June left no doubt that France was fed up with cohabitation. Chirac's center-right coalition (called the Union for the Presidential Majority, or UMP) won a decisive victory, garnering 357 seats to the second-finishing Socialist Party's 140 seats. But the UMP received only about a third of the votes cast and nearly two-fifths of the electorate stayed home. The message of these two elections was mixed but clear: On the positive side, no more divided government, and on the negative side, little confidence in the president. Nonetheless, the extreme right was shut out of the National Assembly, having failed to win a single seat (thanks to the peculiar arithmetic of the French electoral system).[17] And despite the fact that President Chirac's mandate was hollow, he could look forward to five more years in office with a prime minister of his own choosing and a compliant National Assembly.

Problems and Prospects

After World War II, the French adopted an economic strategy that was exactly the opposite of Great Britain's. The working class was made to sacrifice most, while the rich got richer. Marshall Plan aid was used in part for current consumption and indirectly to pay for the Indochina War (which cost more than the Marshall Plan contributed). General de Gaulle rejected the proposal of Prime Minister Pierre Mendes-France to break inflation after the Liberation, so the value of the franc plummeted. Economists in France and abroad wrote the country off. Yet after an initial expansion of the communist vote in a burst of working-class anger, France eventually did achieve its own economic miracle of sorts, and it is now on a par with the United Kingdom.

The French postwar economic miracle gave way to a time of troubles in the 1980s. By odd coincidence, France's economic fortunes started to sputter just as the British economy began to crank up. France's difficulties deepened under Socialist economic reforms aimed at enlarging the role of the state and cutting the size of the private sector. In the early 1980s, France under Mitterrand and Great Britain under Thatcher were moving in opposite directions. However, as we have seen, by the end of the decade, President Mitterrand was looking and sounding a lot like a born-again Reaganite. (Recall that President Ronald Reagan was generally opposed to state regulation of the economy.)

With the movement from "community" to "union" in Europe, President Mitterrand assigned high priority to preparing France for a competitive future, one without the protectionism and state intervention (*dirigisme*) that have been hallmarks of the French economy. It was one of history's ironies that this job fell to a Socialist leader; it was a sign of the times that he seemed to relish the prospect.

Why was it a "sign of the times"? Because in the United States and United Kingdom market-friendly, pro-business economic policies appeared to be working; the electorate was moving to the right; and left-of-center political parties (the Democrats in America and Labour in Britain) were following. This tendency was evident beyond the two countries in which it started. In the ensuing years it turned into a major trend.

Chirac and France's "Highs" The election of Jacques Chirac as president in 1995 appeared to signal a mild shift toward the right in French politics. During the campaign, Chirac pledged to undertake fiscal reform and reduce France's high unemployment rate (which had skyrocketed in recent years). Nor was unemployment the only "high" problem Chirac faced. High taxes and bloated budgets were part of Mitterrand's legacy. But the high jobless rate made it difficult to cut France's budget deficit, as did high wages and pensions for France's 5 million public-sector workers.

Another "high," the high cost of welfare in France — including health benefits, generous unemployment compensation, family allowances, and housing subsidies — also complicated efforts at reform. Between 1990 and 1995, France's welfare system accumulated a huge debt. Attempts to cut welfare benefits were vigorously resisted by workers, but failure to cut the cost of these benefits to business and industry, while keeping the minimum wage at high levels, discouraged employers from hiring new workers. (The system is funded by employers and employees as well as by the state.)

Meanwhile, three weeks of public-sector strikes in late 1995 crippled the economy and cost the country dearly. The strikes were precipitated by the Bank of France's decision to hike interest rates sharply in response to a run on the franc. But workers were also disgusted with government efforts to reduce the budget deficit while doing little to ease the double-digit jobless rate. For President Chirac, who had promised to make unemployment his "priority of priorities and reduce the budget deficit," it was not a promising start.

In April 1997, Chirac dissolved the National Assembly and called new elections, hoping to achieve a larger center-right majority and fortify his own popular mandate in the face of continuing labor unrest and obstruction from both the left- and right-wing opposition over key issues such as unemployment, immigration, and the planned European Monetary Union (EMU). The combined left, led by the Socialists, won a clear majority in the National Assembly. The Socialists alone won significantly fewer votes than the combined total for the center-right (RPR-UDF) but in the workings of parliamentary elections the vote added up to a big victory for the left.

What accounted for the swing to the left? No single problem can explain voting behavior anywhere, but in France it was a knot of interrelated issues with the workplace at the core. French workers are traditionally demonstrative. Organized labor has declined dramatically in numbers, but damaging strikes are still common. The Socialists won the election in 1997 by promising a thirty-five-hour workweek — less work at the same pay. They delivered on this promise but the solution did not make other problems go away; in fact, it made at least one big one — namely, pension reform — decidedly worse.

As mentioned earlier, France's "highs" (for example, high unemployment and high levels of public debt) complicate efforts to deal with pressing social problems. But another high, namely the high expectations and volatility of the workforce, is often the biggest political challenge facing the government. Indeed, implementation of the thirty-five-hour workweek in early 2000 actually prompted a series of protests by some workers loath to give up a two-hour lunch break or unhappy about having to work Saturdays, others (such as postal employees) who objected to having to do the same amount of work in less time, and still others (such as truck drivers) who would lose hours and overtime. To make matters worse, it was not at all clear that the main argument in favor of a shorter workweek — that it would boost productivity and employment — would prove to be true.

At the core of the pension problem is the fact that the state provides generous benefits to France's retirees — that, plus the fact that the money for public pension funds has to come from somewhere. The favored source in France (and nearly everywhere else) has been taxes. But today's taxpayers do not want to pay more today for less tomorrow — and that is precisely what the taxpayers in France feared they would be asked to do. There are only so many ways to keep a sinking ship afloat; the same can be said of a pension fund. Besides raising taxes (always politically risky), the retirement age can be raised or the benefits reduced (for example, by excluding bonuses from the definition of "income" or calculating payments on the basis of the highest paid twenty-five years of service rather than the highest paid ten years).

But none of these solutions is likely to be popular with French employees for obvious reasons. Moreover, the search for policy prescriptions is always conditioned ideology in France. Hence, no Socialist government is likely to tamper with the **special regimes** which give public-sector employees generous pension terms compared with private-sector employees. Nor are the Socialists likely to consider moving toward a system of individual (private) pension funds. (It was the adoption of just such a plan in 1995 that led to the conservative defeat two years later.)

The question of pension reform is emblematic of the type of policy dilemmas facing not only France but also most other modern, postindustrial societies. It remains to be seen whether France will be on the cutting edge — helping to show the way — or get mired in the kind of endless debate and rancor that will give France's friendly competitors in the New Europe an advantage.

France under Chirac remains firmly committed to the European Union (EU). In close partnership with Germany, France is the anchor of EU. French farmers benefit from the system of price supports (subsidies) and tariffs called the Common Agricultural

Policy (CAP), which was adopted at French insistence in the 1960s. In the 1990s, France strongly backed creation of the new European monetary system (the euro), as well as EU enlargement.

After the 9/11 attacks, President Chirac pledged French support for America's war on terrorism. Accordingly, France joined the coalition of states that actively aided the American invasion of Afghanistan in 2001. But France strongly opposed the invasion of Iraq, threatening to use its veto in the United Nations Security Council if necessary. As a result, the Bush administration decided not to seek UN approval. This incident left a bitter taste in the mouths of many Americans — so bitter that French wines virtually disappeared for a time from store shelves, tables, and restaurants in the United States. Perhaps more than anything Washington officials said or did, this public response, which harmed one of France's most important farm exports, made Paris take notice. President Chirac subsequently endeavored to smooth relations with the United States, without, however, recanting or expressing any regrets publicly. France and America have long had a love-hate relationship and still do today.

In Sum . . . Coping with changes at home and abroad presents a challenge to France in the coming years. For example, immigration, especially from North Africa, is changing the character of French society (especially in urban areas), making it more heterogeneous and creating problems of assimilation and social inequality. This problem is also linked to unemployment, the public debt (welfare and education costs), and so on. Dealing with these problems is costly in economic and cultural terms; not dealing with them may be even costlier in political terms, as the rise of the ultraright attests.

In external affairs, the unification of Germany inevitably raised old fears in France, which lost three wars to Germany between 1871 and 1945. The Franco-German agreement to create a joint army corps separate from NATO reflected France's anxiety over the twin prospects of German resurgence and American retrenchment. The launching of the euro (single currency) and creation of a European Central Bank (headquartered in Frankfurt, Germany) has helped reassure France that Germany is permanently enmeshed in Europe.

Germany is no longer a threat to France, thanks in large part to the American military presence there, but three wars between 1870 and 1945 left a legacy of mistrust. Germany's leadership role in building the European Union and its success in building a stable democracy, however, have done much to reassure France and the rest of Europe that the German threat is a thing of the past. We look next at government and politics in Germany.

Germany's Unified Federal Democracy

On October 3, 1990, West Germany and East Germany were united as one country, after more than four decades as separate entities. The East German communist regime was swept away, and the West German system of government was extended throughout the new nation. Thus, despite a tradition of autocratic rule, Germany is today a thriving democracy. Before unification, the Federal Republic of Germany (West Germany)

Germany

comprised ten states, or **Länder** (singular, *Land*), plus West Berlin.[18] It encompassed an area about the size of Oregon. The new unified Germany encompasses sixteen *Länder* and a land area of 137,838 square miles, slightly larger than Montana. Its population has gone from just under 62 million to just over 82 million. (See Table 4.3.) The capital has been officially moved from Bonn back to Berlin, historically the center of Germany's political life, although the process of physically moving the machinery of government will take several years.

Table 4.3 The New German Federation

Land	Capital	Area (square miles)	Population
Baden-Württemberg	Stuttgart	13,803	10,000,000
Bavaria	Munich	27,283	11,600,000
Berlin*	Berlin	341	3,450,000
Brandenburg*	Potsdam	15,044	2,670,000
Bremen	Bremen	156	680,000
Hamburg	Hamburg	291	1,690,000
Hesse	Wiesbaden	8,151	5,900,000
Lower Saxony	Hannover	18,311	7,480,000
Mecklenburg–West Pomerania*	Schwerin	6,080	1,850,000
North Rhine–Westphalia	Düsseldorf	13,149	17,690,000
Rhineland–Palatinate	Mainz	7,658	3,653,000
Saarland	Saarbrücken	992	1,080,000
Saxony*	Dresden	6,839	4,600,000
Saxony-Anhalt*	Halle	7,837	2,800,000
Schleswig-Holstein	Kiel	6,053	2,700,000
Thuringia*	Erfurt	5,872	2,540,000

*Formerly part of East Germany; estimated populations.
Source: Accessed February 5, 2004, on the Web at <http://userpage.chemie.fu-berlin.de/addressen/bl/bundeslaender.html>.

The *Länder* are the building blocks in a system designed to ensure a high degree of political decentralization. *Land* governments have the primary responsibility to enact legislation in specific areas such as education and cultural affairs. They alone have the means to implement laws enacted by the federal government, to command most of the administrative personnel to accomplish this task, to exercise police power (taking care of the health, welfare, and moral well-being of the people), to direct the educational system, and to ensure that the press does not violate constitutional rules.

Although the *Länder* have considerable clout, the federal government is the main repository of political authority in the constitutional system. The central government has the exclusive right to legislate in foreign affairs, citizenship matters, currency and coinage, railways, postal service and telecommunications, and copyrights. In other areas, notably civil and criminal law and laws relating to the regulation of the economy, the central government and the *Länder* share power.

Compared to the United States, Germany's federalism leaves more power in the hands of the states (*Länder*); the *Länder* run more of their own affairs and receive a larger proportion of taxes than American states do. For example, individual and corporate income taxes are split between Berlin and the *Länder* in equal 40 percent shares; the cities get 20 percent. The *Länder* also receive one-third of the value-added tax (VAT), the major source of tax revenue used in Germany and throughout Europe. (The

VAT is a turnover tax levied on all transactions — it is based on the incremental price of an item as it goes from manufacturer to distributor to retailer, paid by the buyer, and collected by the seller.) Thus, the *Länder* in Germany are not reduced to begging the national government for money, as the states in the United States so often are.

In sum, Germany borrowed the idea of federalism from the United States, but modified it to fit a different set of circumstances. The situation was so different, in fact, that the former West Germany gave its charter an unusual label.

The Basic Law

Germany's charter is called the **Basic Law** rather than a "constitution" because it was designed as a temporary document after World War II to be supplanted by a formal constitution (with a capital *C*) at such time as the two Germanys were reunified. Its last article states, "This Basic Law loses its validity on the day on which a Constitution that has been freely decided on by the German people comes into effect." That day has not yet arrived even though Germany is now unified because the German people are quite satisfied with what they have now and because no German government has wanted to open up a Pandora's box by initiating a process that would have an unpredictable and potentially divisive outcome.

The drafting of the Basic Law was extraordinary in part because it was done under the watchful eyes of the powers occupying Germany after World War II. The United States, Great Britain, and France served as models from which the West Germans borrowed freely. From the United States they took the principles of federalism (dividing governmental responsibilities between a national government and state governments) and true bicameralism (having two legislative chambers elected in different ways and playing distinctive constitutional roles). From Great Britain they adapted the parliamentary system. They imitated the French electoral system, using proportional representation to fill some of the seats in the **Bundestag** (lower house). The preamble to the Basic Law proclaims West Germany's right of self-determination, and there is no mention of the Occupation. Remarkably, one decade after World War II, a sovereign, independent, and democratic government became fully operational in West Germany.

The Basic Law and Individual Rights Significantly, the first nineteen articles of the Basic Law deal with the inalienable rights of every West German. As one student of German politics has observed, "The relevant historical experience was that of the Third Reich with its oppressive flouting of all human liberties."[19] The Weimar Constitution (imposed by the victorious powers after Germany's defeat in World War I) made it possible for the government to suspend constitutional rights during times of emergency. Abuse of these emergency powers by the Nazi regime eventually led to the revocation of the constitution itself. Accordingly, Article 19 of the Basic Law proclaims, "In no case may the essential content of a basic right be encroached upon." The guarantees contained in the first nineteen articles are entrenched: No act of the executive, legislative, or judicial branch of government can revoke or abridge them. If a question arises about whether a statutory law conflicts with the Basic Law, the Federal Constitutional Court resolves the issue.

The rights guaranteed under the Basic Law include equality before the law; freedoms of speech, religion, assembly, and the press; academic freedom; freedom of association; freedom from unlawful searches; private property rights; the right of asylum; freedom from discrimination based on race, sex, or political convictions; and the right to refuse military service as a matter of conscience. Article 18 attaches a caveat to these rights, stipulating that they cannot be used "to attack the democratic order." This provision was clearly aimed at the two extremes of left and right, communism and nazism, which have so afflicted German life in the twentieth century. It also reflected the postwar preoccupation with Soviet communism that prevailed throughout the Atlantic community and was particularly pervasive in West Germany. However, fear of the reawakening of neo-Nazi ultranationalism has never been far beneath the surface in the Federal Republic, as evidenced by the fact that neo-Nazi activity has generally been interpreted as constituting an attack on the democratic order.

It is not easy to amend the Basic Law. In fact, some key parts of the German "constitution" are irrevocable (they cannot be changed, period). Can you guess why?

The Amendment Process Amending the Basic Law requires a two-thirds majority vote in both houses of the parliament, but the fundamental principles and guarantees cannot be revoked or amended. In addition to the civil liberties enumerated in the first nineteen articles, the federal, republican, democratic, and welfare state features of the political system are deliberately set in stone to prevent a recurrence of the Nazi nightmare.

Article 23 From its inception, the Basic Law of the Federal Republic looked ahead to a time when Germany would be united. Under Article 23, East Germany (the German Democratic Republic, or GDR) could be merged with West Germany at any time, the only proviso being that the GDR accept the Basic Law. Before 1989, this part of the Basic Law seemed irrelevant in the context of the Cold War. But with the overthrow of communist rule in East Germany at the end of 1989, Article 23 became the vehicle by which the two states were united.

The Chancellor

Germany has a parliamentary form of government with a dual executive. The president is a figurehead, indirectly elected and endowed with ceremonial powers. The true chief executive is the **chancellor,** who obtains the position in the same way as the British prime minister — by being leader of the majority party in the lower house (the Bundestag). If no one party enjoys an absolute majority, as has often been the case in Germany, the leader of the major party in the ruling coalition (that is, a government comprised of two or more parties) becomes the chancellor.

The chancellor, with parliamentary approval, appoints and dismisses cabinet members. Together with the cabinet, the chancellor sets policy guidelines and proposes legislation. As the head of government, the chancellor is responsible for translating policies into operational programs. The chancellor has the power to veto budget measures. In a national emergency, the chancellor becomes commander in chief. In short, the chancellor, like the British prime minister, is the dominant figure in the government.

The Basic Law contains a provision, called the constructive vote of no confidence that would seem to make it very difficult to remove a chancellor. Indeed, this very rule allowed Konrad Adenauer (Germany's first chancellor after World War II) to rule in difficult times with only a one-seat majority. But in this respect Germany resembles Great Britain. Three of Germany's five chancellors — Adenauer (1949–1963), Ludwig Erhard (1963–1966), and Willy Brandt (1969–1974) — resigned between elections when they became a liability to the party they headed. Similarly, since World War II, no fewer than four conservative British prime ministers have stepped down between elections to make way for new party leadership. The leader gets most of the credit when the party's fortunes are rising, and all the blame when they are falling.

The chancellor chooses cabinet members in close consultation with the party's executive committee. Seldom does one of the two major parties win a clear majority in the Bundestag, so it is usually necessary for either the Christian Democratic Union (CDU) or the Social Democratic Party (SDP) to enter into a coalition with the small Free Democratic Party (FDP) or, after the 1998 elections, the Green Party. As a consequence, the allocation of cabinet posts typically reflects the need to entice the coalition partner with some key ministerial appointments. For example, Hans-Dietrich Genscher, leader of the FDP, was for many years the Federal Republic's foreign minister, first as the junior partner in a coalition with the SDP under Helmut Schmidt and then, after FDP broke with the SDP in 1982, in a coalition with the CDU under Helmut Kohl. (Genscher, in poor health, resigned in 1992.) In 1998, Green Party leader Joshka Fisher became the foreign minister in the government headed by the SDP (see below).

Almost all cabinet members are also members of the Bundestag and are active in both roles. In contrast to British cabinet members, German ministers are almost always chosen for their expertise in a particular policy area. There are generally about seventeen cabinet members, the most prominent being the ministers of finance, foreign affairs, defense, and interior. Cabinet members participate in decision making, advise the chancellor on policy matters, direct the formulation of policy proposals and legislation within their own departments, and oversee the implementation of policy by their subordinates.

Directly below the chancellor and the cabinet are the parliamentary secretaries (who are members of the federal legislature) and state secretaries (career civil service employees). The parliamentary secretaries are considered junior ministers — they leave office at the end of the term of the cabinet member they serve. The state secretaries, as professional bureaucrats, provide some continuity from one government to the next — they stay on after cabinet members leave office. The departments tend to be small (in contrast with British departments) because the *Land* governments, as we noted earlier, actually administer most federal programs and enforce federal as well as state laws.

Today in Germany, the power of the executive branch is counterbalanced by the legislative branch. A popularly elected legislature with a vigorous opposition is one key to protecting individual liberties and preventing an adventuristic foreign policy (for example, one seeking to conquer neighboring states by force of arms no matter what the costs and risks). Given its history of political extremism, which led to totalitarian (Nazi) rule between the two world wars, the newly unified German state definitely needs a proactive parliament. Such a body is necessary not only to ensure democracy at home, but also to assure the rest of Europe that Germany no longer poses a threat to stability and peace on the Continent. Hence, it is especially important in Germany's case that its parliament, to which we now turn, can make or break governments — and has.

The German Parliament

Unlike Great Britain, Germany lacks a great parliamentary tradition. Bismarck largely ignored the Reichstag (the forerunner of the Bundestag), and during the Weimar period it was ineffectual. Even after 1949, the Bundestag lacked prestige and was treated with a certain disdain by Chancellor Adenauer (who resembled France's authoritarian President Charles de Gaulle in this respect).

The German parliament is bicameral. The lower house (Bundestag), consisting of 672 members, is directly elected; the 69-member upper house — known as the **Bundesrat** — is indirectly elected. The Bundestag is the primary lawmaking body, although the Bundesrat also plays an important legislative role. The chancellor initiates most bills, but before any bill can become law, the Bundestag must vote its approval. Thus, it functions as one of the principal mechanisms in the constitutional system of checks and balances. The Basic Law underscores the independence of the Bundestag by stipulating that its members are "not bound by orders and instructions and shall be subject only to their conscience."

The Bundestag In addition to choosing the chancellor, the Bundestag acts as a watchdog over the government. The Bundestag has the power to oust a chancellor at any time with a constructive vote of no confidence. On its own initiative, it can also enact legislation binding on the government, conduct public debates on government policy, investigate government actions, and directly question the chancellor and cabinet members. (The latter can be summoned to appear before the Bundestag, but they cannot be forced to disclose information.)

Voting patterns in the Bundestag reflect a strict party discipline. Parliamentary parties are organized into ***Fraktionen*** (factions). The *Fraktionen* meet frequently to decide how to vote on upcoming bills and to discuss legislative strategy and determine the specific responsibility each deputy will assume on each piece of legislation. The assignments and instructions even include the precise arguments that deputies will make. The *Fraktionen* are built into the parliamentary structure: only parties with a large enough block of deputies to form a *Fraktionen* (at least 5 percent of the total membership) can be represented in committees.

In Germany, as in the United States, committees are a principal source of legislative power. Committees generally meet in private, and the opposition has ample opportunity to participate. Most of the nineteen standing committees have identical counterparts in the cabinet. This arrangement facilitates the flow of communications between the government and the Bundestag because cabinet officials are usually deputies in the Bundestag as well. Normally, committees in Germany do not have the kind of investigatory powers found in the U.S. Congress, but the Bundestag can establish special committees of inquiry on the recommendation of one-fourth of the deputies.

The Bundestag elects a presiding officer through a secret ballot. In practice, the majority party actually decides who will be the Bundestag president. There are also three vice presidents selected from opposition parties. Together with other party leaders, these officials form the Council of Elders, which acts as an advisory board to the president of the Bundestag, schedules debates on pending legislation, and allocates speaking time to the parliamentary parties.

The Bundesrat Also known as the Federal Council, the Bundesrat is the main institutional mechanism for adjusting and regulating relations between the *Bund* (federal government) and the *Länder.* It is perhaps the most distinctive feature of the German system. Unlike the relatively powerless British House of Lords, the Bundesrat is a powerful body with exclusive constitutional functions. Directly responsible to the state governments, it has wide-ranging influence on federal policies and procedures. The most imposing institutional expression of German federalism is the Bundesrat, the upper house of the national legislature.

The Bundesrat is not popularly elected; the various *Land* governments, which have three to six seats each (depending on population), appoint its members. Each *Land* government must vote as a block — a provision that reinforces the federal character of the German parliament.

The Bundestag is constitutionally required to submit the legislation it passes to the Bundesrat. All bills that directly affect the *Länder* must be approved by the Bundesrat to become law; in other words, the Bundesrat can veto such legislation. Other bills do not require its approval, but any objections raised by the Bundesrat must be debated in the Bundestag before the bill becomes law. The influence of the Bundesrat over federal policy has increased steadily, giving the *Länder* a role in the political system far exceeding that of the state governments in the United States.

Because the composition of the Bundesrat is not affected by national elections, this house has a special aura of stability. It is also more streamlined and more efficient than the lower house because most of its members hold ministerial posts in their respective *Land* governments and can use their own administrative staffs to help them prepare legislation. In general, Bundesrat members tend to have more technical expertise than Bundestag deputies do, and they can be more specialized. Finally, there is little party influence in the Bundesrat. Members are expected to represent the interests of the *Länder* without regard for party preference. The strict party discipline found in the Bundestag is matched by the tight control *Land* governments exercise over their representatives in the Bundesrat. In sum, the Bundesrat gives the German states a powerful weapon to protect themselves against federal encroachment.

How Laws Are Made

The Basic Law divides legislation into three categories: exclusive, concurrent, and framework law. Article 30 lodges state legislative authority firmly in the *Länder,* and Article 70 stipulates that the *Länder* have all legislative powers not expressly conferred on the federal parliament. Exclusive legislative authority, assigned solely to the *Bund* (federal government), is limited to foreign affairs, defense, currency, and trade. Concurrent legislative authority applies in such areas as criminal and civil law, trade and commerce, and public roads. The *Länder* may legislate in these areas so long as the *Bund* has not already done so. (All federal legislation in this category must be approved by the Bundesrat to become law.) Framework legislative authority limits the *Bund* to providing only outline bills, leaving the details up to the *Länder.* This category includes public services, the environment, and regional planning. Although the most important legislation is given to the *Bund,* administration of programs and implementation of policy are left largely in the hands of the *Länder.*

Bills in the parliament run a familiar gauntlet: formal introduction, committee review, several readings, debate, and final vote. Individual lawmakers in both chambers may introduce measures. The executive branch drafts most legislation. All government bills must be sent to the Bundesrat first, and any changes to a bill must accompany it to the Bundestag. Because the Bundesrat has veto power over all concurrent legislation, the government normally works closely with this body in the drafting stages to avoid potential problems. (On some issues, the Bundesrat has only a suspensive veto— meaning that it can delay passage of a bill but cannot defeat it.)

After a bill has been introduced, it goes to the Bundestag, where it is debated. Next it is sent to a standing committee, where most of the detail work is done. A committee member is usually assigned to prepare a report about the bill, which then goes back to the full house for further debate. This stage is known as the second reading. A third reading usually follows shortly thereafter, and the measure is voted on. If it passes, it is sent to the Bundesrat. In the case of legislation introduced by the government, the Bundesrat gets two reviews. If the Bundesrat and the Bundestag do not agree on the form or substance of a particular bill, the bill goes to a conference committee, as it might in the U.S. Congress. The conference committee has twenty-two members, half from each house of the parliament. Differences in language are usually reconciled through this mechanism. Once a bill has been passed by both houses and has been signed by the president and the chancellor, it becomes law.

Parties and Elections

Under the Weimar Republic, the left- and right-wing parties were separated by a yawning ideological chasm that produced the instability that led Germany down the path to totalitarian rule. Today the vast majority of German voters have crowded around the political center, choosing moderation over extremism.

Since 1949, the Federal Republic has had just two major parties, the center-left Social Democratic Party (SDP) and the center-right (or conservative) Christian Democratic Union (CDU). The latter has formed a permanent alliance with the Bavarian

Christian Social Union (CSU). In addition, the relatively small Free Democratic Party (FDP) has shown remarkable staying power and has played a strategic role as the holder of the balance. Because the two major parties are frequently represented almost equally in the Bundestag, the Free Democrats have often controlled the decisive votes; as a result, the FDP's influence has been disproportionate to its size, and it has been a junior partner in most coalition governments.

Although the SDP is a socialist party and the CDU-CSU is a free-enterprise party, both are relatively moderate. Indeed, the two parties shared power from 1966 to 1969 in what was known as the Grand Coalition.

Smaller parties have a better chance of surviving in Germany than in Great Britain because half of the Bundestag is chosen by proportional representation. Even so, the party system was consciously designed to keep the number of parties at a reasonable level and to prevent small extremist groups from disrupting the orderly democratic process. Parties must receive a minimum of 5 percent of the national vote or must win seats in a minimum of three electoral districts to gain Bundestag representation.

The most successful fringe party in the Federal Republic has been the Greens, a leftist party that focuses almost exclusively on environmental and antinuclear issues. In the spring of 1987, the Greens led a counterculture coalition in protest against a nationwide census. The ostensible issue was the right to privacy; the real issue was the authority of the state, which the Greens generally regard with fear and loathing.

National elections normally occur every four years in Germany. Two different electoral systems are used to choose the Bundestag's deputies — a **first vote** and a **second vote.** Half are elected by a simple majority ("plurality") in single-member districts — the first vote. The other half are elected by proportional representation — the second vote. In the first vote, the individual candidate is featured; in the second vote, the party is paramount. Thus each voter casts two votes, one for an individual and one for a *Land* list put together by the party. The second vote is crucial because it determines the total number of seats a party receives in each *Land.* The party decides who is at the top of the list and who is at the bottom, a practice that enhances the role and importance of political parties in Germany.

A Limited Government

Weighing the cumulative effects of the system prescribed by the Basic Law (federalism, the unique organization of the legislature, the carefully structured party system, the independent judiciary, the explicit guarantees of civil liberties), it becomes apparent that one of the main purposes of the Basic Law was to arrange the institutional furniture in postwar Germany to preclude a reincarnation of prewar Germany. Limited government, more than any other facet of constitutional democracy, was central to the drafters of the Basic Law, who deliberately sought to build into the system safeguards against the concentration of power that had caused so much turmoil leading up to World War II.

The democratic performance of the Federal Republic of Germany (FRG) since World War II has indeed been impressive. The experience of Weimar has not been repeated. Though the Weimar Republic was largely undone by severe economic distress, West Germany's rapid postwar recovery and sustained industrial growth since 1949 have frequently been described as an economic miracle. Spurred on by a remarkable economic resurgence and a firm commitment to constitutional government, the present generation of Germans has given democracy a new lease on life in a land where it was once thought to be unworkable. Moreover, West Germany's economic success no doubt spurred East Germans' dissatisfaction with a communist regime that was unable to match West Germany's performance or even come close to providing a comparable standard of living. Germany had been a microcosm of the Cold War for over forty years; the collapse of communism in East Germany thus symbolized the end of an era in international politics and a new beginning for the German people.

Problems and Prospects

After World War II, the Allies imposed deflationary policies on West Germany. The Germans in turn imposed austerity and hard work on themselves — in contrast to the British, who fell to taking more and more from the state while giving less and less. Helped in part by the American decision to extend Marshall Plan aid to Germany, the German economy revived very quickly. In short order, the Federal Republic created a welfare state far more lavish than anything in Great Britain or France. The West Germans came out winners.

In the 1950s, West Germany's economy surged ahead of most of its neighbors' economies on the Continent (Italy alone kept pace for a time). In the decades that followed, Germany became the standard by which other Western industrial democracies measured their own economic performance. West Germany's extraordinary and sustained record of economic growth would not have been possible without an equally extraordinary record of political stability that lasted through the 1980s.

The Kohl Era In 1982, the center-right Christian Democratic Union–Christian Socialist Union (CDU-CSU) formed a coalition government with the Free Democrats (FDP), who decided to break a thirteen-year alliance with the left-leaning Social Democrats (SDP). Six months later, German voters gave a solid mandate to Helmut Kohl's conservative government.

The victory of Chancellor Kohl's *Koalition der Mitte* (center coalition) in 1983 followed Germany's worst economic slump since the Great Depression of the 1930s. Many German voters blamed the recession on the generous but expensive welfare-state programs favored by the SDP. Kohl and the Christian Democrats promised to reverse the course with a combination of tax cuts, investment incentives, and budget reductions. Although less drastic, Kohl's approach vaguely resembled Reaganomics and the supply-side prescriptions of Great Britain's Prime Minister Thatcher.

Kohl's economic program produced generally positive results: economic growth stopped its downslide, inflation was brought down to its lowest point thirty-four years, and budget deficits were sharply curtailed. In addition, spending for social welfare programs was curbed significantly.

In this auspicious climate, business and industry rebounded. By mid-1986, German factories were operating at 85 percent of capacity, and in some heavy industrial sectors could not keep pace with demand. Capital investment perked up as well. Plant modernization — particularly the use of computers and robots — accelerated rapidly. To top it all off, the balance of payments showed a record surplus in 1986. The one low mark on Kohl's report card was unemployment, which remained high.

In the 1987 parliamentary elections, the CDU came out on top, but the Greens — an antinuclear, environmental party — garnered a million votes more than they had four years earlier. Environmentalists and peace activists got a boost in that election from the 1986 Chernobyl nuclear accident in the Ukraine. The Greens sought to capitalize on popular fears, calling for West Germany's immediate withdrawal from NATO, unilateral disarmament, and the dismantling of all nuclear power stations in West Germany. In so doing, they struck a responsive chord within a slim but significant minority of the German electorate, winning a small block of Bundestag seats in the 1987 elections.

Although Germany is an affluent society, the struggle over how wealth and power are (or ought to be) distributed intensified as a result of German **unification.** Organized labor charged that the Kohl government was blatantly partial to big business, while big business counters by pointing to Germany's notoriously high labor costs (directly related salaries, benefits, and pensions). (See Figure 4.2.)

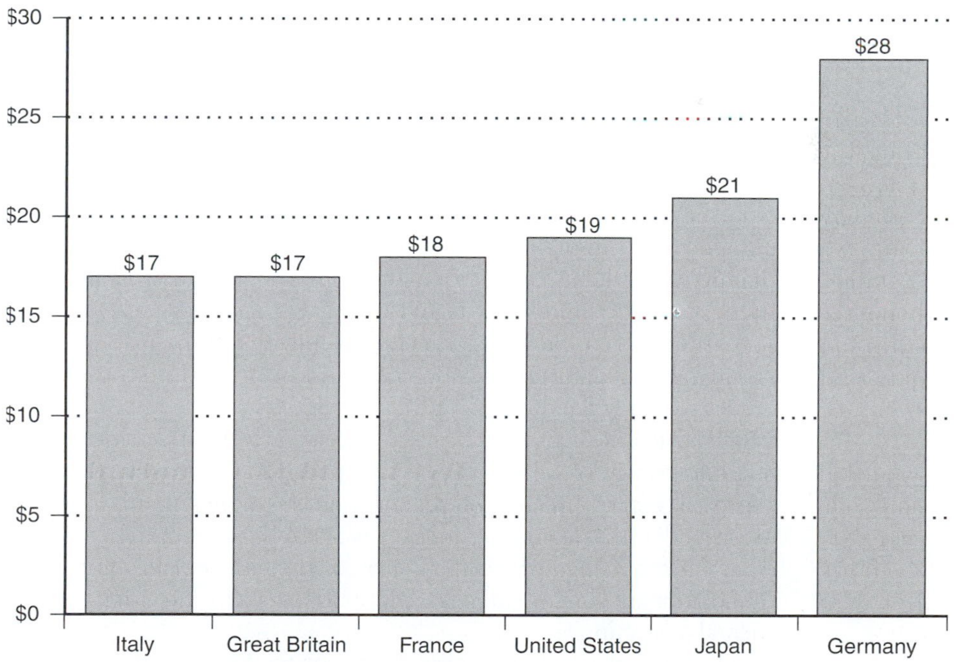

Figure 4.2 Germany's Labor Pains (manufacturing labor costs, wages, and benefits, in U.S. dollars per hour, 1999 estimate)

Source: Organization for Economic Cooperation and Development.

A related problem was the presence of poverty amid plenty. Hit especially hard by what Germans call the "new poverty" were the long-term unemployed, divorced women with children, elderly pensioners, and refugees seeking asylum. Some Germans see a relationship between poverty and policy. For example, the percentage of long-term unemployed rose sharply during the 1980s, a trend that feeds into the poverty issue in Germany because, under existing rules, the longer an individual is unemployed, the less he or she receives in public assistance.

In 1989, West Germany's political world changed abruptly. For several years, all previous policy debates were overshadowed by one overriding concern — how to happily remarry the two Germanys after a half century of bitter divorce.

German Unification The unification issue moved front and center following the dramatic toppling of the communist regime in East Germany at the end of 1989. The conservative East German Christian Democratic Union, which won a plurality (41 percent) of the votes in March 1990, campaigned on a platform calling for rapid merger of the two German states. With his popularity high and rising, West German Chancellor Helmut Kohl went to East Germany and campaigned for the conservatives and for early unification. On October 3, 1990, the two German states formally merged into a single entity. Two months later the first free, all-German elections in fifty-eight years were held. The center-right coalition by the ruling Christian Democrats received a strong mandate to continue in power; the Social Democratic Party, only one-third of the popular vote.

Unification added 16 million Germans to the Federal Republic literally overnight. What would be the political implications of suddenly incorporating so many people who had never lived under constitutional democracy or coped with a free-enterprise system? How long would the process take? How much would it cost? How would it be financed? What sort of compromises would be necessary? The problems associated with making the two states into one were daunting even for a country like Germany with a stable government and a strong economy. Transforming the former East Germany from a police state with a centrally planned economy to a democratic society with a free-market economy proved to be a very costly and rancorous enterprise.

The pace of unification was a primary issue in the early 1990s. The CDU on both sides of the border favored a merger "as soon as possible" pursuant to Article 23 of the Basic Law, which allows regions of prewar Germany to join the Federal Republic upon acceptance of the Basic Law. The SDP, however, called for a new constitution. Drafting such a constitution would obviously take time and involve careful negotiations between the two German governments. The timetable for unity was thus a key question. A closely related issue was how much West Germany would compromise with its GDR "poor relation" in negotiating the precise terms of unification. For example, would West Germany agree to modernize the Basic Law by including such themes as environmental protection?

Having dreamed of a united Germany for four decades, however, West Germans quickly discovered that the dream came with a staggering price tag. Absorbing the influx of East Germans and modernizing the GDR's outmoded factories would be expensive. In addition to unemployment, adjustments associated with a quick monetary union (using the West German mark in all German territory) brought the risk of inflation and recession. Predictably, the government was forced to raise taxes.

Divisions between Germany's western and eastern populations widened at the outset of the 1990s. The economy continued to boom in the west, while unemployment rose rapidly in the east; fully one-third of the workforce was either unemployed or employed part time. *Ossis* (easterners) received less than half the average wages of *Wessis* (westerners), and *Ossis* felt like second-class citizens. This situation was exacerbated by a sharp decline in eastern Germany's GDP. The deepening economic crisis in the east led to angry anti-Kohl demonstrations in eastern cities in March and April 1991, as well as outbreaks of right-wing racist violence (discussed in the next section). At the same time, Kohl came under attack in western Germany for allegedly breaking his promise not to raise taxes to rebuild the former GDR. It was the kind of dilemma that is often the undoing of a democratic leader. Indeed, the CDU did suffer losses in state elections in the spring of 1991. Perhaps the most humiliating defeat for Kohl came in his home state (*Land*) of Rhineland-Palatinate, one that cost the CDU the majority it had held in the Bundesrat since October 1990.

Having embarked on unification, there was no turning back for the Kohl government. But the realities were daunting. For example, East Germany under communist rule had become an ecological nightmare, and the cleanup costs alone were staggering. In addition, the states that once comprised East Germany have 25 percent of the Federal Republic's population and 33 percent of its territory, but in the early 1990s accounted for only about 7.5 percent of its total output. Closing down inefficient enterprises and modernizing others was essential but could not be done without causing high unemployment in the former GDR. After reunification, the jobless rate in Germany as a whole (but highest by far in the east) steadily rose until it reached double digits.

In the meantime, the Federal Republic struggled to absorb the flood of immigrants from Eastern Europe. Some came as asylum seekers; others were ethnic Germans who could expect immediate citizenship under a policy carried over from the Cold War. In all, some 2.5 million people poured into Germany after 1989, including 775,000 Eastern Europeans of German descent and a large number of refugees (former East Germans constituted the majority of new arrivals). This invasion was unsettling to many West Germans — so much so that it opened a debate on the nation's asylum laws and immigration policies. Many observers attributed the rise of an ultraright nationalist movement in Germany in the early 1990s to Germans' growing fear that their country would be overwhelmed by a human tidal wave from the east. The neo-Nazis committed a spate of violent crimes against foreigners, especially Turks, in 1991 and 1992 — behavior reminiscent of Nazi attacks on German Jews in the late 1930s. Popular indignation both within Germany and from the international community prompted a government crackdown on the far right at the end of 1992.

In the 1994 elections, a resurgence of the German economy helped the CDU-CSU overcome Chancellor Helmut Kohl's fading popularity. The center-right coalition won but ended up with a precarious ten-seat majority in the Bundestag and a net loss of fifty-seven seats. But Kohl's political troubles were far from over. In early 1995, Kohl banned neo-Nazi groups in an effort to curb continued far-right racial violence — another sign of the times. In December 1995, unemployment reached a postwar high of

3.8 million — another sign of the times. The likelihood that these two developments were related was particularly disturbing to students of history who recalled the circumstances leading to the Holocaust — the polarization of German society associated with severe economic dislocations of the 1920s and 1930s. (See Chapter 3.)

The German Malaise German voters ended Chancellor Kohl's sixteen-year rule in 1998 when a center-left coalition led by the Social Democrats resoundingly defeated the CDU-CSU. The SDP joined forces with the Greens to form a government. New Chancellor Gerhard Schröder chose Joshka Fisher, leader of the Greens, to head the foreign ministry. For the first time ever, a major European power had a Green foreign minister. Given the Greens' history of vociferous opposition to nuclear weapons and the use of military force, would Germany now become a less reliable ally of the United States? Would the Schröder government ask the United States to close its military bases on German territory? How would NATO be affected? The answer to these questions would become clear in 2002–2003, when George Bush decided to confront Iraq's Saddam Hussein.

Schröder's most controversial appointment was the new finance minister, Oskar Lafontaine (popularly known as "Red Oskar"). Under Lafontaine's influence, German economic policy at first tilted sharply to the left (reminiscent of what happened in France under Mitterrand in the early 1980s). Not only was spending hiked but also a large "ecological" tax was put on gasoline. At the same time, changes in workplace rules favored labor and had a chilling effect on the business climate. As economic conditions worsened and his government's popularity plummeted, however, Schröder abruptly changed directions, adopting a more centrist economic policy called *Sparpaket* (austerity package) in the summer of 2000. The German economy rebounded for a time, and then slowed again. Unemployment hovered around 9 percent (4 million workers), and the German economy underperformed by comparison with the EU average. For Germans, accustomed to being Europe's economic leader, this was a rude awakening.

The SDP barely kept control of the government in the 2002 elections, polling just 6,000 votes more than the CDU-CSU (out of a total electorate of 61.4 million). Schröder capitalized on the antimilitarism of most German voters by opposing the U.S. policy of confrontation with Iraq. In addition, the FDP stumbled going into the 2002 elections. As a result, the Greens finished third in the balloting (ahead of the FDP) supplying the governing coalition with a slim majority in the Bundestag.

Germany remains Europe's economic giant. The German economy — which ranks third in the world behind only the United States and Japan — continues to have many underlying strengths which include innovative and competitive firms, a well-trained workforce, among the highest GDP per capita in Europe, a comprehensive system of social welfare, and a stable democracy. The German economy not only generates investment capital itself, but also attracts venture capital from abroad — especially when the economy's vital signs are strong. Many of its recent troubles stem from the fact that it absorbed a failed state (the former East Germany) in the 1990s — a remarkable achievement by any standards. As the eastern *Länder* catch up, they will cease to be a liability and instead will become a major contributing asset.

In Sum . . . The German economic miracle after World War II re-created the most dynamic economy in Europe. West Germans have long enjoyed a standard of living that is among the highest in the world. In the 1990s, East Germans began catching up (thanks mainly to huge and unprecedented capital transfers from the western part of Germany to the eastern part). As we have seen, Germany displays many economic and social problems common to other postindustrial countries in Europe, but none of these problems is likely to hobble Germany's robust economy or mar Germany's record of political stability in the postwar period. Germans, like the British and French, have a bright future — made all the brighter by the energizing effects of the greatest regional economic structure in world history, the European Union. Beginning in 2002, Germany openly opposed the United States (over the war in Iraq) for the first time since World War II. Whether this newfound foreign policy independence is a temporary expedient or a permanent stance, and what it might mean for the future of Germany (and Europe), are questions of the utmost importance.

The European Union: An Embryonic State?

Any treatment of contemporary European politics is incomplete without a look at Europe's ambitious experiment in supranational institution building.* Since the inception of the Common Market in 1958, Western Europe has moved toward ever tighter economic integration. In the 1990s, the European Community (EC) was transfigured into the European Union (EU) when its members voted in steps for full economic unification complete with a common European currency, the euro. In 2003, the EU comprised fifteen countries (Austria, Belgium, Britain, Denmark, Finland, France, Germany, Greece, Ireland, Italy, Luxembourg, the Netherlands, Portugal, Spain, and Sweden), compared to six at its modest beginning. Ten more countries were set to join in 2004, including Latvia, Lithuania, Estonia, Poland, the Czech Republic, Slovakia, Hungary, and Slovenia, plus Malta and Cyprus. It will increase in total population from 370 million to 460 million. It is the largest trading bloc in the world and rivals the United States as an economic power.

The EU encompasses three separate legal entities dating back to the 1950s: the European Coal and Steel Community (ECSC), the European Economic Community (EEC), and the European Atomic Energy Community (Euratom). It is governed by institutions common to all, including the European Parliament, Council of Ministers, Commission, Court of Justice, and Court of Auditors. The Economic and Social Committee performs an advisory role. In 1999, the European Monetary Union went into effect, creating the single currency (mentioned above) and a new institution, the European Central Bank (ECB) headquartered in Frankfurt, Germany. However, four of the fifteen member states (Britain, Denmark, Sweden, and Greece) opted out. Significantly, the hesitation of these countries did not prevent the 12 governments of the new **Euro zone** from moving forward.

---

*For more information about the European Union, see Thomas Magstadt, *The European Union Today: A Quest for Unity Amidst Diversity,* published as a supplement to the Fourth Edition of this book.

The **Council of Ministers** has the final decision-making authority. It is composed of the foreign ministers of the member states, which in practice means that these states have not given up their right of self-determination or sovereignty. Voting power in the Council of Ministers is weighted according to population; Germany ranks first; France, Italy, and the United Kingdom share the second rank; then Spain; and so on. The European Commission is the administrative arm. Its members (two each from France, Germany, Italy, Spain, and the United Kingdom; and one from each of the other member states) are pledged to independence of national interests. It is accountable to the European Parliament, which can dismiss the commission by a vote of censure (but so far it has never done so). It initiates proposals but must obtain the prior approval of the Council of Ministers before taking action on any new measures. The parliament shares the power of the purse with the Council of Ministers and has the right to reject the budget — a power it exercised in 1979 and 1984 because it disagreed with the council's spending priorities.

An assembly — named the **European Parliament** in 1962 — was envisioned in the original treaties setting up the Common Market, but the first election of members of the European Parliament (MEPs) did not take place until 1973. For several years delegates were appointed from their national parliaments. MEPs were directly elected for the first time in 1979. In 1984, the second direct EU elections involved 120 million voters in ten countries — 60 percent of eligible voters. Turnout varies greatly, ranging from a high of 92 percent in Belgium (where voting is compulsory) to a low of 32 percent in the United Kingdom (where the electorate has always been lukewarm toward the EU).

The European Parliament is truly European. Its administration is located in Luxembourg, weeklong plenary sessions take place monthly (alternating between Strasbourg and Brussels), and the eighteen specialized committees normally meet for two weeks each month in Brussels. The proceedings in full sessions and in committees are simultaneously translated into the EU's nine official languages: English, Danish, Dutch, French, German, Greek, Italian, Spanish, and Portuguese. MEPs sit and vote not as national delegations but as parliamentary factions based on political aims and ideological compatibility. (Table 4.4 shows how seats are apportioned in the European Parliament.)

The EU Council of Ministers considered the plan too radical, however. Instead, in February 1986 they signed the **Single European Act,** which called for greater use of majority voting in the Council of Ministers and a limited increase in the European Parliament's powers. The act went into effect in 1987 following approval by the national

Table 4.4 The European Parliament: One Germany = Six Denmarks

Germany	99	Netherlands	25
United Kingdom	87	Sweden	22
France	87	Austria	22
Italy	87	Denmark	16
Spain	64	Finland	16
Belgium	25	Ireland	15
Greece	25	Luxembourg	6
Portugal	25		

Table 4.5 The EU Council of Ministers: Weighted Voting

	Current	Nice Treaty
Germany	10	29
France	10	29
Italy	10	29
United Kingdom	10	29
Spain	8	27
Netherlands	5	13
Belgium	5	12
Greece	5	12
Portugal	5	12
Austria	4	10
Sweden	4	10
Denmark	3	7
Finland	3	7
Ireland	3	7
Luxembourg	2	4
Total Votes	**87**	**237**

parliaments. The Council of Ministers has since adopted most legislation by qualified majority, rather than by unanimous voting. A system of **weighted voting** is used. (See Table 4.5.) Whereas before adoption of the Single European Act any member state could veto any measure, it now takes a minimum of three member states. Six of the seven small states would have to join forces to block a measure. Furthermore, three of the "big four" — Germany, France, Italy, and Great Britain — were needed to defeat a proposal. This decision-making mechanism is called **qualified majority voting** and is used in all but the most politically charged issue areas (for example, foreign policy, taxation, and the environment) in which unanimity is still required. With the continued enlargement of the EU, this bold effort to facilitate EU decision making, and to avoid deadlock, takes on increased importance.

The Single European Act gave the European Parliament the right to reject or amend legislation, and the Council of Ministers can override its decisions only by a unanimous vote. Also, the importance of coordinating policy in two salient areas, foreign affairs and environmental protection, was formally recognized, giving higher visibility to the European Parliament's debates than in the past.

In early 2002, the EU embarked on one of its most ambitious projects to date: a constitution-drafting convention. Hitherto, treaties have framed the EU's structures and defined its powers, beginning with the Treaty of Rome of 1958 and culminating in the Treaty of Amsterdam in 1997. That the constitution hammered out in Brussels and tentatively endorsed at an EU summit in Greece by the fifteen member states in June 2003 is also a *treaty* is a point of enormous symbolic and practical importance. The new EU constitution will not go into effect until it has been duly ratified by each of the individual member states (including the ten new members) as prescribed in their respective national constitutions. In other words, sovereignty still clearly rests with the member states. So unassailable is this principle that even a tiny member state like Luxembourg (population: 427,000) or Malta (population: 377,000) can, theoretically, prevent the constitution of the new EU (population: 450 million) from going into effect!

Deference to the issue of sovereignty is clearly apparent in the disproportionate power of small states within the EU scheme of things. Every member state is entitled to at least one commissioner and even the largest states get no more than two commissioners. The commission decides by majority vote what policy measures to propose to the Council of Ministers or the European Parliament. Thus, in the decade from 1995 to 2004, the ten smallest member states carried the same voting weight in the EU Commission as the five largest states. The situation in the Council of Ministers was not much different. There, Spain was the holder of the balance of power: if Spain joined the small states, they had an absolute majority of forty-seven votes to forty votes for the big states; if Spain voted with the big states, the balance shifted forty-eight to thirty-nine against the small states. Although voting in the Council of Ministers probably does not strictly break down along big state–small state lines as a rule, nonetheless the decision-making "arithmetic" says a lot about the importance of sovereignty.

Indeed, there is little prospect of a full-fledged European federal government. Decisions continue to be made by a torturous process that combines bureaucracy and diplomacy. National leaders are understandably reluctant to relinquish the sovereignty they are sworn to protect. Moreover, the executive branch (the European Commission and the Council of Ministers) is criticized as undemocratic, especially by the socialists who constitute the largest voting bloc in the European Parliament. In 2001, the voters of Ireland single-handedly defeated a treaty approved at Nice, France, which would have changed the weighted voting system in the EU Council to the advantage of the four largest members — Germany, France, Italy, and the United Kingdom. (See Table 4.5.) That decision by one of the smallest countries in the EU dramatized the difficulties in the path of any future move toward Europe federation.

By contrast, EU public opinion strongly favored the idea of full *economic* union in the 1990s. The widespread acceptance of this idea suggests that the EU's economic benefits are eroding the strong nationalistic tendencies that have so long been the hallmark of European politics. It is doubtful whether the European Union would have come so far so fast if the countries involved were not democratically ruled and politicians did not have to win votes to stay in power.

Europe's Future When the Common Market was established in 1958 it had only six members, a limited scope (abolishing tariffs on trade among its members), and no record of proven results. In 2004, the European Union will encompass twenty-five states in both halves of Europe in a single economy. It is impossible to talk about the problems and prospects for individual European states at present without taking into account whether they belong to the EU and, if not, whether (and when) they are likely to be admitted. The EU advanced down the path of ever-greater integration so far and fast after 1987 that its members have had to renegotiate the basic rules governing its operation several times. (See Box 4.3.)

Contrast and Comparison

BOX 4.3

Tightening the Knot: The Treaties of Europe's Union

Founding Treaties	In Force	Signatories	Main Points
European Coal and Steel Community Treaty (Treaty of Paris, 1951)	1952	Belgium, France, Germany, Italy, Luxembourg, Netherlands	Limited pooling of sovereign powers, first supranational "high authority"
European Economic Community Treaty (Treaty of Rome, 1957)	1958	As above	Wide-ranging treaty fixing principles of a "common market" for goods, plus common farm and trade policies
European Atomic Energy Communty Treaty (Rome, 1957)	1958	As above	Institutions and policies regulating nuclear industry
Later Treaties			
Single European Act (Luxembourg, 1986)	1987	As above, plus Denmark, Greece, Ireland, Portugal, Spain, and the United Kingdom	Extension of qualified majority voting; abolition of last internal barriers to trade
Treaty on European Union (Maastricht Treaty, 1992)	1993	As above	Blueprint for monetary union; launch of common foreign and security policy
Treaty of Amsterdam, 1997	1999	As above, plus Austria, Finland, Sweden	Rules on freedom of movement incorporated into EU treaty law
Treaty of Nice, 2000	2001	As above	New rules for choosing commission and voting in council; treaty base for common defense policy

Source: "Union Pauses for Breath," *The Economist,* February 12, 2000, p. 27.

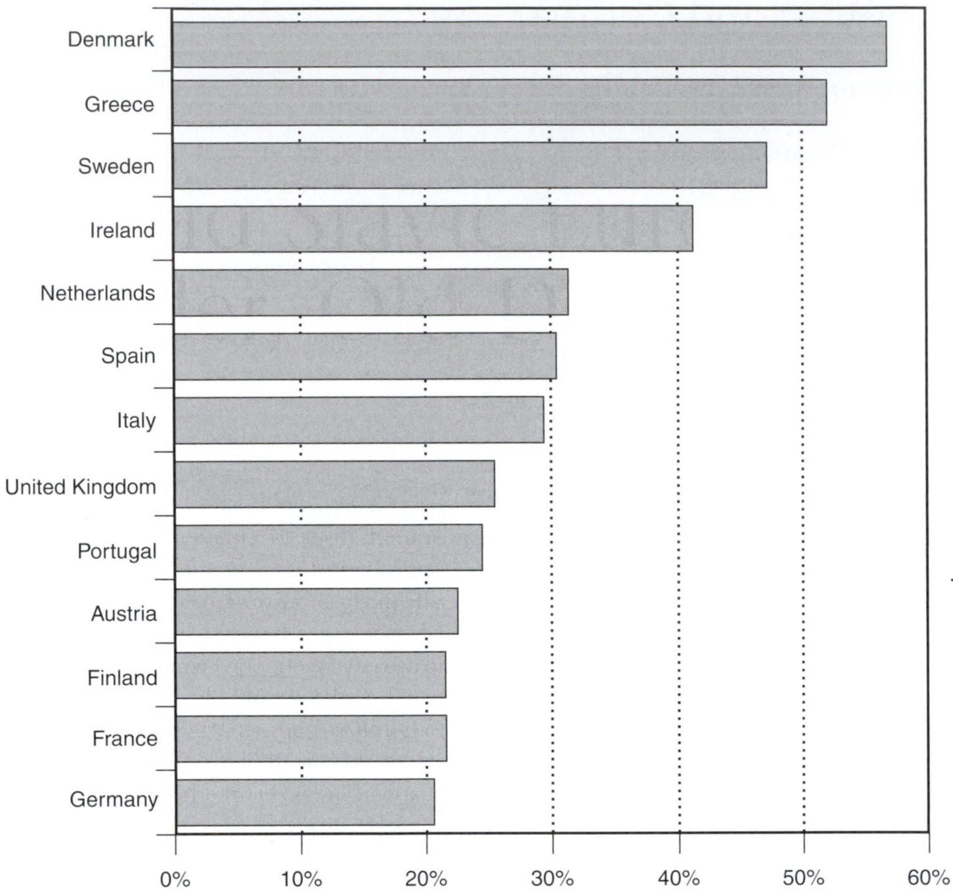

Figure 4.3 Should the EU Expand? (percentage who say it should be "a priority")

Source: "Eurobarometer," *The Economist,* September 9, 2000, p. 40.

In terms of population, the EU is a far larger single market than the United States, and the combined GNP of the current fifteen members is almost as large. There is no end in sight to the EU's growth in membership or economic might, depending on the political will of its member countries. The family fight over the European Monetary System (EMS), which created the single currency (euro), is a preview of the political obstacles to a deeper and wider Europe. Voters in Sweden rejected a government-sponsored proposal to join the Euro zone in September 2003; Danish voters earlier rejected the EMS in a similar referendum, as did the United Kingdom, one of the EU heavyweights. These facts raise the distinct possibility that the old-fashioned politics of nationalism will impede future steps toward further economic integration and preclude any move toward federation. The resounding Swedish no vote (56 percent for; 42 percent against) virtually guarantees that voters in Denmark and the United Kingdom will feel vindicated. These three countries will thus join the ten new EU members slated to join in 2004 as part of a non-Euro bloc, which means that the Euro bloc will actually be outnumbered thirteen to twelve. Finally, the Irish referendum against the Nice Treaty is yet another example of a recent resurgence of a soft nationalism (that is, nationalism not tied to militarism or aggressive aims but rather to self-interest).

In truth, public opinion in the largest EU countries is far less enthusiastic about EU enlargement than the Irish, Danes, Greeks, or Swedes. (See Figure 4.3.) Fear is often the enemy of innovation and change. It is conceivable that, precisely for this reason, national *problems* will hinder regional *prospects* in Europe.

SUMMARY

At present, the political systems of Western Europe display a remarkable consistency: all are based on the principle of government by consent of the governed, all are ruled by civilians who came to power by free elections based on universal suffrage and the secret ballot, and all protect personal freedoms and civil liberties from infringement by the state. This consistent pattern is no doubt one reason why the West has been able to move further and faster toward economic unity (and perhaps political union) than any region of the world.

KEY TERMS

constitutional monarchy
Marshall Plan
North Atlantic Treaty Organization (NATO)
Organization for European Economic Cooperation (OEEC)
European Union (EU)
overdevelopment
reverse development
parliamentary democracy
statutory law
member of Parliament (MP)
House of Commons
House of Lords
common law
custom and convention
works of authority
parliamentary sovereignty
rule of law
unitary system
fusion of powers
collective ministerial responsibility
two-party system
first past the post
corporatist model
stagflation
Keynesian economic theory
Provisional Irish Republican Army (IRA)
Ulster
special relationship
European Monetary Union (EMU)
euro

New Labour
Fifth Republic
plebiscite
National Assembly
divided (dual) executive
two-ballot system
package vote
les grands corps
les grandes écoles
Écoles Nationale d'Adminstration (ENA)
technocrats
prefects
tutelage system
Senate
Gaullist parties
National Front
cohabitation
special regimes
Länder
Basic Law
Bundestag
chancellor
Bundesrat
Fraktionen
first vote
second vote
unification
Euro zone
Council of Ministers
European Parliament
Single European Act
weighted voting
qualified majority voting

STUDY QUESTIONS

1. Given a choice between serving as the president of the United States or as the prime minister of Great Britain, which job would you prefer? Why?
2. How do the electoral systems of Great Britain, France, and Germany differ, and with what consequences?
3. In comparing and contrasting the constitutional powers of the French president and the British prime minister, what features should be stressed?
4. To what extent is the German political system based on the U.S. model? To what extent is it based on the British model? To what extent is it unique?
5. What is the European Union, who belongs to it, and how does it work? How did it get where it is today, and where is it going? Does it have a bright future, or has it outlived its usefulness?

SUGGESTED READINGS

Alford, B. W. *Britain in the World Economy since 1880.* White Plains, N.Y.: Longman, 1995.

Barberis, Peter. *The Whitehall Reader: The U.K.'s Administrative Machine in Action.* Bristol, Penn.: Taylor and Francis, 1996.

Bogdanor, Vernon, ed. *Politics and the Constitution: Essays on British Government.* Brookfield, Vt.: Ashgate, 1996.

Braunthal, Gerard. *Parties and Politics in Modern Germany.* Boulder, Colo.: Westview, 1996.

Delamaide, Darrell. *The New Superregions of Europe.* New York: NAL Dutton, 1994.

Dorey, Peter. *British Politics since 1945.* Cambridge, Mass.: Blackwell, 1995.

The Economist, "What Is Europe?" February 12, 2000, p. 13 (lead); pp. 19–23 (Europe's new left); pp. 75–78 (Europe's new capitalism); p. 27 (EU enlargement); see also, "Euroshambles," September 16, 2000, p. 21 and pp. 91–94 (Europe's economies).

Freedman, Leonard. *Politics and Policy in Britain.* Reading, Mass.: Addison Wesley Longman, 1996.

Jones, Barry, ed. *The European Union and the Regions.* New York: Oxford University Press, 1995.

Keating, Paul. *Class and Inequality in Britain: Social Stratification since 1945.* Cambridge, Mass.: Blackwell, 1997.

Parkes, Stuart. *Understanding Contemporary Germany.* New York: Routledge, 1996.

Studlar, Donley. *Great Britain: Decline or Renewal?* Boulder, Colo.: Westview, 1996.

Waller, Robert. *Almanac of British Politics.* New York: Routledge, 1996.

Wiesenthal, Helmut. *The Grand Experiment: Contrasting Views on Shock Therapy, Transition Theory, and the East German Case.* Boulder, Colo.: Westview, 1997.

SUGGESTED WEB SITES

http://www.gksoft.com/govt/en/europa.html
http://euro-information.com
http://eiop.or.at/europint
http://www.eurunion.org
http://dir.yahoo.com/Regional/Regions
http://www.hri.org/nodes/europe.html
http://www.lib.umich.edu/govdocs/foreur.html

NOTES

1. See the OECD's Web Site at www.oecd.org/about/origins/oeec.htm.
2. Sydney Bailey, *British Parliamentary Democracy,* 3rd ed. (Westport, Conn.: Greenwood, 1978), pp. 4–5.
3. The House of Lords locked horns with the House of Commons in 1991 over a controversial measure (called the War Crimes Bill) that cleared the way for prosecution of several alleged Nazi mass murderers living in Great Britain. That was the first time the Parliament Act of 1911 had been invoked in four decades.
4. See, for example, Bagehot, "A Dangerous Game," *The Economist,* December 7, 2002, p. 56. One issue they disagreed about was whether the United Kingdom should adopt the euro (Blair pushed for it, Brown opposed it). Another issue was whether to give universities authority to set and collect tuition fees (Blair for, Brown against). Normally, policy disputes within the government are kept from public view. There is much speculation that Brown's true ambition is to be the next prime minister.
5. Alexander MacLeod, "Britain's Labour Party Faces Watershed Battle," *Christian Science Monitor,* April 15, 1992, p. 1.
6. Bailey, *British Parliamentary Democracy,* p. 131.
7. R. M. Punnett, *British Government and Politics,* 5th ed. (Prospect Heights, Ill.: Waveland, 1990), p. 68.
8. For example, in 1983 the Conservatives won an overwhelming 144-seat majority with well under half the popular votes. In the 1987 elections, they captured only about 43 percent of the popular vote but still ended up with a 101-seat majority in Parliament. In the 1992 elections, by contrast, the Conservatives won roughly the same percentage of the popular vote but gained only a 22-seat majority — a much smaller magnifier effect but enough to give the Tories more than half the seats. In 1997, the same type of effect worked in favor of the victorious Labour Party.
9. See, for example, Craig R. Whitney, "British Race Is Neck and Neck at the Finish," *New York Times,* April 9, 1992, p. A4.
10. "One More Defeat on Long Retreat," *The Economist,* May 7, 1988, pp. 51–52.
11. In the edition published June 27, 1987, p. 60. *The Economist* appears once a week in the form of a magazine and can be accessed on the Internet at http://www.economist.com.
12. "Tony Two-Timed," *The Economist,* July 22, 2000, p. 53.
13. Howard La Franchi, "French Say 'Non' to Traditional Political Parties," *Christian Science Monitor,* March 24, 1992, p. 1.
14. Suzanne Berger, *The French Political System,* 3rd ed. (New York: Random House, 1974), p. 368.
15. Roy Macridis, ed., *Modern Political Systems: Europe,* 6th ed. (Englewood Cliffs, N.J.: Prentice-Hall, 1986), p. 120.
16. "Jacque Chirac wins by default," *The Economist,* May 11, 2002, pp. 48–49.

17. To qualify for round two in France's parliamentary elections a party either has to come in first or second or win on the ballots of at least 12.5 percent of the registered voters. A low turnout thus hurts smaller parties because it means they must secure a larger share of the vote actually cast to clear the 12.5 percent hurdle.
18. The term *unification* here is used in preference to *reunification* because the latter term suggests a return to the Germany of Hitler's Third Reich, which would be misleading and provocative.
19. Guido Goldman, *The German Political System.* (New York: Random House, 1974), p. 56.

PART III
Russia and Slavic Europe

Russia

Area: 6,592,812 square miles

Population (2004): 144,400,000

Density per square mile: 21–22

Language(s): Russian, many others

Female school enrollment: 100%

Major religion(s): Russian (Eastern) Orthodox, Islam

Monetary unit: ruble

GNP: $392 billion (2003 est.)

GNP per capita: $2,700–$2,800 (2003 est.)

GNP average per capita growth (1990–1998): –7.2%

Recent GNP growth rate: 6.8% (2003)

Inflation (1990–1998): 230%

Recent inflation rate: 14% (2003)

Personal computers per 1,000 people: 40.6

Czech Republic

Area: 49,373 square miles

Population: 10,295,000

Density per square mile: approximately 340

Language: Czech

Female school enrollment: 100%

Major religion(s): Atheist (predominant), Roman Catholic, Protestant

Monetary unit: Czech koruna (crown)

GNP: $91 billion

GNP per capita: $8,800–$8,900

GNP average per capita growth (1990–1998): –0.2%

Recent GNP growth rate: 2.2% (2003)

Inflation (1990–1998): 13.7%

Recent inflation rate: 0.3% (2003)

Personal computers per 1,000 people: 97.3

Yugoslavia

Area: 39,000 square miles

Population: 10,616,000

Density per square mile: 266

Language(s): Serbo-Croatian (majority), others

Female school enrollment: n.a.

Major religion(s): Eastern Orthodox (50%), Roman Catholic (30%), Islamic (9%)

Monetary unit: dinar

GNP (2003): n.a.

GNP per capita (2003): n.a.

GNP per capita growth (2003): n.a.

Recent inflation rate: n.a.

Personal computers per 1,000 people: n.a.

Area detailed
0 Km 800
0 Miles 800
Arctic Ocean
Bering Sea
NORWAY
SWEDEN
GERMANY
Baltic Sea
LITHUANIA
FINLAND
ESTONIA
POLAND
LATVIA
KARELIA
St. Petersburg
BELARUS
Barents Sea
KOMI
SAKHA
Sea of Okhotsk
Moscow
ROMANIA
Marii-el
Chuvashia
UKRAINE
Mordvinia
UDMURTIA
RUSSIA
TATARSTAN
Lena
Volga
Volgograd
BASHKORTOSTAN
Black Sea
TURKEY
KALMYKIA
Omsk
KHAKASSIA
BURYATIA
1. Adygeia
2. Karachai-Cherkessia
3. Kabarda-Balkaria
4. North Ossetia
5. Ingushetia and Chechnya
DAGESTAN
GORNO-ALTAY
Irkutsk
Vladivostok
KAZAKHSTAN
TUVA
Sea of Japan
Aral Sea
Caspian Sea
MONGOLIA
UZBEKISTAN
TURKMENISTAN
NORTH KOREA
SOUTH KOREA
JAPAN
KYRGYZSTAN
IRAN
CHINA
TAJIKISTAN

Part III Outline: Russia and Slavic Europe

Chapter 5: The Other Europe: Russia, Czech Republic, and Yugoslavia

The Slavic Shatter Zone

The Influence of Geography

The Imprint of History

The Bolsheviks: Vanguard of the Proletariat

Ideology and Political Culture

Eastern Europe before 1945

Eastern Europe under Soviet Tutelage

Case Studies: Beyond Russia — Czechoslovakia (the Czech Republic) and Yugoslavia

- Czechoslovakia
- Yugoslavia

Chapter 6: Russia and Slavic Europe: New Order, Old Disorders

Transition or Regression?

The Legacy of Soviet Communism

Postcommunist Russia

Eastern Eruope: From Stalinism to Pluralism

Case Studies: Czechoslovakia (the Czech Republic) and Yugoslavia

- The Czech Republic: Reinventing Democracy
- Yugoslavia: Rejecting Dictatorship

CHAPTER 5

The Other Europe: Russia, Czech Republic, Yugoslavia

The October Revolution of 1917 ushered in the most repressive era in the history of modern Russia. The "ten days that shook the world" — the title of John Reed's famous firsthand account of this momentous event — also set in motion a progression toward totalitarian rule that within thirty years would envelop virtually all the European territories inhabited by Slavic-speaking peoples. In the aftermath of World War II, Poland and Bulgaria fell under the domination of the Soviet Union — these countries were, in effect, annexed to the territory of old Russia and the empire it ruled during the time of the czars (Russia's monarchs), including Ukraine. Although Hungary, Romania, and the Baltic states of Lithuania, Latvia, and Estonia are not ethnically Slavic, they are located along the predominantly Slavic-speaking regions of East-Central Europe and the Balkans. As such, they were critical to Stalin's effort to create a buffer zone against invasion from the west. Prussia (the former East Germany), occupied by the Soviet Army in 1945, also became part of this zone. Among the Slavs, only Yugoslavia — the cobbled-together republic uniting Serbs, Croats, and Slovenes — managed to break away from the Soviet bloc and pursue an independent, albeit communist, course.

The ill-fated *perestroika* (restructuring) campaign launched by Soviet President Mikhail Gorbachev in the second half of the 1980s led to the collapse of communist rule throughout the region. In December 1991, following an abortive coup attempt by hard-liners (who opposed economic and political reforms) in Moscow, the Soviet Union self-destructed.

This chapter examines the political setting in the predominantly Slavic eastern half of Europe. It traces both the precommunist history of the region in broad outline and the communist era, which now has also passed into history. The end of **Pax Sovietica** — a term once used to describe Moscow's hegemony (political-military domination) in Slavic Europe — ushered in a period of ethnic conflict and political instability, which is simply another way of saying that the natural contours of history and political geography, obscured for four decades by the false uniformity of totalitarian rule, have reappeared.

The Slavic Shatter Zone

On March 5, 1946, Winston Churchill gave an address at Westminster College in Fulton, Missouri, in which he spoke darkly of the danger posed by Soviet communism:

> From Stettin in the Baltic to Trieste in the Adriatic, an iron curtain has descended across the Continent. Behind that line lie all the capitals of the ancient states of Central and Eastern Europe. Warsaw, Berlin, Prague, Vienna, Budapest, Belgrade, Bucharest, and Sofia, all these famous cities and the populations around them lie in what I must call the Soviet sphere, and all are subject in one form or another, not only to Soviet influence but to a very high and, in many cases, increasing measure of control from Moscow.[1]

Whether we regard Churchill's words as alarmist or prophetic, the political geography he traced remained a fact of life for more than forty years.

The region behind that iron curtain contained the former Union of Soviet Socialist Republics (USSR), more commonly known as the Soviet Union, plus Bulgaria, Hungary, Poland, Romania, and what were until recently Czechoslovakia, East Germany, and Yugoslavia. **Eastern Europe,** or **Slavic Europe,** today refers to the lands of Central Europe and the Balkans. It encompasses not only the former Soviet republics of Russia, Ukraine, Belarus, and Moldova but also Latvia, Lithuania, and Estonia. It does not include the former Soviet republics of Georgia, Armenia, and Azerbaijan, located in the Caucasus, wedged between Europe and Asia. These countries are not geographically and culturally part of a larger region — they are neither European nor Asian. They exhibit the historical influences of Russia and the Islamic cultures of the Middle East (including Turkey). Tiny Albania has a geographic and political relationship to the Balkans; ethnic Albanians constitute the majority of people living in the Kosovo province of Yugoslavia.

Two-thirds of the peoples of Russia and Eastern Europe are of Slavic origin. Slavs have been the predominant group there since at least the seventh century. They can be divided into three major subgroups: eastern Slavs (Great Russians, Ukrainians, White Russians, and Ruthenians); western Slavs (primarily Poles, Czechs, and Slovaks); and southern Slavs (Serbs, Croats, Slovenes, Montenegrins, and Bulgars).

The Slavic nations are extremely diverse. Cultural and linguistic traditions vary considerably. Christianity spread throughout the region but took different forms: eastern and southern Slavs embraced the Eastern Orthodox rite (related to Greek Orthodox and once based in Byzantium or present-day Istanbul), whereas the western Slavs looked to Rome and the Pope. This explains in part why western Slavs use the Latin alphabet, and eastern and southern Slavs use the Cyrillic.

The non-Slavic groups of Slavic Europe are likewise diverse. The three largest groups are the Magyars, Moldavians, and Germans. (See Box 5.1.) Others are Gagauz, Latvians (Letts), Lithuanians, Estonians, Finns, Jews, Tatars, Bashkirs, Chechens, Ingush, Abkhazians, Meshketians, Albanians, and Mongols. (Georgians, Armenians, and Ossetians live primarily in the Caucasus and therefore do not belong to Slavic Europe as defined earlier.) These groups generally resented Moscow's **Russification** policies of the past (imposing Russian culture on non-Russian peoples) and now abhor

Contrast and Comparison

BOX 5.1

Magyars in a Slavic World

What is a Magyar (pronounced MADJAR)?
Clue: Hungary.

Hungary is a country in Eastern Europe with a population of about 10 million. Most Hungarians are not Slavs — the language they speak is related to Finnish and Estonian. It has no more in common with Slavic languages than with, say, German or French. Hungarians make up nine-tenths of the population of Hungary and one-tenth of the population of Slovakia and Romania. There are also tens of thousands of Serbs, Romanians, and Slovaks — as well as large Romany (Gypsy) and German minorities — mixed into Hungary's population along the borders it shares with those two countries. Two-thirds of the population is Roman Catholic and about one-third is Protestant (Calvinist, Lutheran, or something else), whereas the Eastern Orthodox Church (the Greek branch of Catholicism) is prevalent in Russia, Ukraine, and the Balkans.

How did so many Hungarians happen to settle outside of Hungary? Why do so many people who are not ethnic Hungarians live in Hungary? To answer these two questions is to explain a great deal about the history of Eastern Europe — a history of changing borders and ethnic conflict. From the sixteenth century to the twentieth century, Hungary was part of the Hapsburg (or Austro-Hungarian) Empire, which contained many large and distinct ethnic groups. After World War I, Hungary, Czechoslovakia, and Yugoslavia emerged from the ruins of the defeated Austro-Hungarian monarchy. Both Czechoslovakia and Yugoslavia broke apart after 1989. Hungary has stayed together but has traded allegations of ethnic discrimination with Slovakia, Romania, and Serbia.

These problems are rooted in a time when nation-states did not exist in Europe or anywhere else and when borders were not clearly defined and tightly controlled. From the Golden Age of Rome to the heyday of the Soviet Union, the great empires of Europe were multinational entities. The emergence of nation-states in the modern era awakened nationalistic stirrings throughout Europe — including among ethnic groups (nations) within the Hapsburg Empire. The Hapsburg rulers suppressed nationalism, sometimes brutally. When Austria-Hungary broke up, there was no script to follow in creating new nation-states in its place. Instead, a ragtag process of political bargaining, improvisation, and compromise gave rise to boundary lines that did not always make sense — a problem complicated by a history of settling ethnic and political differences by the sword.

Hungary has several advantages over some other "emerging democracies" in Eastern Europe. First, it was ruled as a monarchy (by Magyar kings) long before it became part of the Hapsburg Empire — thus, Magyars have a clear sense of who they are and deep roots where they are. Second, Magyars greatly outnumber Hungary's ethnic minorities. Moreover, the presence of ethnic minorities, paradoxically, gives the majority an incentive for solidarity. Third, Hungary has a long tradition of looking West rather than East. As a result, it has moved quickly to reestablish cultural and commercial ties with Europe's prosperous democracies and is on the "fast track" to join the European Union. Finally, Hungary's transition to a market-based liberal democracy after 1989 was faster and smoother than that of most of its neighbors.

---

the "pan-Slavic" sentiments often expressed by Russian nationalists. The impact of this non-Slavic presence, particularly in periods of social decay and political instability, is greater than the sum of its parts.

The mutual antagonisms so common to this region have not been confined to relations between Slavs and non-Slavs. The "shatter zone" that is Slavic Europe encompasses a bewildering array of historically deep-rooted ethnic conflicts — between Poles and Russians, Russians and Ukrainians, Czechs and Slovaks, Slovaks and Hungarians,

Hungarians and Romanians, Hungarians and Serbs, Serbs and Croats, Bosnian Muslims and Albanians, and so on. Dozens of such animosities persist.

Although the nations of Eastern Europe are diverse in many ways, their fates have been interwoven. Besides linguistic links and the political fortunes (or misfortunes) that have fused them together in one empire or another at different times, in some cases they have shared religious and cultural experiences. Above all, the forces of history and geography have intruded on these nations and shaped a destiny that is uniquely Slavic.

The Influence of Geography

Early in the nineteenth century, France's most famous student of American democracy, Alexis de Tocqueville, predicted that the United States and Russia were apparently "marked out by the will of heaven to sway the destinies of half the globe."[2] Tocqueville anticipated the bipolar world that emerged after 1945 because he understood the importance of geopolitics: the United States and Russia, he observed, would be able to expand over relatively empty landmasses and incorporate or annihilate the indigenous populations, whereas the Europeans would have no choice but to attempt to knock together overseas empires, which were more difficult to keep under firm political-administrative control for obvious geographical reasons (they were scattered, distant, and inaccessible except by marine transport).

For most of the twentieth century, the Soviet Union dominated the map of Eurasia. Occupying more than 8.6 million square miles (one-sixth of the earth's total landmass), it was by far the largest country in the world, more than twice the size of the United States. (About 25 percent of the USSR was in Europe.) Accounting for about half of the Soviet Union's total population and slightly more than three-fourths of its territory was Russia proper. Russia's 6.6 million square miles dwarf the United States' 3.6 million, but in terms of population the situation is reversed: the United States has over 281 million people, while Russia has less than 145 million.

Russia and Ukraine

If Eastern Europe was dominated by the Soviet Union, the Soviet Union was in turn dominated by Russia. Geography has played a major role in shaping the political traditions of the Russian people. One authority on Soviet politics has written:

> It is indeed easy to see how Russia's geography has influenced the course of its history. To begin with, Russia's original location on the East European plain contributed directly to many of its important historic events. Being relatively close to Byzantium, for example, influenced Russia's choice of Eastern (Greek) Orthodoxy as its state religion (988). Two and a half centuries later, because of its location, Russia fell prey to the Mongol invasion and remained for several centuries almost completely isolated from Europe, which was then going through the Renaissance and Reformation. A result of this isolation was Russia's lagging behind Europe in technology and industrialization.[3]

Three facts of life determined by geography have been crucial in shaping Russian history and culture. First, Russia lies in the northern latitudes, where it is cold much of the year. Second, it is mostly flat (much like Kansas and Nebraska in the United States) and thus presents no natural barriers to invasion or expansion. Third, it is vast, especially the Siberian wilderness: "The immensity of Russia, the absence of boundaries, was expressed in the structure of the Russian soul . . . the same boundlessness, formlessness, reaching out into infinity, breadth."[4]

Russia has been blessed with an abundance of fertile soil, mineral resources, and mighty rivers. Yet nature's bounties have been yielded grudgingly, given the relatively short growing season and the long, cold winters. The Ukraine was the breadbasket of czarist Russia and then of the Soviet empire (due to a growing season long enough for grain crops to mature), but its location on the globe corresponds to that of Ontario, Canada — meaning that it typically experiences harsh winters. The storied resilience of the Russian people in the face of adversity no doubt owes much to the rigors of the climate.

Power Vacuum or Empire?

The sheer size of Russia, resulting in a need to protect boundaries thousands of miles long, and the absence of natural barriers, which leaves the nation open to attack from any direction except the north, have contributed to a pervasive sense of insecurity. This insecurity reaches as far back as the thirteenth century, when the Mongols invaded, pillaged, and plundered Kievan Russia. The Mongol yoke was not removed for nearly 250 years.

In the early sixteenth century, danger came from the opposite direction: Poland. The result was another humiliating defeat and another foreign occupation, this time for only three years. In 1709, Sweden attacked, under Charles XII, a military genius. Russia's Peter the Great, soon to become an empire builder in his own right, rose to the challenge. Under his command, the defending Russian forces defeated the Swedes at Poltava in the Ukraine.

A century later, Napoléon Bonaparte of France invaded Russia and marched all the way to Moscow. However, the onset of winter was a major factor in forcing his army to retreat. Russia's sheer physical size came into play as well. According to historian Nicholas Riasanovsky, "More soldiers of Napoleon died from hunger and epidemics than from cold, for the supply services, handicapped by enormous distances, insecure lines of communication, and bad planning, failed on the whole to sustain the military effort."[5]

Germany invaded twice in the twentieth century. In World War II, Hitler conquered and occupied much of historic Russia west of the Urals. Kiev was destroyed, Leningrad was besieged for two and a half years, and Moscow came perilously close to falling. Twenty million Soviet citizens died; cities, towns, and villages were reduced to rubble and ash; the foundations of the economy were obliterated.

The same geography that has made Russia vulnerable to invasion and instability has also afforded opportunities for expansion. Thus "when not being invaded, Russia itself was often invading neighboring countries, annexing them, building an empire, and pursuing territorial expansion in the quest for greater physical security."[6] Russian rulers themselves thus created stability problems in bordering areas by incorporating non-Russian groups into the empire. The czars never achieved full Russification of these groups.

Aside from the quest for security, there were powerful economic and commercial incentives to engage in empire building, many of them also affected by geography. For example, the desire to gain access to warm-water ports, a major objective of Russian foreign policy, can be traced directly to Russia's geographic predicament. This drive for trading outlets and the strategic importance of the Bosporus straits (the passage between the Black Sea and the Mediterranean) motivated a push to the south that provoked tension between Russia and the Ottoman Empire (now Turkey) and a war with two other Great Powers in the mid-nineteenth century. Russia's humiliating defeat by Great Britain and France in the Crimean War (1853–1856) was a classic example of the danger of "imperial overstretch."[7]

Geography has also influenced Russian political culture. A famous Russian historian, Vasili Kluchevsky, identified "forest, steppe and river" as "the basic elements of Russian nature" and asserted that they "played an active and unique part in the formation of the life and ideas" of the Russians.[8] Many Russians, for example, have a very romantic view of nature, and associate the Russian landscape closely with love of country or the "motherland." This emotional attachment explains why millions of Russians fought so bravely in World War II. Russians did not love Marx or Lenin, nor were they willing to die for an alien ideology (communism). Significantly, even Russia's brutal dictator Joseph Stalin urged Russians to fight for "Mother Russia," not for Marx or Lenin.

Another scholar, Nicholas Berdyaev, argued that "the immensity of Russia" has also left a deep imprint on the culture, society, and general outlook of the Russian people. What is particularly fascinating is the way Berdyaev links geography and politics:

> A difficult problem presents itself ceaselessly to the Russian — the problem of organizing his vast territory. The immensity of Russia, the absence of boundaries, was expressed in the structure of the Russian soul. . . . It might be said that the Russian people fell victim to the immensity of its territory. Form does not come easily, the gift of form is not great among the Russians. Russian historians explain the despotic character of Russian government by this necessary organization of the boundless Russian plain. Kluchevsky, the most distinguished of Russian historians, said, "The state expands, the people grow sickly." In a certain sense this remains true also of the Soviet-Communist government, under which the interests of the people are sacrificed to the power and organization of the Soviet state.[9]

Geography and environment have not predetermined Russia's history, but these physical factors have undoubtedly conditioned and constrained the development of Russian institutions, traditions, and values. The great constants in Russia's history are environmental in the broadest sense of the word: its vast space and daunting distances; its majestic forests; its smooth, flat plains; and its harsh winter climate.

The Imprint of History

Just as geography influences history, the past (particularly memories of a nation's finest and darkest moments) leaves a deep imprint on political culture. History is relevant to politics for as long as it is remembered (a good example is the Mongol invasion of Russia). Moreover, what is remembered is more important than what actually happened. For example, the Russians and neighboring peoples have very different collective memories of the beginning of World War II. The actual events are much less important, politically speaking, than the prevailing cultural mythology about those events.

Decline of the Romanov Dynasty

When Czar Nicholas II abdicated in 1917 amid the turbulence of war and revolution, he brought to an end three centuries of Romanov rule in Russia. Nicholas and his predecessor, Czar Alexander III, had been obsessed with unifying the multinational empire they inherited. However, unlike Peter the Great (1682–1725), Catherine the Great (1762–1796), Alexander I (1801–1825), or Nicholas I (1825–1855), the last two Romanov rulers were unequal to the challenges they faced.

And challenges sprang up like crocuses in spring. First, there were external threats on two sides: to the west, a united Germany; to the east, Japan. Germany had shown its military prowess in victories against Austria in 1866 and France in 1870. Japan's emergence as a great power caught Russia by surprise. In the Russo-Japanese War of 1904–1905, Japan destroyed Russia's Far Eastern fleet with a surprise attack in the outer harbor of Port Arthur (Lüshun). When Czar Nicholas II ordered the Baltic fleet to sail around the globe to save the day, the Japanese dealt Russia's antique armada another crushing blow in the battle of Tsushima Strait in 1905.

The Far Eastern debacle set the stage for Russia's first revolution, just as the October Revolution would do twelve years later. The Revolution of 1905 was precipitated by defeat in war, but war alone does not explain the revolutions. The forces of rebellion and violence had been stirring within Russian society for decades before they erupted in 1905. They first appeared in the 1870s, when anarchism (opposition to all rules) and nihilism (advocacy of destruction for its own sake) mixed with populism (closeness to the people) to produce a homegrown ideology called *narodnichestvo* ("populism"). The leaders of this movement came to be known as *narodniki;* some of the most prominent were Alexander Herzen, Mikhail Bakunin, Nicholas Chernyshevsky, Peter Lavrov, and Nicholas Mikhailovsky.

The *narodniki* inspired a group of fanatical revolutionaries, the *Narodnaya Volya* ("People's Will"), who launched an offensive against the government of Alexander II. Members of this group believed that "because of the highly centralized nature of the Russian state, a few assassinations could do tremendous damage to the regime, as well as provide the requisite political instruction for the educated society and the masses."[10] Alexander II had the misfortune to become their chief target: the ringleaders of *Narodnaya Volya* condemned him to death and began what has been described as an "emperor hunt":

> The Executive Committee of the "Will of the People" included only about thirty men and women. . . . Although the police made every effort to destroy the revolutionaries and although many terrorists perished, the "Will of the People" made one attempt after another to assassinate the emperor. Time and again Alexander II escaped through sheer luck. Many people were killed when the very dining room of his palace was blown up, while at one time the emperor's security official refused to let him leave his suburban residence, except by water![11]

An anarchist finally succeeded in killing Alexander II in 1881. Several years later, revolutionaries also made an attempt on the life of Alexander III. The plot failed, but one of the conspirators arrested by the Okhrana (the czar's secret police) was Alexander Ilyich Ulyanov, the brother of Vladimir Ilyich Ulyanov, who became known to the world as Lenin. Without Lenin, there would probably not have been an October Revolution; without the October Revolution, there would certainly not have been a Soviet Union.

The Bolsheviks: Vanguard of the Proletariat

Lenin's ideas about revolution were a mixture of Russian populism, anarchism, and Marxism. As a self-styled champion of Russia's oppressed masses, Lenin had a certain kinship with the old *narodniki;* as an advocate of revolutionary violence (though not assassination), he was a soulmate of the anarchists; and as the founder of the Communist Party of the Soviet Union, he was a disciple of Marx.

Lenin split the Russian Social Democratic Party in 1903 over the issue of revolution. One faction of the party known as the **Mensheviks** opposed subversion and revolution, arguing that socialism and democracy could be achieved in Russia without violence. The **Bolshevik** faction, led by Lenin, insisted that only a conspiratorial vanguard party, secretly laying the groundwork for all-out revolution, could bring the corrupt czarist order down. Lenin explained this idea in a famous 1902 essay, "What Is to Be Done?":

> The working class exclusively by its own efforts is able to develop only trade union consciousness. . . . Modern social consciousness can be brought to them only from without. . . . [It] can arise only on the basis of profound scientific knowledge. The bearers of science are not the proletariat but the bourgeois intelligentsia. It is out of the heads of members of this stratum that modern socialism originated. . . . Pure and simple trade unionism means the ideological subordination of the workers to the bourgeoisie. . . . Our task is to bring the labor movement under the wing of Social Democracy.

Lest anyone miss the point, Lenin added, "aside from the influence of Social Democracy, there is no conscious activity of the workers."[12]

The working class had become a potent base of power. In the decades leading up to World War I, western Russia had undergone rapid economic growth, thanks to inflows of European capital and to government-promoted industrial development (including state ownership). If the rate of growth had been maintained, and if the Great War had not intervened in August 1914, Russia would have been a major economic power even without a revolution. But Marx's observation that capitalists would be their own grave diggers (by creating an underclass of exploited assembly-line workers) turned out to be particularly prophetic in the case of Russia, where the growth of a manufacturing sector created centers of large-scale industry in key cities such as Saint Petersburg and Moscow. In these cities, the Bolsheviks found the working class, the proletariat that Marx praised in his writings. This industrial component was the underpinning of the revolution.

Marx and Engels had said, "the emancipation of the working class is the task of the working class itself." Lenin's amendment to this Marxist proposition was to have momentous consequences for Russia and the world. The Communist Party (which Lenin called the "vanguard of the proletariat") would supplant the **proletariat** (working class) as the key to the future. An elite corps of "professional revolutionists" would move front and center on the stage of history; the workers would fade into the background. Here, then, are the seeds of the totalitarian Soviet state sown in the fertile revolutionary soil of a society in decay.

Dress Rehearsal: The February Revolution

In February 1905, twelve years before the Russian autocratic system was toppled, workers staged a peaceful march on the Winter Palace to petition Czar Nicholas II. The unarmed demonstrators were massacred by Russian troops in what came to be known as "Bloody Sunday." A revolution without a Leninist "vanguard" (or leading element), this event had little real impact on the way Russia was ruled. Although it did lead to some agrarian reforms under Prime Minister Stolypin, the **February Revolution** also triggered a ferocious government assault on political dissent. Well over a thousand revolutionaries and suspected terrorists were sent to the gallows — victims of Stolypin's policy of "pacification."

Were it not for World War I, Lenin's ideas on revolution would not have borne fruit. The defeat of the Russian army at the hands of the invading Germans, like the defeat of the Russian navy by the Japanese a decade earlier, caused a crisis of confidence in the whole czarist system. The extreme hardships, the death and destruction, and the national humiliation associated with Russia's defeat all contributed to the spirit of rebellion.

The unpopularity of the war was paralleled by a general disintegration of the armed forces in the period leading up to 1917. Aleksandr Kerensky, a moderate socialist, had tried to lead the nation toward a form of parliamentary democracy, but he foolishly insisted that Russia continue to fight even though the war was tearing the country apart. Lenin seized on this issue, promising "peace, land, and bread" if the Russian masses would heed his revolutionary call.

Why did Kerensky's attempt at democracy fail? Two factors stand out. First, like Weimar Germany, Russia lacked a liberal democratic tradition. This is not to say that Russians have no democratic traditions — for example, historically, the city-states of

Kiev and Novgorod were much more liberal than was Moscow. In addition to a council of boyars (merchants and nobles), these medieval cities had local assemblies: when the assembly bell tolled, all free male citizens would gather to discuss issues of public interest. But Muscovite rulers later used brutal measures to repress both the boyars and the assemblies — this is the darker side of Russia's democratic traditions.

Second, chaos reigned in the Provisional Duma (legislature) in 1917, and discontent was rampant in Russian society. There is a certain parallel between Kerensky's difficulties with an unruly Duma and a rebellious public in 1917, and problems former Russian President Boris Yeltsin had with a chaotic Congress of People's Deputies and a Russian people whose patience has worn thin (see Chapter 6).

The October Revolution

Lenin, with the help of fellow Bolshevik Leon Trotsky, masterminded the **October Revolution.** Never known for political moderation, Lenin moved quickly to consolidate his power by scrapping the elected **soviets** (governing councils), banning or suppressing all opposition groups, and putting Bolsheviks in control of the military, the police, the state administration, and the economy. He also established his own dreaded secret police, the Cheka. The Cheka imitated the czarist Okhrana but went further in perfecting a system of state terrorism that included purges against all alleged counterrevolutionaries, expropriations of property, and tight control of all mass communications (radio, newspapers, journals, and publishing houses). Thus, Lenin and Leninism set the stage for Stalin and Stalinism.

The Bolsheviks faced a variety of challenges in the first few years after seizing power. The national government was embroiled in a civil war with the so-called white (anti-Bolshevik) armies during this period, commonly known as **war communism.** The Western Allies — including the United States, Great Britain, and France — intervened indirectly with military and economic aid. They also intervened directly, if halfheartedly, on the pretense of recovering war supplies given earlier to the czarist government. The main aim, however, was to assist the "whites" in overthrowing the Bolshevik "reds."

Lenin's government managed to survive the civil war and Allied intervention, but the harsh policies of war communism alienated many former supporters of the October Revolution. In 1921, when sailors (who had played a key role in the revolution) mutinied at Kronshtadt — a naval base near Saint Petersburg in the Gulf of Finland — Lenin crushed the rebellion. However, the incident apparently made a deep impression on Lenin, who subsequently relaxed the stringent measures imposed earlier. The result was the **New Economic Policy (NEP),** which allowed limited private enterprise, involvement of foreign managers in industry, farming for profit, and considerable literary and artistic freedom.

The Stalin Era: Totalitarianism in Full Swing

To most objective observers, **Stalinism** and totalitarianism are synonyms. Stalin was one of Lenin's close associates. After the October Revolution, he became the commissar for nationalities, a key position in the sprawling multinational Soviet empire. One of

Stalin's jobs was to keep a close eye on non-Russian nationalities and to prevent any organized opposition from developing on the Soviet periphery, which, of course, included the vital border zones. Thus, Stalin played a key role in maintaining internal security and in building organizational-administrative ties between the Kremlin (the seat of the central government in Moscow) and the capitals of the so-called Soviet republics.

When Lenin became incapacitated due to an assassination attempt that nearly resulted in his death and then a severe stroke, there ensued a ferocious behind-the-scenes power struggle. Stalin was considered one of the least likely to succeed Lenin. Paradoxically, the fact that his colleagues on the Politburo (the supreme decision-making body in the Communist Party) underestimated him probably helped him out-maneuver them. Within a few short years of Lenin's death, Stalin would consolidate his absolute power, creating a "cult of personality" in the process and becoming one of modern history's most notorious totalitarian dictators. In the late 1920s, he initiated a brutal campaign designed to transform a backward country into a modern military-industrial state at breakneck speed.

At the height of the Stalin reign of terror in the mid-1930s, nobody was safe. Nearly all the party's "old guard" — comrades of Lenin — fell before Stalin's firing squads. Most of the military high command met a similar fate. Guilt by association became the order of the day. Anyone who was connected in any way with the old czarist government — anyone who had ever held a position of responsibility in the economy or been recognized in any professional field (science, education, letters) before the revolution — was purged.

Stalin even invented subversive groups as a pretext for purging whole categories of "enemies." One class of prosperous peasants known as **kulaki** was completely wiped out — either killed or sent into exile in Siberia. Millions more peasants perished in the early 1930s in a famine actually worsened by Stalin's brutal policy of diverting capital from agriculture to industry and confiscating crops to feed city dwellers. Despite the domestic famine, Stalin still exported grain to the West to earn hard currency during this period.

Why did Stalin wage war against his own society? What did the resulting bloodbath accomplish? Was there a method in his madness? When Lenin became incapacitated by a stroke in 1922, Stalin knew that a succession struggle was inevitable. On Lenin's death in 1924, Stalin began maneuvering against top Bolshevik leaders. His first victim was Trotsky, whom he condemned for advocating "permanent revolution" (working for the overthrow of bourgeois capitalist governments) and expelled from the party with the support of Lenin's other lieutenants. Using "salami tactics," he cut the Bolshevik old guard to pieces, cleverly playing one faction against another, denouncing first the leftists, then the rightists, until he had vilified and discredited them all.

By 1928, Stalin had succeeded in turning the obscure position of general secretary of the Communist Party into a vehicle of autocratic power. But achieving personal sway over a weak nation did not satisfy Stalin's lust for power, nor did it assuage his obsessive insecurity. Russia was weak, he reasoned, because it was economically backward. It would never be strong until it industrialized. In the modern age, industrial development is the key to military prowess and national glory: that was the lesson to be learned from Japan, Germany, and the United States. In Stalin's own words: "We are fifty or a hundred years behind the advanced countries. We must make good this lag in ten years. Either we do it or they crush us."[13] But how could the Soviet Union industrialize? It was poor and agrarian. Worse, it was surrounded by hostile capitalist states.

Trotsky's permanent revolution was all wrong, Stalin asserted, because the Soviet Union was all alone in the world. Encouraging revolution would provoke the nation's enemies and jeopardize the future of the only socialist state then in existence. Under these unfavorable circumstances, Stalin argued, a policy of "socialism in one country" — a euphemism for his highly nationalistic economic development strategy — made more sense than Trotsky's adventurism.

Stalin's solution was simple but brutal: if the West could not be trusted (or was not willing) to provide the capital for Soviet industry, Stalin would squeeze it out of Soviet society. Given that the Soviet economy was largely agricultural, Stalin's go-it-alone strategy — a policy generally known as **autarky** — meant that Soviet farmers would have to bear the brunt of the industrialization drive. But Stalin knew that the peasants would resist confiscatory taxes or forced deliveries to the state. So he decided to collectivize agriculture (take land away from the peasants and reorganize agriculture into large state-controlled farms) more for economic expediency than out of ideological conviction. **Collectivization** was Stalin's way of extracting capital from agriculture for investment in industry — collectivization and forced industrialization were two sides of the same coin.

Stalin's economic development strategy also prompted his bloody campaign against the kulaks. Because the kulaks were the richest farmers, they had the most to lose from collectivization and were therefore the most likely to resist or obstruct. Stalin's *dekulakization* campaign thus appears to have been launched because the hapless kulaks were inconvenient (not, as Stalin claimed, because they were "capitalist bloodsuckers"). Of course, imposing party control over the majority of the population (the peasantry) was another reason for collectivizing agriculture.

It is no coincidence that the first Five-Year Plan and the collectivization of Soviet agriculture were inaugurated in the same year, 1929.[14] (The Soviet Union based all of its economic activity — including production, investment, and consumption — on so-called Five-Year Plans, which were broken down into yearly and monthly plans, containing specific quotas or targets for all enterprises, including industry, agriculture, and services.) Henceforth, Stalin would let nothing (and nobody) get in the way of his crash industrialization program.[15]

Even the Great Terror of the 1930s can be seen as part of Stalin's mad dash for modernization. Millions of citizens were arrested on the flimsiest of pretexts and were sent off to labor camps run by the secret police. Prison-camp labor built a major part of the USSR's industrial infrastructure (roads, canals, bridges, railroads, dams, and power grids). In Siberia, forced labor opened new mines and built new towns. In Moscow, forced labor built the impressive subway system — one of the marvels of the Stalinist era proudly shown to all visitors from abroad.[16]

Forced labor is slave labor. Much of the terror Stalin unleashed in the 1930s was in reality an excuse for enslaving much of the Soviet workforce in order to industrialize the nation without having to pay for it. Is this scenario too diabolical to be true? No one familiar with the show trials of the 1930s, in which the old Bolsheviks who had been

Lenin's comrades in arms publicly confessed to heinous crimes and denounced themselves as spies and traitors, would doubt Stalin's capacity for cruelty. (After they had confessed, Stalin's rivals were taken out and shot.)

In sum, Stalin created a rigidly centralized system of rule in which state terror was used to mobilize society and enforce strict conformity with his will. He brought the entire economy under a central plan that consistently gave greater priority to industrial development than to agriculture or the production of consumer goods. This dogmatic insistence on the primacy of heavy industry became one of the hallmarks of Stalinist economy policy, not only in the Soviet Union but in Eastern European satellite states as well.

World War II and the Soviet Phoenix

In Egyptian mythology, the phoenix is a beautiful bird that lives for five hundred years before voluntarily consuming itself in flames, only to emerge from the ashes and start a new life cycle. The legendary rebirth of the phoenix is an appropriate metaphor for the Soviet experience in World War II.

On June 22, 1941, Hitler's army invaded the Soviet Union and rolled relentlessly toward Moscow. By October, German forces had encircled the city on three sides at a distance of twenty miles. Although Hitler's troops did not actually enter Moscow, they came much too close for comfort.

Without question, the Soviet Union was the main victim of German aggression in World War II. The Red Army did emerge victorious but as historian Isaac Deutscher noted:

> Against this backdrop must be set the price Russia paid for the victory: the seven million dead, officially counted — the losses may in fact have been much larger [twenty million]; the uncounted millions of cripples; the devastation of most cities and towns, and of much of the country-side in European Russia; the destruction of industry, exemplified by the total flooding of the coal-mines of the Donets; the complete homelessness of twenty-five million people, living in caves, trenches, and mud huts, not to speak of the latent homelessness of many more millions of evacuees in the Urals and beyond.[17]

Soviet industry, bought at a terrible human price in the 1930s, lay in shambles. Between 1941 and 1945, Soviet industrial might was cut nearly in half; despite the Stalinist emphasis on steel production, the USSR was producing only about one-eighth as much steel as the United States in 1945. Soviet agriculture, too, had to be rebuilt "almost from scratch."[18]

But for all the death and destruction, the Soviet Union did not disintegrate. On the contrary, the war strengthened Soviet patriotism and made the survivors determined to do whatever was necessary to rebuild the country. West Germany's postwar reconstruction is generally considered an economic miracle. Similar "miracles" occurred in Italy and Japan, but what is more remarkable (though less frequently remarked on) is the Soviet economic miracle. Soviet workers, unlike their German, Italian, and Japanese counterparts, had to rebuild without economic aid from the United States.

Most of the Soviet recovery is attributable to two factors: Stalin's draconian system of labor conscription (the war and its aftermath provided a steady flow of fresh recruits to the gulags, or labor camps) and a centrally planned economy that permitted all resources and energies to be concentrated on strategic industries (coal, steel, electricity, machine tools, and armaments).[19]

By 1950, the Soviet Union had consolidated its hold on Eastern Europe, successfully tested an atomic bomb, and rebuilt much of its heavy industry. Stalin had the largest standing army in Europe (indeed, the largest in the world), and the Soviet Union was less than a decade away from entering the space age. (In 1957, the USSR became the first country to put a satellite — its name was *Sputnik* — into orbit.)

The Cold War Roller Coaster

The Cold War had a major impact on Soviet and Eastern European politics after World War II. The tenor of relations between the United States and the Soviet Union set the limits of East-West cooperation in all areas, including trade, tourism, technology, and cultural exchange. For this reason, we need to look at the general pattern of superpower relations since 1945.

In retrospect, the Cold War began before the Great Patriotic War (as the Soviets call World War II) ended. The Big Three — Churchill, Roosevelt, and Stalin — met several times as the war wound down, at Tehran, in Persia (Iran); Yalta, Ukraine; and Potsdam, Germany. On the surface, these meetings were conducted in a spirit of mutual trust as befits allies in a great and noble cause. Below the surface, mistrust guided the maneuvers of both Stalin and Churchill. Only Roosevelt appears to have entertained illusions about the possibilities for postwar collaboration between the Soviet Union and the West.

President Roosevelt did not live to see the end of World War II or the visible outbreak of the Cold War; he died suddenly in April 1945. His successor, Harry Truman, took a dim view of Stalin from the start. When the United States dropped the atomic bombs on Hiroshima and Nagasaki in August 1945, Truman's desire to stop the Russian advance into Manchuria (northern China) may have been a factor (although defeating Japan without having to invade the main islands was of course the primary consideration).

The United States abruptly cut off aid to the Soviet Union and turned down a Soviet loan request. Stalin then refused to withdraw Soviet troops from northern Iran and reneged on wartime promises to allow free elections in Soviet-occupied Eastern Europe. Instead, Stalin moved to consolidate Soviet control over Poland, East Germany, Romania, Hungary, Bulgaria, and, finally, in early 1948, Czechoslovakia.

Against the backdrop of Stalin's expansionism in Eastern Europe, a great debate unfolded in the United States about policy toward the Soviet Union. The Cold War would not emerge clearly until 1948. But a telegram dispatched by George Kennan from the U.S. embassy in Moscow in February 1946 presaged the policy of containment, which after 1948 became the cornerstone of the United States' national security strategy for four decades. (See Box 5.2.)

Democracy in America

BOX 5.2

The Great American Crusade: "Containing" Communism in Eastern Europe

Isolationism has deep roots in the political culture of the United States. In the nineteenth century, America followed the admonition of George Washington in his farewell address to avoid "entangling alliances" and, specifically, to remain aloof from Europe's wars. The outbreak of World War I, however, pulled a reluctant America into what was essentially a European war in order to prevent the balance of power from tilting decisively to Germany.

After World War I, isolationist tendencies again came to the fore. The outbreak of World War II saw American public opinion and the U.S. Congress against American entry into the war in Asia or Europe. President Roosevelt's hands were tied, in effect, until the Japanese attack on Pearl Harbor on December 7, 1941 — "a date which will live in infamy" in FDR's memorable words.

The end of World War II saw the Soviet military forces in control of Eastern Europe and the armed forces of the United States (together with British forces) in control of Western Europe. There was nothing to hold the wartime alliance of the Big Three together after the defeat of Germany (and Japan). Stalin imposed Soviet-style communist governments in Eastern Europe; only in Czechoslovakia were the communists actually voted into office.

The communist takeover in Czechoslovakia triggered new alarm bells in Washington and helped to secure passage of the Marshall Plan in the U.S. Congress in the spring of 1948. It also set the stage for the establishment of the North Atlantic Treaty Organization (NATO) in 1949. Both were preceded (in 1947) by the Truman Doctrine, which pledged U.S. support for governments (Greece at that time) threatened by communist subversion. Clearly, the United States had shed its isolationist skin, so to speak.

America's role in the world was guided by a concept called "containment" for the next four decades. A professional diplomat named George Kennan developed the idea. In an article entitled, "The Sources of Soviet Conduct," published in the prestigious journal *Foreign Affairs* in July 1947, Kennan laid out the basis for a policy aimed at preventing the spread of communism by patiently and persistently resisting Soviet expansion. Western Europe was considered the most important "battlefront" in the Cold War, which explains why all Marshall Plan monies were dedicated to the rapid economic reconstruction of "free" Europe (to the exclusion of Asia and other regions).

In retrospect, containment appears to have worked. However, with the collapse of communism in Europe during 1989–1991, the Cold War ended and the United States suddenly found itself without an "enemy" or a clear sense of its purpose in the "new world order."

Stalin's actions in Poland and Czechoslovakia were particularly alarming to the American public. There was a sizable Polish community in the United States — Chicago still boasts the second-largest concentration of Polish people in the world (exceeded only by Warsaw). Stalin had assured Roosevelt that the Soviet Union would respect Polish sovereignty. Czechoslovakia was a special case because it had been a showcase of democracy between the two world wars. In early 1948, leaders of the Czechoslovakian Communist Party, subservient to Stalin, staged a coup — with Stalin's backing and very likely on his orders. In the course of the communist takeover, Jan Masaryk, the country's popular foreign minister and son of the beloved first president of Czechoslovakia, Tomás Masaryk, died under mysterious circumstances — he fell or was thrown from a window. Capitalizing on the furor created by the latest Soviet land grab, President Truman asked Congress to back the **Marshall Plan** (a massive, multibillion-dollar aid program aimed at speeding the economic recovery of Western Europe from the devastation of World War II). Though it was by far the biggest foreign-aid package ever proposed, funding was approved in short order.

The year 1948 also saw the first Berlin crisis. Before World War II, Berlin had been the capital of Germany. After the war, when Germany was divided into zones occupied by each of the victorious Allies, Berlin, located inside the Soviet-occupied eastern zone, was likewise divided. Stalin wanted all of Berlin under East German (Soviet) jurisdiction. He decided to force the issue by blockading Berlin. The United States responded with an airlift that kept West Berlin alive. Stalin was checkmated: either he could shoot down the U.S. supply planes and touch off a new hot war, or he could back off. He backed off.

In 1949, the United States established the **North Atlantic Treaty Organization (NATO),** the first peacetime U.S. alliance in 150 years. The Soviet Union responded by forming the **Warsaw Pact.** In 1949, two other landmark events occurred: the Soviet Union conducted its first successful atomic bomb test, and the pro-Western government of Chiang Kai-shek was driven off China's mainland onto the island of Taiwan by the forces of Chinese communist leader Mao Zedong.

Despite a slight thaw following Stalin's death in 1953, the Cold War persisted. The Soviet Union faced major challenges at home and abroad. After Communist Party Secretary Nikita Khrushchev renounced Stalinism in 1956, uprisings against communist rule occurred in Poland and Hungary. Khrushchev sent troops into Hungary in 1956; the communist government in Poland weathered the storm without direct Soviet intervention. But the lessons on both sides were clear: Moscow would not permit defection of the Eastern European satellites from the Warsaw Pact; for Moscow, the price of empire was eternal vigilance.

Between 1958 and 1961, the issue of Berlin heated up again, resulting in an on-again, off-again crisis that culminated in August 1961 in the building of the Berlin Wall to stop the flood of escapees to the West. A year later came a crisis over Soviet offensive missiles stationed in Cuba that brought the two superpowers to the very brink of nuclear war. The confrontation had a sobering effect on both sides. The upshot was the establishment of a telephone "hotline" between the White House and the Kremlin and the signing of the Partial Nuclear Test Ban Treaty in July 1963.

But as tensions were stabilizing with the West, they were heating up on the other Soviet flank. In the early 1960s, a rift in relations between the USSR and its former communist ally, the People's Republic of China, escalated into a war of words. Throughout the 1960s, the two communist giants traded insults. The spat turned ugly in 1969 when fighting broke out along the border demarcated by the Amur and Ussuri rivers. There were relatively few casualties, but Sino-Soviet relations remained frigid, and Moscow found itself engaged in two cold wars at once.

Even within Eastern Europe — Moscow's own special sphere of influence — the Soviets faced challenges. In 1968, Czechoslovakia attempted defiance. With the "Prague spring" came the flowering of a democratization movement ("socialism with a human face"). Led by Alexander Dubcek, the communist regime proposed to open up the political system to opposition parties. Moscow would not tolerate such "bourgeois" heresy. At the order of General Secretary Leonid Brezhnev, Soviet troops rolled into Prague and crushed Dubcek's government. Brezhnev justified the intervention on the grounds that socialist states have an obligation to aid any member of the socialist commonwealth beset by counterrevolution. In other words, once a socialist state, always a socialist state. Elsewhere this policy, which came to be known as the **Brezhnev Doctrine,** was roundly condemned.

The early 1970s witnessed the opening scene in a dramatic realignment: the United States and Communist China buried the hatchet after more than two decades of hostility. Moscow looked on in dismay but should not have been surprised: one of the oldest principles of international politics — the enemy of my enemy is my friend — was working to bring together these strange bedfellows.

With relations between Washington and Beijing warming, the Soviet Union decided it was time to seek accommodation with the United States. In 1972, the two superpowers signed a strategic arms limitation agreement — SALT I. They also moved to improve their trade relations. East-West trade had already developed outside the Soviet-American relationship. In the early 1970s, West Germany, under the center-left government of Chancellor Willy Brandt, pursued an independent foreign policy (*Ostpolitik*) that sharply increased trade and other ties between East and West Germany and between Eastern and Western Europe.

Superpower relations in the 1970s were uneven. Progress in strategic arms limitation was not matched in other areas. The decade ended on a discordant note with the Soviet invasion of Afghanistan, a punitive grain embargo imposed on the Soviet Union by the Carter administration, and a boycott of the Moscow Summer Olympics (by the United States, Communist China, Japan, and other nations). The election of Ronald Reagan, a staunch anticommunist, seemed likely to bring a resurgence of the Cold War as the 1980s unfolded.

American distrust of Moscow and a string of Soviet leaders who lacked vision and vigor (because of old age or failing health) prevented progress. The accession of Mikhail Gorbachev in 1985 and Reagan's desire to finish his second term with a flourish broke the standoff. In November 1987, the two superpowers signed a treaty eliminating intermediate-range nuclear forces in Europe. Moscow had made several unilateral concessions in the negotiations. This conciliatory attitude in matters of arms control, combined with Gorbachev's liberal domestic reforms, raised the first prospect of a true thaw in the Cold War.

Stalin's Heirs: From Khrushchev to Gorbachev

Stalin's death in 1953 provoked a succession crisis. Following several years of bitter infighting, Nikita Khrushchev emerged as the winner. He lost little time in distancing himself from the deceased dictator.

At the Twentieth Party Congress in 1956, Khrushchev delivered his famous **Secret Speech.** The four-hour address contained a blockbuster: the pronouncement that Stalin had made serious errors in the 1930s and had committed excesses in the name of building communism. Of course, many who heard this shocking "revelation" already knew about the Stalin terror (not a few from firsthand experience). But before Khrushchev's speech, nobody in the Soviet Union dared whisper a word about it.

Khrushchev's **de-Stalinization** drive was his most significant contribution to the development of the Soviet state. Not only did he denounce government based on fear and Stalinist terror, but he also emptied the labor camps and dismantled most of the vast camp system (the "gulag archipelago," in Aleksandr Solzhenitsyn's memorable phrase).

Other attempts at reforming the Stalinist state, however, were destined to fail. In agriculture, Khrushchev launched the **virgin lands campaign** under which millions of hectares of land in Kazakhstan and eastern Russia were to be plowed and planted for the first time. It seemed like a good idea at the time, and at first it seemed to be working. But within a decade it turned to disaster as the fragile topsoil was blown away by fierce winds. In the spring of 1963, according to one account:

> Dust clouds hid the sun for several days, irrigation canals were choked, and along some stands of trees drifts of soil more than two meters high were formed. Many towns and villages were covered with dirt, and from thousands of hectares the arable layer was so completely removed by the winds that the underlying bedrock was exposed. Precise data on the damaged areas were not published, but millions of hectares were involved. . . . It will take at least one to two centuries before the arable layer is restored to these areas.[20]

Khrushchev's other attempts at economic and administrative reform were equally ill-fated. In an effort to decentralize the cumbersome state bureaucracy, he abolished most of the Moscow-based economic departments, creating regional economic councils (*sovnarkhozy*) in their place. But officials with a vested interest in preserving the power and status of Moscow resisted this change. He also introduced a plan for the regular rotation of party personnel (thus threatening the job security of party bosses) and tried splitting regional party committees into agricultural and industrial sectors, again in the name of increased efficiency.

What resulted was confusion and probable sabotage by disgruntled functionaries and administrators. When Khrushchev was ousted in 1964, his successors cited his "harebrained schemes" as justification. His detractors also accused him of trying to create a "cult of personality" (a Stalinist sin) and thus violating the Leninist principle of collective leadership. Accordingly, Leonid Brezhnev, Khrushchev's successor as general secretary, did not assume the post of premier. (Khrushchev, like Stalin, had simultaneously held the top post in both party and government.) Alexei Kosygin became the new premier, while Nikolai Podgorny served as the new president. Thus, a kind of triumvirate, with Brezhnev as "first among equals," replaced one-man dictatorship for the first time in Soviet history. (Brezhnev ousted Podgorny and assumed the post of president, as well as party chief, in 1977.)

Brezhnev's long tenure (1964–1982) brought a return to policies and methods reminiscent of the Stalinist era. State terror was not resumed on a massive scale, but some dissidents were placed in psychiatric hospitals and subjected to chemical and electric shock "therapies," while others were harassed by the secret policy or imprisoned for long periods. This **neo-Stalinism,** as it is sometimes called, was evident in both cultural and economic policy. In the economic sphere, the Brezhnev regime briefly toyed with market-oriented reforms, based on the proposals of Soviet economist Evsei Liberman. But the reforms were soon abandoned in favor of a return to the Stalinist system of central planning with its emphasis on quotas, artificial prices, and top-down management. In the cultural sphere, censorship, which Khrushchev had relaxed in the early 1960s, was restored. In 1968 two writers, Andrei Sinyavsky and Yuli Daniel, were convicted of "anti-Soviet agitation," a political crime under Soviet law that typically carries a penalty of seven years in prison. The trial sent a chill throughout artistic and literary circles in the Soviet Union.

Two events led to the emergence of a human rights movement in the USSR in the late 1960s: the Israeli victory in the Six-Day War in 1967 and the Soviet invasion of Czechoslovakia in 1968. The first event inspired Soviet Jews to seek permission to emigrate to Israel (or the West); the second focused attention on repressive Soviet policies both at home and abroad and gave rise to protests (even from devout communists) throughout Eastern and Western Europe. In the Soviet Union, a small but vocal group of dissidents took up the cudgels for liberalization of Soviet politics and culture.

The human rights movement was given a boost by the Soviet signing of the Helsinki Accords in 1975. Part of the agreement obligated the signatories to respect personal rights and civil liberties. **Détente,** the rapprochement between the two superpowers — crowned by SALT I and a new trade pact in the early 1970s — was a major factor. But Soviet-American relations, always tense and tentative, soured in the late 1970s. The Soviet invasion of Afghanistan in 1979 drove relations between Washington and Moscow to the lowest low point in a decade. (The SALT II treaty, which subsequently stalled in the U.S. Senate, was one of the casualties.)

One manifestation of the hardening Soviet attitudes toward both the West and internal liberalization (the two policy tracks tended to move in tandem) was a crackdown on dissent. Several prominent human rights activists and so-called **refuseniks** (Soviet Jews who were refused permission to emigrate) were arrested and put on trial. The most famous, Anatoly Shcharansky, was both a human rights activist and a refusenik, thus symbolizing everything the Brezhnev regime sought to suppress. He was accused not only of anti-Soviet agitation but also of being a spy. The punishment for treason in the Soviet Union was death. Shcharansky's life was spared but he was sentenced to thirteen years in a labor colony. (In 1986, he was exchanged for several East German spies, and he now lives in Israel.)

After 1979, Jewish emigration was reduced to a trickle, and the political climate discouraged manifestations of dissent or nonconformity. The Kremlin's neo-Stalinist social and cultural policies were matched by a strict, orthodox approach to economic problems. The prescribed remedies for inefficiency continued to have one common denominator: overcentralized management within the rigid framework of economic planning. (An in-depth analysis of the Soviet economic malady is presented in Chapter 6.) In the early 1980s, the ossified Soviet system, like its geriatric leaders, showed clear signs of old age.

The ebb and flow of political repression during the Brezhnev years obscured the steady erosion of central authority. Several forces were causing this growing instability. First, the steel sword of Stalin's totalitarian system had been the secret police, or **KGB.** After Khrushchev's Secret Speech in 1956, the KGB was demoralized, discredited, and partly defanged. Still formidable, it nonetheless ceased to inspire the kind of fear it had in Stalin's day.

The fact that Western visitors were allowed to enter the country and move about specific "open" cities relatively freely, especially after the Soviet-American détente of the early 1970s, was a symptom of the Kremlin's weakening hold on society. At the same time, more Soviet academicians, scientists, and other professionals were permitted to venture abroad. Accompanying this "travel revolution" was a "communications revolution." With the waves of tourists coming to the USSR came Western ideas, clothing, music, magazines, tapes, records, and gadgets. Some young people learned to speak English by approaching Americans (and other English speakers) on the street and striking up a conversation. They would offer their services as unofficial tour guides, asking only for an opportunity to speak English in return.[21]

When Brezhnev died in 1982, former head of the KGB Yuri Andropov succeeded him. Andropov moved quickly to revitalize the Soviet economy, relying primarily on exhortation and admonition; his watchword was discipline. Anyone caught skipping work ("absenteeism"), avoiding work or malingering on the job ("parasitism"), getting drunk or causing a public disturbance ("hooliganism"), dealing on the black market ("speculation"), or engaging in other corrupt practices would be punished to the limits of the law.

Soviet citizens were both optimistic and apprehensive about the new regime. There was widespread recognition that stagnation had set in and that only a strong leader with a clear vision of the future could pull the nation out of its doldrums. But there was also an unspoken fear that Andropov might resurrect the Stalinist police state.

These hopes and fears were for naught, however. Andropov fell ill and died in the spring of 1984. His successor, Konstantin Chernenko, old and frail from the start, died a year later. The Soviet Union had now been without energetic leadership for years. For nearly three decades, one iron-fisted ruler — Joseph Stalin — had held sway in the Kremlin. Then, between 1982 and 1985, the country would have four different "bosses" (Brezhnev, Andropov, Chernenko, and Gorbachev) in one three-year period. Something had to be done about the Soviet gerontocracy. Aging neo-Stalinists whose jaded habits of mind precluded initiative and innovation could not rejuvenate an arthritic economy.

Enter Mikhail Gorbachev. Gorbachev was in his fifties when he took over the reins of power — a youngster by Soviet political standards. Gorbachev's reforms are examined in Chapter 6. For now it suffices to note that he moved boldly on the cultural and economic fronts. In the political sphere, he paid lip service to democratization, but the constitutional changes he proposed did not compromise the Communist Party's power monopoly. As the Soviet state passed the half-century mark in 1987, many observers believed that it was on the verge of a new era. In fact, it was approaching its demise.

Ideology and Political Culture

An **ideology** is an official belief system; in the case of Soviet-type communist states, it was an amalgam of ideas and teachings associated primarily with Marx and Lenin. Political culture is broader, not only encompassing ideology but also values, attitudes, myths, fears, prejudices, perceptions, and preferences that permeate and condition the political thoughts and actions of society's members. This distinction was especially crucial in the Soviet-bloc countries because the ideology was used as a kind of smoke screen concealing the underlying values that actually motivated political behavior.

Marxism-Leninism: A Secular Religion

During the heyday of communism, volumes were written about Soviet ideology. Now that the Cold War is over and the Soviet Union is defunct, **Marxism-Leninism** has faded into the pages of twentieth-century history. Even so, the moral, economic, and political consequences of decades of communist rule are still very much in evidence throughout the region, as we shall see in Chapter 6. To find the intellectual roots of the ill-fated system Lenin and his successors invented, it is necessary to explore the world of Marxist-Leninist thought.

Marxism is not simply a blueprint for revolution. It combines a philosophy of history with an elaborate theory of social development. Karl Marx claimed to have discovered the laws of sociopolitical evolution. The driving force in history, he believed, is economics, the organization of the means of production. Social and political institutions are seen as mere "superstructure," edifices built on economic foundations defined by relationships of production. Control or ownership of the means of production determines political power, social status, and economic well-being. According to Marx, this iron law of history applies at all times and in all places.

Capitalism, in Marx's eyes, is simply a stage in social evolution. Capitalism is a system in which the few ("monopoly capitalists") control the means of production (land, labor buildings, machines, money) and use this control to exploit the many (who have no choice but to work for meager wages). The **law of capitalist accumulation** operates through fierce dog-eat-dog competition to squeeze out small producers and create opportunities for big ones to get bigger. Darwinian-style survival of the fittest prevails: producers must either "get big or get out" of the market.

Profit is the engine that drives capitalism, according to Marx; even non-Marxist economists agree. But Marx believed that profits are robbery. Under capitalism, workers toil long hours for subsistence wages. The difference between the income their labor generates and the pay they receive for that labor is what Marx called **surplus value** (profit based on exploitation).

As the rich get richer, the poor get poorer. The rich also get fewer, while the ranks of the poor swell as industrialization shifts the economy from rural to urban, from farm to factory. A new underclass, the proletariat, is thus created by a relentless process Marx called the **law of pauperization.** As machines replace human labor, unemployment grows, poverty spreads, and domestic markets shrink. The resulting business recession leads to even greater unemployment and eventually to economic depression. Here, in a nutshell, is the Achilles' heel of the free-market system — the inevitable and recurrent "crisis of capitalism" that will eventually cause its total collapse.

The concept of **alienation** plays a central role in the Marxist theory of revolution. As part of an impersonal wage-labor force, workers are estranged from the means (and fruits) of production. Capitalists own the work (labor) they perform; they have no voice in how things are run; the jobs they do are monotonous and menial; they take no pride in good work; mass consumption means that quality is less important than quantity and that producers and consumers do not know each other. Workers are cogs in a machine. Thus, capitalism is dehumanizing.

The *Communist Manifesto* opens with these prophetic words: "A spectre is haunting Europe — the spectre of Communism." Marx wrote this pamphlet (with Friedrich Engels) to explain his thesis that "the history of all hitherto existing society is the history of class struggle." The final class struggle, between the proletariat and the bourgeoisie, would result in spontaneous revolution and usher in socialism, a system of productive relations characterized by public ownership and a fair, though not equal, distribution of goods ("from each according to his ability, to each according to his work"). In time the state would simply wither away. The ultimate form of society would evolve gradually and naturally from socialism to communism ("from each according to his ability, to each according to his needs"). For Marx, equality was the supreme moral value.

Lenin was less interested in theory than practice. He wanted to make a revolution, not philosophize about history. Marx had called for a **dictatorship of the proletariat** as a temporary measure to forestall counterrevolution. It was an unfortunate turn of phrase: Lenin used it as an excuse to create a dictatorship over the proletariat. In addition, as noted, Lenin coined a new term for the Communist Party, exalting it as the **vanguard of the proletariat.** Without the vanguard, the revolution would never get rolling, Lenin argued. In this way, Lenin set the stage for the party dictatorship that became the hallmark of the Soviet state.

Two other Leninist principles deserve mention. First, Lenin invented **democratic centralism,** which governed the organization and operation of the party. As soon as a decision was announced, lower-level discussion within the party would cease. Decisions on important issues were made behind closed doors at the highest level and were strictly binding on all subordinate levels. Second, Lenin placed a ban on factionalism within the party, meaning that any opposition to the party line, no matter how loyal, would be suppressed whenever the leadership found it expedient to do so. Also, any party leader guilty of factionalism risked demotion or expulsion.

Leninism evolved into a state religion. "Despite all the museums of atheism that have taken the place of Russian Orthodox churches throughout the country, the Soviet Union is now less an atheistic country than a Leninist country," wrote one observer just a few years before the collapse of Soviet communism. "Even the most casual visitor to the Soviet Union is overwhelmed by evidence of the religion of Leninism."[22] Every day, thousands of Soviet citizens stood in long lines waiting to file past Lenin's open coffin in a granite mausoleum in Red Square. Pictures, statues, and busts of Lenin were everywhere. Graven images of Lenin set against a background of scarlet to symbolize the Great October Revolution and bathed in a soft halo of light replaced the traditional icons that once adorned special corners in factories and schools.

The Eastern European regimes carried this ideological baggage as well. They continued to pay lip service to Marx and Lenin, but the litany had grown stale. By 1989, when communist governments in the region toppled like dominoes, Marxism-Leninism had more in common with religious ritual than political reality. (The reasons for the decline of ideology in these nominally communist societies will be discussed in the following chapter.)

Soviet Political Culture: Old Wine, New Wineskins

Understanding other cultures requires a certain ability to suspend our own ingrained values and habits of mind. Failure to do so inevitably leads to misconceptions. To cite one example, a journalist named Hedrick Smith, posted to Moscow in the 1970s, expected to find that most Soviet citizens remembered Stalin with fear and loathing. He was surprised to discover that, on the contrary, "so essential was Stalin to the concept of how Russia should be ruled for many middle-aged and elderly people that they no longer recall their panic at the time of his death."[23] Many ordinary Soviet citizens expressed nostalgia for a strong boss.

Smith's observations comparing Soviet (and especially Russian) attitudes toward authority with Western (in particular, American) views are worth quoting at some length:

> [There is] a fundamental difference between Russians and Americans, who are often moved to seek similarities in their national characters. They may share an openness of spirit but Russians and Americans differ sharply in their attitudes toward power and authority — and not just because of Soviet Communism. Inbred mistrust of authority is an American tradition. We are wary as a people of bigness when it is accompanied by unchecked power — Big Business, Big Labor, big anything. . . .
>
> Not so the Russians. Bigness and power are admired almost without qualification. Size inspires awe — huge Kremlins, cannons, churchbells under the czars; huge dams, missiles, atom smashers under the Communists. Marxism-Leninism has provided a rationale for large-scale production and concentrated power in the hands of Party leaders and central planners. But six centuries of authoritarian rule from Ivan the Great and Ivan the Terrible forward had made Russians monarchists in their bones long before Lenin and Stalin came along. . . .
>
> So much has been inherited from the past that a Russian takes for granted elements of political despotism that are instantly an affront to a Westerner. History has conditioned Russians differently. The cruel tyranny of Stalin was prefigured by the bloody reign of Ivan the Terrible in the sixteenth century and the iron rule of Nicholas I in the nineteenth century. Peter the Great, celebrated for opening Russia to the West and introducing a more modern Army and state administration, is well known abroad for having also improved the efficiency of authoritarian controls, some of which survive today. It was Peter who set up the first political police administration and who officially instituted censorship and the practice of issuing internal passports to keep Russians from traveling away from their permanent homes without special permission.[24]

The easy assumption that the virtues of democracy are as obvious to Russians as they are to Americans turns out to be a delusion. For reasons deeply rooted in their history, Russians tend to value security more than freedom (which, before Gorbachev's reform campaign, they had never known); at the same time, they often fear disorder more than tyranny.[25]

Part of the Russian aversion to overt forms of disobedience can probably be explained by their history of draconian rule, the resulting absence of democracy, and a natural fear of the unknown. People accustomed to stern discipline are bound to feel insecure and perhaps disoriented when that discipline is reduced or removed. Of course, not all Soviet citizens feared freedom or equated democracy with disorder, but most probably did.

Russians learned to deal with embarrassing facts by hiding them. Western observers are often struck by the Russian penchant for *pokazukha,* putting up a false front. The practice of deliberately disguising unpleasant realities is a time-honored and highly perfected tradition in Russia. This practice became a trademark of Soviet rule. For example, the Soviet travel agency, Intourist, packaged special tours of showcase cities just for foreigners, provided guides (who did double duty as chaperones), and kept visitors' schedules so jam-packed with excursions, museums, ballet performances, and the like that there was no time to poke around and explore the darker side of Soviet life.

Russians have long believed that Western nations view them as crude and uncultured. "You like to laugh at our misfortunes" is a common sentiment Russians express toward Americans. (Like many other misperceptions we entertain about each other, this one contains a kernel of truth.) The deep-rooted Russian inferiority complex — manifested, for example, in the proclivity of Russian schoolteachers to challenge American visitors to impromptu poetry-reciting contests — was reinforced by Soviet propaganda during the Cold War. The upshot was a kind of reflexive Soviet patriotism that popped up even in nonthreatening interpersonal encounters with the West. Such reactions may strike Westerners as inappropriate, but they are a natural reflection of a deep-seated Russian sense of inferiority vis-à-vis the West.

Patriotism is a universal emotion, but the "blood and soil" Russian variety startles many Western visitors. During the communist era, "Soviet" patriotism was really Russian patriotism with a thin Bolshevik veneer. Signs of patriotism were everywhere; some were transparently contrived by the regime for foreign consumption, but many were spontaneous and heartfelt. Hedrick Smith quoted a young Soviet economist: "We learned from our history that to survive, we must band together." Smith also noted that Suvorov, the great Russian military commander who defeated both Frederick the Great and Napoléon, used to say, "*Pust khuzhe, da nashe*" ("Let it be worse, but let it be ours").[26]

This attitude is akin to "My country, right or wrong," something the Russians call *kvasnoi patriotizm.* Smith explained it this way:

> Like so many essentials of Russian life, the phrase does not readily lend itself to translation, for one has to know that kvas is a fermented peasant drink made from water dripped through burnt bread. Kvas has a malty flavor, and cheap kvas can be like cold coffee — bitter, the color of muddy water, with grounds at the bottom. In cities all over Russia, white-coated women serve up glass mugs of kvas from large, saffron-colored, mobile metal kegs in the summertime. Foreigners usually pass up a second mug, but Russians swear by it, and peasants produce their own home brew of kvas. So kvas patriotism represents the earthy peasantry: an intensely Russian brand of patriotism.[27]

The impact of communism on Russian political culture was (and still is) evident in a phenomenon called ***blat*** — a generic term for the pervasive corruption, cheating, and dishonesty that permeated everyday life in the USSR. *Blat* assumed myriad forms: theft of state property, bribery, embezzlement, moonlighting, dealing on the black market. It involved bending, evading, or breaking the rules in all sorts of subtle and not-so-subtle ways. Almost everybody did it, largely out of necessity, because consumer goods and services were always scarce (and therefore precious) and because prices fixed by the state did not reflect their true (market) value. Thus, the distortions introduced into the Soviet economy by the system of central planning — in particular, the emphasis on heavy industry and defense production at the expense of consumer needs — created a morally ambiguous climate in which widespread dishonesty and underhandedness were rewarded (and tacitly accepted) while honesty and integrity appeared foolish. Moreover, the rigidities of central planning made it expedient for plant managers, too, to cheat, lie, and falsify records on a vast scale, including the use of illegal go-betweens to obtain essential materials on the black market, in a never-ending struggle to fulfill monthly production quotas.

Public morality in the USSR reflected the collectivism that lay at the core of Marxist ethics. This moral propensity contrasted sharply with the individualism so prevalent in countries like France and the United States. In the Soviet Union, the paramount importance of the collective was rarely questioned. Schoolchildren were taught to place group rights above individual rights and to take responsibility for the performance and conduct of their classmates. Similarly, teachers generally held parents responsible for the attitudes and actions of their children in school. Adults were even expected to take responsibility for the conduct of other adults — especially family members, neighbors, and coworkers — to an extent that was startling and alien to Westerners.

Eastern Europe before 1945

The nations of Eastern Europe have historical roots, but the present states emerged as sovereign entities only in the modern age, after centuries of foreign rule. Hungary regained internal independence in 1867 with the establishment of the dual monarchy (the emperor of Austria was also Hungary's king). Romania became independent in 1878, Bulgaria in 1908, and Albania in 1912. Czechoslovakia and Yugoslavia emerged as independent states only after World War I and dissolved shortly after the demise of the Soviet Union. Poland was reconstituted as a sovereign state after the war; Russia, Prussia, and Austria had dismantled it in a series of "partitions" more than a century earlier.

East Germany was a special case. Stalin formed the German Democratic Republic (GDR) from the portion of Germany occupied by Soviet troops after the defeat of Hitler's Third Reich in 1945; it had never aspired to a separate existence, always considering itself part of a single German nation.

Before World War I, four great empires dominated Eastern Europe, all located on the periphery of the region and only one, Russia, anchored in a Slavic culture. By the mid-nineteenth century, the Russian empire encompassed all of Ukraine, part of Poland, and Bessarabia (now part of Moldova). The German and Austrian empires partitioned and ruled Poland from the end of the eighteenth century until 1918. Austria's domain included the territories of what are now the Czech Republic, Slovakia, Hungary, Slovenia, and Croatia from the fifteenth century until its defeat and dissolution in World War I. The Ottoman Empire (Turkey) ruled the present-day Balkan nations of Bulgaria, Romania, Bosnia, Yugoslavia, Macedonia, and Albania.

The most important distinction, politically, is between the Eastern European countries once ruled by Austria and Germany and those ruled by the Ottoman Turks. Most of the former were greatly influenced by Western Europe and made important contributions to the high culture of the West (consider, for example, the impact on classical music of Czech composers such as Dvořák, Smetana, and Janáček or the Polish composer Chopin). The Balkans developed in relative isolation from the West, and hence the cultural contributions of its peoples are generally less widely known outside the region.

Although all Eastern European countries had limited autonomy, the northern-tier Slavic nations generally experienced less oppression and abuse than did their neighbors to the south, who endured religious persecution and heavy taxation while benefiting from little or no economic and political development well into the twentieth century.

In the turbulent period between World War I and World War II (1918–1939), many Eastern European governments had a democratic veneer, but only Czechoslovakia was a true democracy. Other nations in the region lacked experience in democratic self-government. Many also lacked moderate leadership and faced enormous economic and social problems. Anti-Semitism and extreme nationalism were prevalent throughout the region, as were divisions over religion, social reform, and national aspirations. The leaders of Hungary, Romania, and Bulgaria saw the Nazi totalitarian model as a solution to their desperate domestic circumstances. (All three countries later joined the Hitler-led Axis.) Widespread hostility to both Russia and communism also reinforced this perverse inclination to embrace Nazi Germany.

All the nations of Eastern Europe lost their independence in World War II. Poland, Czechoslovakia, and Yugoslavia were conquered by Nazi Germany (though in Yugoslavia, Tito's Partisans waged a ferocious guerrilla war against the Germans).

In 1939, Hitler and Stalin signed a nonaggression pact under which they split Poland. Two years later, Hitler tore up the agreement, overran Poland, and attacked the Soviet Union. Later, when Stalin turned the tide, the advancing Red Army waited on the eastern bank of the Vistula River while German troops crushed the Polish underground. (The Polish government in exile had called for the Warsaw uprising in the belief that it would hasten the defeat of the Germans; rather than helping the Polish fighters, Stalin kept his army on the sidelines.) In due time, Soviet troops crossed the Vistula and pursued Hitler's retreating forces into Germany. Thus in an ironic twist, Hitler ended up giving the USSR a golden opportunity to dispatch Soviet troops into Poland. After the war, the Red Army occupied Poland and ensured Soviet domination of that country until 1989.

The story of Poland is tragic but not without precedent. In 1772, Prussia and Russia annexed major portions of Polish territory in the First Partition of Poland. According to Ivan Volgyes, "Poland then tried to re-create its former greatness by reforming the obsolete workings of its government." In the Second Partition in 1793, Poland was further reduced. "Even though the Poles, under the brilliant general Tadeusz Kosciuszko, fought valiantly against partition, the dream of Polish independence was brutally crushed by the invading Prussian and Russian armies." The Third Partition, involving the Austrians, in 1795 marked "the end of Poland as a political entity, as a state."[28]

Hungary, Romania, and Bulgaria were first seduced and then subjugated by Hitler. As accomplices of Nazi Germany, they could expect little sympathy from the Allies after the war. (This point is often underemphasized in historical treatments of this period.) Thus, the postwar Soviet land grab in Eastern Europe was actually facilitated by the very nations that eventually fell victim to Stalin's megalomania.

One of the most important consequences of World War II was the unification of Eastern Europe into a military and political bloc under the Warsaw Pact, led by the Soviet Union. Thus one Slavic nation, Russia, the nucleus of the USSR, succeeded in bringing Eastern Europe's Slavic peoples under a single political authority for the first time in history. But in so doing, Stalin made the same mistake the czars had made in earlier centuries: he overextended the empire.

Eastern Europe under Soviet Tutelage

The Soviet grip on Eastern Europe was probably never as firm as it appeared to the West, as periodic revolts in Poland and attempted defections by Hungary and Czechoslovakia revealed. In addition, the "captive nations" resisted Soviet rule in a number of subtle ways. In the first place, most people seldom paid more than lip service to the official ideology. It was the subject of jokes and sarcasm in private, even as it was treated with mock reverence in public. In the second place, an undercurrent of anticommunist (anti-Russian) sentiment bubbled just beneath the surface throughout Eastern Europe. The extent of this rejection of the communist ideology was dramatically revealed in 1989, as one communist government after another simply abandoned the ship of state.

According to one scholar, "The failure of the Soviet Union to Russify the area and convert the population to its brand of 'Marxism-Leninism' should not overshadow the enormous moral, spiritual, and cultural damage inflicted upon the East European nations." The Soviet model was "superimposed on natural diversity," and no aspect of life was left untouched:

> The extent of damages and the degree of recovery naturally vary from country to country, but in all of them deep-rooted feelings of having been robbed and degraded by an alien superpower are still very live issues. Indeed it is hardly an exaggeration to say that nationalism constitutes the heart of the challenge to Soviet domination and that external and internal emancipation from the Soviet Union is the central theme of East European political life.[29]

Remarkably, these words were written two decades before the great "emancipation" of which they spoke came to pass.

Widespread anti-Sovietism was reinforced by another universal element in Eastern Europe: ethnic particularism, or nationalism. Each group is highly conscious of its heritage. When the Soviet Union interfered (or worse, intervened) in the internal affairs of the various countries, it stirred strong nationalistic impulses. Moscow's heavy-handed treatment of its satellites in Eastern Europe helped heterogeneous states like Czechoslovakia and Yugoslavia overcome ethnic tensions within their own societies. The dissolution of these states following the Soviet withdrawal from Eastern Europe strongly supports this conclusion.

In the absence of Soviet hegemony, nationalism is again playing a major role in Eastern Europe, both within and between states. Historic rivalries were submerged but never dissolved by ideology or alliance ties. Even during the heyday of the Cold War, these rivalries occasionally came to the fore:

> Witness, for example, the glee with which the East Germans and Poles intervened in Czechoslovakia in 1968, the pressures for military intervention in Poland in 1981 expressed by the East Germans and Czechoslovaks, or the problems between Hungary, on the one hand, and Czechoslovakia and Romania, on the other, regarding the presence of significant Magyar minorities in the latter two states.[30]

One commonality that may have helped ease the pain of adjustment to the Stalinist system after World War II is the tradition of authoritarianism that pervades most of Slavic Europe. The fact that, of all the nations of Eastern Europe, only Czechoslovakia has ever tried democracy with any degree of success has taken on new relevance with the collapse of communism in the region.

In retrospect, the underlying problem throughout the Soviet bloc was more spiritual than material, more psychological than economic. What ultimately determines the success or failure of a society or an economy (especially one endowed with the natural resources and population base necessary for sustained growth and prosperity) is the heart and soul of a nation, the intangible factors that account for the vigor and vitality of a country. Japan, for example, achieved its postwar economic miracle even without the natural resources that would seem to be a prerequisite.

Chiang Kai-shek, the pro-West leader of Nationalist China, once described communism as a disease of the heart. In the 1980s, the communist leaders of the Soviet Union and Eastern Europe were forced to confront the fact that Chiang might have been right. As the events of 1989–1991 were to show, the disease was ultimately to prove fatal.

Case Studies: Beyond Russia — Czechoslovakia and Yugoslavia

Slavic ("Eastern") Europe encompasses the former Soviet Union west of the Urals, East-Central Europe, and the Balkans. We have already examined the USSR in this chapter; here the focus is on the Czechoslovakia in East-Central Europe and Yugoslavia in the Balkans — both of which have broken up into smaller states in the 1990s.

Poland and Hungary are also strong candidates for special consideration in this section. (See Box 5.3.) Like the Czech Republic, both are relatively homogenous societies

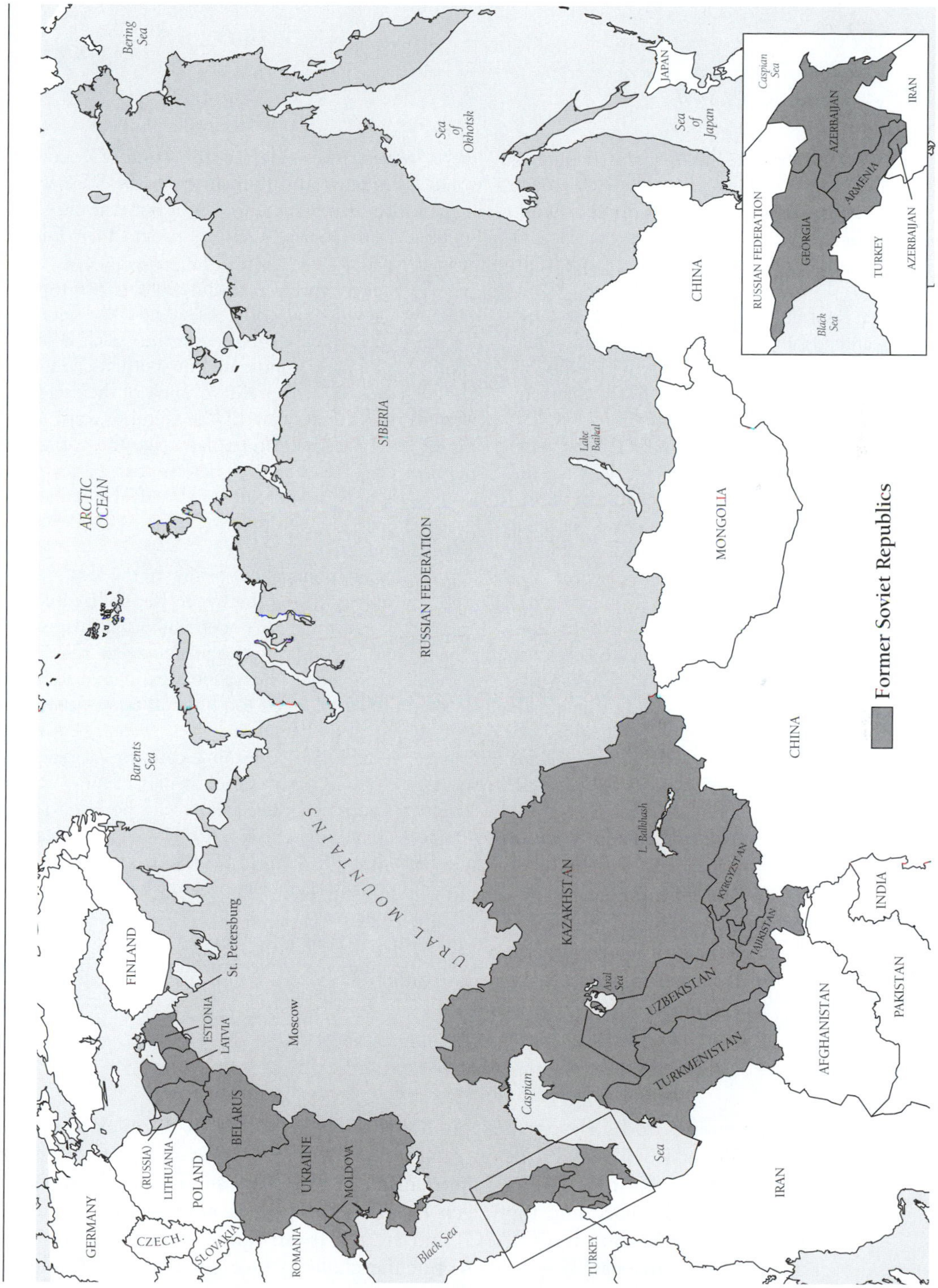

Russian Federation

What if?

BOX 5.3

What if Czechs Spoke English?

In the Netherlands, for example, many people—including cab drivers and shopkeepers—do speak English. In fact, there are quite a few countries in Western Europe, Asia, and sub-Saharan Africa where lots of people speak English. But this is not the case in Eastern Europe.

The Czech Republic could adopt English as a second language and add an English language requirement to the public school curriculum. It would probably boost the Czech Republic's fortunes faster than any other single policy measure. Think about it.

First, English is the world language. It is not only the language of diplomacy, but also the language of business. In addition, it is the universal language of professional sports, medicine, music, and many other fields of endeavor. Moreover, it is the language of people-to-people contacts nearly everywhere in the world. For example, when a person from Finland is sitting next to a person from Japan on a transoceanic flight from London to Delhi they will typically communicate in English or not at all. So if the Czech Republic made English proficiency mandatory in the schools it would be giving the next generation of Czechs a big competitive advantage over Poles, Hungarians, and other Slavic-speaking nations—especially in light of the fact that, unlike French, German, or Spanish, Slavic languages (except for Russian) are rarely spoken by nonnatives.

Second, if the Czech Republic were to adopt English as a second language it would have enormous symbolic significance. There is little doubt that Western countries would suddenly embrace the Czech Republic with a new ardor. The European Union would certainly take notice and any questions about whether the Czech Republic is ready to enter the EU would fall away. Most likely, foreign investment in the country's economy would also jump. And tourism from the West would increase, as well, once the word got out that the Czech Republic is the most "Western" country in Eastern Europe.

The logic of this move applies with equal force to Hungary, Poland, or any other Slavic country. But if one country in the region were to do it, the Czech Republic would be a likely candidate, or perhaps Hungary. Although most Czechs prefer to think of themselves as Western rather than "Slavic," they tend to resist learning (or speaking) any foreign language (be it English, German, or Russian) and to be less than patient with "foreigners" who are not fluent in Czech. Of course, the Czechs are not alone in resisting the idea of adopting a second language.

Apart from political opposition to the idea, there is no practical reason why the Czech Republic could not do it. Of course, there are not enough English-speaking primary and secondary schoolteachers in the Czech Republic to implement such a measure immediately, but it would probably not be too difficult to attract young, well-trained ESL (English as a second language) teachers from English-speaking countries to spend a year or two in a Czech school as part of an exchange program. Czech schoolteachers could be given incentives to seek retraining in English-language instruction. In a few years, the Czech Republic would have a self-sustaining English language program as its own university graduates would fill the vacancies created by the departure of foreign teachers. The Czech Republic would become widely recognized as Eastern Europe's most "Western" nation—and that, in turn, would trigger a flood of new foreign investment.

with populations and governments committed to the painful and complex transition from totalitarianism to liberal democracy. Hungary is not Slavic—a fact that helps underscore the point that there are important non-Slavic groups in Eastern Europe. All three (Poland, Hungary, and the Czech Republic) have been admitted to the North Atlantic Treaty Organization (NATO) and are the frontrunners in the race for early entry into the European Union (EU). But the challenges of economic and political liberalization are daunting. At the same time, the difficulties discussed here — restructuring, privatization, corruption, inflation, unemployment, currency convertibility, foreign investment, and external trade — are in many cases magnified in other parts of the region (for example, Moldova and Ukraine) where efforts to reinvent the state and economy in the 1990s have met with little success.

Czechoslovakia

Czechoslovakia is located in East-Central Europe, bordered by Poland, Germany, Austria, Hungary, and Ukraine. The Czechs are widely considered to be the most Western-oriented people in Slavic Europe. Dr. Tomas G. Masaryk (1850–1937), Czechoslovakia's principal founder, was both a product of this tradition and its perpetuator.

The First Slavic Democracy Czechoslovakia came into being after World War I. Established in 1918 as an independent republic it was the only functioning democracy in Slavic Europe during the interwar period. Masaryk succeeded in melding the two parts of the country — Bohemia and Moravia, the Czech lands to the west, and Slovakia in the east — into a single state under a constitution that provided for a freely elected parliament which in turn elected the president. Appropriately enough, Masaryk became Czechoslovakia's first and most beloved president. He was perfect for the job: his father was a Slovak, his mother a Moravian, and his wife an American. A philosopher and teacher by profession, he was an extraordinary leader who displayed both wisdom and moral courage throughout his long life.

Carved out of the Austro-Hungarian Empire, Czechoslovakia was a hybrid state from the beginning. The Czech lands were part of Austria before World War I, and Slovakia was part of Hungary. The Czechs were more numerous than the Slovaks (by almost two to one), more Western, and industrially more advanced. Although the languages they speak are so similar they have no difficulty communicating with one another (indeed, both use the Roman rather than the Cyrillic alphabet), both Czechs and Slovaks insist that Czech and Slovak are distinct languages rather than one language spoken in slightly different dialects. So from the outset, the political institutions of Czechoslovakia had to bridge economic, cultural, ethnolinguistic, and geographic divides.

Totalitarianism Right and Left Czechoslovakia's golden age of democracy ended in 1938 following the infamous **appeasement** of Hitler by British Prime Minister Neville Chamberlain at Munich. Chamberlain conceded the Sudetenland, a part of Czechoslovakia inhabited by 3 million ethnic Germans, to Hitler in return for the Nazi leader's false promise of peace. The Nazi occupation lasted from 1939 to 1945 and helped set the stage for a new kind of totalitarian dictatorship by brutalizing the society and introducing police-state methods into a country that had been governed by good and decent leaders committed to constitutionalism and the rule of law.

After World War II, the fate of Czechoslovakia was in the hands of the Soviet Union, reflecting the fact that the Soviet army had played the largest role in liberating the country from Nazi rule. The communists staged a coup in February 1948, ousting President Eduard Benes and establishing the Communist People's Republic (changed to Socialist Republic in 1960). Subservient to Moscow from its inception, communist Czechoslovakia became a federal system in 1969 following the Prague Spring uprising, a popular uprising against communist rule put down by invading Soviet forces the previous year. Until the demise of communist rule at the end of 1989, Czechoslovakia had a reputation as one of the most rigidly Stalinist states in the Soviet bloc.

The story of how and why Czechoslovakia committed political euthanasia a few years after the return of democracy will have to wait until the next chapter. Suffice it to say that the "o" connecting the Czech lands and "Slovakia" was a wedding ring that no longer fit.

Yugoslavia

The Balkans have proved to be a particularly unstable subregion of Europe in the twentieth century. In this area, Yugoslavia had long been considered the country most likely to disintegrate. That it stayed together for more than four decades after World War II was the result largely of the leadership skills of one man, Josip Broz Tito.

Tito's Fragile State The largely Slavic population of Yugoslavia consisted of eight primary ethnic groups speaking one of four languages (Serbo-Croat, Macedonian, Slovenian, and Albanian) and comprising three distinct religious communities (Eastern Orthodox, Roman Catholic, and Muslim; see Table 5.1).

After World War II, Marshal Tito, the popular leader of the communist-inspired Partisans who fought valiantly against the Axis powers, created one of the most complex political and economic systems anywhere in the world. This complexity was a reflection of the fragile ethnic and historical basis for the Yugoslav state, which had come into being after World War I. Tito himself was the glue that held the country together. After his death in 1980, the country began to come apart. Before its violent breakup in 1991–1992 there were six constituent republics and two autonomous provinces, each with its own governmental apparatus (presidency, prime minister and cabinet, indirectly elected assembly, and judiciary (see Table 5.2).

Table 5.1 Composition of the Population of Prebreakup Yugoslavia

Ethnic Group	Share of Population (percent)	Religion
Serbs	37	Eastern Orthodox
Croats	20	Roman Catholic
Bosnian Muslims	9	Muslim
Slovenes	8	Roman Catholic
Albanians	8	Muslim
Macedonians	6	Eastern Orthodox
Montenegrins	3	Eastern Orthodox
Hungarians	2	Roman Catholic

Table 5.2 Prebreakup Yugoslavia

Republic or Province (capital)	Area (square miles)	Population
Republics		
Bosnia-Herzegovina (Sarajevo)	19,741	4,116,439
Croatia (Zagreb)	21,829	4,578,109
Macedonia (Skopje)	9,928	1,913,571
Montenegro (Titograd)	5,333	583,475
Serbia (Belgrade)	21,609	5,666,060
Slovenia (Ljubljana)	7,819	1,883,764
Autonomous Provinces		
Kosovo (Pristina)	4,203	1,584,558
Vojvodina (Novi Sad)	8,303	2,028,239

Between East and West Tito's decision to break with Stalin in 1948 was a turning point in the history of world communism. It ensured that Moscow would use its control over the rest of Eastern Europe to try to isolate Belgrade and force Tito out. This left Tito little choice but to turn to the West for trade and aid.

But how could Tito, a fervent communist, expect a sympathetic hearing in the industrial democracies, particularly the United States? Communism and capitalism are antithetical, and Europe in 1948 was feeling the chill of the Cold War. Tito's solution was to complicate the picture enough so that the leaders of the "free" (noncommunist) world could deal with Yugoslavia without seeming to be consorting with the enemy.

In addition, Tito no doubt wanted to show the Soviets that he could find a way between communism and capitalism that would be a model for the newly emerging nations of Africa and Asia. Indeed, Tito established himself as an early leader of the nonaligned movement — Third World nations that sought to avoid choosing sides in the East-West conflict and to redefine global issues along North-South lines (that is, developed versus developing countries).

Building the Workers' Paradise Tito's reforms were aimed at decentralizing decision-making authority — the antithesis of the highly centralized Stalinist system. One of the first and most dramatic steps in this direction was the introduction of **workers' self-management.** The idea was to give the workers control over production (and hence responsibility for it) via freely elected workers' councils and management boards. Even the enterprise manager was to be elected by the workers.

Workers' self-management, Tito reasoned, would remove one major obstacle to labor productivity: workers' alienation. On the positive side, workers would take greater pride in their work, leading to improved quality of goods; they would better understand the problems of management and thus would avoid unreasonable demands and expectations; and they would develop a greater loyalty to the collective — both the enterprise and their coworkers.

Within this system evolved **indicative planning** to set overall targets for the various sectors of the economy. These targets were guidelines, not obligatory goals. In agriculture, too, the state relinquished direct control: collectivization was halted, and the state reprivatized most farmland in the 1950s.

In the 1960s, the Yugoslav leadership gave greater autonomy to plant managers and further reduced the role of central administrators. As in the West, the market forces of supply and demand set prices, and profitability became the test of efficiency. A state planning agency remained active in Belgrade, but production targets were set at the republic level and were coordinated by the federal agency. Under the impact of these reforms, Yugoslavia developed the most consumer-oriented economy in Eastern Europe.

How well did these reforms work? The results were mixed. While Tito was alive, the economy remained healthy; but in the 1980s a number of chronic problems emerged, including mounting external debt, a falling standard of living, and rising unemployment. In addition, despite workers' self-management, low productivity caused prices to climb, and energy costs were high. And even harder times lay ahead.

Federalism without Democracy Economic reforms in Yugoslavia were accompanied by changes in the formal structures of the government. These changes were designed to create the appearance of decentralized, democratic republicanism.

Under Tito, it did not matter much who held what official position. As founder and chief architect of the nation, Tito called the shots, and no one expected otherwise. This extraordinary consensus enabled Tito to experiment with various forms of political power sharing without having to relinquish any personal power. He designed an elaborate set of institutions that shrouded the dominant role of the Yugoslav Communist Party (officially the League of Yugoslav Communists) in the trappings of federalism and democracy. Under this unique system, Yugoslavia had a rotating collective chief executive that consisted of nine persons, one from each of the six republics and the two autonomous provinces, and one ex officio member representing the Communist Party. The Federal Assembly elected a chairman to a one-year term. Under a special constitutional provision, Tito served as president until his death in 1980. The system was therefore never really tested during Tito's lifetime.

The thirty-three-member Federal Executive Council (the cabinet) was the functional equivalent of the Council of Ministers in the USSR. The collective presidency nominated a member of the bicameral Federal Assembly to be president of the Federal Executive Council, and the Federal Assembly then voted confirmation. The Yugoslav premier was thus chosen in a manner similar to that of many parliamentary democracies. The council was responsible for the government's day-to-day operations.

The Federal Assembly was a bicameral legislature made up of the Federal Chamber and the Chamber of Republics and Provinces. The electoral process was Byzantine in its complexity, but during Tito's lifetime it mattered little because elections were stage-managed (and all candidates were screened) by a communist front organization called the Socialist Alliance of Working People of Yugoslavia (SSRNJ). Ultimately, local assemblies chose delegates to the Federal Chamber and provincial or republic-level assemblies chose delegates to the other chamber.

The basic unit of local government, the commune, had considerable administrative authority and some autonomy in matters not expressly delegated to the federal government, the constituent republics, or the autonomous provinces. Government at this level involved extensive citizen participation. One student of Yugoslav politics reported in 1977:

> The communes have become key local units that have several primary concerns. One of these is economic, including planning, investments, internal trade, and supervision over economic enterprises. Another concern is municipal services, such as water supply, sewers, streets, and public utilities. A third comprises the area of "social management," that is, citizen control over public utilities.[31]

Administration of municipal services and public utilities is certainly relevant to the quality of life, but such matters are trivial compared with the momentous issues that confront whole societies and nations. The Communist Party did not relinquish its right to address those issues.

The Party Vanguard Thus, despite the elaborate façade of federalism and democracy, political power remained a Communist Party monopoly to the end. Other political parties were banned, and dissent was kept to a minimum. Marxist-Leninist dogma pervaded the press, the arts, and propaganda. In the final analysis, Yugoslavia, though not in the Soviet sphere, was nevertheless a communist state not too different from the Soviet model.

Nearly a decade after Yugoslavia split with the Soviet Union, Milovan Djilas, Tito's former comrade in arms and perhaps the most famous inside critic of Soviet-style communism in the postwar period, published a book called *The New Class.* (Djilas was in prison at the time for expressing the ideas contained in the book.) "The greatest illusion," he wrote, "was that industrialization and collectivization in the USSR, and destruction of capitalist ownership, would result in a classless society." Instead, he argued, a "new class" emerged in place of the old one:

> The roots of the new class were implanted in a special party of the Bolshevik type. Lenin was right in his view that his party was an exception in the history of human society, although he did not suspect that it would be the beginning of a new class. . . .
> This is not to say that the new party and the new class are identical. The party, however, is the core of that class, and its base. . . . The new class may be said to be made up of those who have special privileges and economic preference because of the administrative monopoly they hold.[32]

Nonetheless, thanks to Tito, the Yugoslav Communist Party had a stronger bias toward collective leadership than its Soviet counterpart.

Thus, Tito balanced regional and ethnic interests in the top party organs much as he did in the collective presidency and the Federal Executive Council. This system may have ensured representation of the major parts of Yugoslavia's diverse multiethnic society, but it did not constitute a participatory democracy. Nor could such a façade resist, once the iron hand of Tito was gone, the centuries-old resentments of those various ethnic groups.

SUMMARY

Slavic Europe has developed along quite different lines from Western Europe. Powerful intellectual and cultural movements such as the Renaissance and Reformation never penetrated much of Eastern Europe; it remains a Slavic world. The history of the region bears scant evidence of fraternal ties among Slavic nations beyond ethnolinguistic similarities. On the contrary, outbreaks of ethnic conflict have been quite common except during the period of Soviet domination. The Soviet Union ruled most of the Slavic world for four decades after World War II; Russia, in turn, dominated the Soviet Union. All the nations of Eastern Europe have almost always been dominated by an imperial power — Russia, Germany, Austria-Hungary, the Ottoman Turks. In 1989, one Communist regime after another fell in a wave of popular discontent and brought an end to the period of Pax Sovietica — stability enforced by Soviet military might. In December 1991, the Soviet Union itself collapsed following an abortive coup by hardliners. In the next chapter, we turn our attention to the new political institutions now being put to the test in the former Soviet Union and Eastern Europe.

KEY TERMS

Pax Sovietica
Eastern Europe
Slavic Europe
Russification
Mensheviks
Bolsheviks
proletariat
February Revolution
October Revolution
soviets
war communism
New Economic Policy (NEP)
Stalinism
kulaki
autarky
collectivization
Marshall Plan
North Atlantic Treaty Organization (NATO)
Warsaw Pact
Brezhnev Doctrine
Secret Speech
de-Stalinization
virgin lands campaign
neo-Stalinism
détente
refuseniks
KGB
ideology
Marxism-Leninism
law of capitalist accumulation
surplus value
law of pauperization
alienation
dictatorship of the proletariat
vanguard of the proletariat
democratic centralism
blat
appeasement
workers' self-management
indicative planning

STUDY QUESTIONS

1. How did geography influence the Soviet Union's history, political traditions, economy, and political culture (its attitudes, beliefs, myths, prejudices, hopes, fears, and the like)?
2. What impact did the Cold War have on East-West relations in such areas as arms control, trade, investment, and conflict management?
3. What, if anything, is distinctive about the geography and cultures of Eastern Europe? How have these factors influenced the region's history? Has a sense of Slavic solidarity been present throughout the region in modern times, or is today's nationalism more particularistic?
4. What were the main tenets of Soviet ideology? How did both Lenin and Stalin bend Marx's ideas to fit the political circumstances that each faced?
5. What were the most significant developments in the Soviet Union after Stalin's death in 1953? What reforms are associated with Nikita Khrushchev? With Leonid Brezhnev?

SUGGESTED READINGS

Brent, Jonathan, and Naumov, Vladimir P. *Stalin's Last Crime: The Plot Against the Jewish Doctors, 1948–1953.* New York: HarperCollins, 2003.

Cohen, Philip J. *Serbia's Secret War: Propaganda and the Deceit of History.* College Station: Texas A&M University, 1996.

Dziewanowski, M. Kamil. *A History of Soviet Russia and Its Aftermath.* Englewood Cliffs, N.J.: Prentice-Hall, 1997.

Kabakov, Ilya. *The Man Who Never Threw Anything Away.* New York: Abrams, 1996.

Lafeber, Walter. *America, Russia and the Cold War, 1945–1996.* New York: McGraw-Hill, 1996.

Lees, Michael. *The Rape of Serbia: The British Role in Tito's Grab for Power.* San Diego: Harcourt Brace, 1990.

Leff, Carol. *The Czech and Slovak Republics.* Boulder, Colo. Westview, 1996.

Lieven, D. C. B. *Nicholas II.* New York: St. Martin's, 1966.

Lukes, Igor. *Czechoslovakia between Stalin and Hitler: The Diplomacy of Edward Benes in the 1930s.* New York: Oxford University Press, 1996.

Martin, Janet. *Medieval Russia, 980–1584.* New York: Cambridge University Press, 1996.

Mironov, Boris N. *A Social History of Imperial Russia, 1700–1917.* Boulder, Colo.: Westview, 1997.

Montefiore, Simon Sebag. *Stalin: The Court of the Red Tsar.* London: Weidenfeld and Nicholson, 2003.

Narodni Muzeum V Praze Staff. *A Thousand Years of Czech Culture: Riches from the National Museum in Prague.* Winston-Salem, N.C.: Old Salem, 1996.
Pipes, Richard. *Russia under the Old Regime.* New York: Viking Penguin, 1997.
Raleigh, Donald J., ed. *The Emperors and Empresses of Russia: Rediscovering the Romanovs.* Armonk, N.Y.: Sharpe, 1996.
Robson, Roy R. *Old Believers in Modern Russia.* DeKalb: Northern Illinois University Press, 1996.
Thurston, Robert W. *Life and Terror in Stalin's Russia, 1934–1941.* New Haven, Conn.: Yale University Press, 1996.

SUGGESTED WEB SITES

http://www.departments.bucknell.edu/russian/history.html
http://www.valley.net/~transnat/
http://www.utoronto.ca/serap/
http://news.bbc.co.uk/hi/english/static/map/yugoslavia/

NOTES

1. Quoted in Louis J. Halle, *The Cold War as History* (New York: HarperCollins, 1991), pp. 103–104.
2. Alexis de Tocqueville, *Democracy in America* (New York: Knopf, 1945), p. 452.
3. Vadim Medish, *The Soviet Union* (Englewood Cliffs, N.J.: Prentice-Hall, 1987), p. 23.
4. Nicholas Berdyaev, *The Origin of Russian Communism* (Ann Arbor: University of Michigan Press, 1960), p. 9.
5. Nicholas V. Riasanovsky, *A History of Russia,* 4th ed. (New York: Oxford University Press, 1977), p. 347.
6. Medish, *Soviet Union,* p. 22.
7. See, for example, Paul Kennedy, *The Rise and Fall of the Great Powers* (New York: Vintage Books, 1987), pp. 70–77.
8. Medish, *Soviet Union,* pp. 22–23.
9. Berdyaev, *Origin of Russian Communism,* pp. 8–9.
10. Riasanovsky, *History of Russia,* p. 425.
11. Ibid., p. 426.
12. Robert Conquest, *V. I. Lenin* (New York: Viking Penguin, 1972), p. 32.
13. Quoted in Isaac Deutscher, *Stalin: A Political Biography* (New York: Vintage Books, 1960), p. 550.
14. In the Stalinist tradition, five-year plans were documents that set forth general economic goals. These plans, drawn up at five-year intervals, provided the framework for the annual plans that prescribed detailed production targets (quotas) for each industrial and agricultural enterprise.

15. See, for example, Robert Conquest, *The Harvest of Sorrow: Soviet Collectivization and the Terror-Famine* (New York: Oxford University Press, 1987); and Adam B. Ulam, *Stalin* (Boston: Beacon, 1989).
16. See Edward Crankshaw, *Khrushchev: A Career* (New York: Viking Penguin, 1966).
17. Deutscher, *Stalin,* pp. 550–551.
18. Alexander Werth, *Russia at War, 1941–1945* (New York: Avon, 1964), pp. 904–906.
19. On the question of forced labor, one eyewitness estimates that at least a million Russian refugees were "perfidiously returned by Allied authorities into Soviet hands" in 1946 and 1947. The same writer records many other instances of mass arrests and banishment to the gulags during this period. See Alekandr Solzhenitsyn, *The Gulag Archipelago, 1918–1956* (New York: Harper & Row, 1973), p. 85.
20. Roy A. Medvedev and Zhores A. Medvedev, *Khrushchev: The Years in Power* (New York: Norton, 1978), p. 121.
21. See J. Philip Rogers, *The Future of European Security* (New York: St. Martin's, 1993).
22. Stanley Meisler, "For Kremlin Rulers, Lenin Is Only God," *Los Angeles Times,* October 25, 1987.
23. Hedrick Smith, *The Russians* (New York: Ballantine, 1984), p. 332.
24. Ibid.
25. See David K. Shipler, *Russia: Broken Idols, Solemn Dreams* (New York: Viking Penguin, 1983), p. 200.
26. Smith, *Russians,* pp. 410–411.
27. Ibid., p. 411.
28. Ivan Volgyes, *Politics in Eastern Europe* (Homewood, Ill.: Dorsey, 1986), pp. 29–30.
29. Paul Lendvai, *Eagles in Cobwebs: Nationalism and Communism in the Balkans* (Garden City, N.Y.: Anchor/Doubleday, 1969), p. 15.
30. Volgyes, *Politics in Eastern Europe,* p. 297.
31. Richard F. Starr, *Communist Regimes in Eastern Europe,* 5th ed. (Stanford, Calif.: Hoover Institution, 1988), p. 194.
32. Milovan Djilas, *The New Class* (New York: Praeger, 1957), pp. 37–40.

CHAPTER 6

Russia and Slavic Europe: New Order, Old Disorders

Many of the elements of both Leninism and Stalinism survived several post-Stalin reform campaigns and continued to influence political patterns and practices in the USSR and Eastern Europe even in the waning years of communist rule. After 1985, the policies and practices associated with Mikhail Gorbachev's "new thinking"—including ***glasnost*** (openness), ***perestroika*** (restructuring), and ***demokratizatsiia*** (political pluralism)—led first to the relaxation of police state controls on society and then, at the end of 1991, to the breakup of the Soviet Union. In the years that followed, Gorbachev's successor, Boris Yeltsin, led the attempt to create a democratic republic on Russian soil for the first time in history. In 2000, Vladimir Putin was elected to succeed Yeltsin as Russia's president: for the second time in Russian history leadership changed hands in a manner consistent with constitutional democracy. (Yeltsin's election to the Russian presidency in 1991 was the first.)

The tidal wave of popular uprisings that rolled across Eastern Europe in 1989 swept away communist regimes in Poland, Hungary, East Germany, Czechoslovakia, and Romania. (Communist governments in Bulgaria and Albania soon fell by the wayside as well.) In East-Central Europe, new leaders with popular mandates moved rapidly to democratize the political processes and reorient domestic and foreign policies. But the pace of change in Poland, Czechoslovakia, and Hungary was not matched in Russia, Ukraine, or the Balkans (Romania, Bulgaria, and Yugoslavia). In the former Soviet Union, the old order was replaced by a new disorder. As a consequence, the East-West conflict quickly faded from the vernacular of European politics, but the Slavic world rapidly divided into parts going in different directions at different speeds.

Chapter 5 demonstrated the distinctive religious, ethnic, and cultural experiences of the Slavic nations. Although the iron curtain has fallen away, the lingering effects of Stalinist rule remain. Europe today is not a single region any more than it is a single nation. The most important division is still the jagged line that separates the West from the rest of Europe. Many of the problems facing the former communist states of Europe are the product of rigid economic policies that stifled all initiative for more than four decades. The new political systems cannot be implemented overnight, nor can ruined economies be easily restored, but hopeful signs of an economic revival have appeared from Lithuania in the north to Slovenia in the south. In Poland, the Czech Republic, and Slovakia, the winds of change have brought in foreign investment — the vital seeds of growth for emerging markets. But in other countries such as Serbia, Romania, and Ukraine the fruits of reform (like the reforms themselves) are slow to materialize or nonexistent.

Transition or Regression?

Economically, Slavic Europe has lagged far behind Western Europe throughout modern history. In recent times, however, the gap has become a chasm. Indeed, in the mid-1990s, the German economy alone dwarfed the combined gross domestic product of the entire Slavic world. (See Tables 6.1 and 6.2.)

Table 6.1 Eastern Europe's Economic Profile in the 1990s

Country	Gross National Product, 1998 (millions of U.S. dollars)	Real per Capita Growth Rate, 1990–1998 (percent)	GNP per Capita, 1998 (U.S. dollars)	GNP per Capita (PPP*)	GNP per Capita Growth Rate, 1985–1993 (percent)
Russia	331,776	−7.2	2,260	6,180	−5.0
Ukraine	49,207	−11.4	980	3,130	−3.9
Belarus	22,332	4.0	2,840	6,360	−0.2
Moldova	1,652	−8.3	380	1,995	−5.4
Poland	78,938	1.5	1,050	3,725	−1.8
Czech Republic	53,034	−0.2	5,150	12,197	−2.0
Slovakia	19,941	1.1	3,700	9,624	−2.6
Hungary†	45,660	0.9	4,510	9,832	0.0
Romania†	30,596	−0.6	1,360	5,572	−6.5
Bulgaria	10,085	−1.8	1,220	4,683	−2.8
Yugoslavia‡	—	—	—	—	—
Slovenia	19,385	4.4	9,780	14,400	—
Croatia†	20,786	0.5	4,620	6,698	—
Germany	**2,179,802**	**0.9**	**26,570**	**22,026**	**2.2**

*Purchasing power parity: denotes the equivalent goods and services that the dollar amount in the previous column would purchase in the relevant country.

†Not a Slavic country, but located in the predominantly Slavic region of Europe.

‡Mainly Serbia; except for Macedonia, all major parts of the former Yugoslavia — including Croatia, Slovenia, and Bosnia-Herzegovina — have broken away. The 1993 GNP figures for Yugoslavia in columns one and three are taken from the *World Almanac 1996.* Bosnia is not included in this table; statistics are not available because of the civil war that raged for several years in the 1990s.

Source: International Bank for Reconstruction and Development, *The World Bank Atlas* (Washington, D.C.: Author, December 2000).

Table 6.2 Population Dynamics: Slavic Europe

Country	Population, 1998 (thousands)	Growth Rate, 1990–1998 (percent)	Life Expectancy, 1998	Infant Mortality Rate, 1998 (per 1,000 live births)
Russia	146,909	−0.1	67	17
Ukraine	50,295	−0.4	67	14
Belarus	10,239	0.0	67	28
Moldova	4,298	−0.2	68	23
Poland	38,666	0.2	73	10
Czech Republic	10,323	0.0	72	10
Slovakia	5,391	0.3	73	9
Hungary*	10,114	−0.4	71	10
Romania*	22,761	−0.4	69	21
Bulgaria	8,257	−0.8	71	14
Yugoslavia	10,616	0.1	72	13
Slovenia	1,982	−0.1	75	5
Croatia*	4,501	−0.9	73	8
Bosnia*	3,768	−2.4	73	13

*Not a Slavic country but located in the predominantly Slavic region of Europe.

Source: International Bank for Reconstruction and Development, *The World Bank Atlas* (Washington, D.C.: Author, December 2000).

The impediments were the Stalinist system of central planning, a domestic climate generally inhospitable to technological innovation and foreign investment, and a lingering Cold War rivalry that barred Soviet-bloc countries from full participation in the global economy. After 1989, the leaders of Poland, Hungary, and Czechoslovakia moved quickly to replace the police state organs that underpinned communist rule for four decades. The movement toward a free-market economy was now unhampered by ideological strictures or the threat of Soviet intervention. In Poland, the government boldly adopted a strategy called **shock therapy** — austerity measures (budget cuts, wage restraints, and reduced state subsidies), an end to price controls, and rapid privatization of the economy. In Czechoslovakia, an alternative strategy aimed at a less jarring — but no less complete — transition to a free market.

In the Balkans, however, the pace of change was much slower and the ghost of totalitarianism lingered longer. Any hope of a peaceful evolution toward a new order was shattered by the bloody civil war in Yugoslavia, where tens of thousands of people were killed, and millions more were left homeless. The war, which was sparked by ethnic hatred in Bosnia-Herzegovina, gave rise to a kind of déjà vu in the West.* No sooner was the "dirty war" in Bosnia brought to a bitter end than another one broke out in Kosovo, a province of Serbia inhabited mainly by ethnic Albanians. Elsewhere in the Balkans, Romania sank deeper into a political and economic morass, while Bulgaria engaged in cautious reforms and withdrew into an isolationist shell.

*Recall that World War I was triggered by the assassination of Archduke Ferdinand of Austria at Sarajevo, the capital of Bosnia, by a Bosnian-Serb nationalist in June 1914.

The danger that instability in one country would spill over into neighboring countries, possibly causing cross-border conflicts, could not be discounted. Massive population movements — refugees, asylum seekers, and immigrants in search of jobs — were (and are) a major concern for neighboring states, one that is not confined, however, to Eastern Europe. A rich region is a natural magnet for the poor and downtrodden of poor regions. (This age-old phenomenon explains how the American "Wild West" was populated.) During the Cold War, the Soviet Union kept the populations of Eastern Europe (often called "captive nations") from migrating to the West — precisely the reason why the Soviet Union and East Germany built the Berlin Wall in 1961.

There were many ironies in Europe's new international order in the 1990s. For centuries, the Balkan nations wanted to get the Great Powers (later the two superpowers) out. In the past, these nations had important strategic interests in southern Europe, but times were changing. In the early 1990s, outsiders (especially the United States, the European Community, and Russia), interested mainly in stability, were reluctant to intervene in Yugoslavia's civil war even after reports of atrocities and human rights violations (especially by the Serbs) in Bosnia-Herzegovina were reported in the press and condemned by the United Nations.

The Western powers were particularly anxious not to do anything that might provoke the Russians into intervening on the side of the Serbs (as they did in World War I). As long as Yeltsin — who has a history of illness, including alcoholism and heart disease — remained in power, that was highly unlikely. But in the chaos and uncertainty enveloping Russia, one danger was that Russian generals would join forces with extreme nationalists (including neocommunists) and take action with or without Yeltsin's approval. It was alarmist perhaps, but the great powers (Austria, Germany, and Russia) had a hand in creating the Balkan tinderbox that sparked World War I. Who could say for certain that history was not repeating itself?

Clearly, democracy has not been a panacea for Slavic Europe. In fact, it brought to the surface ethnic tensions forcibly suppressed during more than four decades of communist rule after World War II. In the process, it opened a Pandora's box in economically distressed societies, thus creating the danger that demagogues parading as patriots and populists would seek to ride to power on a rising crest of nationalism, fed by public fear, anger, and despair.

The turmoil resulting from the collapse of the Soviet empire occasioned a great debate in the West. According to one theory, stability in Eastern Europe and the Balkans, as well as in the former Soviet Union itself, was purely a function of Moscow's hegemony (dominance) in the region. When Mikhail Gorbachev pulled the props from under the structures that his predecessors had built (the Warsaw Pact, Comecon), the whole thing collapsed like a house of cards. Subscribers to this theory tend to be pessimistic about the long-term prospects for peace in the region.

The consequences of the Soviet withdrawal are obvious, but cause and effect are much more difficult to establish. For example, Yugoslavia was never under Soviet domination and might well have disintegrated even if the Cold War had not ended. Nor is it a foregone conclusion that the conflict there will spill over. Significantly, Czechoslovakia went through a bloodless breakup very different from Yugoslavia's violent one. Moreover, the Slavic nations are not alone in fighting wars with neighboring states — witness the innumerable conflicts in Western Europe following the emergence of the nation-state

Table 6.3 Elections and Parties: The Early Winnowing Effect

Country	Election Date	Number of Parties in Election	Number of Parties in the Parliament
Bulgaria	October 13, 1991	37	5
Czech Republic	June 5, 1992	21	6
Hungary	March 26, 1990	45	7
Poland	October 27, 1991	67	29
Romania	September 27, 1992	7	7*
Slovakia	June 5, 1992	5	5

*Excludes thirteen seats for national minorities.

system in the sixteenth century. And it is quite possible that a stable order will emerge in Slavic Europe after all. With the partial exception of Poland, the winnowing effect of elections quickly narrowed the number of viable political parties in the early 1990s, thus reducing the danger of parliamentary fragmentation and governmental paralysis. (See Table 6.3.) Given the long period of enforced conformity they have just gone through, it is not surprising that the former socialist countries are having some difficulty containing pent-up collective emotions, coping with newfound liberties, and reaching consensus on the best solutions to the problems that are the legacy of communist rule.

The Legacy of Soviet Communism

From World War II until the watershed events of 1989, Moscow sought to impose the Soviet model of "scientific socialism" on its client states in Eastern Europe. That model shaped the region's approach to politics, government, and economy for nearly half a century (longer in Russia and its empire). To understand politics in contemporary Russia, therefore, it is essential first to get a sense of how Russia was ruled under communism. As you read what follows, try to imagine how living in such an oppressive society would affect you personally. How might it change your values, work habits, and relationships with family and friends? If you were deprived of the freedom Westerners take for granted would you be more idealistic, trusting, and ambitious, or less? What would be the cumulative effect on society as a whole? Would it pay to be honest, trustworthy, and hardworking, or would deceit and sloth be more rational? Questions of this kind are crucial to an analysis of what's wrong with Russia today, why the Russian economy has fallen into a deep slump, and why "democracy" gets mixed reviews (at best) from most Russians now.

The Soviet System: A Bird's-Eye (Re)View

The Soviet constitution proclaimed the Communist Party-Soviet Union (CPSU) the "leading and guiding force of Soviet society and the nucleus of its political system." As previously noted, the party operated according to the Leninist principle of "democratic

Table 6.4 Soviet Leaders, from Lenin to Gorbachev

Leader	Years in Power
V. I. Lenin*	1917–1924
Josef Stalin*	1922–1953
Nikita S. Khrushchev	1953–1964
Leonid I. Brezhnev	1964–1982
Yuri V. Andropov	1982–1984
Konstantin U. Chernenko	1984–1985
Mikhail S. Gorbachev†	1985–1991

*As chairman of the Council of People's Commissars, Lenin was the de facto head of the party and the government: although Stalin was named general secretary of the party in 1922, he was unable to assert unquestioned control over the party until after Lenin's death in 1924.

†In 1989, the office of chairman of the presidium of the Supreme Soviet was strengthened and renamed "chairman of the Supreme Soviet." Gorbachev was elected to this new office and served until the Congress of People's Deputies created the executive presidency in March 1990. The office of chairman of the Supreme Soviet remained, but its executive and ceremonial functions were transferred to the executive presidency.

Note: All top Soviet leaders, whatever specific title(s) they may have preferred or position(s) they may have held, presided over the Politburo.

centralism" (an oxymoron if ever there was one). The preamble to the party rules unequivocally stated, "monolithic cohesion" and "a high degree of conscious discipline on the part of all Communists are an inviolable law of the CPSU."[1]

Since 1918 the CPSU had been the sole repository of legitimate authority in the Soviet Union and throughout Slavic Europe. For seven decades after the October Revolution of 1917, the party was an all-pervasive presence in Soviet society. Its tentacles reached deeply into four key structures: the state bureaucracy, the secret police (KGB), the economy (a kind of giant corporation), and the military.

The party's leading role was rooted in Leninist ideology, which stressed the need for a "vanguard of the proletariat." Karl Marx used the word *proletariat* to designate the oppressed working class, which, he theorized, would eventually seize power in a revolutionary takeover. Lenin asserted that strong leadership — in the form of the Communist Party — was necessary to galvanize the masses into revolutionary action. These two seminal ideas — that revolution is the path to working-class power and that the Communist Party is the necessary catalyst — are basic tenets of Marxism-Leninism. No Soviet leader before Gorbachev had dared (or cared) to renounce them. (See Table 6.4.)

Soviet "Democracy" and Potemkin's Ghost

As students of Russian history know, any mention of a "Potemkin village" refers to something that appears to be true or real but in fact is only an illusion. Grigory Potemkin (1739–1791) was the favorite minister of Catherine the Great, who, according to a celebrated legend, contrived to please and impress the all-powerful czarina by showing her a supposedly typical village in the country. But the "village" was a ruse: it consisted of false fronts and a cast of characters in costumes playing well-rehearsed roles — like a Hollywood set. The story of Potemkin's trickery may or may not be true, but it has become part of Russia's rich folklore, and it accurately depicts what Soviet "democracy" was (and was not) all about.

On its face, the Soviet government looked much like Western democracies. All citizens at least eighteen years of age were eligible to vote; election to local and regional soviets (or councils) were held every two years, and elections were held every four years for the **Supreme Soviet** (national legislature). The latter functioned like a parliament; its 1,500 members were elected to two chambers of equal size, the Soviet of Nationalities and the Soviet of the Union. The Supreme Soviet chose the **Council of Ministers,** which implemented the laws it passed. The same pattern was replicated on lower levels all the way down to the local soviets.

Elections to the Supreme Soviet and thousands of soviets at the republic, provincial, and local levels were held with much fanfare. Everyone was required by law to vote; the government claimed that 99.99 percent of all eligible voters cast ballots in national elections. (According to official figures, one election in the Turkmen SSR was almost perfect: only one voter out of 1.5 million failed to vote!)

But real power resided elsewhere. The Communist Party (CPSU) monopolized control of all key positions in the state bureaucracy, secret police (KGB), and military. This control was exercised through an interlocking directorate made up of two bodies — the **Politburo** and the **Secretariat.** The term *interlocking* is apt here because the same individuals were often members of both groups. The Politburo (or "political bureau") and the Secretariat (comprising party chieftains called "secretaries") were actually twin organs of the Communist Party and, in theory, were not part of the "government" at all. The General Secretary was the most powerful figure in the government (although a premier who presided over the Council of Ministers was the formal head of government and a president "elected" by the Supreme Soviet was the head of state). In practice, a dozen or so party bosses ruled the country. Even the party's own "legislative" body, known as the **Central Committee,** existed largely to rubber-stamp the Politburo's decisions. Thus, the Soviet regime was an oligarchic dictatorship disguised as a democracy.

Gorbachev's "Democratization" Campaign

Any type of reform is risky in a country accustomed to repressive rule. Pushing for political change threatens the power and privilege of the ruling class and risks opening the floodgates of popular unrest. By 1990, Mikhail Gorbachev's democratization campaign had gone past the point of no return. Although he certainly never intended to dismantle the whole system, Gorbachev did take dramatic steps to reconstitute the Soviet parliament and to allow the first meaningful elections in Soviet history, at the same time breaking the Communist Party's monopoly and relaxing press censorship.

Gorbachev had apparently decided that a greater measure of popular participation was the price the party had to pay to get the country out of its economic doldrums and lure trade, aid, and investment from the West. His reforms involved converting the Supreme Soviet into an unwieldy new **Congress of People's Deputies,** which elected a smaller, full-time parliament and a president. The president would assume the power previously exercised by the Communist Party leader. (Gorbachev already held both positions.)

The government delivered on its promise to hold multicandidate elections in 1989 and 1990. An open process of nominating candidates sparked an enthusiastic popular response. Meetings, at times, were raucous. Although the Communists won a majority of the seats (as expected), many independents also won and some highly placed Communist officials were, in fact, defeated. Moreover, such outspoken opposition figures as Andrei Sakharov and Boris Yeltsin (who had been removed as Moscow party chief for criticizing Gorbachev) were elected handily. Yeltsin, running as an at-large candidate for all of Moscow, won by a landslide. The popular election was followed by a second vote within the Congress to choose members of the smaller Supreme Soviet. When Yeltsin was not elected to this body, such a hue and cry arose from an awakened citizenry that he was quietly given a seat.

For the first time ever, the new Soviet parliament gave voice to an opposition with an agenda of its own, including a demand to end the Communist Party's monopoly on power. (Article 6 of the constitution guaranteed the Communist Party's "leading and guiding" role in Soviet society.) Under mounting pressure from parliament, public opinion, and Western governments, Gorbachev finally renounced this icon of Soviet rule at a historic meeting of the Central Committee in early 1990, foreshadowing the collapse of Soviet power the following year.

Precisely what Gorbachev meant by "democratization" was always a mystery. He made it clear from the outset that Western-style democracy was not what he had in mind, denouncing attempts to "use democratic rights for undemocratic purposes." As examples, he mentioned efforts aimed at "redrawing boundaries" or "setting up opposition parties."[2]

It is difficult to say whether Gorbachev moved too fast or too slow, whether he willed the complete demise of the Stalinist system or was swept along by swift political currents he could not control. Clearly, he vacillated between accelerating the pace of reform and applying the brakes. His failure to define his terms and detail his policies was perhaps a case of calculated ambiguity. If so, the strategy failed miserably.

The main problem, however, was not political, but economic. The model of **central planning** that Stalin had brutally imposed first on the Soviet Union and, after World War II, on Eastern Europe did not work. As a consequence, the communist states were falling further and further behind the capitalist states — the exact opposite of what Marx had predicted. The failure of this prophecy also discredited the prophet.

Stalin's Legacy: Dysfunctional Economies

In the closing decades of the twentieth century, the rulers of Slavic Europe's communist countries — joined in a kind of East bloc "common market" called Comecon — had to ask whether state planning was appropriate for industrially developed socialist nations. The specter of a stagnant workers' state had haunted the Soviet Union and its Warsaw Pact allies at least since the early 1960s. As noted in Chapter 5, Nikita Khrushchev launched a series of ill-starred reforms in industry and agriculture (as well as a radical reorganization of the party-state machinery) before he was ousted in 1964. Later in the decade, Hungary experimented with market-style reforms, and Czechoslovakia tried to introduce multiparty democracy. In the Soviet Union, Premier Alexei Kosygin tried to restart the stalled reform effort. In so doing, he was guided by the theoretical writings of Soviet economist Evsei Liberman.

The **Liberman reforms** were designed to decentralize economic decision making. Managers were to be given considerable discretion in making microeconomic production and investment decisions. Enterprises were even to be charged interest on the capital they used. Given more latitude, "managers were expected to take risks, innovate, reduce costs, and thereby increase the sales and profits of their enterprises."[3]

Had Libermanism triumphed, Soviet managers would have had to operate much as Western entrepreneurs do. But the entrenched party-state bureaucracy, at whose expense the reforms would have come, quickly aborted the embryonic reform movement. In retrospect, the failure of the reforms in the 1960s sealed the fate of the Soviet Union and its satellites in Eastern Europe.

Marxism versus the Marketplace According to the Soviet constitution, the nation's economy was "based on the Socialist ownership of all the means of production," including the land. Two forms of socialist ownership were recognized in the USSR: state ownership and collective, or cooperative, ownership. The former was considered a higher form because it encompassed the entire society, whereas the latter was a lower form because it was limited to relatively few people. This distinction was clearly evident in agriculture, which was divided into *collective farms (kolkhozy)* and state farms *(sovkhozy)*. The farmers themselves technically owned the collective farms, whereas state farms were owned by society at large and were run by the government, which gave them preferential treatment (more funds, better equipment). State farms were huge, averaging well over 90,000 acres — five or six times the size of the average collective farm. They were operated like an assembly line in an industrial enterprise and were managed by professionals trained in such fields as agronomy, animal husbandry, and horticulture. State farmers, like industrial workers, were specialized by function and paid an hourly wage. In effect, the Soviet government sought to industrialize agriculture.

The state also owned all industrial enterprises, public utilities, banks, transportation systems, and mass-communication facilities, as well as most retail outlets and repair shops. As a result, nearly everybody (approximately 85 percent of the workforce) worked for the state. Those who did not work for the state belonged to cooperatives or collectives, which, though not state-owned, were tightly controlled by the state.

This employment monopoly gave the state enormous control over the individual. Furthermore, a so-called antiparasite law made it a crime not to work. If you were fired for any reason (including unauthorized political activity), where could you go to find another job? The employer who dismissed you from one job could bar you from another and at the same time put you on the wrong side of the law — a kind of double jeopardy that very effectively kept Soviet workers in line.

The Concept of Central Planning The idea of central planning is simple enough: decide what society needs, put the people to work, and distribute material benefits fairly. Nobody owns anything but transportable personal possessions — for example, clothing, furniture, and books. (It was possible to own a car in the Soviet Union, but most people either could not afford one or were put on a waiting list for years.)

Prices are set by the state; they do not fluctuate in response to the market forces of supply and demand, as under capitalism. The Soviet economy — the largest ever to adopt this system — was thus planned and managed from the top, whereas a market economy is driven from the bottom, by consumers.

The State Planning Committee — or **Gosplan** — had primary responsibility for charting the course of the Soviet economy but had to coordinate its work with a number of other bureaucratic entities, including the State Committee on Prices, the State Bank (Gosbank), the Ministry of Finance, the State Committee on Material and Technical Supplies (Gossnab), and nearly fifty central ministries (as well as 750 in the fifteen union republics) that ran the various industries.

The complicated planning process involved both long-range (five-year) and short-range (one-year) plans. These plans set production growth targets for the various sectors of the economy, which were then translated into **output quotas** for individual enterprises. The short-range plan contained the growth targets for the whole economy for the current year. The various ministries then broke down this general blueprint into monthly plans with quotas for every factory, plant, enterprise, and association in the Soviet Union. (If you think this process sounds complicated and cumbersome, you are quite right.) The plans always reflected the political priorities of the top leadership in the interlocking directorates of the Politburo, the Secretariat, and the Council of Ministers. Unlike market-based economies, what they did *not* reflect was popular priorities and consumer preferences.

Such detailed economic planning would be daunting under any circumstances. To keep factories humming and assembly lines moving, it was necessary to determine in advance how many parts, in what exact sizes, would be needed to turn out the quota of, say, tractors at a given plant; how many train cars, trucks, or barges would be needed to deliver the right quantities of iron and steel and other components on schedule; how much energy would be needed to run the plant during different times of the year; and on and on. Innumerable calculations were made for every single item manufactured or processed.

Under the Stalinist system of economic management, the state planning mechanism made millions of supply-and-demand calculations each year and set prices on hundreds of thousands of industrial and consumer items.[4] Obviously, if material allocations were miscalculated or if suppliers' and producers' timetables were not synchronized or if a key transportation pipeline got disrupted or clogged, the system would break down. Indeed, bottlenecks were one of several generic problems that plagued Soviet central planning. Rare attempts to more directly link producers, suppliers, and consumers failed miserably.

Problems of Planning The absence of market mechanisms was at the root of many, if not most, Soviet economic problems. Take performance indicators as an example. Output quotas (rather than the profits that drive capitalism) were used to measure success in the Soviet economy. Every factory was expected to fulfill its quota every month. If a factory overfulfilled its quota for the year, its workers and managers were rewarded with pay bonuses. Underfulfillment blocked promotions for plant managers and dashed workers' hopes for a year-end windfall. Thus the primary objective of every plant manager was not to improve efficiency but rather to overfulfill the quotas by a small margin (overfulfilling by large margins would lead to higher quotas the next year, thus creating new pressures).

Plan fulfillment became an all-consuming end. To achieve it, plant managers typically hoarded supplies and deliberately inflated labor requirements to provide a cushion in case vital materials were not delivered on time or it should become necessary to speed up production to meet the monthly quota. These widespread practices caused planning distortions and supply bottlenecks.

Moreover, as performance indicators, quotas themselves were problematic. Imagine that a factory produced nails. Nails of all sizes, weights, and types were needed, but there was always a dilemma: if the quota was based on gross weight, the manager had an incentive to produce big, heavy nails rather than small, lightweight ones; but if the quota was based on quantity, the manager would produce lots of little nails.

Another economic fact of life in the USSR was low labor productivity, resulting mostly from the paucity of incentives. Workers were all paid about the same, no matter how much or how little they produced. Everyone was guaranteed a job, and rarely was anyone fired (except for political reasons). In short, the system did little to encourage efficiency.

The collapse of communism was primarily the result of economic failure. Stalin imposed this inefficient system on all the satellite states of Slavic Europe after World War II. Many of the problems these countries face today are rooted in the economic deformities caused by central planning.

The Gorbachev Reforms

Gorbachev inherited an economy that had been declining steadily for at least two decades. (See Table 6.5.) By the mid-1980s, Soviet economic growth had fallen to less than 2 percent a year, about half what it had been a decade earlier. One out of every nine industrial enterprises and nearly a third of the farms were losing money, and such essentials as food, housing, medical treatment, and transportation were being heavily subsidized by the state (indeed, these subsidies, it is now clear, had become a crushing burden). The irony of this situation is glaring: Soviet propagandists had long boasted that central planning, the heart and soul of "scientific socialism," would solve the problems of "boom and bust" economic cycles, which plagued (and ultimately doomed)

Table 6.5 The Shrinking Soviet Economy, 1961–1985 (average annual growth in net material product, percent)

Years	1961–1965	1966–1970	1971–1975	1976–1980	1981–1985
Official statistics	6.5	7.8	5.7	4.3	3.2
CIA* (GNP)	4.8	4.9	3.0	1.9	1.8

*U.S. Central Intelligence Agency.
Source: Anders Aslund, *Gorbachev's Struggle for Economic Reform* (Ithaca:, N.Y.: Cornell University Press, 1991), p. 17.

capitalism. Indeed, a blustering Nikita Khrushchev, the same Soviet "boss" who earlier denounced the crimes of Stalin, warned the West that "we will bury you" in the late 1950s. But when Gorbachev walked in Khrushchev's footsteps thirty years later it was exactly the other way around.

The Soviet Economy before the Crash In the waning years of Soviet rule, annual increments in food production barely kept pace with population growth, and despite heavy investment in agriculture, the Soviet Union continued to spend billions of rubles to import meat and grain. Even so, the supply of meat and butter was so far short of demand nearly three years after Gorbachev's rise to power that severe rationing of both remained in force in many provincial cities.[5]

Investment priorities in agriculture, ironically, reflected terrible planning. Farm-to-market roads and facilities for storage, processing, packaging, and retailing were woefully neglected. Nearly one-third of Soviet farm output (including a quantity of grain equal to what the government was buying on the world market) spoiled or was eaten by rodents. In 1987, for example, well over half of the entire potato crop rotted in the fields when heavy rains disrupted the harvest (potatoes and bread are the two most important staples in the Russian diet).

General living standards were abysmal compared with those in the industrial democracies of the West. Housing was always in short supply. In the cities, many lived in communal apartments, sharing bathrooms and kitchens with other families.

A growing technology gap with the West accentuated the Soviet economy's downslide. The gap widened in the 1970s and 1980s as the computer revolution, like the Renaissance and the Reformation centuries earlier, eluded the East and energized the West. The consequence, in Gorbachev's own words, was to create "pre-crisis conditions" that forced the USSR to change the way it worked in order to ward off decline and decay. Soviet economists conceded shortly before dissolution of the USSR that "no more than about 10 percent of the country's industrial production measures up to world standards of quality and technological advancement."[6]

Perestroika: *Deconstructing the Soviet Economy* The conventional wisdom within the Soviet bloc long held that Moscow was the model for the other socialist countries, but with the advent of Gorbachev's "new thinking," the Soviet Union showed a willingness to learn from the experience of other socialist states, especially Yugoslavia, Hungary, and the People's Republic of China (PRC). Gorbachev's dilemma was acute: how to reconstruct the economy without first destroying it.

At a Communist Party meeting in early 1986, Gorbachev endorsed a radical restructuring *(perestroika)* of the Soviet economy. Later in the year, the official gazette of the Supreme Soviet published a list of thirty-eight measures to be implemented before the end of 1990; the new laws' concerns ranged from voting and plebiscites to economic incentives, pricing, the press, governmental reorganization, and the activities of the KGB. In November, the Supreme Soviet approved a law allowing citizens to moonlight for extra cash (many had been doing so illegally for decades).

The moonlighting law, which took effect in the spring of 1987, was the first to ease the ban on private enterprise since Lenin's short-lived New Economic Policy in 1921.

Any Soviet citizen could now ask local authorities for permission to start what would amount to a small business. However, the Kremlin warned that it was not sanctioning "free-enterprise activities." Its ostensible aim was to tap the energies of Soviet citizens who were not in the workforce, including housewives, pensioners, invalids, and students.

This new attitude toward private initiative was in truth an attempt to alleviate the woeful lack of services in the Soviet Union. Moreover, it represented a first tentative step toward recognition of individuals' economic rights by a regime long hostile to the idea of private property. But jealousy proved to be a problem, for many Russians resent entrepreneurs who make a lot of money. In this and other ways, the political culture spawned by Marxist-Leninist ideology and a cradle-to-the-grave system of social welfare impeded efforts at economic reform.

The 1987 Law on Soviet Enterprise provided the legal framework for *perestroika* by mandating major changes in the management of state-owned enterprises. The changes were aimed at simulating market conditions without actually creating a free market. In 1988, another new law permitted individuals to produce and sell consumer goods for a profit at free-market prices. By the end of 1988, thousands of new businesses were operating. Although these new cooperatives typically produced consumer goods of better quality than those made by state-run enterprises, shoppers complained that the prices were prohibitively high. The cooperatives in turn complained that the government policies (including high taxes) made it impossible to lower prices.

Gorbachev promised to decentralize the Soviet economy further by changing the regulations governing external trade. Many industrial enterprises and even some governmental departments were empowered to make deals with foreign firms. (Previously, all international commerce was conducted through a state monopoly.) Moreover, these enterprises and departments were to be allowed to retain some of their profits.

In the end, Gorbachev's halting economic reforms failed miserably. *Perestroika* turned out to be a series of halfway measures that had the effect of disrupting the centrally planned economy without laying the foundations for a true market economy. In short, the economy was in limbo and Gorbachev was to blame.

Worse, the Soviet economy showed no signs of reviving. During the first half of 1989, for example, productivity rose less than 3 percent, according to official Soviet figures. Against a backdrop of unprecedented inflation and all-too-familiar empty shelves, Soviet consumers complained bitterly that the shortages were worse than at any time since World War II, despite a looming foreign-trade deficit that threatened to bankrupt the state.

Glasnost: *Building a Civic Culture* *Perestroika* was overshadowed in the late 1980s by *glasnost* ("openness") and democratization, which eased the political controls that were the hallmark of Communist Party rule. Even before the landmark political reforms of 1989–1990, Gorbachev had allowed greater public candor. This new freedom of expression was an integral part of Gorbachev's strategy for economic revitalization, but it carried considerable risks.

Gorbachev declared that "to unleash the latent human potential necessary to make national restructuring a success, each citizen must undergo a personal *perestroika*."[7] That would necessitate a fundamental change in the social psychology of a nation unaccustomed to personal freedom or individual initiative, encumbered by a discredited ideology, and inhibited by centuries of political and religious oppression. There was a "cultural fear of spontaneity here dating back to the czars, a tendency to see Western-style individual freedom as the first, inevitable step toward anarchy."[8] Breaking this pattern without breaking up the political system was the challenge. Far from abandoning the system, Gorbachev hoped to breathe new life into it.

Glasnost was thus a kind of grand experiment in behavioral engineering. Soviet society became a giant laboratory for testing new forms of cultural expression and political activity. Writers and books long banished were "rehabilitated." Many films and documentaries that had been blocked by censors for decades were cleared for Soviet audiences in 1987 and 1988. Even previously banned American films began appearing in Soviet movie theaters.[9]

The Soviet press also enjoyed a new openness, publishing articles on such previously taboo subjects as prostitution, drug abuse, homosexuality, and even the misuse of psychiatry to punish dissidents. Embarrassing statistics about infant mortality and life expectancy, withheld for years by Soviet authorities, were again made available. Negative news — crime statistics, industrial accidents, traffic mishaps, and official corruption — began to transfigure the Soviet mass media: the old formula combining Pollyanna and propaganda gave way to accuracy, honesty, and realism.

Reform this . . . Westerners tend to assume that people everywhere want democracy. The reality is not so simple. In fact, Russians have good reason to be skeptical of government, pessimistic about progress, wary of reforms, and indifferent to democracy. Russians' fear of anarchy often overshadows any yearning for democracy.[10] Russians "repeatedly remind a foreigner" that Russian history

> is replete with illustrations that authority cannot be eroded only a little but is swept away completely when weakened and overwhelmed. . . . And in the milieu of Russia's upheaval and chaos, revolutions have been made.[11]

There are also pragmatic reasons why people were cynical about reforms. Reformers in the Soviet Union had always failed. Furthermore, the surface changes associated with *glasnost* "failed to bring any substantial change in the everyday life of people or the functioning of the system."[12] On the contrary, the first effects of *perestroika* were to bring a cut in pay for many workers, price increases for food and other state-subsidized essentials, and the disturbing possibility of unemployment. Suddenly the great advantage of state-centered socialism — security — gave way to a new and nagging sense of precariousness. This problem persists right down to the present and has, if anything, worsened with the passage of time.

To succeed in revitalizing the Soviet economy, Gorbachev had to revitalize Soviet society; to succeed in revitalizing society, he had to overcome widespread fear that radical reforms would only mean longer food lines and emptier shelves. Gorbachev's successors faced the same challenge. In sum, democratization paradoxically deepened popular cynicism in Russia due to (1) a moribund economy; (2) pervasive corruption in both government and business; (3) collusion between the two; and (4) the rise of a new class of Russian robber barons and "mafia" (organized crime) bosses.

Why Gorbachev Failed

As the architect of the reforms that vanquished Stalinist rule, dissolved the Soviet empire, ended the Cold War, and ushered in a new era, Gorbachev's place in world history is secure. But his place in *Russian* history is a different story. Many Russians still blame Gorbachev for the country's current problems. Very few express any sympathy for what he tried to do. What he actually did, as they see it, was to destroy the old order, which, for all its flaws, was better than the new one. But Russians (understandably) tend to see things from a personal rather than a systemic perspective. Looking at the big picture, Gorbachev inherited an arthritic and debilitated economy, as we have already seen.

Stalinist central planning had the great advantage of giving the state total control over the economy. As a result, the command economies of the Soviet bloc generally experienced very low inflation. (See Table 6.6.) Only in the 1980s did this begin to change significantly in certain countries; until the late 1980s, price stability was a given in the Soviet Union, East Germany, Czechoslovakia, and Romania.

However, as we have already seen, the advantages of central planning were offset by even bigger disadvantages. For example, growth rates slowed perceptibly between 1951 and 1988, not only in the Soviet Union but also in the other member states of **Comecon** (the name of the Soviet-inspired trading organization in Eastern Europe). (See Table 6.7.) This downward trend in the face of dynamic market economies in Western Europe, Asia, and North America forced Gorbachev's hand. In a real sense, then, in embracing economic reforms he was simply making a virtue of necessity.

In addition, Gorbachev faced formidable opposition, not least from within his own party and the government he headed. Take the mammoth Soviet state bureaucracy, for example. At the upper echelons, bureaucrats constituted a privileged elite under Stalinism. Of course, they had little to gain and much to lose under the Gorbachev reforms. As part of the planned restructuring, half of these functionaries would be fired, as ministries consolidated and streamlined. Party bureaucrats also felt threatened. The party's

Table 6.6 Comecon Inflation Rates, 1970–1990 (percent)

Country	1970	1975	1980	1985	1990
Soviet Union	0.0	0.1	0.1	1.0	10.0
Bulgaria	–0.4	0.3	14.0	1.7	64.0
Czechoslovakia	1.7	0.7	2.9	2.3	10.0
East Germany	–0.3	0.2	0.5	0.0	–3.0
Hungary	1.3	3.8	9.3	7.0	28.3
Poland	1.2	2.3	9.4	15.1	584.7
Romania	0.4	0.2	1.5	–0.4	4.7

Sources: Domenico Mario Nuti, "Perestroika," *Economic Policy* 3 (October 1988), p. 369; Vienna Institute for Comparative Economic Studies, ed., *Comecon Data 1988* (London: Macmillan, 1989), p. 157; Vienna Institute for Comparative Economic Studies, ed., *Comecon Data 1990* (London: Macmillan, 1991), p. 159.

Table 6.7 Sinking Together: Comecon at a Glance, 1951–1988 (annual average GDP expansion at constant prices, percent)

Country	1951–1973	1974–1982	1983–1988
Soviet Union	5.0	2.1	1.9
Bulgaria	6.1	2.4	1.4
Czechoslovakia	3.8	1.8	1.8
East Germany	4.6	2.6	2.1
Hungary	4.0	1.9	1.4
Poland	4.8	0.5	4.2
Romania	5.9	3.7	2.9

Sources: International Monetary Fund, *World Economic Outlook,* May 1990 (Washington, D.C.: Author, 1990), p. 65; International Monetary Fund, *International Financial Statistics Yearbook 1991,* vol. 54 (Washington, D.C.: Author, 1991), pp. 160–163; Development Centre of the Organization for Economic Cooperation and Development, *The World Economy in the 20th Century* (Paris: Author, 1989), p. 36.

power was inseparable from its watchdog function in all areas of Soviet life — social, cultural, political, economic, and military.[13]

Ethnic diversity was another obstacle in the path of Soviet reform. The Soviet state encompassed eleven time zones, one-sixth of the earth's surface, 120 official languages, and over a hundred separate nationalities. Russians constituted a bare majority (52.4 percent) of the total Soviet population at the time the union splintered apart. For decades, the Russian-dominated and highly centralized Soviet government had suppressed expressions of cultural and linguistic particularism. Marxist-Leninist ideology was a convenient (though not very satisfactory) substitute for the various cultures contained within this vast empire.

Gorbachev's policies unwittingly aroused nationalistic rumblings all over the Soviet periphery. In the Baltic States, Latvians, Estonians, and Lithuanians looked back nostalgically to the period before World War II, when they were self-governing. In the Transcaucasus, Azerbaijanis, Georgians, and Armenians retained a strong sense of national identity; ethnic tensions in Nagorno-Karabakh, a part of Azerbaijan populated mainly by ethnic Armenians, touched off violent clashes, mass demonstrations, and bloody rioting in 1988–1989.[14] In Ukraine, with a population nearly equal to that of France or Great Britain, nationalism and separatism were reinforced by a rich cultural legacy, a history that predates the Muscovite era, and a long-standing resentment of Russian dominance. Finally, in Soviet Central Asia, Turkmen, Kirghiz, Uzbek, Kazakh, and Tajik nationalities continued to observe their own customs and practices, despite Soviet efforts to "modernize" them; all except the Tajiks speak Turkic languages, and all are Muslim.

Nationalism and the rekindling of old ethnic rivalries gave rise to violence in various places. For a brief time, Gorbachev attempted to contain these conflicts and to demonstrate that the center (Moscow) was still strong enough to maintain law and order wherever and whenever necessary. Then in August 1991 an event of seismic proportions suddenly threw the door to independence wide open.

The August Coup: Prelude and Aftermath The rebellious mood of the republics posed a danger to the survival of Gorbachev's reform movement and ultimately to the union. The other danger lurking in the background was the faltering economy, as Soviet GNP started to shrink in 1990 and plunged sharply in 1991. Ominously, the state budget deficit escalated during this period and inflation reached near-panic levels, as Soviet printing presses were stamping out ruble notes around the clock.[15] Meanwhile, Soviet debt to the West mushroomed, leaving the Kremlin in the humiliating position of owing tens of billions of dollars to its "capitalist" Cold War rivals and being too broke to keep up the interest payments.[16]

Gorbachev's failure to revive the economy had two immediate consequences. First, it brought further hardships to long-suffering Soviet consumers who, thanks to *glasnost,* now had a voice. In 1990 and 1991, Gorbachev faced growing public hostility to *perestroika;* as his popularity plummeted, the danger of a coup by hard-liners rose commensurately. Second, Gorbachev's vacillation on the conversion to a free-market economy damaged his prestige in the West. The combination of disaffection at home and disillusionment abroad made Gorbachev vulnerable. His carefully cultivated public image had been his greatest political asset; now that image was badly tarnished.

The unresolved nationalities problem ultimately proved to be Gorbachev's Achilles' heel. In the spring of 1991, Gorbachev convened a conference at which he concluded a compact with the nine participating republics, granting them internal autonomy under a proposed new constitution that would establish the "Union of Soviet Sovereign [rather than Socialist] Republics." Gorbachev was to meet with the nine republics to sign the new union compact on August 20; Kremlin hard-liners tried to preempt this action by staging a coup on August 18.

Gorbachev failed to heed the warning signs and paid a high price: he was kidnapped and placed under house arrest at a retreat in the Crimea. The person best positioned to challenge Gorbachev for preeminence was Boris Yeltsin, a popular maverick who had been elected president of the Russian Republic in June 1991. Yeltsin moved quickly into the breach, emerging from the crisis a national hero. With his chief rival in captivity, Yeltsin bravely rallied the nation, at one point climbing onto a tank to read a ringing proclamation of defiance against the would-be destroyers of Russia's fledgling democracy.

The **August coup** quickly fell apart. Ironically, it accelerated the processes of national decay. With the now politically bankrupt Gorbachev standing alone against the republics, the dissolution of the Soviet Union was only a matter of time (four months, to be exact). Unlike Gorbachev, Yeltsin claimed the right to rule Russia as a result of winning a legitimate election. The formal dissolution of the USSR, accompanied by Gorbachev's ignominious departure from the political scene, left Yeltsin in sole charge of Russia's destiny.

Postcommunist Russia

The **Russian Federation** is easily the largest and most powerful remnant of the old Soviet empire. Russia's population numbers roughly 147 million, or about half that of the former USSR. Ukraine, with a population of some 50 million, is the other large

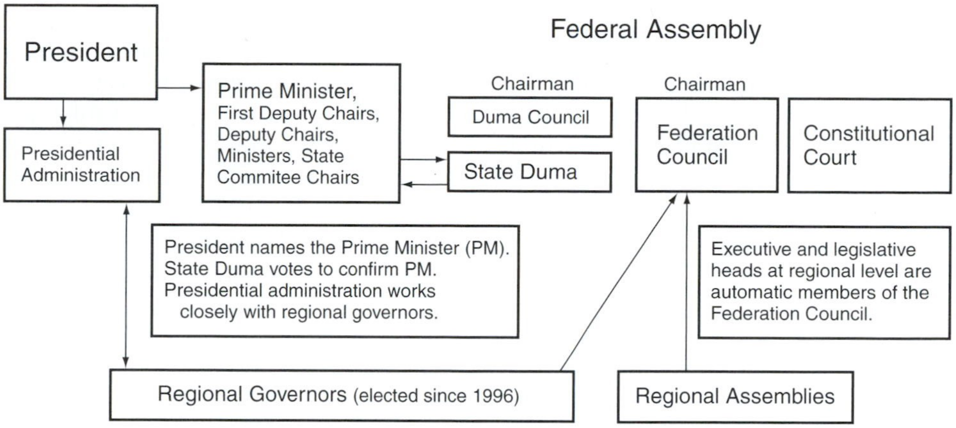

Figure 6.1 Russia's "Presidential Republic"

successor state. Both have witnessed a net population loss due largely to out-migration in recent years. In terms of territory, Russia occupies 76 percent of the former USSR and continues to be the world's largest state in geographic size. Governing such a vast territory is a challenge under the best of circumstances; governing it democratically is an even bigger challenge. In trying to meet this challenge, the authors of Russia's current constitution borrowed features from the French, German, American, and British models, among others.

During Boris Yeltsin's tenure as president (1991–1999), Russia was governed democratically but not very effectively. The present constitution, adopted in December 1993, came in the wake of a bitter struggle between Yeltsin and his opponents (opposed to radical reform), which culminated in an abortive coup attempt by leaders of the Yeltsin opposition in the Supreme Soviet. These dramatic events were televised by CNN and watched by a world audience. The climax came when the army decided to back Yeltsin, staging an artillery attack on the Russian White House (parliament building) and killing several dozen people in the process. Soon thereafter, Russian voters elected a new parliament and approved Yeltsin's proposed new constitution.

The Yeltsin constitution buttressed presidential powers at the expense of the legislature and gave the central government enhanced authority over Russia's twenty-two republics and sixty-eight regions. (See Figure 6.1.) The new political system, which Yeltsin called a "presidential republic," most closely resembles that of the French Fifth Republic.

Russia's French-Style Presidency

As in France, a directly elected president appoints a government — headed by the prime minister (officially, the Government Chairman) — which must maintain the confidence of the parliament to stay in power. The Russian president also has the right to dismiss the prime minister (again, as in the French system). Moreover, the president can dissolve the parliament (lower house) if it rejects his choice of prime minister three times in a row. This "hammer" is only available in certain circumstances. The parliament cannot be dissolved in the first year of its election, or after it has filed impeachment charges against a sitting president, or once a state of emergency has been declared, or, finally, in the last six months of a president's term.

The Russian president can veto laws, although the legislature can override the veto with two-thirds majorities in both houses. (Here, a page was taken from the American system of checks and balances.) Moreover, the president may declare martial law or a state of emergency and may rule by decree with legislative approval. The president can also issue decrees (laws, for all practical purposes). Presidential decrees, however, must meet two tests: (1) they must not violate existing laws; and (2) they must have enough support within the parliament to avoid a vote to override. (See Box 6.1.)

The parliament, in turn, can bring down a government (as in other parliamentary systems) but with this caveat: *it takes not one but two no confidence votes* to force the president's hand (the president can ignore the first one). If the government loses on a second vote of confidence the president must either dissolve parliament (and set new elections) or dismiss the government. Also, parliament can impeach the president if a two-thirds majority in both the upper and lower houses vote to do so. The process also involves Russia's two highest courts (Supreme Court and the Constitutional Court) and is therefore similar (but not identical) to that used in the United States.

In at least one other respect, Russia's presidency under the 1993 constitution reminds us of France's under the Fifth Republic. Like France's Charles de Gaulle, Yeltsin avoided any direct association with a political party. (French presidents after de Gaulle, however, did not follow this precedent.) Yeltsin's successor, Vladimir Putin, also did not run as the candidate of any particular political party (although he endorsed a coalition of liberal reformers called the Union of Right Forces). This precedent in Russia is likely to continue until the Russian political party system evolves into one more nearly resembling Western models — that is, having relatively few parties (say, five or six) with a clear identity and enough financial and popular support to survive for more than one or two elections.

Russia's German-Style Parliament

The *Federal Assembly* (parliament) comprises two chambers, the *Council of the Federation* (upper house) and the *State Duma* (lower house). The Council has 176 members (two from each of the republics and regions) and the State Duma has 450 members. Half the State Duma is elected by proportional representation (but parties must get at least 5 percent of the total votes cast to win any seats); the other half is chosen by the first past the post system (simple-majority voting in single-member districts) used in the United States and Great Britain. Note that the dual system of electing delegates resembles that used today in Germany, as does the "indirect" way the upper house is constituted (in contrast to the U.S. Senate, for example, which is directly elected).

The two houses of the Federal Assembly differ greatly in the way they are chosen and how they operate. The State Duma initiates most legislation (the exceptions are

Democracy in America

BOX 6.1

The American Presidency: Bully Pulpit but Not for Bullies

President Theodore Roosevelt called the presidency a "bully pulpit." He was referring to the president's unique power to persuade the American people to support his domestic and foreign policies. With the advent of television, the American president's political advantage in the U.S. system of government has grown far beyond the bounds imagined even by Teddy Roosevelt.

Constitutionally, the American president plays an important but limited role in the governance of the country. Among the powers he exercises alone are the following:

- Serves as commander in chief of the armed forces
- Commissions officers of the armed forces
- Grants reprieves and pardons for federal offenses (except impeachment)
- Receives ambassadors
- Takes care that the laws be faithfully executed
- Wields the "executive power"
- Appoints officials to lesser offices

Among the powers the president shares with the Senate are:

- Treaty making
- Appointment of cabinet members, judges, ambassadors, and other high officials

In addition, the president shares with the Congress as a whole the power to propose and approve legislation. The president exercises the latter power by either signing or vetoing laws passed by Congress.

By itself, this list is surprisingly unimpressive. In fact, the presidency has evolved into a more powerful institution than it was in George Washington's day. The man for whom the nation's capital was named wanted to make sure future presidents would not become dictators. Indeed, the fact that the president was (and, technically, still is) chosen by "electors" meeting in an institution called the Electoral College was a safeguard against a demogogue who could get into office by deceiving or tricking the people.

The office has changed in other ways as well since Washington's time. For example, presidents can only serve for two terms (Twenty-second Amendment, 1951). On the other hand, presidents have expanded executive powers in certain areas. During the Cold War, several presidents sent U.S. troops into battle without a formal declaration of war, starting with President Truman in the Korean "conflict" (1950–1953); likewise, Presidents Lyndon Johnson and Richard Nixon waged an undeclared (and highly unpopular) war against Vietnam (1965–1972).

Unlike Russia's president, however, the American president cannot dissolve a Congress that he or she finds inconvenient, nor issue "decrees" or declare martial law and rule as a virtual dictator. However, the American president — as both head of government and head of state — is far more powerful than presidents or constitutional monarchs in most parliamentary systems where they are often little more than figureheads.

enumerated in the constitution and apply to certain policy areas of special importance to the regions represented by the Federation Council). When a bill passes in the Duma it is sent to the Federation Council. If the upper house rejects the bill it goes back to the Duma where a commission (similar to a conference committee in the U.S. Congress) tries to iron out any differences. When the differences cannot be resolved, the Duma may override the Federation Council's action (if it can muster a two-thirds majority) and send the bill directly to the president.

When a bill clears the parliament it goes to the president to be signed. The president, as mentioned earlier, may refuse to sign a bill into law (veto), instead sending it back to the Duma with proposed changes. The Duma can either accept the presidential version of the bill and approve it by an absolute majority, or reject the president's amendments (override) by a two-thirds majority vote. The measure then goes to Federation Council, which has essentially the same options (approve by a simple majority or reject by two-thirds).

The Duma has occasionally overridden presidential vetoes and more often overrides Federation Council rejections. Generally, the president and parliament have sought to avoid provoking a constitutional crisis, although the State Duma initiated impeachment proceedings against Yeltsin in 1998 based on rather extravagant charges including treason (for his role in dissolving the USSR in 1991), violating the constitution (illegally waging war in Chechnya and illegally dissolving the Russian Congress and Supreme Soviet in 1993, destroying Russia military capabilities, and committing genocide against the Russian people by implementing ruinous economic policies. Ultimately, none of the charges got the required 300 votes (two-thirds) but the Chechen War charge failed by only 16 votes.

The Not-So-British Prime Minister

The new Russian government combines features of presidential democracy with features of parliamentary democracy. Russia has borrowed sparingly from the British model. Thus, for example, the prime minister is the formal head (chair) of government and he (she) is responsible to the parliament (that is, subject to approval and removal by the lower house). There are obvious differences even here, however. First, the Russian prime minister has no popular mandate and is not automatically chosen by being the head of the party that wins parliamentary elections (as in Great Britain). Second, the Russian prime minister can be dismissed by either the president or by the parliament.

Because Russia does not have two large political parties that alternate in power, the prime minister is unlikely to have a strong power base either within the parliament or within the electorate. That leaves only the bureaucracy itself as a potential source of leverage. At least two of Yeltsin's five prime ministers — Victor Chernomyrdin and Yevgenii Primakov — rose to the top ranks of the state administration prior to becoming prime minister, but Yeltsin dismissed both when he saw fit. For its part, the Duma twice rejected Chernomyrdin when Yeltsin tried to give him a second chance.

Given the fact that the Russian constitution (like its French counterpart) does not clearly define the relationship between the two executives or who (which one) can do precisely what, when, and how, it is possible that a future prime minister will be able to play a more assertive role in the policy process than past prime ministers have played so far. At present, the prime minister has been the chief executive in economic policy and bureaucratic management while the president has taken the lead in foreign policy and national defense. What this has meant in practice is that the president can sack the prime minister when the economy fails rather than taking the blame himself.

In all likelihood, the relationship between the two chief executives will evolve and the position of prime minister will gradually be strengthened relative to that of both president and parliament. As myriad upstart political parties of the early democratic period are winnowed out and replaced by a few parties with staying power, the workings of the Russian parliamentary system will probably come to bear a closer resemblance to the British model. The reason is simple: a majority party (or a two-party coalition led by one of two major parties) can demand that the president name its own leader to be the prime minister. If the president refuses, he (she) would run the risk of provoking a constitutional crisis. Thus, the French experience in cohabitation is one of several possible faces of Russian democracy in the future.

Putin's Surprising Rise to Power

In August 1999, Yeltsin named Vladimir Putin, a former KGB officer and political unknown, to be his new prime minister. None of Yeltsin's first four prime ministers had lasted long in office, so Putin's sudden elevation to this post might have been no big deal. In fact, it was a big deal: eight months later Putin was the newly elected president of Russia. The story of Putin's meteoric rise to power says a great deal about the promise and unpredictability of Russia's experiment in democracy.

As background, President Yeltsin's second term proved to be only slightly less turbulent than the first (see "Policy and Prospects"). His continuing problems with the economy and a dirty war in Chechnya (discussed later) were compounded by episodes of serious illness. Through it all, Yeltsin somehow managed to cling to power. His daughter and other members of his personal entourage (called "the Family" by political insiders) were instrumental in keeping the ship of state afloat when Yeltsin himself was incapacitated. Miraculously, he always bounced back. In retrospect, Yeltsin's decision to make Putin prime minister was the first scene in the final act of a drama that had begun almost a decade earlier. To the end, Yeltsin displayed an extraordinary sense of political theater.

If Yeltsin's plan was to position Putin for succession to the presidency, the December 1999 parliamentary elections were critical. Putin, for his part, did two things that bolstered his standing with the voters. First, he quickly won over many Russians with a "get tough" approach to the conduct of the war in Chechnya after a long period of dithering and indecision on the part of his predecessors (and, of course, President Yeltsin). Second, he boldly endorsed two upstart political parties — Unity (also called *Medved,* which means "bear"), a last-minute coalition with no known program, and the Union of Right Forces, a party of liberal reformers. Unity nearly finished in first place, only slightly behind the front-running communists, while the Union of Right Forces finished a respectable fourth. Together these two parties garnered about one-third of the popular vote and just a few seats fewer than the communists in the new Duma. For the first time, the Russian parliament had two blocs — one on the left and one on the right — facing each other. Was the Russian political party system at long last becoming less chaotic, perhaps even normal?

Not exactly. At the first meeting of the newly elected Duma, the Communists and Unity (the main pro-Putin party) formed an alliance of odd bedfellows, dividing up the chairmanships of the key committees between them. The Communists came out best, retaining the post of Duma speaker (leader) and getting nine committee chairs, but in return pledged to support the new government — in other words, to accept Putin's choice of prime minister and reform program. The opposition parties cried foul (one former prime minister, Yevgeny Primakov, called the deal a "desecration"). Nonetheless, the arrangement was a first for Russia's young democracy.

In sum, Russia's new constitution looks democratic. The real test, however, is not how a constitution looks on paper but how it works in practice. We will examine how well Russian democracy is meeting this test in the following section.

Problems and Prospects

Russia's economic problems did not evaporate with the passing of the Soviet Union. Nor did the prospects for Russia or the other former Soviet republics suddenly improve — for the vast majority, things went from bad to worse in the 1990s. But President Putin, tough and energetic, is slowly turning the economy around. Turning Russian society around will take longer.

Economic Performance — A Dismal Decade At the very outset, the Russian Federation found itself in an economic crisis. In January 1992, consumers rioted in many cities, protesting against the lifting of price controls. It was a harbinger of things to come. As the year wore on, the economy continued its tailspin, incomes and output plummeted, inflation soared, and the government was powerless to reverse the trends. Meanwhile, it appeared as though only profiteers and criminals were prospering while millions of law-abiding citizens were once again forced to wait in long lines for sugar, flour, and other staples. (See Table 6.8.) It was the disappointment of democracy — the fact that it brought hardship rather than hope — that quickly became paramount in the minds of the vast majority of Russians.

In part because of reckless monetary policies, Russia teetered on the brink of hyperinflation. Massive government subsidies to failing state enterprises were financed by a flood of freshly printed rubles. The inflation rate reached such dizzying heights by the end of 1992 that the ruble was fast becoming worthless.

With paltry foreign reserves (gold and convertible currency), the Kremlin was forced to seek a moratorium on repayment of its external debt. The International Monetary Fund (IMF) agreed to extend a new multibillion-dollar loan to Russia in April 1993 but made the deal conditional on implementation of market reforms. Meanwhile, Russia was also running up large multibillion-dollar trade deficits and foreign debts to Germany, the United States, and other Western countries. Russian nationalists found it humiliating for Moscow — still a nuclear superpower, after all — to be financially dependent on the West. Small wonder that Yeltsin was no longer a hero to most Russians.

Under enormous cross-pressures from the international community on the one hand, and from his domestic critics on the other, Yeltsin temporized. In the aftermath of the 1993 political crisis, Yeltsin turned over management of the economy to his Prime Minister Viktor Chernomyrdin. Never known as a market enthusiast, Chernomyrdin nonetheless adopted a pragmatic monetary policy aimed at restricting growth of the money supply and curbing consumer demand. In response, the inflation rate fell sharply by the mid-1990s, although it was still exceedingly high by Western standards.[17]

Table 6.8 Russian per Capita Consumption, 1990–1993 (kilograms)

Product	1990	1991	1992	1993
Meat	75	69	60	56
Milk	386	347	281	279
Eggs (number)	297	288	263	246
Fish	20	16	13	10
Sugar	47	38	34	35
Vegetable oil	10	8	7	8
Potatoes	106	112	118	114
Vegetables	89	86	77	83
Grain products	119	120	125	130

Source: Official statistics; see U.S. Central Intelligence Agency, *Handbook of International Economic Statistics* (Washington, D.C.: Author, September 1995), pp 34–35.

Yeltsin was understandably reluctant to shut down many of the country's woefully inefficient medium-size and large factories knowing that to do so would cause massive layoffs. His dilemma was the greater because under the old communist system, everybody (except "parasites") had a job, unemployment was anathema, and nobody was ever fired. As a result, in the first three years of Yeltsin's presidency, industrial growth rates in Russia actually fell faster than GNP as a whole. (See Table 6.9.)

The price of Yeltsin's ambivalence was a failing economy. For example, light industry declined overall by almost one-third, and the chemicals sector (including petrochemicals) fell by nearly one-fourth. Agriculture production also dropped steadily during this period. Russia's per capita GNP in 1995 was roughly a tenth of Belgium's and barely half of Hungary's.

Table 6.9 Russia: Selected Economic Indicators

Indicator	1991	1992	1993	1994
GDP, 1991–1994 (percent change)				
Real growth	–13.0	–19.0	–12.0	–15.0
Per capita real growth	–13.0	–19.0	–11.0	–15.0
Industrial output (change in total)	–8.0	–19.0	–16.2	–22.8
Agricultural output (change in total)	–5.0	–8.0	–2.0	–9.0
Energy				
Oil (thousand BPD)	—	7,880	6,935	6,320
Natural gas (billion m^3)	—	639	618	607
Coal (million MTS)	—	329	296	271
Electricity (billion kWh)	—	1,002	950	876

Source: Official statistics; see U.S. Central Intelligence Agency, *Handbook of International Economic Statistics* (Washington, D.C.: Author, September 1995), pp. 34–35.

Table 6.10 Russian Economic Performance, 1992–2002 (percentage annual change)

	1992	1994	1996	1998	2000	2002	2004
GDP	−14.5	−12.6	−6.0	−5.0	9.0	4.1	5.7
Inflation	2323	202	21.8	82.0	20.2	14.9	10.8

Sources: World Bank and "Emerging Market Indicators," *The Economist,* July 1, 2000, December 7, 2002, and March 27, 2004.

Thus, when Yeltsin ran for reelection in 1996, he was courting voters whose average wages (about $150 per month) and living standards had fallen during his first term in office. However, the economy was showing some signs of reviving thanks in part to fresh loans from the IMF; inflation decelerated; the value of the ruble stabilized; and foreign investors were beginning to take notice. Russians were not better off than they had been four years earlier, but there was new hope. That plus a well-timed lull in the war in Chechnya proved to be enough to put Yeltsin over the top one more time as he trounced Gennady Zuganov, the Communist Party's lackluster candidate, in a runoff election. Russia's great campaigner had done it again.

Russia's economy perked up in 1996–1997 but plummeted again in 1998. (See Table 6.10.) The reversals were due in part to external circumstances — lower oil prices and a crisis that started in Asia's emerging markets and spread. But Yeltsin was also to blame. In return for financing his campaign, Yeltsin allowed a few tycoons to gain a stranglehold on the commanding heights of the economy — banking, energy, and mining, among other areas. These so-called oligarchs demanded (and got) all sorts of special privileges, including "privatization on favorable terms, and a virtual tax holiday which starved the exchequer and kept interest rates high."[18] Yeltsin proved in spades that skilled politicians do not always make good presidents.

Under Putin, Russia's economic picture brightened considerably. Putin subdued Russia's powerful pseudocapitalist oligarchs using both the police and the legal system to cut them down to size. He also made moves to curb corruption, control inflation, balance the budget, improve Russia's trade relations, and attract foreign investment. The results were not miraculous, but Russia's economic performance did improve markedly thanks to Putin's firm hand – perhaps at last a real start on the long road to recovery.

Russia's Nettlesome Nationalities Post–Soviet Russia remains a multiethnic Eurasian empire stretching from the Gulf of Finland to the Sea of Japan. By itself, it still boasts roughly three-fourths of the total land area of the former Soviet Union and one-half of its population. Although over four-fifths of the Russian Federation's population consists of ethnic Russians, many ethnic minorities (including Tatars, Ukrainians, Chechens, Germans, and Poles, among others) live there as well. Under the old Bolshevik structure (which survives intact), Russia comprises twenty constituent republics representing relatively large ethnic groups and a plethora of smaller administrative entities.

Contrast and Comparison

BOX 6.2

The War in Chechnya: Shades of Nixon

Nineteen ninety-five brought new turbulence to a society already in turmoil. After President Yeltsin signed a peace accord with the Chechen rebels in July, the State Duma passed a vote of no confidence in the government. Yeltsin was hospitalized with a heart ailment in October. The fighting in Chechnya resumed in December. Yeltsin agreed to give the Chechens enhanced autonomy. Chechens went to the polls to elect a homegrown government. But in January 1996, the Russian army bombarded a village on the Chechen border where 250 Chechen separatists were holding 100 hostages. At least 150 Chechens died in this assault, which prompted renewed outrage abroad. In March 1996, Yeltsin declared a cease-fire, but the fighting continued. In May, after Chechen leader Jokar Dudayev reportedly was killed in a Russian rocket attack, Yeltsin struck a deal with Dudayev's successor, Zelimkhan Yandarbiev. It was no mere coincidence that Yeltsin sued for peace on the eve of the presidential elections. In the United States in 1972, with the unpopular war in Vietnam raging, President Richard Nixon, campaigning for reelection against a "peace" candidate (Senator George McGovern), did exactly the same thing for exactly the same reason.

The War in Chechnya The virus of nationalism infected some of these republics, especially Chechnya, where a bid for independence in November 1991 triggered a crisis and led eventually to a protracted war. When Yeltsin decreed a state of emergency in the rebel area and dispatched special Interior Ministry troops to enforce it, a majority in the Russian parliament refused to back this move and called instead for negotiations under parliamentary auspices.

The opponents of Yeltsin's action charged that it was no different from Gorbachev's failed attempts to settle ethnic conflicts by force, while defenders warned that if Yeltsin failed to act decisively, Russia would suffer the same fate as the disintegrating Soviet Union. The issue split the Democratic Russia movement, a pillar of Yeltsin's political support. "In the ensuing uproar," wrote one reporter, "the Russian government backed down, leaving an uneasy truce in which the Chechen government issues statements as if it were independent and the Russian government ignores them."[19] This armed rebellion, which culminated in a ferocious war a few years later, was a stark reminder that the new Russia would face many of the same problems that had undone the old Soviet order.

Unlike his predecessors (including Gorbachev), when President Yeltsin decided to get tough in Chechnya, he had to justify the use of force to the press, the parliament, and the public. (See Box 6.2.) His inept handling of the ensuing war in the mid-1990s nearly cost him the presidency; worse, the war badly divided Russian society and threatened to crack the very foundations of Russia's none-too-sturdy democratic institutions. During the course of that conflict, with horrific battle scenes being broadcast around the world on satellite television, Yeltsin vacillated between the extremes of conciliation and vengeance. As a result, he appeared indecisive, alienating doves and hawks alike, while the international community widely condemned the Kremlin's brutal intervention.

After a bloody two-year war that left the diminutive Chechnya in ruins but unconquered — a war that exposed Russia's weakness to an incredulous world — Yeltsin decided to negotiate a settlement. As a result, free elections were held in Chechnya in January 1997. Chechnya's leadership continued to demand full independence from Russia, but Moscow remained publicly silent on this all-important question, despite having signed the peace agreement.

The silence was broken in the fall of 1999 with bombs and artillery fire: in the twilight of his presidency, the ever-unpredictable Yeltsin launched a second war in Chechnya. But this time the military operations were better planned and executed. As noted earlier, Yeltsin put Vladimir Putin, his new prime minister, in charge of the war effort. Putin quickly proved himself to be the right man for the job, ruthlessly directing a massive assault against Chechnya's rebel strongholds, and the Russian public responded with a patriotic outpouring of gratitude. Putin's surging popularity in the polls was the immediate result. (See Figure 6.2.)

Although Putin had subdued Chechnya and installed a puppet government, low-intensity conflict continued. Rebels resorted to guerrilla-style tactics, sniper fire killed Russian soldiers daily, and Chechen leaders, including the ousted president, remained at large. After September 11, 2001, President George W. Bush's "war on terrorism" in effect gave Putin a green light to intensify Russia's military solution to the Chechen problem. But the rebels refused to surrender.

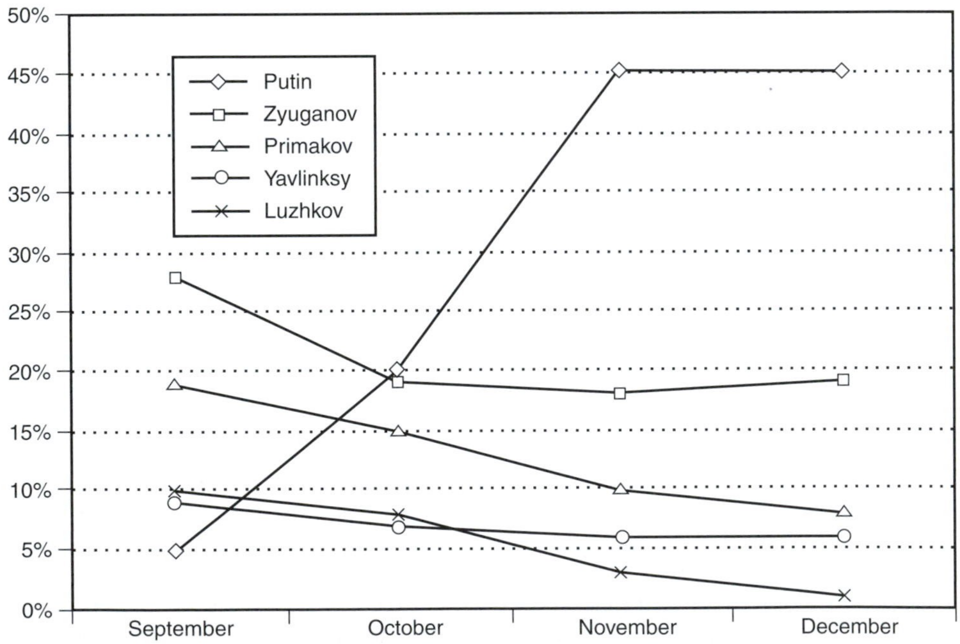

Figure 6.2 Putin's Surging Popularity, September–December 1999

In October 2002, Chechen fighters seized a Moscow theater and held 700 people inside hostage. After a standoff that lasted for two and half days Russian commandos moved in, using a presumably nonlethal poison gas to render the hostage-takers (and the hostages) unconscious. But when the gas killed many of the hostages, the government refused to name the gas (allegedly for security reasons) and would not tell doctors how to treat the victims. The incident further incited hatred on both sides.

A Russian-choreographed referendum the following spring adopted a new constitution and formally declared Chechnya part of Russia, but it settled nothing. In the summer of 2003, a suicide bomber drove a truck packed with explosives into a Russian military hospital, killing many of the hospital's staff and patients. The Kremlin blamed Chechen rebels and painted them as criminals in the same mold as the perpetrators of the 9/11 terrorist attacks on America. By linking Moscow's Chechen problem with Washington's terrorism problem, Putin gained the diplomatic leverage he needed to keep Western powers from protesting the Russian army's brutal efforts to crush the Chechen rebellion. In March 2004, Putin was re-elected in a landslide (over 70% of the vote).

The two Chechen wars pushed Moscow's troubled relations with other minorities off the stage. The Tatarstan's dispute with Moscow, unlike Chechnya's, ended peacefully in 1994. Tensions between Russia and other former Soviet republics remain, as well. Flash points include Georgia, where the South Ossetians wanted to secede to join Russia; Moldova, where ethnic Russians were fighting native Romanians in a Russian-majority enclave in the Dnestr region; and Nagorno-Karabakh, a relatively large chunk of territory that is legally part of Azerbaijan but politically and militarily controlled by Armenia.

Russian or Citizen? Russia has an endemic "federal" problem that the United States does not have. Although the majority of its population is ethnic Russian, Russia remains a multiethnic empire. The distinction between ***Russkye*** (ethnic Russians) and ***Rossianiye*** (citizens of Russia) in the vernacular reflects this diversity. When the parliament proposed calling the country just plain "Russia," objections were raised on the grounds that this name refers only to the *Russkye* — the *Rossianiye* would have been left out. This may seem like an abstruse point to outsiders, but the ethnic wars in the former Yugoslavia, as well as Russia's war in Chechnya, serve as grim reminders that, in this part of the world, such matters are anything but academic.

As its name declares, the Russian Federation is a federal (as opposed to unitary) system. The Soviet Union was also a titular "federation," but the key to its survival for more than seven decades was the existence of a monopoly of force at the center rather than any division of powers between the center and the provinces. By contrast, the rulers of the current Russian Federation are duty-bound to accept constitutional constraints on the power they exercise. Such constraints are often severely tested in times of crisis (even for well-established federal republics) — especially if a secession movement provokes the crisis. The American Civil War is a case in point. In the United States, constitutional rules have always been restored (and often strengthened) following conflicts and crises. Whether Russia's fledgling and fragile democracy will slide into dictatorship as it faces an uncertain future remains to be seen.

India and Nigeria are two other countries where federalism has been adopted as a solution to the problem of governing a diverse population scattered over a large territory. Significantly, in both countries (and also in Canada) the spirit of secession has, at one time or another, shattered the calm. The United States put that issue to rest nearly a century and a half ago. India and Nigeria still have not done so, and neither has Russia.

Eastern Europe: From Stalinism to Pluralism

From 1945 to 1989, Eastern Europe consisted of nine sovereign nations: Albania, Bulgaria, Czechoslovakia, East Germany, Hungary, Poland, Romania, Yugoslavia, and the USSR. After World War II, the Red Army occupied all of them except Albania and Yugoslavia. By 1948, Stalin had imposed the Soviet model everywhere; in Yugoslavia, Marshal Tito rebuffed Stalin but in many ways imitated Stalinism. Monolithic rule prevailed until an avalanche of popular demands for democratic reforms swept it away in 1989 and 1990 — and more than doubled the roster of nations in the Slavic Europe.

Stalin insisted that the governments of the "outer empire" in Eastern Europe be modeled on his own, featuring these four elements:

1. a Communist Party dictatorship
2. a government apparatus democratic in appearance but highly centralized and hierarchical
3. a socialist command economy in which patterns of production and consumption reflect political priorities rather than market forces
4. a foreign policy based on fraternal relations with other socialist states

However, the "outer empire" changed dramatically after the deluge of 1989.

Eastern Europe during the Cold War

Throughout Eastern Europe, the Communist Party dominated politics. In some cases, other political parties existed (for example, in Poland and Hungary), but they were empty shells designed to hide the fact that the ruling party was all-powerful.

Party organization in Eastern Europe mirrored Soviet practice. The size of party membership in each country was kept at 6 to 12 percent of the total population, ensuring that the party remained an elite organization. Elitism was apparently necessary for party morale, political recruitment, ideological integrity, and internal discipline.

Communist parties in Eastern Europe also imitated the Soviet insistence on political and intellectual conformity. Like the Communist Party of the Soviet Union (CPSU), they were intolerant of dissent and used censorship, surveillance, intimidation, coercion, and incessant propaganda to suppress freedom of artistic and literary expression, as well as political free speech.

Czechoslovakia, East Germany, Bulgaria, and Romania were hard-line Stalinist regimes. Poland and Hungary were the two most permissive communist regimes (not counting Yugoslavia). Hungary actually attempted to break away from Moscow in 1956, as did Czechoslovakia in 1968. Both attempts came to grief when the Soviet Union sent in tanks and troops to restore communist rule. Yugoslavia was the one major exception to this portrait of Soviet domination over Eastern Europe.

Moscow's Clones

Government structures in the East European nations differed superficially from the Soviet model, but in all of them executive authority was centralized, and the state apparatus was subservient to the party. In these countries, as in the Soviet Union, responsibility for day-to-day administration rested with the premier and a council of ministers handpicked by the party leadership. Rubber-stamping was the primary function of Eastern European parliaments, much as the Supreme Soviet legitimized Politburo decisions in the Kremlin.

Cloned Economies, Too

Following World War II, Moscow imposed Stalinist economic as well as political structures on Eastern Europe. Hence the entire region simultaneously embarked on the adventure of central planning, nationalization of industry, and collectivization of agriculture. Only in Poland did stiff peasant resistance keep most land in private hands.

In design and function, the command economies of Eastern Europe were clones of the Soviet economy. Developmentally, however, they lagged behind the Soviet Union (which itself fell further and further behind the West, as we have already noted). Moscow was content to buy raw materials from these countries and sell manufactured goods back to them — not exactly a good deal for the East European satellites. To add insult to injury, Soviet manufactures were relatively expensive, and the quality was notoriously poor.

The problem with central planning, in a nutshell, was that the system did not produce prosperity anywhere and, as a result, an ever-widening gap opened up between standards of living on opposite sides of the so-called iron curtain. That central planning was fundamentally flawed was most vividly illustrated by divided Germany where the capitalist western part blossomed — an "economic miracle" it was said — in stark contrast to the prevailing gloom in the Stalinist eastern part.

Rulers who kept popular discontent at bay only by police-state vigilance became one of the hallmarks of the Cold War. Not surprisingly, "reform" was whispered long before Gorbachev gave it Moscow's stamp of approval. First Hungary and then other countries (especially Poland) began experimenting with market mechanisms. These experiments were cautious and tightly controlled, but they suggested that the Stalinist model was a major impediment to economic growth and technological progress.

Why did East Europeans wait so long before finally scrapping a system that did not work? In a word, fear. When Hungary tried to break away in 1956, the Kremlin dispatched tanks and troops to crush the rebellion, executing its popular leader as a traitor to the cause of "socialism." When another reform-minded leader promised "socialism with a human face" in Czechoslovakia during the ill-fated **Prague Spring** of 1968, the Soviet Union again launched a brutal military intervention, ousting the reformers and restoring neo-Stalinists to power. Soviet pressures on the Polish government to crack down on dissent in 1956 and again in 1980 and 1981 did not go unnoticed in the other "satellite" states either.

One of the bitter lessons of Hungary, Czechoslovakia, and Poland was that Moscow would not allow any Eastern European member state to withdraw from the Warsaw Pact; Hungary had tried and failed. Nor would the Soviet Union allow opposition parties to exist. Czechoslovakia's move in this direction in 1968 jeopardized the party's monopoly on power. That, in turn, led to the Soviet invasion and the enunciation of the **Brezhnev Doctrine,** which asserted Moscow's right to intervene in Eastern Europe to defend socialism against "counterrevolution." Finally, the Soviet Union would not tolerate independent power centers (such as the Solidarity trade-union movement in Poland in the early 1980s) that threatened or challenged the party's monopoly on power. As the events of 1989 demonstrated, Soviet domination was the only glue holding the "socialist commonwealth" together.

The Revolutions of 1989

The year 1989 was a turning point in the long struggle between two irreconcilable ideologies — communism and capitalism. As it happened, Eastern Europe was the stage for Act I of this great drama. The year began with steps toward free elections in Poland and Hungary; it ended with the ouster of East Germany's communist dictator, the subsequent opening of the intra-German border (and the dismantling of the Berlin Wall), the resignation of the communist leadership in Czechoslovakia, and the overthrow of a particularly corrupt and brutal tyrant in Romania.

During 1989, Poland and Hungary introduced a series of political reforms aimed at democratization. In Poland, the eight-year ban against the independent trade union **Solidarity** was lifted. The government permitted relatively free elections in June. Solidarity was allowed to contest all of the seats for the Senate (upper house) and won an overwhelming majority in that body. It also won all of the seats it was allowed to contest in the Sejm (lower house). Although the communists enjoyed a guaranteed majority in the Sejm (nearly two-thirds of the seats), the June elections were a ringing mandate for the opposition (mainly Solidarity). In August, the Polish parliament chose the first noncommunist prime minister in a Soviet-bloc country.

In a similar move, the Hungarian parliament voted to allow freedom of association and assembly in January 1989. The following month, the ruling Hungarian Socialist Workers' Party (HSWP) approved formation of independent political parties. Hungary thus became the first Eastern European state since the Stalinist takeover to relinquish the Communist Party's monopoly position and embrace a competitive multiparty system. In May 1989, Hungary dismantled the barbwire fence separating it from neutral Austria — an act of immense symbolic significance in a country where freedom of movement was so long denied to its citizens. The communist era in Hungary was rapidly drawing to a close.

The communist regimes of East Germany, Czechoslovakia, and Romania tumbled in a kind of chain reaction. The crisis in the German Democratic Republican (GDR) began with the flight of East Germans, vacationing in Hungary, to West Germany. Soon East Germans were clamoring for freedom to emigrate, freedom of speech, freedom of assembly — in a word, for democracy. Some fled through Poland; others sought refuge in the West German embassy in Prague, Czechoslovakia. Spectacular mass demonstrations occurred in Leipzig, East Berlin, and other East German cities throughout the fall of 1989. Under intense popular pressure and increasingly isolated (even Gorbachev offered no support), the Communist Party leadership replaced its hard-line chief. In a further effort to placate a society now in open revolt, the beleaguered GDR first gave Prague permission to allow thousands of East Germans in Czechoslovakia to go west and then caved completely, throwing open the intra-German border and allowing East Germans to travel freely to West Germany.

Next came one of the twentieth century's unforgettable moments: people from both halves of Berlin, a city divided for nearly three decades, began tearing down the Berlin Wall, first with hand tools, then with heavy equipment, celebrating around the clock atop the wall, in the streets, and at popular gathering places. People came from all over the world to celebrate with them, and millions more joined the party via satellite television. German youths on unscheduled holiday from school danced and sang, laughed and cried. Strangers embraced. For anyone who had grown up during the Cold War, it was an unforgettable scene.

In short order, the East German government resigned. In the elections held soon thereafter, the communists suffered a humiliating defeat, as East Germans endorsed an early merger of the two German states — the key plank in the winning Christian Democrats' platform. Unification came quickly in October 1990.

In neighboring Czechoslovakia, the conservative communist government steadfastly resisted major economic and political reforms until it was swept away by popular discontent in late 1989. In an amazing role reversal, Vaclav Havel, a dissident writer languishing in a Czech prison at the beginning of the year, accepted the presidency in December.

Romania was the last domino to fall. It had had the most repressive regime in Eastern Europe. The army captured its fleeing dictator and his wife (an accomplice in his crimes), staged a perfunctory trial, and executed them on the spot. Romania's new leaders — so-called reform communists — set up the Council of National Reconciliation to run the country until free elections could be held. Critics denounced the new government for including members of the fallen dictator's inner circle and for operating too much like the old government.

Oddly enough, the last dictatorship to fall in Eastern Europe was to be in Yugoslavia, the only communist country in Europe that had successfully pursued an independent and remained friendly toward the West throughout the Cold War. Indeed, Yugoslavia (Serbia and Montenegro) would not be rid of Slobodan Milosevic's tyranny for another decade.

During the first half of 1990, East European voters rejected not only the communists but also other parties of the left and center-left (most notably the Social Democrats). *The Economist* noted: "In one country after another, 'reform communism' proved empty."[20] The surprising popularity of center-right parties touting free enterprise reflected widespread disillusion with the Stalinist system of central planning. But rising expectations associated with market reforms put the new leaders under the gun to produce quick results.

The transition from communism to constitutional democracy has not been easy or painless anywhere. Czechoslovakia quietly split in 1992. The relatively homogeneous societies of Poland and Hungary were in no danger of breakup but they displayed a common set of weaknesses that added up to a kind of postcommunist syndrome—official corruption, weak civic cultures, and badly fragmented party systems. (Initially, Poland and Romania each had eighteen parties represented in parliament; Hungary and the Czech Republic had seven and six, respectively). On the plus side, however, the emerging democracies abolished the old Stalinist order, moved to create a free press, extended civil liberties widely, and held free parliamentary elections. And chaotic parliaments did not necessarily lead to chaotic governments. In Poland, for example, despite frequent changes of prime ministers and cabinets, economic policy has been strikingly consistent.

Economic Revival in East-Central Europe?

Many of the problems plaguing the former Soviet Union are also present elsewhere in Eastern Europe. The economic dilemmas and dislocations associated with making the transition from central planning to the free market are regionwide. And the ethnic animosities that police-state controls suppressed before 1989 have resurfaced in the Balkans and in parts of what was the USSR.

Despite these nagging problems, Poland, Hungary, the Czech Republic, and Slovakia did take giant steps toward creation of a competitive market, breaking up and "privatizing" many inefficient, outmoded, and uncompetitive formerly state-owned industries. Moreover, all four economies showed signs of economic revitalization. The steep decline in industrial output in the early 1990s reflected this painful but necessary adjustment. (Economists agree that state-owned enterprises under communism generally wasted labor and energy, produced inferior goods, and excessively polluted the environment.)

Although direct foreign investment in the region rose sharply in the early 1990s, the wait-and-see attitude of Western and Japanese investors impeded rapid economic recovery. During the 1990s, Hungary and Poland attracted the lion's share of all foreign investment in the region. The Czech Republic and Slovenia were next in line, followed distantly by the others. A clear commitment to market reforms and evidence of political stability were the two most important factors. For example, in the mid-1990s when a newly elected Polish president (an ex-communist) gave reassurances that he intended to continue Poland's market reforms, foreign investors responded by pouring about $2 billion into Poland's reviving economy.[21] By contrast, in the Czech Republic hopes of enticing private foreign investors were dampened in 1997 when scandals and a currency crisis brought down the conservative government of Vaclav Klaus.

A comparison with other **emerging markets** suggests that at the end of the 1990s, Poland, Hungary, and the Czech Republic were on the right track, economically. (See

Table 6.11 Emerging Markets in 1999–2000: A Performance Comparison*
(percentage of change from a year earlier)

	GDP	Industrial Production	Consumer Prices
Asia			
China	8.1	11.5	0.1
India	5.8	12.2	5.5
Indonesia	3.2	34.8	1.2
Malaysia	11.7	18.6	1.2
Thailand	5.2	4.2	1.7
Latin America			
Argentina	0.9	5.8	−1.0
Brazil	3.1	3.3	5.3
Chile	5.5	2.9	3.6
Mexico	7.9	5.1	9.3
Eastern Europe			
Czech Republic	4.4	2.8	3.7
Hungary	6.8	20.3	9.1
Poland	6.0	12.3	10.0
Russia	7.5	10.6	19.4

*The precise reporting periods represented in this table vary slightly from country to country, but the data all pertain to the one-year period 1999–2000, and therefore provide a reasonable basis for a comparison of relative economic performance.

Source: "Emerging Market Indicators," *The Economist,* July 1, 2000, p. 116.

Table 6.11.) Slovenia was another bright spot in the region; Slovakia, still playing catch-up, was showing signs of vitality, too. More recently, the Baltic States have come on strong; in fact, in 2002, Lithuania had the fastest growth rate in Europe (nearly 7 percent), followed closely by Latvia and Estonia. As a result, all of these countries are slated for admission to the European Union in 2004. Keep in mind, however, that national economies vary greatly in size. For example, Brazil's GNP in the late 1990s was twice the size of Russia's, according to World Bank statistics. It was also roughly seventeen times larger than Hungary's, fourteen times the size of the Czech Republic's, and five times larger than Poland's. Hence, Brazil's growth rates, although slower than, say, Poland's in 1999, were nonetheless more impressive than they seem at first glance, while the Czech Republic's were just the opposite.

The prospect of entering the EU is a major incentive for these countries to work for change and stability simultaneously. It may also help governments facing vociferous opposition parties to encourage pragmatism and moderation rather than ideological posturing and confrontation.

Table 6.12 After Communism: Economic Performance in Eastern Europe, 1990–1998

Country	Average Annual Real Growth (percent)	Average Annual Inflation Rate (percent)
Bulgaria	–1.8	117
Croatia	0.5	131
Czech Republic	–0.2	14
Hungary	0.9	22
Poland	4.4	27
Romania	–0.6	114
Slovakia	1.1	11
Slovenia	4.4	27

Source: International Bank for Reconstruction and Development, *World Bank Atlas 2000* (Washington, D.C.: Author, 2000).

Overall, Poland and Slovenia achieved the highest average annual economic growth rates in the region during the decade of the nineties, followed by Hungary and Slovakia. (See Table 6.12.) Czechs, however, enjoyed single-digit inflation and low unemployment, in contrast to Poland and Hungary, where unemployment was unacceptably high. On the negative side, many formerly state-owned enterprises in the Czech Republic continued to keep redundant and inefficient workers on the payroll — a short-term solution impeding the long-term process of adjustment to a competitive business environment.

Case Studies: Czechoslovakia and Yugoslavia

Czechoslovakia and Yugoslavia both suffered a similar fate after 1989 — both split apart into separate entities. Unlike Yugoslavia, Czechoslovakia was able to accomplish the separation without great turmoil and entirely without bloodshed.

The Czech Republic: Reinventing Democracy

At the end of 1989, after the Soviet-installed regimes in Poland, Hungary, and East Germany had fallen, Czechoslovakia also rose up against its communist rulers. But the Czech uprising was mild compared with what occurred in other communist countries.

What If?

BOX 6.3

Prisoners of Conscience

When Czechslovakia's communist dictators abdicated power at the end of 1989, Vaclav Havel, the conscience of the nation, was hailed both at home and abroad as the hero of the Velvet Revolution. As the leader of a coalition of opposition groups called Civic Forum, Havel played a key role in bringing down the beleaguered communists without a shot being fired. At the beginning of 1989, Havel was a playwright, a pariah, and a prison inmate; at the end, he was the president. Havel's personal triumph in 1989 was rich in symbolism for the region as a whole: democracy, too, had been rehabilitated. What if the Stalinists who ruled Eastern Europe had not persecuted writers and artists like Havel? What if they had not made heroes and martyrs of talented men and women whose only "crime" was artistic self-expression? Paradoxically, communism would probably have survived longer had its leaders not used censorship as a means of staying in power.

The Velvet Revolution

The leaders of the revolt were moderates who opposed violence (hence the name **Velvet Revolution**). Without question, Vaclav Havel was the major inspirational force behind the uprising. (See Box 6.3.) Alexander Dubcek, a Slovak, who had spearheaded the ill-fated attempt to introduce a multiparty system free of police state controls ("socialism with a human face") during the 1968 Prague Spring, was another key figure.

That earlier episode ironically helped seal the fate of Czechoslovakia's rulers. Having crushed the 1968 reform movement and conducted widespread purges of reformers (ultimately affecting half a million party members) from 1969 to 1971, the perpetrators of these draconian policies could not easily jump on the reform bandwagon even if they had wanted to do so. Thus, in March 1987 President Gustav Husak declared, "no one is forcing Soviet ideas on Czechoslovakia." When Husak was replaced as party leader in December 1987, Gorbachev publicly urged his successor, Milos Jakes, to proceed with the "democratization of public and political life." Gorbachev's *perestroika* campaign had put Czechoslovakia's communist leaders on the defensive.

A Cumbersome Constitution

The new short-lived Czech and Slovak Federal Republic (CSFR) created in 1990 as the successor to the Soviet-style federal state formed in 1969, inherited a cumbersome constitution ill-suited to the new era. At a meeting with the leaders of Civic Forum, a flash-in-the-pan opposition party hastily created to negotiate the transition to democratic rule in late November 1989, the tottering dictatorship agreed to delete all references to the Communist Party's "leading role" and a few other provisions. For the most part, however, the government after 1989 continued to operate within the preexisting constitutional structure. (A new constitution was being drafted, but it turned into a race against the clock as the two halves of the CSFR started splitting apart in 1991.) The big difference, of course, was that the communist rulers treated the constitution as an ornament, whereas the new democratic leaders were obliged to take it seriously.

The system set up by the inherited constitution created a division of powers between the federal government on the one hand and the two national governments on the other. It established Prague as the capital of the Czech Republic and Bratislava as the seat of government in the Slovak Republic. Each of the component republics was given separate political institutions, including a National Council (or legislature) and an executive (prime minister and cabinet), to operate concurrently with the federal government in Prague.

The bicameral Federal Assembly, consisting of the Chamber of Nations and the Chamber of the People, was the highest organ of state power (although in practice, of course, the Communist Party enjoyed a de facto power monopoly until 1989). The Federal Assembly elected a president (under the communists this was pro forma), who in turn appointed a head of government and cabinet. Hence, Czechoslovakia had both a head of state (the president) and a head of government (the prime minister), an arrangement common elsewhere in Europe. The Federal Assembly chose the Supreme Court judges, and the National Councils chose judges for regional and district courts.

The federal structure was more complicated than the unitary systems of Western Europe, but it was necessary because of the ethnic makeup of Czechoslovakia. The federation's political problems after 1989 were to some degree attributable to procedural difficulties built into the inherited constitution.

One Country, Three Governments?

Under Czechoslovakia's original 1918 constitution, a three-fifths majority in the Federal Assembly elected the president. This stringent majoritarian requirement was no doubt adopted to ensure that the president would have a clear mandate and could therefore speak with moral authority. It was not a problem in 1918: Tomas Masaryk was the unchallenged leader of the country. (He was elected to a seven-year term and exempted from the constitutional ban against self-succession.) But the three-fifths majority rule was a potential problem in the future. A fragmented Federal Assembly might not be able to agree on a worthy candidate, which could lead either to a constitutional crisis or the election of a weak compromise candidate. In some circumstances, it might even result in the election of a demagogue (that is, a politician who pandered to public opinion to gain power but did not believe in democracy).

The inherited constitution also prescribed legislative procedures that made it relatively easy for opposition parties in a fragmented parliament to block legislation and in general play an obstructionist role. Both legislative chambers had to approve legislation before it could become law — not an unreasonable rule. The 150 seats in the Chamber of the People were allocated in proportion to population (giving the Czechs a two-to-one advantage); the 150 seats in the Chamber of Nations were split equally between the two republics. The Chamber of Nations also voted in a peculiar way: the two parts voted separately. Legislation had to be approved not only in both chambers but also in both parts of the Chamber of Nations. Hence, a relatively small opposition (as few as thirty-eight members) in one part of this chamber could block all government policy and federal legislation, which meant that the will of the majority in the Federal Assembly could be thwarted by one-eighth of its delegates. Moreover, certain actions (such as election of a president) required a three-fifths majority in both houses of the Federal Assembly. In this case, it took not only 180 votes total for approval but also forty-five members in both parts of the Chamber of Nations: in other words, thirty-one members (10 percent of the whole body plus one) could kill a measure.

Finally, the existence of the two National Councils created an institutionalized tug-of-war between three governments of more or less equal weight (although the political balance shifted decisively against the federal government in 1992). In such a compact country (about 15 million people inhabiting a territory the size of New York State), it was an open invitation to a schism between the federal government in Prague and the Slovak National Council in Bratislava. Intended by the communist regime to give the appearance of autonomy to Czechs and Slovaks, it had the effect of magnifying the points of contention between the two parts of the country once the communists were gone and paving the way for two separate nation-states.

One Government, Two Heads?

The Czech constitution establishes a parliamentary system with an indirectly elected president who appoints the prime minister — both can lay serious claim to the role of "chief" executive. The constitution also creates a bicameral legislature, but political foot-dragging delayed creation of the upper house (Senate). As a result, several years after the Czech Republic came into being there were still major unresolved constitutional issues affecting the basic functions of government. Nevertheless, seen through Western eyes, the Czechs adopted a reassuring charter because it is admirably concise and democratic, offers a broad spectrum of human rights guarantees, and protects private property rights.

The president of the Czech Republic is elected by the parliament for a five-year term and can hold office for no more than two terms in succession. The president has the power to appoint and dismiss the prime minister and cabinet, as well as to dissolve the Chamber of Deputies (lower house). These presidential powers only become operative, however, when (1) the parliament fails to pass a measure the government considers a matter of confidence or (2) the parliament itself initiates a no-confidence vote and passes it by an absolute majority of all the deputies. The Czech president thus does not have the discretionary power of, say, the French president to dismiss the prime minister at will. If the Chamber of Deputies fails to approve the president's choice of prime minister after two attempts, the president must appoint the prime minister proposed by the chairman of the Chamber of Deputies — the reverse of the rule in the Russian constitution.

The president's powers of appointment are extensive but, with few exceptions, not exclusive. The president has impressive powers of judicial intervention, as well. Thus, he can issue pardons, reduce penalties, preempt or discontinue criminal proceedings, and nullify punishments. In addition, he has the right to grant amnesty.

Under Article 63, the president represents the Czech Republic in the world and "concludes and ratifies international treaties." The president is also the "supreme commander of the armed forces." In general, presidential powers in the foreign policy arena would appear to be extensive, but Article 63 later stipulates: "Decisions by the President of the Republic made in accordance with Paragraphs (1) and (2) require for their validity the cosignature of the Prime Minister or another member of the government entrusted by him." Thus, the president's hands can effectively be tied in the exercise of the powers enumerated in Article 63 if the prime minister chooses to tie them.

The real substance of executive power for the most part resides in the prime minister, who, under Article 77, organizes the activity of the government, chairs its meetings, acts on its behalf, and carries out the duties entrusted by the constitution and law. Article 67 (1) makes it clear that the "government is the supreme organ of executive power"; Article 67 (2) further states that the "government consists of the Prime Minister, deputy prime ministers and ministers." Under Article 74, the prime minister has the real power to form a government; the president's apparent power to appoint and recall ministers turns out to be a mere formality.

Although the constitution appears to give the president extensive powers, these powers on closer examination are rather illusory. Another way to view the executive powers under the Czech constitution is to recognize the ambiguities (perhaps deliberate) surrounding the president's role and the built-in tensions (almost certainly deliberate) between the roles of president and prime minister. The precedent set by President Havel gives the prime minister virtually a free hand in the conduct of the country's domestic affairs, while responsibility for diplomacy and foreign policy is divided between the president's office and the foreign ministry.

The dual executive came under attack in the late 1990s, when the Czech parliament passed a law aimed at drastically reducing the powers of the president. Former Prime Minister Vaclav Klaus, leader of the opposition ODS party, instigated the action but he had the support of the governing Social Democrats. The next move was President Havel's, who challenged the law's constitutionality, placing the matter in the hands of the high court.

Problems and Prospects

The big question in 1992 was whether Prague would continue to be the capital of a federal state with two republics or whether Bratislava would become the capital of an independent Slovak state. A decade later, few Czechs or Slovaks expressed nostalgia for a bygone time when they were all part of one not-so-happy "family."

The Best of the Worst Before 1989, Czechoslovakia and East Germany had been the two most rigidly Stalinist states in the Soviet bloc. They also had the healthiest economies in the communist world. In the early 1990s, about one-half of the Czechoslovak labor force was employed in industry, producing machinery and machine tools, chemical products, textiles, and glassware. The principal crops were wheat, potatoes, barley (a prime ingredient in beer, for which the Czechs are famous), and sugar beets. Czechoslovakia had been a net exporter of food since the early 1970s.

By 1980, economic tremors prompted the government to call for greater efficiency, cuts in subsidies to state enterprises, the gearing of wages to productivity, and advances in quality control to boost Czechoslovak imports to the West. But economic performance during the 1980s resembled a roller coaster ride.

Economic figures do not tell the whole story, however. Anyone who had spent a few days in Moscow or Leningrad (Saint Petersburg) and then visited Prague could see the sharp contrast in living standards. In Prague, unlike Moscow, one did not see people waiting in long lines to buy food and other necessities. Nor did one see empty shops or bare shelves. Czechs and Slovaks generally ate and dressed well, possessed various household appliances, frequented pubs and restaurants, and attended the theater, cinema, and concerts. Most Czech and Slovak families owned an automobile, whereas most Russians could only dream of having a private car. And the national health system in Czechoslovakia was much better than in the Soviet Union.

In sum, if the Czechoslovak economy was not vibrant in the 1980s, neither was it bleak. To the extent that economic factors contributed to public disenchantment with communism, it probably reflected the fact that the Western-oriented Czechoslovaks tended to use the West rather than the East as a yardstick for comparison. The fact that Czechoslovakia shared a border with prosperous West Germany might well have been a contributing factor (as it certainly was in East Germany). Also relevant is the famous J-curve theory, which holds that the greatest danger of mass revolt occurs not during progressively worsening conditions, as one might expect, but rather when steadily improving conditions are followed by a leveling off or a downturn. As living standards improve, there is a natural surge of rising expectations; and if those expectations are not met, disappointment may be manifested in the spirit of rebellion.

A Velvet Divorce The Czech and Slovak republics formally split into two separate states at the end of 1992. The separation was accomplished peacefully but not painlessly. For many Czechs and Slovaks, the divorce was unwanted. Polls showed that a majority in both republics opposed it. There were many wrenching issues to resolve, including how to divide Czechoslovakia's assets and liabilities (including military facilities and weapons, foreign reserves, the external debt, and foreign embassies); what to do about the flag, anthem, and other important symbols of the former nation; and whether to create a customs union or retain a common currency.

Nonetheless, the breakup occurred without lasting bitterness between the two former partners and the country called "Czechoslovakia" soon became a fading memory. Slovakia was always the junior partner, living within the shadow of the bigger and richer Czechlands. The loss of subsidies from Prague was a sharp blow to the Slovak economy, and a corresponding boost to the Czech Republic. By the same token, Czechs benefited from the stabilizing effect of the soft-spoken, internationally acclaimed President Havel. By contrast, inept leadership and acrimonious politics hampered Slovakia's economic rebuilding program until the defeat of the combative and controversial Prime Minister Vladimir Meciar in 1998.

The Panacea of Privatization Despite the disruptive effects of the breakup, Czechoslovakia's GDP stabilized in 1992 and began rising again. Led by conservative Prime Minister Vaclav Klaus, the Czech Republic initiated an ambitious privatization scheme during this period. The objectives of this plan were to abolish the huge, inefficient state-owned enterprises of the communist era, make ordinary Czechs shareholders in new companies, and create a competitive free-market economy. Unfortunately, the plan fell victim to corruption, mismanagement, opposition, and obstruction from various quarters. Nor was the nation's top policy maker blameless. Prime Minister Klaus was at best inconsistent (at worst cynical), extolling the virtues of free enterprise and striking Thatcher-like poses in public but letting expedience rather than principle be his guide in practice.

In early 1997, the country was rocked by a financial crisis with multiple causes, including the bungled privatization program, a continuing succession of bank failures, government scandals, and a general economic malaise. In July 1997, the Czech Republic, along with Poland and Hungary, was formally invited to join the NATO alliance at the Madrid summit meeting, but this historic event was overshadowed by a natural disaster — the worst flooding in Czech history. One-third of the country was deluged and several dozen people were killed. Many towns and villages were awash; early estimates of the damage put the total at $1.5 billion or higher.

By the end of the year, the public mood had turned from sour to bitter amidst a scandal involving the campaign finances of the ruling ODS party. Prime Minister Klaus denied any personal involvement but as party leader he could not escape responsibility. At the end of 1997 the laconic Klaus was forced to step down in the face of mounting public criticism and crumbling support within the government's party coalition in parliament.

Winners Not Quite In, Losers Not Quite Out With Klaus out and no other party leader in parliament willing or able to form a new government, President Havel appointed a caretaker pending preparation for new elections in mid-1998. The Social Democrats led by Milos Zeman won the election, gaining more popular votes and parliamentary seats than Klaus's ODS, but fell far short of a clear majority. The inconclusive outcome of the election left key questions unanswered. Would Zeman (or anybody else) be able to form a government? If so, would it be able to govern? Zeman's options were severely limited: a coalition of the left that included the unpopular Communists or coalition with small center-right parties. The first option was undesirable and the second proved to be impossible. That left only one possibility for the Social Democrats — a minority government dependent on a benign opposition. But would the former prime minister in defeat make a deal?

Klaus pledged not to play the role of spoiler, but ODS would not become the junior partner in a coalition government either. As the opposition, ODS would freely criticize but not obstruct the new government, this was the essence of the so-called **Opposition Agreement.** In return, Zeman obviously had to resolve not to pursue a policy course or press for legislation unpalatable to the center-right. The result was a government with a gun held to its head by the opposition. Klaus was holding the gun, of course, but there was always the danger that it would backfire: if he pulled the trigger, would he look like an alternative or an assassin? Would the electorate reward or punish his party at the next election?

Taking a Stab at Stability: The Opposition Agreement Not surprisingly, the Zeman government stayed the course, undertaking few new initiatives and banking on a reviving economy to boost the Social Democrats' popular support. There was more common ground between government and opposition than might have been expected. Zeman, an economist by training, pursued privatization with no less vigor (arguably more) than Klaus had. In general, his economic policies had the effect of reassuring potential foreign investors. In foreign policy, too, Zeman followed the course charted by his predecessor. As leader of the opposition, Zeman had been cool to the idea of NATO membership; as leader of the nation he put any earlier doubts aside. He also continued to press for entry into the European Union, but on terms that would protect new members' fragile emerging markets.

Perhaps the most important long-term consequence of the Opposition Agreement was a cooperative effort to scrap the existing system of proportional representation in favor of an Anglo-American first past the post system (single-member districts, plurality vote) and to weaken the office of the presidency. As we noted in a previous chapter, this type of system weakens the link between popular votes and parliamentary representation and tends to favor large parties while shutting out small ones altogether. Obviously, the Social Democrats and ODS stood to gain the most from this change. Alarmed by this development, the smaller parties in parliament formed a four-party coalition in an attempt to stop the political freight train bearing down on them.

It is easy to question the motives behind these two changes in the Czech Republic's political system. Discriminating against small parties appears to violate the spirit of political fair play and the intent of democracy — to give voters the right to choose among meaningful alternatives. On the other hand, governmental stability — or even paralysis — is the price societies often have to pay for such a wide-open system. The confusion, disarray, and improvisation that characterized Czech government in 1997–1998 provide a classic case in point.

A rather bizarre episode at the end of 2000 provided new evidence that all was not well in the Czech transition to democracy. When a council established by parliament named a new head of the Czech state television, journalists at the facility — unhappy with the choice — barricaded themselves inside. They argued that the new director was unfit for the position due to his close ties to former Prime Minister Vaclav Klaus. The issue, they insisted, was journalistic independence and integrity — not personalities. Normal programming was disrupted (for example, there was virtually no news or weather presented) and the disgruntled employees broadcast an alternative news show every night accessible to about 10 percent of Czech households with satellite and cable television. Apparently, many Czechs agreed with the strikers — every night for weeks on end crowds gathered in Wenceslas Square or at the television station on the outskirts of Prague to demonstrate solidarity. And, in traditional Bohemian fashion, people brought food and drink to the rebels who hoisted it up to second-story windows in plastic buckets.

Following the 2002 elections, the Social Democrats joined with two smaller parties to form a fragile coalition government. The coalition had a razor thin one-seat majority in parliament, and even that disappeared in July 2003 when a disgruntled MP announced he was leaving the Social Democratic Party's parliamentary caucus. Whether the government could limp along without a majority until the next election was in serious doubt. The government's disarray would likely play into the hands of the unreformed Communists, the third largest party in the Czech parliament. Many older Czechs especially could not help but remember that the Communists had come to power after World War II as a result of winning an election. Meanwhile, the Czech

Republic was due to join the EU in 2004 – a major milestone that placed a premium on firm leadership.

The *economic* consequences of political instability for Europe's emerging democracies cannot be ignored. The stakes for these countries, including the Czech Republic, are extremely high. When it comes to enticing foreign investment, vital for rapid economic redevelopment, the first hurdle is political, not economic. By the same token, few things are more important to trade expansion in this part of the world than access to Europe's huge single market, but full membership in the EU (including the single currency) will depend, above all, on solid evidence of democratic maturity.

In Sum . . . The Czech Republic's transition to a market economy remains incomplete, but not without its successes. It has not only managed to keep both inflation and interest rates at moderate levels but also partially restructured the economy while avoiding mass worker dislocations. By the end of the decade, real gross domestic product (GDP) was growing at modest but steady rates and industrial production was rising more steeply. Economic forecasts for 2003 were even rosier. (See Table 6.13.) At the same time, Czechs have enjoyed the second highest per capita GDP in the region (first-ranking Slovenia is far ahead, however). Better yet, inflation was nearly nil in 2003, and foreign companies were investing heavily in the Czech economy, leading to rising productivity and higher wages. Budget deficits, a legacy of the communist era, continued to be a problem; it was this issue that animated Czech politics (and caused dissension within the governing coalition in 2003).

The picture was similar in neighboring Poland, where inflation was brought under control but big budget deficits and a weak zloty policy clouded Poland's prospects as a soon-to-be member of the EU. Chronic budget shortfalls were also a big problem in Hungary (exploding to more than 6 percent of GDP in 2002), but the economy continued growing at a modest pace despite the government's strong currency policy, which was a necessary brake on inflation. Overall, Eastern Europe was gradually emerging from the economic doldrums. There were no model democracies to be found, perhaps, but the dictatorships of the past were long gone, with few exceptions. One of the last countries to oust a dictator was Yugoslavia — oddly enough, the very country that had been closest to the West during the Cold War.

Table 6.13 Central Europe's Brightening Prospects: Forecasted Growth in Real GDP (percentage of annual change)

Country	2000	2004
Czech Republic	2.6	3.6
Hungary	5.6	3.2
Poland	5.0	4.2

Sources: "Emerging Market Indicators," *The Economist*, October 14, 2000, p. 148; and "The World in 2004," *The Economist*, pp. 85–86.

Yugoslavia: Rejecting Dictatorship

Serbians have chosen to call what remains of the multinational state Marshall Tito founded after World War II the Federal Republic of Yugoslavia (FRY). It is an egregious misnomer. In point of fact, Yugoslavia was neither federal nor a republic. Indeed, the international community did not recognize the FRY's debut in 1992. Despite the trappings of federalism and representative government, Serbian leader Slobodan Milosevic ruled the rump state of Yugoslavia with a heavy hand until he was finally forced out of office by a popular uprising in September 2000. The breaking away of Slovenia, Croatia, Macedonia, and Bosnia-Herzegovina at the outset of the 1990s left only Serbia and Montenegro in the phony federation.

The Yugoslav Experiment

Yugoslavia broke with Moscow in 1948 and looked westward for friendship and assistance. Recall that Yugoslavia was the only Eastern European state not occupied by Stalin's armies in World War II, having had the good fortune not to share a border with the Soviet Union.

Yugoslavia's pioneering efforts to decentralize administration and to institute workers' self-management, as well as its welcoming approach to trade with the West, were widely admired.[22] Workers' councils were the cornerstone of Yugoslavia's "socialist democracy" from 1950, when Tito promised "factories to the workers" as the first step toward repudiating the Stalinist model. The councils were intended to ensure democratic self-management at the enterprise level in order to avoid the stultifying effects of party-state control.

But in the 1950s, reality failed to catch up with the rhetoric of self-management; and in the 1960s, reformers made repeated attempts at economic liberalization. They sought "to end arbitrary political intervention in the economy in order to allow the market to work freely."[23] Self-management finally came of age in the 1970s, by which time Yugoslav workers did, at least in theory, manage the means of production and make decisions about product distribution. The social and political significance of this system was once described as follows:

> Within Yugoslavia, self-management provides the foundation for the "democratization of social life" and the "construction of a political system" that expresses the plurality of interests in society and allows contradictions inherent in such a society "to be resolved democratically by dialogue and consultations." . . . Self-management affects almost every facet of Yugoslav life.[24]

The Failure of "Self-Management"

Up to 1989, Yugoslavia was the most innovative state in Eastern Europe. Yet its experimentation with market-oriented, pseudodemocratic reforms failed to revitalize its lethargic economy or solve its political problems. The attempt to combine a free-market economy (including free emigration and free trade) with socialism and a one-party state foundered. Efforts to close unprofitable factories threatened workers with unemployment even as soaring inflation reduced purchasing power. Austerity measures implemented in 1987, including price increases and a wage freeze, led to widespread strikes.

Social unrest, spurred by ethnic tensions, was nothing new in Yugoslavia. The rivalry between Serbs and Croats was legendary. But in the 1980s, conflict between Serbs and Yugoslavia's ethnic Albanians broke out. In 1981, thousands of young Albanians demonstrated in the Serbian province of Kosovo, chanting anti-Yugoslav slogans and demanding political emancipation from Serbia. Such subnational particularism was never far below the surface in Yugoslavia, but the upheaval in Kosovo also had economic causes: Yugoslavia had piled up a huge multibillion-dollar foreign debt, price inflation was spinning out of control, and unemployment was in double digits.[25]

In Sum . . . Yugoslavia's economic outlook remained bleak throughout the decade, although it did manage to reduce its foreign debt (thanks to trade surpluses in the mid-1980s). But evidence of remaining structural problems was easy to find: inflation approached triple digits, one worker in seven could not find a job, and state control was increasing.[26]

Almost predictably in this economic climate, ethnic strains reached crisis levels. Milovan Djilas, Yugoslavia's most famous dissident, aptly summed up the situation: "We now face a choice. Either we go forward, become freer and join the rest of Europe, or we will fall backward and become the underdeveloped state we were before World War II."[27] What follows is a brief chronicle of Yugoslavia's fall backward.

Problems and Prospects

The 1992 constitution provided for a directly elected federal assembly consisting of a Chamber of Citizens (120 members chosen by proportional representation) and a Chamber of Republics (with an equal number of deputies for Serbia and Montenegro). The presidents of Serbia and Montenegro were elected by popular vote, but the assembly elected the federal president, who was a virtual figurehead. In theory, both member states are equal, with a guarantee that if the president is from one republic, the prime minister will be from the other. In reality, Serbia dominates the "federation," and the promise of parity has been ignored.

Yugoslavia under Slobodan Milosevic Freedom of the press is guaranteed by the constitution, but under Milosevic, the government often treated civil liberties, including free speech, with disdain. Indeed, Milosevic tightly controlled the news media and the leading newspapers were strictly censored. *Vreme,* an independent newsweekly, was the one major exception. In all probability, Milosevic allowed this single bastion of free speech to exist as a way to mollify or confound his critics.

A virtual dictator, Milosevic was totally out of step with the times, preferring force and intimidation to persuasion, negotiation, and compromise. But he had a keen instinct for personal political survival. In the postcommunist era, he managed to hang onto power longer than others who played by the rules of democracy. Ultimately, he failed to keep even the rump state he inherited united, but in that he was not alone. No East European leader succeeded in maintaining a national consensus during the difficult transition from communist dictatorship to democracy. However, the bitter legacy of Milosevic's rule is not only dissension and disunity but also an economy in ruins and a society with a badly tarnished reputation in the world.

The Failure of Leadership: Yugoslavia's Violent Breakup Ever-increasing economic problems, including hyperinflation (more than 1,000 percent for a time in 1989–1990), accelerated Yugoslavia's disintegration. On July 2, 1990, democratically elected governments in Slovenia and Macedonia declared their independence ("full sovereignty") within Yugoslavia, and Croatia approved constitutional changes having basically the same effect. On the same day, a majority of Serbs approved a referendum on a new constitution that made the formerly autonomous provinces of Kosovo and Vojvodina parts of Greater Serbia (in violation of the federal constitution). Meanwhile, the Kosovo assembly approved a measure making Kosovo a sovereign republic within Yugoslavia. Serbia then dissolved the Kosovo legislature.

Former communists won by landslides in Serbia and Montenegro but lost decisively in Bosnia-Herzegovina. Ethnic tensions were thus reinforced by a political and ideological rift between the Serbs and Montenegrins on the one hand and the rest of the crumbling Yugoslav federation on the other. (A similar phenomenon occurred in Czechoslovakia in 1992, with the Czechs being led by free-market enthusiasts and the Slovaks by a leftist politician who opposed rapid privatization.) The Serbian government further exacerbated the situation by issuing, without National Bank approval, $1.4 billion in new money to ease its own financial straits. Branded as "stealing from the other republics," this action triggered the beginning of the end for the Yugoslav federation.

A bitter civil war broke out, with the first round pitting Serbia against Croatia. The fighting brought extensive loss of life and damage to Croatia; when the smoke cleared, Serbia had annexed Krajina (formerly part of Croatia). Many towns and cities, including Vukovar and Dubrovnik, had endured heavy bombing and artillery attacks by the Yugoslav (Serbian) armed forces. International mediation and a United Nations peacekeeping force brought a cease-fire but not a settlement.

Tragically, there was no containing the conflict. Bosnia-Herzegovina was to be the next battleground.

A Dirty Little War: The Bosnia Crisis In Bosnia-Herzegovina the tragedy was compounded by the fact that **Bosnian Muslims,** although numerically the largest ethnic group there, were caught in the cross fire between Serbs and Croats. After months of bloody fighting and a particularly brutal artillery assault on Sarajevo, the capital, Serbs (31 percent of Bosnia's population) controlled 65 percent of the territory, and Croats (17 percent of the population) held about 30 percent. That left the Muslim population (44 percent of the total) with only 5 percent of the territory. Some well-informed observers feared that the upshot of the war would be to divide Bosnia between Serbia and Croatia, leaving the Bosnian Muslims a nation without a state. Worse, it was not entirely clear who was doing what to whom. The Yugoslav army made a pretense of neutrality, but it was widely reported that the army was supplying Serbian guerrillas with arms and ammunition. Although Yugoslav forces were withdrawing from Slovenia, Croatia, and Macedonia in April 1992, the army was reluctant to withdraw from Bosnia-Herzegovina because 65 percent of its arms industry and installations were concentrated there.

The **Bosnian war** worsened in 1992 and 1993. Egregious human rights violations by all three warring sides — Bosnian Muslims and Croatians, as well as Bosnian Serbs — characterized the conflict from the beginning. Reports of **ethnic cleansing** — the systematic deportation or slaughter of Muslims by Bosnian Serbs, allegedly with the covert support of Belgrade — caused outrage in the West and led to calls (especially in the United States) for economic sanctions, no-fly zones, and even military intervention. As stories of atrocities (concentration camps reminiscent of the Holocaust and the systematic rape of Muslim women) piled up, pressures built for effective measures to punish the Serbs, who nonetheless remained defiant in the face of growing diplomatic isolation.

Former U.S. Secretary of State Cyrus Vance and former British Foreign Secretary David Owen, representing the United Nations and the European Union, respectively, attempted to broker a cease-fire based on a proposed division of Bosnia into ten autonomous regions, some controlled by Serbs, some by Croats, and some by Bosnian Muslims — all supervised by a UN peacekeeping force. But the warring sides rejected this plan, and the Bosnian Serbs continued their relentless ethnic cleansing in the widening areas under Serb military control. Fears that Macedonia and Kosovo would be the next battlegrounds added to the sense of alarm in the international community.

The war in Bosnia dragged on despite continuing efforts by UN peacekeepers, the European Union, and the United States to mediate. Nor did NATO air strikes stop it. Serbia was widely condemned for its role in aiding and abetting the Bosnian Serbs. The effects of the Yugoslav war and the international trade embargo against Serbia were devastating. Critical shortages of many food staples forced the Serbian government to introduce rationing. Inflation reached a staggering 1 million percent in 1993, prompting Belgrade to adopt a new currency, "the super dinar" in January 1994. In the summer of 1994, two-thirds of all working-age Serbs were unemployed, mainly because of plant closings caused by the embargo.

When the war finally ended in 1995 there was still a big question mark over Bosnia's future, and, ironically, over Serbia's as well. Only the fate of the old Yugoslavia was beyond question: its existence was now nothing more than a fiction maintained solely for the self-gratification of Serbian nationalists.

Whistle While You (Skip?) Work: Serbia in Revolt The government of Slobodan Milosevic, Serbia's authoritarian president, faced mounting popular discontent in 1996. In November, a mass antigovernment movement emerged in response to Milosevic's decision to cancel the results of local elections after opposition candidates won in fourteen communities. With national elections just around the corner, Milosevic and his followers had good reason for concern. In Belgrade, thousands of peaceful demonstrators streamed into the streets, ignoring the government's warnings, threats, and entreaties.

Milosevic was especially loath to relinquish the state monopoly of the mass media. A swelling tide of protesters began to drown out the government's lies by going outside or simply opening a window and banging on pots, pans, and garbage can lids every evening during the censored nightly news broadcasts on state television. They also began blowing whistles. Soon the whistle became a symbol and a badge, as well as the "weapon" of choice. People of all ages, including schoolchildren, started wearing whistles around their necks. The din and roar of the movement literally overwhelmed the voice of official authority.

Finally, Milosevic made a concession, allowing some of his opponents to take office. In one such community south of Belgrade police barricaded themselves in local radio and television stations in January 1997 to prevent these facilities from falling into the hands of the duly elected officials. Miraculously, incidents of violence between police and protesters had so far been few. But how much longer the tension could continue to build up without erupting was anybody's guess.

Another Dirty Little War: Kosovo In November 1995, the United States brokered the **Dayton peace accord,** which halted the fighting in Bosnia-Herzegovina. The Serbian government played a constructive role, finally accepting the principle of a separate Bosnia and Croatia. In return, the United States lifted economic sanctions against Serbia. Notwithstanding, there remained a serious question about whether — or how long — conflict in the neighborhood of the former Yugoslavia could be contained. Would Bulgaria, Romania, Hungary, Albania, Greece, and Turkey stand by if Serbia attempted to incorporate more territories of the former Yugoslavia into "Greater Serbia"? For example, hundreds of thousands of Hungarians lived on the "wrong" side of the border (in a region of Serbia called Vojvodina), as well as in Slovakia and Romania. By the same token, some 2 million Albanians lived in **Kosovo** (part of Serbia). Macedonia also had a large Albanian minority.

The answer was, unfortunately, not long in coming. Another war in the name of Greater Serbia broke out, this time in Kosovo, a province of Serbia inhabited by mostly ethnic Albanians but highly prized for historical and cultural reasons by the Serbs. The Serbian army cracked down brutally in Kosovo after ethnic Albanian Kosovars revolted. The **Kosovo Liberation Army (KLA)** offensive was spurred by Serbian refusal to grant an acceptable degree of autonomy to the province.

But Serbian arms were far superior and the Serbian army showed no mercy in Kosovo. Quite the contrary: Serbian forces began systematically driving Kosovars out of their homes, villages, and, ultimately, out of Serbia (Kosovo, that is) into neighboring Macedonia, Albania, and other neighboring states. The aim of this strategy, to the world's horror, appeared to be "ethnic cleansing." Faced with this unfolding human tragedy and an uncompromising Milosevic, NATO (bolstered by the United Nations) initiated a bombing campaign — belatedly in the opinion of critics — against Serbia in the spring of 1999. By the time NATO's intervention finally brought the Milosevic government to its knees well over 1 million Kosovars (roughly three-fifths of the entire ethnic Albanian population) had been driven from their homes.

The joyless end of the fighting was accompanied by an imposed "peace." The United Nations put its own "interim administration" in charge with NATO troops on the ground as a kind of police force. The declared aim was "substantial autonomy and self-government" for the province, whatever that meant. The UN-NATO regime disarmed the KLA and promised to protect the tiny (5 percent) Serbian minority in Kosovo against recriminations by angry ethnic Albanians. It was a promise not perfectly kept, as many Serbians in Kosovo were attacked or threatened.

In sum, nothing was settled. There was no end in sight for the UN protectorate so long as Milosevic was in power. For all its good intentions, the United Nations once again proved itself ill equipped to govern. UN administrators were unfamiliar with local customs and struggled with a baffling language barrier. NATO forces now in the odd role of protecting Serbians met with hostility from the outraged Kosovars. Meanwhile, there was an institutional and legal vacuum with neither laws, nor courts, nor local police to fight ordinary (and not-so-ordinary) crime.

Milosevic the Loser The economic impact of the war on Serbia was devastating. After years of enduring economic sanctions imposed by the United Nations and the European Union, the effects of NATO bombing raids on infrastructure and strategic industries were severe. Serbs had grown accustomed to a relatively high standard of living during the previous decades of the Cold War but were now facing hardships and shortages. Nonetheless, the Serbian people were divided politically. Because Milosevic blamed the West all along for interfering in Serbia's domestic affairs, the NATO air raids against Serbia, and the imposed "peace" in Kosovo that followed, fed the government's propaganda machine. On the other hand, many Serbs wanted the kind of democratic reforms that had been realized elsewhere in Eastern Europe and opposed Milosevic's dictatorial rule. That Milosevic was a dictator could not be denied: he controlled the press, rigged elections, and dealt harshly with all manifestations of opposition. The upshot was a divided and ambivalent populace, with fear and anger mixing to create a volatile situation.

Milosevic was forced to back down in Kosovo, but not humbled. It was not long before new war clouds were gathering over Montenegro, the only one of the original Yugoslav republics to remain within the rump federation. Taking a cue from Milosevic's eroding support in the aftermath of the fiasco in Kosovo, Montenegro's popularly elected president sought closer ties to the West and posed as a counterweight to Milosevic. The possibility of yet another dirty war in the Balkans once again set off alarm bells in Western capitals.

Meanwhile, Milosevic attempted to boost his popularity by promising an election in the fall of 2000 — an election that he probably expected to win (by hook or crook), but lost. Although his opponent, Vojislav Kostunica, clearly won the election, Milosevic refused to step down claiming Kostunica had gotten just under the 50 percent needed to win outright and calling for a runoff. Serbs knew what that would mean. Milosevic would do a better job of stuffing ballot boxes the second time around. So Serbs surged into the streets. Riot police could not deter antigovernment demonstrators who gathered in Belgrade's main Republic Square by the thousands. Milosevic was also under tremendous pressure from abroad. When the Serbian Army decided to back Kostunica and even the Putin government in Russia deserted him, Milosevic bowed to the inevitable, defiantly telling the Serbian people in a televised address that he was conceding defeat but not getting out of politics.

What followed was a bizarre drama in which remnants of the fallen government, including the interior minister (who controls the national police in Serbia), refused to give up their posts. But the newly elected president, buoyed by a wave of enthusiastic popular support and backed by Western governments, stood firm. And when general elections were held in December 2000 a coalition of eighteen parties, the **Democratic Opposition**

of Serbia (DOS), led by Zoran Djindic won easily, gaining 176 out of 250 parliamentary seats. The election removed all doubt about the extent of the former dictator Milosevic's unpopularity — his disgraced Communists captured only 14 percent of the popular vote. So now Serbia at long last had a popularly elected president, parliament, and prime minister, but little else. The economy was in a shambles and the government was stalemated.

In Sum . . . The prospects for Yugoslavia remain highly uncertain, but the departure of Milosevic created the possibility for a new beginning. It would not be easy, however. Yugoslavia's current problems can be seen as an extension of the policy failures of the past. Milosevic pursued reckless and misguided policies aimed at self-aggrandizement in terms of both personal and national power. He did so at the expense of constitutional integrity, economic development, and international respectability. Ultimately, he failed miserably even on his own terms. The Yugoslavia he bequeathed was physically smaller, economically poorer, and militarily weaker than the one he inherited. Moreover, Milosevic's mania for creating a "Greater Serbia" at all costs made Belgrade the capital of a pariah state in the eyes of the world — a world to which his successor(s) would have to turn for trade concessions, investment, and other favors. As for Milosevic, his fate was left to an international court at The Hague to decide when Kostunica ordered his arrest and extradition to the Netherlands to stand trial for war crimes.

SUMMARY

The Soviet state developed an elaborate set of highly centralized political institutions. The Communist Party — including the Politburo, Secretariat, and the Central Committee apparatus — was the organizational backbone of the Stalinist system. An all-encompassing state bureaucracy carried out the will of this monolithic party. Political dissent was suppressed by the secret police (KGB), which operated outside the normal legal framework of Soviet society during Stalin's long reign of terror. This system mellowed perceptibly after Stalin's death in 1953 but continued inhospitable to open dissent until Gorbachev's accession to power in 1985. By that time, the Soviet economy had stagnated. Mikhail Gorbachev called for new thinking and launched a series of bold economic and political reforms. His own vacillations; resistance from vested interests within the party, state bureaucracy, secret police, and military; and the sheer magnitude of the tasks combined to bring the reforms to grief. The "outer empire" unraveled in 1989; the "inner empire" disintegrated in 1991 after an abortive coup by hard-liners. Today, Russia is ruled as a constitutional democracy, but many Russians still face hardships, and the nation must overcome a wide array of obstacles if freedom is to survive. The former Soviet-bloc countries in Eastern Europe have also adopted liberal constitutions. Although Poland and Hungary have successfully made the transition to democratic rule, the Czech Republic is the most stable, liberal, democracy in the region. The rump state of Yugoslavia, by contrast, remains an ill-disguised authoritarian regime that has yet to undergo a political or economic transition.

The former communist states of Europe are going through a difficult transition period from central planning and police-state controls to market economies and multiparty democracy. In Russia, as elsewhere in the former Soviet Union, this process has been tumultuous, and the outcome remains indeterminate. In East-Central Europe, the reforms have progressed rapidly but not always smoothly. Poland, Hungary, and the Czech Republic, along with Slovenia, have managed the smoothest transitions in the region. In recent years, the Baltic States have also shown signs of economic vitality. All seven (plus Slovakia, Cyprus, and Malta) will join the European Union in 2004. Yugoslavia was torn asunder by ethnic conflict and civil war in the 1990s, but NATO intervention in Kosovo conflict and the subsequent ouster of Serbian dictator Slobodan Milosevic in 2000 brought an end to the fighting. Serbia now has a new democratically elected government, but the Serbian economy is still a basket case.

The problem of ethnic conflict is not confined to the Balkans. Ethnic rivalries continue to threaten peace and stability in many regions of the former Soviet Union, as well.

KEY TERMS

glasnost
perestroika
demokratizatsiia
shock therapy
Supreme Soviet
Council of Ministers
Politburo
Secretariat
Central Committee
Congress of People's Deputies
central planning
Liberman reforms
Gosplan
output quotas
Comecon
August coup
Russian Federation
Russkye
Rossianiye
Prague Spring
Brezhnev Doctrine
Solidarity
emerging markets
Velvet Revolution
Opposition Agreement
Bosnian Muslims
Bosnian War
ethnic cleansing
Dayton peace accord
Kosovo
Kosovo Liberation Army (KLA)
Democratic Opposition of Serbia (DOS)

STUDY QUESTIONS

1. Why did the founders of the Soviet state opt for federalism, and what does the term mean in the Soviet context? How has federalism been affected by Gorbachev's reforms? (Hint: focus on the role of the new Soviet legislature.) How have recent events threatened to reshape the Soviet federal system?
2. What is the traditional relationship between ideology and economics in Soviet-type systems? What leader most left his imprint on the Soviet economy? (Identify spe-

cific ideas and institutions associated with this leader.) What are the comparative advantages and disadvantages of central planning (versus market economies)?

3. What were the major structural elements and operating principles of the Soviet system in the pre-Gorbachev era?
4. How and why did Mikhail Gorbachev attempt to reform the Soviet system, and what were the consequences? How can the collapse of the Soviet system be explained? What were the key internal factors that undermined the Soviet state? Could anybody or anything have saved it?
5. In what sense was 1989 a watershed in the political history of Eastern Europe? What were the major events of that year, and how have those events transformed the region's politics?
6. What were the principal challenges facing Russian President Boris Yeltsin in 1992 and 1993? What sort of political opposition did Yeltsin encounter in his efforts to reform Russia? Evaluate his performance in dealing with his political opponents and moving the country forward. Compare Yeltsin and Putin as leaders.
7. What were (are) the causes of the conflict in the former Yugoslavia?
8. What general transition problems do all the former Soviet-bloc states face? What are the prospects for this region? How much of a difference will joining the European Union make to these countries? In your view, is it likely to effect relations between Russia and its former East European satellites very much?

SUGGESTED READINGS

Aslund, Anders. *Gorbachev's Struggle for Economic Reform.* Ithaca, N.Y.: Cornell University Press, 1991.

Brzezinski, Zbigniew, ed. *Russia and the Commonwealth of Independent States: Documents, Data, and Analysis.* New York: Sharpe, 1996.

Colton, Timothy J. *Moscow: Governing the Socialist Metropolis.* Cambridge, Mass.: Harvard University Press, 1996.

Colton, Timothy J. and Michael McFaul. *Popular Choice and Managed Democracy: The Russian Elections of 1999 and 2000.* Washington, D.C.: Brookings Instititution, 2004.

Dedek, Oldrich, ed. *The Break-up of Czechoslovakia: An In-Depth Economic Analysis.* Brookfield, Vt.: Ashgate, 1996.

Dragnich, Alex N. *Serbs and Croats: The Struggle in Yugoslavia.* San Diego: Harcourt Brace, 1992.

Glenny, Misha. *The Fall of Yugoslavia: Yugoslavia at War.* New York: Viking Penguin, 1993.

Goldman, Marshall. *The Piratization of Russia: Russian Reform Goes Awry.* New York: Routledge, 2003.

Hahn, Jeffrey W., ed. *Democratization in Russia: The Development of Legislative Institutions.* Armonk, N.Y.: Sharpe, 1996.

Huskey, Eugen. *Presidential Power in Russia.* Armonk, N.Y.: Sharpe, 1997.

Ivanov, Igor S. *The New Russian Diplomacy.* Washington, D.C.: Brookings Instititution, 2002.

Karahasan, Dzevad. *Sarajevo, Exodus of a City.* New York: Kodansha America, 1994.

Kullberg, Judith S. *Legislative Politics in Russia: From Soviets to Parliaments.* Armonk, N.Y.: Sharpe, 1997.

Laquer, Walter. *The Long Road to Freedom: Russia and Glasnost.* New York: Macmillan, 1990.

McRaul, Michael, Mikolai Petrov, and Andrei Ryabov. *Between Dictatorship and Democracy: Russian Post-Communist Political Reform.* Washington, D.C.: Carnegie Endowment for International Peace, 2004.

Nogee, Joseph L. *Russian Politics: The Struggle for a New Order.* Englewood Cliffs, N.J.: Prentice-Hall, 1996.

Rothschild, Joseph. *Return to Diversity: A Political History of East Central Europe since World War II.* New York: Oxford University Press, 1989.

Satter, David. *Darkness at Dawn: The Rise of the Russian Criminal State.* New Haven, Conn.: Yale University Press, 2003.

Shevtsova, Lila. *Putin's Russia.* Washington, D.C.: Carnegie Endowment for International Peace, 2004.

Shevtsova, Lila. *Yeltsin's Russia: Myths and Realities.* Washington, D.C.: Carnegie Endowment for International Peace, 1999.

Slider, Darrell L. *The Politics of Russia's Regions.* Armonk, N.Y.: Sharpe, 1997.

Trenin, Dmitri and Aleksei Malashenko, with Anatol Lieven. *Russia's Restless Frontier: The Chechnya Factor in Post-Soviet Russia.* Washington, D.C.: Carnegie Endowment for International Peace, 2004.

SUGGESTED WEB SITES

http://www.columbia.edu/cu/sipa/REGIONAL/ECE/homepage.html
http://www.EINnews.com/centraleurope
http://www.nato.int/
http://www.grip.org
http://members.valley.net/~transnat/
http://www.rferl.org/
http://www.ucis.pitt.edu/reesweb/

NOTES

1. Gordon B. Smith, *Soviet Politics: Continuity and Contradictions* (New York: St. Martin's, 1987), p. 365.
2. Paul Quinn-Judge, "Gorbachev Presses for a Rollback of Party's Power," *Christian Science Monitor,* June 29, 1988, p. 1.
3. Stanley Rothman and George W. Breslauer, *Soviet Politics and Society* (St. Paul, Minn.: West, 1978), p. 242; see also E. G. Liberman, *Economic Methods and Effectiveness of Production* (White Plains, N.Y.: International Arts and Sciences Press, 1971).

4. Robert Gillete, "Perestroika: Bold Shift in Economy," *Los Angeles Times,* October 27, 1987.
5. Ibid.
6. Ibid.
7. Dan Fisher and William J. Eaton, "Rumbles of Change Stir Soviet Union," *Los Angeles Times,* October 25, 1987.
8. Ibid.
9. Dan Fisher, "Glasnost: Soviets Try to Open Up," *Los Angeles Times,* October 29, 1987.
10. See Hedrick Smith, *The Russians* (New York: Ballantine, 1984), pp. 320–362; and David Shipler, *Russia* (New York: Viking Penguin, 1983), pp. 301–346.
11. Shipler, *Russia,* p. 326.
12. Alex Goldfarb, "Testing Glasnost: An Exile Visits His Homeland," *New York Times Magazine,* December 6, 1987, p. 49.
13. Shipler, *Russia,* p. 324. The pervasiveness of the surveillance system nurtured and maintained by the party since 1917 was suggested in this sardonic (and thoroughly Russian) condensation of the Soviet constitution: "Whatever is not forbidden is compulsory."
14. Bill Keller, "Riots' Legacy of Distrust Quietly Stalks a Soviet City," *New York Times,* August 31, 1989, p. 1.
15. Paul Hofheinz, "Let's Do Business," *Fortune,* September 23, 1991, p. 62; Amy Kaslow, "Swedish Adviser Says Soviet Republics, West Are Squandering Chance to Solve Problems," *Christian Science Monitor,* October 23, 1991, p. 1; Gerald F. Seib and Alan Murray, "IMF Effort to Reform Soviet Economy Runs Many Daunting Risks," *Wall Street Journal,* October 15, 1991, p. 1.
16. Ibid.
17. "Emerging Market Indicators," *The Economist,* June 1, 1996, p. 102.
18. "Russia's Flawed Reformer," *The Economist,* January 8, 2000, pp. 19–21.
19. Daniel Sneider, "Yeltsin Struggles to Keep Russian Federation Intact," *Christian Science Monitor,* March 25, 1992, p. 1.
20. *The Economist,* March 24, 1990, p. 21.
21. "Tinker, tailor, soldier, party leader . . . ," *The Economist,* February 3, 1996, p. 43.
22. See Bogdan Denitch, "The Relevance of Yugoslav Self-Management," in *Comparative Communism: The Soviet, Chinese, and Yugoslav Models,* Gary K. Bertsch and Thomas W. Ganschow, eds. (New York: Freeman, 1976), pp. 268–279.
23. April Carter, *Democratic Reform in Yugoslavia: The Changing Role of the Party* (Princeton, N.J.: Princeton University Press, 1982), p. 5.
24. Wayne S. Vucinich, "Major Trends in Eastern Europe," in *Eastern Europe in the 1980s,* Stephen Fischer Galati, ed. (Boulder, Colo.: Westview, 1981), p. 5.
25. Darko Bekic, "Yugoslavia's System in Crisis: Internal View," *Problems of Communism,* November-December 1985, p. 71.
26. Jackson Diehl, "Yugoslavia's New Leader Has Yet to Take Hold," *Washington Post,* December 8, 1986, p. A17.
27. William Echikson, "Top Dissident Now Free to Go Abroad: Yugoslavia 'Faces a Choice,'" *Christian Science Monitor,* January 22, 1987, p. 12.

PART IV
Asia

China

Area: 3,691,521 square miles

Population: 1.3 billion

Density per square mile: 325–350

Language(s): Chinese (Mandarin) Cantonese, local dialects

Major religion(s): Confucianism, Buddhism, Taoism, Islam

Monetary unit: yuan

GDP: $1.388 trillion (2003)

GDP per head: $1,120 (2004 est.)

Annual GDP growth rate: 6.7% (Q2, 2003)

Inflation rate: 0.3% (June 2003)

Foreign direct investment (% of GDP): 4.6 (1998)

Japan

Area: 145,856 square miles

Population: 127.2 million

Density per square mile: 860

Language: Japanese

Major religion(s): Buddhism, Shinto

Monetary unit: yen

GDP: $3.942 trillion (2003)

GDP per head: $34,350 (2004 est.)

Annual GDP growth rate: 2.6% (Q1, 2003)

Inflation rate: –0.4% (June 2003)

Foreign direct investment (% of GDP): 0.1% (1998)

India

Area: 1,266,595 square miles

Population: 1.1 billion

Density per square mile: 775–800

Language(s): Hindi (official), English (associate official), 14 others listed, plus many unlisted

Major religion(s): Hindu (83%), Islam (11%), Christianity (3%), Sikh (2%), others

Monetary unit: rupee

GDP: $538 billion

GDP per head: $593 (2004 est.)

Annual GDP growth rate: 4.9% (Q1, 2003)

Inflation rate: 4.7% (May 2003)

Foreign direct investment (% of GDP): 0.6%

Russia
Kazakhstan
MONGOLIA
Uzbekistan
Kyrgyzstan
Turkmenistan
Tajikistan
Gobi Desert
Beijing
NORTH KOREA
SOUTH KOREA
JAPAN
Tokyo
CHINA
AFGHANISTAN
Iran
PAKISTAN
TIBET
Himalayas
Delhi
NEPAL
BHUTAN
INDIA
TAIWAN
MYANMAR
BANGLADESH
LAOS
THAILAND
VIETNAM
CAMBODIA
PHILIPPINES
SRI LANKA
BRUNEI
MALAYSIA
SINGAPORE
INDONESIA
Papua New Guinea
Australia

Part IV Outline: Asia

CHAPTER 7

Civilizations and Empires

Think of Asia as an awakening giant. It is immense — it accounts for 30 percent of the earth's landmass and is home to 60 percent of the earth's inhabitants. But it is demography rather than geography that makes Asia a colossus. Wealth in the world is grossly maldistributed, most of it concentrated outside of Asia during the lion's share of the twentieth century. But several nations, led by Japan, are in the process of redressing the global economic balance in Asia's favor. According to some prognosticators, the twenty-first century may well belong to Asia.

Of the six regions explored in this book, Asia is the most difficult to treat as a single area because of its size and diversity. Geographically, the Asian continent extends from the Mediterranean Sea and the Ural Mountains in the west to the Pacific Ocean in the east. Thus, it encompasses most of the countries of the Middle East (see Part VI) and more than half of the former republics of the Soviet Union (see Part III). In addition to Southwest Asia (Iran and Arabian peninsula), we can identify four overlapping regions on the vast continent of Asia:

1. **Northeast Asia** (China, Japan, and the Russian Far East)
2. **Southeast Asia** (Vietnam, Laos, Cambodia, Thailand, Malaysia, Indonesia, and Myanmar (formerly Burma)
3. **South Asia** (India, Pakistan, Bangladesh, and Sri Lanka)
4. **Central Asia** (Afghanistan, Kazakhstan, Kyrgyzstan, Tajikistan, Turkmenistan, and Uzbekistan)

The countries of Asia range in size from mainland China and India, with a combined population of 2.4 billion (about 40 percent of all people in the world) to tiny Brunei, with a population of 240,000. Put Japan, Bangladesh, or Pakistan in Europe and they would dwarf every country except Russia. Even Vietnam, a medium-sized country in Asia terms, is nearly as large as Germany, a behemoth in Europe. Indonesia, with a population of over 2 million, ranks fourth in the world behind only China, India, and the United States; it is bigger by far than Russia. Clearly, the population dynamics of Asia are a world apart from those of Europe.

Although these disparate nations defy easy generalization, certain patterns are distinctive to Asia or large parts of it. First, until the middle of the twentieth century, no

Democracy in America

BOX 7.1

The Idea of Natural Rights: Cornerstone of America's Political Culture

The idea of "natural rights" did not originate in America, but it is closely identified with the American Revolution and the subsequent evolution of America's political traditions and institutions. The basis for natural rights is natural law. The most famous exponent of natural law was English philosopher John Locke (1632–1704). In a famous passage from his essay "Concerning Civil Government," Locke wrote:

> Man being born . . . with a title to perfect freedom and an uncontrolled enjoyment of all the rights and privileges of the law of Nature, equally with any other man, or number of men in the world, hath by nature a power not only to preserve his property — that is, his life, liberty, and estate, against the injuries and attempts of other men, but to judge of and punish the breaches of that law in others, as he is persuaded the offence deserves, even with death itself, in crimes where the heinousness of the fact, in his opinion, requires it. (II *Civil Government*, VII, 87–89)

Civil government is the "proper remedy for the inconveniences of the state of Nature," Locke reasoned. However, the commonwealth (or political society) "is constituted only for procuring, preserving, and advancing . . . civil interests." Locke defined the latter to include, "life, liberty, and health . . . and the possession of outward things, such as money, lands, houses, furniture, and the like" (from Locke's "Letter Concerning Tolerance"). Locke also defended the right of the people to revolt against any arbitrary and unjust rulers.

No wonder the American revolutionists were fans of Locke. Indeed, Thomas Jefferson, the author of the Preamble to the U.S. Consitution, could almost be accused of plagiarism when he wrote:

> We hold these truths to be self-evident: That all men are created equal; that they are *endowed by their Creator* with certain unalienable rights; that among these are life, liberty, and the pursuit of happiness; that to secure these rights, governments are instituted among men, deriving their just powers from the consent of the governed; that whenever any form of government becomes destructive of these ends, it is the right of the people to alter or to abolish it. . . .

Today, the triumph of natural rights philosophy in America is so complete that the notion of civil and political rights does indeed seem perfectly natural to Americans. In fact, most Americans find it puzzling that people everywhere do not "fight for their rights" and consider any form of government other than democracy to be positively *unnatural.*

nation in Asia had experienced democratic rule. None had any indigenous democratic or republican institutions. There was no tradition of "natural rights." (See Box 7.1.) A dynastic type of authoritarianism was the basis of all politics.

The archetypal Asian political system was that of Imperial China, long described by Western historians as **oriental despotism** and generally thought to be a pattern repeated, with local variations, throughout Asia. Although this Western stereotype ignores the fact that there were important differences from place to place, China, Korea, Japan, Vietnam, Cambodia, and India all had hereditary autocratic rulers who governed through centralized administrative systems embedded in hierarchical societies with no concept of political or civil rights.

Moreover, these rulers were the products of advanced civilizations with complex writing systems, scholars and scribes, monumental architecture and public works (especially roads and irrigation systems), and impressive religious and philosophical traditions.

Thus, to speak of Asian societies as "underdeveloped" was never appropriate except in a narrow sense of the word, one that equated development with Westernization.

To survey Asian politics, we will feature three countries selected on the basis of size, relative importance, and overall impact on regional patterns: China, Japan, and India. Choosing three countries in a region as large and populous as Asia is bound to raise eyebrows no matter how it is done. Still, it is important to recognize that there are distinct regions within the area commonly called "Asia." Indeed, Asia is as rich and varied in geography, culture, history, and ethnicity as Europe, if not more so.

Mainland China — officially known as the People's Republic of China (PRC) — is the potential hegemon (ruler) of Asia. China's large and industrious population, technological ingenuity, cultural prowess, and imposing geopolitical traits have long thrust it onto Asia's center stage. China is one of three potential great powers in Northeast Asia; Russia and Japan are the other two. Unlike Japan, however, Russia is both European and Asia from a geographic standpoint. Politically and culturally, Russia is Eurasian — a unique mixture of the two.

Japan is Asia's greatest success story in the post–World War II period. It is tempting to view Japan as an exception to the trends and patterns of political and economic development in the rest of Asia. Until recently, Japan seemed economically and politically to belong more to the West than to the East. Indeed, the **Trilateral Commission,** a private foreign-policy interest group founded by David Rockefeller in 1973, consists of representatives from the United States, the European Community, and Japan. But today, Japan is no longer an isolated example of Western technology in an Asian setting: South Korea, Taiwan, Hong Kong, and Singapore have become important producers of high-tech exports, and even mainland China has begun moving toward an export-oriented model of development.

Finally, India is the dominant power in South Asia. Pakistan is India's longtime rival in South Asia. Pakistan is an Islamic society, whereas India has a large Muslim minority. Kashmir — geographically situated between the two countries and claimed by both — is a bone of contention. Both India and Pakistan are technologically advanced and both possess nuclear weapons. Pakistan has been ruled by military strongmen for most of the period since independence in 1947. By contrast, India is a democracy. However, India faces daunting problems related to overpopulation; regional and communal strife; vulnerability to natural catastrophe; pervasive poverty; uneven growth; and excessive regulation of the economy. However, this list of problems conceals certain underlying strengths that significantly improve India's prospects for the future.

Physical Environment and Population

Stereotypes of Asia revolve around size and scale — teeming masses of people and vast deserts, mountain ranges, rivers, and jungles. These images are part imagination and part truth. In area and population, Asia is gigantic. It is nearly twice the size of North America, the second largest continent. And, as noted, three-fifths of all people on earth live in Asia (two-thirds of them in China and India).

Environment

Because of its huge size, Asia has climates of every kind, from the frozen tundra of Siberia to the steamy jungles of Indochina and the tropical lowlands of Indonesia. In between lie temperate zones, which encompass northern China, Korea, Japan, and Taiwan; a massive desert in western China and the semiarid plains of Central Asia; the high plateaus and snowy, craggy wilderness of Tibet, Bhutan, and Nepal; and the huge subcontinent of South Asia, with the Great Indian Desert in the northwest and the semitropical Deccan peninsula in the south.

The topography, too, offers great variety — forbidding mountain ranges, fertile river valleys, coastal lowlands, and flowing plains. Much of Asia's deep interior is inhabited either sparsely or not at all. In fact, Asia supports well over half of the world's people, but much of its surface area is mountain, desert, or jungle terrain that makes human habitation difficult. For example, mainland China has more than one-fifth of the world's population, yet two-thirds of its territory is uninhabitable.

We might expect an abundance of natural resources in so large and diverse a territory, but Asia is not particularly well endowed in this respect. Only mainland China, Indonesia, and Brunei produce oil, in modest amounts. Japan, the richest nation in Asia, imports all of its petroleum. Malaysia produces about one-third of the world's tin and rubber, and Indonesia exports various raw materials. In general, however, no Asian nation has extraordinary mineral resources.

Human beings are Asia's most abundant resource. Japan has proved that human resources are more vital to economic growth and development than natural resources. Although burgeoning population has been a liability for many Asian nations, South Korea, Taiwan, Hong Kong, Singapore, and the PRC have harnessed their human potential and made impressive economic gains. By contrast, India and Indonesia have failed to do so, and nations like Bangladesh, Burma, Vietnam, Laos, and Cambodia remain among the most economically stagnant in the world.

Population

Extraordinary efforts to control the population explosion in the People's Republic of China brought the growth rate down to a level similar to Ireland or Switzerland today (below 1 percent a year) by the mid-1980s, though it has risen since. In India, however, growth rates remain very high compared to Japan or South Korea, for example. (See Table 7.1.) Other populous Asian nations also face demographic pressures, especially Indonesia, Bangladesh, Vietnam, Malaysia, and Pakistan. Significantly, the most highly developed Asian nations have the lowest population growth rates: Japan, followed by South Korea. Fertility rates (births per woman) also range widely (compare Japan and Pakistan in Table 7.1).

The population base is so enormous in Asia that even moderate growth will keep the trend lines climbing rapidly well into the twenty-first century. Statistical projections for Asia are truly alarming. By 2020, Asia's population is projected to reach nearly 4.5 billion — equivalent to the population of the whole world in 1980.

Table 7.1 Demographic Facts: Selected Asian States

Country	Population, 1998 (thousands)	Annual Growth Rate, 1980–1991 (percent)	Annual Growth Rate, 1990–1998 (percent)	Fertility Rate, 1992 (births per woman)
Bangladesh	125,629	2.3	1.9	4.0
Cambodia	11,498	—	3.3	4.5
China	1,238,599	1.5	1.2	2.0
India	979,673	2.1	2.0	3.7
Indonesia	203,678	1.8	1.9	2.9
Japan	126,410	0.5	0.3	1.5
Malaysia	22,180	2.4	2.8	—
Pakistan	131,582	3.1	2.8	5.6
South Korea	46,430	1.1	1.1	1.8
Thailand	61,201	1.8	1.4	2.2
Vietnam	76,520	—	2.1	3.7
United States	270,299		1.1	

Source: International Bank for Reconstruction and Development, *The World Bank Atlas* (Washington, D.C.: Author, December 1995 and 2000).

We will explore the disparities in economic development and income distribution in Asia in Chapter 8; here we are interested mainly in the links between population dynamics and development. Besides Japan, the Asian "tigers" (Hong Kong, Singapore, South Korea, and Taiwan), China, and several other countries, including India, Malaysia, and Thailand have all made notable gains. The rest lag behind; indeed, Bangladesh and Burma are among the poorest countries in the world. The close interrelationship between demographic factors and economic development is suggested by stark differences in key quality-of-life indicators. (See Table 7.2.)

These figures indicate the dimensions of the challenge Asia faces. Even Japan, with its booming economy, has a demographic quality-of-life problem related to **overdevelopment:** its population is stable, but 126 million Japanese are now living in a country smaller than California (which many Americans consider overpopulated). Over one-third of Japan's population lives on 1 percent of the land. The Tokyo-Yokohama metropolitan area alone contains more people than all of California; the Osaka-Kobe-Kyoto metropolitan area is also huge. A deteriorating lifestyle is a grim reality for millions of Japanese city-dwellers despite Japan's renowned economic success. Japan is not alone in failing to find a magic formula for softening the impact of urban overcrowding, but for the Japanese the dilemma is deepened by Japan's unforgiving geography.

Table 7.2 Development Profile: Selected Asian States

Country	Life Expectancy at Birth, 1998	Infant Mortality Rate, 1998* (percent)*	Female Primary School Enrollment, 1997 (percent)	Female Labor Force, 1998 (percent of total)
Bangladesh†	59	73	70	42
Cambodia‡	54	102	100	52
China	70	31	100	45
India	63	70	71	32
Indonesia	65	43	99	40
Japan	81	4	100	41
Malaysia	72	8	100	37
Pakistan	62	91	—	28
Singapore	77	4	91	39
South Korea	73	9	100	41
Thailand	72	29	89	46
Vietnam	68	34	100	49
United States	77	7	100	46

*Infant mortality rate (per 1,000 live births).

†In 1993, the share of females in the labor force (last column) was a mere 7 percent; the dramatic change is due largely to the efforts of a young Westernized Bengali entrepreneur who started a bank in Bangladesh with the purpose of making small loans to largely unschooled women with marketable skills (for example, basket weaving) but no money to buy jute (for baskets) or other supplies.

‡After the Khmer Rouge (communist) takeover in April 1975, Cambodia was renamed Kampuchea; the monarchy was reestablished in 1993 with the aging Norodom Sihanouk (in exile during the period of communist rule) as king, and the country is again called Cambodia.

Source: International Bank for Reconstruction and Development, *The World Bank Atlas* (Washington, D.C.: Author, December 2000).

Economic Development: The Three Faces of Asia

Levels of economic development vary widely from one part of Asia to the next. (See Table 7.3.) Japan has one of the most highly developed economies in the world. On the basis of gross national product (GNP), only the United States ranks above Japan. In qualitative terms, Japan's dynamic high-tech multinational corporations, its strong currency, its powerful financial institutions, its huge trade surpluses, its status as a major creditor nation, and, finally, its paltry spending for defense since World War II (only about 1 percent of GNP), combine to make it an economic superpower, despite serious setbacks in the 1990s.

Following in Japan's footsteps are the so-called **Asian tigers** — South Korea, Taiwan, Hong Kong, and Singapore. (In Asia, tigers are at once admired and feared — the image suggests both beauty and danger.) All four countries adopted strategies patterned on the Japanese model: accelerated industrialization, export promotion, and heavy protectionism. All four, like Japan, are now mass-consumption societies and

Table 7.3 Contrasting Economies: Selected Asian States, 1998

Country	Share of Agriculture in GNP (percent)	Share of Investment in GNP (percent)	Personal Computers*
Bangladesh	22	22	—
Cambodia	47	15	0.9
China	21	43	8.9
India	31	25	2.7
Indonesia	19	31	8.2
Japan	2	31	237.2
Malaysia	16	33	58.6
Pakistan	25	21	3.9
Singapore	0	44	65.1
South Korea	7	34	156.8
Thailand	12	39	21.6
Vietnam	29	21	6.4
United States	2.1	19	458.6

*Per 1,000 people.

Source: International Bank for Reconstruction and Development, *The World Bank Atlas* (Washington, D.C.: Author, December 2000).

exporters of high-tech manufactured products as well as other, more traditional goods. Besides exporting motor vehicles and electronic equipment, Japan has become a major international financial market. South Korea also exports cars, and both South Korea and Taiwan produce many other consumer products that compete directly with Japanese exports. At the end of the 1990s, Japan's per capita income was one of the highest in the world, comparable in purchasing power parity to that of Germany; Singapore and South Korea trailed behind Japan but led most the other non-Western countries by a large margin. (See Table 7.4.)

Elsewhere in Asia, countries undertaking basic economic development (road building, mining, steel making, electric power generation, and so on) have all they can do to keep pace with population growth. The poorest Asian nations have abysmal annual per capita income levels: it is probably lowest in Myanmar but no figures are available; otherwise, Bangladesh, Cambodia, Laos, Vietnam, and (surprisingly) Pakistan rank as the poorest of the poor in Asia.

Economic statistics do not necessarily give an accurate picture of conditions. For example, Sri Lanka (formerly Ceylon) has a low per capita GNP by Western standards, and the number of people living in poverty is still rising, but other indicators — infant mortality, life expectancy, literacy, nutrition, and employment — show significant gains. At least in some cases, these are more meaningful measures of development than financially based Western standards.

Some experts argue that the greatest need in poverty-stricken developing countries is more and better jobs. How, they ask, can overpopulated, undercapitalized nations advance unless they can put their most abundant resource, their people, to work? And

Table 7.4 Economic Profile: Selected Asian States

Country	GNP 1998 (millions of dollars)*	Per Capita GNP, 1998 (dollars)*	Average Annual per Capita Growth Rates (1990–1998)
Bangladesh	44,244	350 (1,407)	3.2
Cambodia	2,945	260 (1,246)	2.0
China	923,560	750 (3,051)	9.6
India	427,407	440 (2,060)	4.3
Indonesia	130,600	640 (2,407)	4.0
Japan	4,089,140	32,350 (23,592)	1.3
Malaysia	81,311	3,670 (7,699)	4.8
Pakistan	61,451	470 (1,652)	1.5
Singapore	95,453	30,170 (25,295)	6.7
South Korea	398,825	8,600 (13,286)	4.9
Thailand	131,916	2,160 (5,524)	4.4
Vietnam	26,535	350 (1,689)	6.5
United States	**7,902,976**	**29,240 (29,240)**	**2.1**

*Figures in parentheses represent purchasing power parity (PPP); PPP is the real value of U.S. dollar amounts at local prices in local markets.

Source: International Bank for Reconstruction and Development, *The World Bank Atlas* (Washington, D.C.: Author, December 1995).

how can they create good jobs without capital and without markets, both domestic and foreign? Finally, how can they afford to produce for domestic consumption unless people have incomes that let them translate needs into demand? A large population creates the potential for demand-driven economic growth, but only if the majority of people have purchasing power.

Thus, from the standpoint of political economy, Asia presents three faces to the world: one is affluent and technologically sophisticated, another is impoverished and tradition-bound, and a third is in transition.

Cultural and Historical Patterns

Asia provided the setting for several ancient civilizations. For millennia, empires flourished in China, India, and Indochina. An urban civilization with an as yet undeciphered writing system evolved in the Indus valley and may have been ruled as a single empire between 3000 and 2500 BCE. It had geometric cities with underground sewers and huge granaries. Bronze was used, and graphic arts were highly developed. Aryan invaders from the north overran this early civilization around 1750 BCE. The latter spoke an Indo-European language from which the modern languages of Pakistan, North India, and Bangladesh descend. An Aryan civilization spread from the west as far as the Ganges valley by 500 BCE.

Culture and Religion

Regarding the dissemination of culture, Asia is to some extent analogous to Europe. Just as the cultures of Western Europe were in many cases heavily influenced by the Greek and Roman civilizations, many of the cultures of Asia were influenced by the Chinese and Indian civilizations. And just as Russia was insulated by physical, cultural, and linguistic barriers from European intellectual and spiritual movements (such as the Renaissance and the Reformation), India was cut off from Chinese influence by the world's highest mountain range, the Himalayas.

China's cultural and political influence explains some of the similarities among Asian nations. For example, the imprint of the Chinese writing system is clearly evident in the written languages of Vietnam, Korea, and Japan. **Confucianism** (an ethical system emphasizing the family and respect for authority) spread well beyond the borders of Imperial China. Japan, Korea, and the Vietnamese kingdom in Indochina, which gradually displaced the great Khmer Empire (889–1434), imitated the Chinese system. Indeed, China dominated the Vietnamese culturally and politically for 1,000 years.

The religions of Asia also show cultural influences. India was the cradle of a number of religions, including two of Asia's three great religious traditions, Buddhism and Hinduism. Buddhism spread from India to China and from there, to Japan. It also found its way to Southeast Asia. Hinduism spread across India to Sri Lanka, Malaysia, and Indonesia. Islam, the continent's third great religion, is prevalent in much of South and Southeast Asia; in fact, more of the world's Muslims live in Afghanistan, Pakistan, India, Bangladesh, Malaysia, and Indonesia than in the Middle East.

Cultural grandeur is common throughout Asia. In every part of the region, magnificent shrines, temples, palaces, and gardens bear witness to the greatness of bygone ages. These architectural remnants are reminders that many Asian societies have a history of economic prosperity and political stability.

Historical Patterns

The past reveals striking political patterns. First, **empire building** has been a dominant motif throughout Asia for well over 2,000 years. Early examples include the Asoka Empire in India (250 BCE), followed by the great Mogul Empire. In China, the Han

Empire prospered around 200 BCE — the first of many dynastic empires that dominated East and Southeast Asia until the second half of the nineteenth century. In Indochina, the Khmer Empire controlled vast territories and built the monumental Angkor Wat temple center (1113–1150). Japan was first united under the House of Yamato sometime between the second and fourth centuries AD. From the late sixteenth century until the Meiji Restoration (1868), Japan was ruled as one nation by the Tokugawa shogunate. In World War II, the Japanese attempted to establish an Asian empire that would have included Korea, China, Taiwan, Vietnam, Laos, Cambodia, Malaysia, Indonesia, and the Philippines. Imperialism is thus a major motif in Asian history.

Second, Asia's indigenous political institutions and traditions are rooted in **dynastic authoritarianism**. Its characteristics include the concentration of power in a single potentate who claims to rule by divine authority. In Japan, the emperor was worshipped as a god; in China, autocrats ruled with the Mandate of Heaven; the Khmer rulers were Hindu god-kings; and the Mogul emperors of India based their legitimacy on the teachings of Islam. Dynastic rule is an integral element in this pattern, and the great empires of Asia were assembled and administered by royal families. Power was passed from one male heir to the next (though in the absence of a male heir, empresses did occasionally ascend to the throne). This pattern of rule varied somewhat from place to place and from time to time. For example, in China, a merit-based civil service system was established, and in Japan, administrative positions were reserved for the feudal nobility.

Labor regimentation for large-scale construction projects was also a salient characteristic of dynastic authoritarianism. The flood control and irrigation systems of China and Vietnam, the Angkor Wat temple in Cambodia (mentioned earlier), and the famous Taj Mahal in India are examples of the use of conscript labor to build on a grand scale. Centralized administration for political control, law enforcement, and tax collection was also typical of Asian autocracy. For example, during the eighteenth century, the golden age of the Qing (Manchu) dynasty, a cadre of only 20,000 civil servants governed a population of 300 million. (At lower levels, officials depended on the cooperation of local landowners and on the greed of nonofficial functionaries to get things done.) Finally, advanced methods of food production, epitomized by the Chinese system of **permanent agriculture,** allowed Asia to sustain relatively large populations in premodern times.

None of these characteristics — religion-based authoritarianism, centralized administration, labor regimentation, and advanced agriculture — was unique to Asia. Yet the pattern of highly centralized authoritarian rule reinforced by effective administrative control radiating to the periphery of the political system made it possible to mobilize peasants for massive public-works projects. This pattern was typical of Asian rule until recent times; it was even used, with some modifications, by the Maoist regime in mainland China until the mid-1970s.

A third facet of Asia's traditional political culture is the prevalence of **patron-client relations.** Such sociopolitical arrangements are informal, affective (based on friendship or familiarity), and particularistic (excluding all but kinfolk or members of some in-group) rather than formal, cognitive, and universalistic. In other words, Asian society has traditionally preferred personal relationships based on mutual trust and loyalty over organizational ties based on abstract values. The natural setting for patron-client relations is the village, whereas the city is the natural setting for impersonal, formalistic ties such as political parties, civic associations, and trade unions.

Higher levels of economic development are generally associated with greater urbanization, and vice versa. Thus, we might expect patron-client networks to be eroded by the social changes that accompany modernization. The case of Japan, however, casts doubt on this proposition. As we shall see in Chapter 8, the Japanese have assimilated traditional patterns of patron-client relations into the democratic process, resulting in a distinctive "patron-client democracy."[1] They have managed to combine Western form with Japanese substance.

Finally, **colonialism** and **neocolonialism** directly affected nearly every Asian nation. (Neocolonialism refers to the economic domination and alleged exploitation of former colonies by industrially developed nations such as the United States, France, and Great Britain.) Historically, Asian colonization of other Asians preceded the arrival of European powers in the regions. In the nineteenth century, Europe established its dominance throughout much of Asia. India was among the first nations to be colonized; China was the last (and even then incompletely). Japan escaped domination by a European power. It did so by adapting to the Western challenge. As already noted, Japan's genius was to absorb Western technology and imitate Western institutions while keeping the essence of its own culture intact.

The British colonized present-day India, Pakistan, Sri Lanka, Burma, Singapore, Malaysia, and Hong Kong. The Dutch colonized Indonesia, and the Portuguese, Goa, Timor, and Macao. The French colonized present-day Vietnam, Cambodia, and Laos. (Thailand was never colonized; Korea was controlled first by China and then by Japan.)

The effects of colonization are still debated. Some scholars stress the benefits that it brought to the colonies; others maintain that the burdens far outweighed any benefits. One school argues that the cumulative effects of colonialism have been to impede economic development in the Third World by creating a harmful dependency:

> Dependency theorists point out that during the nineteenth-century industrialization of the West, there were no already developed nations whose economic power could effectively control or manipulate the paths of development. . . . Japan, the one Asian nation that successfully industrialized in the late nineteenth century, did so by first fighting off Western imperialism and by prohibiting foreign investment from coming into Japan; in current jargon, it "delinked" itself from the world capitalist system in order to independently develop its economy from internal sources and under leadership of a native entrepreneurial class. Only then did Japan join the European powers in imperialist exploitation of China and Southeast Asia.[2]

Other observers disagree. The nations of Africa and Asia that have developed most rapidly, they argue, did so by absorbing Western capital and technology, developing export-oriented industries, and aggressively entering overseas markets. In this view, nations that responded to colonialism by withdrawing into a protectionist shell and pursuing a strategy of economic self-reliance fared the worst.

Asians do not wax nostalgic about colonial days. Regardless of the effects on economic development, the political effect of colonialism was to impose a degrading foreign dominance on proud, once relatively independent and even powerful nations.

Decolonization also left an indelible imprint. The nations and states of the Asian subcontinent are the products of conflict associated with the end of the colonial era. For example, after the British left, India and Pakistan separated along religious lines.

Pakistan originally consisted of two ethnically and linguistically dissimilar territories on opposite sides of India, separated by nearly 1,000 miles. When East Pakistan demanded autonomy in 1970, West Pakistan refused. There ensued a bloody war in which India — West Pakistan's archrival — became deeply involved. East Pakistan ultimately won independence as the new nation of Bangladesh, but the Indo-Pakistani conflict, an unintended consequence of the way in which the subcontinent was decolonized, smolders even today.

The struggle on the subcontinent continues. In the 1990s, India beat back bloody secessionist uprisings not only in Kashmir, but also in the remote northeastern provinces of Assam, Mizoram, Manipur, and Tripura. At the end of the decade, tensions between India and Pakistan raised the specter of war — an alarming prospect, as both countries now possess nuclear weapons.

The political division of Indochina was another legacy of decolonization. The French did not leave Vietnam gracefully. Communist leader Ho Chi Minh led the nation in a war for independence that ended with the French defeat at Dien Bien Phu in 1954. At the Geneva Peace Conference later that year, Vietnam was divided temporarily into North and South, with the understanding that national elections would occur within two years. The Western powers reneged on the agreement when it became obvious that Ho Chi Minh and his Communist Party would win. The resulting civil war escalated into an international conflict that raged on for two decades. It finally ended in 1975, with North Vietnam unifying the nation militarily and colonizing Laos and Cambodia as well.

Clearly, colonialism and decolonization have left scars in Asia, especially in the subcontinent and Indochina. Decolonization accentuated the artificiality of cultural and ethnic bonds in most Asian nation-states, and conflicts inevitably followed independence. Since 1945, wars have pitted Indians against Pakistanis, North Koreans against South Koreans, Vietnamese against Cambodians, and Chinese against Russians, Vietnamese, and Indians. To some extent, these wars can be attributed to actions taken (or not taken) by Western powers during the hasty decolonization process. Politically and psychologically, the colonial experience will continue to affect Asian politics for years to come.

In sum, a survey of Asian history reveals a tradition of empire building; a pattern of centralized, bureaucratic, authoritarian rule; an intricate web of patron-client ties; and a struggle to overcome the detrimental effects of colonialism, decolonization, and neocolonialism. None of these elements by itself is uniquely Asian. The combination of the four, however, has produced a distinctive Asian political culture. Furthermore, despite the cyclical rhythms of Asian social and political history, most of Asia has exhibited extraordinary resilience and continuity from ancient times to the present; as we shall see, parts of Asia, led by Japan, have also shown remarkable adaptability in the modern era.

Case Studies: China, Japan, and India

Geography, physical environment, resources, levels of economic development, and history vary greatly among the three countries examined here. Each is distinctive, and yet each shares features with other parts of Asia.

China: The Middle Kingdom

In area, the People's Republic of China is the third largest country in the world, after Russia and Canada. It is the largest nation wholly in Asia. China claims both Tibet and Taiwan as provinces. The mainland's long coastline extends from the mouth of the Yalu River in the northeast to the Gulf of Tonkin in the south. The PRC's

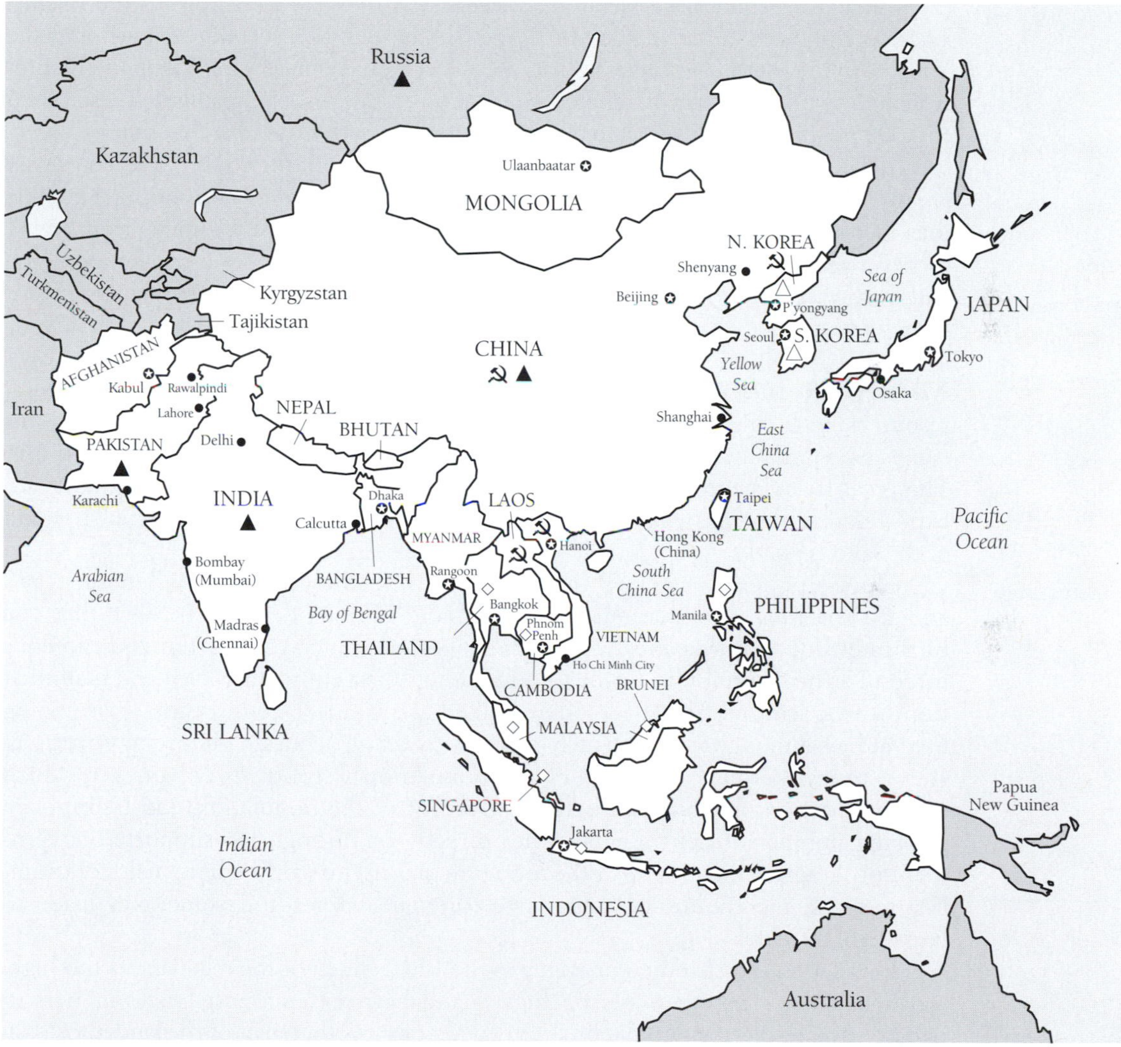

◇ **Association of Southeast Asian Nations (ASEAN):** Brunei, Cambodia, Indonesia, Malaysia, Philippines, Singapore, Thailand
☭ **Communist Governments:** China, Laos, North Korea, Vietnam
▲ **Nations with Nuclear Weaponry:** China, India, Pakistan
△ **Threshold Nuclear States:** North Korea, South Korea
✪ **Capital**

Southeast Asia

total perimeter measures over 17,000 miles; its boundary with Russia alone is 3,500 miles long.

Topographically, China consists of coastal lowlands in the east (where 90 percent of the population lives) and mountains and plateaus in the west. From the eastern seaboard, the land rises to plateaus in central China and Mongolia; beyond these lie the high plateaus of Tibet and the great mountain ranges, most notably the Kunluns and the Himalayas. China has several great rivers that flow eastward toward the Pacific. These include the Amur in the north, the Yellow (China's second longest), and the Yangtze in the south (the longest). In 1976, an earthquake measuring 8.2 on the Richter scale hit the northern city of Tangshan, ninety miles east of Beijing, killing an estimated 650,000 people (roughly equal to the population of South Dakota at that time).

Most of mainland China lies in the temperate zone, but the country's climates vary greatly with the topography. Northern areas have colder winters and shorter summers than southern areas. Rains are heaviest in the south and southeast, ranging from eighty inches a year in Guangzhou (Canton) to about twenty-five inches a year in the north and northeast. In the Gobi Desert of the northwest, rainfall averages only about four inches a year.

Natural Resources and Population The PRC is well endowed with natural resources, including huge oil reserves, iron, coal, lead, and a variety of other minerals (tungsten, antimony, mercury, manganese, molybdenum, potash, phosphates, and tin). The great rivers make hydroelectric power abundant. China is a major producer and exporter of silk and has achieved food self-sufficiency, even though only a small fraction of the land is arable.

China's population passed the billion mark in the early 1980s. Between 1950 and 2000 China's population doubled to 1.2 billion, despite the fact that the birthrate dropped dramatically during this period, which reflects the government's forceful efforts to stabilize China's population. Apparently, starvation and malnutrition — two scourges that have often stalked the Chinese countryside — are being held at bay, although it is extremely difficult to get an accurate picture of poverty in China today. Perhaps one-third of the population is fourteen or younger, which means that working adults (roughly 60 percent of the population) must support a growing number of dependents, either directly or through tax-supported government programs. China is one of the few countries in the world where males outnumber females; the traditional preference for male babies still sometimes leads to female infanticide.

Population is distributed unevenly in the PRC. Much of the mainland is too high, too hot and dry, or otherwise too rugged and barren to support large numbers of people. As a result, the population is crowded onto less than half of the land, mostly in eastern and southeastern China.

The largest ethnic group by far is the Han (94 percent of the total), who predominate in the densely populated parts of China but remain a minority in Inner Mongolia and Tibet. Fifty-five recognized ethnic minorities make up the remaining 6 percent of the population. These minorities have an importance disproportionate to their numbers because they are located in strategically sensitive zones around the country's periphery — securing these borders against incursions and preventing rebellion are two of Beijing government's age-old obsessions.

Various Chinese dialects are spoken, but Mandarin is the official language. Written Chinese is a highly refined form of calligraphy; it consists of thousands of ideographs — characters that represent concepts as well as words. There is no Chinese alphabet.

China's Heritage Modern China traces its origins back to Xia (Hsia)[3] dynasty (about 2200–1700 BCE). A millennium later, the second (or Eastern) Zhou (Chou) dynasty (770–256 BCE produced the famous Chinese philosophers Kongfuzi (K'ung Futzu, known to the West as Confucius) and Laozi (Lao-tzu). This Golden Age in China overlapped with the Golden Age of Greece.

Between 475 and 221 BCE, the great Qin (Ch'in) dynasty emerged. Shi Huangdi (Shih Huang-ti), the first Qin emperor, ended the feudal fragmentation of China, organizing it into a system of prefectures and counties under central control. During his reign (221–210 BCE), work was begun on the Great Wall as a defense against nomadic Mongolian tribes. Under the Qin, the Chinese developed an elaborate irrigation system in the fertile Yellow River valley and began cultivation in the Yangtze valley. Supported by a system of intensive farming, China's population grew to an estimated 40 million.

The Qin were displaced by the Han dynasty (206 BCE–CE 220), after which time China broke up into three kingdoms. The empire was reunited under the Sui (581–618) and Tang (618–907) dynasties. Under the Tang, China reached its zenith as the cultural and commercial center of Asia. Poetry and painting also flourished during this era.

A period of partition under the Five Dynasties (907–960) was followed by the Song (Sung) dynasty (960–1279), which is notable for its achievements in literature, philosophy, and science. The Song rulers saw the invention of movable type, gunpowder, and the magnetic compass. Beginning in the twelfth century, Mongol and Tatar tribes forced the Chinese to abandon their capital and move it to a new, safer site. In the thirteenth century, the Mongols under Genghis Khan (c. 1155–1227) subjugated all of China. The Great Canal, begun under the Sui and Tang dynasties, was completed during the reign of Kublai Khan (1279–1294), the first ruler of the Mongols' Yuan dynasty (1260–1368). No doubt impressed by Chinese culture and technology, the Mongols accommodated to the ways of China rather than attempting to displace or destroy them.

After nearly a century of foreign rule and domestic turmoil, the Mongols were supplanted by the native Chinese Ming dynasty (1368–1644). During the reign of Yongluo (Yung-Lo, or Ch'eng Tsu, 1403–1424), the heyday of the Ming dynasty, the capital was moved to Beijing (Peking, or Peiping). It was during the Ming dynasty that Europe discovered China: the Portuguese arrived in 1516, followed by the Spanish, Dutch, and English.

The Ming dynasty was overthrown in 1644 by invaders from the northeast, the Manchus, who established the last imperial dynasty, the Qing (Ch'ing, 1644–1912). The Manchus proved effective administrators as well as warriors. Like the Mongols, the Manchu conquerors adopted Chinese culture, laws, and administration. At its peak, their dominion extended to all of China proper, plus Manchuria, Mongolia, Tibet, Taiwan, and Turkestan — a far-flung empire of 300 million people.

China long remained mysterious and impervious to Europe. Until the 1840s, only one Chinese port, Guangzhou (Canton), was open to foreign merchants, and trade was tightly restricted. British demands for more trade and Chinese anger over illegal opium imports from British-controlled India led to the **Opium War** (1839–1842), which China lost. The **Treaty of Nanjing** (1842) forced China to open five major seaports and to cede Hong Kong to Great Britain. At mid-century, the prolonged and bloody **Taiping Rebellion,** aimed at overthrowing the Manchus, reduced southern China to ruins. A second war with Britain (1856–1860), joined by France, opened another major port to foreign trade. From this point forward, the empire was weak, and a series of unequal treaties resulted in territorial losses to Russia and Japan. (After the Sino-Japanese War of 1894–1895, Japan annexed Korea.) In 1898, Britain, France, and Germany all "leased" major ports in Shandong (Shantung), the concessionary terms dictated by the Europeans. In 1900, the **Boxer Rebellion,** a xenophobic uprising, was crushed by the joint intervention of British, French, German, American, Russian, and Japanese troops. China's humiliation was complete, but its nightmare was far from over.

Plans to relinquish control of a Chinese-owned railway to European interests in 1911 precipitated the downfall of the Manchu dynasty. Following a brief period of republican rule under Sun Yat-sen, a strongman named Yuan Shikai took power. Yuan died in 1916, whereupon warlords ruled in Beijing. Meanwhile, Sun Yat-sen, having consolidated his Nationalist Party, or **Kuomintang,** set up a government in the south at Guangzhou. China endured four decades of domestic turmoil until the Chinese Communist takeover unified and pacified the country in 1949.

The Chinese Civil War Although the Beijing regime joined the Allies in World War I, it was not rewarded at the Versailles peace conference. The powers refused to accede to Chinese demands for an end to all foreign "extraterritorial" privileges. (Some foreign rights were abolished at the Washington Naval Conference in 1922; also, Japan and Great Britain agreed to evacuate the Shandong peninsula.)

Following Sun Yat-sen's death, Chiang Kai-shek, the party's new leader, succeeded in unifying part of the country. The Kuomintang (or Nationalist Party) was founded on Western democratic principles, but it evolved into an instrument of Chiang's dictatorial power. In 1927, he tried to destroy the Chinese Communist Party; its remnants fled to southern Jiangxi Province and set up a rural "soviet," gaining valuable experience in governing. Following repeated Nationalist attacks, the communists again took flight, embarking on the legendary **Long March** during 1934 and 1935. Moving north and gaining recruits along the way, they eventually arrived in Shaanxi Province and, now under the firm leadership of Mao Zedong (Mao Tse-tung), set up headquarters at Yenan.

Japan's military leaders watched with keen interest as the Chinese civil war dragged on. In 1931, Japan occupied Manchuria, China's industrial heartland. (Recall that Japan had won control over neighboring Korea before the turn of the century, following a war with China.) The Japanese kept up the pressure in northern China, and in July 1937 war broke out. The hostilities merged into World War II, and Japan soon occupied much of the mainland. Chiang, forced to abandon the Nationalist capital at Nanjing, took his government to the southwestern hinterland, beyond the reach of Japan's armies. Meanwhile, Mao's guerrilla forces stood their ground in the northwest and fought the Japanese invaders to a stalemate.

Time was on Mao's side: in 1945, a defeated Japan was occupied by American forces under General Douglas MacArthur and was forced to evacuate China. The

United States became the new nemesis of the Chinese communists. After Japan's departure, the Chinese civil war had resumed with fury. Despite massive U.S. support, the Nationalists could not mount an offensive, and in 1949 the Communists won a near-total victory. Chiang Kai-shek took refuge on the island of Formosa (Taiwan), where he set up a rival regime and pressed an increasingly feeble claim that his was the legitimate government of all China. Meanwhile, on October 1, 1949, the Chinese Communists proclaimed the People's Republic of China and made Beijing its capital.

Japan: Land of the Rising Sun

The Japanese archipelago is located off the eastern coast of the Asian continent and has a total area about the size of California. Japan is divided into five districts: Honshu, Hokkaido, Kyushu, Shikoku, and Okinawa. Each consists of one main island and many smaller surrounding islands. The principal district is Honshu, which is in turn divided into five administrative units.

Like Great Britain, Japan is an island nation near a large continental landmass, but that is where the similarity ends. Consisting of the peaks of a vast, mostly submerged mountain range in the Pacific Ocean, much of Japan's terrain — over 70 percent — is steep and rugged. Twenty-five mountains rise 10,000 feet or more; the highest is the majestic Mount Fuji. Of Japan's nearly two hundred volcanoes, thirty are still active. Earthquakes are also a constant threat: in 1923, a quake that devastated Tokyo and Yokohama claimed 140,000 lives.

At first glance, Japan appears to suffer from severe natural disadvantages. Most of its land is unsuitable for cultivation, and its mineral resources are negligible. Less than one-third of the terrain is flat, and these plains lie mostly along the seacoast, where Japan's population is concentrated. Thus, urban development and agriculture compete intensely for the same scarce real estate.

The climate varies from north to south, but most of the nation is fairly humid and gets abundant rainfall. Two major ocean currents — a warm one from the south and a cold one from the north — affect weather patterns. Typhoon season runs from May through October, and several storms sweep through the islands each year. Environmental pollution related to the large and concentrated population threatens Japan's ecological balance.

Japan ranks seventh among the world's most populous nations; it is fifth in terms of population density. In terms of density per unit of arable land, however, Japan ranks first, with about eight persons per acre. As noted, the population is very unevenly distributed. Four out of five Japanese live on the island of Honshu.

Japan's Homogeneity In terms of culture, language, and ethnicity, Japan is one of the world's most homogeneous nations. The spoken language is unique to Japan, but the written language was borrowed from the Chinese. Japan's religions are **Buddhism** and Shinto. The former originated in India and migrated eastward; the latter is a native religion involving worship of natural spirits that developed under the influence of Chinese Confucianism and eventually grew into an instrument of Japanese nationalism. After the Meiji Restoration in the nineteenth century, **Shinto** became the state religion.

It was taught in the schools, and all Japanese were required to belong to a state Shinto shrine. State religion was abolished after Japan's defeat in World War II, but Shintoism remains an integral element of Japanese culture.

Buddhism is often considered Japan's most important religion. It was introduced from China and Korea in the sixth century and spread rapidly throughout the country. Its influence can be seen in the fine arts and in many social institutions. Japan's temples and gardens, its unique tea ceremony, and such arts as flower arranging *(ikebana)* are all derived from Zen Buddhism.

Confucianism has helped shape Japanese religious, cultural, and social institutions. For example, one offshoot of Confucianism, a cult known as Soka Gakkai, controlled an important political party in Japan (Komeito) until a 1970 law required the strict separation of politics and religion.

The Origins of Modern Japan Mythology holds that Japan's emperors descend from the sun goddess and that Emperor Jimmu Tenno ruled all of Japan in 660 BCE, but there is no evidence of this legendary empire. The present emperor is a direct descendant of the House of Yamato, which established hegemony over Japan during the first centuries CE. Contacts with mainland China in the fifth century led to wholesale cultural borrowing: the Japanese imitated or adopted the Chinese industrial arts, script, medical texts, and calendar; they even embraced Buddhism. Japanese rulers also copied China's political administration, with one notable exception: they did not adopt the Chinese merit system, preferring to apportion power on the basis of heredity. The imperial capital was established at Kyoto in 784.

During the twelfth century, powerful military clans arose outside the capital. Yoritomo, leader of the Minamoto clan, set up a military regime at Kamakura and forced the emperor to recognize him as the **shogun,** or chief military commander. Thus began the famed Japanese **shogunate,** a feudal form of government based on hereditary land ownership, vassalage, and military prowess that prevailed for seven hundred years. The emperor remained as a figurehead, but the dominant military clan held the real political power.

Isolated from Asia by the Sea of Japan, the nation developed a strong military tradition, as rival feudal lords, **daimyo,** kept the nation in a nearly continuous state of civil war until the sixteenth century. The Japanese professional warrior class called **samurai** developed during this era. At the same time, Japan's first contact with Europe occurred: Portuguese traders arrived in southern Japan in 1543, and Saint Francis Xavier introduced Christianity a few years later. Spanish and Dutch traders were not far behind.

The emperor elevated a powerful leader of the Tokugawa clan to the position of shogun in 1603. Thereafter, the **Tokugawa shogunate** ruled Japan until 1868. The Tokugawa shoguns moved the capital to Edo (modern Tokyo), closed Japan to all foreigners except Chinese and Dutch traders (who were restricted to Nagasaki), and banned Christianity. Under Tokugawa rule, Japan enjoyed 250 years of unaccustomed peace and internal order. With domestic tranquility came the flowering of culture.

Opening to the World Japan's insularity ended abruptly with the arrival of Commodore Matthew C. Perry and his American fleet of "black ships" in 1853. The following year, Perry extracted a treaty of peace and friendship between Japan and the United

States, and similar treaties soon followed with Russia, Great Britain, and the Netherlands under Japan's new **open-door policy.** The forced opening of Japan to foreigners led to a decade of turmoil. In 1868, samurai from several southern clans forced the Tokugawa shogun to abdicate, and they restored the emperor Meiji to power. With the **Meiji Restoration,** Japan embarked on a modernization drive that brought it to a position of preeminence in Asia by the end of the nineteenth century.

Spurred on by a new elite of modernizing samurai, Japan industrialized rapidly. It also abolished feudalism and established a modern army and navy, universal military conscription, and compulsory education. State-led economic development based on imported technology propelled Japan toward the twentieth century. In 1889, a new constitution set up a bicameral legislature, the Diet. The reforms created a parliamentary system in theory but not in practice: the new civilian cabinet, headed by a prime minister, was made responsible only to the emperor.

Japan's ascendancy was signaled by spectacular victories over China (1895) and Russia (1904–1905). As a result, Japan began to acquire the elements of an Asian empire, including the island of Formosa (Taiwan), part of Sakhalin Island, and railway and port rights in Manchuria. China also recognized Korea's independence; this led to a Japanese protectorate in 1910.

Though not a major participant in World War I, Japan was one of the five chief powers at the treaty signing in Versailles, and at the 1922 Washington Naval Conference, it was recognized as the third-ranked naval power in the world. The economy advanced rapidly in the 1920s, and Japan was transformed from an agricultural to an industrial nation. Japanese industry was organized into huge combines, ***zaibatsu,*** controlled by the families of samurai who had spearheaded modernization fifty years earlier. In 1925, universal male suffrage introduced democracy, and political parties arose for the first time. But when Emperor Hirohito ascended the throne the following year, the military seized the initiative and swept the political parties aside; in 1931, still acting independently of the government, the Japanese army invaded Manchuria. Japan had embarked on a course of military adventurism and empire building that would end in the atomic tragedy of Hiroshima and Nagasaki fourteen years later.

Japan's Bid for Hegemony in Asia On the eve of World War II, Japan entered into a military pact (the infamous Axis Alliance) with Germany and Italy. The goal of Japan's militarists was to conquer all of Asia and create a Japanese-ruled **co-prosperity sphere.** Viewing the formidable U.S. Navy as the only obstacle to this aim, Japan decided to launch a surprise attack on the American Pacific naval fleet at **Pearl Harbor,** Hawaii, on December 7, 1941; simultaneously, the Japanese attacked American forces in the Philippines and British forces in Hong Kong and Malaya.

The attack on Pearl Harbor was a preemptive strike, designed to deliver a knockout blow to the U.S. Seventh Fleet. The United States was caught utterly off guard. At Hawaii, five battleships and three cruisers were sunk or severely damaged, three other battleships sustained some damage, many smaller vessels were sunk or crippled, and 177 aircraft were destroyed on the ground. The casualties shocked the nation: several thousand dead or missing and hundreds more injured.

What happened at Pearl Harbor aroused American indignation like nothing

Table 7.5 Aircraft Production of the Powers, 1939–1945

Country	1939	1940	1941	1942	1943	1944	1945
United States	5,856	12,804	26,277	47,836	85,898	96,318	49,761
USSR	10,382	10,565	15,735	25,436	34,900	40,300	20,900
Great Britain	7,940	15,049	20,094	23,672	26,263	26,461	12,070
British Commonwealth	250	1,100	2,600	4,575	4,700	4,575	2,075
Total Allies	**24,428**	**39,518**	**64,706**	**101,519**	**151,761**	**167,654**	**84,806**
Germany	8,295	10,247	11,776	15,409	24,807	39,807	7,540
Japan	4,467	4,768	5,088	8,861	16,693	28,180	11,066
Italy	1,800	1,800	2,400	2,400	1,600	—	—
Total Axis	**14,562**	**16,815**	**19,264**	**26,670**	**43,100**	**67,987**	**18,606**

Source: Paul Kennedy, *The Rise and Fall of the Great Powers* (New York: Vintage, 1987), Table 34, p. 354.

Table 7.6 Armaments Production of the Powers, 1940–1943 (billions of 1944 U.S. dollars)

Country	1940	1941	1943
Great Britain	3.5	6.5	11.1
USSR	–5.0	8.5	13.9
United States	–1.5	4.5	37.5
Total of Allied Combatants	**3.5**	**19.5**	**62.5**
Germany	6.0	6.0	13.8
Japan	–1.0	2.0	4.5
Italy	0.75	1.0	—
Total of Axis Combatants	**6.75**	**9.0**	**18.3**

Source: Paul Kennedy, *The Rise and Fall of the Great Powers* (New York: Vintage, 1987), Table 35, p. 355.

before and cleared all domestic political hurdles to America's entry into the war in both Asia and Europe. In time, it was America's great economic capacity (see Tables 7.5 and 7.6) and the fact that the territory of the continental United States was not subjected to any direct attacks during the war that turned the tide decisively in the Pacific (as well as in the European theater).[4] The United States dropped two atomic bombs (the entire American "stockpile") on Japan. The very existence of these bombs was a secret until the day they wiped out two large Japanese cities, **Hiroshima and Nagasaki,** killing hundreds of thousands of people (mostly civilians, many of whom died agonizingly from burns and radiation) and destroying everything in a wide radius. (See Box 7.2.) The war's Armageddon-like end in August 1945 found Japan totally defeated, exhausted, and demoralized. Japan was now at the mercy of the United States — specifically, of General Douglas MacArthur, commander in chief of U.S. forces in the Pacific.

What If?

BOX 7.2

Dropping the Bomb(s): Right or Wrong?

It has been more than half a century since the United States dropped atomic bombs on two Japanese cities, killing and injuring hundreds of thousands of civilians. The burden of that decision fell on the shoulders of President Harry S Truman. What if Truman had decided against using these weapons of mass destruction?

The decision to drop the two most destructive bombs ever used in war — against a civilian population, no less — is still controversial to this day. Some critics argued that Truman should not have used atomic bombs at all because these weapons are simply too powerful and too cruel. Other have argued that the United States did it for the wrong reason — that the real purpose was to stop the Soviet Army (and dictator Joseph Stalin) from taking control of Manchuria (in northern China), and perhaps the Korean Peninsula as well. Or perhaps, the United States simply wanted revenge for the Japanese "sneak attack" on Pearl Harbor.

Truman himself had a different explanation. He insisted that the decision to drop the two bombs was designed to save American lives. How? The idea, he said, was to so shock the Japanese leaders and send them into such a panic that they would sue for an immediate peace. If so, it worked. Did it save American lives? Undoubtedly. An invasion of Japan by American forces of Japan would have been bloody and possibly prolonged. As it happened, no invasion was necessary — thanks to the atom bombs' shock effects.

When Truman saw pictures of the death and destruction his decision had caused, did he have any second thoughts or pangs of conscience? He said not — in fact, he remained convinced to the end of his life that he had done the right thing.

What if you had been the president? Even if you had decided to use "the bomb," would you have dropped them *both?*

The iron-willed general compelled the Japanese to abandon emperor worship (which American leaders associated with Japanese ultranationalism), renounce war, and draft a new liberal democratic constitution. Japan was quickly transformed from America's all-time Asian nemesis into America's number-one Asian partner.

India: From Raj to Republic

The Republic of India is the world's most populous democracy and the second largest country wholly in Asia (only China is bigger). About one-third the size of the United States, India's territory encompasses most of the Asian subcontinent, which it shares with Pakistan, Nepal, Bhutan, and Bangladesh. (See Box 7.3.)

The southern half of India is bounded by the Bay of Bengal to the east, the Indian Ocean to the south, and the Arabian Sea to the west. In the north, the Himalayas effectively insulate India, climatically and politically, from the rest of Asia. India shares borders with Pakistan to the northwest; with China, Nepal, and Bhutan to the north; and with Burma and Bangladesh in the east. Between the northern mountains and the southern peninsula lies fertile lowland. In addition, there is a slender coastal plain along the Arabian Sea and a wider one along the Bay of Bengal. These five surface features — the mountains, the Ganges floodplain, the peninsula, and the two coastal plains — have shaped India's economic and political history for thousands of years.

Contrast and Comparison

BOX 7.3

Pakistan

Pakistan is the other large country created when the British left the Indian subcontinent in 1947. Territorially, it is only about one-fourth the size of India. Although its population of 135 million is dwarfed by India's, it ranks seventh in the world (only slightly behind Russia) and its population growth rate is one of the highest in Asia. These comparative statistics are especially important on the subcontinent because India and Pakistan are bitter rivals.

Pakistan's population is far less diverse than India's but it is by no means homogenous. About one-half the population is Punjabi. The major minorities are Sindhi, Pashtun, Baluch, and the Muhajir people of India. The official languages are Urdu and English. Pakistan is a Muslim country, about four-fifth Sunni and one-fifth Shiite. Differences in ethnicity, language, and religion between India and Pakistan were behind the split in 1947 and have inflamed relations between these two countries ever since.

By most objective standards, Pakistan trails behind India. For example, life expectancy and literacy rates are higher in India than in Pakistan, while the infant mortality rate in Pakistan is higher than in India.

Pakistan's government contrasts sharply with that of India. An indirectly elected president (chosen by the national and provincial legislatures) has broad powers and has often acted as a virtual dictator. Under Pakistan's constitution, the president has the power to dismiss the prime minister and dissolve the parliament. Military intervention in politics has been a fixture of Pakistani political life.

Throughout the Cold War, Pakistan was a friend and ally of the United States while India often leaned toward the Soviet Union. The United States rewarded Pakistan with economic and military aid, including help in developing a supposedly peaceful nuclear capability. At present, both India and Pakistan are believed to possess nuclear weapons.

India's spectrum of climate types range from the arid Rajasthan Desert in the west to the rain-drenched Khasi Hills of Assam in the east, from winter snowfalls in the northern mountains and the Kashmir valley to scorching spring dust storms in the Deccan Plateau to the south. Monsoon winds govern the weather patterns, dividing the year into four seasons: rainy (southwest monsoon, June to September), moist (retreating monsoon, October and November), dry and cool (northeast monsoon, December to March), and hot (no monsoon, April and May).

India is not particularly rich in minerals but does possess sizable deposits of iron, coal, bauxite, manganese, mica, salt, and gypsum. Oil reserves are small but significant. As in China, India's huge population is its most abundant natural resource and presents both problems for the present and potential for the future.

A Human Mosaic: People, Language, Religion At the beginning of the 1990s some 865 million people lived in India; by the end of the decade India's population had surpassed 1 billion. The increase was equivalent to incorporating a country slightly larger than Japan over the course of a single decade! (By comparison, when wealthy West Germany absorbed a "mere" 16 million East Germans during the same period, its public finances were severely strained.)

India's population began to explode after World War I, quadrupling by the end of the century. The dynamics of this "population bomb" are well-known to demographers: the death rate fell much faster than the birthrate thanks to improvements in health care, nutrition, and sanitation. The birthrate was slashed in the 1970s, but only through an aggressive program of family planning, contraception, and sterilization instituted by then Prime Minister Indira Gandhi. Nonetheless, the population growth rate remains high; in absolute numbers, India's annual population increase is the largest in the world, exceeding even the PRC's.

The age structure in India, as in all societies with rapidly growing populations, is skewed toward youth. Like China, more than 40 percent of India's population is fourteen years of age or younger. The remainder of the population has to support the hundreds of millions who are too young (or too old) to work. The challenge of providing jobs for millions of new workers every year strains the nation's political, economic, and social systems.

Despite nuclear power plants and modern steel mills, India remains a traditional society in many ways. Three-fourths of its population is rural, living in villages with fewer than 10,000 residents (most villages have a population of less than 1,000). When observers contemplate rural life in Third World countries, they often think of India, where a person can be born, live, and die in the same village and never travel beyond its horizons.

India's tremendous cultural, religious, and ethnic diversity is perhaps its most striking feature. Ethnically, India is one of the most complex societies in the world. Linguistically, it is one of the most prolific, boasting hundreds of different languages and dialects. Of the more than two hundred distinct languages, no fewer than sixteen are recognized by the constitution. Nearly everyone in India speaks at least one of these "official" languages.

The two principal native languages are Hindi and Urdu. Hindi is spoken by about half the population (mostly Hindus), and Urdu is the primary language of India's huge minority Muslim population. Hindi is written like Sanskrit, whereas Urdu is written in Arabic-Persian script and contains many Arabic and Persian words. Other northern Indo-Aryan languages include Assamese, Bengali, Gujarati, Kashmiri, Marathi, Oriya, Punjabi, Rajasthani, Sanskrit, and Sindhi. In the south, the languages are of Dravidian origin; examples include Telugu, Tamil, Kannada, and Malayalam. English is the language of government, diplomacy, education, science, communications, and industry.

Language has played a major role in determining India's internal boundaries, and efforts by the central government to make Hindi the national language have met with resistance. In some cases, linguistic differences have magnified cultural and religious rivalries. Punjab is a case in point. Punjabi-speaking leaders (mostly Sikhs) demanded that the province be divided in two. The result was the creation of Haryana, the part of the former state inhabited primarily by Hindi-speaking people. (The "new" Punjab is, of course, the part inhabited by Punjabi-speaking people.) Many such examples of the interaction of linguistics and politics could be cited.

India is the birthplace of several religions, including **Hinduism** and Buddhism. Hinduism can be traced back to 1500 BCE. The Buddha taught in the fifth century BCE., around the time that **Jainism,** another distinctively Indian religion, appeared. **Sikhism,** a monotheistic Hindu sect founded in the fifteenth century, is the dominant religion in Punjab. Originally an effort to reconcile Muslim and Hindu doctrine, Sikhism evolved into a militant sect that violently opposes Islam.

Over four-fifths of India's population is Hindu; the largest minority is Muslim (about 11 percent). Though Hinduism is clearly preponderant, India's Muslim community is the third largest in the world, after Indonesia's and Pakistan's. Buddhism has died out in India — there are actually more Christians than Buddhists. Religion-based violence — between Hindus and Muslims, Sikhs and Muslims, Sikhs and Hindus, and so forth — has been a recurring problem, resulting in thousands of deaths, since India's independence in 1947. Indeed, religious differences led to the creation of Pakistan, and tensions still remain unresolved.

India's **caste system** is prescribed by Hinduism but proscribed by Indian law. A clearer case of conflict between sacred and secular values would be difficult to find. Every Hindu baby is born into one of four castes, or classes: Brahman (priests and scholars), Kshatriya (warriors and rulers), Vaisya (artisans, shopkeepers, farmers), and Sudra (farm laborers and menial workers); an underclass of outcasts are the Panchamas, known as **untouchables.** These castes, in turn, are divided into as many as 3,000 subcastes (jatis) based on occupation, geographic location, and other factors. The Indian constitution abolished discrimination based on caste (especially untouchability), but the caste system is so deeply ingrained in India's culture that outlawing it has had little effect. However, ex-untouchables — called **Dalits** — have become an important block of voters in contemporary India (see Chapter 8).

India's Heritage: Splendor amid Poverty The Indus valley is one of the oldest continuously inhabited regions in the world. It was civilized long before the Aryans (Hindus) began invading from the northwest in 2400 BCE. For centuries thereafter, small states and larger kingdoms came and went in various parts of the subcontinent as a steady procession of would-be conquerors struggled for power. Over this long period, enduring patterns of village and family life evolved, as did the caste system.

When Alexander the Great invaded in 326 BCE, the region already had a population of 30 million, two-thirds of whom lived in the Ganges Basin. A new Aryan dynasty followed under Chandragupta, who subdued most of northern India and established the **Maurya Empire;** his successor, the great Asoka (273–232 BCE), unified all of India. Asoka converted to Buddhism, and his rule brought outstanding administrative, legal, and cultural achievements. Many of India's most impressive ancient Buddhist *stupas* (shrines), pillars, and temples date from this time. After Asoka, invaders from the northwest again overran India, and the empire again disintegrated into separate kingdoms. Caste Hinduism now prevailed over Buddhism, which almost completely vanished from the land of its origin.

Although Brahmanic states had been present in peninsular India for a long time, genuine Hindu kingdoms first appeared there after the fourth century CE and Hindu Rajput princes did not reach the height of their power until 700 or later. Descendants of these rulers retained power and influence until well after the British arrived in the seventeenth century. Magnificent Hindu structures dating from long before the time of Christ can be found throughout the peninsula, and many of them are still places of worship.

The Hindu epoch was followed by a long period of Muslim rule no less glorious or grandiose. Muslim invaders began streaming through the northeast mountain passes in the eighth century; in the early eleventh century, Mahmud of Ghazni led seventeen forays into Hindustan over the course of three decades. The first Muslim sultan (king) of Delhi held sway in the thirteenth century, and Muslim power reached its pinnacle under the **Moguls** during the sixteenth century. Babur (1483–1530), who invaded Punjab in 1526, was the first Mogul despot to proclaim himself emperor of India, a title he thought he had earned by defeating the Afghan sultan of Delhi. Babur's grandson, Akbar (1542–1605), ruled the Ganges Basin and became the first Muslim emperor to attempt to create a national state through alliances with Hindu kings. Art and literature flourished under Akbar, though the emperor himself was illiterate. Akbar's successors were no less illustrious. Two of them, Shah Jahan (1628-1658) and Aurangzeb (1658–1707), were especially renowned and left legacies of splendid palaces, fortresses, mausoleums, and gardens. The Taj Mahal epitomizes the grandeur of the great Mogul rulers, but it is only one of many dazzling works of architecture from this period. Under the despotic rule of Aurangzeb, the frontiers of the Mogul Empire were pushed to new limits, but the emperor's repressive policies prompted armed revolts, and the empire fell into decline.

In the eighteenth century, one form of alien rule replaced another as the British *raj* (rulers) reduced India to a colony through the agency of the **British East India Company.** (The company itself was brought under British government control in 1784; the first British governor-general was appointed in 1786.) When the Indian army revolted in the **Sepoy Mutiny** (1857–1859), which has been called "the most dramatic event in nineteenth-century India," the British crown abolished the powers of the East India Company and assumed direct control over India in 1858. Long the object of imperialistic designs, India was the "crown jewel" of the British Empire until 1947, when the subcontinent reverted to indigenous rule.

India's "Exceptionalism": Blessing or Curse? Every country is unique, but the uniqueness of India stands out. India's highly evolved Hindu civilization has produced masterpieces of art, architecture, music, and literature. As we have seen, India is the birthplace of several of the world's great religious and philosophical traditions. Indian cuisine is a widely appreciated "export." Indian music, too, is popular outside of India. Finally, India's people have migrated to many other countries, including the United States, where they have often prospered and made important contributions in education, science, business, and other fields.

On the other hand, the so-called brain drain from India is a measure of the challenges India has faced and will continue to face in the coming century. There are still far too few jobs to go around, and not enough opportunities for young, educated adults. At the same time, there are still many children in poor, rural areas whose parents are illiterate and who have no chance (or parental encouragement) to go to school. These are problems of economic development and "social engineering" that only prudential public policy supported by private investment — including foreign capital — will solve in the long run. In the final analysis, it is for India alone to decide whether India's exceptionalism is a blessing or a curse.

SUMMARY

There is no single Asian civilization, nor is Asia itself easily divided into a single region. Indeed, there are a great many distinctive civilizations in Asia, the largest being the Chinese, the Indian, and the Japanese. There are at least three distinct regions within Asia: Northeast Asia, Southeast Asia, and South Asia. Central Asia can be considered a fourth region, although its history (especially in the case of Afghanistan) is closely linked with that of South Asia. Except for Islam, which spread across much of South and Southeast Asia from the Middle East, the civilizations and cultures from Arabia westward to the Pacific are essentially homegrown. They did interact with and influence one another, but they borrowed virtually nothing from non-Asian societies before the modern era. In Chapter 8, we will examine the political systems of Asia, again focusing on China, Japan, and India.

KEY TERMS

oriental despotism
Trilateral Commission
overdevelopment
Asian tigers
Confucianism
empire building
dynastic authoritarianism
permanent agriculture
patron-client relations
colonialism
neocolonialism
Opium War
Treaty of Nanjing
Taiping Rebellion
Boxer Rebellion
Kuomintang
Long March
Buddhism
Shinto
shogun
shogunate
daimyo
samurai
Tokugawa shogunate
open-door policy
Meiji Restoration
zaibatsu
co-prosperity sphere
Pearl Harbor
Hiroshima and Nagasaki
Hinduism
Jainism
Sikhism
caste system
untouchables
Dalits
Maurya Empire
Moguls
British East India Company
Sepoy Mutiny

STUDY QUESTIONS

1. To what extent is China a victim of circumstances, such as scarcity of natural resources, overpopulation, unfortunate geography, and a harsh environment?
2. How has geography influenced Japan's cultural and political development? What features of contemporary Japanese society can be traced to Japan's unusual physical environment (topography, land scarcity, resources, climate)?

3. What are the salient characteristics of Indian society and culture, and how do such factors as ethnicity, religion, and language constrain or facilitate the political process?
4. How do the historical experiences of China, Japan, and India compare in terms of (a) empire building, (b) forms and methods of rule, (c) foreign intrusion, and (d) sociocultural unity or diversity?

SUGGESTED READINGS

Burke, Samuel M. *The British Raj in India: An Historical Review.* New York: Oxford University Press, 1995.

Buruma, Ian. *Inventing Japan,* 1853–1964. New York: Modern Library, 2003.

Cohn, Bernard S. *Colonialism and Its Forms of Knowledge: The British in India.* Princeton, N.J.: Princeton University Press, 1996.

Cohen, Paul. *History in Three Keys: The Boxers as Event, Experience, and Myth.* New York: Columbia University Press, 1997.

Eiji, Takemae. *Inside GHQ: The Allied Occupation of Japan and Its Legacy.* New York: Continuum, 2002.

Fairbanks, John K. *The United States and China.* 4th enlarged ed. Cambridge, Mass.: Harvard University Press, 1983.

Gordon, Andrew. *A Modern History of Japan: From Tokugawa Times to the Present.* New York: Oxford University Press, 2003.

Hutchings, Graham. *Modern China: A Guide to a Century of Change.* Cambridge, Mass: Harvard University Press, 2001.

King, Robert D. *Nehru and the Language Politics of India.* New York: Oxford University Press, 1997.

McClain, James L. *Japan: A Modern History.* New York: Norton, 2001.

Moore, Ray A. and Robinson, Donald L. *Partners for Democracy: Crafting the New Japanese State under MacArthur.* New York: Oxford University Press, 2002.

Nishiyama, Matsunosuke, and Groemer, Gerald. *Edo Culture: Daily Life in Urban Japan.* Honolulu: University of Hawaii Press, 1997.

Peers, Douglas M. *Between Mars and Mammon: Colonial Armies and the Garrison State in 19th-Century India.* New York: St. Martin's, 1995.

Perry, Elizabeth J. *Challenging the Mandate of Heaven: Social Protest and State Power in China.* Armonk, N.Y.: Sharpe, 2001.

Reischauer, Edwin O. *Japan: The Story of a Nation.* 4th ed. New York: Knopf, 1991.

Robb, Peter. *A History of India.* New York: Palgrave, 2002.

Roy, Denny. *Taiwan: A Political History.* Ithaca, N.Y.: Cornell University Press, 2003.

Vohra, Ranbir. *The Making of India: A Historical Survey.* Armonk, N.Y.: Sharpe, 1997.

Wolpert, Stanley A. *A New History of India.* 3rd ed. New York: Oxford University Press, 1989.

Zakaria, Rafiq. *Communal Rage in Secular India.* Mumbai: Popular Prakashan, 2002.

WEB SITES

http://history.hanover.edu/eastasia/ea.html
http://www.fordham.edu/halsall/eastasia/eastasiasbook.html
http://www.cnd.org/fairbank/
http://etext.lib.virginia.edu/japanese/
http://www.asiasource.org/
http://users.snowcrest.net/jmike/asianhist.html

NOTES

1. See Nobutaka Ike, *Japanese Politics: Patron-Client Democracy* (New York: Knopf, 1972).
2. John Nagle, *Political System Performance in Three Worlds* (Chicago: Nelson-Hall, 1985), p. 230.
3. The system for transliterating Chinese into English was changed in the 1950s. We use the modern spellings here but give the traditional versions in parentheses.
4. See Paul Kennedy, *The Rise and Fall of the Great Powers* (New York: Vintage, 1987), pp. 347–357.

CHAPTER 8

Asia: Continuity and Change

Asia's political traditions are strictly authoritarian, but except for the kingdoms of Nepal, Bhutan, and Brunei hereditary monarchies have vanished. Today, many Asian governments have adopted democratic institutions in principle, though few have abandoned authoritarian methods. The precise forms and mixes of democracy and authoritarianism, however, vary from country to country.

Constitutional democracy has made significant inroads since World War II. Although clear-cut cases of popular rule are few, two of Asia's three major powers — India and Japan — qualify as full-fledged democracies. Sri Lanka and the Philippines are also democratic republics. Prosperous Singapore is a parliamentary democracy in form, but its government features a strong executive committed to promoting business and enforcing law and order even at the expense of civil liberties. South Korea and Taiwan have both moved toward genuine constitutional rule and demonstrated newfound respect for civil liberties in recent years.

At the end of the 1990s, only a few Asian nations were still ruled by communist regimes, most notably the People's Republic of China (PRC), North Korea, and Vietnam. The end of the Cold War led to the liquidation of communist rule in the former Soviet republics and Afghanistan and a transitional regime in Cambodia.

Southeast Asia was home to several semidemocracies with emerging markets at the end of the 1990s, including Thailand, Malaysia, and Indonesia. Democracy and markets alike were still submerged in Myanmar (formerly Burma) and Afghanistan. In South Asia, Bangladesh remained desperately poor, while Pakistan continued to be dragged down by governmental instability, corrupt civilian and military leadership, religious fundamentalism, and a perennial conflict with India over Kashmir. Meanwhile, Central Asia also remained a trouble spot. In Afghanistan, American and British armed forces ousted the fundamentalist Islamic Taliban regime following the 9/11 terrorist attack on the United States. Subsequently, a U.S.-installed Afghan government existed largely on paper, having little or no control (or legitimacy) in much of the country beyond the capital (Kabul) and owing its survival to the presence of American and other foreign troops.

The Impact of War and Revolution

Although it is changing with each passing year, the current map of Asia is a product of epoch-making upheavals. Politically speaking, World War II was the most important event in modern Asian history. Japan's attempt to unite nearly all of East and Southeast Asia under a new Greater East Asian empire ended in defeat at the hands of the U.S. military.

Japan's constitution, in effect since 1947, was prepared under the watchful eye of General Douglas MacArthur, U.S. proconsul in Japan after World War II and the architect of Japanese democracy. Thus, Japan's current political system was imposed from outside, a consequence of losing the war. Because the Japanese constitution was based on Western principles and imposed by the United States, Japan became part of America's postwar military-strategic system in the western Pacific. This meant that Japan would provide bases for U.S. forces, that the United States would be Japan's chief trading partner, and that Japan would never again threaten its neighbors or fall prey to extremism (indeed, the constitution prohibited two alleged causes of Japanese aggression: military forces and emperor worship).

World War II also put mainland China on the road to communism. When Japan invaded and occupied much of China in the 1930s and early 1940s, the Chinese Nationalist government of Generalissimo Chiang Kai-shek was discredited; only Mao Zedong's communist guerrilla forces had any success against the Japanese. After Japan's withdrawal, Mao's forces continued to wage war, now against the Nationalist government rather than the Japanese. This civil war lasted until 1949, when Mao's communists drove Chiang's Nationalists (the Kuomintang) off the mainland. Chiang took his rump government to the island of Formosa (Taiwan), where his successors continue to monopolize political power. Mao took over China, setting up the highly authoritarian communist state currently in place.

India's present political system is the result of a largely nonviolent national independence movement led by Mahatma Gandhi. Gandhi's strategy of nonviolent resistance (or civil disobedience) was highly successful, but World War II played a role as well: the British were too weary and preoccupied with domestic reconstruction after the war to resist Indian demands for self-rule. In fact, Great Britain dismantled nearly all its colonial empire after the war. In Asia, Pakistan obtained independence when India did, in 1947; Burma and Ceylon (Sri Lanka), in 1948; and Malaya (now part of Malaysia), in 1957.

The creation of a parliamentary-style democracy in India reflects the strong British influence. At the same time, however, India's extreme diversity made democracy as essential as it was difficult. The only other option capable of holding the nation together would be a highly centralized police state. Thus, by establishing popular self-rule, the founders of independent India made a virtue of necessity.

Pakistan was an afterthought in the British rush to decolonize. When Muslim leaders objected to becoming part of a Hindu-dominated independent India, the British took the course of least resistance and allowed Pakistan to become a separate dominion — actually two separate states, West Pakistan and East Pakistan (now Bangladesh). Much of the conflict that has plagued the subcontinent since independence derives from the national boundaries drawn in 1947.

War and revolution were closely related to the decolonization process elsewhere in Asia as well. Despite the urgent tasks of reconstruction at home, the French clung tenaciously to their colonial possessions in Indochina. The Vietnamese, led by Ho Chi Minh, waged a protracted "war of national liberation" against France (emulating Mao's guerrilla strategy and tactics) and emerged victorious in 1954. It took another long struggle in Vietnam — this one against the U.S.-backed Saigon-based regime in the south — and two more decades to reunite Vietnam under communist rule. The Hanoi government quickly consolidated its control in the south and in 1979 invaded and conquered Cambodia, ousting the bloody, pro-Chinese dictatorship of Pol Pot.

Korea was also divided after World War II, with the communists in control of the North and a U.S.-backed anticommunist government installed in the south. This temporary expedient became permanent after the Korean War (1950–1953) ended in a draw. North Korea, the territory controlled by Soviet troops in August 1945, was set up as a pro-Soviet communist dictatorship, while South Korea became a pro-American, anticommunist military-authoritarian regime thinly disguised as a democracy. Following widespread protests and rioting in 1987, the military rulers agreed to permit direct popular election of the next president. A civilian who had strongly criticized military rule was elected. However, the military held veto power over policy formulation, and mass demonstrations, often violent, kept the country on the brink of civil war. Although reunification is the declared intention of both Korean governments, any prospects for a breakthrough were diminished in 2003 when North Korea vowed to press ahead with its nuclear weapons research and development program in open defiance of world opinion and vague American threats of retaliation.

Indonesia and Thailand are unusual, for different reasons. Indonesia was the only major Dutch colony in Asia. The Japanese occupied Indonesia in World War II; after they left, a war of independence ensued, much as in Indochina. When the Netherlands quit the fight in December 1949, Sukarno, who spearheaded Indonesia's liberation struggle, took over the reins of government and ruled as a dictator until his overthrow in 1965. The leader of that coup, General Suharto, dominated Indonesian politics until 1998, when he was finally forced to step down in the face of mounting opposition at home and diplomatic pressure from abroad. Subsequently, Indonesia remained a trouble spot in Southeast Asia. Following the 9/11 terrorist attacks on the United States, there were reports that Osama bin Laden's al-Qaeda terrorist organization, thought to be responsible for the attacks, had active cells operating in Indonesia. Islamic terrorists bombed dozens of churches on Christmas Eve 2000, and killed over two hundred people in a bombing attack on Bali in October 2002. In East Timor, the Indonesian military reportedly massacred hundreds of civilians in 1999. A special UN Serious Crimes Unit indicted sixty-three members of the Indonesian armed forces in 2003, but the Djakarta government refused to prosecute them. The United States preferred to use its limited influence in Djakarta to go after Islamic terrorists rather than human rights violators. Thus, nearly all remained safe in Indonesia, including the commander in charge.

Thailand (Siam) was never colonized. Although Japan occupied all of Southeast Asia in 1941, Thailand returned to self-government after World War II. The military seized power in 1948 and ruled most of the time until the early 1970s. During the Vietnam War, Thailand placed a major air base at the United States' disposal, and the nation has generally pursued a pro-Western foreign policy. In recent years, Thailand's economy has been consistently among the most dynamic in the region.

Patterns and Trends

There is no specifically Asian model of democracy. Although the governments of Japan and India are patterned after the British parliamentary system, they both deviate from it in important ways. For example, the British two-party system has no counterpart in Asia. As we shall see, Japan's ruling Liberal Democratic Party has dominated Japanese politics and government since the mid-1950s; similarly, although it relinquished power in the 1990s, India's Congress Party ruled India almost continuously for nearly half a century after independence, and remains the party to beat in national elections. Thus, rule by a single party, rather than alternation in power by two or more parties, seems to be one aspect of Asian democracy.

If there is no Asian model of democracy, neither is there a contemporary Asian model of authoritarianism. Oriental despotism is a thing of the past. Most authoritarian governments in Asia today have at least a patina of popular rule and use a mixture of new and old methods to stay in power. The former include control of the mass media, public education, and welfare-state benefits; the latter involve political patronage, corruption, and police-state repression.

Military dictatorship is a common form of government in Asia — as, for example, in Pakistan, South Korea before 1988, Myanmar, and Bangladesh before 1991. Thailand has experienced seventeen coups in the last seventy years, most recently in 1991. But when the general who led that coup tried to install himself in power, an outraged public backed by the king (normally a figurehead) forced the military to step aside in favor of civilian rule. For a long time, Taiwan and Indonesia were civilian authoritarian regimes set up by military strongmen (Generalissimo Chiang Kai-shek and General Suharto, respectively). Regimes of this type, quite common in the Third World, might be termed *civilitary* government, a hybrid form of rule in which the leader is a civilian president but the military has a primary role in government.

A second pattern is Marxist-Leninist government, as in the PRC, Vietnam, Laos, Cambodia, and North Korea. The fall of Soviet communism left all these countries except China isolated and excluded from world trade. Of the five, only China has prospered in the 1990s. All (including North Korea) have taken steps both internally and externally to gain acceptance by the international community.

Since the 1970s, there has been a gradual trend in Asia toward democratization and greater respect for human rights. Indonesia, Malaysia, Thailand, Singapore, Taiwan, and South Korea are best described as mixed regimes today because they combine new democratic institutions with old authoritarian political cultures. These countries feature market economies and all have benefited greatly from the rapidly growing volume of world trade in recent decades.

In terms of political economy, Asian nations have been moving away from central planning and state intervention and toward greater reliance on market forces. This trend is not simply a move in the direction of laissez-faire economics, however. Rather, it involves an alliance between the state and private enterprise for the purpose of coordinating public and private investment, attracting foreign capital, and developing overseas markets. Japan's success has made a strong impression throughout Asia. A modified "Japanese model" of development first produced impressive results in South Korea, Taiwan, Hong Kong, and Singapore — the Four Tigers, or Four Little Dragons, as they came to be known in the 1970s and 1980s. Following suit, Communist China also adopted a market-oriented, export-driven strategy, as did Malaysia, Thailand, and Indonesia. All enjoyed rapid economic growth in the 1990s, except for the "Asian flu" banking crisis of 1997–1998.

Economic Development: A Study in Contrasts

Contemporary Asia exhibits extreme contrasts in economic development. Japan and Singapore are the two richest countries in Asia. Several other Asian countries, including South Korea, Taiwan, and Thailand have made major economic gains and now enjoy a relatively high standard of living. In addition, the People's Republic of China and Malaysia are two other countries that have made impressive gains; these gains are particularly significant in the case of PRC because of the sheer size of the Chinese population. However, some less developed countries in South and Southeast Asia face serious problems arising from food shortages, land and resource scarcity, natural disasters, and the like. In Bangladesh, Myanmar, Vietnam, Laos, and Cambodia, for example, efforts to meet basic human needs absorb virtually all resources available.

The Wealth of (Some) Nations The richest nation in Asia is Japan. Its GNP ranks second in the world (surpassed only by that of the United States), and the Japanese economy was the most dynamic among industrially developed nations until 1992, when a sharp downturn occurred. (See Table 8.1.) However, it is noteworthy that Japan is now facing a major challenge from China.[1] In addition, one measure of Japan's success — huge annual current-account trade surpluses—became a major source of friction between Japan and its main trading partners, especially the United States, in the 1990s.

Table 8.1 Growth in Four (plus One) of Japan's Asian Challengers* (percent per annum)*

Country	GDP 1970–1983	GDP 1980–1991	Per Capita, 1980–1991	Per Capita, 1985–1993	Fourth Quarter GDP 2003
China†	7.8	9.4	7.8	6.5	9.9
Hong Kong‡	8.7	6.9	5.4	5.3	5.0
Singapore	8.9	7.1	4.9	6.1	4.9
South Korea	7.1	10.0	8.8	8.1	3.9

*The "plus one" is Taiwan (Republic of China), also one of Japan's challengers in Asia. Figures for Taiwan are not published by the World Bank in deference to the political objections of the PRC, which considers Taiwan a province of China; boasting a GNP of $224 billion (PPP) in 1993 and a per capita GNP of $10,600 (PPP), Taiwan has long been one of the world's ten leading economies. In 1995–1996, Taiwan's advanced economy was growing at a rate of 6 to 7 percent a year.

†In the mid-1990s, China's economy was again growing at the more rapid rate achieved in the period 1980–1991 — roughly 10 percent a year.

‡Under a hundred-year-old treaty, Hong Kong reverted to China's control in 1997; during the entire twentieth century, it was a British colony.

Source: Data for 1980–1991 are from the International Bank for Reconstruction and Development, *The World Bank Atlas* (Washington D.C.: Author, 1992); data for 1985–1993 are from *The World Bank Atlas* (1995); data for 4th quarter 2003 are from "Emerging Market Indicators," *The Economist*, March 27, 2004, p. 106.

Nor is Japan the only prosperous country in Asia at the beginning of the twenty-first century. South Korea, Taiwan, Singapore, and the People's Republic of China, have all shown remarkable economic vitality. (See Table 8.1.) These so-called newly industrialized countries are not only emulating Japan but also exporting to Japan, producing a variety of consumer goods at lower costs than the Japanese. This "import invasion" poses a challenge to Japan that is potentially as formidable as Japan's own challenge to the United States has been since the 1960s.

Until quite recently, Taiwan's economic miracle contrasted sharply with the troubled economic history of mainland China since the communist takeover in 1949. In the 1980s, the economy of tiny Taiwan was ten times richer than that of PRC. Taiwan bustles with economic activity of all kinds. Per capita GNP in 2003 was nearly $13,000 (well above South Korea's), and consumer durable goods are available at affordable prices. Taiwan's economy has absorbed new technology like a sponge; the result is prosperity built on a foundation of massive exports. With a population of only 22 million, Taiwan is one of the world's leading traders, and the fifth-largest trading partner with the United States. In 2003, its foreign-exchange reserves were more than $175 billion, significantly larger than even those of South Korea.[2] On the mainland, the PRC is now replicating Taiwan's economic miracle, and doing so in the face of far greater obstacles.

Just as Japan has set an example for countries like South Korea and Taiwan, they in turn have set an example for other Asian nations. Indonesia, Malaysia, the Philippines, and Thailand are now competing with Japan in foreign markets. Between 1984 and 1986, this export surge halved the annual combined trade deficit among the members of the Association of Southeast Asian Nations (ASEAN; members are Indonesia, Malaysia, the Philippines, Thailand, and Singapore). These states (and a few others) have been called *newly exporting countries* because they rely heavily on foreign investment and access to foreign markets.

The Marxist-Leninist states in Asia are North Korea, the PRC, Vietnam, Laos, and Cambodia. The PRC has shifted from a near total reliance on central planning to an approximation of free-market conditions, especially in the agricultural sector; indeed, the vast nation has achieved food self-sufficiency thanks to market-oriented economic reforms instituted since 1979. Vietnam appears to be following suit. North Korea remains an unreconstructed Stalinist state with a largely autarkic economy; until the PRC's recent economic resurgence, it was probably the most economically viable Marxist-Leninist state in Asia.

As elsewhere in the world, the poorest Asian countries tend to be in the southern tier — India, Pakistan, Bangladesh, Myanmar, Laos, Cambodia, and Vietnam — where per capita incomes are the lowest in Asia and where population growth rates are the highest. Putting India and Pakistan in the same category as Bangladesh and Myanmar is misleading, however, because the former have extensive manufacturing sectors, large pools of university-educated scientists and engineers, and some high-tech industries (including nuclear-weapons development programs), while the latter have nothing of the sort.

The Population Bomb As noted in Chapter 7, the population explosion has been a pattern throughout Asia and one of the chief obstacles to net gains in economic growth (annual GNP growth minus population growth).

Contrast and Comparison

BOX 8.1

The Other Asian Bomb: Which One Is More Deadly?

The population explosion in Asia is somewhat less dramatic than in sub-Saharan Africa and Central America, where population growth rates have long exceeded 3 percent. Nevertheless, Asia's growth is spectacular when compared with Europe's, which is well below 0.5 percent. To understand the implications of these statistics, consider the time it takes to double the population at a constant growth rate: at 0.5 percent annually, it takes 139 years; at 1 percent, it takes 70 years; at 2 percent, it takes 35 years; and at 3 percent, it takes a mere 23 years.

In Pakistan, for example, annual population growth rate averaged nearly 3 percent in the 1990s, while the GNP per capita was less than $500. For the situation to improve significantly, Pakistan's economy would have had to grow at a much faster rate than the 1.5 percent a year it registered during this period. In India, the picture is still rather bleak. India's annual population growth rate is lower than Pakistan's, but India's population base is more than 7 times larger. At current rates, the population of the two nations will double to 2 billion in about twenty-five years. (See Box 8.1.)

Myanmar and Bangladesh are even poorer and population growth rates are high. To make matters worse, Myanmar is a military dictatorship racked by domestic political turmoil, and Bangladesh in recent times has been devastated by floods that have left millions homeless, cost countless lives, overwhelmed relief efforts, and reduced the nation's chronically stagnant economy to ruins.

The Poverty Trap Other demographic characteristics also have important implications for Asia's future. There are generally more males than females in Asian society (the opposite is true in industrially developed nations). The reasons reflect cultural as well as economic factors: deaths caused by frequent pregnancies, poor female hygiene and health care, and a preference for male babies. Some of these problems arise from poverty; others are related to the lower social status of females in many developing countries.

In societies with rapidly growing populations, the age composition changes dramatically. As the number of babies born each year rises and the infant mortality rate drops, the population gets younger. In most Asian societies, children under fifteen years old account for at least 40 percent of the total population. By comparison, this number in the industrial democracies (including Japan) is consistently below 25 percent. The implications for developing countries are enormous. First, more health care services are required, for both childbearing women and their infants. A large proportion of the very young in Asia suffer from malnutrition, a problem that is likely to worsen as the number of infants increases. Survivors will constitute the future labor force; but because malnutrition at an early age affects physical and mental development, it has an impact on later productivity and health care needs. As preschool populations grow, governments have to increase educational expenditures, diverting resources from development projects that could improve the standard of living.

Second, it is inescapable that the larger the proportion of children, the greater the burden on productive adults. This notion can be expressed as a dependency ratio: number of dependents (under age fourteen and over age sixty-five) in relation to the economically active population (between fifteen and sixty-four). Dependency ratios are generally higher in Asia than elsewhere (with the exception of Japan). In addition, high unemployment typically hits young adults hardest. When unemployed young adults (fifteen to twenty-four years old) are factored in, the dependency ratio worsens considerably.

Third, the prospects for many of Asia's youth are still dim. Adolescents and young adults are typically rebellious, and students everywhere are loath to accept the status quo, even if it is favorable. Education without opportunity can be dangerous, especially for societies that are beset by problems which they lack the resources to address. Will Asian youth accept this plight? Or will frustration boil over — as it already has in Communist China, Myanmar, and South Korea — thus further impeding economic growth and development? How can Asia's overpopulated and underdeveloped nations escape this poverty trap?

Finally, the demographic conundrum affects all of Asia's nations, rich and poor. Dependency ratios come into play at both ends of the age spectrum. As life expectancy increases and the birthrate comes down, the proportion of elderly pensioners also rises. This problem is only beginning to have an impact in most of Asia, but it is already being felt in Japan, which is one of the fastest-aging countries in the world. In the future, however, the PRC, with its billion-plus population despite its policy of promoting one-child families, faces the heaviest burden in Asia as the birthrate drops and life expectancy climbs. India, the only other country with a billion-plus population, faces similar challenges.

Dilemmas of Development in Asia Economic development and population control pose major challenges for most of Asia. Both encompass a host of interrelated problems. For example, if left unchecked, population growth affects future economic prospects. Underdevelopment also puts obstacles in the path of population control. Education is one essential ingredient in any formula for reducing the birthrate. It is no coincidence that societies with low birthrates also have high literacy rates. By the same token, affluent societies whose governments can afford to provide a wide range of social services, including pensions and medical care for the aged, typically have lower birthrates. In contrast, the poor and needy in developing countries cannot rely on government to provide for them in their old age; having a large family is the only form of "social security" available. Hence, what appears to be irresponsible behavior for society as a whole may be entirely rational behavior for individuals.

Large families also make sense in societies where wage-earning jobs are few and farming or running a small business is a family affair. Children, especially males, ensure that the head of the household will have help with the arduous labor needed to eke out a living in an agrarian society where plots are too small and capital is too scarce to permit the use of modern farm machinery.

This incentive to have large families will not change unless most Asians become wage earners — they must be able to get jobs for fair wages and benefits that are taken for granted in industrial nations. The poor countries of Asia are still predominantly agrarian: roughly 70 percent of the total population is engaged in subsistence farming, and many of the rest survive by working, often on a seasonal basis, for subsistence wages.

Asia's developing countries account for more than half of the world's population but only 10 percent of its wealth and production, and that meager share is actually shrinking. South and Southeast Asia, along with much of sub-Saharan Africa, are the most impoverished regions in the world. United Nations statistics support this conclusion: several of the world's least developed countries (including Afghanistan, Bangladesh, Nepal, Bhutan, Cambodia, Laos, and Vietnam) can be found in Asia.[3]

In Asia as elsewhere, endemic poverty translates into massive unemployment. No one knows for certain how many of Asia's working-age adults are actually unemployed (most official figures greatly understate the problem), but the figure is probably in the range of 15 to 20 percent. Worse still, underemployment is much higher than unemployment in most of developing Asia.* In reality, perhaps half of the working-age population lacks steady employment.

Asia's poorest nations face the challenge of modernizing, integrating traditional methods of production with new technologies, and adapting to regional and global competition without losing the social cohesion and cultural identity that are so vital in human terms. In other words, Asia must learn to manage change rather than be swept along by it. Change is inevitable; its pace and direction will either be dictated by chance or be molded by conscious choice.

Lacking such choice in public policies, Asia may or may not reap the benefits of modernization, but it will definitely experience most of the burdens: pollution, traffic congestion, overcrowding, escalating crime rates, and the other ills of most advanced industrial societies. Less obvious is the moral and spiritual erosion that accompanies modernization as the family gives way to the cult of the individual, as values and virtues are reduced to materialism, and as affluence leads not to leisure but rather to a rat race in which keeping up replaces happiness as a goal.

Japan is a case in point. Affluent and admired, many Japanese now seek the spiritual and cultural values that they set aside in order to climb up the economic ladder. Although Japan is an Asian society, it responded to the challenges of modernization with extraordinary resourcefulness and ingenuity, becoming outwardly Westernized in the process. It is in a class by itself, and yet for millions of Japanese, life is hard and the rewards are disappointing.

Case Studies: China, Japan, and India

Among Asia's giants, China stands out. Its imposing landmass and population, immense armed forces, and geographical position place it center stage in the region. Recent economic strides have strengthened Beijing's claim to a central role in regional affairs. By contrast, Japan's claim to regional leadership rests almost exclusively on its

*Underemployment exists when people are overqualified for the jobs they are doing or when they can get only part-time or seasonal work.

People's Republic of China

economic prowess. For centuries, Japan existed in splendid isolation, separated and insulated from the Asian mainland, in contrast to Korea and Vietnam, which lived in the cultural and political shadow of neighboring China. Today, Japan boasts one of the most advanced, export-oriented economies in the world and continues to rank second behind the United States, according to most estimates. But China is gaining fast. Indeed, some recent estimates based on purchasing power parity (PPP) rather than on exchange-rate values actually place Communist China ahead of Japan. More likely, the PRC today ranks about even with Germany — impressive enough. (However, on a per capita basis, it still ranks as one of the world's poorest countries.) Japan and China, so different in many ways, have several competitive advantages in common, including highly stable societies and cultures that are conducive to entrepreneurship.

India enjoys neither the stability nor the economic vitality associated with the kind of entrepreneurial cultures found in Japan and China and lags behind Thailand and Indonesia as well. Despite its certain disadvantages (for example, linguistic, cultural, and religious barriers to internal consensus, communication, and commerce), India has managed to function as a democratic society and to develop an impressive array of modern industries, including steel production, nuclear power, and computer technology.

China: Reversing the Great Leap Backward

World War II unleashed forces that transformed the political map of Asia. Within two years of the war's end, India became independent, and Pakistan sprang into being as its rival. Within four years, the **People's Liberation Army (PLA)** of Mao Zedong drove the U.S.-backed Nationalist government of Chiang Kai-shek off the Chinese mainland. Japan renounced war and adopted a democratic constitution (under American military tutelage). All across Asia, European power was receding, and the two superpowers — the United States and the Soviet Union — filled the power vacuum.

The United States established a massive military presence in Japan and the Philippines, and Mao's communist forces controlled all of China, though they were isolated and needed foreign assistance. Stalin waited until the Chinese civil war was over and then offered economic aid to Mao in return for allegiance. In Korea, as mentioned earlier, a Soviet-installed communist government ruled north of the thirty-eighth parallel, while a U.S.-backed anticommunist regime ruled in the south. This uneasy arrangement exploded into the Korean War (1950–1953) after North Korea invaded South Korea. (The United Nations condemned the North Korean invasion and voted to intervene on the side of South Korea.)

The French tried to hold on in Indochina, and a slow war of liberation dragged on until the Vietnamese communist-led insurgents delivered a knockout blow in the 1954 battle of Dien Bien Phu. Both superpowers sought a toehold in South Asia, but India's great postindependence leader, Prime Minister Jawaharlal Nehru (1947–1964), chose a policy of nonalignment — friendly relations with both, obligations to neither.

Nonetheless, Asia became an arena of superpower competition, second only to Europe. Often, such basic questions as who would govern and how remained unresolved. Nowhere was this uncertainty more explosive or significant than in China. After 1949, the

Maoist regime quickly consolidated power and launched an aggressive program of industrialization and collectivization, getting significant, though limited, economic aid from the Soviet Union. In 1957, Mao proclaimed the **Hundred Flowers movement,** an invitation to the country's professionals and intellectuals to criticize the political system. This unprecedented thaw was followed by an antirightist campaign against those who had previously attacked the system. The tumult was a prelude to the **Great Leap Forward,** one of history's most ambitious experiments in social transformation.

Mao's "Great Leap Forward"

In the Great Leap, launched in 1958, Mao attempted to catapult China into full communism, ahead even of the Soviet Union. Khrushchev had denounced the "crimes of Stalin" in his Secret Speech at the Twentieth Party Conference in 1956. His daring move had led directly to unrest in Eastern Europe, particularly in Hungary and Poland. Mao observed these events with chagrin, and he concluded that the Soviet Union had strayed from the revolutionary path. Communist China, he vowed, would show the way. The Great Leap was an effort to do that.

Although Mao claimed to be a good Marxist-Leninist, he added his own twist, much as Lenin had done. But **Maoism** stood Marx on his head. Mao asserted that human will was capable of overcoming all material obstacles, and he placed leadership above economics as the driving force in society. In Marxist terms, Mao considered the superstructures — a revolutionary party, inspired leadership, a mass-mobilizing ideology — more important than the economic base. The Great Leap Forward was designed to prove that revolutionary will had the power to reshape society. Thus, Maoism was the antithesis of Stalinism: Mao sought to harness the "hurricane force" of the people and thereby prevent a privileged elite from evolving.

Mao's experiment in mass mobilization turned out to be a great leap backward rather than forward. It enlisted some 70 million peasants in a bizarre undertaking that, among other things, involved a futile attempt to produce steel from backyard furnaces. Meanwhile, the fields remained unattended, even though agriculture had been reorganized into huge communes where groups performed all work and every aspect of private life was collectivized. Life in the communes was regimented to the point of being militarized; for example, food was prepared in communal kitchens, meals were eaten in mess halls, and men and women slept in segregated barracks.

The scale of impending disaster was not immediately apparent as overzealous cadres, eager to please Chairman Mao, vied with each other by falsifying production figures. Once the dimensions of the debacle became clear, leadership split between utopians (Mao's supporters), who stressed social and moral perfection, and pragmatists, who favored economic efficiency. Mao purged top leaders in the party and military who did not fully endorse his radical vision, including a proposal to turn the "people's army" into an instrument of ongoing social and political revolution, rather than a Soviet-style army led by professional officers and trained solely for combat.

Although the infighting was concealed, the dire consequences of the Great Leap Forward became increasingly obvious as the PRC plunged into an economic abyss. The period from 1960 to 1962 was known as the "three bitter years," as production dropped sharply and famine stalked the countryside. Chairman Mao retreated from daily management of domestic affairs, which were now handled by other top lieutenants. Between 1962 and 1966, these more pragmatic leaders spearheaded the PRC's economic and political recovery while Mao concentrated on foreign affairs and conducted ideological warfare against the Soviet Union.

The Cultural Revolution

In 1966, Mao reasserted his leadership by launching the **Great Proletarian Cultural Revolution,** an even stranger campaign than the Great Leap Forward. Mao was apparently troubled by the decline in revolutionary élan among party cadres, the masses, and especially youth. He believed that the only way to keep the revolution alive was to infuse the next generation of leaders with the kind of revolutionary spirit that had sustained the communist revolutionaries through the Long March and the years of struggle with the Kuomintang. The only way young people could learn the meaning of revolution was to experience it firsthand; otherwise, Mao feared, they would become complacent and elitist. What was needed was a new revolution, created by Mao himself, to purify the party ranks and educate the next generation.

Mao's shock troops were the **Red Guards,** mostly high school and university students inspired by a little red book containing the "thoughts of Chairman Mao." The Red Guards regarded this pocket-sized publication as their catechism and Mao as their hero. Directed by a group of zealots later condemned as the **Gang of Four,** the Red Guards stormed the bastions of authority, waving the book in the faces of their teachers as they dragged them into the streets, hung insulting signs around their necks, and paraded them for the masses to ridicule.

At first, intellectuals bore the brunt of the Red Guards' fury, but soon others in authority, including party and state officials, came under scrutiny. At the height of the Cultural Revolution, no one who had ever held a position of authority was safe from the rampaging students. In the meantime, Mao purged the party leadership, including Deng Xiaoping (secretary general of the Central Committee since 1954) who would one day return to power, and transform the PRC's economy in the process. Few senior leaders survived the Cultural Revolution unscathed. Mao's aim was to remove entrenched elites who had "taken the capitalist road." The Cultural Revolution thus set the party against itself and ushered in a decade of infighting and polarization, which ended only with Mao's death in September 1976.

By 1969, the country lay in ruins. The entire educational system had shut down, the party was demolished, food production and distribution were severely disrupted, and it was unclear who, if anybody, was in charge. Perhaps 2 million people died as a direct result of the Cultural Revolution, although there is no way of knowing the exact number.

The Rise of Deng Xiaoping

After Mao's death in 1976, a succession struggle ensued. In one of the great comebacks of all time, Deng Xiaoping, who had been shunted to the sidelines in an earlier showdown, returned to center stage. Deng stressed practice over theory, expressing his view in a now-famous metaphor: "it does not matter whether the cat is black or white as long as it catches mice." The tug-of-war between Deng and die-hard Maoists was only the latest expression of what had become a perpetual battle between two conflicting tendencies within the Chinese Communist Party.

The culmination came in 1978 when Deng and his "practice group" emerged the clear winners at a key meeting of the top Communist Party leadership from all over the country. The plenum adopted the formula of "emancipating the mind" by making "practice the sole criterion of truth." This decision proved to be a turning point in the history of the PRC: from then on, practical policies that could be measured by economic results were given priority over revolutionary actions that lacked focus or attainable aims.

Democracy Wall

For a time, perhaps to underscore the break with the legacy of the Cultural Revolution, party leaders relaxed restrictions on free expression. Public debate and open criticism of the government, past and present, suddenly appeared. Huge posters bearing democratic slogans, displayed on Democracy Wall in the center of Beijing, attracted much attention. At first this popular agitation was useful to the reform-minded Deng, but soon it became a threat to the regime and provoked a crackdown.

Deng subsequently issued four guidelines for political discussion, stressing the primacy of the socialist road, the dictatorship of the proletariat, the vanguard party under the banner of Marxism-Leninism, and the obligatory **Mao Zedong thought.** However, Deng revised the history of the party and corrected some distortions of the past. The new party history still presented Mao in a positive light, but it criticized him for creating a cult of personality and for leftist tendencies in his last twenty years. The Cultural Revolution was denounced as a prime example of Mao's reliance on theory over practice, but the extreme Maoist Gang of Four (including Mao's wife) got the blame for the worst excesses and were sent to prison. (Other Maoists sentenced to death were given no clemency.)

How China Is Ruled

In the post-Mao era, personal rule has been replaced by institutionalized rule. Although the 1982 constitution is the nation's fifth since 1949, formal government structures continue to be based on the Stalinist model — dual hierarchy of party and state organs. (See Table 8.2.) Political-administrative extensions of these bodies radiate from the center outward and downward through regional levels to local units of government. In theory, at least, the party formulates and coordinates policy, and the state bureaucracy implements it. The ever-present local party committee monitors the implementation of party policy.

Under the principle of **dual rule,** adopted in 1956, state organs were responsible both to the next higher level of state administration and to the party organization on the same level. In practice, this meant that managers at any given level had to serve two

Table 8.2 China's Centralized Political System: Parallel Party-State Structures
Head of State: President of the PRC (Hu Jintao)

Government Structures	Party Structures
Executives	**Executives**
Premier (Wen Jiabao)	General Secretary (Hu Jintao)
State Council Standing Committee (11)	Politburo Standing Committee (7)
State Council (39)	Politburo (24)
Central Military Committee (7)	Central Military Commission (7)
Chairman (Jiang Zemin)	Chairman (Jiang Zemin)
Administration	**Administration**
State Council General Office	Secretariat
Government Ministries and Commissions	Party Departments
Judiciary	**Judiciary**
Supreme People's Court	Discipline Inspection
Supreme People's Procuratorate	Commission
Representative Bodies	**Representative Bodies**
National People's Congress Standing Committee 155	Central Committee 344
National People's Congress 2,979	National Party Congress 2,108

Note: Numbers in parentheses indicate the size of each body, for example, the State Council has 39 members. These numbers change slightly from time to time but this table gives an indication of how the centralized PRC State is structured at the very top.

masters. This stultifying setup tended to stifle initiative and to demoralize the very bureaucrats whose efforts are essential to success.

The Party's Over . . . Everything Maoist China's approach to administration was a legacy of the long civil war, when necessity required that the functions of party, state, and army be fused into an efficient instrument of mass mobilization. This tradition of **guerrilla administration** was reflected in a peculiar blend of civil and military functions, on the one hand, and party and state functions, on the other — one of the trademarks of Chinese communism. This blurring was always discernible, but it assumed new extremes during the Cultural Revolution, when party and state organizations from the provincial level down were dissolved and replaced by so-called revolutionary committees representing the PLA, "revolutionary mass organizations," and "revolutionary state and party cadres." Separate party organizations were reestablished in 1971, but state administration remained in the hands of revolutionary committees until 1979. The 1980s gave a new impetus to the separation of party and state and, in general, to a regularized and rationalized policy-making process.

The party monopolizes power in contemporary China (but experts and technocrats, rather than generalists and ideologues, now run the governmental and party apparatuses). It is built on the Leninist principle of democratic centralism (see Chapter 5). In theory, the highest-level policy-making body is the **National Party Congress,** which normally convenes every five years to elect the **Central Committee** of roughly 350 members (only 60 percent of whom can vote). The Central Committee in turn elects the **Politburo.** Unlike its former Soviet counterpart, the Chinese Politburo is not the most powerful decision-making body; this distinction is reserved for the **Standing Committee,** an inner circle of six or seven leaders who set economic priorities, formulate defense and foreign policies, and direct the pursuit of these priorities and policies. (See Figure 8.1.) The Central Committee chooses the **Secretariat,** which administers the party's daily affairs.

The **general secretary,** as head of the Secretariat, is the highest-ranking party official. (The position of chairman, preeminent in Mao's day, was abolished in the early 1980s.) Deng Xiaoping was clearly the most powerful figure in the PRC after 1978, but his authority as "paramount leader" had little or nothing to do with a high office or title — in fact, he never held the top office in either the government or party.

The Overshadowed State The **State Council** is the chief executive organ of government. It is headed by the premier, who is theoretically appointed by the president with the approval of the **National People's Congress (NPC)**. The presidency is essentially a ceremonial office. Presidents are necessary symbolically even when they are expendable in a practical sense; hence, the Chinese president performs such formal duties as receiving foreign heads of state and diplomats, as well as promulgating laws and decrees, ratifying treaties, and appointing members of the State Council. The president serves a maximum of two 5-year terms and is assisted by a vice president, who becomes president if that position is vacated.

The premier heads the State Council (or government) and is assisted by a secretary general and two or three vice-premiers (reduced from thirteen in 1982). The State Council comprises the heads of the various ministries, commissions, and agencies (roughly halved in number in 1982). The State Council drafts laws for approval by the NPC, supervises the state bureaucracy, devises economic plans, and constructs national budgets. (Under the 1982 constitution, the PLA falls under the control of the State Council; it had reported directly to the Politburo.)

The 1982 constitution declared the National People's Congress "the highest organ of state power," but in reality it is a rubber stamp for the ruling organs of the party and the state. Provincial people's congresses and units of the PLA elect its members. The term of office is normally five years, and the NPC is supposed to convene once a year. (Because of the upheaval of the Cultural Revolution, the NPC did not meet from 1965 to 1975.) As a deliberative body with roughly 3,000 members, the NPC is unwieldy; moreover, it meets for only a few days at a time. Hence, it (like the presidency) is largely symbolic. When the NPC is not in session, the Standing Committee performs its duties; with approximately 150 members, the committee is much better suited to act than the

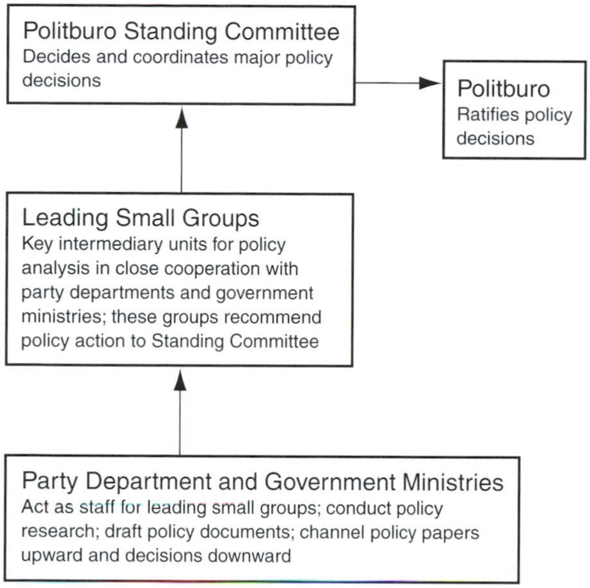

Figure 8.1 China after Mao: How Decisions Are Made

NPC itself. In theory, it possesses several important legislative, judicial, and executive powers, including the right to nullify laws it deems unconstitutional. Nevertheless, its functions appear to overlap with those of the State Council, and its actual role in the governing process is ambiguous.

Courts: A "New Legality"? The PRC does not have an independent judiciary. Since the late 1970s, however, there has been renewed emphasis on socialist legality, a policy that fits the attempt to foster stability, creativity, and productivity. After a short period of liberalization in 1978, the government clamped down on dissent in 1979 and 1980. The 1982 constitution devotes twenty-four articles to the "fundamental rights and duties of citizens," including freedom of speech, assembly, religion, and privacy. However, Article 51 introduces a caveat: the exercise of citizens' rights "may not infringe on the interests of the state, of society, and of the collective." Thus, true liberty in the PRC remains elusive. (See Box 8.2.)

There is much talk now about the **new legality** in China encouraged by efforts to create law codes after 1978. Incredibly, for the first three decades after the PRC's founding there was no criminal law. This void has been filled, but critics are not so sure the job is done (or done right). They point out that crimes punishable by death in China include smuggling, theft, and official corruption, as well as murder. Periodically the government decides to crack down on crime and a rash of executions follows. Moreover, court procedures are severely skewed against the accused (the guilty verdict having been decided by the pretrial "investigation"); the trial is inquisitorial (meaning the

Democracy in America

BOX 8.2

America's Bill of Rights

The first ten Amendments to the U.S. Constitution comprise the Bill of Rights. The Framers of the Constitution envisioned a far more limited national (federal) government than exists today: it would be able to do only that which it was specifically empowered to do and no more. Also, most of the original thirteen states (former colonies) already had bills of rights so another one at the federal level was thought to be unnecessary by some delegates to the Philadelphia Convention. Nonetheless, ten of the twelve proposed amendments adopted by Congress were later ratified by the states and went into effect in 1791.

The First Amendment protects the right of citizens to participate in the political process, including freedom of religion, speech, press, and assembly; it also guarantees the right to petition the government.

The Second Amendment gives citizens "the right to bear arms"; the Third Amendment prohibits the government from quartering troops in homes in peacetime; finally, the Ninth Amendment stipulates that unlisted rights are not necessarily denied to citizens.

The Fourth through Eighth Amendments protect citizens against arbitrary policy and court action:

Amendment 4: No unreasonable searches and seizures

Amendment 5: Rights of accused

- Grand jury indictment required to prosecute a person for a serious crime.
- No "double jeopardy" (cannot be tried twice for the same crime)
- No person can be forced to testify against him-self/herself (prohibits forced self-incrimination)
- No loss of life, liberty, or property without due process of law

Amendment 6: Right to "speedy trial" by impartial jury with defense counsel and right to cross-examine witnesses

Amendment 7: Jury trials in civil suits involving more than $20

Amendment 8: No excessive bail or fines, no "cruel and unusual punishments"

With regard to states' rights, the Tenth Amendment provides that powers not delegated to the United States or denied to states are reserved to the states.

This impressive laundry list of political and civil liberties has been a model for many contemporary constitutions. Experience shows that principles on parchment are no guarantee: only a strong and independent judiciary, supported by a political culture sympathetic to individual rights, can ensure against the arbitrary use of state coercion.

judge asks the questions), the main purpose is to decide the severity of the sentence. Finally, the government still puts dissidents in jail sometimes; the existence of political prisoners in any country is a sure sign that the rule of law is not firmly established, say most legal experts.

China's Economic Reforms

Reform in the PRC has had little to do with political change. Rather, it has been focused on the economy. Deng Xiaoping identified four areas as having the highest policy priority — agriculture, industry, science and technology, and national defense. In keeping with Mao's practice of reducing policy to simple slogans for mass consumption (a necessity in earlier times when illiteracy was the rule), he called this strategic plan the **Four Modernizations.**

The Four Modernizations in Practice The most impressive early results came in agriculture. Between 1979 and 1981, the rural economy was completely converted from collectivized production to family farming. Long a net importer of food, feed, and fiber, the PRC quickly became a net exporter of grain and cotton.

The present farm system operates on a few simple principles. Land ownership is public rather than private, but peasants lease the farmland for fifteen years or more. Beyond a certain quota that must be delivered to the state each year, peasants are free to grow anything they wish. Many specialize in various agricultural services and participate in profit-making peripheral enterprises. Peasant incomes doubled in just a few years under this quasi-free-enterprise system. And as the rural economy became more diversified and more specialized, the proportion of the population directly dependent on agriculture (roughly 80 percent in the late 1970s) began to decline.

Economic reforms in industry were introduced more cautiously. At first, industrial managers were allowed to market only a small amount of the output that exceeded plan targets; the rest continued to go to the state. The main aim in this first phase was to bring about more balanced growth (agriculture versus industry, heavy industry versus light industry, manufacturing versus services, and consumption versus accumulation).

In October 1984, new arrangements were designed to decentralize industrial decision making — in effect, to dismantle the system of central planning. In all but a few strategic industries, taxation replaced quotas as the means of giving the state its due. Managers were, in theory, granted more discretion in making production, marketing, and investment decisions. Instructions from above were to be replaced by guidelines, and plan fulfillment was to be replaced by profit. The state would not withdraw entirely but would seek to control the operation of the market.

The most delicate and most difficult adjustments involved prices and wages. Under central planning, great distortions occurred. Prices reflected the government's priorities rather than the realities of the marketplace. Wages were set by the state, and labor had no means of organizing to improve pay, benefits, working conditions, or other concerns. Switching to a system in which prices and wages respond to market forces is bound to be destabilizing, both economically and politically. The state must relinquish some control over the economy; at the same time, workers' hopes for higher wages and a better life can lead to rising expectations that, if unmet, can provoke civil unrest. Thus, in a previously controlled society, even purely economic reforms are politically risky.

Legal and Administrative Reforms China's economic reforms were accompanied by legal and administrative reforms aimed at normalizing politics. Many new laws, decrees, and regulations were enacted, including the Criminal Law and the Law of Criminal Procedure. The civil rights supposedly protected under the 1982 constitution, however, are severely jeopardized by a law against "disruption of the socialist system." Nonetheless, the PRC's present political and legal systems have lasted longer than any others in its history.

In February 1980, the Secretariat of the Central Committee was resuscitated. At the insistence of Deng Xiaoping, lifelong tenure for top party leaders was abolished. Equally important, the party was enjoined to take a hands-off approach to state administration, that is, to stop interfering in executive management. This reflected the new emphasis on pragmatism and professionalism in economic matters. As part of a purge of Maoist remnants, the position of chairman was abolished in 1982, and the office of president was restored. The normalization of Chinese politics was now complete.

Major changes in party leadership occurred in September 1985 when the party held its first national congress in four decades. The results represented a victory for Deng, who wanted to rejuvenate and professionalize the top leadership as part of his plan to modernize the economy. A landmark Central Committee meeting exactly one year later sought to bring party ideology into line with the new pragmatism. One resolution adopted at this meeting called for greater freedom of expression. It also reaffirmed the open door in foreign policy, especially in trade and investment. Finally, it defended the reforms against attacks by conservative critics within the old guard.

During this period, Deng also restructured, streamlined, depoliticized, and professionalized the army; retired older officers; and made promotion dependent on merit (in particular, outstanding performance in military academies). The armed forces were cut by 25 percent (1 million men), and military regions were reduced from thirteen to seven. Above all, Deng and his confederates redefined the army's mission to exclude domestic functions; the military was now clearly focused on national defense. Deng Xiaoping and the new civilian leadership thus reclaimed China's government in full. (Significantly, the only formal office Deng held was chairman of the Central Military Commission.)

The Limits of Change By early 1986, at least part of the PRC's leadership had apparently decided that continued economic revitalization, especially in urban industrial sectors, was impossible without some sort of political restructuring. During the first nine months of 1986, articles appeared in the Chinese press advocating greater autonomy for plant managers in decisions regarding consumption, production, and research — precisely the areas that the party had reserved for itself. Moving in this direction would thus diminish the powers of the party. Some advocates of liberalization went even further, maintaining that China's rapid transition from feudalism to socialism had bypassed the capitalist stage altogether. Consequently, according to this view, China lacked the capital accumulation that normally occurred during the capitalist stage; the only way to make up for this deficiency was to extend the open-door policy further — to allow greater competition, give more play to market forces, and even create a stock exchange to facilitate the raising of venture capital.

An ideological struggle erupted within the party leadership following massive demonstrations in December 1986 by students demanding democracy and Western-style freedoms. In one camp were the reformers, presumably led by Deng Xiaoping and his top lieutenant Zhao Ziyang; in the other were the conservative old guard. Because Deng had expressed his intention to retire in 1987, the leadership struggle was in effect a succession crisis; the future direction of the country was at stake. In January 1987, Beijing's behind-the-scenes power brokers replaced a reform-minded premier with a hardliner: The recent student uprising had clearly alarmed the leadership. The fallen leader was a scapegoat. In fact, he had been faithful to Deng's wishes. Why was he ousted? In a word, tradition: Communist China's political culture calls for somebody to take responsibility when things go wrong so that the ruler(s) who remain can save face. Anything less, in this view, would undermine the political and moral authority of the state.

The Chinese leadership remained divided over the pace and scope of reform. A Party Congress held later in 1987 brought a further rejuvenation of the PRC's leadership, as aging members of the top party organs bowed out to make room for a new generation of leaders. Seven new members were added to the Politburo. Among the five members of the Politburo's prestigious Standing Committee, only General Secretary Zhao Ziyang was a carryover from the previous ruling group.

The former premier who had been purged in 1987, died in 1989 while attempting a political comeback. His death triggered another rash of student demonstrations that led directly to yet another struggle for power within the PRC's top leadership. Subjected to a thinly veiled attack in the official *People's Daily* for engineering a "planned conspiracy," Zhao Ziyang publicly defended the students as "well intentioned and patriotic." In the end, Zhao himself was purged, and the hard-liners once again gained the upper hand — but not before the bloodiest crackdown since the Cultural Revolution: Beijing's **Tiananmen Square massacre** resulted in the death of several thousand demonstrators and dashed all hopes for the triumph of liberal reforms. Hard-liner Jiang Zemin now replaced Zhao, the reformer. (In 1993, Jiang also became president.) Deng Xiaoping, China's paramount leader, died in February 1997 at ninety-two. His advanced age and failing health, mingled with the bitter memories of Tiananmen, raised questions about China's political future — and with it the future of economic reform — in the last years of his life.

Why There Was No Chinese Gorbachev The Chinese leadership watched the drama unfolding in the Soviet Union closely and critically. Gorbachev's promises of economic reform had almost certainly been inspired by the Chinese example. But he made economic reform secondary to rapid political and cultural liberalization. By Beijing's lights, Gorbachev thus put the cart before the horse: he created the conditions for political dissent without first attacking the underlying economic causes of growing social unrest. The social fabric of the Soviet Union quickly unraveled, and the once-impregnable fortress of the Bolshevik party-state collapsed.

In stark contrast to the failed Gorbachev strategy, China's reforms have been confined to the economic realm. Measures such as decollectivization of agriculture, liberalization of foreign trade, and encouragement of free enterprise have not been accompanied by parallel reforms in the cultural and political spheres. China's approach to reform may thus be less gratifying to Westerners, but it appears to be succeeding spectacularly.

Problems and Prospects

The puzzle of Chinese politics has never been solved, often making it difficult to predict or explain twists and turns in Beijing's domestic or foreign policies. This generalization is particularly appropriate relative to the new market-oriented economic policies that are rapidly changing the face of Chinese society.

Beijing's Roller-Coaster Reforms In the late 1970s, Deng Xiaoping launched a program of market-oriented reforms. These prefigured Mikhail Gorbachev's much-touted restructuring campaign *(perestroika)* in the USSR and may have inspired it. The original intent was to decentralize economic decision making and allow market forces to determine prices, profits, and investments. But the drive for marketplace efficiency turned into a roller coaster ride that ended in disaster.

The PRC's shift toward market principles was most dramatic in agriculture, where average annual productivity more than quadrupled during the early 1980s, compared with the previous quarter century. Rural income also rose sharply during these years. The decision to allow private farming was the key. Now for the first time since the communists rise to power peasants managed the land they cultivated, decided what to plant, and did not have to sell everything they harvested to the state.

Of far-reaching importance is the land-use policy that separates public ownership of land from the private right to use it. Once a farmer has obtained the right to use land, the state cannot take it away. Furthermore, land-use rights are transferable, meaning that they can be kept in the family. Individual households have a guaranteed land tenure of at least fifteen years. (Legal ownership is not as important in Chinese culture as it is in the West.)

In industry, decentralization and a shift from bureaucratic strangulation to economic regulation was to be the cornerstone of the PRC's reform efforts, but central planning remained the rule in heavy industry. Beijing's vacillations over (and ambivalence toward) market reforms reached new heights in 1988. On the one hand, the government unveiled a comprehensive package of new market-oriented reforms, including an enterprise law aimed at giving managers greater autonomy. On the other, it reimposed economic controls intended to curtail the role of the free market and local decision making. The government also froze the prices of basic foods, agricultural supplies, and raw materials; curbed the proliferation of private traders; and cut back capital spending by localities. Soaring inflation in 1988 (running at an alarming 50 percent) caused widespread discontent. At the same time, the new flush of capitalism was accompanied by official corruption at all levels.[4]

Despite major gains, the PRC in the late 1980s was still among the poorest nations in the world in terms of per capita gross national product. Three-quarters of China's teeming population was rural and used hand tools rather than machines to make a living. Illiteracy remained high, affecting one-fourth of the population. And the disparity between rising expectations and disappointing results threatened the stability of the system and eroded the credibility of the reforms themselves.

Interlude: The Tiananmen Square Massacre The stage was set for a confrontation in May 1989 when students and workers launched a mass march in Beijing to demand democratic reforms. Protests continued throughout the month of May and coincided with a visit to Beijing by Soviet leader Mikhail Gorbachev — the first Chinese-Soviet summit in three decades. As the protest movement gathered momentum, demonstrations were mounted in at least twenty other cities, and Beijing declared martial law — to little avail.

Army troops entered Beijing with tanks and armored personnel carriers. They brutally attacked the demonstrators — now a million strong — in Tiananmen Square, outside the Great Hall of the People, crushing the revolt, killing and injuring thousands of demonstrators, and arresting many more. Security forces later rounded up as many as

10,000 dissenters, and at least 31 were tried and executed. The bloody crackdown was all too reminiscent of the awful days of totalitarian rule.

The government was widely condemned by the international media and there was a drum roll of diplomatic protest as well. China was shut out of the General Agreement on Tariffs and Trade (GATT; later the World Trade Organization) for another decade following Tiananmen. It was part of the price an unrepentant Beijing was apparently willing to pay. In any event, it was soon (literally) business as usual — the lure of China's huge market proved again to be irresistible to the West.

China's Half-Open Door The PRC more than doubled its foreign trade (primarily with the West) between 1981 and 1986, and reversed its long-standing ban on foreign loans and direct foreign investment. China borrowed billions of dollars from the West (and Japan) in the 1980s. The decision to seek direct foreign investment — absolutely taboo when Mao was alive — was even more remarkable. Deng Xiaoping's most controversial and innovative step was the creation of **special economic zones (SEZs)**, which were intended not only to attract foreign capital but also to stimulate exports and improve access to modern technologies and management methods. Although obstacles to foreign companies remained formidable, the new policy brought in much needed investment capital.

In 1986, Beijing took several steps to lure more capital into the country, including incentives such as preferential tax treatment, priority access to supplies at guaranteed prices, and loans for export-oriented or technologically advanced projects. But these new measures did not remove the bureaucratic obstacles, legal impediments, distorted prices, and political uncertainties, and foreign investment fell short of expectations.

In the absence of massive infusions of foreign investment, the PRC's best hope for prosperity is boosting exports. Japan's economic growth in the 1970s was export-driven, and the Japanese example probably played a role in inducing the PRC to adopt an export-oriented open-door policy after Mao's death. As a result, the PRC's two-way foreign trade grew rapidly after the reform program was launched, as did the number of organizations permitted to engage in foreign trade.

The PRC's attempt to generate export-led growth in the 1980s met with only limited success, however. At the peak of the reform campaign, only a small fraction of China's labor force was employed in export industries, and exports accounted for just 15 percent of national output (compared with 55 percent in Taiwan and 37 percent in South Korea). [5] China was also running relatively large trade deficits in the late 1980s. Along with rising inflation, this trade shortfall undermined economic reform. (See Table 8.3.)

Despite the ups and downs of the 1980s, a legal framework to regulate foreign commerce gradually emerged. Laws covering joint ventures, contracts, land-use rights, taxes, copyrights, patents, and SEZs were promulgated. In 1986, Beijing applied for membership in the GATT, later renamed the World Trade Organization. As we noted earlier, that goal was set back in 1989.

Beijing became a major arms supplier in the 1980s, ranking in fourth place behind the Soviet Union, the United States, and France. China's billions of dollars in arms sales have loomed large in the PRC's trade statistics, raising not a few eyebrows in the West.

Table 8.3 Inflation Rates: Japan, China, and Three Asian NICs, 1970–1995 (percentages)

Country	1970	1975	1980	1985	1990	1995	2004
China	−0.2	0.2	7.4	11.9	2.1	10.1	2.1
Japan	7.7	11.8	7.7	2.0	3.1	0.4*	−0.4
Singapore	0.4	2.6	8.2	−1.4	3.4	0.8	1.6
South Korea	16.1	25.3	21.3	2.8	8.6	5.1	3.3
Taiwan	3.6	5.2	19.0	−0.2	4.1	4.6	0.6

*July 1995 to July 1996.

Sources: International Monetary Fund, *Government Finance Statistics Yearbook 1991,* vol. 54 (Washington, D.C.: Author, 1991), pp. 116–119; Executive Yuan, *Statistical Yearbook of the Republic of China 1991* (Taipei, Taiwan: Directorate-General of Budget, Accounting and Statistics, 1991), p. 152; Alvin Rabushka, *The New China* (Boulder, Colo.: Westview, 1987), p. 216; *China, North Korea Country Report* no. 4 (London: *The Economist* Intelligence Unit, 1991), p. 3; *The Economist,* February 10, 1996, p. 112; September 7, 1996, p. 98; March 27, 2004, p. 106.

Although China's principal trading partners are Asian, Western Europe and the United States have accounted for significant shares in recent years. Two Asian trading partners, Japan and Hong Kong, accounted for nearly half of China's trade in the 1980s.

The PRC is no longer merely an exporter of primary products. Since 1990, Beijing has registered substantial trade surpluses every year except 1993 (an eye-popping $29 billion in 2000).

Despite these positive signs, China's foreign trade remains modest compared with that of Japan, South Korea, or Taiwan. One scholar sums up China's predicament this way:

> If Chinese exports are to lead Chinese economic development, they will have to compete with the other export-oriented economies of the Pacific, economies in which skillful exploitation of world technology trends is a key factor. For instance, Taiwan is now the world's third largest producer of personal computers (PC's), after the United States and Japan, and South Korea is number four.[6]

Nonetheless, the surge in China's exports, especially to the United States, has caused a stir among the PRC's trading partners led, not surprisingly, by the United States. The Chinese trade bonanza came in large part at America's expense. In 2002, China surpassed Japan as the number one exporter to the United States. (See Figure 8.2.) The PRC's twelve-month trade balance surplus was over $22 billion in mid-2003, while the United States was running $519 billion in the red by the same measure. (The U.S.-Japan trade imbalance was even worse, however.) Nevertheless, the United States finally agreed to admit China to the World Trade Organization (WTO).

The Dragon Stirs: A Chinese Economic Miracle? The Chinese economy grew at an average annual rate of 9 to 10 percent a year in the 1990s, continuing an ascent that began in 1978. (See Table 8.4.) China appeared to be replicating the economic miracles of Japan, Taiwan, and South Korea.[7] However, the exuberant estimates

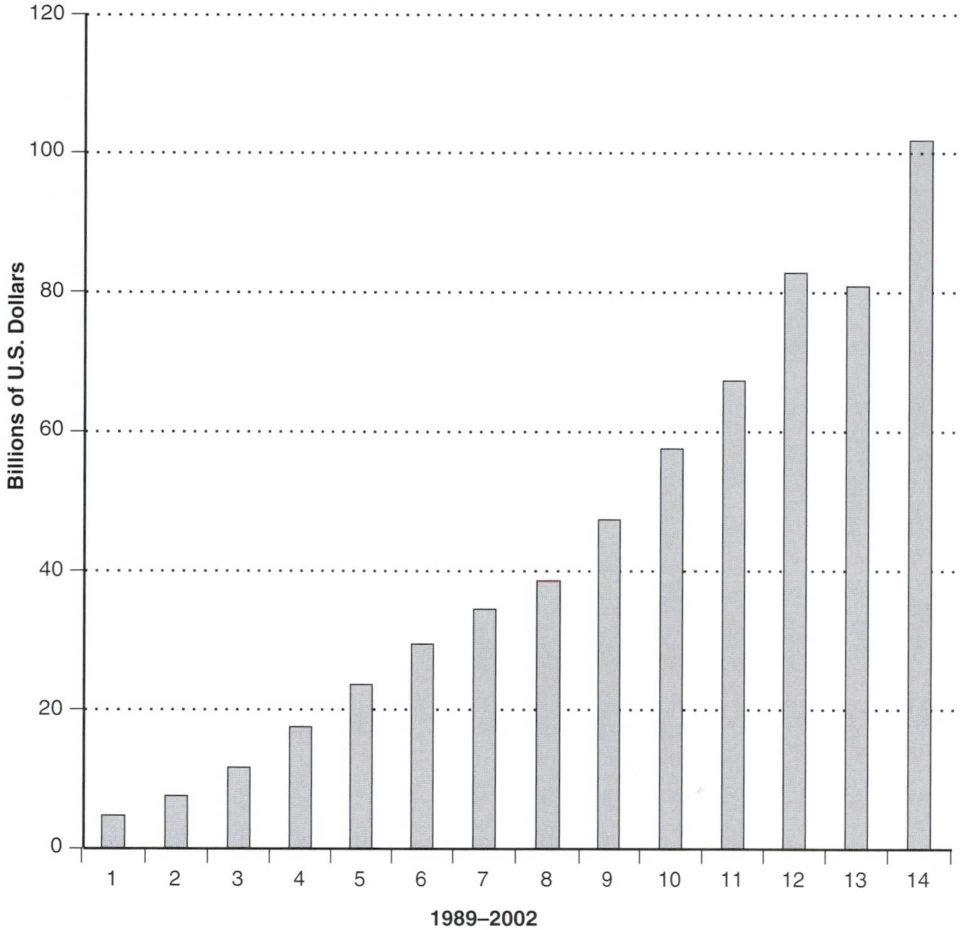

Figure 8.2 Through the roof: China's Trade Surplus to U.S. ($ billions)

Source: Compiled by the author from official statistical data.

of the early 1990s were later called into question when revised World Bank figures reduced the size of the Chinese economy by 25 percent and put the number of Chinese living in poverty at about a third of the population (as opposed to its earlier estimate of 7 percent). (See Box 8.3.)

Some 800 million Chinese, roughly 75 percent of the population, still labor on the land. Even so, the transformation of China has surpassed anything Mao Zedong achieved in his lifetime. Rural China depended heavily on agriculture for its income in 1978; by 2000, agriculture accounted for only about 18 percent of the PRC's gross domestic product. At the same time, private firms and foreign-owned firms have sprouted alongside state enterprises. The share of state-owned firms accounted in all industrial output and nonagricultural employment dropped steadily in the two decades after 1978.

Table 8.4 Comparison of Real GNP Growth per Capita in Six Leading Economies (percent per annum)

Country	1980–1991	1985–1993	1990–1998	2003*
China	9.4	6.5	9.6	8.0
France	1.8	1.8	1.2	2.1
Germany	2.2	1.9	0.9	2.0
Great Britain	2.6	1.3	2.0	2.1
Japan	3.7	3.6	1.3	1.5
United States	2.1	1.2	2.1	2.6

*GDP forecasts, *The Economist,* The World in 2003, pp. 93–94, 96.

Source: Data for 1980–1991 are from the International Bank for Reconstruction and Development, *The World Bank Atlas* (Washington D.C.: Author, 1992); data for 1985–1993 are from *The World Bank Atlas,* 1995; data for 1990–1998 are from *The World Bank Atlas,* 2000.

Some Get Rich First By various measures, Chinese consumers have experienced an unprecedented leap in general living standards. A surge in the availability of everything from seafood, meat, and poultry to color television sets, washing machines, and refrigerators has already transformed the lives of millions of Chinese people.

China has experienced the fastest economic growth in the world, real per capita income has more than doubled, and the number of people living in poverty has certainly declined (although by just how much remains debatable). Although an overall growth rate of nearly 10 percent is in itself quite remarkable, the fact remains that China's economy must grow rapidly if it is to feed, clothe, house, educate, and employ its people. There is also an increasingly nettlesome issue of growing inequality to be dealt with.

The last two decades have witnessed the state-encouraged emergence of an entrepreneurial middle class in China. Especially in the cities, examples of conspicuous consumption can be easily spotted: successful businessmen (often automatically assumed by the public to be crooks) drive big cars, sport cellular phones, wear expensive imported clothing, and dine in posh restaurants. This appearance of a new class is part of an official **some get rich first** policy. The slogan suggests that others who trail behind will also get rich eventually. Whether "eventually" will be in time to prevent jealousy and resentment from spilling over remains to be seen.

The flip side of letting "some get rich first" is the breaking of the **iron rice bowl** — the state's guarantee of permanent employment and basic benefits to all. Restructuring (mergers and downsizing) and the closing of inefficient state enterprises has already put millions of industrial workers in China out of jobs, often without severance pay. Fear of social unrest sparked by angry furloughed workers has induced the state to keep inefficient industrial plants operating (by extending bank credits), contradicting official economic policy.

Indeed, structural deformities continue to hamper economic performance. Most key industries are still dominated by about 100,000 state-owned firms. These firms con-

What If?

BOX 8.3

The Number of "Poor" Chinese (Who's Counting?)

China alone accounts for about one-fifth of the world's entire population. If 1 billion Chinese left the country, China would still rank third in the world (behind only India and the United States)! The number is so large — estimated at 1.3 billion in 2003 — that any miscalculation is magnified to an astonishing degree. What if certain "facts" are wrong? What if the definition of poverty is slightly adjusted? Consider the following.

In recent years, China has been widely portrayed as a superpower in the making. Experts have predicted that China's economy would be the largest in the world by 2001. In a 1996 report, the World Bank put the percentage of China's teeming masses living in poverty at "only" about 7 percent (approximately 84 million people). Later that same year, the bank drastically revised the statistics in its previous publications. The new figures downsized the Chinese economy by 25 percent and consigned nearly a third of the population (or roughly 400 million people) to poverty. More specifically, the1996 *World Development Report* put Chinese GDP per person, based on purchasing power parity (PPP), at around U.S. $2,500 in 1994; the newer report lowered the figure to U.S. $1,800. (Imagine if a bunch of statisticians suddenly gave us a 28 percent "pay cut.") However, by 1998, China's robust economy had made the earlier (apparently false) numbers look true — GDP per person according to the World Bank's own numbers had raced past $2,500 and reached a new plateau of $3,000.

How poor is China? The answer is that all depends on who you talk to and how poverty is measured. Using current exchange rates rather than purchasing power parity to calculate income levels makes a huge difference, as does the definition of "poverty." Is the Chinese poverty line set at sixty cents a day (the Chinese standard) or is it set at a dollar a day (the World Bank standard)? It was this forty-cent difference that made the World Bank decide it had underestimated the number of poor people in China by some 316 million souls.

sumed well over half of all investment capital in the mid-1990s, although many actually lose money in any given year. State-owned banks lend state-owned firms money for political rather than commercial reasons, which means that a large chunk of the nation's finances goes into nonperforming loans. Pressure from local governments, which control eight out of ten state-owned firms, is partially to blame. But the central government also has a motive for its complicity: if state-owned firms were squeezed, even the healthiest among them would have no choice but to lay off millions of redundant workers. The sickest would go bankrupt and shut down. Paying for housing, education, and health care of unemployed workers obviously would place a heavy financial burden on the central government, which, in any event, incurs large budget deficits every year. The solution to this problem, in turn, depends on effective implementation of recent, overdue reforms in the PRC's obsolete tax system.

Changing of the Guard Communist China remains an enigma to the outside world. Little is known about the personalities, politics, and decision-making procedures within the top leadership. Jiang Zemin retired from office in 2002 (as he said he would), and was succeeded as party secretary and president by Hu Jintao, about whom the outside world knew little. (Jiang retained the powerful position of commander in chief of

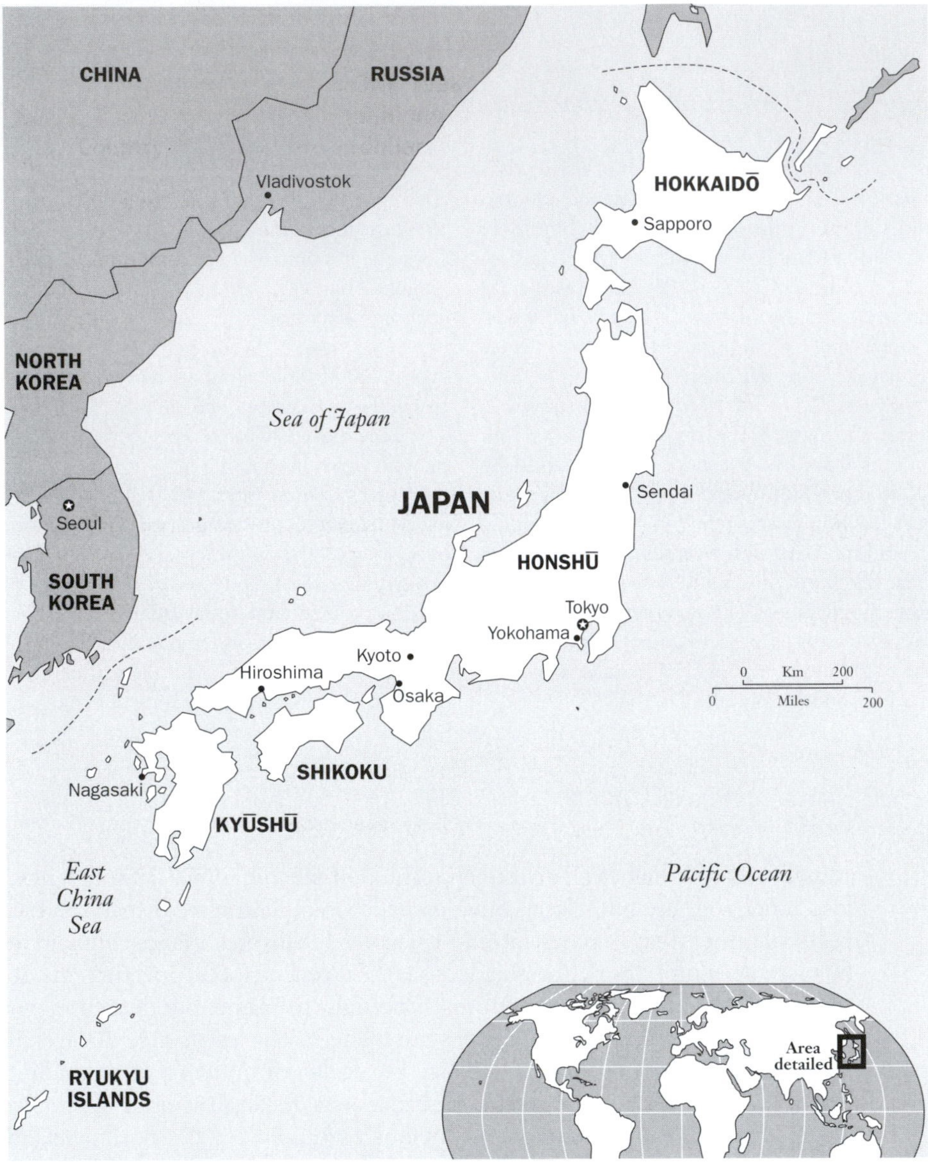

Japan

the armed forces as Deng Xiaoping had done.) In April 2003, the world learned about an epidemic involving a potentially deadly but mysterious respiratory disease called SARS (Severe Acute Respiratory Syndrome) that infected hundreds of Chinese people of all ages. The world also learned that the Beijing government had first tried to conceal the problem and then grossly underreported the number of victims. When cases of

SARS began to show up in Hong Kong and Toronto, the PRC cover-up became a major political and diplomatic embarrassment, as well as a possible medical catastrophe. Such fears proved unfounded, but heads rolled nonetheless as high-level Chinese officials, including the health minister and the mayor of Beijing were dismissed for incompetence. This marked perhaps the first time ever in PRC history that high-level officials were fired for reasons other than alleged ideological heresy. Thus, the SARS incident suggests that in some ways the political process in the PRC is changing, but in others, to borrow a saying from the French, "the more things change, the more they stay the same."

In Sum . . . A dynamic, new China is stepping onto the global stage after a century of turmoil and humiliation. What kind of a world citizen will China be? China finally signed the Nuclear Non-Proliferation Treaty (NPT) in 1995. Whether Beijing will stop secretly helping nuclear have-nots build weapons of mass destruction, for example, remains open to question. Although it has adopted market-friendly economic policies and opened China to foreign investment, Beijing has not softened its repressive political policies against its own dissidents or against Tibet. Hong Kong has been reincorporated in a relatively smooth transition from British to Chinese control, but there continues to be a potential for armed conflict over the status of Taiwan, over which China still claims sovereign rights. Finally, it remains to be seen how an unreconstructed communist dictatorship will deal with the "bourgeois" values of the rising middle class that its market-oriented policies have nurtured. China is undergoing profound changes that will have profound effects on Asia and the world — this much is clear, and little else.

Japan: Asian Phoenix

As noted in Chapter 7, Japan had little experience with democracy before the 1940s. Its history and culture were in many ways antithetical to Western democratic ideas. Today, a half century after its crushing defeat in World War II, Japan is a shining example of democracy and capitalism in Asia. At the same time, its politics and government reflect Japan's unique cultural heritage.

The 1947 Constitution

The United States was in a commanding position in Japan after World War II. The 1947 constitution, still essentially unchanged, embodied U.S. resolve never to permit a resurgence of Japanese militarism. The American influence on the Japanese constitution is especially apparent in its preamble:

> We, the Japanese people, acting through our duly elected representatives in the National Diet, determined that we shall secure for ourselves and our posterity the fruits of peaceful cooperation with all nations and the blessings of liberty throughout this land, and resolved that never again shall we be visited with the horrors of war through the action of government, do proclaim that sovereign power resides with the people and do firmly establish this Constitution. . . . Government is a sacred trust of the

> people, the authority for which is derived from the people, the powers of which are exercised by representatives of the people, and the benefits of which are enjoyed by the people.

The framers of the 1947 constitution sought to construct an elaborate system of representative government for Japan. In addition to a wide range of civil liberties, the constitution guarantees the right of citizens to an equal education and the right of workers to organize and engage in collective bargaining.

Article 9 "renounces war as a sovereign right of the nation and the threat or use of force as means of settling international disputes" and pledges, "land, sea, and air forces, as well as other war potential, will never be maintained." Japan has taken this pledge seriously; until recently, it spent less than 1 percent of its GNP on defense. Ironically, this has given the Japanese a competitive edge in world trade: with the United States assuming the security burden, Tokyo has been free to concentrate on industrial development.

So-called **self-defense forces** are permitted. The role and mission of Japan's armed services became the focus of political controversy in 1992, when the Liberal Democratic Party, under pressure from other governments (especially the United States), moved to allow Japanese forces to be deployed outside Japan. Although these forces were to be restricted to humanitarian missions, the opposition charged that any dispatch of Japanese soldiers to foreign soil would be a violation of Japan's constitution.

Basic Institutions: Western Style, Japanese Substance

Japan has a parliamentary form of government. The emperor is nominally the chief of state, but his duties are strictly ceremonial. The real chief executive is the prime minister, who is chosen by the majority party in the **Diet** (parliament). In theory a powerful figure, the prime minister must in practice mediate among various factions in the majority party to function effectively. The prime minister has the constitutional power to choose and dismiss the twenty or so cabinet ministers. Only civilians may serve in the cabinet (to prevent a recurrence of militarism), and a majority of members, including the prime minister, must hold Diet seats.

The cabinet prepares and submits the annual budget to the Diet, formulates domestic and foreign policies, manages the bureaucracy, negotiates treaties, and reports to the Diet on national and international affairs. In short, the cabinet heads the executive branch of the government. As in Great Britain, the principle of collective responsibility is observed — all cabinet members are jointly responsible for all policies and decisions of the government. In keeping with Japanese tradition, decisions are usually made by consensus; taking a formal vote, especially in the intimacy of a small group, is alien to Japan's political culture. Personal bonds of mutual trust play a major role in social, political, and even economic transactions. By the same token, the legalism so prevalent in Western constitutional democracies is almost entirely lacking in Japan.

The authors of the constitution intended to place supreme power in Japan's bicameral Diet. This legislature is divided into the House of Representatives (511 members serving four-year terms) and the House of Councilors (252 members serving six-year terms). Members of each house were, until 1994, elected by universal suffrage from multimember districts in which voters made only one selection from a list of candidates put forth by various political parties (often five or more). Smaller parties, such as the Clean Government Party and the Communist Party, could obtain seats in the Diet quite easily; for example, in a four-member district, a candidate could win by coming in fourth.

In such an electoral system, the distribution of votes was crucial. If the dominant **Liberal Democratic Party (LDP)** put up candidates for all the seats in a given district and one candidate attracted most of the votes cast for the LDP in that district, strong candidates from smaller parties had a good chance of securing seats. (As a strategy, small parties could run a single candidate to make every vote count.)

The constitution declared that popular sovereignty was to be expressed through the Diet, the only institution empowered to make laws. Whereas the prime minister and cabinet had been answerable to the emperor, they were now responsible to the Diet, "the highest organ of state power." (See Figure 8.3.) The House of Representatives alone has the power to choose a prime minister, pass (or reject) the budget, and ratify treaties. The House of Councilors has equal weight in passing ordinary laws, however. The distribution of power between the upper and lower houses, therefore, falls between the U.S. Senate (maximal) and the British House of Lords (minimal). Also, in

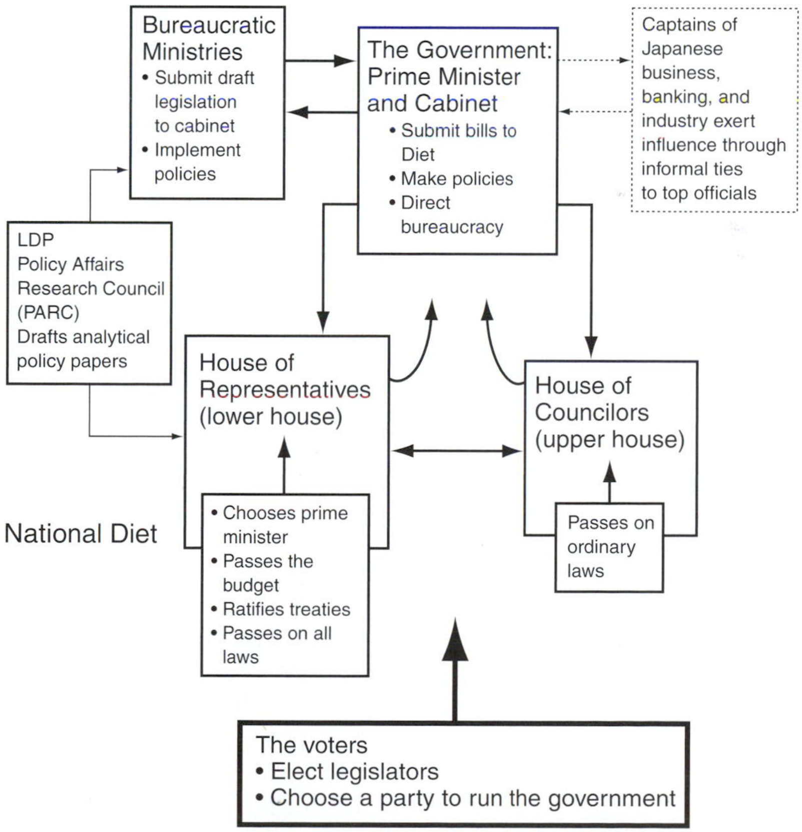

Figure 8.3 How Japan Is Ruled

contrast to the German system, which gives the Bundestag (upper house) only a "suspensive veto" over legislative proposals (meaning the lower house can vote to override), Japan's lower house has no choice but to accommodate the upper house in most legislation (the budget being the big exception).

The Japanese parliamentary system closely resembles the British system. For example, the lower house of the Diet can force a government to resign through a vote of no confidence. (Alternatively, the cabinet can dissolve the lower house and call for new elections following a no-confidence vote.) But appearances are sometimes deceiving, for the Japanese have adapted Western institutions to their own political culture. For example, internal bargaining among Liberal Democratic Party **factions** is a key to understanding the policy process as is the LDP's **Policy Affairs Research Council (PARC),** the party's potent policy-making apparatus. The result is a unique system that combines democratic politics and market economics with Japanese traditions such as **consensual decision making,** economic conglomeration, and social discipline.

The distinction between formal (constitutional) powers and informal (real) power is crucial to understanding the Japanese political system (and all others). Informal power relationships cannot be depicted in a diagram, unfortunately. Although sovereignty is vested in the people by the constitution, and formal lawmaking power is vested in the Diet, the country is actually run by a "revolving door" triad of top bureaucrats, corporate leaders, and LDP chiefs.

Japan's Ruling Party and Its Rivals

The LDP dominated Japanese politics from its inception in 1955 until 1993, when for a short time it was out of power. Its chief rival is the Japan Socialist Party, which typically has about half as many seats in the Diet as the ruling Liberal Democrats.

The LDP is a classic catchall party: instead of depending on a particular social class, it draws support from a wide range of interest groups. The secret of its success is three-pronged: co-opting much of the opposition, satisfying a multiplicity of interests, and seeking broad popular appeal rather than ideological purity.

The internal power structure of the LDP becomes especially crucial during biennial party conferences, when the party's power brokers elect a leader (president), who becomes (or remains) the prime minister so long as the LDP is the majority party. This method would be highly undemocratic but for the fact that Japanese voters are guaranteed the right to choose a new government every four years. (Elections have actually occurred more frequently — every two years, on average.) Moreover, LDP conferences are nothing like the staged and orchestrated party conclaves held in Communist China. In Japan, the outcome of presidential balloting is the result of intense bargaining by factions, each of which has its own leader, its own constituencies, and its own policies.

Japan has retained some elements of its patron-client system. Before World War II, Japan had been ruled by powerful heads of factions and cliques who built and maintained power bases by dispensing personal favors and rewards. This aspect of the political system has endured, in less pronounced form. Perhaps the most important vehicle for perpetuating Japan's patron-client tradition has been the LDP itself.

Because the LDP held power for four decades and because it still embraces an assortment of political interests, powerful factional leaders have emerged within the party organization. They "feed" their factions with money and influence obtained through personal support groups known as ***koenkai.*** As the political fortunes of party leaders rise and fall, the faction leaders act as power brokers, deciding who will become prime minister and which cabinet post will go to whom. By contemporary Western standards, this system may seem neither open nor democratic, but by Japanese standards, it is remarkably Americanized. Even so, the "paradox of Japan's being an open society made up of closed components" continues to set Japanese democracy apart from its counterparts in the West.[8]

Despite LDP dominance, Japanese voters have traditionally not lacked party choices. The Socialists (recently renamed the Social Democratic Party of Japan, or SDPJ), the Communists (JCP), and the Clean Government Party (Komeito) — an offshoot of a very large (and very rich) Buddhist religious sect known as the Value Creation Society (Soka Gakkai) — have presented Japanese voters with clear alternatives to the ruling LDP. (A ruling by the Japanese Supreme Court barring religious sponsorship of political parties forced the Komeito to sever its formal ties with Soka Gakkai, but the public continues to identify the party with the religion that spawned it.) In addition, several new political parties sprang up in the early 1990s after a series of political scandals involving top LDP leaders badly tarnished the party's image.

The LDP's Short Fall from Grace After World War II, Japan did not face the kind of political instability that often mars attempts to move from authoritarian to democratic rule in other countries. Japan admired and imitated the bureaucracy of Imperial China; like the Chinese, the Japanese have an extraordinary record as institution builders. The Japanese genius for creating durable institutions has helped to make Japan's politics highly stable, conservative, and predictable. "They invent or borrow from others, adapt, refine, but never so rigidly that the rules obstruct rather than facilitate the achievement of their objectives."[9]

But things changed abruptly in the late 1980s. When one LDP leader succeeded another as party president and prime minister in the fall of 1987, it was a textbook example of a Japanese-style power transfer. Similarly, the new leader selected his cabinet in accordance with the unwritten rules of the game, which meant that key posts in the new government were distributed on the basis of factional strength, seniority, and other well-established criteria. In retrospect, however, it was the calm before the storm — one that hit the LDP with full force in the early 1990s.

What happened to the LDP is a kind of David-and-Goliath story, except that in this case Goliath's fatal wound was self-inflicted. Prime Minister Tanaka resigned in 1989 after a bribery scandal badly damaged his reputation. His successor was in office only a few months when he was forced to resign following allegations of adultery. Nonetheless, the LDP's new leader led the party to victory in the 1990 elections. Trying to buff the LDP's badly tarnished image, he named a new cabinet with no political baggage: only the foreign and finance ministers were carryovers from the previous cabinet. But his advocacy of electoral reform and honest government ruffled powerful figures in his own party, and in October 1991 the party's "old guard" replaced him with a timeserver named Miyazawa. The old politics came roaring back. In 1992, over a hundred politicians were implicated in a new financial scandal. The following year witnessed the onset of Japan's worst recession in the postwar era.

These reversals came in the face of spreading disillusionment within Japanese society. The Japanese people work long hours for wages that afford them, at best, a modest lifestyle in an environment of astronomically high prices for housing and other essentials. Recognizing this problem and its implications for the future of his ruling party, the new prime minister came to office in 1991 promising an improved standard of living for middle-income Japanese families. "It's been said we Japanese live in rabbit hutches, and, unfortunately, its true," Miyazawa mused.[10] He was not being comical: people living in Tokyo have only about one-half as much living space as people in Munich, Paris, or London and only about one-third as much as people in Washington, D.C. Public spaces are crowded in Japanese cities, too. Residents of Bonn, Germany, for example, have ten times more park area per capita than do residents of Tokyo; residents of London and New York have five or six times more park area per capita.

Among other things, Miyazawa promised to bring the cost of a home in Tokyo from eight times the annual salary of a worker to five. He also promised to reduce the number of hours employees spend at work, too. These promises, however, turned out to be too little, too late.

The clamor for electoral reform — that is, for a fundamental change in the rules of the game — grew ever louder. Indeed, it was the loss of a confidence vote on this very issue that prompted Miyazawa to resign and call for new elections in 1993. The main issue in the campaign was the LDP itself, which many voters believed had monopolized political power through corrupt practices engendered by an insatiable appetite for campaign funds to feed the party's greedy and powerful factions.

Political Reform and Party Realignment In national elections that followed the extraordinary no confidence vote against Miyazawa in 1993, the LDP lost its legislative majority for the first time in nearly forty years. This reversal led to the formation of a seven-party coalition headed by the leader of the upstart New Japan Party, which, captured a mere thirty-five parliamentary seats. (Although it was a watershed, the outcome of that vote was not a resounding defeat for the Liberal Democrats; only twenty-eight votes short of majority, the LDP remained by far the largest party in the Diet.)

The new government comprised a fragile coalition of centrist, center-left, and leftist parties. Mutual enmity toward the LDP was about the only common denominator for these strange bedfellows. Neither this governing coalition nor its two successors proved to be viable.

A historic political reform package passed in November 1994. The old electoral system magnified the LDP's plurality enough to give it a clear majority in the Diet through a Japanese-style gerrymandering scheme that involved manipulating district boundaries in order to favor farmers, who traditionally support the LDP. The new electoral law replaced the previous system of multimember voting districts with a combination of single-member (first past the post) seats and proportional representation. As a result, 60 percent of the seats in the lower house are now filled from single-member districts.

Would this change in the electoral rules finally open up the political party system to vigorous competition? If the 2000 elections are any indication, the answer is no. In the race for the 180 proportional representation seats the Democratic Party of Japan won 20 more seats than the ruling coalition, but the LDP cleaned up in the 300 single-member districts. The fact that as many as six or seven political parties may contest a given seat generally redounds to the advantage of the LDP because a larger field means fewer votes are needed to win. (Recall that in single-member districts a candidate needs only one vote more than the next highest vote getter to win.)

The LDP ended up with a slim 3-seat majority in the 480-member lower house, but its two junior coalition partners added another 41 seats to the government's bloc in the parliament. The main opposition party, the Democratic Party of Japan (DPJ), won 115 seats. Another 60 seats were distributed almost equally among three other opposition parties, including the Communists. Thus, the unfinished business of party realignment in Japan had not yet produced a second major party, but the Democrats (DPJ), a product of the turbulent 1990s, showed some promise of eventually playing that role.

Toward a Two-Party System? The split in the LDP in 1993 led to the creation of a new opposition group known as the **New Frontier Party (NFP),** a year or so later. This new party was the handiwork of Ichiro Ozawa, one of several key figures to defect from the LDP. After a very promising start, the NFP itself splintered and then disbanded in 1997. Electoral reform gave the new parties a fighting chance; however, the leaders of these parties did most of the fighting amongst themselves. As a consequence, the frenetic and futile attempts at party realignment during this period bewildered (and probably alienated) voters, ironically helping the LDP to return to power.

In the 1996 elections, the LDP staged a comeback of sorts, boosting its strength in the Diet, but still falling well short of a clear majority. At the same time, LDP's main rival, the NFP, stumbled badly. Voters, however, also rebuffed the LDP's coalition partners. The upshot was that the new LDP-led coalition government faced the grim prospect of governing with a slim majority of only five or six seats. A wild card also emerged in this election in the form of the Democratic Party of Japan (DPJ), formed only weeks before the election by two Clean Government Party mavericks. The DPJ won fifty-two seats, making it the third-largest party in the parliament.

Elections to the House of Councilors in 1998, at which half the seats were at stake, dashed the LDP's hopes of being restored its former position of preeminence any time soon. Winning only about 37 percent of the seats available, the LDP was still the largest party in the upper house, but it had fewer seats than before. It was a particularly humiliating defeat for the Prime Minister (Hashimoto), who promptly announced he would resign.

In the spring of 2000, the next cookie-cutter LDP prime minister suffered a stroke and was incapacitated. A month later, former prime minister named Takeshita announced he was retiring from the House of Representatives, where he had served for over four decades. These two events were linked. Takeshita it was said had been "running Japan's ruling Liberal Democratic Party from his pillows — shaping political events, big and small, throughout the land."[11] Takeshita played a key role in choosing Japan's prime ministers. A lot of what we call "politics" takes place behind the scenes in every democracy. How much of that sort of thing goes on is one way to measure how democratic (or undemocratic) a given country really is. By this standard, Japan is not very democratic, but then neither, arguably, is the United States.

Takeshita's departure from the scene threw the future of the LDP (not to mention the country) into question. The party's rising "young Turks" asserted that the LDP's poor showing in the lower-house election in June 2000 proved the LDP needed rejuvenating. But the party's entrenched elders would not be easy to dislodge — the seniority system that regulates the power struggles among the party's competing factions remains unchallenged. Indeed, the successor to the stricken prime minister was an old-style patron of special interests whose popular rating in opinion polls was abysmal. In April 2001, with public discontent reaching the boiling point, the LDP named a populist reformer, Koizumi, as its new leader and Japan's new prime minister.

In power, Koizumi gave the LDP and the Japanese government a whole new look. He also sounded very different from his stodgy predecessors. His modish personal appearance, charisma, and candor were atypically for a Japanese politician. But faced with strong opposition from the antireform LDP old guard Koizumi decided to buy time rather than push hard for a "Japanese perestroika," prompting critics at home and abroad to express bitter disappointment.

In 2003, the DPJ merged with the Liberal Party. These two parties together still had only 137 seats in the lower house, but DPJ leader Naoto Kan promised a new campaign manifesto and announced his intention to seek an electoral alliance with Japan's Social Democratic Party as well. With the possibility of parliamentary elections looming in November, the DPJ-Liberal Party merger was clearly aimed at creating a viable alternative to the Liberal Democrats (and reducing the number of opposition candidates running in the new single-member districts). After more than a decade of economic stagnation, Japanese voters appeared ready for a change, but it was still a good bet that the inertia of Japanese politics would keep the LDP on top.

In Sum . . . Government in Japan was tumultuous in the 1990s. The tumult gave rise to a paradox. In one view, the Japanese political system has changed forever and the LDP now confronts a new competitive political environment. Because three hundred Diet seats are decided in single-member districts, the emergence of a second major party that can rival the LDP is possible; but because two hundred Diet seats are decided by proportional representation, it is likely that Japan will remain a multiparty system with a less-than-dominant LDP as the first among equals in the Japanese Diet. In another view, the more things change, the more they stay the same. Despite the electoral reforms earlier in the decade, the Japanese political system has not changed fundamentally: gerrymandered voting districts continue to give rural voters (traditional LDP stalwarts), three times the voting power of town-dwellers. The LDP, in turn, continues to reward Japan's farmers with tax breaks and tariff protection. It is still by far the largest party in both houses of parliament and will most likely continue its dominant role for many years to come. However, one thing does appear to be changing, namely the practice of naming geriatric old men to run the government. Japan needs an energetic and popular government no less than any other country, and perhaps more, given Japan's recent economic malaise. As the LDP's first reform-minded leader, it is significant that Koizumi said that if he won a second term as party leader (as seemed likely) the party should adopt his ideas for reforming Japan's closed economy as its election manifesto.

LDP lawmakers and rank-and-file members reelected Koizumi as party leader in September 2003. Koizumi won on the first ballot against three challengers, a mandate in most democracies. Whether he would at last be emboldened to launch a program of far-reaching economic and political reforms depended in part on the outcome of the general elections in November and on the upper house elections set for July 2004.[12]

Problems and Prospects

Japan's very success has created problems. Most of these problems are essentially internal, but one of the biggest is external. Even problems that are primarily domestic in nature, however, have international ramifications because Japan's economy is so thoroughly enmeshed with the global economy. We begin this section with a brief review of Japan's success and then we look at current problems facing the country.

Asia's First "Miracle" The **Japanese economic miracle** began in the mid-1950s. From then until the oil crisis of 1973–1974, Japan did not rely heavily on exports to sustain its accelerating economic growth; on the contrary, an expanding domestic market energized Japan's economy. Exports rose rapidly, but so did imports of raw materials and fossil fuels.

The oil crisis brought dramatic changes. Japan's yearly economic growth rate was cut in half, which triggered a reduction in imports. The energy crisis led to conservation efforts, as well. At the same time, leaders of government and business — always closely linked in Japan — began looking in earnest to foreign markets as a way to cope with sluggish domestic demand.

Other trends also pushed Japan toward an export orientation in the 1970s and 1980s. Japan's steel, shipbuilding, manufacturing, synthetic textile, motor vehicle, petrochemical, and home appliance industries — once the engines of Japanese economic growth — became depressed. Foreign competition, especially from Asia's new industrial countries (NICs), contributed to the slump in heavy industry. Many Japanese consumers opted to save rather than spend. Japan turned increasingly to high-technology industries for the export market. The economy again surged ahead. (See Figure 8.4.)

By 1980, Japan had become the largest automobile producer in the world, overtaking the United States, Japan's leading trade partner. The United States absorbed fully a third of Japan's exports, while Japan's imports from the United States lagged. This gap has been reflected in huge trade imbalances between the United States and Japan ever since. The U.S. trade deficit with Japan soared in the 1990s, leading to friction between previously close friends. In particular, Japan's success in penetrating the American automobile and consumer electronics markets elicited a public outcry in the United States against "unfair" Japanese trading practices.

Fairness versus Japan Bashing Japan's critics cited the need for a wide range of internal economic reforms. First, deregulate the banking system and money markets to end Japan's policy of low interest rates and thus attract overseas assets back into the country. Second, put an end to agricultural protectionism (especially for rice). Third, break up state-supported monopoly arrangements in the distribution system, which

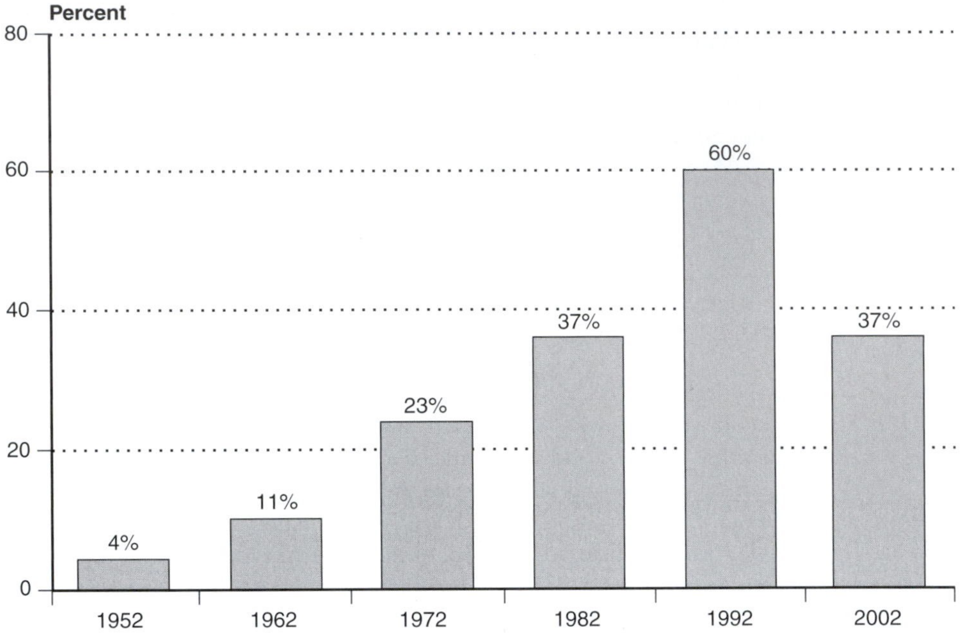

Figure 8.4 Japan's Gross Domestic Product (GDP), as a Percentage of U.S. GDP

Source: Compiled by author from official statistical data.

make it extremely difficult for foreign manufacturers to penetrate Japanese markets even without tariffs, import quotas, and other barriers. Fourth, actively combat the unfair trade practices of enterprise groups that discriminate against foreign firms. Fifth, do away with closed bidding for government contracts, which traditionally go almost exclusively to a handful of Japanese construction firms. Finally, tighten the interpretation of Japan's antimonopoly laws, further opening Japan's economy to free-market forces and foreign competition.

Japan was also urged to institute tight-money policies (to push up interest rates and thus keep capital at home) and to implement expansionary fiscal policies, including tax cuts (to encourage imports and absorb more domestic production internally, thereby reducing exports). Instead, Japan did just the opposite. Meanwhile, the United States pursued "Reaganomics" — the very mix of policies that many of Japan's critics asserted Japan needed to put into effect.

For both economic and political reasons, Japan faced pressure from the international community to make major policy adjustments that might require sacrifices. For example, developing nations have amassed foreign debts totaling more than a trillion dollars, while Japan has become the world's leading creditor nation. It is inevitable that governments and international agencies will look to Japan for leadership, loans, and debt relief, much as the world once looked to the United States as benefactor and backbone of the international monetary system. Moreover, Japan's affluence raised expectations of free-flowing foreign aid. Japan recognized this fact and boosted Japanese public and private assistance to developing countries accordingly. Most Japanese foreign aid goes to Asian countries.

As noted earlier, there was a growing chorus of criticism, led by the United States, of Japan's purportedly **unfair trade practices** at the beginning of the 1990s. For example, the United States has demanded that Japan lift its strict quotas on beef and citrus fruit, and rice-producing countries want Japan to abandon the protectionism that has long prevented foreign rice (and other foodstuffs) from entering the Japanese market. Nonetheless, Japan continued to impose "special tariffs in industries that [were] considered vulnerable to foreign competition."[13]

Nontariff barriers (NTBs) posed another problem. For example, the tariff on foreign cigarettes is only the tip of the protectionist iceberg. Imported tobacco products may be sold by only 10 percent of Japan's 250,000 tobacconists, and importers are allowed to advertise only in English-language publications. Such NTBs are common in Japan. Restrictions like these were especially upsetting to foreign competitors because Japan has been so aggressive in developing overseas markets for its own exports.

During the early years of Japan's export push, the Ministry of Finance waived taxes on up to 80 percent of a company's export earnings; depreciation allowances pegged to export earnings were later substituted for tax exemptions, but the net effect was the same. The Finance Ministry continued to control big banks that direct loans to industries favored by the government. For this purpose, the Japan Development Bank could draw on huge Post Office savings accounts that grew to immense proportions due to tax exemptions and generous interest rates. At the same time, the **Ministry of International Trade and Industry (MITI),** charged with promoting the nation's export industries, "targets countries and markets to be penetrated" and "[could] also bring together large producers into one company to achieve economies of scale — a practice U.S. antitrust law would prohibit." Finally, Japan was accused of being "willing to go to extreme lengths, subsidizing vulnerable items in foreign markets by raising domestic prices and shielding home markets."[14]

Japan's Perilous Fortune Japan faced several major challenges in the 1990s. Extreme scarcity of land had produced runaway real estate inflation in metropolitan areas, making urgent the need for an effective land-use policy. (One idea was to construct office complexes underground.) Many Japanese have come to regard Tokyo, with its high-rise landscape, as a "concrete desert."

Japan's economic bubble burst early in the decade. Real estate and stock values plummeted. The pace of bankruptcies quickened dramatically, and unemployment climbed to dizzying heights in a society unaccustomed to layoffs.

Evidence of a deepening recession was not hard to find. The Japanese economy actually shrank in 1993 and managed little more than a zero growth rate in 1994 and 1995. The government ran large budget deficits each year. By the fall of 1996, the national debt nearly equaled Japan's annual GDP.

One problem was the tax structure. Income taxes, particularly on the wealthiest Japanese, were sky high. High taxes and the collapse of private-sector investment slowed economic growth. In an effort to revive the economy, the government lowered interest rates repeatedly in the early 1990s and introduced a variety of stimulatory measures, including tax cuts, investment grants, and public-works projects. Even so, Japan's slide into recession continued unabated.

The Japanese economy bounced back in 1996 following a massive infusion of funds into the public sector the previous year, but it fell back into recession after the government allowed one of Japan's four largest stockbrokers and a large bank to collapse in 1997. This was a stunning development in a society accustomed to: (1) vertical ties that linked manufacturers, wholesalers, and retailers in a (perfectly legal) cartel-like arrangements called ***keiretsu;*** (2) collusive relationships between government and business that virtually guaranteed unlimited credit on soft terms; and (3) government bailouts of faltering giant-sized companies.

The 1997 shocks eventually led to policy changes that reflect a long overdue rethinking of Japan's basic economic institutions. Depending on how far (and fast) the process goes, these changes could usher in an economic transition hardly less profound than the transitions occurring in Eastern Europe and elsewhere.

Japan's Dual Economy There are really two Japanese economies. One is the economy of robust, highly competitive companies known so well to the outside world — Sony, Honda, and Matsushita, to name a few. These companies cluster in a few industries, such as cars, car parts, industrial machinery, and consumer electronics. The other economy, largely unknown outside of Japan, is highly inefficient. This economy includes a long list of industries that could not compete on a level playing field with industries of the same kind in the West. It is kept going by government protection and it, in turn, keeps workers employed in labor-intensive businesses. In many sectors, such as shipbuilding and chemicals, price-fixing and bid rigging are common. These practices are among various anticompetitive methods of perpetuating the dual economy on which Japan's consensual sociopolitical order is built.

To make matters worse, the first-tier, competitive economy is shrinking as Japan's leading export manufacturers are setting up factories abroad to avoid the high cost of land, labor, and energy at home. These companies are also facing stiffer competition from American and European manufacturers with each passing year. In Japan, stultifying regulations hamper key service industries such as information technology and finance that have powered economic growth in America and Europe. Upstart entrepreneurial companies have difficulty competing for labor and capital with big, established firms, which try (often unsuccessfully) to diversify into new "growth" industries.

Japanese Perestroika? Many government and business leaders in Japan recognize that the Japanese economy requires restructuring. As indicated earlier, several steps toward economic reform were taken after 1997. These steps include efforts to attract direct foreign investment (which means opening up the hitherto closed Japanese economy to the outside world). Another step involves banking reform. Until the failure of one of Japan's major banks in 1997, there was virtually no competition among the top twenty banks in the country. The banks, in turn, kept Japan's "welfare" industries in the second-tier economy afloat through a steady flow of soft loans based on *keiretsu* ties between the banks and the loan recipients. A third step involves the reform of accounting practices that, in the past, have allowed Japanese companies to hide losses and use various methods to "cook the books."

The restructuring of Japan's **dual economy** is still in its infancy. But bolder attempts at reform, weaning unprofitable industries away from dependence on easy credit and government protection, have so far proved elusive. Nonetheless, in 1998, the government did reduce the top rate of income tax from 65 percent to 50 percent. This change was aimed at encouraging homegrown wealth accumulation in the form of savings and investment in Japan's emerging new economy. Policy-wise, it was a step in the right direction; by itself, however, it was like putting a bandage on an injury that required stitches and a hospital stay.

Over the next five years, the Japanese economy slowed and steadily deflated — an especially ominous trend for a trade-based economy like Japan's. Japanese manufacturers began looking to relocate operations to China to keep costs down and gain better access to China's expanding markets. For example, Toshiba was making television sets on the mainland, which meant that jobs, incomes, and investment capital were going abroad. Some observers started talking about a new kind of problem. The Japanese economy, they said, was in danger of being hollowed out.

However, in 2003, after more than a decade of decline, Japan's economy showed signs of reviving: the Tokyo stock market rallied strongly for the first time in many years; a wide array of Japanese companies (other than banks) reported strong profits; real gross domestic product was rising by 2 to 3 percent, and employment and wages were following suit; and big business was poised to make large capital expenditures (investments). The timing of this mini-recovery appeared fortuitous in a political sense for Prime Minister Koizumi. If renewed optimism boosted his personal popularity perhaps he would at last have the political clout within the LDP to overcome entrenched opposition to his long-promised (and much-needed) reform program.

Too Much of a Good Thing Ironically, the stability of the Japanese political system, long a major asset, could become a liability if the entrenched forces of business and government obstruct necessary political, economic, and social change. The same goes for Japan's foreign policy.

Japan has little choice but to redefine its role in Asia and the world. As it does so, it will be walking through a political minefield. For example, clamor in the United States over the cost of maintaining U.S. forces in the western Pacific has been growing. Critics ask why the United States should continue to foot the bill for Japan's defense while Japan runs up a massive trade surplus with the United States. In response to such pressures, Tokyo has increased military spending, but the U.S. security umbrella remains in place.

Japan has the potential to be a military as well as an economic superpower, a fact that makes the rise of Japanese nationalism in recent years especially noteworthy. In 1989, this trend was accentuated by the passing of Emperor Hirohito, whose reign of more than sixty years encompassed the rise of Japanese militarism in the 1930s, the achievement of Japanese supremacy in Asia during World War II, Japan's abject defeat in the wake of the cataclysms at Hiroshima and Nagasaki, the adoption of Western-style democratic rule during the U.S. occupation, and the resurgence of Japan as an economic colossus after the mid-1950s. The outpouring of affection for the emperor — the most

India

important symbol of Japan's political heritage — demonstrated that the majority of Japanese people remain emotionally attached to traditional values.

In the wake of the Persian Gulf War, the question of whether Japanese military forces ought to participate in future UN peacekeeping operations was hotly debated in

Japan. (Japan had contributed money and transport planes to the war effort but not troops.) In 1992, a controversial bill was passed allowing future Japanese governments to dispatch self-defensive forces abroad for humanitarian purposes. After the Bush administration launched a preemptive war against Iraq in 2003, the Koizumi government sought parliamentary approval to send roughly 1,000 troops to help American and British occupation forces there. If and when it happens, it will be the largest overseas Japanese troop deployment since World War II. For Japan, the stigma of that war lingers in Asia much as it does for Germany in Europe — making such issues as defense spending, troop commitments, and military capabilities extremely sensitive.

In Sum . . . Despite occasional riots, demonstrations, and even violent outbursts in the Diet, Japan's democratic government was remarkably stable prior to the turbulent 1990s. This is all the more impressive considering that Japan's political traditions before 1947 were authoritarian. Economics has played a key role, for Japan's economic revival after World War II was little short of miraculous.

Close cooperation between political and business elites was one major reason for the Japanese postwar prosperity, but a drive to penetrate overseas markets and massive infusions of American aid during the Korean War were also crucial. Within two decades, the alliance of government, business, and labor that became a Japanese trademark produced huge advances in industry and technology. Today Japan is an economic superpower, second only to the United States. But Japan's past strengths have become its present weaknesses. Its future depends on whether it can adapt to an ever-changing world by changing the cultures, as well as the structures, of Japanese business and politics.

Despite recent troubles, Japan's political and economic success, like Germany's, indicates that democratic self-government can work in a variety of social and cultural contexts. India, too, illustrates that representative democracy can function even in a country that is ethnically diverse, overpopulated, and impoverished.

India: Democracy amid Diversity

Although it is a democracy like Japan, India is beset by chronic economic and social problems. On the surface, the country seems ill prepared for democracy: In the words of one wise observer:

> I have the impression that when we talk so confidently of liberty, we are unaware of the awful servitudes that are created by the ancient enemies of mankind: the servitude of poverty when means are so small that there is literally no choice at all; the servitude of ignorance when there are no perspectives to which the mind can open because there is no education . . . ; the servitude of ill-health which means that the expectation of life is almost too short to allow for any experience of freedom.[15]

Such doubts about the appropriateness of democracy for the Third World seem especially relevant to India, a nation of one billion people encompassing a bewildering array of cultures, languages, religions, and ethnic identities.

India's Drive for Independence

India's quest for self-rule can be traced back to the nineteenth century. Great Britain had originally ruled India indirectly, through Indian intermediaries and allies, but in the process it introduced various institutions that the British found useful, including property laws and notions about the nature and functions of government. Indians chosen for minor posts in colonial administration were first sent to England to receive a "proper classical education." Familiarity with Western ideas of equality, liberty, social justice, and representative democracy spread among India's English-speaking elites — merchants, landlords, public officials, doctors, lawyers, teachers — whose common interests transcended caste, religion, or region. After 1885, they began to meet annually in a conference called the **Indian National Congress,** the seed from which the independence movement would spring.

The British yielded power in India gradually and reluctantly. World War I strained Britain's resources, and London conceded that it would be necessary to transfer power (but not sovereignty) to Indian hands. Beginning in 1919, the National Congress, led by Mahatma Gandhi, conducted nationwide campaigns of **civil disobedience** *(satyagraha),* or passive resistance to British rule. Periods of confrontation (1919–1922, 1929–1932, 1942) alternated with periods of Congress participation, first in a power-sharing arrangement known as *dyarchy* and, after 1935, in provincial self-government.

The last thirty years of British rule saw the National Congress grow steadily in stature and strength, evolving into a major force in Indian politics — at once a mass movement, a political party, and an alternative government. Under the leadership of Mahatma Gandhi and Jawaharlal Nehru, the Congress became the vehicle of Indian independence.

The rise of the Congress, however, created a schism between Hindus and Muslims; the latter came to regard the Congress as just as dangerous to Muslim interests as the British themselves. Bloody communal riots occurred in the 1940s.

When the British quit India after World War II, they chose the easy way out by partitioning the subcontinent along religious lines. The most contentious issue involved the future of Jammu and Kashmir. Located between India and Pakistan, Kashmir was partitioned between them in 1947, but both claimed the entire territory. A local Hindu maharaja ruled Kashmir, but the population was predominantly Muslim and sought union with Pakistan; the maharaja favored merger with India. Hostilities erupted almost immediately, the first of three major wars between India and Pakistan (1947, 1965, and 1971). Kashmir was divided with half the territory on the Pakistani side of the line of control (LOC) and half on the Indian side. Communal violence between Hindus and Muslims has been a recurring problem in other parts of India as well.

The Indian Constitution

Although India gained independence from Great Britain in 1947, it took nearly three years to complete the new constitution. India's diverse society and sprawling geography necessitated not only a federal model but also the specific delineation of how power would be parceled out. The resultant constitution was a long and intricate document, containing not one list of powers but three: the **Union List,** enumerating powers of the central government; the **State List,** reserving certain powers to the provincial government; and the **Concurrent List,** spelling out the powers to be shared by both.

The division of power is laid out in painstaking detail. The Union List contains ninety-seven items covering national defense, the armed forces, atomic energy, foreign affairs, transportation, communications, banking, currency, insurance, regulation of industry and mining, income taxes, customs duties, and other areas. Enumerated in the State List are sixty-six items of primarily local interest: legal administration, public health and sanitation, education, agriculture, forests, fisheries, burials, duties on alcohol, and a variety of taxes (especially land taxes). The Concurrent List contains forty-seven items that fall into gray areas: marriage and divorce, contracts, bankruptcy, civil suits, trade unions, social security, labor welfare, price controls, and so on. States may pass their own laws dealing with these matters, but the constitution stipulates that national law always prevails over state law.

Federalism: Overcoming Language Barriers

The Indian federal system divides the country into twenty-three states and eight union territories. It strongly favors the central government to counterbalance the centrifugal tendencies inherent in India's cultural and linguistic diversity.

Because language was a potential source of civil strife, India's states were deliberately drawn along linguistic lines. The Indian Federal Union was reorganized in 1956; the number of states was reduced, and all but two of the new states were based on regional language patterns. English, a vestige of colonialism, has remained the language of privilege and power. Although the 1949 Constitutional Assembly specified that Hindi would become the national language after 1965, regional opposition was so violent that this timetable had to be abandoned. Rather than one national language, India has adopted a three-language formula: schoolchildren learn to read and write in their native tongue but also study English and Hindi.

A Centralized Federal Democracy

India's independence leaders were well aware of the dangers inherent in the nation's cultural diversity, so they designed a highly centralized federal democracy. For example, the central government is vested with elaborate emergency powers under the constitution. A national state of emergency can be declared in cases of imminent war or revolution. (Under this provision, Prime Minister Indira Gandhi, facing a challenge to her political authority, suspended the constitution in 1975 and assumed dictatorial powers for a period of nineteen months.) In addition, through a special declaration of emergency, the central government can take over any state that is threatened with a breakdown of law and order. Finally, if a state becomes financially insolvent, the central government can declare an economic emergency and can step in to run state affairs until the situation is under control.

The legislature, called the **Federal Parliament,** is divided into two houses. The upper house, known as the Council of the States or **Rajya Sabha,** has considerable legislative power, except in budget matters, where it has only the power to delay. Far more powerful is the House of the People, or **Lok Sabha,** modeled after the British House of Commons. An interesting aspect of the lower house is that it reserves a certain number of seats for groups that were victims of past discrimination, including former untouchables (outcasts).

As in other parliamentary systems, India's executive is divided. An electoral college made up of officials from the Federal Parliament and state assemblies chooses the president, or chief of state. The majority party or senior coalition partner in the House of the People elects the prime minister, who as the head of government appoints the cabinet, directs policy formulation, and represents the nation abroad. Except for brief spells, the prime minister has traditionally been the head of the **Congress Party** (or a successor with a slightly different name).

The Judiciary, Civil Liberties, and Social Rights

India has an independent judiciary that acts as a bulwark against official abuses of human rights. However, during periods of **presidential rule,** the federal government can dismiss an elected state government and rule directly until order and stability are restored. At such times, New Delhi can suspend civil liberties in the troubled state, and even jail political opponents at will. The most notorious use of emergency powers occurred in the mid-1970s when Indira Gandhi ruled as a virtual dictator for nineteen months. These powers have most often been used by the central government when instability in a particular state has led to a breakdown of law and order. But ordinarily, India's citizens enjoy freedom of speech, the press, assembly, religion, and so on.

Of particular interest is a section of the constitution that sets forth basic "social" rights (as opposed to the more familiar civil rights). These can be found in the "directives," of which Article 39 is a prominent part. It stipulates:

> The State shall, in particular, direct its policy toward securing
>
> a. that the citizens, men and women equally, have the right to an adequate means of livelihood;
> b. that the ownership and control of the material resources of the community are so distributed as best to subserve the common good;
> c. that the operation of the economic system does not result in the concentration of wealth and means of production to the common detriment;
> d. that there is equal pay for equal work for both men and women;
> e. that the health and strength of workers, men and women, and the tender age of children are not abused and that citizens are not forced by economic necessity to enter avocations unsuited to their age or strength.[16]

A new national party emerged from the old Congress coalition — Prime Minister Gandhi's **New Congress Party,** later renamed the Congress I (I for "Indira"), which was essentially a reincarnation of the one-party-dominant system under Gandhi's personal tutelage. Against fragmented and ineffectual opposition, she was able to remain in power despite growing disenchantment with her methods and policies.

When Gandhi declared the state of emergency in 1975, she had many opposition leaders arrested. At the end of martial law in 1977, new elections were announced, and the revitalized opposition parties formed an umbrella organization known as the **Janata Party.** This loose-knit coalition won a parliamentary majority and formed a government, but its fragile unity was predicated on little else than hostility toward Gandhi. Lacking consensus or a coherent program, the coalition lasted only two years. As India's foreign and domestic problems mounted, the need for a strong leader became more and more apparent; in the 1980 parliamentary elections, Congress I won impressively and again fashioned a coalition that enabled Gandhi to form a government. The Janata Party faded into oblivion, and the other parties once again became part of a fragmented and ineffectual opposition.

Communal Violence: India's Slow-Motion Civil War

Gandhi's return to power was plagued with misfortune, turmoil, and tragedy. First, her son Sanjay, who won a seat in the Lok Sabha in 1980, was killed in an airplane crash. Then a resurgence of caste and communal violence threatened Indian society as religious and regional separatism racked the federal structure. In Assam and northeast India, hatred of Bengalis and immigrants was expressed in murders, bombings, strikes, and civil disobedience. Hundreds of lives were lost in 1982 and 1983. When Prime Minister Gandhi tried to hold new elections rather than prolong presidential rule, the violence escalated, and New Delhi was forced to make concessions to the militants.

Violence between Hindus and Muslims breaks out regularly; hundreds of incidents are reported each year. Tensions boiled over in 1984, when Hindu-Muslim rioting occurred throughout the year in Hyderabad, and in Bombay where an alleged insult to Muhammad touched off the worst communal fighting since partition. In December 1992, a Hindu mob destroyed an ancient Muslim mosque in the northern Indian town of Ayodhya. The ensuing riots and violence prompted Prime Minister Rao to dismiss the governments in four states run by the Hindu-nationalist Bharatiya Janata Party (BJP). A decade later, Hindus and Muslims again killed each other in violent clashes precipitated by a terrorist act involving the still-simmering dispute over Ayodhya. The pattern was sickeningly familiar: Muslim radicals staged a vicious terrorist attack in Gujarat, killing fifty-eight Hindus on a train as they returned from Ayodhya, and Hindus (both the Indian army and angry mobs) retaliated by murdering Muslims.

Tensions between Sikhs and Hindus also run high. A Sikh secessionist movement has existed in the Punjab for decades. At first, the secessionists represented a small minority, but Punjabis became polarized as hundreds of people, most of them Hindu, were killed by terrorists. Hindus understandably urged the central government to intervene. The violence escalated in 1984 when a militant Sikh leader converted the Golden Temple at Amritsar into a terrorist sanctuary. Soon murders were occurring regularly, and a military reaction was inevitable. The assault on the temple lasted three days. The Indian army stormed the citadel, killing the leader and hundreds of his backers and damaging sacred buildings. An army blockade and curfew followed. Bitterness over this incident led directly to the assassination of Indira Gandhi by two Sikh security guards in 1984 and subsequent bloody reprisals by Hindus against Sikhs. Anti-Sikh riots in New Delhi and elsewhere, left more than 2,700 people dead.

Meanwhile, Sikh separatism continues to simmer in Punjab, India's wealthiest state. Sikhs constitute about half the population, but the balance is shifting against them as entrepreneurial Sikhs move out and Punjab's flourishing agriculture draws in Hindu laborers. As a result, the Sikhs often express fears that Sikh culture, religion, and language are endangered.

Separatism is a problem elsewhere in India as well. In the geographically isolated and strategically vulnerable northeast, rebels have mounted an insurrection since 1947. Tribalism and secessionism combine to produce an extraordinarily volatile situation in the states and territories of this region. Attempts by New Delhi to placate the various tribal and secessionist groups — for example, by creating the states of Nagaland in 1963 and Mizoram in 1972 — have not succeeded.

In Assam, foreigners are the issue. The immigration of Bengalis from neighboring Bangladesh has alarmed the Assamese, who fear becoming a minority in their own state (as indeed they may already be). Religion is a factor too: the Bengalis are Muslim, while the Assamese are Hindu. The northeast is not wealthy, like Punjab, and has long felt neglected by New Delhi. The slogan, "Assam is not India's colony," indicates how economic grievances combine with ethnic concerns in the bubbling cauldron that is India.

Kashmir is another hot spot in India, but one that periodically threatens to erupt into a full-scale war with Pakistan. An insurgency that started in Jammu and Kashmir in the late 1980s has claimed some 40,000 lives and continues to be fuelled by militant Muslim separatists who infiltrate across the line of control (LOC) — the border separating the two parts of Kashmir — to carry out terrorist attacks against Hindus. At least forty people died in a suicide attack on the state legislature in Jammu and Kashmir on October 1, 2001. New Delhi blamed Pakistani-sponsored terrorist groups for the atrocity. In December 2001, terrorists struck again, this time at the heart of India's democracy, assaulting the Indian parliament and killing fourteen people. Tensions subsequently reached the boiling point. India and Pakistan appeared headed for another war in the spring of 2002, but now they were (are) both armed with nuclear weapons, which is probably why both sides backed away from the brink. Despite the lingering war danger, terrorist attacks continue in Jammu and Kashmir and there is no final settlement of the Kashmir question in sight.

In sum, festering animosities among rival religious and social communities pose perhaps the greatest threat to India's long-term political stability. Problems in Jammu and Kashmir, rooted in long-standing Muslim-Hindu animosity, also point to the ever-present possibility of war with Pakistan. Unfortunately, with the exception of the American Civil War (1861–1865), India has been the scene of the worst and most frequent outbreaks of mass violence found in any modern democracy.

The Last Gandhi

The assassination of Indira Gandhi came at a time when her popularity was at low ebb, but Congress I and the country rallied around her surviving son, Rajiv, who had entered politics after his younger brother's untimely death in 1980. In the elections of

December 1984, Congress I won a landslide victory, capturing all but 19 of the 508 seats contested.

Rajiv Gandhi won early respect for his conciliatory gestures both at home and abroad. But the success of the Congress I Party at the national level was not matched by similar success in state elections. These defeats undermined Rajiv's credibility, as did continuing communal violence and a resurgence of Sikh separatism. In the summer of 1987, Sikh militants launched a new terrorist offensive. Such intractable problems, plus charges of high-level corruption within the government, a personally damaging conflict over constitutional issues with the outgoing president, and a series of cabinet resignations, raised doubts about the fate of India's democracy.

Charismatic leaders are a political tradition in India. The great Mahatma Gandhi was the first in a succession of dominant Congress figures. After him, both the party and the nation came to be dominated by a new dynasty. Nehru ruled from 1947 to 1964; Indira Gandhi, his daughter, from 1966 to 1977 and from 1980 to 1984. When she was assassinated and her son Rajiv succeeded her, the tradition of dynastic rule appeared to have returned in a new guise, adapted to the structures and processes of constitutional democracy. The presence of firm leadership throughout the postwar period was one key to India's success with democracy. In late 1989, however, political scandals and social unrest forced Rajiv Gandhi to step down, ushering in a period of governmental instability, which continued into the 1990s. Rajiv Gandhi was assassinated in May 1991 while campaigning to regain his position as prime minister. It was the end of the Gandhi era. For the first time since independence, India faced the future without a strong leader at the top.

Problems and Prospects

That India can be so poor and yet remain a relatively stable democracy is a marvel that rivals even the magnificent Taj Mahal. The durability of democracy attests to the coercive power of India's central government, to the resolution of strong leaders like Jawaharlal Nehru and Indira Gandhi to preserve the union, and to the success of a single national political party in integrating the nation's extremely diverse society. Finally, Indian democracy has survived despite a burgeoning population that would strain any nation's resources.

Development or Decline? India's development record has been checkered. Since 1947, the Indian economy has grown steadily but too slowly to get very far ahead of rapid population growth. As a result, per capita gains have been sluggish since 1947. The many causes of India's plight read like a laundry list of obstacles to growth: inadequate consumer demand, poor management, too little investment in the public sector (schools, roads, and so on), high capital-output ratios, overregulation, high production costs, and low productivity.[17] At the top of any such list belong two dynamic problems: the dynamics of population growth and India's lagging adaptation to the dynamics of the new global economy.

Table 8.5 Economic Performance: India, China, and Japan

	1998 GNP (millions of U.S. dollars)	1998 Per Capita GNP* (U.S. dollars)	1990s Average Annual Real Growth (percent)
India	427,407	440 (2,060)	4.3
China	923,560	750 (3,051)	9.6
Japan	4,089,140	32,350 (23,592)	1.3

*Figures in parentheses are PPP equivalents.
Source: International Bank for Reconstruction and Development, *The World Bank Atlas* (Washington, D.C.: Author, 2000).

Mixed Results A striking feature of India's development experience has been its failure to achieve a steady pattern of high growth. The golden decade of development, from 1956 to 1966, has not been matched since. India remains a very poor country with a per capita GNP of $543 in 2004, one of the lowest levels in the world. The pace of per capita growth quickened in the last two decades of the century, but a simple statistical comparison of India, China, and Japan in the 1990s shows just how far behind Asia's other giants India has fallen. (See Table 8.5.)

Although nearly 80 percent of its population is rural, India has more industrial infrastructure than most developing countries. Major basic industries include coal mining, electricity generation, steel, cement, petroleum, and chemicals, including synthetic fertilizers needed to grow wheat, rice, and other grains. By the 1980s, India was producing a wide array of industrial and capital goods, from traditional textiles to heavy machinery and transport equipment. Much of India's heavy industry is in the public sector. There is also a diversity of light (consumer) industries. Indians who have the money can buy a wide variety of domestically made consumer goods. The continued growth and diversification of the industrial economy in the 1990s made India a potential NIC. In recent years, India has developed a dynamic new growth (and export) industry in computer software. But these gains have done relatively little to alleviate India's economic and social problems.

India's Poor (but Not Silent) Majority The persistence of widespread poverty continues to challenge the Indian government and mar its record. Income distribution is uneven and rural poverty — affecting two-thirds of the population — is widespread. Millions of people earn just enough to stave off starvation. Estimates of the number of Indians living in poverty vary greatly. India's government set the figure at about 19 percent of the population in 1993–1994, but an independent estimate by a respected group of Indian economists, using the government's own data from household surveys, put the figure nearly twice as high. These sterile statistics, however, do not tell the real story. In human terms, the difference between the two divergent estimates is 166 million souls — more than the entire population of Russia.[18]

What does this extraordinary demographic profile mean for its prospects of strengthening and deepening India's democratic institutions? First, the obstacles are formidable. Perhaps 30 percent of the Indian population has no access to daily news in any form and nearly a third have never heard of the United States. Second, India is living proof that poverty is not always lethal to democracy. Sixty percent or more of all eligible voters in India cast ballots in national elections (a significantly higher rate of participation than in the United States). In the 1999 election, half the voters were visited by a canvasser and more than one in five voters attended an election meeting. Moreover, rates of participation are highest among the downtrodden: Dalits (ex-untouchables) and rural villagers are more likely to vote than upper-caste Indians and urbanites. Dalit support accounted for fully a third of the victorious anti-Congress alliance's popular votes in 1999. Commenting on the results of a 1999 survey which it cosponsored, *The Economist* observed: "Indians use their votes to demolish barriers to the advancement of their caste or community, to secure protection and patronage, and very often, to punish."[19]

Human Resources or Wasted Assets? One irony of underdevelopment in a populous country like India is that so much of the nation's most abundant resource — its people — is wasted. Despite considerable economic strides, India has been losing ground in the battle to provide gainful employment for a large segment of its adult population. This negative trend has actually accelerated as the labor market has expanded too slowly to absorb the number of young people seeking entry each year.

As fits the pattern for LDCs, **underemployment** (part-time or seasonal work) is even more prevalent than unemployment in India. And because the social service "safety net" found in wealthier countries is virtually nonexistent, having or not having a full-time job can literally be a matter of life and death for many low-caste members of Indian society.

Sick Industries The chronic employment deficit in India is a major stumbling block to the solution of another problem — the existence of many extremely inefficient industries. The state owns and operates capital-intensive industries such as steel and mining, and state-owned banks finance most industrial expansion. As a result, India has thousands of money-losing enterprises that successive governments sheltered for fear of exacerbating unemployment.[20]

When Narasimha Rao became prime minister in 1991, the signs that India's economy was failing were clear. So were the causes. The state had expanded continuously since independence. It had done so by taxing and borrowing as much as possible. India was on the verge of bankruptcy. Foreign-exchange reserves fell to near zero in 1990. The budget deficit soared and inflation, already in double digits, was rising. Facing default, India's ability to borrow abroad was in jeopardy.

India had accumulated a crushing external debt by the early 1990s, a fact that underscored the country's vulnerability to pressure from the international community — the IMF, the World Bank, the World Trade Organization (WTO), and the Commonwealth. The government needed billions of dollars in IMF loans to cover the principal and interest payments each year. At one point, Delhi sold twenty tons of confiscated black-market gold in order to meet these payments, a move "akin to selling the family jewels," in the eyes of some Indians.[21]

Indian Perestroika Prime Minister Rao's response to this crisis was a package of radical market-oriented reforms. One essential step was to devalue the rupee, which made Indian exports more competitive and imports more expensive. Another step was to abolish industrial licensing, which removed a bureaucratic obstacle to the creation of new businesses. A third was to slash import tariffs, which exposed India's industries to foreign competition. Also, in many cases importers were no longer required to obtain licenses. However, India still has a long way to go to catch up with the competition. (See Figure 8.5.) Finally, the Rao government allowed private — including foreign — investment in roads, power, ports, telecommunications, and aviation, thus ending the era of public-sector monopolies in India. At the same time, Rao eased the rules of entry for foreign investors.

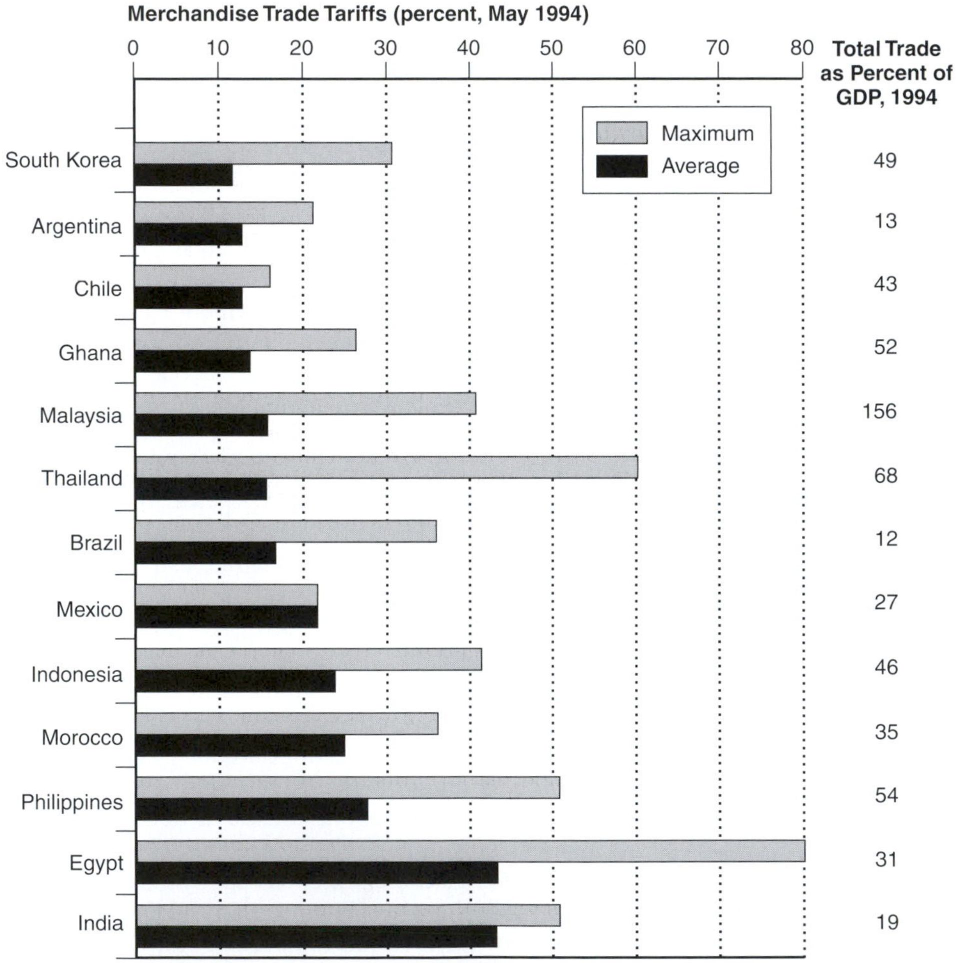

Figure 8.5 India's Average Tariff Was Still at Least Twice as High as the Average Tariff in Most East Asian and Latin American Countries a Decade Ago, and Remains High to This Day

Source: International Monetary Fund (1994). Reprinted with permission.

Although inflows of foreign capital increased in the1990s, India still trails far behind China. In 1998, for example, net private capital flowing into China's economy was seven times greater than the amount coming into India. Similarly, direct foreign investment in India was a mere $600 million compared to the $4.6 billion China captured.

Rao recognized the need to liberalize the economy, but he adopted a prudent, cautious approach that hit corrupt bureaucrats (accustomed, for example, to receiving bribes for licenses) and inefficient managers. He avoided antagonizing bankers, workers, and farmers. He stopped well short of privatizing public-sector companies. He did not allow even the worst public-sector companies to go under, nor did he do away with many subsidies.

Rao's critics dismissed his reforms as too little, too late. Whatever the case, Rao deserves credit for initiating the process of reform without causing mass unemployment or other dislocations that would have risked turning the public against the whole idea of reform. In the process, he left the Indian economy in better shape than he found it in.

Nonetheless, India remains less open to trade and investment than many other Asian countries. The contrast between the Indian economy and the vibrant economies found in other parts of Asia — most notably, China and the Asian tigers — suggests that India today stands at a crossroads: either it will have to push economic restructuring to another level, or it will fall dangerously far behind.

Too Many Wild Parties India's economic problems are exacerbated by a fragile and fragmented party system reflecting deep divisions within Indian society and a political ethos that places a low value on party loyalty. The original Congress Party split in 1969 and again in 1978. Breakaway elements and opposition parties tried to come together in 1975 and again in the late 1980s, but both of these coalitions soon fell apart. Kaleidoscopic changes of party affiliation by Indian politicians led in 1985 to an extraordinary constitutional amendment dubbed the **antidefection bill,** the aim of which was to disqualify members of parliament (and state legislatures) who switched party allegiance. But in politics, as in law, there are often loopholes: for example, when V. P. Singh organized the People's Front in October 1987 after his break with Rajiv Gandhi, he characterized it as a "nonparty political forum."

Singh was later instrumental in the formation of the **National Front (NF),** a coalition of odd groups including Singh's Janata Dal, the Communist Party of India (CPI), and the Communist Party of India-Marxist (CPI-M). The National Front failed to outpoll the Congress I in 1989 but managed to form a government with the support of the Hindu fundamentalist **Bharatiya Janata Party (BJP)**. That government, like the anti-Gandhi Janata coalition of the late 1970s, proved too unstable to rule (as did its successor). In 1991, Congress I returned to power as the senior partner in an alliance that won the election but captured less than a clear majority of seats in the Lok Sabha.

Given the difficulties inherent in India's fractious party system, Prime Minister Rao (1991–1996) turned out to be a surprisingly effective leader, as we noted earlier. Rao's relative success in handling the economy, however, did not extend to a healing of the deep divisions within Indian society — divisions expressed in the great profusion of regional political parties. Indeed, even Congress — the party of Mahatma Gandhi and Jawaharlal Nehru — was able to win only 30 percent of the vote in the 1996 election.

The results of the 1996 election left no party in a commanding position. The BJP could not find allies in the parliament. The efforts of BJP leader Atal Behari Vajpayee to form a viable government failed within a few weeks. But Congress, having received a clear vote of no confidence in the election, was in no position to step into the breach. That left only the National Front, a loose grouping of thirteen regional and leftist parties. The Front and the Congress parties, in turn, formed an alliance for the sole purpose of ousting the BJP from power.

The alliance accomplished its intended purpose, but the result proved to be nothing like the hoped-for new beginning its supporters had envisioned. In 1998, after two years of governmental disarray, the National Front suffered an electoral defeat at the hands of the resurgent BJP, led by A.B. Vajpayee. But Vajpayee's first attempt to form a government also fizzled. In the new elections held in October 1999, the voters gave the thumbs up to a BJP-led multiparty coalition (consisting of no less than twenty-four parties).

The 1999 Election Rechristened the **National Democratic Alliance,** the BJP alliance demonstrated a nationwide appeal for a second time in 1999, actually winning more seats than in 1998 (but a slightly smaller percentage of the popular votes). (See Table 8.6.) It was the first election since 1984 in which a party alliance won a clear majority in the parliament and the first time a prime minister won back-to-back elections since Indira Gandhi did it in 1971.

But the outcome of the election did not give Vajpayee much cause for complacency. In nearly half the constituencies, the party that won in 1998 lost in 1999, meaning that a huge number of voters were not committed to *any* political party. Even so, at the end of the 1990s, it appeared as though India's political system was maturing and perhaps moving toward a stable two-party configuration. There were many parties represented in the Indian parliament but only the BJP and Congress could claim to be truly national parties. All but a few of the other parties were confined to one or two of India's twenty-five states and seven territories.

Remarkably, policy did not become a victim of politics during this era of fluid party realignment. Despite the bewildering parade of governments and the circus created by so many political parties in the parliament, India remained on a steady path of reform during the 1990s. Prime Minister Vajpayee promised a government of moderation and consensus and laid out dozens of measures aimed at launching a second round of reforms, as well as completing the first. Two goals of the government's program for the economy were to boost the growth rate closer to Chinese levels and to raise direct foreign investment threefold.

Vajpayee's minister for disinvestments (a former World Bank economist) led an effort to privatize state-owned companies, eventually selling off more than a dozen of them. These sales, especially one involving India's largest automaker, helped to buoy the Bombay stock market in 2003 and to boost India projected GDP growth for the year by a percentage point or two (but still below the government's own target of 8 percent for the five-year period ending in 2007). They also helped to offset India's huge annual budget deficits. One other bright spot in the economy: India's foreign reserves surged to over $80 billion in 2003 (enough to cover more than a year's worth of imports) thanks to high rupee interest rates attracting new deposits from foreigners and Indians living abroad.

A Tough Neighborhood Conflict between India and Pakistan continues to smolder over the issue of Kashmir.[22] Mutual mistrust has exacerbated the problems in Punjab, where India frequently accuses Pakistan of trying to stir up trouble. India and

Table 8.6 India's 1999 National Elections: Vajpayee Back in the Saddle Again

Party	Seats	Votes (percent)
BJP Alliance	299	40.8
Congress Alliance	134	33.8
Other	104	25.4

Source: "How India Voted," *The Economist,* October 16, 1999, p. 75.

Pakistan have fought three wars since partition — 1947, 1965, and 1971. Communalism is again a factor: Pakistan is a Muslim nation, whereas India is predominantly Hindu. India has successfully tested an atomic bomb, and Pakistan also has an advanced program of nuclear-weapons building. Is the conflict over Kashmir really worth a nuclear confrontation?

India has a history of troubled relations with other neighboring states, too. From 1959 to 1962, it fought a major border war with China. More recently, India faced off against Sri Lanka over the latter's handling of an insurgency by Tamils. India also sent troops to thwart a coup in the Maldives and has feuded with Nepal over its relations with China. Tensions with neighboring Bangladesh continue to mount as illegal Bengali immigrants flood into India.

India is widely viewed as the bully of the neighborhood and as a potential threat to the regional balance. Pakistan alone can act as a military counterweight to India on the subcontinent. Herein lies the paradox: India is too strong to live comfortably with its neighbors and too weak to compete in the larger global community.

Events took a potentially dangerous turn in May 1998 when the BJP government became the first in India to undertake nuclear tests (five in all) explicitly for reasons of national security. Hitherto, Indian governments had maintained the fiction that its nuclear test in 1974 had been strictly "peaceful" — that is, not related to any military-strategic capability or plan. The nationalist BJP, however, dispensed with this fiction, in effect telling the world that India has as much right as any other sovereign state to do what it deems necessary in its own national interest.

Pakistan countered with a series of nuclear tests of its own, as the world watched in alarm, but the worst did not happen. In fact, the two governments deescalated the rhetoric of confrontation and began negotiations over confidence-building measures. Tensions abated for a time, but rose again in the fall of 2001 when a series of terrorist attacks allegedly supported by Pakistan killed dozens of Hindus and once again brought the two rival nuclear states to the brink of war.

The relationship between foreign and domestic policies is often neglected. In this case, the consequences of India's decision to "go-nuclear" with no apologies led to an international backlash. The world community, led by the United States, expressed sharp disapproval of both India and Pakistan. The United States is the largest provider of direct foreign investment in both countries; putting bilateral relations at risk jeopardizes India's drive to galvanize its creaky economy. This unresolved policy dilemma is a classic example of how governments sometimes pursue incompatible aims. It also shows how globalization has blurred the line between domestic and foreign policy.

In Sum . . . To survive as a constitutional democracy, India will need an international support system for many years to come. India's most famous modern poet, Rabindranath Tagore (1861–1941), summed up the situation as clearly as anyone:

> Power has to be made secure not only against power, but against weakness; for there lies the peril of its losing balance. The weak are as great a danger for the strong as quicksand for an elephant. . . . The people who grow accustomed to wield absolute power over others are apt to forget that by so doing they generate an unseen force which some day rends that power to pieces.[23]

Indian society has not become secularized, despite the efforts of such great Indian leaders as Gandhi and Nehru. The importance of secularization in the context of a multicultural society like India has little to do with religious piety and much to do with political stability. The contrast between India, on the one hand, and Japan or China, on the other, is stark. India's continuing social and political instability, caused above all by its communal divisions, is a major obstacle to domestic tranquility. Without civil order, there is little chance that India will be able to solve its pressing economic problems or compete with other up-and-coming Asian nations.

In sum, the ever-present danger of communal violence, the patchwork parliament, and the absence of a leader of great stature capable of uniting India's fractured society, combine to cast some doubt over the country's future, but the danger of disintegration ought not to be exaggerated. Against all odds and for half a century now, India has sustained itself as a federal democracy with a relatively sparing use of the state's police powers and a respect for human rights that is indeed rare in Asia.

SUMMARY

The political traditions of Asia are distinct from those of Europe. Although Asian political traditions and systems have been predominantly authoritarian, many Asian societies display a remarkable propensity to assimilate and adapt certain features of Western society (such as secularization and the emergence of a large middle class) and Western political economics (including market economies, liberal trade policies, mass consumption, technological innovation, free elections, and parliamentary democracy). India is a notable exception because it has not become secular nor is it becoming a mass-consumption society (in contrast to its even more populous neighbor China). Also, Asia displays a greater maldistribution of wealth than any other region in the world.

Compared with other regions, Asia has experienced remarkably uneven rates of development, with some countries ranking among the fastest-growing economies in the world and others continuing to be among the poorest. The success of Japan, South Korea, Taiwan, Hong Kong, Singapore, and, most recently, the People's Republic of China may spur similar successes elsewhere in the region. Thailand has moved ahead of some other countries in South and Southeast Asia, followed by Malaysia and Indonesia. India has also shown signs of economic dynamism. Rapid population growth clouds the prospects for much of the region, but the success of the PRC in raising living standards for the majority of China's people and drastically reducing the numbers who live in absolute poverty suggests that the demographic obstacles to social progress need not be insuperable. China's economic miracle holds out hope not only for other overpopulated and impoverished nations of Asia but also for other developing regions. In addition to poverty, inequality, and a fragmented party system, India is still plagued by communalism and separatism.

KEY TERMS

People's Liberation Army (PLA)
Hundred Flowers movement
Great Leap Forward
Maoism
Great Proletarian Cultural Revolution
Red Guards
Gang of Four
Mao Zedong thought
dual rule
guerrilla administration
National Party Congress
Central Committee
Politburo
Standing Committee
Secretariat
general secretary
State Council
National People's Congress (NPC)
new legality
Four Modernizations
Tiananmen Square massacre
special economic zones (SEZs)
some get rich first
iron rice bowl
Article 9
self-defense forces
Diet
Liberal Democratic Party (LDP)
factions
Policy Affairs Research Council (PARC)
consensual decision making
koenkai
New Frontier Party (NFP)
Japanese economic miracle
unfair trade practices
nontariff barriers (NTBs)
Ministry of International Trade and Industry (MITI)
keiretsu
dual economy
Indian National Congress
civil disobedience
Union List
State List
Concurrent List
Federal Parliament
Rajya Sabha
Lok Sabha
Congress Party
presidential rule
New Congress Party (Congress I)
Janata Party
underemployment
antidefection bill
National Front (NF)
Bharatiya Janata Party (BJP)
National Democratic Alliance

STUDY QUESTIONS

1. What effects did the outcome of World War II have on political systems in China, Japan, and India?
2. What was China's Great Leap Forward? Was the Cultural Revolution a second "great leap" or was it qualitatively different? Why did Mao believe it was necessary to launch periodic revolutions from above? Is Maoism dead or does the ghost of Mao continue to haunt the PRC?
3. How is the People's Republic of China governed? What, if anything, changed after Mao's death?
4. How does Japan's political system work? How is it similar to Western parliamentary government? How is it different?
5. Given the multiethnic nature of Indian society, how can India function as a parliamentary democracy? What features of other political systems did India borrow? What features are unique to India?
6. Of the three countries featured in Chapters 7 and 8 — Japan, China, and India — which one, in your view, has dealt the most successfully with the problem of managing change without eroding the values that define what it means to be Japanese, Chinese, or Indian?
7. Explain the Japanese economic miracle as best you can. Is Japan a market economy like the United States or not? Explain.
8. Do you think Japan or China will be a stronger competitor — economically, politically, and militarily — for the United States ten years from now? Explain.

SUGGESTED READINGS

Armacost, Michael H. *Friends or Rivals? The Insider's Account of U.S.-Japan Relations.* New York: Columbia University Press, 1996.

Bernstein, R., and Munro, R. H. *The Coming Conflict with China.* New York: Knopf, 1997.

Bose, Sugata, ed. *Nationalism, Democracy, and Development: State and Politics in India.* New York: Oxford University Press, 1997.

Chang, David Wen-wei. *China under Deng Xiaoping: Political and Economic Reform.* New York: St. Martin's, 1991.

Chang, Gordon. *The Coming Collapse of China.* New York: Random House, 2001.

Dandekar, V. M. *The Indian Economy, 1947–92: Population, Poverty and Employment.* Thousand Oaks, Calif.: Sage, 1996.

Argy, Victor, and Stein, Leslie. *The Japanese Economy.* New York: New York University Press, 1997.

Dickson, Bruce J. *Red Capitalists in China: The Party, Private Entrepreneurs, and Prospects for Political Change.* New York: Cambridge University Press, 2003.

Dreze, Jean. *India: Economic Development and Social Opportunity.* New York: Oxford University Press, 1996.

Finkelstein, David M. and Kivlehan, Maryanne, eds. *China's Leadership in the Twenty-first Century: The Rise of the Fourth Generation.* Armonk, N.Y.: Sharpe, 2003.

Jharta, Bhawana. *Women and Politics in India.* Columbia, Mo.: South Asia Books, 1996.

Johnson, Chalmers. *Blowback: The Costs and Consequences of American Empire.* New York: Holt, 2000.

Hardgrave, Robert L., Jr., and Kochanek, Stanley A. *India: Government and Politics of a Developing Nation.* 5th ed. Orlando, Fla.: Harcourt, 1993.

Howe, Christopher, Kueh, Y. Y., and Ash, Robert, eds. *China's Economic Reform: A Study with Documents.* New York: Routledge Curzon, 2003.

Lardy, Nicholas R. *Integrating China into the Global Economy.* Washington, D.C.: Brookings Institution, 2002.

Meisner, Maurice J. *Mao's China and After.* New York: Free Press, 1997.

Miles, James. "Out of Puff: A Survey of China," *The Economist,* June 15, 2002.

Ogden, Suzanne. *Inklings of Democracy in China.* Cambridge, Mass.: Harvard University Press, 2002.

Pye, Lucian W. *The Spirit of Chinese Politics,* 2nd ed. Cambridge, Mass.: Harvard University Press, 1992.

Roberti, Mark. *The Fall of Hong Kong: Britain's Betrayal and China's Triumph.* New York: Wiley, 1997.

Sato, Kazuo. *The Japanese Economy: A Primer.* Armonk, N.Y.: Sharpe, 1997.

Studwell, Joe. *The China Dream: The Quest for the Last Great Market on Earth.* New York: Atlantic Monthly Press, 2002.

Terrill, Ross. *The New Chinese Empire: Beijing's Political Dilemma and What It Means for the United States.* New York: Basic Books, 2003.

Thomas, Raju. *Democracy, Security, and Development in India.* New York: St. Martin's, 1996.

Varshney, Ashutosh. *Ethnic Conflict and Civic Life: Hindus and Muslims in India.* New Haven, Conn.: Yale University Press, 2002.

Waters, Harry J. *China's Economic Development Strategies for the Twenty-first Century.* Westport, Conn: Greenwood, 1997.

NOTES

1. "Fit to Rule?" *The Economist,* August 31, 1996, p. 15; see also Robert Cottrell, "A Vacancy Awaits (A Survey of China)," *The Economist,* March. 18, 1995.
2. The statistics in this paragraph are found in *The Economist*, "The World in 2003," p. 97. The figure for Taiwan's foreign reserves is from *The Economist,* July 5, 2003, p. 90.
3. Gunnar Myrdal, *Asian Drama: An Inquiry into the Poverty of Nations,* 3 vols. (New York: Twentieth Century Fund, 1968).
4. Ibid.
5. See Harry Harding, *China's Second Revolution: Reform after Mao* (Washington, D.C.: Brookings Institution, 1987).
6. John Frankenstein, "Chinese Foreign Trade in the 1980s," *Current History,* September 1988, p. 258.
7. "When China Wakes," *The Economist,* November 28, 1992. According to the author, "China's economic performance has brought about one of the biggest improvements in human welfare anywhere at any time."
8. Robert H. Scalapino and Junnosuki Masumi, *Parties and Politics in Contemporary Japan* (Berkeley: University of California Press, 1962), p. 153.
9. Haruhiro Fukui, "Japan's Takeshita at the Helm," *Current History,* April 1988, pp. 173–175, 185–186.
10. "The Test for the LDP," *The Economist,* July 25, 1992, p. 17.
11. "Japan's New Politics," *The Economist,* May 6, 2000.
12. Norimitsu Onishi, "With a Big Victory, Japanese Premier Gains Momentum," *New York Times,* September 21, 2003, online edition; see also, "A Stimulating Contest," *The Economist,* September 13, 2002, pp. 35–36, and "Keeping Koizumi," *The Economist,* September 6, 2002, pp. 37–38.
13. David Brock, "Fortress of Mercantilism Still Wary of Competitors," *Insight,* July 18, 1988, p. 17.
14. Ibid.
15. Barbara Ward, *The Rich Nations and the Poor Nations* (New York: Norton, 1962), pp. 158–159.
16. Note the emphasis on gender equality in the workplace — a contrast with the common image of India as a society in which women are oppressed. Actually, the picture regarding gender rights is rather contradictory. On the one hand, India's most powerful prime minister in recent decades was a woman (Indira Gandhi), and the wife of her slain son (Rajiv Gandhi) now leads the New Congress Party. On the other hand, most Indian women, especially those in lower castes that constitute the great majority, are typically trapped in traditional subordinate female roles.
17. Robert J. Hardgrave, Jr., and Stanley A. Kochanek, *India: Government and Politics of a Developing Nation,* 4th ed. (Orlando, Fla.: Harcourt, 1986), p. 329.
18. "How Poor Is India?" *The Economist,* April 13, 1996, p. 30.
19. "How India Voted: A Cacophony of States," *The Economist,* October 16, 1999, p. 75. This article is also the source of the data cited in the same paragraph in the text.

20. "Tiger or Tortoise?" *The Economist,* April 27, 1996, pp. 21–23.
21. Sheila Tefft, "Economic Woes Besiege India," *Christian Science Monitor,* June 4, 1991, p. 5; Sheila Tefft, "India Deals with Economic Crisis," *Christian Science Monitor,* July 3, 1991, p. 7.
22. See, for example, "The stand-off on the roof of the world," *The Economist* (special report), January 19, 2002, pp. 20–21, 24; see also, "Kashmir: Summer Pleasures," *The Economist,* July 5, 2003, p. 36.
23. Rabindranath Tagore, in *Aspects of Our Foreign Policy: From Speeches and Writings of Indira Gandhi,* All-India Congress Committee, ed. (New Delhi: All-India Congress Committee, 1973), p. 72.

PART V
Latin America

Mexico

Area: 761,604 square miles

Population (2004): 105,200,000

Language: Spanish (official)

Female school enrollment: 100%

Major religion(s): Roman Catholicism

Monetary unit: peso

GNP: $641 billion (2003 est.) (1998 = $368 billion)

GNP per capita: $6,200 (2003 est.) (1998 PPP = $7,450)

Average annual GNP per capita growth: 0.6% (1990–1998)

Recent growth rate: 2.3% (2003, Q1) (2000, Q2 = 7.6%)

Average annual inflation rate: (1990–1998): 19.5%

Recent inflation rate: 4.3% (June 2003)

Personal computers per 1,000 people: 47 (1998)

Brazil

Area: 3,286,470 square miles

Population (2004): 179,000,000

Language: Portuguese (official)

Female school enrollment: 94%

Major religion(s): Roman Catholic (70%), Protestant (15%)

Monetary unit: cruzeiro

GNP: $514 billion (2003 est.) (1998 = $767 billion)

GNP per capita: $4,630 (1998) (PPP=$6,460)

Average annual GNP per capita growth: 1.7% (1990–1998)

Recent growth rate: 2.0% (2003, 1Q) (2000, Q2 = 3.9%)

Average annual inflation rate: 347.4% (1990–1998)

Recent inflation rate: 16.6% (June 2003)

Personal computers per 1,000 people: 30.1 (1998)

United States
MEXICO
CUBA
HAITI
DOMINICAN REPUBLIC
PUERTO RICO
VIRGIN ISLANDS
GUADELOUPE
ST. LUCIA
BARBADOS
ST. VINCENT
TRINIDAD AND TOBAGO
BELIZE
HONDURAS
JAMAICA
GUATEMALA
EL SALVADOR
NICARAGUA
COSTA RICA
PANAMA
VENEZUELA
GUYANA
SURINAME
FRENCH GUIANA
COLOMBIA
ECUADOR
BRAZIL
PERU
BOLIVIA
PARAGUAY
CHILE
ARGENTINA
URUGUAY

Part V Outline: Latin America

Chapter 9:
The Spanish Conquest and Its Aftermath

Land, Population, and Resources

Historical Background

Political Culture

Latin American Development and Dependency

Case Studies: Mexico and Brazil

- Mexico
- Brazil

Chapter 10:
Caudillos, Coups, and Constitutions

The Latin Authoritarian Model

Winds of Change: Democracy and Debt

Troubled Transitions: Civilians Take Charge

Foreign Debt: The Lost Decade

Reforms, Regionalism, Recession: The 1990s

Case Studies: Mexico and Brazil

- Mexico: Only One Fox, So Many Hounds
- Brazil: Lula to the Rescue?

CHAPTER 9

The Spanish Conquest and Its Aftermath

Latin America owes its name to the Latin-derived languages spoken there (Spanish and Portuguese). The region encompasses Mexico, Central America, the Caribbean, and South America. Its thirty-four sovereign states range in size from Brazil, which is larger than the contiguous United States, to tiny Caribbean island-states such as Barbados (about one-tenth the size of Rhode Island). The actual Latin countries, in which Spanish or Portuguese is the principal language, number only twenty; of these, all except Brazil, colonized by Portugal, were once under the colonial rule of Spain.

Central America comprises seven independent countries: Belize, Costa Rica, El Salvador, Guatemala, Honduras, Nicaragua, and Panama. Mexico, though usually considered part of Central America, is historically and geographically apart from it. Two years after they broke from Spain in 1823, Guatemala, Honduras, El Salvador, Costa Rica, and Nicaragua formed the United Provinces of Central America. This union lasted until 1838. Since then, repeated attempts to restore the union — some twenty-five in all — have failed.

South America is the world's fourth largest continent. (North America's landmass is larger.) South America boasts some of the world's highest mountains (the Andes), its largest rain forest (the Amazon Basin), and one of its oldest advanced civilizations (the Incan). South America's multiplicity of native cultures complements its geographic diversity. It includes two populous states with relatively advanced economies, Argentina and Brazil, and two smaller but relatively prosperous states, Chile and Uruguay, as well as poor states such as Bolivia, Ecuador, Paraguay, and Peru. Other states – most notably Colombia and Venezuela – fall somewhere between the rich and the poor. Guyana continues to be the poorest of the poor in South America.

The Caribbean region consists of hundreds of islands in a chain running from northern South America to just south of Florida. The southernmost islands are Trinidad and Tobago; the northernmost are the Bahamas. Cuba is by far the biggest of these islands. Some, like Cuba and the Dominican Republic, are Spanish-speaking; in others, the primary language is English, French, or Dutch. The Caribbean islands are culturally diverse and only tenuously connected by strands of history or commerce to the rest of Latin America. Geographer David Lowenthal aptly characterized the difficulty of generalizing about these islands, known as the **West Indies:**

> Alike in not being Iberian [Hispanic], the West Indies are not North American either, nor indeed do they fit any ordinary regional pattern. Not so much undeveloped as overdeveloped, exotic without being traditional, they are part of the Third World yet ardent emulators of the West.[1]

Although language is a common denominator throughout most of the region, Latin America as a whole is a diverse mixture of nations and cultures, to which Spain, Portugal, England, France, Italy, the Netherlands, Africa, and indigenous peoples have all contributed. Even the experts differ on the extent to which Latin America comprises a single unity. Some, like Chilean historian Claudio Veliz, argue that the Iberian inheritance is an essential part of Latin American life. Others, like U.S. political scientist Lawrence Graham, disagree. In Graham's view, "generalizations about Latin American cultural unity are no longer tenable." But he notes that nationalism is a powerful force in the region and that "one of the effects of nationalism has been to . . . lead growing numbers of individuals within the region to identify with their own nation-state before they think in terms of a more amorphous landmass called Latin America."[2]

Stereotypes and generalizations about Latin America often do impede understanding and it is true that every state in the region has distinctive features. But, as we are about to discover, the region *does* have a common heritage, rooted in the historical influence of Spain and Portugal and Iberian cultures. This European — Iberian — connection has not resulted in carbon-copy cultures, but with few exceptions it has profoundly influenced each individual culture.

Land, Population, and Resources

In Latin America, geographic factors have often hindered economic development and impeded state building — the spread of the state's administrative and political institutions, popular recognition of the state's legitimate authority, and growth of a sense of citizenship as evidenced in identification with the state's symbols, aims, and interests. Throughout much of the region, the progression from local to national loyalties so essential to state building has been blocked by physical barriers — mountains, jungles, and sparsely inhabited plains. In Bolivia, for example, most natives identify themselves not as Bolivians but as members of a tribe, village, or region. The same is true in Guatemala, in Peru, and elsewhere.

Geography

The most important aspect of Latin America's geography is its location in the Southern Hemisphere, for a host of climatic, political, economic, diplomatic, and cultural reasons. Generally speaking, the climate is warmer and wetter than in North America. The vast rain forests of South America's Amazon Basin, for example, are enormously important from an environmental standpoint and have no true counterpart on other continents. Temperature, rainfall, and altitude also set South America apart environmentally. The geographic diversity within Latin America is equally striking.

South America The continent of South America divides quite naturally into three main parts: the northern Andean countries of Venezuela, Colombia, Ecuador, Peru, and Bolivia; the Southern Cone countries of Argentina, Uruguay, Paraguay, and Chile; and Brazil (which occupies almost the entire eastern half of the continent), plus, to its north, the small states of Guyana (formerly British), Suriname (formerly Dutch), and French Guiana (an overseas department of France).

The majestic Andes, with peaks reaching nearly 23,000 feet in Chile and Argentina, stretch all the way from Venezuela to the tip of the Southern Cone. This massive mountain range bisects South America, separating the narrow western coastal plain from the rest of the continent. It also divides the countries it passes through into separate regions, with important political, economic, social, and cultural consequences. From the standpoint of settlement patterns, South America is a "hollow" continent. Most large cities are situated on the Atlantic and Pacific coast. Historically, harbors and port facilities were the key to trade and travel, giving the wealthy elites of these states a natural outward orientation, while widening the social and economic gulf between rich and poor. Unlike North America, interior development has lagged far behind and remains minimal in much of the region.

Mexico and Central America The Andes are justly famous; less famous is the chain of volcanic mountains that extend from Mexico through Central America. These mountains have influenced history in several ways. As barriers to communication, for example, they have complicated the process of national integration. Because their terrain is difficult or impossible to cultivate, they have also impeded economic development. The mountains that form the spine of Middle America rise along major fault lines. Volcanic eruptions and earthquakes have reduced thousands of villages and nearly every major city in this region to rubble and ash at one time or another. In recent years, massive earthquakes have devastated Mexico City in the north and Managua, the capital of Nicaragua, farther south. Disastrous floods are also common, because of heavy rains from May to October, and along the coast, hurricanes are a familiar threat as well.

A kaleidoscope of microclimates and environments, Central America can be divided into four geographic subregions: northern Guatemala and Belize (an extension of Mexico's Yucatán peninsula); the Caribbean coasts of Guatemala, Honduras, and Nicaragua; the Pacific volcanic region, and the Costa Rica–Panama isthmus. The cultural and political history of Central America is anchored in the highlands and Pacific plains, the areas most hospitable to human habitation.

Population Patterns

The people of Latin America are as diverse as the land. Except in the West Indies, descendants of the Spanish or Portuguese colonial rulers form the nucleus of a social and economic elite throughout most of the region. At the bottom of the socioeconomic order is Latin America's large and culturally differentiated Indian population. For the most part, the Indians of Latin America have clung tenaciously to their traditional values and beliefs and have resisted modernization schemes drawn up by urban elites, who remain foreigners in their eyes. Attached to a particular locality and oriented toward village and family, native inhabitants still do not view themselves as Guatemalans, Nicaraguans, or Peruvians. They typically live in rural poverty, often far from the center of government, victims of benign neglect or even official abuse.

The elites are European or Europeanized, urban in outlook, university-educated, sophisticated, and stylish. They typically live in affluent neighborhoods, and in the capital or some other large city. They constitute the professional class — politicians, businesspeople, bureaucrats, lawyers, doctors, engineers, academics, and the like. The cities are also home to absentee landlords, the heirs of old money for whom land ownership is not only a source of wealth but also a status symbol and proof of pedigree, which is important to many elites in any culture.

The Mixing Bowl South Americans have a three-layered ethnic heritage — Iberian, Indian, and **mestizo** (mixed blood) — but intermarriage has blurred ethnic distinctions. Ethnic commingling is most dramatic in Chile, which is 95 percent European and Spanish-Indian; it is least evident in Argentina and Uruguay, which are overwhelmingly Spanish-European. Unassimilated Indians are most prevalent in the Andean countries of Bolivia, Peru, and Ecuador, a reminder of the Incan civilization that once flourished there. (For example, over half the population of Bolivia is Indian.) In Venezuela and Colombia, mestizos, who constitute about 60 percent of the population, outnumber Spanish and Indians. Mestizos are a major segment of society in most of Latin America. There is little or no stigma attached to mixed blood, and mestizos, though not Indians, are prominently represented among social, political, and economic elites.

In Central America, a similar pattern holds, with one notable exception: here **Ladinos** are a major element in the population. The word *Ladino* refers to anyone who has been latinized, but it means different things in different places. In Guatemala, it is synonymous with *mestizo,* a person of mixed blood; elsewhere in Central America, it refers to an Indian who has adopted European ways. Initially, Ladinos were caught between two cultures and were rejected by both — they looked Indian and "acted white." But they excelled as entrepreneurs and became agents of social change, modernization, and national integration. Today, Ladinos are local leaders in Guatemala, Nicaragua, Honduras, and El Salvador.

Urbanization, Migration, and Poverty Since the Spanish conquest, culture in Latin America has been inseparable from city life. A bias against the harsh, remote, and "uncivilized" world beyond the city gates permeates the thinking of the elites and middle class who dominate Latin society and define its values. Latin culture is highly social — networks of families and constant interaction with friends and neighbors are the norm. In fact, there are more cities with a population of over half a million in Latin America than in the United States, even though the United States is far more advanced industrially (urbanization and industrialization are often viewed as inextricably entwined).

In recent decades, Latin America has been the scene of major population shifts from the countryside to the cities. This migration cannot be explained by cultural factors or by the lure of bright city lights alone. Rather it is driven by land scarcity, population pressure, insurgency, rural poverty, and the promise of a better life. The appeal of an improved situation in the city turns out to be an illusion for most migrants.

The influx of people from impoverished rural areas has been particularly heavy in the cities of Middle America. The population of Mexico City, for example, exceeded 20 million by 1990 and continues to grow at an alarming rate. The government's capacity to provide essential services such as running water, electricity, sewage disposal and treatment, garbage removal, street maintenance, neighborhood schools, and fire and police protection is overwhelmed. Shantytowns have sprung up on the outskirts of mushrooming urban centers like Mexico City; living conditions in them are wretched by any standard. Such overcrowding and urban poverty no doubt contribute to the steady flow of illegal immigrants coming from Mexico to the United States every year — mass migration is almost always a symptom of social and economic ills.

In 1992, Mexico sought a customs union with the United States and Canada. It was an idea whose time had come. Whether the new North American Free Trade Association (NAFTA) will energize the economy and improve the wretched lives of Mexico's poor is still anybody's guess. In Central America, El Salvador has experienced the most intense population pressure. There is simply too little land to go around now that the population is growing at a rate of 2.9 percent a year — second only to Nicaragua (3.0 percent) in Central America. Most of the land is devoted to export crops — primarily cotton and coffee — or to cattle ranching. Thus, it is little wonder that land reform has been a burning issue in El Salvador and that a rural insurgency has torn apart the country. Nor is the problem of land scarcity in El Salvador likely to be resolved: even if agrarian reform were implemented (which is highly unlikely), there would still be too little land to go around.

Thousands of Salvadorans migrated to Honduras in the 1960s in search of land or jobs in commerce and industry. By the end of that decade, some 75 percent of all foreigners in Honduras were from El Salvador. The resulting tension was a contributing cause of the two-week war that broke out between the two countries in 1969.

Depopulation of the countryside is also occurring in South America. Peru and Bolivia provide striking illustrations. In both cases, people from the impoverished highlands, facing famine, have fled to the cities. In the case of Peru, natural disasters and a vicious guerrilla war in the southern Andes have played a role as well. At present, 6 million people, or nearly one-third of Peru's population, live in Lima, the capital. Most newcomers have no money, no education, no job, and therefore no choice but to become squatters, settling in squalid suburban communities that Peruvians euphemistically call *pueblos jovenes* ("new towns").

Although migration is not acute everywhere, it is pervasive throughout Latin America. Where the grass looks greener on the other side of the border, immigrants (and refugees) flock to neighboring countries. Venezuela has had an immigration problem somewhat analogous to that of the United States' problem with Mexico. Since the early 1970s, when Venezuela experienced an oil-export driven economic boom, Colombians have been crossing into Venezuela illegally in search of high-paying jobs.

Thus, population movements pose serious problems for many governments in the region. If the trend reflected positive marketplace conditions — economic growth and labor shortages — this geographic mobility would be healthy. Unfortunately, in contemporary Latin America, it reflects negative conditions — poverty, hunger, insurgency, and despair.

Natural Resources

In resources, Latin America is neither rich nor poor. Mexico and Venezuela are both significant petroleum producers and exporters. Chile, Brazil, and Colombia have many kinds of minerals. Brazil and Colombia also have precious gemstone deposits. Colombia, for example, supplies 90 percent of the world's emeralds, and Brazil has diamonds. Both countries produce gold.

In addition to mining, Latin America has rivers that produce hydroelectric power, and Brazil has the world's largest rain forest. (See Box 9.1.) Also, the region has long been a major food producer. Although some states in Central America are sometimes derisively labeled "banana republics," they are also important producers of such export crops as cotton, sugar, and coffee. The same holds true for South America. For example, coffee accounts for 50 percent of Colombia's annual legal exports, and Brazil produces more coffee than any other nation in the world. Argentina is a leading producer of beef and feed grains.

Colombia, Bolivia, Peru, and Ecuador are the world's leading coca producers and supply most of the cocaine sold in the United States. Although coca may not be considered a commodity by many observers, it is the major export crop for several countries in the region. Coca plants are extremely hardy, grow in a variety of climates and at different altitudes, and yield by far the highest income for the peasants who cultivate them. South America's illegal drug trade is estimated in the billions of dollars.

Historical Background

Many studies dealing with the development of Latin American political institutions begin at the wrong point — the Spanish conquest or the start of the independence movement in the early nineteenth century. But the Spanish could not impose new institutions until they had displaced, destroyed, adapted, or assimilated the cultures and civilizations that were already there.

Latin America's Original Civilizations

The **Incas,** the **Mayas,** and the **Aztecs** developed the three most advanced native cultures in the Americas. The Incan Empire stretched 2,000 miles along the high mountains and plateaus of the Andean range in South America. It was based in what is now the city of Cuzco in southern Peru, north of Lake Titicaca. From Cuzco, the Incan monarch controlled a highly centralized empire.

When the Incas expanded their territories, the peoples they conquered were fully integrated into the political system and were required to learn the Incan language,

What If?

BOX 9.1

Brazil's Disappearing Forests

The tropical rain forests of South America and sub-Saharan Africa generate not only oxygen but also exports worth a total of $8 billion a year. Brazil's rain forest, the world's largest, is being destroyed at an alarming rate. Vast tracts of jungle forest are being burned, adding to already dangerously high carbon dioxide levels, thinning the ozone layer over the Antarctic, and contributing to the "greenhouse effect," or global warming.

Much of the devastation of the Amazon rain forest is the result of government policies aimed at encouraging Brazil's land-hungry peasants (70 percent of the rural population is landless) to resettle in Amazonia, a "land without men for men without land," as a way to sidestep the politically delicate issue of land reform (large landowners possess 43 percent of the cultivated land area).

Brazil's disappearing rain forest provides a clear illustration of the tensions that exist between environment and development in the Third World, and suggests that, in a conflict between the two, the environment is likely to lose unless something is done to change the public's perceptions and policy makers' priorities. So far, efforts by environmental groups outside Brazil to save the rain forest have no doubt had some impact on the Brazilian government. Although cause and effect in the policy arena is always difficult to measure, environmentalists' efforts can be useful because they focus worldwide attention on a problem that otherwise seems remote to people who have never set foot in South America. On a personal note, having spent time in the Amazon rain forest, the author can attest to the magnificence of this region. Its continued degradation is a tragedy, not only for Brazil, but also for the entire globe.

Quechua. The empire was served by extensive transportation and communication systems of roads, supply posts, and runners and an advanced water system of aqueducts, irrigation ditches, and reservoirs. Incan agriculture was innovative and efficient, and the administrative system was sophisticated, penetrating as far down into society as the family. The Incas had been established at least four hundred years by the time Francisco Pizarro arrived in the 1520s.

The Mayan civilization, anchored in the Yucatán peninsula of present-day Mexico, had existed for at least a thousand years before Hernán Cortés came and conquered it in 1519–1521. The Mayas, like the Incas, were architects and scholars. They built large stone temples, developed an accurate calendar, and had a writing system (which the Incas did not have). The Mayas also surpassed the Incas in mathematics and astronomy. Religion was a vital part of Mayan life, and priests actually ruled for a time, turning the Mayan political system into a kind of theocracy.

In contrast to the peace-loving Mayas, the Aztecs were warlike, often attacking weaker neighbors. Entering Mexico in the 1200s, they too were empire builders, making alliances with neighboring tribes that they could not easily subjugate and collecting tribute wherever possible. They worshipped various deities and practiced human sacrifice. The pictorial writing system they developed was less advanced than that of the Mayas. Their administrative system was also inferior, but they excelled at architecture and sculpture, building immense religious pyramids and a capital city, Tenochtitlán, which was an engineering marvel. Situated in the center of a large lake, the fortress city, adorned by imposing temples and statuary, could be reached only by three causeways. It supported a population of 60,000 families.

Many other less advanced Indian tribes inhabited the Americas. Millions of Native Americans lived within territorial and cultural boundaries etched into mental maps that had guided their ancestors and governed their way of life for centuries. One thing that all the indigenous peoples had in common was that they did not want to be liberated, converted, conquered, or enslaved. Yet there was no stopping the Iberian juggernaut borne by the winds from an alien world.

The Spanish Conquest

Christopher Columbus arrived in the New World in 1492 while on a quest for King Ferdinand and Queen Isabella of Spain to find a new route to the East Indies. The first Spanish settlements were established in the Caribbean, where the colonists had little difficulty subduing the native populations and forcing them into a slavery-based tribute system. Attempts to gain a foothold on the mainland were less successful, however; more advanced Indians attacked and killed some of the first explorers and slave catchers. Spain had only recently become a unified state under Ferdinand and Isabella after a long war to oust the Moors (Arabs). As a consequence, a generation of Spaniards knew no life other than war. Unfortunately for Native Americans, many Spaniards became soldiers of fortune and journeyed to the New World in pursuit of adventure and riches.

Hernán Cortés first conquered Cuba, then cast about for another challenge. Against the governor's orders, he set sail for the mainland in February 1519 with eleven ships and six hundred men. After two years of bloody battles, Cortés finally conquered the Aztecs. His triumph redeemed his image as a rebel, and he was appointed Spanish proconsul in Mexico. The Spanish built Mexico City on the ruins of Tenochtitlán, the great Aztec capital.

Cortés also sent armed expeditions into other parts of Mexico and Central America. In 1523–1524, a force led by Pedro de Alvarado defeated the Mayas. A second empire had fallen.

The conquest of the Incan Empire took longer, even though it was aided by conflict among the Incas themselves. Francisco Pizarro set out from present-day Panama in 1524 to explore South America. Having discovered the wealth of the Incas, he sought and received permission from the Spanish court to conquer and colonize the continent. Pizarro's charging horsemen and thundering artillery terrified the Incas, who had never seen horses or firearms; they panicked and fled.

Spain then progressively colonized the Andean empire of the Incas and moved into what are now Colombia and Venezuela in the north and Paraguay, Uruguay, and Argentina in the south. At the same time, the Spanish were also colonizing Central America. (They concluded in the 1540s that North America held nothing that would attract settlers.) (See Box 9.2.)

Spanish Colonial Rule Colonizing Latin America proved to be more difficult than conquering it. The conquest brought chaos to areas where organization had once flourished. Now Spain had to build new institutions on the ruins of those it had destroyed. Governance was not Queen Isabella's only concern; converting the Indians to Christianity was a high priority from the outset.

Democracy in America

BOX 9.2

Cockney Colonialism: The English Conquest of North America

The Spanish conquered South America and left an indelible imprint on the peoples and history of that region. The same might be said of the English "conquest" of North America, but the differences between these two European invasions of the Western Hemisphere are more striking than any similarities. First, the English were latecomers. The Spanish were the first Europeans to stake a claim to territories in North America — present-day Florida and Alabama, for example — and were there long before the Pilgrims landed at Plymouth Rock. Second, English rule never penetrated very far beyond the thirteen colonies huddled on the Atlantic coast. The interior was under Spanish and French control (Alaska was "owned" by Russia). As every schoolchild in America knows, the United States acquired much of the land west of the Mississippi from the French during the presidency of Thomas Jefferson through the famous Louisiana Purchase (at a total cost of just $15 million to the government). Thus, the conquest of North America was done more gradually than that of South America, and the job was far from finished when the colonists gave the English the boot in 1776.

The eminent historian Charles A. Beard wrote that "the English migration to America was in one fundamental respect unique." Whereas the Spaniards had "conquered and exploited," such was not to be England's "fate in the new world":

> Instead of Natives submissive to servitude . . . the English found an immense continent of virgin soil and forest, sparsely populated by primitive peoples who chose death rather than bondage. To this continent the English . . . transported their own people, their own economy, and the culture of the classes from which they sprang, reproducing in a large measure the civilization of the mother country. Unlike the Spaniards and other empire builders, the English succeeded in founding a new state, which became vast in extent, independent in government, and basically European in stock. That achievement is one of the capital facts of world history.*

Whether Beard's interpretation is entirely correct or not is, of course, a matter for reflection and (perhaps) contention. Clearly, however, the English conquest of North America was a very different operation than the Spanish conquest of South America.

*Charles A. Beard, *American Civilization* (New York: Macmillan, 1930), p. 11.

The Spanish needed laborers to build their cathedrals and cities and to work on their plantations, so they conscripted the Indians. The ***encomienda* system** was designed to compel the Indians to do what was supposedly in their own best interest: to work for pay while learning the Christian religion. Indian laborers were organized by villages where an ***encomiendero*** — who supervised work, religious instruction, and welfare — had virtually unlimited authority. He also collected all fruits of the land and labor he managed.

Had the system worked as intended, the Indians' dignity and freedom would have been respected. But flagrant abuses occurred. Many of the *encomienderos* were petty tyrants. The Indians, forced to do grueling work, became slaves. The hard labor killed many conscripts, especially in the Caribbean islands, where entire native populations were wiped out. (They were replaced with slaves from Africa, which is why blacks now make up the majority of the population throughout much of the Caribbean.)

In most of Latin America, Indians remained the primary labor source, particularly in the high elevations to which they were adapted. In these areas, the Spanish divided villages into sections and forcibly drafted about one man out of every seven to work in the mines or elsewhere until another section relieved them. Laborers were supposed to be paid, and there were limits on the distance they could be taken from home. But abuses were common, and Indians were frequently overworked and poorly fed, housed, and clothed. Many died in the mines.

Despite efforts of the Spanish crown to protect Indians' rights and prevent their exploitation, the colonists always prevailed. The *encomienda* system lasted well into the eighteenth century, when it was finally outlawed. By this time, however, colonial overlords had imposed Spanish culture and Christianity on the Indians, leaving a legacy of hatred and prejudice that remains a major cause of civil strife in parts of the region (especially Peru and Guatemala).

Nor did exploitation of the Indians end with the demise of the *encomienda* system. Ironically, the natives were forced to help destroy their own empires and build a new one. Persecuted and proselytized, they found their cultures, languages, and identities threatened with extinction. That cultures are often more resilient than political systems is evident in the fact that the Spanish Empire is long gone but some of the Indian cultures have survived. For example, 30 percent of the people in Peru do not speak Spanish; they speak Quechua, the language of the Incas.

The basic problem inherent in Spanish rule was that the crown wanted to maintain direct control over its colonial empire, but its proconsuls had to make decisions and react to conditions on the spot. (Communication between the colonies and the royal court, dependent on ship traffic, took months.) To resolve this dilemma, a system was eventually established whereby an official appointed by the crown exercised full authority within a designated territory. The **viceroys** (and their captains general) were responsible for enforcing laws, collecting taxes, running the government, spreading Christianity, and commanding the Spanish army within their jurisdiction.

Besides being inefficient in structure and practice, the colonial administration of the Spanish Empire became corrupt to the core. Some Spanish officials served with honor and distinction, but they were the exceptions. More commonly, unqualified people of poor character curried favor with the crown in order to get a colonial post in the Americas. By the end of the sixteenth century, positions were simply awarded to the highest bidder. Political favors, promotions, the legal system, and tax collection — all had their price. Property ownership came with no guarantees of permanence, and even inspectors sent to check on officials were not above taking bribes. In the words of one historian, "Corruption was universal and in most cases unpunished. The public treasury was defrauded in countless ways, and justice (or more frequently injustice) was for sale in the courts."[3]

The Role of the Catholic Church Under the Spanish colonial administration, a special relationship between church and state developed. Catholicism had been the official religion in Spain since the heyday of the Roman Empire, and the Spanish crown was determined to export the "one true faith" to the New World. To this end, Spain barred from the colonies all non-Spanish and non-Catholic immigrants.

With a near-homogeneous religious population in colonial Latin America, the Catholic Church became very powerful, overseeing baptisms, weddings, registration of births and deaths, religious processions and festivals, holidays, and charities. It built and managed the schools, hospitals, asylums, missions, and cemeteries and operated its own system of civil and criminal courts. The church amassed great wealth, receiving 10 percent of the taxes as well as bequests of money and land from the estates of the rich. It also controlled much of the banking system, many mortgages on personal property, and much land in its own right. Church revenues were tax-exempt.

The power of the church reached its zenith during the **Spanish Inquisition** of the sixteenth century. The Spanish crown established tribunals in Lima in 1570 and in Mexico City in 1571 to punish heretics and other religious offenders with property loss, imprisonment, exile, or even death, sometimes by burning. Other repressive measures included press censorship and book burning.

The church eventually came to be perceived as a threat to the state. In 1767, Charles III expelled the **Jesuits** — a Roman Catholic religious order founded in 1534 that had played a leading role in the colonial phase of the Spanish Inquisition — from Spain and the colonies. This battle was only the beginning of a long struggle between church and state in Latin America. The conflict pitted liberals, who wanted to reduce church power and enact religious reforms, against conservatives, who supported minor church reforms but generally aligned themselves with the clergy.

The church-versus-state dispute lasted until the 1820s — well beyond the period of Spanish rule — and became particularly acute in Mexico, Central America, Colombia, and Ecuador. The liberals, who eventually won out, instituted religious reforms that abolished many of the church's privileges. Years of struggle, however, were largely for naught:

> In most instances . . . all that the people obtained from the expensive, bloody, and prolonged conflict was a little more freedom in religion — in which they were not seriously concerned, since they were content to remain Roman Catholics — and somewhat broader opportunities for education.[4]

In the end, the Catholic Church retained its religious monopoly and much of its prestige, but its power and wealth were curbed.

Control of Trade Despite the tension between the church and the Spanish crown, religion was an instrument of Spanish imperial rule. Another was a crude form of mercantilism — the plundering of the region's natural resources. Spanish indifference to the material well-being of the colonies contrasted sharply with the crown's solicitude for the spiritual welfare of the Indians. Spain actually discouraged economic development in Latin America, concentrating instead on extraction and export of raw materials, particularly gold and silver. The crown never even took full advantage of potentially profitable cash crops, such as sugar, indigo, and cacao.

Besides neglecting economic growth in the colonies, Spain also imposed severe trade restrictions on them. Only two Spanish ports, Seville and Cádiz, were allowed to carry on trade with the colonies, and all imports had to pass through New Spain (Mexico) or Peru. Tough restrictions also governed trade among the colonies themselves. Foreign powers or pirates would often capture lone ships sailing between Spain and the New World, so after 1550 almost all trade was done in fleets of merchant ships or convoys sailing under the protection of the Spanish navy.

Class Conflict Spanish colonial administrators also had to deal with tensions between newly developing social classes. Of particular concern was the animosity between **Creoles,** Spanish descendants born in the New World, and the **peninsulares,** immigrants from Spain. The crown persisted in giving preferential treatment to "pure" Spaniards whose ties to Spain were most direct; Creoles greatly resented this discrimination.

The mestizos ranked next in the Latin American caste system. Intermarriage between Spaniards and Indians occurred partly because few Spanish women emigrated to the New World. Mestizos were not accepted as equals by the Creoles, although some white fathers succeeded in conferring upper-class status on their children of mixed blood.

Next in rank came the **mulattoes,** of mixed Spanish and African blood, and the **zambos,** of mixed African and Indian blood. Both groups held lower status than the mestizos, but none of the mixed races suffered from open discrimination. The lowest classes were the Indians, free Africans, and African slaves, in that order. Members of these groups were discriminated against in education, employment, and other areas.

Class conflicts thus became a natural part of the Spanish Empire in Latin America. Government policy was flawed and unenlightened from start to finish. Having discovered the New World by accident, the Spanish crown did not know what to do with it. By the time Spain finally decided that its highest priority in the colonies was to keep other powers out, its conquistadors had already destroyed three native civilizations. Overlooking Latin America's long-range economic potential, Spain adopted a short-range policy of exploitation that favored extraction over cultivation. Meanwhile, the Spanish left the "Indian problem," as well as the social and cultural development of the colonies, to the Roman Catholic Church, which itself exploited the Indians and resented every intrusion of secular authority.

The Spanish colonists could accept the sad state of affairs in Latin America out of blind loyalty. But a new class of native-born Latin Americans was emerging to challenge colonial rule. One of the most urgent tasks of the new leaders would be to fill the vacuum the Spanish would leave behind.

Coming of Age: Independence and Self-Government

The conquest of Spain by Napoléon and the abdication of Charles IV at Bayonne in 1808 undercut the authority of the Spanish proconsuls in the colonies. Most of the colonists, even the rising Creole and mestizo classes, had no desire to exchange Spanish tutelage for French. Latin America's turbulent independence movement grew out of the confusion and disarray that followed Spain's fall. (By contrast, Brazil, a Portuguese colony, made a peaceful transition to independence, which probably accounts for the relative stability that has characterized Brazil's political development.)

Latin America's Liberation Simón Bolívar, the most famous of Latin America's early freedom fighters, led an abortive revolt against Spanish rule in the summer of 1811. Two years later, he captured Caracas, the capital of Venezuela, and earned the title "the Liberator." After the British defeated Napoléon in 1815, however, Ferdinand VII ascended to the Spanish throne and sent a force of 10,000 men to crush the New World revolution. Other early insurrections met a similar fate. But the virus of revolt spread like an epidemic, and Spain could not contain it.

The conflict pitted not only Spain against the colonies but also colonist against colonist. More than a war of national liberation against Spain, the independence struggle was actually a series of civil wars. As the ranks of revolutionaries swelled, a nearly equal force of colonists loyal to Spain rose up to defend the crown's interests. Much of the fighting was thus between local royalist and revolutionary forces, a split that persisted even after independence had been won.

The New Order (and Disorder) Independence from Spain was achieved in the mid-1820s, but the newly independent states soon encountered many of the same problems as the Spanish had had in establishing stable systems of government. The first turbulent decades after independence were marked by power struggles in which **caudillos** (local dictators) played a prominent role in many countries. Brazil and Chile enjoyed relatively stable government, but other countries — notably Argentina, Mexico, Colombia, and Venezuela — were torn by civil war. Freed from the commercial restrictions imposed by Spain, Latin America (particularly Argentina, Brazil, and Chile) became more actively involved in international trade. However, Middle America and much of South America sank into a deep torpor. In general, the period from 1820 to 1870 brought more turmoil than prosperity to the region, and the population remained predominantly rural, illiterate, and poor.

Beginning in about 1870, Latin America entered the takeoff phase of its modern development as international capitalism expanded and opened up new markets around the globe. Latin America's exports consisted of foodstuffs and raw materials, for which demand was rising in Europe's rapidly industrializing nations (and later in the United States). Many Latin American nations, enjoying an unprecedented export boom, could now finance imported manufactured goods. Transportation and urban life were modernized. Argentina's economic development was especially rapid during this period. In other countries, too, national leaders saw export-driven growth and foreign capital as the keys to progress.

The new economic vitality stimulated social change. Cities grew, literacy spread, and a middle class came into being. At the same time, a new urban proletariat (and labor movements) also sprang up, especially in countries where a surge in exports created new domestic markets for consumer goods that could be manufactured locally. Social diversification accompanied urbanization in the early stages of industrial development, with important consequences for political life. The state became better organized. As new social groups (especially the industrial labor force) emerged to challenge traditional landowning elites, the stage was being set for future domestic tensions and power struggles.

The Struggle for Independence A major change in hemispheric relations occurred with the rise of the United States as a great power. The emergence of the "colossus to the north" was dramatically evidenced in the Mexican-American War (1846–1848), the Spanish-American War (1898), and the seizure of Panama (1903).

Numerous military interventions in the first three decades of the twentieth century confirmed the new patterns of power and influence in the Western Hemisphere.

The worldwide depression of the 1930s, followed by World War II, greatly disrupted the preexisting system of international trade. The export-driven economies of the region saw their foreign markets dry up. Without export earnings, the Latin nations could not service their overseas debt and were soon cut off from foreign financial markets. Every country except Argentina and Haiti defaulted. The crisis led directly to greater state intervention in the economy, and "import-substituting industrialization" now became a prominent strategy.

World War II brought a new surge in the region's exports that in turn helped finance industrialization. By 1960, Argentina, Brazil, and Mexico had become the leading industrial nations in the Third World, with Chile and Colombia close behind. The smaller nations, however, remained dependent on agriculture and mining. All the while, the role of the state — particularly in banking, market development, and industry — continued to grow.

As industrialization advanced, the process of social differentiation also accelerated. The middle class and organized labor gained political power, although viable multiparty systems did not develop (except in Chile). Broad-based populist coalitions ruled for extended periods in some countries — for example, in Brazil under Getúlio Vargas and in Argentina under Juan Perón. In Mexico, one-party rule became deeply entrenched.

From the 1930s to the 1960s, Latin America displayed a variety of political systems, including civilian democracies and military dictatorships. Whatever the specific disposition, however, the shadow of the caudillo and the possibility of a coup were ever present.

Political Culture

The past impinges on the present through its power to shape the values, perceptions, and predilections of a nation or, as in Latin America, of an entire region. Many Latin leaders and academicians, as well as outside observers, blame Latin America's failure to keep pace economically with Western Europe, North America, and East Asia on basic attitudes brought from the Iberian peninsula during the period of Spanish and Portuguese colonial rule.

The Lingering Effects of Spanish Rule

Some scholars argue that a culture inhospitable to liberal democracy and innovation is to blame for Latin America's eclipse. In contrast to the settlers who colonized the United States and Canada, according to one cultural theory, the colonists of Latin America

> arrived with the notion of power and authority as invariably centralized, owing to the hierarchical organization of the Spanish crown and the conservative Spanish Catholic

> Church, which gave birth to the Inquisition. They saw wealth as something to be distributed rather than to be created.
>
> The English settlers of the north, on the other hand, already were used to the idea of shared power and authority and had begun to believe in the primacy of the individual, as well as the capitalistic notion of making money to make more money.[5]

The colonial experience gave Latin America a unique moral unity that was reinforced by the pervasive influence of the Roman Catholic Church and the dissemination of Spanish language and culture. The colonial administration was staffed at the highest levels by crown-appointed peninsular officials through the Council of the Indies at Seville. (After their tenure, top officials were subject to the *residencia*, an evaluation of their performance in office.)

Religious Conflict and Caudillismo

As mentioned earlier, when the Spanish Empire crumbled in the 1820s, a struggle developed between liberals, who were generally associated with republicanism and anticlericalism, and conservatives, who wanted to preserve the privileges of the traditional elites and saw defense of the established church as one way to do it. Liberals also came to be identified with demands for local autonomy, whereas conservatives favored a strong, centralized state. The role of Napoléon in weakening the Spanish monarchy and destroying its mystique in the colonies is significant here: Napoléon himself became a kind of model for the fledgling Latin America republics, and military prowess became the principal source of political legitimacy. Hence, the military caudillo was institutionalized throughout the region in the first half century after independence.

Caudillismo was idiosyncratic — it depended on the personality of the leader. Simón Bolívar, liberator of Venezuela, Colombia, Ecuador, Bolivia, and Peru, epitomizes the historical importance of the charismatic leader in Latin politics. Unlike Bolívar, however, most caudillos were pragmatic military figures who cared little about ideas, ideals, or ideologies. Constitutions were used to legitimize power seizures rather than to constrain aggressors. Venezuela, in 1811 was the first to draft a constitution, and has since had no fewer than twenty. Historically, law has been subordinated to order, and order has been a function of military rather than civilian leadership. A prominent military role in domestic affairs, even under civilian rule, has thus become a trademark of Latin America.

Warlords Unlimited: The Politics of Localismo

Localismo — a strong identity with a particular geographic area — is another key feature of Latin American politics. Typically, caudillos asserted their local dominance first and only then challenged the existing ruler, if they dared. The extent of a caudillo's power depended on his personal charisma, which in turn reflected his military exploits, machismo, and local reputation. If he could recruit a large enough personal army, he had a chance of toppling the current strongman (who may or may not have come to power by similar means). More likely, he would be content to rule his fiefdom as part of a larger and relatively loose-knit political system based on local patron-client networks.

Local political bosses were not universally loved. They were often pejoratively called **caciques** in Hispanic Latin America and ***coronels*** in Brazil. The term ***caciquismo*** is a local variant of caudillismo — both imply corruption and arbitrary rule.

Militarism and localism were thus deeply embedded in the culture and even, to some degree, in the geography, which isolated small areas and made communication difficult. Tropical jungles also impede communication in both Central and South America. Geographic isolation reinforced tendencies toward local particularism and created barriers to political integration, which helps explain why civil and, more recently, guerrilla wars have been so much a part of Latin America's history.

Hostility toward the United States, or **anti-*yanquismo,*** also permeates Latin American politics. This sentiment is expressed in literature as a rejection of North American materialism and in politics as a radical, sometimes revolutionary, brand of left-wing extremism. The Cuban Revolution (1959), which dramatized Cuba's break with the United States, might have become a symbol throughout the region had it not been for Castro's clumsy attempts to "export revolution" by subverting other governments in Latin America. (See Box 9.3.) After Che Guevara, a revolutionary *compadre* of Fidel Castro, was killed in Bolivia in 1967, fear of communism caused a chain reaction of military coups and repressive countermeasures that wiped out all threat of revolution in most places; the anti-Americanism that helped spawn it, however, remained intact.

Damn Yankees: Good Neighbors or Bullies?

The United States is viewed with a mixture of admiration and resentment in Latin America — admiration for U.S. military prowess, power, and prestige; resentment for its **big-stick diplomacy** (interventionism), which has often overshadowed U.S. efforts to be a good neighbor. The foundation of U.S. foreign policy toward Latin America was laid in the 1820s with the enunciation of the Monroe Doctrine, which declared the Western Hemisphere off-limits to the great powers of Europe. In effect, the United States was replacing Spain as the dominant power in Latin America; it is no coincidence that the promulgation of the **Monroe Doctrine** coincided with the crumbling of the Spanish Empire in the New World. The only time the European powers violated the U.S. ban on outside interference was in Santo Domingo and in Mexico during the 1860s, when the United States was momentarily preoccupied with its own Civil War.

The United States made Mexico relinquish Texas in 1836, and after the Mexican-American War (1846–1848), it came away with Texas and the entire Southwest (California, Nevada, Utah, and most of New Mexico and Arizona). Half a century later, the United States acquired Cuba, Puerto Rico, and the Philippines in the Spanish-American War (1898). In 1904, President Theodore Roosevelt cast a covetous eye on the Isthmus of Panama, wrested the desired territory from Colombia, and began construction on the Panama Canal.

Since then there has been no waning of U.S. interest or intervention in Latin American affairs. The U.S. government sent marines into Nicaragua and Honduras in 1912

Contrast and Comparison

BOX 9.3

Cuba: Communist Hold-Out

Cuba became a virtual U.S. protectorate after the Spanish-American War in 1898. In 1952, Fulgencio Batista seized power and established a repressive dictatorship. Seven years later, Fidel Castro led a successful guerrilla insurgency movement against Batista.

Castro denounced American imperialism and nationalized industries and banks in Cuba, including over $1 billion in U.S.-owned properties. These actions prompted the Eisenhower administration to organize a force of Cuban exiles in a covert plan to overthrow Castro. The resulting Bay of Pigs invasion, ordered by President Kennedy in 1961, was a debacle of the first order. Not only did Castro survive it, he emerged with enhanced prestige in the eyes of most Cubans.

The United States suspended trade with Cuba and refused to recognize Castro's regime. Facing diplomatic and economic isolation, Castro declared himself a Marxist and turned to the Soviet Union for help. In return, Castro agreed to allow the Soviet Union to place medium-range nuclear missiles in Cuba. This decision led to the Cuban Missile Crisis of 1962 — the closest the two superpowers ever came to nuclear war.

Thereafter, the United States used its economic and military might to make Cuba the pariah of the Western Hemisphere. Dependent on Moscow, Castro allowed Cuba to be used as an instrument of Soviet foreign policy, especially in Africa. Cuban "proxy" forces were inserted into various regional conflicts, mostly notably in Ethiopia and Angola.

At home, Castro's government was autocratic. Cuba became a closed society. Castro was an absolute dictator, but apparently not an unpopular one, despite perennial allegations of human rights violations. Castro blamed Cuba's ills on the Americans.

Although Castro is secretive about such matters, it is obvious that Cuba's economy is failing. By contrast, Cuba's social policies have apparently been quite successful. Annual population growth in the 1990s averaged 0.6 percent (in Honduras, for example, it was almost 3 percent). Life expectancy (seventy-six years) and infant mortality (7 deaths per 1,000 live births) were the same as in the United States; female primary school enrollment was 100 percent in 1998; and illiteracy was a mere 5 percent (compared to 45 percent in Guatemala and around 30 percent in Honduras and El Salvador).

The dissolution of the Soviet Union deprived Cuba of its patron and protector. Cuba, however, has continued to resist liberalization and the U.S. government continues to shun Castro as a pariah. The importance of Florida in American presidential elections was dramatically underscored in 2000, when a few contested votes there determined the eventual winner. If Cuban-American relations change any time soon, it is a safe bet that President George W. Bush will not be the one to make the first move.

(and kept a military presence in Nicaragua until the late 1920s); it sent forces to the Dominican Republic and Haiti in 1915–1916. After Pancho Villa conducted a raid against a border town in New Mexico in 1916, President Woodrow Wilson ordered a military expedition headed by General John J. Pershing into Mexico; the troops stayed nearly a year. The president of Mexico, though Villa's adversary, denounced the U.S. action; the venture accomplished little more than to solidify Mexican sentiment against U.S. interventionism. Anti-U.S. feeling in Mexico around this time was so intense that Mexico sided with Germany in World War I.

After World War II, the United States intervened against Guatemala's government (1953), attempted to overthrow Fidel Castro in Cuba (1961), sent marines into the Dominican Republic (1965), armed Nicaraguan rebels against Daniel Ortega's Sandinista regime (1980s), invaded Grenada (1983), and ousted Panamanian dictator Manuel

Noriega (1989). In addition, the United States supported Great Britain against Argentina in the Falkland Islands War (1982).

But big-stick diplomacy is only one side of U.S.–Latin American relations; the **Good Neighbor Policy** is the other. After World War II, the United States created the **Organization of American States (OAS)** to provide a multilateral framework for hemispheric collaboration. In the early 1960s, President John Kennedy launched the **Alliance for Progress,** aimed at fostering economic cooperation and development in Latin America. More recently, the Reagan administration sponsored the **Caribbean Basin Initiative,** designed to promote prosperity, trade, and free enterprise in the Caribbean.

Today the United States is Latin America's major trading partner. Moreover, U.S. aid and investment have played a key role in the region's development efforts. U.S. banks, encouraged by the government, made billions of dollars in loans available to Latin America in the 1970s, as did other Western countries. The result was a Latin American foreign debt that topped $400 billion at the end of the 1980s. The United States and the International Monetary Fund agreed to debt relief and rescheduling schemes in a number of cases, but the price that these debtor states have had to pay is high: unpopular austerity programs that put severe strains on recently established democratic institutions.

The debt crisis in Latin America gave rise to renewed North-South tensions and gave new ideological ammunition to the critics of "world capitalism." In Latin America, even more than other developing regions, world capitalism was synonymous with American "imperialism." We look briefly at the origins of anti-imperialism in the twentieth century and then explore the specific form it assumed in Latin America beginning in the 1970s.

Latin American Development and Dependency

In a 1916 essay titled "Imperialism: The Highest Stage of Capitalism," V. I. Lenin advanced a thesis about the economic causes of nineteenth-century imperialism. He characterized the processes of advanced capitalist development as follows:

> The concentration of production and development of capital to such a high stage that monopolies come to dominate economic life.
>
> 1. The merging of bank capital with industrial capital; the resulting "finance capital" gives rise to a powerful "financial oligarchy."
> 2. The export of capital becomes more important than the export of commodities.
> 3. The internationalization of monopoly capitalism; world markets are shared for mutual profit.
> 4. The territorial division of the entire globe by the greatest capitalist powers is consummated.[6]

Lenin argued that imperialism could generate higher profits for monopoly corporations by exploiting cheap Third World labor and pirating natural resources. Part of these profits, in turn, could be used to buy off potentially militant unionized workers in the West (Lenin called them the "labor aristocracy").

Closely related to this line of analysis is the leftist view that Western-based multinational corporations (MNCs) have, in effect, created a new kind of colonialism, or neocolonialism, by substituting corporate economic domination for control by imperialist powers. The MNCs allegedly manipulate Third World governments by co-opting leaders, exploiting elite fears of leftist revolution, subverting the military with arms aid, and interfering in domestic politics. An oft-cited case in point is Chile in the early 1970s. The U.S. government, in conjunction with U.S. corporate interests, mounted a covert operation to destabilize the government of Chile's popularly elected socialist president, Salvadore Allende. According to one critic:

> MNCs have attempted, through privileged links to the State Department, the CIA, and the Pentagon, to undermine policies and overthrow regimes that threaten their interests. . . . The MNC would of course prefer not to have to "get tough" in order to assure a favorable investment climate; but in fact it does get tough when its profit margins are at stake, and it can call in some pretty powerful friends to help it get its way.[7]

This vehement criticism of Western governments, banks, and corporations, including such U.S.-dominated world organizations as the International Monetary Fund and the World Bank, has been echoed in the writings of the so-called dependency theorists. The genesis of this school of thought, which has been extremely influential among Latin American political and intellectual elites, is instructive:

> Special hopes and much publicity had been given to the Alliance for Progress, a United States–sponsored investment and aid program of the 1960s, the goal of which was to achieve a breakthrough to sustained and independent economic development for at least several Latin American nations. The spectacular failure of the Alliance (judged by both friends and critics) led to a thorough critique of conventional Western models (Rostow, Kuznets) of economic development, which spelled out a general "do it like we did it" approach. This critique in turn led to a new theory of dependency, which accounted for the failure of Western-style development to appear in Latin America and also predicted that real development would not appear as long as the dependency syndrome lasted.[8]

Significantly, dependency theory was first propounded by a group of Latin American economists. It has since been applied to Africa and Asia as well. Unfortunately, dependency theory tends to obscure the extremely inequitable conditions that socioeconomic elites have both created and perpetuated. Dependency theorists consider these elites to be part of a **comprador** class, created by foreign imperialists and capitalists who needed the help of local elements. Seen in this light, dependency theory is a self-serving rationalization for homegrown inadequacies and failures.

It is difficult to generalize about development in Latin America because the picture differs considerably from one state to the next and even from one part of a state to another. Many Latin American nations have made great strides politically, economically, socially, and culturally, but much remains to be done to spread the benefits of economic development to millions and millions of Latin Americans living in extreme poverty.[9]

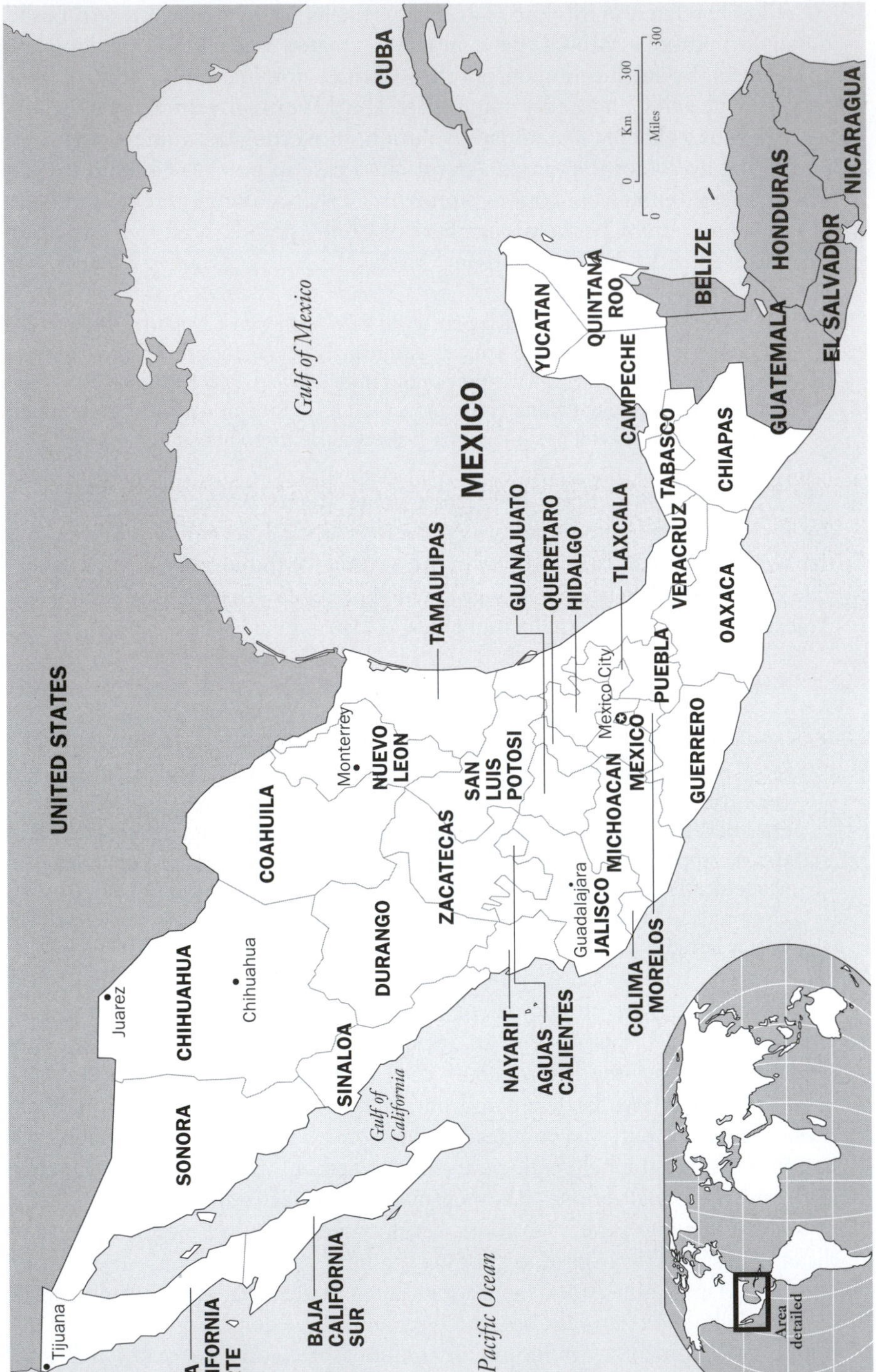
UNITED STATES
CUBA
Gulf of Mexico
MEXICO
Pacific Ocean
Gulf of California
BAJA CALIFORNIA NORTE
BAJA CALIFORNIA SUR
SONORA
CHIHUAHUA
COAHUILA
NUEVO LEON
TAMAULIPAS
SINALOA
DURANGO
ZACATECAS
SAN LUIS POTOSI
NAYARIT
AGUAS CALIENTES
JALISCO
COLIMA
MICHOACAN
MEXICO
MORELOS
GUANAJUATO
QUERETARO
HIDALGO
TLAXCALA
PUEBLA
GUERRERO
OAXACA
VERACRUZ
TABASCO
CHIAPAS
CAMPECHE
YUCATAN
QUINTANA ROO
BELIZE
GUATEMALA
HONDURAS
EL SALVADOR
NICARAGUA
Tijuana
Juarez
Chihuahua
Monterrey
Guadalajara
Mexico City
Km 0 300
Miles 0 300
Area detailed

Mexico

Case Studies: Mexico and Brazil

Now we will look closely at two large Latin American countries: Mexico and Brazil. In many ways, they are representative of the region's political patterns and trends, which is not to say that the other countries in the region, including Venezuela, Colombia, Peru, Chile, and Argentina, are not distinct and important in their own right. Chile, for example, has the most successful economy in Latin America today (but in that sense, unfortunately, Chile is not representative of the region).

Mexico

Under Spanish rule, Mexico was known as New Spain, a tribute to the flagship colony of Spain's New World empire. At independence in 1821, Mexico had the largest population in Latin America and produced two-thirds of the world's silver. Mexico City was not only the largest city in Latin America but also its cultural center. Despite these advantages, the new nation of Mexico got off to a troubled and turbulent start.

Mexico's first two constitutions were short-lived. The first election (1829) was nullified when the losing party, refusing to accept the outcome, revolted and ousted the victorious party, with help from the military. Thus, precedent was set at an early stage: elections must be held for the sake of appearances, but the outcome is not sacrosanct. If the results are not satisfactory, resort to violence rather than submit; better yet, manipulate the elections to ensure the desired results.

Tug of War over Texas The greatest figures in Mexico's political history before the Revolution of 1911 are Antonio López de Santa Anna, Benito Juárez, and Porfirio Díaz. Santa Anna, the first successful leader after independence, came to power following a revolt in 1829 and dominated politics for the next twenty-five years. He dissolved the congress and discarded the constitution. He was a tough-minded pragmatist, but his rule was destined to coincide with one of the greatest humiliations in modern Mexican history.

In 1835, the settlers of Texas revolted against Mexico City. They defeated the Mexican forces the following year and captured Santa Anna, who was forced to sign a treaty granting Texas independence from Mexico. In 1838, after several foreign powers accused Mexico of offenses against their nationals, France sent a fleet to Veracruz and demanded restitution in the form of a large cash payment. The fighting that followed is known as the Pastry War because France claimed that a baker's shop had been ransacked. Britain mediated the dispute, and Mexico paid the claim.

Worse was yet to come. In 1845, the United States annexed Texas despite a clear warning from the Mexican government that such a move would be considered an act of war. Mexico attacked but lost again. Disgraced, Santa Anna stepped down and went into exile. Mexico signed the **Treaty of Guadalupe Hidalgo** in 1848, officially making Texas, New Mexico, Arizona, Nevada, Utah, and California part of the United States. For Mexico, the loss of this vast territory was traumatic and humiliating. Nonetheless, Santa Anna returned from exile in 1853 and resumed his former role as dictator until a revolt a year later forced him to flee, thus closing one of many unhappy chapters in Mexico's history.

Mexico's Other War The struggle between liberals and conservatives in Mexico festered. The conservatives, who identified with the church and the landed aristocracy, were in the ascendancy in the 1820s. Under Santa Anna, pragmatism had eclipsed ideology (Santa Anna and many of his contemporaries switched sides opportunistically). With the end of the Santa Anna era, the liberals, who sought to rein in the church and extend civil rights, gained the upper hand. Led by a caudillo named Juan Álvarez, the new liberal government embarked on major reforms aimed at reducing the power and wealth of the church. The new reforms, along with sundry individual liberties and protections, were enshrined in the constitution of 1857. But this liberal triumph did not put an end to class conflict in Mexico.

The period from 1857 to 1876 was a time of troubles for Mexico — civil war, foreign intervention, economic collapse. In 1876, Porfirio Díaz staged a caudillo-style military coup and embarked on the longest career of personal dictatorial rule in Mexican history (1877–1911).

The Porfiriato The **Porfiriato,** as Díaz's rule was called, represented the triumph of pragmatism over ideology and ushered in a period of accelerated economic development. Díaz ruled as a benevolent dictator, placing prosperity ahead of liberty. Elections were rigged, and opposition was co-opted or crushed. "Plenty of administration and no politics" was a popular slogan during this period. Díaz stressed a state-energized market system as the key to economic revitalization. Always the pragmatist, he refused to let anti-*yanquismo* or nationalism interfere with his development strategy. He attracted foreign capital by allowing foreign investors to develop — and profit from — mining ventures, railways, and commercial agriculture.

Mexico's economic recovery under the Díaz dictatorship is the bright side; there was a dark side as well. In rural areas, the rich got richer as enterprising landlords gobbled up smallholders' lands, and protest was smothered by local *jefes,* politicos (political bosses) loyal to the Porfiriato. The result was a rising agrarian discontent. In the cities, too, the burgeoning middle class, educated and prosperous, resented being excluded from the political process. In the waning years of the Díaz dictatorship, the surface tranquility was deceiving: underneath, an upheaval was in the making.

The Mexican Revolution The upheavals that rocked Mexican society between 1911 and 1917 left the country in shambles. Francisco Madero, the leader of the revolution, wrote a widely circulated book urging the Mexican voters to reject Díaz in the 1910 election. During the presidential campaign, Díaz jailed Madero for allegedly fomenting a revolt. Díaz "won" the election, but facing the threat of civil war, he subsequently resigned.

A popular hero, Madero was elected president of Mexico in November 1911. He had little time to savor his triumph, however. The very next year, two simultaneous revolts broke out, one led by Emiliano Zapata in the south, the other led by Pancho Villa in the north. In 1913, the commander in chief, General Victoriano Huerta, overthrew Madero and assumed the presidency. Madero was killed, allegedly during an attempted escape while awaiting trial for treason.

The Mexican Revolution did not die with Madero, however. Civil war ravaged the country for several more years before the smoke cleared and Venustiano Carranza emerged as victor and president. In 1917, following seven years of turmoil, Carranza promulgated a new constitution, built on the liberal foundation of the 1857 constitution. It prescribed an impressive array of radical reforms in government, education, labor, and land tenure. For example, the new constitution prohibited presidential self-succession; embraced the principle of universal compulsory education as a responsibility of the state (rather than of the church); created a labor code that guaranteed workers' rights to organize, strike, and engage in collective bargaining; expropriated all property of religious orders; and restored communal lands to the Indians. The constitution also reduced the role of the church in political life. By secularizing Mexican society, it sought to undercut the moral authority of the power elite, whose legitimacy depended on the church, and at the same time to remove a major impediment to modernization.

Sonoran Rule and More Civil War Scintillating in theory, the 1917 constitution was never fully observed in practice. In 1920, Álvaro Obregón, a caudillo from the state of Sonora who had earlier defeated Pancho Villa, came to power following the overthrow and assassination of President Carranza. His successor, Plutarco Elías Calles, dominated Mexican politics for a decade. The "Sonoran dynasty" pared down the army and drastically reduced the military budget. It sought the support of urban workers and land-poor *campesinos* as a counterweight to the military, which revolted on three separate occasions (1923, 1927, and 1929) without success.

Sonoran policies combined conservative and liberal elements. Moderate land reform and anticlericalism coexisted with a preference for a strong centralized state, a capitalist economy, and a placid, productive society. In many respects, Sonoran rule resembled Porfirian rule. For example, foreign investment was encouraged, although it was more closely regulated than during the Díaz dictatorship. The 1920s brought economic progress, tarnished at times by violent social and religious strife.

A civil war over the issue of church rights raged for three years (1926–1929). In 1928, Obregón was elected to a second term as president but was assassinated by a Catholic fanatic before his inauguration. This act prompted former President Calles to found the **National Revolutionary Party** (PNR), precursor of the **Institutional Revolutionary Party** (PRI), which has dominated Mexican politics since its inception in 1946. By further institutionalizing civilian rule, the PNR in effect demilitarized the political system.

The Cárdenas Era The PNR helped Calles maintain his dominance until 1934, when Lázaro Cárdenas, a Calles protégé, was elected president but proved to be too independent and too radical for his mentor. Cárdenas won decisively the resulting power struggle (Calles was sent into exile), and a period of genuine agrarian reform began.

Cárdenas also courted organized labor. In 1936, the Confederation of Mexican Workers (CTM) was founded and became an integral part of a newly constituted official party. Cárdenas pleased labor by arbitrating generous wage settlements, nationalizing the railways, and expropriating foreign oil companies (1938). Cárdenas was thus instrumental in building a broad farm-labor coalition and paving the way for Mexico's economic resurgence after 1940.

Since World War II, Mexico has undergone substantial economic development. With the PRI monopolizing power and setting priorities, the Mexican government was able to launch a modernization drive with single-minded determination. The results

Brazil

were extraordinary: industry surged ahead of agriculture, and manufacturing displaced mining as Mexico's economic engine. Between 1940 and 1965, the overall economy grew fivefold, agricultural output quadrupled, and population doubled. Mostly fortuitous events kept the bubble from bursting until the 1980s. We will look at more recent developments in Chapter 10.

Brazil

Portugal's colonial claim to Brazil dates back to the middle of the fifteenth century, but the first settlement was not established there until 1530. Phillip II of Spain extended his royal authority to Portugal in 1580, and after a war between the Spanish and the Dutch, the latter dominated Portugal for a time. This period coincided with the heyday of the Dutch East India Company, which effectively controlled Brazil after overcoming some resistance by Portuguese settlers. The Dutch opened up trade with Brazil, but the colonists continued to revolt, eventually with Portugal's aid. The ensuing struggle ended in 1654, and the Dutch abandoned claims to Brazil in 1661.

Portugal's interest in Brazil was desultory. Gold was discovered in 1695, and diamonds were found in 1729. Settlements had been confined to the coast, but the gold rush sent a flood of fortune seekers into the interior, and towns sprang up there. In contrast to the Spanish colonies, the church in Brazil was poor and thus less politically influential. Britain helped Portugal hold Brazil in the 1700s in return for trade privileges.

When Napoléon invaded Portugal in 1807, the royal family took refuge in Brazil. This happenstance helped reverse Brazil's status as a benighted colonial backwater. Under direct rule of the Portuguese monarch, Rio de Janeiro became the capital of Portugal, and a colonial culture blossomed, complete with schools, libraries, newspapers, and banks. The king returned to Portugal in 1821, but his son, Prince Pedro, stayed behind.

Pedro, Emperor of Brazil Back in Portugal, the ruling council tried to enact restrictions that would be harmful to Brazil. When Pedro was ordered to return to Portugal, he refused, and with a rallying cry of "Independence or death!" he declared himself emperor of Brazil on October 12, 1822. Brazil thus achieved independence without bloodshed or upheaval — in sharp contrast to the turbulence of Spanish America. Pedro ruled until 1831, when, having lost a short war with Argentina and alienated Brazilians in various ways, he abdicated in favor of his five-year-old son.

A single regent replaced the triumvirate-style regency that succeeded Pedro in 1835. Five years later, the parliament ousted the regent and pronounced the youngster, age fourteen, old enough to rule. The coronation of Pedro II, who reigned for the next half century, ushered in a period of stability and economic development.

The First Republic The monarchy ultimately became arthritic and inflexible in the face of social change, which, ironically, it had done much to foster. A military coup was mounted in November 1889, and a republic replaced the empire. The new regime adopted a constitution patterned after the federal government of the United States. The first five years, however, were characterized by power struggles among oligarchies controlling the various states. For the winner, the prize would be control of the national government. After 1894, three civilian presidents, all from São Paulo, brought a period of peace and prosperity to Brazil — the golden age of the first republic.

In 1922, a group of radical young army officers rebelled; in 1924, another army revolt occurred, but loyal troops suppressed it and established martial law. The first republic collapsed in 1930, a casualty of both the Great Depression, which devastated Brazil's export-dependent economy, and an increasingly chaotic political system. The military's power seizure this time was intended in part to avert civil war. Fractious rivalries among the politicians themselves finally doomed the republic.

The Vargas Presidency and the Estado Novo The 1930 revolution put Getúlio Vargas in the presidential palace, where he remained until 1945. He was elected president in 1933, in Brazil's first secret ballot. In 1937, he suspended the constitution rather than relinquish the presidency. From that point on, he ruled as a relatively benevolent dictator, banning political parties, censoring the press, and creating a corporatist state, the **Estado Novo** ("New State"), in which the interests of business, labor, landowners, and bureaucrats were fused.

Brazil sided with the United States and the Allies in World War II and even sent troops to fight on the Italian front. After the war, Vargas agreed to free elections, but the military was not taking any chances: believing that Vargas would not give up power without a fight, the generals plotted a successful coup d'état and established a democratic republic that lasted until 1964.

Brazil's Short-Lived Democracy The most important figure during this period was President Juscelino Kubitschek, who took office in 1955 vowing to give Brazil "fifty years' progress in five." During his tenure, industrial production rose sharply, and the economy grew apace. Brazil became self-sufficient in auto production and operated an international airline. Kubitschek's most flamboyant project was building a new capital city, Brasília, in the interior of the country on a previously barren site. But Kubitschek's profligate spending (financed, in part, by heavy international borrowing) led to debt-servicing problems and spiraling inflation. The resulting disillusionment brought a surprise winner in the 1960 election — an independent candidate named Jânio Quadros.

Quadros had a reputation for integrity and competence; for reasons that remain unclear, however, he resigned after less than a year in office, handing over the reins of power to his vice president, João Goulart. As the economy declined and inflation soared, Goulart pursued a vaguely leftist course that antagonized not only the military but also the upper and middle classes. In the spring of 1964, the military staged a coup that had widespread civilian support. Critics saw Goulart as incompetent and politically inept; others viewed him as an embattled figure who paid a high price for trying to rid his country of undue U.S. influence. More than two decades were to pass before civilian rule was restored.

From Repression to "Decompression" It gradually became apparent that what appeared to be just another military coup was in fact a revolution. The military junta proceeded to centralize power, drive the traditional parties into the political wilderness, and ruthlessly rid Brazil of subversive and leftist elements. Newspaper editors were harassed, all dissent was suppressed, and opponents were arrested. Torture and death squads were the junta's gruesome trademarks.

Old guard politicians were muzzled, but the military called on civilian technocrats to engineer Brazil's economic recovery. The result was a short-lived economic miracle in the early 1970s, fueled by new loans, foreign investment, and debt retirement. Thus reinvigorated, the economy perked up, inflation slowed, and Brazil finally began exporting manufactures.

The oil crisis, however, soon spoiled Brazil's economic recovery. Output declined and inflation again soared. After 1974, the military regime, now headed by Ernesto Geisel, a pragmatist, moved to ease the repressive measures still in effect. His successor, another general, continued on this course, allowing an independent trade union movement to develop and lifting the ban on political parties. This process culminated in the election of a civilian president in 1985. We look at the rest of the story — Brazil in Latin America's age of democracy — in the next chapter.

SUMMARY

The countries of Latin America still bear the imprint of the brutal Spanish conquest and of repressive Spanish rule. The United States has long since replaced Spain as the dominant power in the region; the U.S. habit of military intervention in Latin America, inspired by the Monroe Doctrine and reinforced by the perceived Soviet threat after World War II, has left a residue of bitter anti-American feelings in many Latin American societies.

Unlike other former colonial areas of the world, the Americas came to be dominated by descendants of the European colonizers rather than by indigenous political elites. Historically, the most important local rulers, the caudillos, came to power by force and fraud more often than by free elections. The native peoples became oppressed minorities in their own homelands both in the United States and in Latin America. After World War II, the military juntas that have traditionally ruled throughout most of Latin America often enjoyed the support of the United States, despite egregious violations of human rights in some cases. This U.S. policy was an outgrowth of the Cold War: basically, any anticommunist government in Latin America, especially if it was threatened by a left-wing insurgency, could count on American military and economic aid.

Mexico faced similar nation-building problems — how to stitch separate regions into a tightly knit union. In all three countries, the military played a major role in domestic politics. A major difference, however, is that Mexico managed to demilitarize the political process in the twentieth century; the same cannot be said of Brazil and Argentina.

Latin America does have a weak tradition of democracy, but throughout most of its history, military juntas or personal dictatorships have ruled nearly every country in the region. The military plays a much larger role in Latin American politics than it does in the United States or in Europe. In the 1980s, one South American government after another switched from dictatorship to democracy. Why and how are taken up in Chapter 10.

KEY TERMS

- Latin American
- Central America
- South America
- West Indies
- mestizos
- Ladinos
- Incas
- Mayas
- Aztecs
- Quechua
- *encomienda* system
- *encomiendero*
- viceroy
- Spanish Inquisition
- Jesuits
- creoles
- peninsulares
- mulattoes
- zambos
- caudillos
- caudillismo
- *localismo*
- cacique
- *coronels*
- *caciquismo*
- anti-*yanquismo*
- big-stick diplomacy
- Monroe Doctrine
- Good Neighbor Policy
- Organization of American States (OAS)
- Alliance for Progress
- Caribbean Basin Initiative
- comprador
- Treaty of Guadalupe Hidalgo
- Porfiriato
- National Revolutionary Party (PNR)
- Institutional Revolutionary Party (PRI)
- Estado Novo

STUDY QUESTIONS

1. How do Latin American political traditions and institutions differ from those of the United States?
2. Compare and contrast political development in Mexico, Brazil, and Argentina. What role did the military play in the history of these countries? How did the world wars and the Great Depression affect political development in these countries?
3. Does Latin America have abundant natural resources? Fertile farmland? Temperate climates? Or is Latin America destined by latitude and topography to be poor? (Use the case studies as focal points in developing a thoughtful response.)
4. What do you think it means to be Mexican, Brazilian, or Argentine? Do Mexicans see the world much differently than Argentines or Brazilians? What similarities and differences would you expect among citizens of these countries?

SUGGESTED READINGS

Bianciotti, Hector. What the Night Tells the Day (trans. of *Ce Que la Nuit Raconte au Jour*). New York: New Press, 1995.

Burns, E. Bradford. *A History of Brazil.* 2nd ed. New York: Columbia University Press, 1980.

Cohen, Youssef. *Radicals, Reformers, and Reactionaries: The Prisoner's Dilemma and the Collapse of Democracy in Latin America.* Chicago: University of Chicago Press, 1994.

Gallup, John Luke, Alejandro Gaviria, and Alejandro and Eduardo Lora, eds. *Is Geography Destiny? Lessons from Latin America.* Palo Alto, Calif.: Standford University Press, World Bank, 2003.

Goñi, Uki. *The Real Odessa: Smuggling the Nazis to Peron's Argentina.* New York: Granta Books, 2002.

Hess, David J., and Da Matta, Roberto, eds. *The Brazilian Puzzle: Culture on the Borderlands of the Western World.* New York: Columbia University Press, 1995.

Keeling, David J. *Contemporary Argentina: A Geographical Perspective.* Boulder, Colo.: Westview, 1996.

Kraay, Hendrik. *Race, State, and Armed Forces in Independence-Era Brazil: Bahia, 1790s–1840s.* Stanford, Calif.: Stanford University Press, 2001.

Page, Joseph, A. *The Brazilians.* Reading, Mass: Addison Wesley Longman, 1995.

Maxwell, Kenneth. *Naked Tropics: Essays on Empire and Other Rogues.* New York: Routledge, 2003.

Meyer, Michael C., and Sherman, William L. *The Course of Mexican History.* 4th ed. New York: Oxford University Press, 1991.

Postash, Robert A. *The Army and Politics in Argentina, 1928–1945.* Stanford, Calif.: Stanford University Press, 1980.

Rock, David. *Authoritarian Argentina: The Nationalistic Movement, Its History and Its Impact.* Berkeley: University of California Press, 1993.

Romero, Luis Alberto. *A History of Argentina in the Twentieth Century,* translated by James P. Brennan. University Park: Pennsylvania State University Press, 2002.

Van Young, Eric. *The Other Rebellion: Popular Violence, Ideology, and the Mexican Struggle for Independence, 1810–1821.* Stanford, Calif.: Stanford University Press, 2001.

Veloso, Caetano. *Tropical Truth: A Story of Music and Revolution in Brazil.* New York: Knopf, 2002.

Verbitsky, Horacio. *The Flight: Confessions of an Argentine Dirty Warrior,* translated by Esther Allen. New York: New Press, 1996.

Vinson, Ben III. *Bearing Arms for His Majesty: The Free Colored Militia in Colonial Mexico.* Stanford, Calif.: Stanford University Press, 2001.

SUGGESTED WEB SITES

http://lanic.utexas.edu/
http://darkwing.uoregon.edu/~atlas/
http://www.brasilemb.org
http://www.politicalresources.net/brazil.htm
http://countrystudies.us/brazil/82.htm
http://www.brazilbrazil.com/politics.html
http://www.exploitz.com/brazil_government-and-politics-cg.php
http://www.mexonline.com/mexagncy.htm
http://questia.com/popularsearches/mexican_politics_and_governments.jsp

NOTES

1. Quoted in Paul B. Goodwin, Jr., *Latin America,* 3rd ed. (Guilford, Conn.: Dushkin, 1988), pp. 81–82.
2. Quoted in ibid., p. 3.
3. Dana Gardner Munro, *The Latin American Republics: A History* (Englewood Cliffs, N.J.: Prentice-Hall, 1950), p. 81.
4. J. Fred Rippy, *Latin America: A Modern History* (Ann Arbor: University of Michigan Press, 1958), p. 185.
5. Eugene Robinson, "The Battle for the Soul of Latin America," *Washington Post,* November 3, 1991, p. 1.
6. See V. I. Lenin, *Imperialism: The Highest Stage of Capitalism* (New York: International Publications, 1969), p. 16.
7. John D. Nagle, *Comparative Politics: Political System Performance in Three Worlds* (Chicago: Nelson-Hall, 1985), p. 229.
8. Ibid.
9. Lucrecia Lozano, quoted in David Clark Scott, "Ibero-Americans to Move toward Integration," *Christian Science Monitor,* July 17, 1991, p. 4.

CHAPTER 10

Caudillos, Coups, and Constitutions

Latin America differs from North America in many ways. The region's authoritarian political traditions and the extreme maldistribution of wealth found in most Latin societies are two of the most striking contrasts. But in the 1980s the political landscape changed as one Latin American country after another switched from military rule to civilian government based on popular election. Economic liberalization received lip service everywhere but lagged behind democratization in most countries (Chile is one notable exception). When reforms did not lead to a quick economic turnaround, hopes for a better future were dashed. In the words of one Latin Americanist: "The late 1990s were supposed to be the years in which the long period of austerity and adjustment to world market norms would pay off for the majority of Latin America's people . . . [but] many Latin Americans again wonder if the region is the innocent victim of irrational forces."[1] Nonetheless, Latin America has changed dramatically in the past two decades. To understand the extent of this change, we will begin with a look at the traditional model of politics and government in Latin America.

The Latin Authoritarian Model

Throughout Latin America, authoritarian regimes, often dominated by or dependent on the military, restricted civil liberties and paid lip service to free elections. In most cases, dictators or military juntas were closely linked to a deeply entrenched economic elite, and the most common method for replacing a government was the military coup d'état.

Patterns of Military Rule

There are several identifiable patterns of military involvement in Latin American politics. In countries such as Brazil and Uruguay the army ruled in coalition with civilian leaders. In other countries, including Peru and Ecuador, military and civilian rulers have tended to alternate in power. In still others, among them Argentina and Bolivia, the military is entrenched in the political system, but military rule, when it occurs, is unstable. Personalistic rule by a general turned president is yet another familiar pattern; recent examples include Panama under Noriega, Chile under Pinochet, and Paraguay under Stroessner. Finally, in countries such as Venezuela, Colombia, Mexico, and Cuba, the military plays a key role but has not actually ruled for many decades. Costa Rica is a genuine exception to the militarism found throughout the region: it has no standing army.

Until the 1960s, most military dictatorships fit the personalistic caudillo model to the extent that their legitimacy depended heavily on the prestige and personal authority of a single individual. During the 1960s and 1970s, the military in many Latin American countries entered into a limited partnership with civilian politicians, holding elections or plebiscites without giving up real power. In the 1980s, the military stepped back (except in Panama, Chile, and Paraguay) and let the politicians grapple with growing domestic problems.

Manipulated Elections

Dictators or juntas sometimes held elections, but these were seldom either free or fair. More often, the government banned opposition parties (and jailed their leaders); muzzled the press; harassed, threatened, and intimidated voters; stuffed ballot boxes; manipulated voter registration rolls; bought votes; and, if all else failed, falsified election returns. (See Box 10.1.)

Before the historic election of 2000, Mexico provided a notorious example of how not to run national elections. For decades, the dominant Institutional Republican Party (PRI) manipulated the outcome of elections to ensure its own continued control of Mexico's government. The Mexican model was not perfectly replicated anywhere else, but the practice of using phony elections to legitimize military dictatorships was common until the 1980s.

Human Rights and Wrongs

Corruption has been rampant in Latin American politics. Election fraud is just one example; bribery and extortion have also been pervasive. Worse still, politically motivated violence has afflicted many Latin American societies. At various times in recent history, horrendous government repression has occurred in Argentina, Brazil, Chile, El Salvador, Guatemala, Nicaragua, and other places. The most notorious case was Argentina's **dirty war** (1976–1982) in which as many as 30,000 people vanished. In Argentina, as elsewhere, repression came in response to a leftist threat. Earlier in the 1970s, a military junta seized power in Uruguay after the civilian president turned to the army for help in fighting urban guerrillas. In both countries, repressive state policies had probably played a role in bringing the insurgencies into being; the insurgencies in turn prompted the governments to step up the repression. Thus, in Latin America power struggles between ruling oligarchies and disaffected leftist groups have led to violence on both sides.

Democracy in America

BOX 10.1

U.S. Elections: Model or Muddle?

Americans often look at election fraud in Latin America and elsewhere with a mixture of disdain and disbelief. How, we wonder, could other nations be so cynical, corrupt, or incompetent to let such a thing happen time and time again? However, people around the world watch elections in the United States with no less dismay.

First, there is the whole question of campaign finance rules that force candidates for office to raise money privately while allowing corporations, unions, and wealthy donors to spend unlimited sums (called "soft money") as they see fit. In the 2000 U.S. elections, the total amount spent ran into the billions of dollars. In the eyes of the world, this "run for the money" debases the process at the very heart of democracy and undermines America's claim to be a model for others. America, they say, has the best government that money can buy.

Second, elections in America are complex and confusing by any standards. There are basically two kinds of elections in the United States: *general elections,* used to fill elective offices, and *primary elections,* used to select candidates for elective offices. However, not all primary elections are the same. In *closed primaries* (the most common type), voters must indicate a party preference before casting their ballots; in *open primaries,* voters can choose any party's ballot they wish on Election Day, but only one — in other words, Republicans can vote in the Democratic primary and vice versa. A variant of the open primary is the *blanket primary* (used in Alaska and Washington), in which voters can actually choose, race by race, which party contest they wish to vote in (for example, choosing the Republican primary for governor and the Democratic primary for the seat in Congress).

The *presidential primary* constitutes a special case, which is no less complicated. It is used to pick delegates to the *national party conventions,* which are used to nominate (or annoint) presidential candidates. These primaries take a multitude of forms. To simplify, there are three basic variants:

1. Delegate selection only — only the names of the delegates (not the candidates) appear on the ballot; delegates may or may not indicate a personal preference.
2. Delegate selection with advisory presidential preference — voters both choose delegates and indicate their own personal preference; delegates are not bound by the voters' wishes.
3. Binding presidential preference — voters indicate their presidential preferences; delegates are bound by these preferences and may be chosen in primaries, caucuses, or state conventions.

The complexity (and sheer length) of American elections, combined with the high cost of modern campaigns (especially media advertising), make for a confusing process that often produces muddled results (neither party in firm control of the national or state governments). Add the Electoral College into the mix, and there is even the possibility that the candidate who wins the election will lose the presidential "sweepstakes" (as happened to Al Gore).

Insurgencies are a fact of political life in many Latin American countries. In the 1990s, guerilla groups continued to engage in armed struggle against the governments of Guatemala, Colombia, and Peru, in particular. The persistence and magnitude of the guerilla problem has varied from country to country—for example, in Nicaragua, El Salvador, Venezuela, Uruguay, and Argentina, the guerillas have been defeated. In Colombia, where several insurgent groups are active, kidnapping and other terrorist acts occur regularly. In Peru, a vicious Maoist guerilla movement, ***Sendero Luminoso*** ("Shining Path"), terrorized the countryside and the capital starting in 1980, and tens of thousands of civilians were massacred by both guerrilla and government forces.[2] After the capture of Shining Path leader Abimael Guzman in 1992, there was a lull in the violence when the guerrilla organization collapsed. But terrorist attacks, including car bombs (a favorite method of Shining Path), resumed in mid-1995. In December 1996, another Peruvian terrorist group, Tupac Amaru (MRTA), seized control of the Japanese ambassador's residence in Lima during a diplomatic reception — the most spectacular terrorist act in recent Peruvian history (discussed later).

Even Mexico, a stranger to insurgency since the Revolution of 1911, was no longer immune. In the mid-1990s, the government — not once, but twice — sent troops into the southeastern state of Chiapas in an attempt to quash an armed rebellion by the **Zapatista National Liberation Army (ZNLA);** and in 1996 a group calling itself the People's Revolutionary Army (EPR) kindled a second insurgency in the Pacific state of Guerrero.

Winds of Change: Democracy and Debt

Until recently, to speak of Latin American democracy was almost a contradiction in terms. Excluding the Caribbean, only three nations in the region — Costa Rica, Colombia, and Venezuela — had a democratic tradition. Costa Rica is a small, neutral country with no army whose president, Oscar Arias Sánchez, was awarded the Nobel Peace Prize in 1987 for his Central American peace plan. Colombia is a country plagued by insurgency, terrorism, and violent crime, but has nonetheless managed to function as a constitutional democracy with a two-party system and an elected president since the end of a twelve-year civil war (1946–1958). Venezuela is an oil-rich nation with a democratic federal system that closely resembles that of the United States.

Other nations in the region began converting to civilian democratic rule in the late 1970s, and dictatorships toppled like dominoes. In South America, the new democracies included Brazil, Argentina, Uruguay, Peru, and Bolivia. In Central America, four nations — El Salvador, Honduras, Nicaragua, and Guatemala — have instituted fragile democratic processes, but the military is still waiting in the wings in case the civilian leaders falter. Mexico remains a mixed regime, half democratic and half authoritarian; although elections occur at regular intervals, the dominant Institutional Revolutionary Party (PRI) has not lost an election in more than six decades.

But all was not well despite the flowering of democracy. The economic dynamism of the 1960s and 1970s gave way to an epidemic of debt and decline that weakened the social fabric and threatened the stability of the region's fledgling democracies. These problems were exacerbated in some countries by high birthrates. (See Table 10.1.) This bad economic news was accompanied by an epidemic of crime and corruption. Drug trafficking and money laundering became inseparable from the image of Latin America in the minds of North Americans and a source of continuous tension in hemispheric relations between North and South.

In the 1980s, two opposing trends shaped politics in Latin America. The violent forces of revolution and repression that ravaged the region for nearly two decades were finally subdued, as moderate civilian governments replaced military regimes in

Table 10.1 Demographic Facts: Selected Countries in Latin America

Country	Population, 1998 (thousands)	Annual Growth Rates, 1990–1998 (percent)*	Fertility Rate (births per woman)	Infant Mortality Rate, 1998 (per 1,000 live births)†
Argentina	36,125	1.5	2.8	17
Bolivia	7,950	2.7	4.7	60
Brazil	165,874	1.6	2.9	33
Chile	14,822	1.8	2.7	10
Colombia	40,804	2.2	2.7	23
Costa Rica	3,526	2.3	3.1	13
Guatemala	10,799	3.0	5.1	42
Mexico	95,846	2.0	3.2	30
Nicaragua	4,794	3.2	4.4	36
Panama	2,764	2.0	2.9	21
Peru	24,801	2.0	3.3	40
Venezuela	23,242	2.5	3.6	21

*Compare these rates to the United States, where the population growth rate growth is 1.1 percent per year.

†The infant mortality rate in the United States is 7 per 1,000 live births; it is even lower in some Western European countries.

Sources: International Bank for Reconstruction and Development, *World Bank Atlas* (Washington, D.C.: Author, 2000). Data for fertility rates are for the early 1990s and are from the *World Bank Atlas,* 1995.

Guatemala, El Salvador, Honduras, Ecuador, Bolivia, Peru, Brazil, Uruguay, and Argentina. To this list add countries where civilians have long ruled — Mexico, Costa Rica, Venezuela, and Colombia — and a clear pattern emerges. The role of the military in Latin America receded, and popular self-government made unprecedented gains. In South America, this trend signified a dramatic turnabout from just a decade or two earlier, when military rule and brutal repression were the norm. In recent years, elections in Latin America have been free and unfettered. Candidates have had access to newspapers, radio, and television and have campaigned without interference. Political rallies are no longer considered subversive, and elections have been intensely competitive.

A third trend emerged in the 1990s as Latin American countries moved toward greater regional economic integration. This development was inspired by the success of the European Community and by the need of recently reinstituted democratic governments to chart a new economic course. The first Iberian-American summit, which brought together leaders from nineteen Latin American countries plus Spain and Portugal, was convened in Guadalajara, Mexico, in mid-1991 and is now an annual event. Argentina, Brazil, Paraguay, and Uruguay have created a common market known as *Mercosur,* while Colombia, Mexico, and Venezuela have taken steps to create a free-trade zone. In addition, Colombia, Venezuela, Ecuador, Peru, and Bolivia resurrected the **Andean Pact,** an all-but-forgotten 1960s integration plan. Finally, regionalism in the Western Hemisphere gained new impetus when Mexico joined with the United States and Canada in the North American Free Trade Agreement (NAFTA).

Troubled Transitions: Civilians Take Charge

The onset of an economic crisis throughout the region in the early 1980s sent the military scurrying for cover. In Argentina, the generals, looking for a diversion, conjured up the Falkland Islands War in 1982, which they lost to Britain. Elsewhere, they bowed out more gracefully. Nearly everywhere, the key question was not whether the military would relinquish power but precisely when and how.

South America

By the mid-1980s, the transition from dictatorship to democracy and from military to civilian rule was well under way. The last country in South America to make this switch was Chile, where General Pinochet was defeated in a plebiscite and so allowed free elections near the end of 1989. As we will see, Brazil's generals allowed a civilian chief to take charge in 1985.

Could the newly chartered governments consolidate power when doing so meant having to overcome a daunting array of domestic, social, and economic problems? (See Table 10.2.) We look first at Peru, where a vicious insurgency movement sprouted in the remote, rural, and poverty-stricken southern province of Ayacucho in the early 1980s, then infiltrated into the capital, Lima, and challenged the very survival of the country's fragile new democracy.

Peru's Violent "Path" Peru was an important test case. There, a charismatic young politician, Alan Garcia Pérez, was elected president in 1985. His victory was impressive for several reasons. Only thirty-six years old, Garcia was the head of the Popular American Revolutionary Alliance (APRA), a left-leaning party with a history of opposition to the military. Never before had Peru's generals allowed an APRA candidate to assume the presidency. His election marked the first time in many decades that power had been transferred by free election and without fraud or foul play from one civilian president to another. But Peru faced excruciating economic difficulties, including runaway inflation, massive unemployment, and a burdensome foreign debt. In addition, the nation was in the midst of a bloody and protracted guerrilla war waged by the *Sendero Luminoso* (Shining Path).

After a promising start, however, Garcia stumbled. The problems that had plunged the nation ever deeper into poverty — hyperinflation, budget deficits, stagnant output, strikes, and trade deficits — were once again ravaging the country. President Garcia's popularity faded, and the future of Peru's fledgling democracy was cast into the shadows.

Garcia's successor, Alberto Fujimori, the son of Japanese immigrants, promised to turn the country around, but he also failed to reverse Peru's economic decline or to stop the Shining Path's relentless offensive. In the spring of 1992, Fujimori suspended the constitution and dissolved the congress. "Chaos and corruption" in the congress and the judiciary, the president declared, meant that the state "could not combat the combined power of terrorism and drug traffickers." He vowed to "defeat terrorism before 1995."[3]

But it was not to be. In December 1996, a small guerrilla band known as the **Tupac Amaru Revolutionary Movement (MRTA)** paralyzed the Fujimori government by seizing the Japanese Embassy and taking three hundred hostages, including two government ministers, the head of the Supreme Court, the head of the antiterrorist police and his prede-

Table 10.2 Indicators of Economic Change in Latin America, 1998

Country	Percentage of Agriculture in GDP	Personal Computers (per 1,000 people)	Percentage of Females in Labor Force
Argentina	6	44.3	36
Bolivia	15	7.5	38
Brazil	8	30.1	35
Chile	7	48.2	33
Colombia	13	27.9	38
Costa Rica	15	39.1	31
Guatemala	23	8.3	28
Mexico	5	47.0	33
Nicaragua	34	7.8	35
Panama	8	27.1	35
Peru	7	18.1	31
Venezuela	5	43.0	34
United States	1–2	458.6	42

Source: International Bank for Reconstruction and Development, *World Bank Atlas* (Washington, D.C.: Author, 2000).

cessor, and seventeen ambassadors. The hostage takers demanded immediate release of some four hundred imprisoned MRTA comrades. Fujimori vowed not to deal with terrorists. Most of the hostages were let go within a few weeks, but the fate of the eighty who remained captive, including President Fujimori's younger brother, was uncertain until April 22, 1997, when the government retook the embassy in a commando raid that resulted in the safe rescue of all the hostages and the annihilation of the hostage takers.

This was to be Fujimori's finest hour. In 2000, Fujimori won a third term in a controversial election but a major scandal involving his top aide led to a clamor for his ouster. He resigned while on an official trip to Japan; rather than accept his resignation, the Peruvian Congress voted to remove him from office. His aide fled to Venezuela but was arrested there, extradited, and sentenced for abuse of power. Fujimori was later charged with complicity in a series of killings perpetrated by a paramilitary death squad in 1991–1992. Fujimori remained in exile in Japan, the country of his ancestors.

In sum, the strange cases of Garcia and Fujimori, both extremely popular presidents at one time, illustrates an important point about Latin American politics, namely its volatility. Radical mood swings in public opinion are the norm, as are revelations of spectacular malfeasance on the part of political leaders. It is no exaggeration to say that anything can happen — and sooner or later, it probably will.

Three "Civilitary" Governments In Uruguay, Bolivia, and Ecuador, civilians were in charge, but the military stood ready to intervene at any time. Until the late 1980s, Chile and Paraguay were authoritarian holdouts. Isolated internationally and facing wide opposition at home, the Chilean regime held a plebiscite on a new constitution in 1989 that would automatically renew General Augusto Pinochet's term in office for another decade. (Pinochet had seized power in a military coup in 1973.) Voters rejected the new constitution, which then paved the way for national elections in November 1989. In Paraguay, a military coup ousted aging dictator Alfredo Stroessner, who had ruled since 1954. The general who led the coup subsequently won a multicandidate presidential election and vowed that his successor would be a freely elected civilian.

Drugs and Thugs South America's only two traditional democracies, Colombia and Venezuela, were not immune to destabilizing forces. In Colombia, where *"la violencia"* claimed 200,000 lives in Colombia from 1948 to 1958, the country reeled from the combined impact of natural disasters (including a major volcanic eruption in 1985), multiple guerrilla insurgencies, kidnappings for ransom, terrorist acts, illegal drug trafficking (Colombia is the world's primary source of cocaine), and rampant political corruption. When the government's domestic peace initiative collapsed in 1985, guerrillas stormed the Supreme Court building in Bogotá, seized scores of hostages, and executed some of them (including eleven justices) before being killed themselves by security forces. In 1989, the ruling party's presidential candidate for the 1990 election was assassinated in retaliation for the government's crackdown on Colombia's illicit drug cartels; in 1990, drug traffickers assassinated two other presidential candidates.

During the 1990s, the drug trade flourished under the protection of left-wing guerrillas in an alliance based on the existence of a mutual enemy. Meanwhile, high-placed army and police officers were widely suspected of accepting bribes from drug kingpins to look the other way, making right-wing paramilitary groups the government's only available option for fighting terrorists and drug traffickers. The United States authorized $1.3 billion in antidrug aid to Colombia in 2000 and the government in Bogotá again cracked down on leftist guerrillas in 2002 following the collapse of talks with the rebels. All efforts at negotiating a cease-fire in the civil war have failed, as have efforts to eradicate the illegal drug trade and prevent domestic terrorism. The stalemate hangs over Colombian society like a menacing volcano on the verge of erupting. (In fact, both volcanoes and earthquakes have claimed thousands of lives in Colombia in the past two decades.)

Venezuela, once awash in oil profits, had to adopt austerity measures after oil prices plunged in the early 1980s. A declining standard of living threatened to crack the broad consensus supporting Venezuelan democracy since the late 1950s. Similarly, economic problems prompted center-left President Carlos Andrés Pérez to institute belt-tightening measures that provoked a coup attempt in February 1992. The coup failed, however Congress removed Pérez on corruption charges. (He was convicted of mismanaging a $17 million secret state security fund in 1996.) His center-right successor suspended civil liberties for a time in the mid-1990s. In 1998, a self-styled populist and former army general named Hugo Chávez, one of the 1992 coup leaders, was elected president. The next year Chávez succeeded in getting a constitutional assembly to slash the power of Congress, and voters approved a new constitution granting the president much-enhanced powers. At first, the swarthy Chávez appealed to the poor, but his controversial economic and political reforms alienated the upper classes, including the very rich, people in business, the professions, and the mass media, and even the military (whence Chávez himself had come). A mass protest in April 2002 ended in pandemonium and tragedy when gunshots were fired and seventeen people died in the melee. Chávez was forced to step down, but the interim government that replaced him lacked legitimacy: decrees

Contrast and Comparison

BOX 10.2

Central America: Still Poor

Central America forms the land bridge between North America and South America. Excluding Mexico, the area formerly had a population roughly equal to half that of the United Kingdom or Italy, but in recent decades, population growth rates in this region have been among the highest in the world.

Central America is impoverished, but it is not as blighted as sub-Saharan Africa. Life expectancy ranges from around sixty-five in Guatemala and El Salvador to seventy-five in Costa Rica. Infant mortality rates are high by Western standards but generally much lower than in sub-Saharan Africa. Nutritional standards are also much lower than in the West but far better than in the poorest countries on the African continent. In some Central American countries today, the majority of children get only a primary education. Illiteracy is highest in Guatemala (perhaps more than 50 percent) and lowest in Costa Rica and Panama.

Women still make up less than one-third of the labor force in Central America (compared with nearly one-half in many industrially developed countries). The percentage of women in the labor force (one objective measure of social justice) is more than twice as high in the four Scandinavian countries than in Central America.

The combined GNP for the region (minus Mexico) is smaller than that of the Czech Republic and Slovakia (formally Gechoslovakia), which have less than half the population. In the 1980s and 1990s, the economies of Central America barely grew at all and yearly real per capita growth rates were actually negative everywhere except the tiny nation of Belize. The economies of Nicaragua, Honduras, Costa Rica, and Belize still depend heavily on agriculture, and most countries in the region export no manufactured products. Monoculture — growing a single cash crop (mainly bananas) for export — has long been the only means of earning hard currency in Guatemala, Nicaragua, and Honduras. Excluding Belize and Costa Rica, investment as a percentage of gross national product in Central America has been much lower than that of many Asian economies, which are growing faster.

were issued suspending the constitution and dissolving the legislature, causing Chávez supporters to stream back into the streets — and Chávez to slip back into power.

Once again, a political crisis in a Latin American democracy proved to be more like a soap opera than an exercise in constitutional government. And, once again, the story involves an Andean country where coca is the main cash crop and thugs rule.

Central America

In Central America, only Costa Rica has a well-rooted democratic tradition. El Salvador and Nicaragua were consumed by civil war in the 1980s, and both countries are still struggling with that bitter legacy. Honduras and Guatemala are nominal democracies in which the military continues to play a prominent political role and reports of human rights violations are common. El Salvador and Nicaragua struggled to overcome the bitter legacy of civil war. In Panama, civilian government was restored after a U.S. expeditionary force seized military dictator Manuel Noriega, who had been indicted by two U.S. federal grand juries on drug-trafficking charges. In a kind of vicious cycle, social and economic problems in these countries can only be overcome through basic reforms, but the elected governments most likely to institute such reforms are too easily destabilized when they fail to produce quick results — a virtual impossibility in light of the challenges and obstacles implicit in Central America's bleak development profile. (See Box 10.2.)

In sum, throughout the region democracy has made significant gains but the tradition of authoritarian rule and military intervention in politics is far from dead. Consolidation of democracy hinges above all on economic reforms and solid results. Mounting foreign debt continues to be a serious stumbling block for many of Latin America's new democracies.

Foreign Debt: The Lost Decade

By the end of the 1980s, the region's total debt had climbed to hundreds of billions of dollars.[4] Paying off this debt strained the economies of Mexico, Venezuela, Brazil, Argentina, and Peru — the major Latin American debtor nations — and, according to some observers, placed debt and democracy on a collision course. Many Latin American countries still depend heavily on a single export (not counting cocaine): copper (Peru), oil (Venezuela and Mexico), bananas (Honduras), coffee (Colombia), and sugar (Cuba). For Colombia, Peru, Bolivia, and Mexico, another commodity — illegal drugs — became a major source of export earnings. The debt crisis that started in 1982 when Mexico defaulted led to Latin's America's so-called lost decade.

Losing Interest

During the 1980s, Latin America suffered the worst recession in half a century. (See Table 10.3.) Exacerbating Latin America's economic problems was the debt burden being borne by Mexico, Brazil, Argentina, Venezuela, Chile, Colombia, Peru, and Ecuador. The region's debt-to-export ratio — a measure of repayment capacity — deteriorated rapidly in the early 1980s. As a result, over one-third of Latin America's export earnings were devoted to interest payments.

Beginning in 1981, the outflow of funds for interest payments and repatriated profits of foreign firms exceeded the inflow from new loans and investments — in other words, Latin America had a net loss of capital every year. Between 1981 and 1987, the region transferred about 5 percent of its GNP in debt service to the industrial democracies. Interest payments cut deeply into savings, and capital flight further reduced both consumption and domestic investment (which was shrinking rapidly).

The **debt crisis** thus set up a vicious cycle. Devoting savings to debt service rather than to investment stunted economic growth. Slow growth, in turn, meant that debtor nations had to choose between external and internal priorities (loan repayment versus wage concessions, tax cuts, subsidies, and so on). This predicament generated much politically charged controversy. In 1985, Peru's President Garcia bitterly denounced the IMF and the United States and announced that Peru would limit its loan repayments to one-tenth of its annual export earnings. The IMF withdrew Peru's borrowing privileges, and the United States declared outstanding loans to Peru "value-impaired," blocking future credit from U.S. commercial banks. Garcia's unilateral solution to Peru's debt problem was less drastic than it might have been: there had been fears that Peru might actually default. President Garcia seemed to be launching a debtors' revolt, with the enthusiastic endorsement of his compatriots.

Table 10.3 Economic Profile: Selected Countries in Latin America

Country	GNP, 1993 (million of dollars)	GNP Growth, 1995*	GNP Growth Rate, 1980–1991	GNP per Capita, 1993 (dollars)	Per Capita Growth Rate, 1985–1993 (percent)
Argentina	244,013	–3.2	–0.2	7,290	1.4
Bolivia	5,472	—	0.5	770	1.4
Brazil	471,978	2.3	2.5	3,020	–0.6
Chile	42,454	9.0	3.4	3,070	6.1
Colombia	50,119	3.8	3.2	1,400	2.3
Costa Rica	7,041	—	3.4	2,160	2.6
Guatemala	11,092	—	1.0	1,110	0.8
Mexico	324,951	7.2	1.5	3,750	0.9
Nicaragua	1,421	—	–1.4	360	–6.2
Panama	6,621	—	0.3	2,580	–0.7
Peru	34,030	—	–0.4	1,490	–3.5
Venezuela	58,916	2.2	1.1	2,920	1.0

*Data in this column are taken from *The Economist,* September 14, 1996. For Argentina, Chile, and Colombia, the data represent the percentage change from the first quarter of 1995 to the first quarter of 1996; for Brazil and Mexico, the period covered is from the second quarter of 1995 to the second quarter of 1996.

Sources: International Bank for Reconstruction and Development, *World Bank Atlas* (Washington, D.C.: Author, 1992 and 1995).

The political impact of the debt issue pervaded Latin America. Economic ills led to the downfall or decimation of incumbent governments in Mexico, Brazil, Argentina, Peru, Ecuador, Venezuela, and Bolivia. The message from the voters was clear: provide economic relief, or do not expect any more self-sacrifice.

By the end of 1987, eight Latin American countries were substantially behind on their external debt payments, and governments were under mounting pressure to take drastic action. A single default could touch off a chain reaction.

New hope came from the north in the form of an American debt-relief package called the **Brady Plan.** A drop in world interest rates also helped ease the burden on financially strapped governments. Inflation slowed dramatically throughout the region, and economies revived. For example, Mexico's net external debt, which equaled 60 percent of its GNP in 1988, shrank to 20 percent of GNP in just four years.[5] Unfortunately, as time passed the Brady Plan proved to be unequal to the task at hand.

Economic Stirrings

The economic picture has not been entirely bleak since the mid-1980s. In some parts of the region, foreign-debt pressures were alleviated by the end of the decade. Mexico negotiated a sizable new loan package; Uruguay signed a multiyear restructuring agreement and obtained new capital from abroad; and Venezuela succeeded in restructuring its public-sector debt. Other countries — including Brazil, Argentina, and Peru — also maneuvered for international debt relief.

The financial dilemma for most of Latin America, however, was not to be resolved soon. To avoid losing IMF borrowing privileges and to obtain new loans from the World Bank, foreign governments, and overseas commercial banks, the debtor nations were under great pressure to adopt IMF austerity programs. These generally involved budget cuts, constricted money supplies, tax increases, wage restraints — any belt-tightening measures that might restore solvency and stability. But there was a serious downside to this formula:

> Since the debt crisis, the poor in Latin America have gotten poorer and the middle class has moved down a peg or two; austerity policies have been unpopular. Letting off steam, voters kicked unpopular austerity-minded governments out of office in Colombia (1982), Venezuela (1983), Ecuador (1984), Peru (1986), and the Dominican Republic (1986).[6]

Thus, severe income maldistribution — extremes of wealth and poverty — remained (and remains) a threat to stability in the class-ridden societies of Latin America.

Reforms, Regionalism, Recession: The 1990s

Under pressure from international creditors, the World Bank, and the United States government, many governments in Latin America instituted market-oriented reforms during the 1990s. The results were mixed, but on the whole the region's economies improved somewhat for a time. (See Table 10.4.) Inefficient state-run corporations were privatized throughout the region. Chile and Costa Rica led the way, followed by Argentina and Mexico. Chile was the star performer in the region, as its economy grew at a brisk pace during 1990–1995 and continued to advance thereafter. Argentina's government lightened its debt load by many billions of dollars in a few short years by selling off airlines and telephone companies to private investors, as did Mexico. In the late 1990s, Brazil followed suit. Other countries in the region moved at varying paces toward more competitive market conditions, less state regulation, and reduced deficit spending.

Trade patterns shifted to reflect a greater intraregional emphasis in the 1990s, as well. At the beginning of the decade, for example, Brazil's exports within South America climbed steeply, while its exports to the United States fell. Brazil and Argentina formed a common market called **Mercosur** (the "Southern Cone Common Market") in 1986, which Paraguay and Uruguay joined in 1991. The four nations agreed to eliminate internal trade barriers in 1995 and levy a common tariff on imports from outside. Mercosur is potentially a powerful engine of economic growth.

Mexico entered into the **North American Free Trade Agreement (NAFTA)** with the United States and Canada in 1992. This pact eliminated customs duties on tens of thousands of items "from car windshields to tomatoes" and promised to "make it possible for a Mexican trucker earning $7 a day to climb into an 18-wheeler in Monterrey and drive a load of auto parts all the way to Detroit."[7]

NAFTA was hotly debated in the 1992 presidential election campaign. President George H. W. Bush strongly favored the treaty, but his Democratic challenger, Bill Clinton, while generally for NAFTA, wanted to renegotiate certain parts. Ross Perot, a

Table 10.4 Before the Slide: The Hopeful 1990s

Country	GNP, 1998 (millions of U.S. dollars)	GNP Growth, 2000*	GNP Growth per Capita, 1998 (dollars)	Average Yearly GNP Growth, 1990–1998 (percent)
Argentina	290,261	0.8	8,030	4.2
Brazil	767,568	3.9	4,630	1.7
Chile	73,935	6.1	4,990	6.5
Colombia	100,667	3.5	2,470	1.7
Mexico	368,059	7.6	3,840	0.6
Peru	60,491	—	2,440	4.0
Venezuela	82,096	7.6	3,530	−0.1

*Data in this column are taken from *The Economist,* October 14, 2000.

Sources: International Bank for Reconstruction and Development, *World Bank Atlas* (Washington, D.C.: Author, 1992 and 1995).

third-party 1992 presidential candidate, vigorously opposed NAFTA, arguing that there would be a gigantic "sucking sound" as investment dollars drained out of the United States into Mexico. NAFTA did pay off in a big way for Mexico even before the agreement was signed — in 1991, foreign investment nearly doubled over the previous year. The inflow of foreign investment accelerated even more as the agreement came closer to completion. Nonetheless, Perot's dire warnings, and the fears they nourished, turned out to be unfounded. The bottom line: NAFTA created a single market of 360 million consumers, somewhat larger than the EU's head count at that point in time.

Latin America as a region experienced an economic turnaround of uncertain proportions in the 1990s. With a few notable exceptions (Venezuela, for example), inflation fell sharply. In addition to tariff reduction, many governments adopted market-oriented reform strategies, cutting back on public expenditures and reducing the role of the state in the economy (especially by selling off state enterprises). The regionwide results were encouraging, if less than spectacular. (See Table 10.5.) In Chile, one of the first to institute reforms, the poverty rate fell by 23 percent between 1987 and 1996.

But new storm clouds soon appeared. The economies of Mexico and Argentina, for example, went on a roller coaster ride, plunging into deep recession in 1995. A few years later, Brazil and Latin America as a whole were thrown into financial turmoil by developments external to the region.

Various global factors conspired against Latin America's vulnerable economies. First, recession in Asia drove down commodity prices, especially for oil and copper, two of the region's most important exports. Second, financial crises in Asia and Russia in 1998 induced a stampede out of Latin American securities as investors sought safer havens (notably, Wall Street and other Western stock and bond markets). Throughout Latin America, **current account deficits** rose considerably during this period. (Current account refers to trade in goods and services, including interest payments.) At the same time, capital flight confronted Latin governments with the stark choice of raising interest

Table 10.5 Not Good, But Getting Better
Social Indicators in Latin America and East Asia

Country	Circa	Life Expectancy at Birth	Infant Mortality per 1,000 Live Births	Literacy (percent)	Access to Safe Water (percent)
Brazil	1960	54.9	177	61.0	32
	1980	62.7	80	74.5	56
	2001	68.3	36	87.3	87
Mexico	1960	57.3	134	65.0	38
	1980	66.8	74	82.2	50
	2001	73.4	29	91.4	88
Latin America	1960	56.5	154	74.0	35
	1980	64.7	79	79.9	53
	2001	70.6	34	89.2	86
East Asia	1960	39.2	198	—	—
	1980	60.0	82	68.8	68.8
	2001	69.2	44	86.8	76

Sources: Kuczynski and Williamson; World Bank

rates (defending the value of the national currency) or devaluation; the resulting interest-rate hikes, in turn, raised the cost of government borrowing at the same time that the economic slowdown reduced revenues — knocking badly strained budgets further out of balance.

Whatever the pathology, Latin America suffers from a kind of economic malady with several distinct symptoms. First, the region is still heavily dependent on commodity exports, which are susceptible to severe price fluctuations. Second, as the economies of the region grow, imports rise rapidly, which creates strong private sector demand for hard currency or "foreign capital." Third, most governments in the region are supported by weak tax structures with high rates of evasion, which means that governments often make up revenue shortfalls by borrowing from abroad, thus sharing financial "dependency" with the private sector. [8]

Reforms without Recovery

Imagine that the fragile economies of Latin America are precariously situated on a series of fault lines. Fault lines do exist in Latin America, but the most serious ones are economic rather than geological (though the latter are bad enough).

Throughout the region, there are frequent tremors that cause panic to spread and investors to flee. From time to time, upheavals are triggered by a combination of governmental misfeasance, social unrest, and a collapsing currency — the economic equivalent of earthquakes that are powerful enough to wreak havoc on the nation's infrastructure (roads, bridges, and buildings). Instead, these economic upheavals wreck the political and psychological "infrastructure" of prosperity, meaning that they cause a

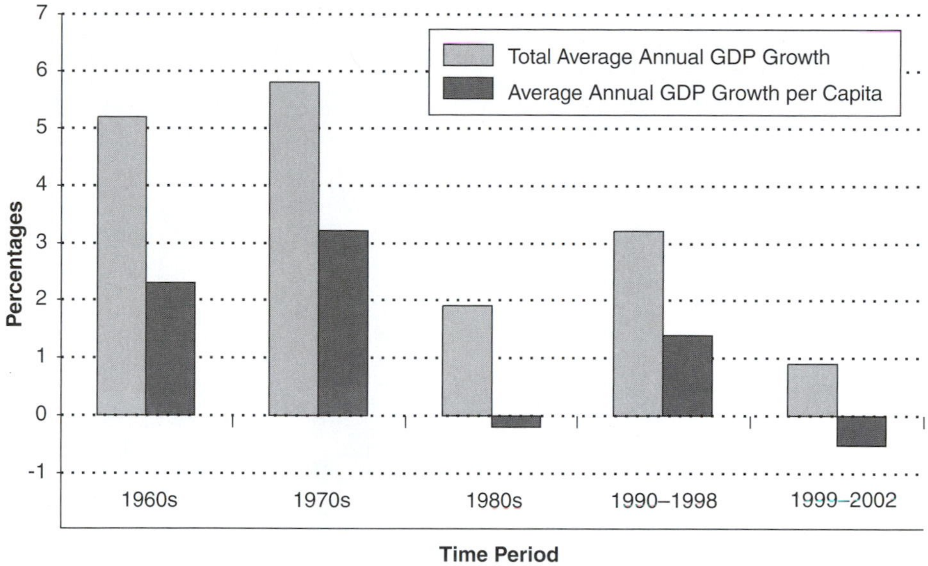

Figure 10.1 Lagging Latin Economies

Sources: World Bank; Economic Commission for Latin America and the Caribbean (ECLAC).

general crisis of confidence in both the economy and the government on the part of consumers, producers, and investors alike. This pattern occurred once again in Latin America between 1998 and 2003. (See Figure 10.1.) The economic mudslide affected the entire region, not just a few countries. In 2002, Latin America's economy actually shrank slightly and per capita income stood at 2 percent below 1997 levels, according to the UN Economic Commission for Latin America (ECLAC). In the 1990s, the countries of the region made modest progress toward reducing a poverty rate that approached 50 percent at the beginning of the decade, but the number of poor and very poor was again on the rise in 2001. (See Figure 10.2.) The region's economies grew rapidly in the 1960s and 1970s (as Figure 10.1 shows), plummeted in the 1980s, and then rallied in the 1990s, only to slide precipitously after 1998.

On balance, even compared to countries considered "poor" by Western standards (Greece, Portugal, and Turkey, for example), Latin America's growth in the second half of the twentieth century has been unimpressive. (See Table 10.6.) Compared to a country like Singapore, however, Latin America's economic performance looks abysmal.

What was wrong with Latin America's economies? Perhaps the best way to answer this question is to look at the kinds of economic reforms that rejuvenated the region for a time in the 1990s. Governments privatized steelworks, factories, and public utilities; spent more on education and health; and in some countries (including Brazil and Mexico) launched new antipoverty programs.

However, Latin America remained highly vulnerable to balance-of-payments shocks (a legacy of the 1980s that has not been laid to rest). Latin America's dependency on highly volatile capital inflows means that the region can be hit by a shock wave at any

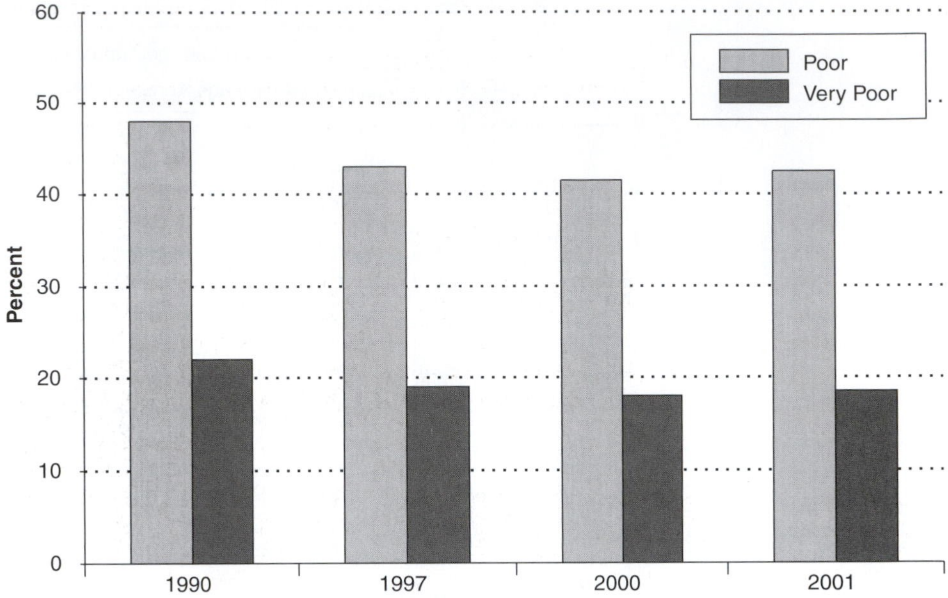

Figure 10.2 Going Nowhere Fast: Latin America's Persistent Poverty Rate

Source: Pedro-Pablo Kuczynski and John Williamson, eds., *After the Washington Consensus: Restarting Growth and Reform in Latin America* (Washington, D.C.: Institute for International Economics, 2003). Adpated by Tom Magstadt.

Table 10. 6 An Embarrassing Comparison

	Projected per capita GDP, 2003*	Ratio of 2000 to 1950†
Argentina	$ 2,580	2.1
Brazil	$ 2,900	3.4
Chile	$ 4,500	2.0
Colombia	$ 1,730	1.9
Mexico	$ 6,210	2.6
Venezuela	$ 3,772£	0.8
Greece	$15,060	5.4
Portugal	$14,070	7.1
Turkey	$ 2,850	2.9
China	$ 1,070	—
Singapore	$22,180	13.6

*The figures in this column are from *The Economist, The World in 2003,* pp. 93–94 and 96–98.

†Pedro-Pablo Kuczynski and John Williamson, eds., *After the Washington Consensus: Restarting Growth and Reform in Latin America* (Washington, D.C.: Institute for International Economics, 2003).

Note: This figure represents actual GDP per capita in 2002, and was declining at the rate of 29 percent in the first quarter of 2003, thus continuing a five-year downward trend; Venezuela's economy shrank by 15 percent between 1998 and 2003.

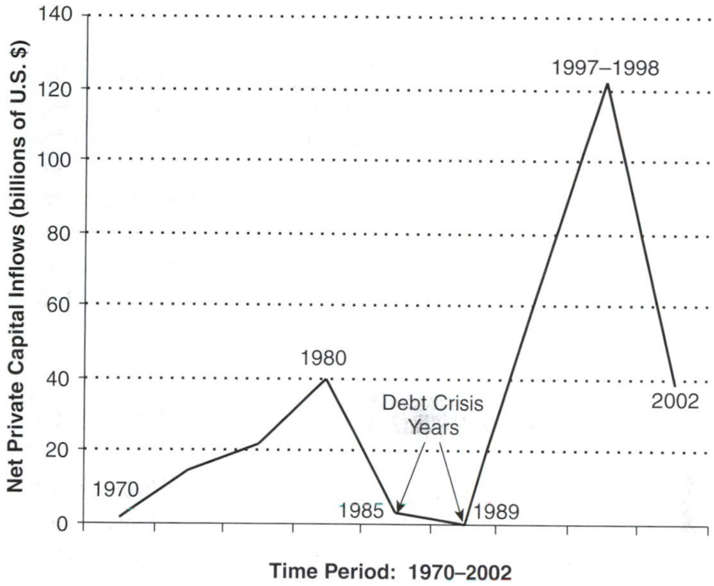

Figure 10.3 Back into the Abyss?

Source: International Bank for Reconstruction and Development.

time. The region's growth spurt in the 1990s was fueled by capital inflows that reached a peak in 1997–1998. (See Figure 10.3.) Hence, the "Asian flu" and the subsequent Russian default, by causing a virtual shutoff of capital flows, precipitated Latin America's economic collapse and Argentina's eventual default.

At the same time, macroeconomic reforms were often halfhearted and badly handled. Then, too, "second generation" reforms such as improving education are often costly to implement and slow to yield tangible social benefits. As a result, the political rewards for such reforms are lacking.

In sum, the mantra of "market reforms" is easy to mouth but translating theory into practice has proven to be as difficult as predicting earthquakes or volcanic eruptions. Mexico and Brazil, the two countries featured in this part of the book, exhibit the symptoms of the Latin American "malady" described above in various degrees. We turn now to a closer look at these two potential powerhouses in Latin America.

Case Studies: Mexico and Brazil

Mexico and Brazil exemplify the political traditions and institutions of Latin America. Prior to the historic 2000 presidential election (discussed later), Mexico was ruled by the same party for seven decades, a party that stayed in power by systematically rigging elections, winking at corruption, silencing its opponents, and repaying its supporters with myriad forms of patronage. Brazil switched from military dictatorship to civilian democratic rule only recently (in 1985, to be exact).

How important is Latin America? The United States long treated its southern neighbors as a stern parent might treat ill-behaved children, lecturing them on human rights, punishing them for not obeying (through military interventions and trade sanctions), or rewarding them with praise, foreign aid, and trade concessions for doing the "right" thing (for example, opposing communism during the Cold War). But there are now signs this tradition of unequal relations will almost certainly change in the future. For example, the combined population of Mexico and Brazil has caught up with that of the United States. Because population growth in Latin America is considerably higher than in the United States, the region as a whole represents a market potentially larger than the U.S. domestic market for products stamped "made in America." It also represents a potential competitor much as the People's Republic of China and South Korea have become Japan's competitors in Northeast Asia.

Mexico has already become a serious competitor in North America, thanks to NAFTA. But the process of institutional reform in Mexico is still incomplete. How far economic rejuvenation can go without such reform, or whether it can survive if the political system reverts, remains to be seen. In the next section, we look at how Mexico is governed, how Mexican policy makers are prioritizing problems, and where Mexico appears to be heading.

Mexico: Only One Fox, So Many Hounds

As we already noted, Mexico's political system originated in the Revolution of 1911; the 1917 constitution was forged in the wake of a protracted and violent struggle. Recall that the Mexican Revolution was a class struggle — not between "proletariat" and "capitalists" but between wealthy, landed aristocracy and impoverished peasants who were much like serfs in a semifeudal order. The excesses associated with the revolution reflected the extremes that spawned it — extreme inequality, extreme poverty, extreme injustice, and extreme indifference to mass suffering. This was the legacy of General Porfirio Díaz (1876–1911), Mexico's last and most infamous military dictator.

The long and bitter fight against a tyrant who ruled with an iron fist for thirty-five years (a lifetime for the Mexican underclass in that dark age) produced a generation of revolutionary leaders who were determined to create a just social order. The constitution of 1917 was the instrument designed to achieve that lofty aim.

The Constitution of 1917

In theory, Mexico is a federal republic comprising thirty-one states and one federal district (around Mexico City, the capital). The constitution of 1917 assigned legislative power to the bicameral National Congress, elected by universal adult suffrage (all nationals eighteen and older who have "an honorable means of livelihood"). The Senate (upper house) has sixty-four members (two from each state and the Federal District), who serve a six-year term. The Chamber of Deputies (lower house) has five hundred members directly elected to a three-year term. Three hundred seats are filled from single-member districts.

The majority Institutional Revolutionary Party (PRI) wins in most of these first past the post contests. In 1986, Congress doubled the number of multimember district seats to two hundred, giving minority parties a realistic chance to compete for one hundred more seats. It was a cautious ruling-party concession to pressure for institutional reform.

Executive power is given to the president, directly elected to a single, nonrenewable six-year term. He appoints both the Council of Ministers (cabinet), whose members head the various government departments, and senior military and civilian officers. The constitution of 1917 also created an independent judiciary. The federal Supreme Court has twenty-six members including a chief justice. The president appoints Supreme Court justices with Senate approval. The thirty-one state governors are popularly elected to a six-year term; like the president, they can never serve again. Under Article 76 of the constitution, the president can ask the Senate to remove the governor of any state in which law and order has broken down.

In sum, the constitution of 1917 set up a federal democratic republic in which powers are clearly separated among the three branches of government. The constitution also enshrined the aims of the Mexican Revolution by mandating radical land reform, drafting a labor code, and sharply curtailing the power of the Catholic Church. Its provisions dealing with religion, education, and the exploitation of mineral wealth reflect the long struggle against dictatorship, the church, large landowners, and "economic imperialism."

Mexico's constitution is a thoroughly democratic document. Drafted just months before the October Revolution in Russia, it outdid even the Bolsheviks in putting workers on a pedestal. For example, Article 123 deals with labor rights. Its provisions include an eight-hour workday, a minimum wage, twelve weeks' pregnancy leave, two extra rest periods each day for nursing mothers, equal pay for equal work regardless of sex or nationality, profit sharing for workers, double pay for overtime, and appropriate compensation for job-related injuries or diseases. This list of workers' rights sounds impressive today; in 1917, it was groundbreaking.

Leaders of a party in power often pretend that things are better than they actually are. Nowhere is the contrast between appearance and reality sharper in Mexican life than in the difference between the formal workings outlined in the constitution and the informal workings of the system.

The Mexican System

"Effective suffrage, no reelection"—this was democracy in a nutshell for Francisco Madero, president of Mexico from 1911 to 1913. Half of this formula — no reelection — has been put into practice. The idea behind the one-term rule was to prevent dictatorships like that of Porfirio Díaz. The rule also prohibits members of the Congress, the state legislatures, and municipal councils from serving two consecutive terms, again to prevent an entrenched elite from regaining a monopoly on power and wealth. But almost every rule can be circumvented. In Mexico, this rule is observed in a formal sense; informally, however, the system is a game of musical chairs in which majority-party politicians rotate from one position to another.

Though different in practice from the original intent of its authors, this system produced a prolonged period of political stability in Mexico. For the entire period, one political party — the Institutional Revolutionary Party (PRI) — controlled the government through a powerful coalition comprising labor, business, and landowning elites.

The president is the pivotal figure in the system. To become president, a politician must have previous experience as a cabinet member; be male, youthful, and physically vigorous; and be able to mediate between the left and right wings of the PRI. The party's inner circle, headed by the incumbent president, chooses the nominee, who is always elected. In effect, the outgoing president handpicks his successor. There is no vice president; if necessary, the National Congress chooses an interim chief executive. Since 1946, every president of Mexico has been a civilian.

Although the constitution gives the National Congress extensive power to make laws, in reality the president dominates the legislative branch. He can introduce legislation directly into both houses and can set the legislative agenda. He can also veto legislation but has never had to do so because no law that was opposed by a sitting president was ever enacted.

The president can also make laws by decree in most areas of public policy. For example, Mexico's income tax was created by decree; only years later did the Congress get around to enacting it formally. Presidential decrees have created cabinet ministries, government departments, public corporations, and major public-works projects. The budget, family planning, and nuclear energy are all areas in which policy — later to be rubber-stamped by the National Congress — has been effected by presidential fiat.

The most important cabinet officer is the *secretario de gobernación* (minister of internal affairs), who supervises intragovernmental relations, liaison with the National Congress, elections, voter and party registration, immigration and emigration, motion-picture production, radio and television airtime, the federal police, and federal prisons. Other key cabinet positions include planning and budget, finance, commerce and industry, public enterprises, foreign affairs, and labor.

Because the PRI dominated the National Congress until 2000, it debated the form rather than the substance of legislation. Floor debates are often vigorous but have little effect. Opposition party leaders frequently voiced criticism of government policies, but the media, which pandered to the all-powerful PRI-dominated state, typically muted such criticism.

The judiciary is independent, but judgeships are awarded on political grounds, which meant that the PRI handpicked federal judges. Since 1929, every Supreme Court justice has belonged to the PRI. Although corruption is endemic throughout the government, justice is frequently served anyway. The major restraint on presidential power is the **writ of amparo** (protection), by which federal judges can protect citizens from violations of their constitutional rights by stopping a government agency from taking action until the Supreme Court has ruled on appeal. The court may halt government action, compel officials to carry out constitutional obligations, or force judges to specify or clarify the charges against a defendant in a criminal case. Some 5,500 writs of amparo were issued against the president or cabinet ministers between 1917 and 1980; the Supreme Court ruled against the government in about a third of these cases.

The PRI's control extended to the thirty-one states as well. Governors were popularly elected, but the PRI inner circle, dominated by the incumbent president, decided whose name appeared on the ballot. Nomination was tantamount to election; between 1929 and 2000, every state governor was a member of the PRI. In all but six states, governors' terms do not coincide with the presidential elections, which means that each new president inherits twenty-five governors who were chosen by his predecessor. Before 1964, presidents frequently exercised the right to remove state governors from office; after 1964 this practice tapered off.

We have already alluded to the importance of the PRI in Mexico's political life. The next section explains just how dominant that party was, until very recently.

Political Parties

For much of the twentieth century, the Institutional Revolutionary Party in Mexico had no serious rivals. Every six years the PRI's candidate for president would be "popularly" elected in what became a monotonous charade. The elections were free but not fair. Although election fraud was common, the opposition was powerless to stop it and often afraid to protest. That began to change in the 1980s, when the upstart **National Action Party (PAN)** made a series of strong showings at the polls. As we will see, that popular surge culminated in the election of the PAN's candidate for president in 2000. Although party competition is gaining ground, it is far too soon to count the PRI out. To understand Mexican politics, it is necessary to look more closely at how the PRI managed to hold onto power for so long, as well as what it stands for.

The PRI Machine The federal government (controlled by the PRI) sets the rules for the creation and operation of political parties. These rules are fairly liberal, but parties must obtain 1.5 percent of the national vote to retain their legal status. The fact that as many as nine parties have been represented in the National Congress at any given time suggests that the right of free association is respected and that minority parties do not have to overcome insurmountable legal or bureaucratic obstacles. At the same time, however, the PRI's organizational machine reached everywhere in the country and was quite capable of fabricating the results it wanted at election time. Consequently, although regular elections were held, the PRI was always assured of winning control of the government.

Prior to the historic 2000 presidential election, the PRI enjoyed a virtual power monopoly in Mexican party politics. As its name suggests, the party claims to be the permanent custodian of an ongoing "institutionalized revolution." As such, it embraces welfare-state policies (even though the state lacks the resources to support them), state ownership of major industries, and individual or communal ownership of land. Two of the party's most fundamental principles are "no reelection" and the right of all workers (including public employees) to strike. Starting in 1933, the party developed six-year plans for the economy. Each new plan became the basis for the government's official program.

The PRI stresses Mexico's independence. Distancing itself from the U.S. imperialism was a major motif of Mexican foreign policy until recently. The PRI was long sympathetic to left-wing, anti-imperialist regimes in Cuba, Nicaragua, and Peru. The fact that Mexico lost about half its total area to the United States in the Mexican-American War accounts for some of the tension between these two "distant neighbors," as journalist Alan Riding once called them.[9] Beginning in the early 1980s, Mexico entered into a new era of goodwill and cooperation with the United States, epitomized by the North American Free Trade Agreement (NAFTA), which was formally launched in 1993.

For seven decades prior to the 2000 election, Mexico was a prime example of a one-party-dominant system. It is still too soon to pronounce that system dead, but it now appears that Mexico is evolving toward either a competitive multiparty system or, perhaps, a two-party system. We look at the other potential major party in Mexico next.

Mexico's Opposition Parties Minority parties in Mexico run the gamut from conservative to collectivist. The PRI's main rival is the right-of-center National Action Party (PAN), which in the 1980s emerged as a serious challenger to PRI control in several northern states (adjacent to Texas, New Mexico, and Arizona). In the 1990s, PAN became a serous threat to PRI domination on the national level. In 2000, Vicente Fox, running as the PAN's candidate, was elected president. It was the end of an era in Mexican politics — and possibly also the beginning of one.

Like most democracies (and unlike the United States), Mexico has long had a variety of political parties running the gamut from far right to far left. The hard-right Party of Mexican Democracy (PDM) advocates reprivatization of the economy, reduction of welfare programs, an end to the PRI patronage system, and a "union of church and state." On the far left, various Marxist parties compete for a share of the staunchly anti-establishment vote. The main left-wing opposition is the Party of Democratic Revolution. Other socialist and workers' parties include the formerly pro-Soviet Communist Party of Mexico (PCM), also known as the Unified Socialist Party of Mexico (PSUM), and a Trotskyite party called the Revolutionary Party of the Workers (PRT). Historically, the dogmatic and uncompromising nature of Mexico's left-wing parties has played into the hands of the PRI.

Elections

In the 1980s, the PRI's popularity fell to historically low levels, and the trend continued into the 1990s. The clearest way to track this change is to look at the vote totals for the PRI's presidential candidates over time. (See Figure 10.4.) History will record the 2000 election as the one that turned the tide against the PRI. In retrospect, however, it actually happened twelve years earlier.

A Tale of Two Elections The left was the beneficiary of labor unrest in the late 1980s. Until then, the government and organized labor worked hand in glove, but economic difficulties led to serious friction between the PRI and the Confederation of Mexican Workers (CTM). Independent labor unions made rapid gains and for the first time posed a potential challenge to the traditional PRI domination of the political system.

In the 1988 presidential election, the PRI managed to keep its grip on power but not without manipulating the ballots. Voting fraud is nothing new in Mexican politics. What made this election unique was that a populist politician who had challenged the PRI's candidate might actually have won had it been a fair contest. The challenger was a disaffected former PRI leader who had forged his flash-in-the-pan "party" out of more than fifteen center-left groups. The coming together of the left in 1988, albeit temporarily, was unprecedented in Mexican politics.

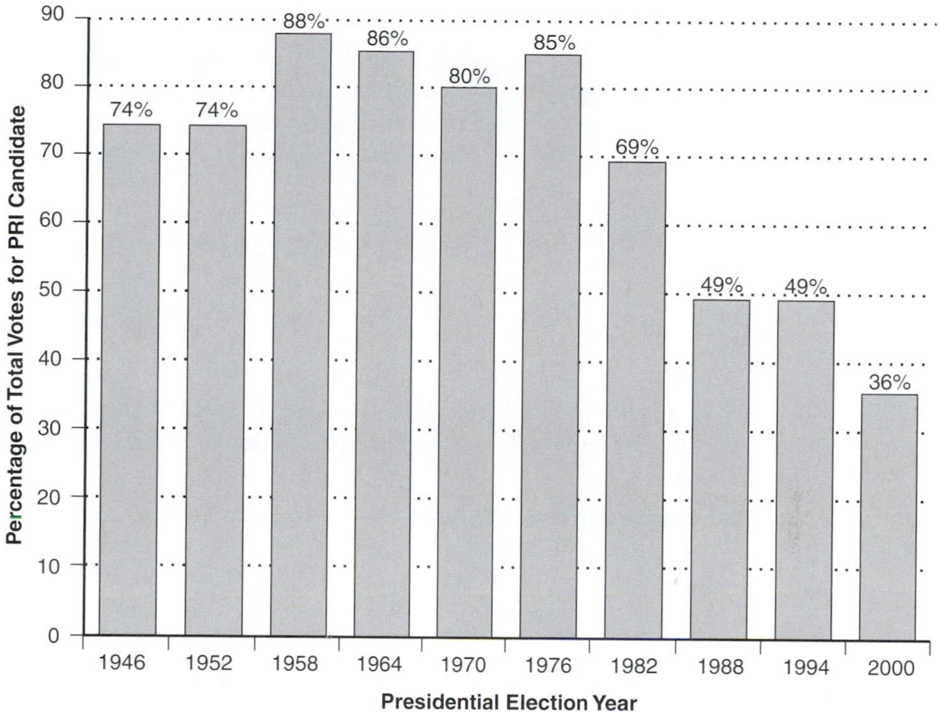

Figure 10.4 The Rise and Fall of the PRI

Sources: Data from Comision Federal Elector (1934–1988); Instituto Federal Electoral (1994); *The Economist,* July 8, 2000, p. 59.

In 1990, the government sponsored an election reform bill designed to perpetuate PRI's hegemony. The new law barred any future electoral alliance of the kind that nearly brought the PRI down in 1988. It also provided that any party receiving 35 percent of the vote would be guaranteed a majority (50 percent plus one seat) in the Chamber of Deputies. With the opposition splintered, this law stacked the deck heavily in favor of the PRI.

Nonetheless, the PRI used a fig leaf to cover its shame. This fig leaf consisted of measures aimed at curbing ballot-box fraud, compiling a new voter roll, and creating an independent election commission. These steps, among other factors, boosted President Carlos Salinas de Gortari's personal popularity. In the 1991 state and federal elections, the PRI's candidates officially won over 60 percent of the votes and all six of the governorships at stake — how free and fair those elections were, as always in Mexico, was open to question.

President Salinas continued and even accelerated the economic reforms initiated by his predecessor. He privatized many state-owned enterprises; drastically reduced tariff barriers that were long among the highest in the world; brought down inflation from triple digits in 1987 (the year before he took office) to just 7 percent in 1994 (the year he left office); and worked closely with Washington to reduce Mexico's mammoth foreign debt. He also made life difficult for corrupt trade unions and drug traffickers.

But a dark cloud hung over Salinas's accomplishments. Some 250 anti-PRI political activists were killed between 1988 and 1994. The PRI's fading popularity was reflected at the polls in July 1992 when, for only the second time in sixty-three years, it lost control of Chihuahua State. Bad luck played a role: public outrage over a catastrophic sewer-line explosion in Guadalajara the previous April was expressed through the ballot box.

The man the PRI picked to succeed Salinas was assassinated campaigning for office in March 1994. His replacement, Ernesto Zedillo Ponce de León, went on to win the election in the fall. Unlike Salinas, Zedillo appeared to have won without cheating. He then oversaw an election in 1997 that ended in a stunning defeat for the PRI and the loss of its parliamentary majority.

The legacy exemplified by the Salinas presidency — a legacy of Machiavellian politics — would cast a long, dark shadow over the PRI in the days to come. It was precisely that legacy which Vicente Fox ran against and defeated in 2000.

Out-Foxing the PRI: The Historic Election of 2000 The political face of Mexico changed in 2000. In July, the voters went to the polls in what close observers characterized as the cleanest election in Mexican history and rejected the PRI's presidential candidate in favor of Vicente Fox, a newcomer to the political scene. Fox, who ran as the candidate of the National Action Party, promised during the campaign to run the government like a business using total quality management and performance indicators to evaluate results (no mean task in a country with an entrenched and venal bureaucracy). Fox won by a substantial margin, and although the PAN also defeated the PRI in the legislative elections, it fell short of a clear majority. (See Figure 10.5.) Breaking sharply with the Mexican tradition of cronyism, the president-elect said he would choose a cabinet based on merit not personal ties and would include all parties and parts of the country in a "government of national unity" to oversee the "democratic transition."

Was it possible that the politics of patronage and favoritism would now give way to a new era of clean government in Mexico? The reform agenda was easy enough to set — stamp out official corruption, professionalize the bureaucracy, devolve power from the federal level to the states, and get the state out of the economy (see "Problems and Prospects"). Whether the new president could do the things that needed to be done without a majority in the Chamber and with PRI governors in control of more than half of Mexico's thirty-two states was open to question. (See Figure 10.6.)

We look next at the economic and social problems that Mexico faces today. We also consider whether political and economic reforms will be accelerated, and, if so, what that might mean for the country's future.

Problems and Prospects

Mexico has changed. When the PRI first came to power in 1929, two-thirds of the population was rural. Today, three out of four Mexicans are urban and the population will soon reach 100 million. In the past fifteen years, the pace of change has accelerated. The economy is no longer state-dominated and protectionist. In fact, it has become one of

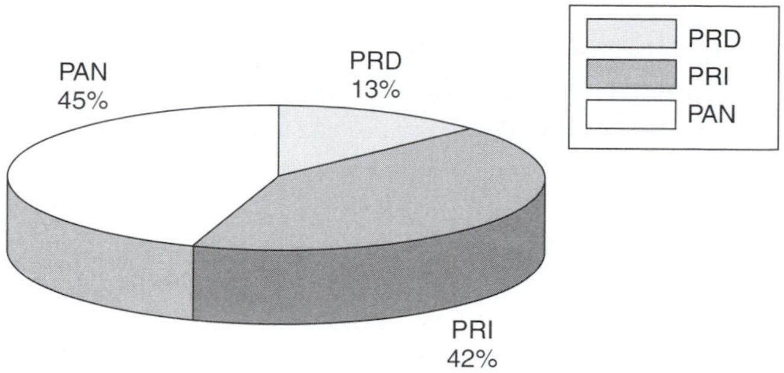

Figure 10.5 Seats in Mexico's Chamber of Deputies after National Elections in 2000

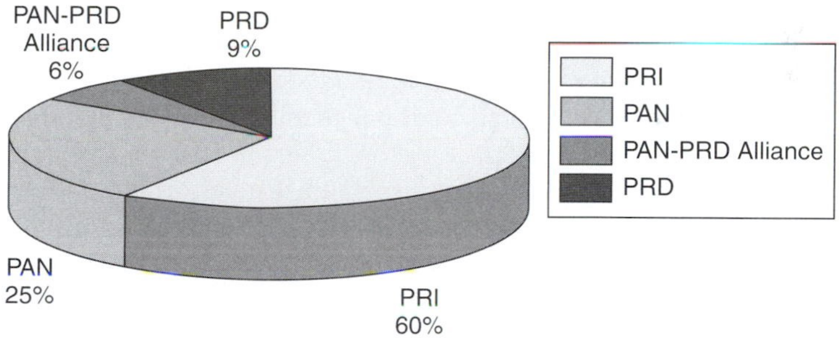

Figure 10.6 State Governorships after Mexico's Elections in 2000

the most open in Latin America. Today, Mexico ranks in the top ten among the world's leading exporters (counting the EU as one) and is the second biggest trading partner of the United States (only Canada is bigger). In 2000, moreover, the economy was growing at a brisk pace (7 percent) and inflation was below the official target (10 percent). However, Mexico's longer-term inflation goal — to match the United States by 2003 — was not achieved. At a modest 4 percent in 2003, inflation was not a serious problem. Mexico's exports continued to grow steadily from 2001 to 2004, but Mexico was losing market share to China in nearly one-third of the 152 main U.S. import categories. Thus, competition from China, India, and other Asian states has become a major issue for Mexico in recent years.

Prior to the 2000 election, changes in Mexico's economy were more dramatic than changes in the political system. But the political scene, too, was in transition. These two arenas — the economic and the political — played off each other. Trying to decide which one was more important is like trying to answer the question, Which came first, the chicken or the egg?

As we noted earlier, 1988 was a turning point in Mexican politics. What caused the change in voting behavior? For answers, we turn to the sad state of Mexico's economy in the 1980s.

A Roller Coaster Economy Between 1950 and 1970, Mexico's economy flourished. Its per capita GNP nearly doubled, and so did its population. The growth curve continued to rise steeply in the 1970s, but signs of trouble began to appear. The government was running up large deficits and borrowing heavily. At the same time, it enlarged its own role in the economy. The number of state-owned enterprises increased tenfold between 1970 and 1977. Trade deficits ballooned in this period because companies catered almost exclusively to captive (protected) internal markets and consequently could not compete in world markets. In 1976, the government was forced to devalue its currency for the first time in more than two decades.

At the start of the 1980s, the picture clouded even more as oil prices fell sharply. By this time, Mexico was well on its way to accumulating a $100 billion foreign debt; at the end of 1982, the interest payments alone were devouring close to half the nation's total annual export earnings. Between 1982 and 1988, the economy stalled at zero growth (per capita GNP actually declined), inflation rose to triple digits, and unemployment reached astronomical levels.

The crisis forced Mexico's government to take drastic action. Currency controls had been put into effect in 1982. Under growing pressure from the International Monetary Fund and foreign creditors, then President Miguel de la Madrid Hurtado adopted unpopular austerity measures including reductions in state subsidies for food and fuel. Other spending cuts were also made in an effort to curb the escalating budget deficits. But it was too little too late. If the stability of a country's currency is a barometer of economic health, Mexico was a candidate for intensive care. The value of the peso plunged in 1986.

Mexico was also hit by a natural disaster in September 1985 when a massive earthquake rocked Mexico City and five states. The greatest loss of life and property occurred in the capital, where official estimates put the death toll at 7,000. Other sources estimated as many as 20,000 deaths. Moreover, hundreds of thousands of people were left homeless, and property damage was estimated in the billions of dollars. The government was scathingly criticized for doing too little too late. There were also allegations that international relief funds had been misappropriated by corrupt Mexican officials.

Old Habits That Die Hard . . . The period 1982–1995 witnessed a startling rise in corruption and crime (including drug trafficking, of course). For example, when President Salinas had made the (economically imperative) decision to sell off hundreds of inefficient state-owned enterprises — a policy of "sink or swim" — in order to reduce Mexico's debt he had divested many of these assets in under-the-table deals, giving the PRI's friends a chance to buy companies at bargain prices. Private transactions involving public property are a telltale sign of "crony capitalism." Mexico prior to 1995 was a textbook case of such a system. In 1993, Salinas invited his cronies (mostly wealthy businessmen) to a dinner and asked them to contribute $25 million apiece to the PRI. Among his dinner guests were some of the new owners of Mexico's banks. Some refused, but others felt so indebted to Salinas that they gave twice that amount.[10]

. . . And Create New Problems The way Salinas sold off Mexico's state-owned companies — in haste and without necessary rules and regulatory regimes in place —

set the stage for the problems his successors have had to deal with. Thus, Mexico's newly privatized banks made a lot of bad loans that they could not collect after the economic crisis in 1995. With the banking system on the verge of collapse, the government had little choice but to bail them out, at a huge cost to Mexican taxpayers. Salinas also privatized the state telephone monopoly, Telmex. Its new owners not only bought it at a discount, they had a free hand in running it. In most countries, public utilities are either state-owned or state-regulated — for good reason. There is a lot of money to be made in service industries. Electricity, telephone, gas, and water are public services, meaning that people depend on these services and the economy would grind to a halt without them. In well-governed societies, these services (or "utilities") are regulated by the state in the public interest. In the 1990s, the state ceased to own and operate Telmex, but did not commence to regulate it. Of course, the people of Mexico paid the price.

Other parts of the economy that needed restructuring included the energy sector, including the oil and electricity producers. Mexico's critics also cite archaic labor laws and the power of corrupt union bosses as obstacles to progress. All in all, the remnants of a system that "makes a few people rich while hurting the poor and stifling Mexico's development" are still around.[11]

From Bust to Boom to Bust . . . When President Salinas took charge in 1988, there was little reason to cheer and even less reason to believe that he could slow the slide into economic oblivion. By 1988, multiple devaluations had reduced the value of the currency by nearly 100 percent. (It would continue to plummet into a bottomless pit until monetary reforms were put in place after 1995.) Within a few short years, however, he managed to work a small miracle, revitalizing an economy that had been heading toward collapse for a decade.

Salinas warmly embraced economic liberalism and gave new impetus to the free-trade policies initiated by his predecessor. Mexico had already moved away from traditional protectionism, opening up large parts of its economy to foreign competition. Accordingly, it joined the General Agreement on Trade and Tariffs (GATT) in 1987 and thereafter slashed its import tariffs. It was President Salinas, however, who first proposed a free-trade agreement with the United States and Canada and then spearheaded the negotiations that led to the signing of such an agreement in 1992.

But the good news for Mexico was not confined to trade relations. Real wages in manufacturing rebounded after a dismal six-year backward slide. Inflation fell from triple digits to levels not uncommon in Western countries, thanks to a tough austerity program Salinas put in place. Governmental belt-tightening turned a huge budget deficit into a slender surplus in 1991. In addition, Salinas pushed through an ambitious privatization program, selling off billions of dollars' worth of state-owned industrial assets and using most of the proceeds to reduce the national debt.

The key to Mexico's new export-driven economic development strategy was the North American Free Trade Agreement (NAFTA) with the United States and Canada. Mexico's trade with the United States rose rapidly between 1987 and 1991. At the end of the 1990s, trade with the United States accounted for 90 percent of Mexico's exports. (See Box 10.3.) Mexico's recovery was abruptly halted at the end of 1994. Under a much-needed currency reform, a new peso had been introduced in 1993, but came under strong pressure the following year. The Zedillo government's decision to devalue

What If? BOX 10.3

After NAFTA

What if the United States proposed taking the *N* out of NAFTA — that is, creating a free-trade zone that would encompass all Latin America? In fact, President Bill Clinton actually made such a proposal on February 26, 1997. The occasion was a joint news conference with his Chilean counterpart, Eduardo Frei Ruiz-Tagle. The timing was no mere coincidence: Chile is one of Latin America's economic success stories.

President Clinton argued that the United States could not afford to sit on the sidelines while other economic superpowers develop trade with Central and South America's democracies. "At the crossroad of trade among the world's most dynamic economies, Chile can be a cornerstone of the vibrant free-trade area we are working to build in our hemisphere," Clinton declared. If AFTA comes after NAFTA, the Americas would be the world's largest free-trade zone.

But being "in the zone" is not all that it's cracked up to be, according to NAFTA's opponents. For one thing, U.S. trade deficits with both Canada and Mexico ballooned after the treaty was ratified in 1993.

President Clinton did not manage to push the AFTA measure through Congress before the end of his second term expired, but it is not necessarily dead. Although the war on terrorism monopolized President George W. Bush's agenda after September 11, 2001, a future president could still decide to put his or her stamp on AFTA. If so, will it be the start of something bigger and better, or just bigger?

the peso in December triggered a financial crisis. In the next two days, huge sums of capital rushed out of the country. The exchange rate nose-dived and the stock market lost almost half its value in three months, sending shock waves north (and around the world).

In the postmortem that followed, analysts blamed the Mexican fall on two main factors. First, Mexico's current account deficit in 1994 was running at an unsustainable level. In other words, Mexico was living way beyond its means, borrowing too much short-term money from abroad to meet its obligations. Its current account deficit ballooned sixfold between 1990 and 1994, while its reserves dwindled. Second, a deeper, underlying cause of Mexico's insolvency was the paucity of domestic savings, which were declining by the year.

. . . Back to Boom? With the help of a massive multibillion-dollar rescue package arranged by the Clinton administration, President Zedillo managed to apply the brakes in time to prevent a disastrous crash. Zedillo's draconian measures brought pain in the form of steeply higher interest rates. At the same time, the government raised the value-added tax and cut its own spending. In 1996, foreign capital flowed back into Mexico, and the *bolsa,* Mexico's stock market, shot up. Foreign direct investment (FDI) rose steadily in the last half of the decade. Economic growth averaged more than 5 percent during this same period. Zedillo's "cure" for the country's economic ills was just what the doctor ordered.

Despite President Zedillo's success in restoring stability to Mexico's economy and finances after the collapse of the peso in 1994–1995, the problems facing his successor, Vicente Fox, are daunting. Average real wages in Mexico in 2000 were still lower than in 1982, when Mexico's economic time of troubles began.

In 2003, growth slowed to a modest 2–3 percent due in part to the economic recession in the United States, which absorbs 85 percent of Mexico's exports. The voters naturally blamed "the government" (though not the president). In the mid-2003 national elections for Congress, the PAN and the government lost 52 seats and gained less than a third of the votes cast. The left-leaning Party of the Democratic Revolution was the big winner, gaining 40 seats (going from 56 to 96 seats), and the PRI gained 15 seats (giving a total of 223, only 28 short of an absolute majority). But the biggest loser was democracy itself: almost three-fifths of the voters stayed home.

The outcome put the president in a weaker position to push ahead with badly needed institutional reforms that the previous Congress had resisted. Gone was any immediate hope that a new Congress would vote to allow private investment in Mexico's state oil and gas monopoly or to revise the irrational tax code. Nor would it be likely to shorten the term of the president and permit a second term (as in the United States) — a change that would give voters a stronger sense of democratic "ownership" now that a competitive three-party system has replaced the heavy hand of one-party rule. Thus, the prospects for progress on reform in the second half of President Fox's term were not good in the spring of 2004. The likelihood of a political stalemate that would leave Mexico's half-reformed economy in a holding pattern was far greater.

Mexico's Unfinished Business Mexico is still a developing country in many respects. Even the relatively robust economy of the 1990s brought modest yearly per capita GNP growth rates; too little to make much of a difference in the lives of most Mexicans.

Politically, the tasks of nation building — integrating the various parts of the country into a unified state and society — have not yet been completed. Myriad types of inequality exist in Mexican society. Three types in particular complicate the challenge of integration: economic, ethnic, and regional. The first form is related to class and caste, the second involves the oppressed condition of the Indian population, and the third is the result of geographically unbalanced economic development.

The mestizo population greatly outnumbers both Indian and Spanish elements in Mexico. Nonetheless, distinct Indian tribes or ethnic groups still number more than two hundred and speak some fifty languages and dialects. Indians are often the victims of discrimination, and many Spanish-speaking Mexicans see them as hindering social progress.

Another obstacle to integration is Mexico's regionalism. Many Mexicans identify with a specific region more strongly than with the nation itself. One observer claims there are at least five distinct regions within Mexico: Metromex — Mexico City and its environs; New Spain — the old colonial heartland; Mexamerica — the progressive northern region along the Mexican-American border; South Mexico — the poor, underdeveloped, predominantly Indian nation between Mexico City and Guatemala; and Club Mex — the wealthy resort areas of both coasts.[12] These regions vary a great deal in terms of average income levels and overall economic development.

Mexico City alone accounts for one-half of Mexico's industry and more than one-third of its total GNP. But Metromex also illustrates the sharp class divisions within Mexican society. In addition to the wealthy elite, some 2 to 3 million government employees, entrepreneurs, and unionized workers enjoyed job security and a rising standard of living before the slump in the 1980s eroded the income security of this sizable middle class.

The teeming underclass, however, remained terribly deprived: half of Mexico City's poor lived without running water, 40 percent had no health care, and a quarter had too little to eat. One of Mexico City's worst health problems, smog, was not confined in its effects on the poor. Air pollution in the capital assaulted everyone. Nor were environmental issues confined to Mexico City or even to domestic politics. Mexico's failure to enforce environmental policies was a major issue for some opponents of NAFTA in the United States.

In Sum . . . Mexico made significant progress toward alleviating its large assortment of social, economic, and political problems in the 1990s. The population explosion is being contained — birthrates have dropped steadily since the 1970s (but remain well above Western rates). Under the leadership of Presidents Salinas and Zedillo, Mexico instituted market reforms as part of an export-driven development strategy. At the same time, it exposed its own industries to foreign competition. These measures, together with NAFTA, were a tonic for a society that had fallen into a deep malaise in the 1980s. The election of Vicente Fox as president in 2000 raised the possibility that Mexico was poised — however precariously — on the edge of a new era of democracy and prosperity. Mexico's economy was on a glide path to higher growth and consumer prices were falling to single digits.[13] Cause for optimism faded by 2003, however, as both the reforms and the economy stalled. The outlook turned bleak following the congressional elections of July 2003, when most voters stayed away from the polls and only about 30 percent of those who did cast a ballot voted for the president's National Action Party.

Mexico's liberal constitution is not enough to guarantee meaningful democracy. Similarly, Brazil's movement toward democracy in the 1980s, known as the *aberatura,* did not fix everything that was wrong with Brazilian politics. Even so, free elections in January 1985 signaled the end of two decades of military rule and the beginning of a new political experiment in Brazil. Next we look at how that experiment is working out.

Brazil: Lula to the Rescue

Brazil's motto, *Ordem e Progresso* ("Order and Progress"), has been emblazoned on its flag since the founding of the republic in 1889, and those two aims have been paramount ever since. Liberty is not mentioned, nor is equality, and order comes before progress. The motto sums up over a century of Brazilian history.

A Not-So-Gentle Giant

In many ways, the Amazon is a metaphor for the sprawling giant called Brazil. It is the world's fifth largest country (roughly equal in size to the United States and the fourth largest democracy; it also boasts one of the world's ten largest economies. Brazil accounts for a third of the region's population and around 40 percent of South America's GNP. It has an industrial economy with income levels near the top of developing nations. However, Brazil's political-economic system, like the Amazon rain forest, is a jungle — dense and potentially dangerous. Brazil has been buffeted by the boom and bust tendencies of an evolving market economy at the mercy of maverick business cycles. In the early 1980s, it was an economic recession that induced the military to relinquish power. In the early 1990s, a second recession severely strained Brazil's new political institutions. In the late 1990s, a third one put President Cardoso's ability to lead the country in jeopardy.

Brazil has made significant strides, if not giant steps, into the upper ranks of the world's nation-states. In terms of economic development, it is a middle-income country. In purchasing power parity (PPP), the most meaningful basis for comparison, it had a per capita GNP in the range of $6,500 in 2000. That figure was only about one-half that of Portugal and Greece, the poorest EU countries, but it was three times that of neighboring Bolivia, one of the poorest countries in South America. Measured by the UN human development index (a tool for comparing the quality of life in different countries), socioeconomic standards have improved steadily in recent decades. In 1998, the UN gave Brazil a high rating in human development, ahead of both Turkey and Saudi Arabia.

But Brazil remains a society of extremes. The modern cities and rural areas of south-central Brazil are relatively prosperous and can be compared to the not-so-prosperous parts of southern Europe. But the interior of the northeast is blighted and impoverished. Some 50 million Brazilians (nearly one-third of the population) live in abject poverty. However, as Brazil's President Cardoso remarked in his first inaugural address, the problem is not that Brazil is underdeveloped but that it is unjust. In terms of region, social group, and race, Brazil is one of the most unequal countries in a region noted for its inequalities. A survey in 1995 found that nearly two-thirds of total income went to the top one-fifth (20 percent) of the population; the bottom one-fifth subsisted on a mere 2.5 percent of the income.

Thus, social and economic inequality remains a stark reality in Brazil more than a decade after the arrival of democracy. The cry for land reform has grown ever more vociferous. Thousands of squatters have invaded the fringes of farms and ranches owned by land barons, with the encouragement of a grassroots political action group. Another problem is police violence. The police in Brazil afford little protection for the poor. For example, in April 1996, police shot and killed nineteen people who were demonstrating for land in the Amazon state of Para. There were unconfirmed reports that ten or more of the victims were killed after being arrested and that local landowners contracted for the killings. True or false, allegations of this sort would seem far-fetched in most countries today, particularly democratic ones. In Brazil, given the reputation for brutality the police there have earned, such is not the case.

A Dualistic Political Tradition

In Brazil, the concept of progress has long been linked with a strong state. Throughout Brazil's history, the military has played a key role in domestic politics, but it has not always exercised power directly. Nor has it been a highly conservative force in Brazilian politics (as is often the case in countries with a history of military intervention) — quite the opposite has been the case.

Radicals in Uniform: Military Modernizers In the 1920s, disenchanted middle-class groups joined junior military officers (*tenentes*) in opposing an oligarchy representing the interests of entrenched coffee plantation owners. They believed that the military alone could awaken the nation, unlock its pent-up energies, and spearhead modernization. They wanted to oust conservative politicians who blocked the path of progress. The *tenentes'* program included labor reforms such as recognition of trade unions, a minimum wage and a maximum workweek, and regulation of child labor. It also called for land reform, state ownership of natural resources, and expansion of the public school system.

The *tenentes* faded into history, but Getúlio Vargas, who staged a revolution in 1930, established a fascist-style corporatist state, and ruled as a benevolent dictator until 1945 when the generals forced him to resign, adopted many of their ideas. Brazil was democratically governed and the voting population (electorate) steadily grew in the two decades that followed.

In the 1950s, Brazil's economy improved, foreign investment (especially in auto plants) brought new jobs, and the government moved from São Paulo to Brasília — the new capital built in the interior. In the 1960s, when inflation began rising sharply and the economy stalled, the military watched with growing alarm. Inflammatory rhetoric by leftist President João Goulart was the last straw: when Goulart called for revolutionary changes in Brazilian society and political institutions, the military stepped in.

The 1964 Coup: Revolution from Above For the next eighteen years, Brazil was governed by a parade of civilian presidents. The parade ended abruptly in 1964 when the military — disgruntled by the leftist leanings of the president and by his failure to curb rampant inflation and official corruption — staged a bloodless coup. The military did not view this intervention as anything ordinary; it was the start of a revolution from above. As if to pick up where the *tenentes* and Vargas had left off, the military launched a major modernization drive. They would have order with progress, but it would come at the expense of freedom and dignity. Strict press censorship was imposed, and flagrant abuses of human rights became commonplace.

In the decade following the revolution of 1964, Brazil experienced an economic miracle, with growth rates averaging 10 percent a year. But the benefits went primarily to the upper and middle classes; they did not trickle down to the vast majority of Brazilians, who continued to live in poverty. Brazil's development strategy was flawed: it stressed industrialization, mechanization, and capital-intensive investment, to the detriment of labor-intensive, low-tech enterprises, agriculture, and public-works projects.

During the 1970s, the miracle turned into a nightmare. A worldwide recession triggered by the OPEC oil embargo hit Brazil especially hard. Energy import prices shot skyward, while the price of agricultural products (about 40 percent of Brazil's exports) fell sharply. Meanwhile, the deteriorating rural economy led to a mass migration into overcrowded cities, where basic services could not keep pace. Brazil's military rulers were slowly rediscovering the advantages of civilian government.

The Great *Aberatura*

The reforms of the late 1970s set the stage for a democratic reform movement, the ***aberatura*** (opening). Hundreds of political exiles were allowed to return, and political parties were permitted, as long as they were not ideological and did not target a single class: the Communist Party was outlawed, and a workers' party was expressly forbidden as well. (The ban on parties of the left was lifted in 1985.)

The prohibition against a British-style labor party reflected the regime's preoccupation with order and its awareness that the crippled economy, coupled with the mass discontent this engendered, could be profoundly destabilizing. The situation was alarming, in part because government and labor in Brazil had long enjoyed a relationship of mutual trust and dependency. Organized labor expected the state to protect its interests; demands for democracy were secondary. If the government, be it authoritarian or democratic, could deliver on promises of benefits to the workers, labor would support it. The government's failure in the 1970s and early 1980s to protect the workers in conditions of economic crisis severely strained this long-standing compact. Facing hyperinflation, surging food prices, and massive unemployment, labor defected in 1983, joining the rising chorus of voices demanding direct elections and civilian rule.

The military bowed out quietly in 1985. For the first time in two decades, the Brazilian people were allowed to go to the polls and vote for a civilian president.

Brazil's Political System: Federal and Presidential

Brazil is arguably the only true federal system in Latin America. Its twenty-six states, plus the Federal District of Brasília, play an important role in governing. On the surface, the parallels with the system in the United States are obvious. Each of the states elects a governor, lieutenant governor, and legislators, who serve four-year terms. The elected state assemblies, however, are all unicameral (having only one chamber). In the United States, only Nebraska has a unicameral legislature.

There are other important differences, as well. For example, state governments in Brazil own banks and industrial enterprises. These assets — operated by economic bureaucracies of a kind not found in the United States — give the states considerable clout in dealing with the federal government. In fact, until the 1930s the states had the upper hand. Since then, there has been a tug of war between the state governments and national government. It is a contest neither side ever wins or loses. In a sense, it is the contest that counts because it allows the political system to strike a balance between the need for national unity and the desire for local control.

The National Government Brazil's president is both the head of government (the role played by prime ministers in parliamentary systems) and the head of state. Thus, despite repeated calls for conversion to a British-style parliamentary system, Brazil remains a presidential democracy similar to that of the United States. This pattern is found throughout Latin America.

Brazil's president and vice president are elected for four-year terms. In 1997, President Cardoso seized an opportunity afforded by his strong standing in the opinion polls to push an amendment through the Congress allowing Brazil's chief executive, for the first time in the nation's history, to stand for immediate reelection. Cardoso did so the following year and was elected in a landslide.

Like the U.S. Congress, Brazil's national congress is bicameral, and, like the U.S. Congress, the powers of the two houses are carefully balanced — both can initiate legislation and they share the power to pass on the national budget. Instead of having two senators from each state in the upper house (Senate), Brazil has three, and instead of six-year terms, they serve for eight years. But, as in the United States, Senate elections are staggered so that substantial continuity of membership is ensured. Deputies in the lower house (Chamber of Deputies) are elected according to population but, in contrast to the U.S. House of Representatives, serve four-year terms instead of two-year terms.

Critics often say that representative democracy in Brazil is flawed in at least one important respect. Membership in the lower house, they say, was deliberately designed by the military regime to overrepresent the northeast and the new states of the Amazon — areas of strong traditional support. Although the military has left the political center stage, the problem is still not fixed because representatives of the favored parts can unite across party lines to block any attempts at reapportionment.

The Brazilian congress has powers similar to those of the U.S. Congress, including the right to approve or reject the budget, to initiate and pass on all proposed laws, to reject presidential policy initiatives (including emergency measures), and to override presidential vetoes. The power to conduct investigative hearings into executive-branch activities was demonstrated several times in the 1990s. In 1992, for example, the Congress, under heavy pressure from an outraged public, voted to impeach President Fernando Collor de Mello for his alleged role in a massive corruption scandal (detailed later).

Like the United States, Brazil has both a federal court system and a system of state courts. The supreme court, like that of the United States, has the power of judicial review — that is, it can overturn legislation that it deems "unconstitutional" (at odds with Brazil's constitution). It also has the power to try presidents and members of congress charged with crimes. In 1994, it acquitted former President Collor of criminal charges in connection with the corruption scandal mentioned above, citing insufficient evidence.

The Supreme Court sits atop a federal judicial system that includes several layers of inferior courts — a superior court of justice, regional federal appeals courts, and district judges. In addition, the federal system includes parallel structures comprising labor courts, electoral courts, and military courts. (Perhaps special electoral courts is what the United States needed to resolve the legal disputes in Florida in 2000 when the outcome of the presidential election there was way too close for anybody's comfort.)

A Presidency Ready for Any Emergency . . . Prior to the return of democracy in 1985, the military ruled through hated "decree-laws" — edicts issued from on high without legislative or judicial review. The 1988 constitution incorporated a modified form of that executive rule-making power, allowing Brazil's presidents to resort to so-called provisional measures, which take effect immediately upon publication. The framers of the constitution wanted to make certain the government would not be paralyzed in times of crisis or emergencies. But the constitution does not define the circumstances that qualify as an emergency, thus leaving the door ajar for a strong-willed president who wishes to circumvent the congress. Since the return to democracy,

Brazil's first four presidents have broadly interpreted this power, issuing hundreds of decrees. The congress can nullify these decrees by voting disapproval or simply taking no action for thirty days. In fact, congress rejects (or refuses to endorse) the majority of presidential decrees, but presidents can simply reissue decrees they deem necessary.

Brazil's presidents are well equipped to govern in other ways, too. Most importantly, only the chief executive can initiate appropriations measures. Unlike the U.S. Congress, which has a well-staffed Congressional Budget Office (CBO), Brazil's Congress must rely entirely on the executive branch to draft the annual budget. In addition, only the president can initiate measures related to the size of the armed forces, the cabinet and other public offices, and the pay levels of public employees.

The president also has a power reminiscent of the French presidency. He or she can declare a piece of proposed legislation to be "urgent" and force the Congress to rearrange its own legislative agenda by giving priority treatment to measures the president considers most important. In practice, Brazil's presidents have made extensive use of this rather unusual executive prerogative.

Finally, Brazil's president, like his American counterpart, can veto legislation, either in full or in part. President Clinton asked Congress to give him the power to make a "line item" (partial) veto, but it was denied. By contrast, Brazil's president can strike bits and pieces of budget legislation he does not like without rejecting the whole budget (and potentially bringing the government to a standstill). American presidents, of course, do not have that luxury. Brazil's Congress can override a presidential veto, but attempts to do so fail nine times out of ten (literally).

In Brazil as in the United States, it takes an active legislature with a vigorous opposition to keep the president honest and to prevent the abuse of executive power. One key to having a legislature that functions properly is having a sound electoral system — the link between elections and legislatures is also the main link between government and the people in a democracy. Elections depend on political parties to provide voters with clear and meaningful choices among competing candidates and courses of action.

Parties and Elections

One measure of Brazil's march toward democracy is the number of political parties that now contest elections. Before 1979, two official parties monopolized the political marketplace. In the 1982 elections, there were five parties and immediately after the restoration of civilian rule in 1985 that number more than doubled. The emergence of various new parties with divergent platforms and programs is a crude measure of democracy's advance in Brazil. At present there are more than a dozen political parties represented in the Brazilian congress, and the party spectrum is broad enough to offer something for nearly everyone, from the far left to the far right and various points in between.

The Birth of a Party System From 1965 to 1979, the military regime maintained a virtual party monopoly. There were only two legal parties in Brazil: the progovernment ARENA Party and the opposition Brazilian Democratic Movement (MDB). The generals, however, dictated the extent to which the "opposition" was allowed to oppose the government. In 1979, the military relaxed its ban on new political parties hoping to split the MDB and thereby head off a fast-rising challenge. This divide and conquer strategy was accompanied by an effort to change the government party's image. The ARENA Party was reconstituted as the Social Democratic Party (PDS) in the early 1980s; by that time, the old MDB had become the new PMDB (its founders simply added the word *party* to the name). The worsening economy, domestic discontent, international pressure, and the winds of change wafting across the region in the 1980s all combined to nudge the military over the edge — and out of power.

As the 1985 elections approached, political maneuvering intensified. A dissident faction of the right-wing PDS split away to form the Liberal Front Party (PFL), which subsequently entered into a coalition with the center-left PMDB. The coalition, known as the Democratic Alliance, challenged the PDS in the electoral college and won. José Sarney was the PFL's candidate; when the coalition was formed, Sarney was given the number two spot on the ticket. Tancredo Neves, the PMDB candidate, headed the winning ticket but died before he was sworn in. As the leader of a small splinter party, Sarney became Brazil's first civilian president in over twenty years.

The 1985 Electoral Reform Liberalization was advanced in the spring of 1985 when the congress legislated several significant changes in the electoral system. First, as mentioned earlier, it abolished the electoral college and provided for direct election of the president. Second, it required direct election of state governors and mayors of cities with at least 200,000 voters (if no candidate receives a majority, a runoff election decides the winner). Third, it eliminated literacy as a voting requirement, thereby expanding the electorate by 20 million voters. Fourth, it abolished the party loyalty rule, which obligated members of the congress to vote the party line and penalized party defectors. Fifth, it eased the establishment of new political parties and legalized communist parties.

Brazil uses three different methods of election. We have already noted that presidents, state governors, and big-city mayors are directly elected by absolute majority vote (requiring a runoff if no candidate gets 50 percent. In the second type of election, senators and mayors of cities with less than 200,000 voters are elected in a first past the post system (as in the United States and Britain) — that is, from single-member districts with only a plurality of the vote needed to win. In the third type, deputies at the federal and state levels are elected by "open list" proportional representation (PR) from multimember districts. In an open-list PR system, parties sponsor multiple candidates in each voting district but they cannot rank these candidates (so party leaders cannot reward party loyalty or punish disloyalty at election time). In other words, voters are free to choose the candidates they like and party affiliation is secondary if not irrelevant. In contrast to the closed PR systems used in most countries, Brazil's system gives the voters, not the parties, the right to decide which candidates win seats.

Opening a Pandora's Box The change in Brazil's electoral laws opened a Pandora's box from which all sorts of upstart parties sprang. Two of Brazil's three largest parties occupy the political center — the PMDB and the Party of Brazilian Social Democracy (PSDB), formed in 1998 by the current president, Fernando Henrique Cardoso. Cardoso's party, the PSDB, had the second largest block of congressional seats after the 1999 election, and the PMDB, the main opposition party, came in third. (See Figures 10.7 and 10.8.)

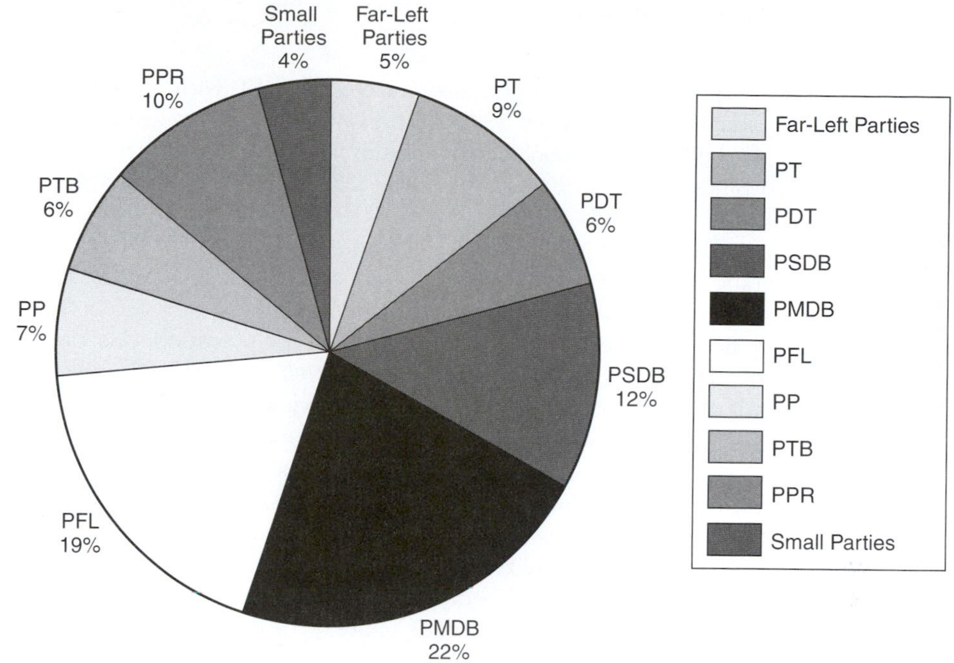

Figure 10.7 Party Representation in Brazil's Congress 1995 Election

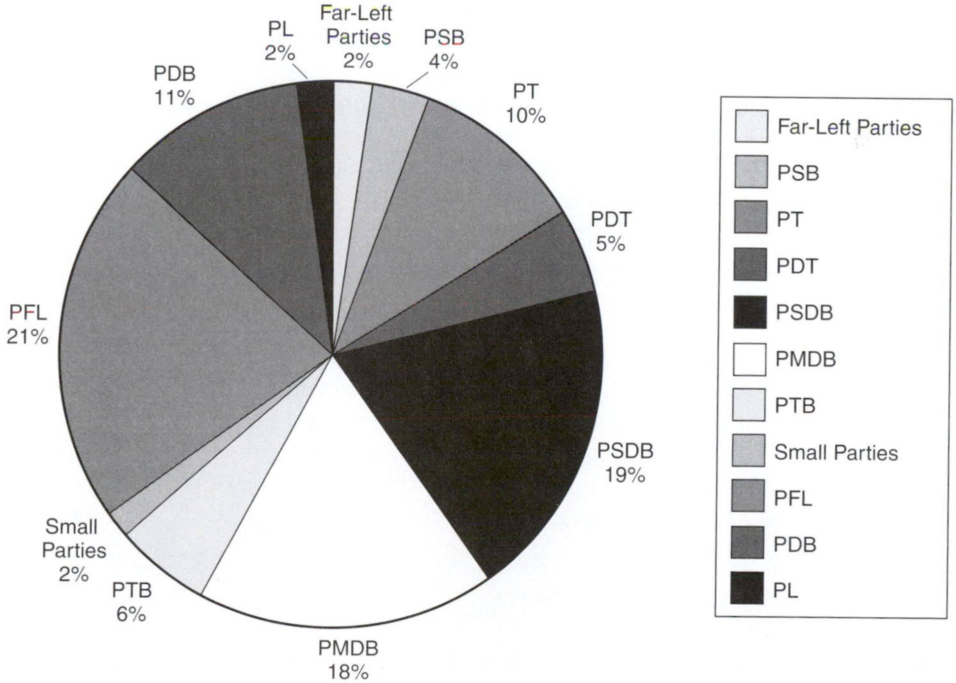

Figure 10.8 Brazil's Party "Pie" after 1999

The main center-right party today is the PFL with roots in the old ARENA Party (later the PDS). In the 1999 elections, the PFL came away with the largest number of seats (about 25 percent of the total) in the congress. Farther to the right is the pro-business Brazilian Progressive Party (PPB) — second largest conservative party. The PFL and the PPB generally back the Cardoso administration.

The most important parties on the left are the Worker's Party (PT) and the Democratic Labor Party (PDT). The PT is not a typical Brazilian political party. It is dominated by an odd combination of intellectuals and workers. Its delegates vote a strict party line, do not cross the isle (switch parties), and do not promise special favors to the party faithful. This rejection of what is known as *clientelism* sets the PT apart from Brazilian parties and the prevailing political culture, which views political favoritism (clientism) as quite normal. Both are center-left, non-Marxist, pro-labor parties. The PDT favors welfare-state policies and considers itself a social democratic party. The PT stresses the need for further democratization of the political process. Farther to the left are the Socialists, who hold twenty-one seats. The Communists have a tiny following but the very fact that they exist, ironically, symbolizes Brazil's new commitment to a political process open to all. In part because the left is so badly fragmented in Brazil (as elsewhere in Latin America), the probability of a serious challenge from this side of the political spectrum is low.

Why Brazil's Parties Are So Weak Brazil's political parties are weak, even when they appear strong. In other words, even the major parties — the PFL, the PSDB, and the PMDB — have shallow roots in Brazilian society. Why? First, as elsewhere in Latin America, politics has always focused on personalities — on the prestige and charisma of individuals rather than on the philosophy (ideas) and program (policies) of competing parties. The culture of personalistic politics is at odds with the culture of party politics because the forces at work in these two cultures are so very different. In the first, the glue that holds a political support group together is a single leader; in the second, the glue is a common set of ideals or interests (or both).

Some critics cite a second reason for Brazil's weak parties, namely the current electoral system in which deputies are chosen by open-list proportional representation. As we noted earlier, that system pits candidates from the same party against each other because voters choose from open lists in voting districts where many seats are up for grabs. This system encourages voters to support a candidate (based on personality) rather a party (based on program). According to one theory of democracy, strong political parties are necessary to give voters opportunities to make clear choices about the direction they want the country to take. Without strong parties, meaningful elections (the most important means of mass participation in democracy) are impossible, according to this view. Do the flaws in its institutions endanger Brazil's democracy? We explore this question as part of a broader look at Brazil's prospects for the future in the next section.

Problems and Prospects

Unlike Mexico, Brazil has endured frequent changes in its political and constitutional system over the past half century — a period that has nonetheless witnessed the transformation of Brazilian society from traditional and agrarian to modern and industrial.

This dramatic change has been engineered by the state, whether in the hands of civilian or military rulers. Today, Brazil is in the process of reinventing its economy — mainly by reducing the role of the state — in an effort to accelerate growth, create new jobs, reduce socioeconomic inequality, and compete successfully in world markets. The task of directing this postindustrial economic revolution has fallen to Brazil's new generation of popularly elected civilian leaders who are simultaneously testing a new set of political institutions. We turn to that topic first.

The Politics of Confusion Brazil's military junta relinquished power to a civilian president in 1985. The promised new constitution was completed in 1988, after the constituent assembly considered more than 10,000 proposals. Two critical issues were resolved. First, the constituent assembly decided to maintain a presidential system rather than switch to a parliamentary system, and second, it extended the president's term from four years to five.

The proceedings of the constituent assembly reflected the nation's confused and chaotic political situation. In November 1986, Brazilians elected 559 delegates (*constituintes*) to the constituent assembly to draft the new constitution. The Brazilian Democratic Movement Party (PMDB) controlled 307 delegates on paper; in reality, nearly three-fourths of the PMDB's original *constituintes* came from the extinct ARENA Party. As a result of opportunistic party switching and reshuffling that took place after the ban on new political parties was lifted in the early 1980s, party affiliations were neither a reliable guide to political convictions nor even a sure sign of party loyalties. The constituent assembly resembled a three-ring circus.

The confusion in drafting the new constitution was mirrored in the government, where the majority PMDB was a hodgepodge of right-wing, moderate, liberal, and left-wing politicians. The PMDB was hampered by intense factionalism, and there was some speculation that it might even break up into rival parties. One Brazilian party had already self-destructed. The Social Democratic Party (PDS), the descendant of the right-wing ARENA Party once headed by President Sarney himself, disintegrated in 1985 when its members defected. Sarney had virtually no power base of his own. Instead, he had to court PMDB chieftains in congress and try to ingratiate himself with the electorate by pretending to be a born-again populist. The result was disarray and drift.

The Debt Moratorium President Sarney's government was chaotic, and so was the economy. His economic cabinet was a revolving door: in the first eighteen months there were three finance ministers, two economic planning ministers, and four central bank presidents. In late February 1987, Brazil suspended interest payments on its huge commercial bank debt, which amounted to roughly 60 percent of its total foreign debt. It was one step away from a default. What motivated him to take such drastic action?

Brazil's mounting debt occurred against a backdrop of hyperinflation, budget deficits, and high unemployment. Even in less extreme circumstances, the debt burden might well have been unbearable. From 1983 to 1986, Brazil made interest payments totaling billions of dollars each year, while imposing austerity measures prescribed by the International Monetary Fund. (During that period, Brazil's debt payments alone accounted for almost 20 percent of Citicorp's profits.) In 1986, Brazil's trade surplus was $2 billion less than its debt-service payments. Meanwhile, the country was enduring a recession and receiving little new money from overseas commercial banks.

President Sarney's initial efforts to deal with the nation's economic problems had an Alice-in-Wonderland quality about them. His stabilization plan created a new unit of currency (the *cruzado*), froze wages and prices, and abolished indexation (pay hikes pegged to inflation). At first, the ***cruzado* plan** seemed to work, but not for long:

> One month after [the plan] was introduced in February 1986, inflation fell to zero. An artificial boom followed as wages temporarily outpaced inflation. Profits soared. The São Paulo stock market doubled in a single month. The unknown Sarney became popular. But by the summer of 1986 acute shortages had appeared. . . . Relative prices became absurd. Typewriters, assuming you could find them, were cheaper than shoes. Meanwhile the Central Bank kept money loose, feeding inflation. By fall inflation was raging. By June 1987 it exceeded 1,900 percent and interest rates were nearly 30 percent a month. The stock market fell 90 percent in real terms. The country's trade surplus nearly disappeared, despite falling prices and interest rates.[14]

In April 1987, Sarney again changed his economic team and unveiled a new stabilization plan, which called for a ninety-day freeze on wages and prices, forbade automatic wage adjustments, and accelerated currency devaluation to spur exports. These measures achieved at least partial success as Brazil's trade balance improved and inflation came down somewhat.

Slight improvements, however, could hardly mitigate the effects of previous policies. Hyperinflation and unemployment had hit labor and the poor in a way that spurred economic crimes such as robbery and shoplifting. Bizarre events suggested the dimensions of social discontent:

> In late May, near São Paulo, hungry people attacked garbage workers and battled them for the garbage. In early June, Rio bus ticket prices were raised by 50 percent, provoking huge downtown riots. . . . The situation has become even worse in . . . Brazil's poorest areas. Each week about 200 buses arrive in São Paulo from northern regions filled with refugees. They survive in makeshift huts, huddled against the city's damp nights.[15]

Changing his mind again, Sarney announced in early 1988 that he would lift Brazil's foreign debt moratorium (and cover at least some overdue interest payments). He also agreed to negotiate an austerity program with the IMF — a clear signal of his intention to shift from confrontation to conciliation.

President Sarney had stepped back from the brink but appeared to be improvising rather than following a rational plan. Lacking a popular mandate, dependent on opportunistic PMDB politicians, and incapable of forging a national consensus, Sarney was not willing or able to administer the medicine Brazil's sickly economy needed. At one point, for example, his economic advisers had urged him to reduce government spending by trimming hundreds of thousands of federal jobs. Sarney refused, expanding the public payrolls instead.

Thus, Brazil had neither order nor progress. Would the generals tolerate the lack of order? Would the public tolerate the lack of progress? Brazil was in dire need of a good national leader at the end of the 1980s. In the 1989 presidential election, Fernando Collor de Mello of the National Reconstruction Party (PRN) won a narrow victory, advocating free-market policies and a crackdown on corruption in high places. Was he the political savior Brazil was looking for?

In Search of Leadership Compared to the United States, Brazil's democracy was unlucky in its infancy. The first American president, George Washington, is often called "the father of his country" — a measure of the public's esteem both then and now. He was greatly trusted by the American people and never betrayed that trust. More than leader, Washington was a legend. John Adams, Thomas Jefferson, and James Madison succeeded him. The prestige of these first presidents was an important factor in helping America's young democracy get its feet on the ground.

By contrast, Brazil's first elected president, Tancredo Neves, died before taking office. His successor, José Sarney, had little prestige, no popular mandate, and no party base. Brazil's next president, Fernando Collor de Mello, proved singularly unworthy of the public's trust and was impeached. What this betrayal meant for a country with a brand new presidential-style democracy merits a closer look.

The Col(l)or of Money After a year in office, Collor had failed to make progress in stabilizing Brazil's economy, and public discontent with his anti-inflation program was rising. In 1991, he announced a new "national reconstruction plan." The plan called for a wide array of tax and administrative reforms, incentives for business, greater privatization, debt renegotiation, and many other bold features — it contained something for everyone. Collor's plan and the swearing in of newly elected governors in twenty-four states raised the hopes of some political analysts. But events dashed the prospects for a new order in Brazil. In August 1991, news reports linked the Bank of Credit and Commerce International (BCCI) to prominent Brazilian citizens. The BCCI scandal did not touch President Collor, but it proved to be the tip of an iceberg of corruption in Brazilian politics. In 1992, another scandal involving millions of dollars in illegal payments and benefits from business interests to Collor and his inner circle outraged the public.[16] The funds were received by a cabal made up of Collor's family and friends in exchange for lucrative government contracts. Collor feigned indignation but resigned in disgrace after congress impeached him and installed Vice President Itamar Franco in his place. The congress banned Collor from political office for eight years; nonetheless, revelations about the Collor family's tawdry dealings had undermined any residue of public trust in government.

Will the "Real" President Please Stand? Brazil's democracy was rattled but not derailed by the Collor scandal. The presidential election in 1994 proceeded smoothly. It was won by the candidate of the Social Democratic Party, Fernando Henrique Cardoso, who as finance minister in the previous administration had earned public confidence by taming the beast of inflation with his ***real* plan** — named after Brazil's new currency, the *real,* which was the heart of the plan. In 1996, Cardoso ran into difficulties getting a proposal to reform the budget-busting national pension system through the congress, and his popularity fell to new lows after the government decided to raise the minimum wage by an amount well below the rate of inflation as part of an overall austerity drive (spending cuts).

Cardoso earned high marks for curbing inflation, which had fallen to about 7 percent in the fall of 2000 (compared to 40 percent a month in mid-1994, when Cardoso's *real* plan first took effect). The economy Cardoso inherited, however, had structural problems similar to other traditional economies in Latin America. State monopolies operated in many strategic sectors, including petroleum exploration and refining, telecommunications, mining, and coastal shipping. At President Cardoso's urging, the constituent assembly voted to end these monopolies in 1995. This bold structural reform was necessary, according to many economists, in order to reinvigorate the economy (which it appears to have done), but it also caused painful adjustments (such as a short-term loss of jobs).

Other old structures were also getting in the way of progress. The welfare system was near bankruptcy in 1996. Government pensioners alone were getting 42 percent of the federal payroll in 1996, more than government employees were paying in by a large margin. (Some public workers have the right to retire at age forty-five on pensions 20 percent above salary.) Cardoso's attempt to fix the public-sector pension problem was overruled by the supreme court in 1999. The tax system and the bureaucracy, too, are due for an overhaul; for example, many public employees are guaranteed jobs for life, making it difficult for a budget-conscious government to downsize the bloated bureaucracy. Without politically unpopular changes in the pension and tax systems, there can be little hope of cutting the troublesome federal deficit.

Belt-tightening is never popular. The biggest obstacles to change, however, are constitutional and political. Many of the Cardoso reforms require amendments to the 1988 constitution. That means the constituent assembly and the supreme court have ample opportunity to defeat, obstruct, or delay the government's initiatives.

How Cardoso "Devalued" Globalization Brazil's economy grew steadily after 1993, leading to a second resounding electoral victory for Cardoso in the fall of 1998. A few months later, emboldened by a fresh mandate and under heavy international pressure, he dropped a bombshell, announcing without warning that Brazil was devaluing its currency, the *real.* Cardoso blamed Brazil's economic ills — in particular, balance of trade (or "current account") deficits and a weak currency — on what he called "asymmetric globalization." These nagging problems, and the resulting need for IMF loans to prop up the *real,* induced the government to fight inflation at the expense of growth by adopting an emergency program of high interest rates, spending cuts, and tax hikes — in the language of Brazilian politics, to opt for "stability" at the expense of "development." According to Cardoso, the free financial markets underpinning the world economy amount to a "protectionism of the strongest" in which "perverse processes" can "turn markets into casinos." (The reader will perhaps recognize the similarity of Cardoso's rhetoric to that of the dependency theorists discussed in Chapter 2.)

The devaluation was done for political as well as economic reasons. The Brazilian economy was growing and most people were better off, but growing unemployment had put the middle class on edge and the business elite was balking at high interest rates. Meanwhile, Cardoso's agenda of reform was far from complete. He could anticipate opposition from the congress, the courts, and the public. His center-right political coalition in the congress (consisting of social democrats, liberals, and conservatives) was far from rock-solid. By taking this bold action and couching it in nationalistic rhetoric, Cardoso probably hoped to blunt attacks from opposition parties, labor unions, and big business and buy precious time for his economic "medicine" to work.

Not surprisingly, the anti-inflation measures mentioned earlier pushed the Brazilian economy into a temporary downturn. Cardoso's rating in public opinion polls dropped to new lows. That, in turn, jeopardized economic reform by weakening the president's hand vis-à-vis both the congress and the supreme court. Nonetheless, the economy recovered quickly, growing at 11–12 percent annually over the next three years (1999–2001).[17] It plunged into negative territory in 2002, however, setting the stage for a populist candidate to win the presidential election in October.

Lula: Poverty to Presidency Everyone loves a rags-to-riches story, but such stories are rare in real life, especially in Latin America where wealth and power are synonymous and few ladders from lower to higher social classes exist. But in 2002, the son of an illiterate farm worker, one of twenty-two children, who started out as a shoeshine boy received some 53 million votes for president — 20 million more than his runoff opponent. Luiz Inácio Lula da Silva was elected in a landslide, but his left-wing Workers' Party won only 91 seats of 513 in the chamber of deputies. Although this total represented an increase of 33 seats (more than one-third), Lula's party was outnumbered by more than five to one in Congress. The good news was that no other party had more seats; the bad news was (and is) that no fewer than eleven parties are represented in the congress, not counting the small bloc of independents.

Lula faced two huge hurdles upon taking office. First, the left orientation of Workers' Party was anathema to the business community and foreign investors who play a crucial role in making or breaking any government's economic program. To succeed in stabilizing the economy, Lula would have to find a way to reassure corporations and financial markets: (1) that he did not intend to default on Brazil's huge public debt; (2) that he would act decisively to cut Brazil's chronic budget deficits; and (3) that he would stay the course of economic reforms undertaken by his predecessor. Second, Lula had to knock together a working majority in Congress without alienating his miniscule coalition partners (the liberals and the communists). Exactly how he might negotiate this hurdle when three of the four largest parties were right-of-center (with a combined total of 207 votes) was a mystery. The fact that the centrist PSDB still held 71 votes in the new Congress appeared to give the opposition the upper hand in any legislative-executive showdown. About the only thing Lula had in his favor was his popular mandate — and that would evaporate if Brazil were to sink into an all-too-familiar morass again.

In Sum . . . To conclude, the history of Brazil is a paradox — progress and injustice have gone hand in hand. Who is to blame for the injustice is less important than what can be done to ensure that progress continues and that rich and poor alike enjoy the benefits of prosperity. Prosperity depends on a robust market economy, but justice depends on good government. By any reasonable standards of justice, Brazil has a history of less-than-good government and millions of Brazil's poor have never had a taste of anything resembling prosperity.

On the positive side, civilian presidents have ruled Brazil since 1985. There have been several peaceful transfers of power based on the outcome of free and fair elections. The military has stayed on the sidelines even in times of political and economic turbulence. Finally, the Cardoso presidency could be a turning point if Brazilians demand the same high standards of decency and competency from Cardoso's successors. However, in early 2004 President Lula de Silva and the governing Worker's Party faced a serious challenge stemming from a damning videotape that showed a senior government official soliciting campaign funds in return for political favors. Lula promptly fired the official involved, but the political fallout was potentially damaging to Lula and the government.[18]

Brazil has enormous untapped human and natural resources, but the future depends above all on a change in political culture. At the risk of trivializing the challenges that lie ahead, it is tempting to say that all Brazil has to do is solve the riddle of politics — how to forge political and social consensus while fostering economic competition — to become a major power in the twenty-first century.

SUMMARY

During the 1980s, much of Latin America underwent a remarkable political metamorphosis from military to civilian rule — in many cases, engineered by the military. The new democratically elected leaders, however, faced daunting tasks. In most countries, the military had badly mismanaged the economy; in a few, a huge foreign debt had accumulated. Economic crisis has contributed to social unrest, exacerbated by the severe maldistribution of wealth and the resulting class tensions that have always characterized these societies. Although the transition to democracy was accomplished without bloodshed or social upheaval, the consolidation of constitutional government continues to be impeded by economic ills, social inequities, and political corruption in many countries. The durability of democracy in Brazil and Argentina, two key countries in South America, is still shaky. By contrast, in Mexico, the election of Salinas de Gortari as president in 1988 ushered in a period of political stability and economic growth there (although the collapse of the peso in 1994–1995 cast a shadow over Mexico's near-term prospects). Given Latin America's many domestic problems, the new democracies must alleviate widespread poverty, gain the confidence of the middle class, and placate the military. Can they do it?

KEY TERMS

dirty war
Sendero Luminoso
Zapatista National Liberation Army (ZNLA)
Andean Pact
Tupac Amaru Revolutionary Movement (MRTA)
debt crisis
Brady Plan
Mercosur
North American Free Trade Agreement (NAFTA)
current account deficit
writ of amparo
National Action Party (PAN)
aberatura
cruzado plan
real plan

STUDY QUESTIONS

1. Describe the kind of political system that is traditional in Latin America. What political and economic trends have predominated in the past two decades? What country (if any) in the region is the major exception to the general pattern?
2. How is Mexico ruled? Is the Mexican political system democratic or authoritarian? Is it repressive or tolerant of dissent? Is it a multiparty or one-party system? Are the leaders civilian or military?
3. How is Brazil ruled? What is the role of the military? How, when, and why did political change come to Brazil? Is the chief executive directly or indirectly elected? Is he or she a president or prime minister? Civilian or military? Constitutionally strong or weak?
4. Compare and contrast politics and government in Mexico and Brazil. What are the most important features that they have in common? What are the most striking differences?
5. If you were hired as a political consultant to diagnose the causes of corruption and bureaucratic mismanagement in Mexico, what would you recommend by way of remedial action. Would your recommendations include major economic and political reforms? Explain. Do the same exercise for Brazil.
6. Discuss the political persuasion and major policies of Brazil's four or five most recent presidents, then rank them in terms of successes and failures.
7. Discuss the historic significance of the 2000 presidential election in Mexico. Why was Vicente Fox elected? Do you think he will be able to reform Mexican politics? Why or why not?

SUGGESTED READINGS

Babb, Sarah. *Managing Mexico: Economists from Nationalism to Neoliberalism.* Princeton, N.J.: Princeton University Press, 2001.

Bulmer-Thomas, Victor, ed. *Regional Integration in Latin America and the Caribbean.* Washington, D.C.: Brookings Institution, 2001.

Cardoso, Fernando Henrique. *Charting a New Course: The Politics of Globalization and Social Transformation,* edited and introduced by Mauricio A. Font. Lanham, Md.: Rowman & Littlefield, 2001.

Colburn, Forrest D. *Latin America at the End of Politics.* Princeton, N.J.: Princeton University Press, 2002.

Corrales, Javier. *Presidents without Parties: The Politics of Economic Reform in Argentina and Venezuela in the 1990s.* University Park: Pennsylvania State University Press, 2002.

Davis, William C. *Warnings from the Far South: Democracy vs. Dictatorship in Uruguay, Argentina, and Chile.* Westport, Conn.: Greenwood, 1995.

De La Balze, Felipe. *Remaking the Argentine Economy.* New York: Council on Foreign Relations, 1995.

Dominquez, Jorge I., and McCann, James A. *Democratizing Mexico: Public Opinion and Electoral Choices.* Baltimore, Md.: Johns Hopkins University Press, 1996.

Font, Mauricio A. *Transforming Brazil: A Reform Era in Perspective.* Lanham, Md.: Rowman & Littlefield, 2003.

Hunter, Wendy. *Eroding Military Influence in Brazil: Politicians against Soldiers.* Chapel Hill: University of North Carolina Press, 1996.

Krooth, Richard. *The Mexican Connection: Crises, Poverty and the New Emperium.* Berkeley, Calif.: Harvest Publications, 1996.

Levine, Robert M. *Brazilian Legacies.* New York: Sharpe, 1997.

Loveman, Brian, and Davies, Thomas M., Jr., eds. *The Politics of Antipolitics: The Military in Latin America.* Lincoln: University of Nebraska Press, 1989.

Martinez-Lara, Javier. *Building Democracy in Brazil: The Politics of Constitutional Change, 1985–95.* New York: Saint Martin's, 1996.

Riding, Alan. *Distant Neighbors: A Portrait of the Mexicans.* New York: Random House, 1984.

Santiago, Silviano. *The Space In-Between: Essays on Latin American Culture.* Durham, N.C.: Duke University Press, 2002.

Wynia, Gary W. *The Politics of Latin American Development,* 2nd ed. New York: Cambridge University Press, 1984.

WEB SITES

http://lib.nmsu.edu/subject/bord/laguia
http://www.usfca.edu/library/databases/hlas.html

http://lanic.utexas.edu/la/region/government/
http://www.soc.jhu.edu/
http://www.georgetown.edu/pdba/

NOTES

1. See James McMahon, "Economic Crisis in Latin America: Global Contagion, Local Pain," *Current History,* March 1999, pp. 105–110.
2. Sally Bowen, "Peru's President Steps Up Battle with Terrorists," *Christian Science Monitor,* May 19, 1992, p. 5.
3. Ibid.
4. "Will Latin America Last?" *The World Today,* April 1987; reprinted in Paul Goodwin, Jr., ed., *Latin America,* 3rd ed. (Guilford, Conn.: Dushkin, 1988), p. 120.
5. David Clark Scott, "South in Transformation: Nations Sell State Firms and Tackle Inflation, Debt," *Christian Science Monitor,* March 18, 1992, p. 10. In the author's words, "Democracy has returned at an inconvenient time: elected governments have had to plunge their countries into unpopular austerity so that they can service the foreign debts piled up by the generals and put their internal economies in order. Standards of living, already miserably low, have gone down almost everywhere. There have been demonstrations and strikes against austerity in Argentina, Brazil, Uruguay, Bolivia, Panama, Guatemala, and El Salvador. Yet extremists of left and right are failing to take advantage of what ought to be a splendid opportunity. Elections are regularly won by middle-of-the-roaders (though left-wing parties seem to be on the rise)."
6. "Will Latin America Last?," p. 120.
7. Keith Bradsher, "Free Trade Accord for North America Is Expected Today," *New York Times,* August 12, 1992, p. 1.
8. McMahon, "Economic Crisis in Latin America," p.110.
9. Alan Riding, *Distant Neighbors: A Portrait of the Mexicans* (New York: Random House, 1989).
10. Gideon Lichfield, "After the Revolution," (A Survey of Mexico), *The Economist,* October 28, 2000, p. 5.
11. Ibid., p. 6.
12. Louis B. Casagrande, "The Five Nations of Mexico," *Focus,* Spring 1987, pp. 2–9.
13. "Emerging-Market Indicators," *The Economist,* July 29, 2000, p. 102.
14. James S. Henry, "Brazil Says Nuts," *New Republic,* October 12, 1987, p. 25.
15. Ibid., pp. 28–29.
16. See, for example, Julia Michaels, "Brazilian President Reels from Charges," *Christian Science Monitor,* May 28, 1992, p. 3.
17. "A Paradox for Cardoso," *The Economist,* July 29, 2000, p. 49.
18. Larry Rohter, "Brazil Threatened by Videotape Showing Graft," *New York Times,* February 16, 2004 (online edition).

PART VI
The Middle East

Israel

Area: 7,847 square miles

Population: 6,700,000

Language(s): Hebrew, Arabic, English

Female labor force: 41% of all workers

Major religion(s): Judaism (82%); Islam (14%);

Christian (2%), Other (2%)

Monetary unit: shekel

GNP: $96 billion (1998); $105 billion (2003 est.)

Average annual GNP growth per head, 1990–1998: 2.2%

Average GNP per head (1998): $16,180 (PPP = $16,861)

Average annual inflation rate, 1990–1998: 11.0%

Recent GNP growth rate (2003): 1.2% (2003, 1Q)

Recent inflation rate: –0.3% (June 2003)

Personal computers per 1,000 people (1998): 217.2

Egypt

Area: 386,659 square miles

Population: 68,000,000

Language(s): Arabic

Female labor force: 30% of all workers

Major religion(s): Islam (94% — mainly Sunni);

Coptic Christian and others (6%)

Monetary unit: Egyptian pound

GNP: $79 billion (1998); $78 billion (2003 est.)

Average annual GNP growth per head, 1990–1998: 2.7%

Average GNP per head (1998): $1,290 (PPP = $3,146)

Average annual inflation rate, 1990–1998: 9.7%

Recent GNP growth rate: 3.1% (2002)

Recent inflation rate: 3.9% (May 2003)

Personal computers per 1,000 people (1998): 9.1

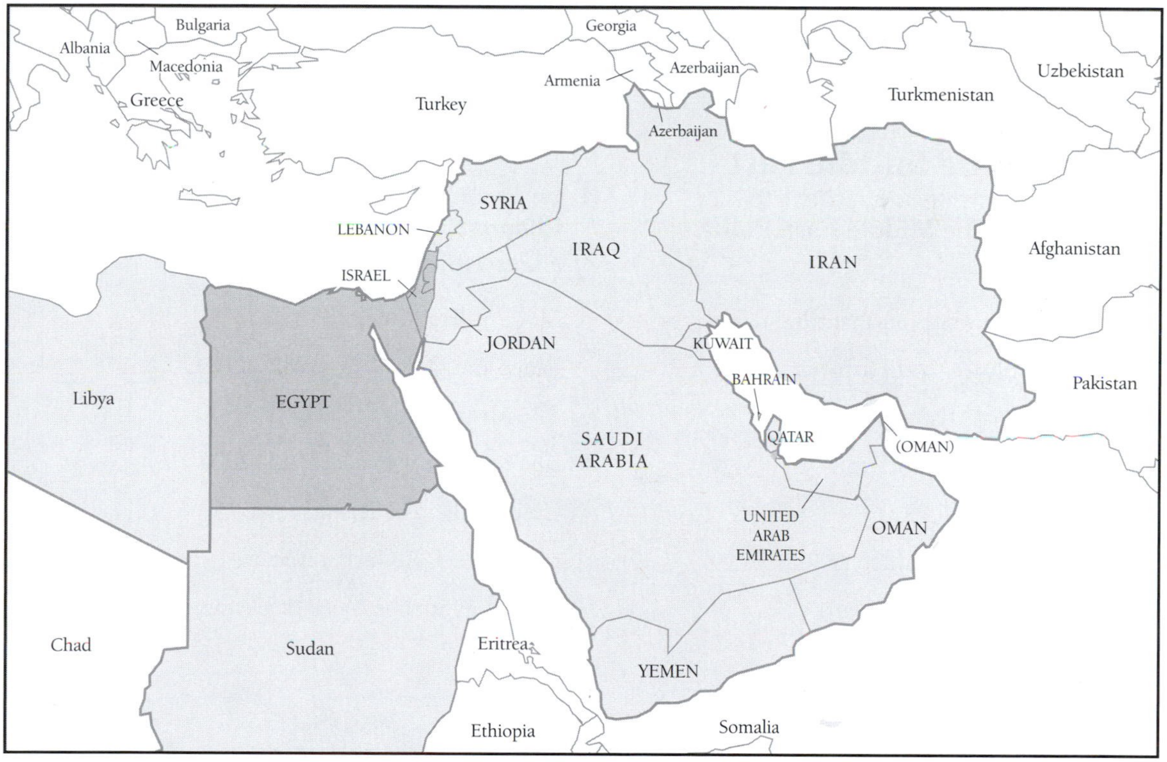
Bulgaria
Albania
Macedonia
Greece
Turkey
Georgia
Armenia
Azerbaijan
Azerbaijan
Turkmenistan
Uzbekistan
SYRIA
LEBANON
ISRAEL
IRAQ
IRAN
Afghanistan
JORDAN
KUWAIT
BAHRAIN
QATAR
(OMAN)
Pakistan
Libya
EGYPT
SAUDI ARABIA
UNITED ARAB EMIRATES
OMAN
Chad
Sudan
Eritrea
YEMEN
Ethiopia
Somalia

Part VI: The Middle East

Chapter 11: The Middle East: Politics and Religion

Geography, Climate, and Natural Resources

Religion, Culture, and History

The Imprint of History

The Challenges of Modernity

An Arab Awakening?

The Arab-Israeli Conflict

The Middle East Chessboard

Case Studies: Israel and Egypt

- Israel
- Egypt

Chapter 12: Monarchies, Dictatorships, and a Garrison State

Modern Arab Regimes

Peace and War, 1977–1982

The Missing Peace, 1983–1993

The Search for Peace, 1993–2004

Case Studies: Israel and Egypt

- Israel: A Garrison State
- Egypt: The Mask of Democracy

CHAPTER 11

Politics and Religion

The **Middle East** is located at the crossroads of three continents — Europe, Asia, and Africa. The region remains a world unto itself, however, as frequent references to the "Arab world" in the Western news media attest. Significantly, similar references to other regional "worlds" are rare. For example, there is seldom any talk of the "African world" or the "Asian world," much less the "European world." The reasons why are explored in this chapter.

The Arab world comprises 280–300 million people who share a culture based on religion (Islam), language (Arabic), and memories of colonial rule. Geographically, this "world" straddles (North) Africa and (Southwest) Asia and is anchored in a vast desert surrounded on three sides by water (a peninsula) known in antiquity as *Arabia.* No other region depends so heavily on the export of a single commodity, which happens to exist there in great abundance.

The imprint of the desert is also important in understanding Arab culture and history. We turn first to the geography of the Middle East, and then take a brief look at the region's climate and natural resources.

Geography, Climate, and Natural Resources

The Middle East encompasses all the Arabic-speaking countries from Morocco in the westernmost corner of North Africa to Iran, whose neighbors to the east are the Asian nations of Afghanistan and Pakistan. Iran is known in the history books as *Persia*, ethnic Persians (about half the total population) speak a language called Farsi. Persians and Arabs are as different culturally and linguistically as, say, Spaniards and Germans. But Persia is an exception in the predominantly Arab Middle East. The other two exceptions are Turkey and Israel.

The Middle East can be subdivided in several ways. For example, the countries of North Africa — Morocco, Algeria, Tunisia, Libya, Sudan, and Egypt — make up the region known as the **Maghreb.** Israel, Lebanon, Jordan, Syria, Iraq, Saudi Arabia, Yemen, and the Persian Gulf ministates are often referred to as the **Near East.** Turkey and Iran (along with Afghanistan) form the **Northern Belt** (or Northern Tier).

The vast Sahara Desert separates **North Africa** from the rest of the African continent, and the Near East, in turn, is separated from North Africa by the Red Sea. Language separates the Arabic-speaking states of the Near East from the Northern Belt states (Turkish is spoken in Turkey, Farsi in Iran, and Pushtun in Afghanistan).

The **Fertile Crescent** comprises Iraq, Syria, Lebanon, Israel, Jordan, and Egypt. The Red Sea region — the vast, arid, and thinly populated **Arabian Peninsula**—contains the world's richest oil reserves. Saudi Arabia occupies most of the peninsula; its neighbors are sheikdoms (some tiny) that, like Saudi Arabia, depend on oil exports for their livelihood. The surrounding waters and the forbidding desert isolate Saudi society from the rest of the world — even from the rest of the Arab world. Consequently, the Saudi monarchy has not been influenced by Europe, and its lands were never effectively colonized.

Egypt, a cradle of civilization, is sustained by the world's longest river, the Nile. Among Egypt's many natural assets is the lush Nile Delta, where three crops a year can be produced; an abundant supply of water; and a propitious location astride a great commercial route. However, Cairo, the capital, is one of the most overcrowded cities in the world, and Egypt is the only Arab country in which the population explosion has become a pressing problem. Yet despite its general poverty, Egypt is one of the most economically advanced countries in the Arab world.

Climate and Natural Resources

As already noted, the heart of the Arab world (both literally and figuratively) is a desert. The desert is surrounded by seas — the Persian Gulf, the Red Sea, and the Mediterranean. For centuries, the desert dictated the way(s) of life available to its human inhabitants. One prominent way of life was **nomadic** (constantly on the move). The Bedouins who were tribally organized nomads constituted perhaps a fifth of the Arab population prior to the twentieth century. Bedouins naturally resisted governmental controls associated with the rise of nation-states in the Middle East. States imply rules and structures — everything from taxes to borders — which are abhorrent to (and incompatible with) a nomadic lifestyle.

How can the fact that advanced civilizations existed in the Middle East be reconciled with this image? First, these civilizations flourished long before ancient Greece and Rome laid the foundations for modern Europe. By the time the European nation-state system emerged, the empires built by the ancient Egyptians or the Persians had faded (or were fast-fading) into history. Second, "[e]ven the settled urban-dwellers, however, were insulated from the weak states that presided over them by a far more dense and complex network of kinship connections than was the case in pre-modern Europe."[1] The climate and desert environment, therefore, provide clues to solving a political mystery of fundamental importance — namely, why weak states were the norm, historically speaking, and why more recent attempts to establish strong states in the region have so often led to turmoil and terrorism. Traditionally, Arab rulers had great difficulty collecting taxes and had to settle for "second best strategies of indirect taxation," for example, depending on the leaders of ethnic, religious, and tribal groups to collect and remit taxes or on "tax farmers" (called *multazims* in Arabic) who were given grants of land (*iltizams*) in exchange for extracting taxes from peasants.[2] Obviously, modern states cannot thrive unless they can perform this "extractive" function efficiently.

Black Gold! But it was a different type of extraction — one made possible by a combination of geological luck and modern technology — that changed the picture in the Arab world. Beneath the barren desert of the Arabian Peninsula lies a gold mine. The petroleum products used to power the modern world's machines are so valuable that oil has been dubbed "black gold." Saudi Arabia's crude oil reserves are the largest in the world — between 165 and 170 billion barrels. The Saudis demonstrated the power of "oil diplomacy" in the 1970s, when they spearheaded the OPEC oil embargo following the 1973 Yom Kippur war. (OPEC is the Organization of Petroleum Exporting Countries —in addition to Arab member-states, most of the important oil-producing countries of Africa, Asia, and Latin America belong).

The presence of so much oil in this part of the world situated as it is at the crossroads of several continents, combined with the extremely high economic and military value of oil in modern societies, placed the Middle East at the center of the Cold War rivalry between the United States and the Soviet Union. Even though the Cold War is over, little has changed to diminish the world's interest in the turbulent politics of this region. Next we look at how geography and geology have conspired to make the Middle East a region of vital importance to the military and economic strategies of the modern world's great powers, including its only superpower.

Geostrategic Considerations

The term *Middle East* is appropriate: the area it describes is located at the crossroads of Europe, Africa, and Asia. The strategic importance of the region derives in part from its proximity to international waterways and "choke points" such as the Turkish Straits, the Suez Canal, and the Strait of Hormuz. During the nineteenth century, the "Near East question" was essentially "a rivalry on the part of the big powers for control of the Turkish Straits until the Isthmus of Suez was pierced by a canal in the latter part of the century."[3] Furthermore:

> The economic significance of these waterways is obvious. Since time immemorial the Turkish Straits have been a vital trade route between the Black Sea shores and the Mediterranean. The prosperity of many a Mediterranean state, such as Genoa or Greece, has been largely dependent upon its ability to trade with the Black Sea hinterland. And, conversely, the Straits have played an increasingly important role in the foreign trade of Russia ever since the latter obtained an outlet to the Black Sea. The commercial significance of the opening of the Suez Canal, which replaced the old Cape route, is so obvious that it does not require elaboration.[4]

The military importance of the Middle East's waterways was amply demonstrated in World War II. Germany and Italy launched various offensives toward Egypt in an effort to seize the Suez Canal; the British, in turn, tenaciously defended the canal.

Meanwhile, Allied efforts to get arms and equipment to the Soviet Union were hampered when Turkey closed the straits. Even in peacetime, "control of these waterways may prove decisive so far as the political independence of Turkey and the diplomatic alignment of Egypt are concerned."[5]

Outside powers have long cast a covetous eye on the Middle East. As dominant naval forces in different eras, Great Britain and the United States have both sought preeminence in the region, and after World War II, the United States and the Soviet Union engaged in intense rivalry there. The USSR made inroads in the 1950s and 1960s, especially in Algeria, Egypt, and Syria. Soviet influence declined dramatically in the 1970s but was partly restored after 1985 by Mikhail Gorbachev. Both superpowers sought a secure grip on the eastern Mediterranean that would guarantee access to the Suez Canal and to Middle Eastern oil. Forty percent of Western Europe's oil and 90 percent of Japan's came from the Middle East — a fact that tipped the balance of interest toward the west. (See Figure 11.1 and Table 11.1.)

Surrounded by the waters of the Mediterranean, the Red Sea, the Arabian Sea, and Persian Gulf, much of the Middle East has been vulnerably exposed. It is more accessible by sea than by land — another reason why the West, with its superior naval and merchant marine fleets, has succeeded at gaining a foothold in the region.

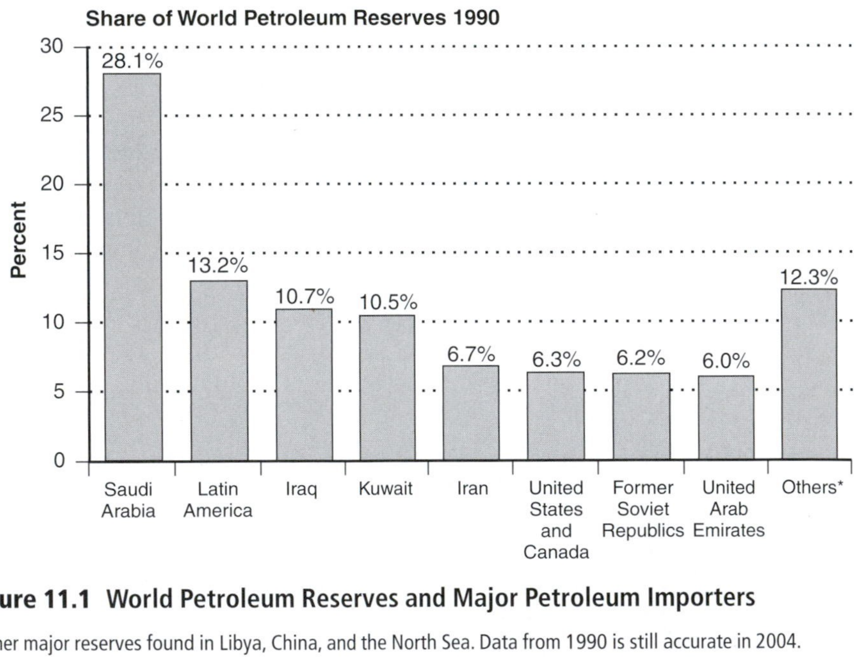

Figure 11.1 World Petroleum Reserves and Major Petroleum Importers

*Other major reserves found in Libya, China, and the North Sea. Data from 1990 is still accurate in 2004.

Sources: Adapted from John Rourke, *International Politics on the World Stage,* 3rd ed. (Guilford, Conn.: Dushkin, 1991), p. 246, and updated with data from the U.S. Central Intelligence Agency (1991).

Table 11.1 World Crude Oil and Natural Gas Reserves (January 2000)

Region	Crude Oil (billion barrels)	Natural Gas (trillion cubic feet)
North America	55.1	261.3
Central & South America	89.5	222.7
Western Europe	18.8	159.5
Eastern Europe & Former Soviet Union	58.9	1,999.2
Middle East	675.6	1,749.2
Africa	74.9	394.2
Far East & Oceania	44.0	363.5
World Total	1,016.8	5,149.6

Source: Energy Institute of America, *Oil and Gas Journal.*

Religion, Culture, and History

Geography is not all that makes the Middle East so pivotal. This region is the cradle of three great monotheistic religious traditions: Judaism, Christianity, and Islam. All three have spanned the globe, but the region remains the center of the newest of the three, **Islam,** which has 1.2 billion adherents worldwide. The Islamic world stretches from Morocco to Malaysia, Indonesia (90 percent Muslim), and the Philippines. The Middle East holds the holiest places of Islam — above all, Mecca, Saudi Arabia, birthplace of the Muslim faith. The Dome of the Rock in Jerusalem is another important Muslim shrine. Believers in all three faiths thus regard Jerusalem, site of the Hebrews' original tabernacle and of Jesus' crucifixion, as a holy city.

In the Middle East, politics and religion are inseparable. The combining of these two elements creates a volatile mixture, which has shaped the history of this region from ancient times to the present. (See Box 11.1.)

Judaism

Judaism and Christianity have even deeper roots in the Middle East than Islam. Like Muslims, Jews and Christians consider Jerusalem the holiest of holy places, and both view Palestine, in which Israel is located, as the Holy Land. The latter is the setting for the action in the Old Testament and encompasses biblical Judea and Samaria (on the West Bank of the Jordan River), which Israel has occupied since its 1967 victory over Egypt and Syria. It is also the setting for the New Testament; such places as Bethlehem, Nazareth, and Galilee are in Palestine. Jews everywhere see Israel as the embodiment of the long-awaited Zionist state, a refuge from political and religious persecution. Because Jews and Christians share the Old Testament and because the West is steeped in the Judeo-Christian tradition, Islam and Arabs seem more arcane and exotic to Westerners than the two older religions and their adherents.

Democracy in America

BOX 11.1

Church and State — How Separate?

The United States has a political tradition of keeping church and state separate — in theory. The First Amendment provides that Congress shall make no law(s) prohibiting the "free exercise" of religion or "respecting an establishment of religion." Exactly what this language means, however, is unclear and hotly debated. The U.S. Supreme Court has handed down dozens of erudite rulings in an effort to clarify what the Constitution requires or permits in the area of religion.

The free exercise clause is relatively unambiguous in its protection of religious practices, however weird or obnoxious to the majority, so long as these do not harm others. Human sacrifice or the use of illegal drugs, for example, is not allowed.

The establishment clause is more ambiguous and, consequently, more controversial. The Supreme Court has quite consistently held that the Constitution erects a "wall of separation" between church and state. (Thomas Jefferson, who opposed making the Church of England the established church of Virginia, coined the phrase.) Does this concept prohibit states as well as the national government from adopting an official religion? The First Amendment is unclear on this crucial point, but the Supreme Court has interpreted the clause broadly to apply to all levels of government.

Maintaining a secular state in a religious society has opened a Pandora's box of litigation over the years. For example, can teachers in tax-supported public schools start or end the day with a prayer? If not, can children be required (or even allowed) to sing Christmas carols on school premises? Is the Pledge of Allegiance permissible? Can state laws ban the teaching of evolution in public schools? Finally, what if any, form(s) of state-support (or involvement) in parochial, private education is permitted by the Constitution? The number and variety of cases inspired by these questions is bewildering to all but the most brilliant constitutional scholars.

In an effort to devise a clear standard, the Court has said that state involvement in religion is constitutional if it meets three tests:

1. It has a secular purpose.
2. Its primary effect neither advances nor inhibits religion.
3. It does not foster excessive government entanglement with religion.

The American experience shows that separating church and state is not the same as separating politics and religion. The controversy continues, but the "battles" are fought in the courts, not in the streets.

It is sometimes forgotten that **Judaism** and Christianity have common origins. Both are monotheistic, and both regard books of the Old Testament as sacred texts. Judaism traces its origins to a Sumerian named Abraham, his son Isaac, and Isaac's son Jacob. Jacob took his own sons (including Judah, after whom the faith is named) to Egypt. According to legend and biblical history, Moses led the Hebrews out of Egypt and through the wilderness to the Promised Land (modern Israel). The religion of the Hebrews became monotheistic by the acceptance of Yahweh — the god of the patriarchs, Abraham, Isaac, and Jacob — as the one true God. This monotheism was symbolized by a covenant between Yahweh and Abraham, confirmed by the rite of circumcision, and reiterated to Moses on Mount Sinai when the Ten Commandments were handed down from on high, according to Jewish and Christian teachings.

The foundations of Judaism are contained in the Pentateuch, or Torah (first five books of the Old Testament), and in the **Talmud,** the collected decisions and opinions of the **rabbis** (scholars) concerning civil and religious law. After thousands of years as a monolithic religious community, Jews in the late nineteenth century began to divide into several branches, the two most prominent being Orthodox and Reform. Judaism has an elaborate set of rites and religious holidays that differ from those of Christianity, and its places of worship are called synagogues (not churches or cathedrals, as in Christianity, or mosques, as in Islam).

Christianity

Christianity is an offshoot of Judaism. It dates back nearly 2,000 years to the birth of **Jesus Christ,** an event that has since become the great divide in world history, often separating time into BC ("Before Christ") and AD (*anno Domini,* Latin for "in the year of our Lord").* According to Christian teaching, Jesus is the Son of God, born of a virgin, Mary, through a miracle known as the Immaculate Conception. As an adult, Jesus roamed Palestine, at the time a Roman province, to preach. His teachings are recorded in the New Testament, written primarily by twelve early believers, known as apostles. Jesus was executed for heresy by crucifixion, a typical Roman punishment.

Judaism and Christianity differ sharply on whether Jesus was the Christ — the Messiah prophesied in the Old Testament. From that, many doctrinal differences flow. For example, Christians believe that Jesus died on the cross to save sinners from eternal damnation (hence the idea of Jesus as Savior); Jews believe that forgiveness of sins depends on one's willingness to repent and do good deeds.

Tensions between Christians and Jews have been most apparent in Europe. In the Middle East, the religious differences that have led to extremism, zealotry, and terrorist violence have involved Zionism on the one hand and Arab nationalism (or Islamic fundamentalism) on the other.

Islam

Islam and the culture that grew up around it have permeated the Arab world, including the countries of the periphery — Turkey (98 percent Muslim) and Iran (95 percent Shiite, a major Muslim sect). Although Islam has spread beyond the Middle East proper, it is first and foremost the religion of the Arabs:

> In many ways, the Arab world today is a religious empire. It encompasses eighteen countries and 4.6 million square miles, an area 25 percent larger than the United States. The largest country, Sudan, is more than three times the size of Texas; the smallest, Bahrain, would fit neatly inside the boundaries of New York City.[6]

Muslims outnumber Jews and Christians in the Arab world by about ten to one. For the faithful, Islam is more than a religion; it is a way of life. Its scripture, the **Koran,** covers politics, law, and social behavior and even sets forth procedures for divorce, loans, and wills.[7]

*To avoid this Christian bias, the designations CE ("Common Era") and BCE ("Before the Common Era") are sometimes used, as in this book, instead of AD and BC, respectively.

Religion has played a central role in the Middle East conflict. Arabs (especially Palestinians) and Jews have fought for control of land that both claim as their own. In truth, the conflict is about territory more than religion, but religious issues have inflamed passions on both sides. Religion played an even more direct role in the Iranian Revolution and in the subsequent war between Iran and Iraq, which pitted Arab against Persian and Shiite against Sunni (the two main branches of Islam).

Historically, in the Middle East, Christians and Muslims have clashed far more extensively than Muslims and Jews. The hostility reached its zenith in the Crusades, three centuries of Christian expeditions intended to wrest the Holy Land from the Muslims.

The House Muhammad Built on Five Pillars Islam dates back to the seventh century CE, when **Muhammad,** a merchant from Mecca, received revelations from God through the angel Gabriel, according to Muslim belief. Mecca was a trading center to which the Arabian nomads of the time would make pilgrimages to worship their various deities (more than two hundred of them). Muhammad taught that only one god, **Allah,** was the true God and that Allah spoke through him. Thus, Muhammad was merely a messenger, the Prophet of Islam. His revelations, passed along to his followers over a period of twenty-two years (610–632), constituted the Way (*Sharia* in Arabic) and are recorded in the sacred text of Islam, the Koran.

Islam's five basic tenets, the Five Pillars, can be summarized as follows:

1. The confession of faith: "I testify that there is no God but God, and Muhammad is the Messenger of God."
2. Prayer five times daily, facing in the direction of Mecca, the holy city
3. Fasting during the daylight hours in the month of Ramadan (the time of Muhammad's revelations)
4. Almsgiving (at least 2.5 percent of one's income) to the community for relief of the poor
5. Pilgrimage to Mecca at least once in one's lifetime

Muslims have much in common with Jews and Christians — belief in one God, in the power of prayer, and in an ethic of compassion. They believe that God revealed himself to many prophets before Muhammad, including Abraham, Moses, and Jesus. But Muslims do not accept Christian beliefs in the divinity of Jesus (that Jesus was God), the Resurrection (that Jesus rose from the dead), or the Trinity (that God consists of God, Jesus, and the Holy Spirit responsible for the Immaculate Conception). Judaism and Islam have much in common, including strict dietary rules and reliance on an authoritative body of scholarship to interpret divine law.

Muhammad was not only a religious figure but also a powerful political leader. Forced to flee Mecca (his escape is called the Hegira), he went to Medina and there established a power base from which he came to rule Arabia. Muhammad mixed politics and religion and created a kind of **theocracy**—a pattern still discernible in some parts of the Middle East (especially Iran).

Muslims consider Muhammad's life a model. His decisions and revelations constitute the Sunna ("Beaten Path"). Muhammad did not have an heir apparent. Although most of his followers favored an elective caliph ("successor"), some believed that Muhammad had intended his cousin Ali to assume leadership. This minority was adamant that only someone of the same bloodline could succeed Muhammad. These Shiite ("sectarian") purists thus originated as the partisans of Ali. Most Muslims are **Sunni,** followers of the Sunna.

Sunni versus Shiite Thus the division between Sunni and **Shiite** is almost as old as Islam itself. About 90 percent of all Muslims are Sunni; most of the rest are Shiite, and most Shiites are Iranian. The split in the seventh century was a bloody affair. Ali was eventually elected caliph, only to be murdered; one of his sons was poisoned; another was ambushed and killed on the orders of Ali's rival, who established his own dynastic rule. Through it all, the Shiite Muslims, though outwardly obedient, never changed their beliefs.

Shiite Muslims generally recognize a line of twelve direct descendants of Muhammad as Islam's spiritual guides called **imams.** Most Shiites believe that the twelfth imam is alive but invisible and that he will reveal himself on the Day of Judgment. Until the "hidden imam" reappears, the religious leaders — **mullahs** — have the right and duty to interpret God's will and guide Shiite true believers in the Way. Thus, the Shiite tradition gives religious leaders (like the late Ayatollah Khomeini in Iran) more power over Shiite Muslims than Sunni religious leaders have over Sunni Muslims.

The barbarism exhibited by both sides in the Iran-Iraq War of the 1980s was motivated partly by opposing nationalisms and partly by Arab-Persian animosity. It was also a reflection of Islam's religious schism and the mutual suspicions it has spawned. A majority of Iraqis are Shiite Muslims (55 percent), but the Sunni minority (40 percent) is politically dominant; Saddam Hussein, Iraq's Sunni ruler, feared the spread of Khomeini-style Islamic revolutionary fervor in Iraq and believed that Khomeini was out to conquer Iraq for Shiite Islam. The two leaders loathed each other. This example demonstrates the difficulty of disentangling religious, political, and even personal factors in the conflicts that have rocked the Middle East since World War II.

Jihad and Islamic Fundamentalism The concept of **jihad** is now well known to Westerners, who equate it with holy war and terrorism. One meaning of the word is "holy war," but it can also mean "sacred struggle" or simply a personal "striving" to carry out God's will. In its violent form, jihad can be directed against external or internal enemies. The assassins of Egyptian President Anwar al-Sadat claimed at their trial that they had acted out of religious principle, insisting that Egyptian law was at odds with Islamic law and that Sadat's 1979 peace treaty with Israel betrayed the Palestinians, whose cause concerns Muslims everywhere. Similarly, Muslim militants who seized the Great Mosque in Mecca in 1979 did so in the name of God — in their view, the secular Saudi monarchy was illegitimate and only halfheartedly Islamic.

Although the West has come to associate jihad primarily with the Shiites of Iran, Sunni Muslims also embrace the concept. For example, the **Muslim Brotherhood** is a militant Sunni secret society that seeks to establish a single universal Islamic state. It has been especially active in Egypt and Syria. It has assassinated Alawi officials in Syria and committed other violent acts.

The Shiite tradition admires martyrdom, a trait traced all the way back to the murder of Ali's son. Consequently, some terrorist attacks have been carried out by Shiites on suicide missions. Similar motives led Iranian children to walk through minefields ahead of soldiers during the war against Iraq: the Ayatollah Khomeini assured them that martyrdom in the jihad against Iraq would give them immediate entry to heaven.

The concept of jihad, which Westerners commonly associate with terrorist acts in the Middle East, stresses individual striving to carry out God's will rather than the killing of innocent people (which the Koran, in fact, strictly forbids). Islam is closely linked with Palestinian nationalism; with the drive to create an independent Palestinian state; and, in the eyes of the West, with Palestinian terrorism. In its extreme form, Islam is not so much a religion as an ideology; in this form, it is more properly known as **Islamism,** rather than Islam per se. On the other side, some extreme right-wing Israeli Jews also justify acts of violence on religious grounds, but here, too, tradition and extreme nationalism are inseparable. And here, too, it is necessary to distinguish between Judaism as religion and Judaism as ideology. When religion becomes the captive of the community's most aggressive members it is politicized, and in the process typically changes to the point where moral constraints fall away — in other words, it becomes indistinguishable from ideology.

The Imprint of History

The Arab world's golden age dates back to the seventh century, when Muhammad founded Islam. His successors, the caliphs, conquered new territories and welded disparate tribes into a single state inspired by Islam. The tide of Arab conquest rolled over Iraq, Persia (Iran), Syria, Egypt, Cyprus, and North Africa. In 711, the Arabs surged into Spain, and six years later they nearly seized Constantinople (Istanbul).

At its fullest extent, the Arab empire extended from the Pyrenees to India. In contrast to the Western stereotype of Islam as a militant, proselytizing creed (reinforced by the Ayatollah Khomeini and his followers after 1979), Arab rulers showed considerable religious tolerance, permitting conquered peoples who chose not to convert to Islam to practice their own religions under certain civil arrangements. Arabs everywhere established themselves as the ruling aristocracy and absorbed the flourishing cultures of Persia, Syria, and Egypt. Arabic became the dominant language of a brilliant new culture.

The Arab empire was doomed to be short-lived, however; it expanded too fast and soon burned itself out. It was torn apart by such internal forces as sectionalism and schism, still apparent in the Arab world today. One fundamental weakness was the lack of an accepted rule of succession to the caliphate. One dynasty moved the seat of government to Damascus, and the next moved it to Baghdad. By the ninth century, the empire had become a commonwealth of independent and often contentious states. Attacks from external enemies hastened its disintegration after the eleventh century.

Thus, the Arabs created a flourishing Islamic civilization that was concurrent with the Christian medieval period in Europe. Arab culture made major contributions to world literature, philosophy, historiography, art, and science.[8] Pride in this former grandeur may in part explain Islam's resistance to the West.

The Ottoman Intrusion

For hundreds of years before World War I, the history of the Middle East was dominated by the Ottoman Empire and European colonialism. By the late fifteenth century, the Black Sea had become a "Turkish lake," and the tentacles of the empire reached into three continents. Yet the Ottomans had to contend with "the involvement of practically every great European power in its foreign and domestic affairs in the course of the last three hundred years."[9] Under Suleiman I, the Magnificent (1520–1566), the Ottoman Turks expanded their domain well into the Balkans, Armenia, and Mesopotamia (Iraq). A formidable navy allowed Suleiman to conquer Aden and the southeastern coast of Arabia and to project his power into the Mediterranean and Adriatic seas and North Africa. It was quite a performance:

> At the time of Suleiman's death the Ottoman Empire stretched from the Danube to the Persian Gulf and from the Ukrainian steppes to the Tropic of Cancer in upper Egypt. It included the mastery of the great trade routes of the Mediterranean, of the Black and Red seas, and of parts of the Indian Ocean. It had an estimated population of fifty million as against some four million in England and embraced some twenty races and nationalities.[10]

The Ottoman Empire declined toward the end of the seventeenth century following a failed attempt to defeat Austria and conquer Vienna in 1683. After that, Russia pushed southward toward the Near East, and the British established a toehold in Egypt. France, too, under Napoléon Bonaparte, made a play for the land of the Nile at the end of the eighteenth century, without success.

European Colonialism

Imperialism characterized the second half of the nineteenth century, when the major powers of Europe scrambled for colonial territories in Africa and Asia. The Middle East was not spared. The French were interested in the area before the British, mainly because France looked on the Ottoman Turks as natural allies against their archrival, Austria. But as imperial Russia encroached on the periphery of the Middle East in the second half of the eighteenth century, British interest in the region grew.

Napoléon's misadventure in Egypt drew British attention even more strongly. As the preeminent naval and mercantile power in the eighteenth and nineteenth centuries, Great Britain was anxious to control strategic waterways and choke points, including the Strait of Gibraltar, the Turkish Straits, the isthmus of Suez, the Bab el Mandeb, and the Strait of Hormuz. Furthermore, the waterways of the Middle East were the shortest route to India, the "Jewel of the British Empire." It thus became "an axiom of British foreign policy to uphold the independence and integrity of the Ottoman Empire, in order to prevent the undue strengthening of Russia and to protect the imperial life line."[11]

Despite British goodwill, the Ottoman Empire continued to decline in the nineteenth century, and Russia was the main beneficiary. Britain (allied with France) and Russia came to blows in the Crimean War (1854–1856), after Russia and France quarreled over control of the holy sites in Palestine. The British won the war, and thus Russian encroachment was effectively stopped, but Western imperialism continued to erode Ottoman rule in the Near East until displacing it entirely after World War I.

The two main rivals for colonial control in the Middle East were Great Britain and France. The French were able to annex large territories in North Africa, directly across the Mediterranean from France's southern coast, taking Algeria (1830), Tunisia (1883), and Morocco (1906–1912). France also had formal ties to the Levant (Syria and Lebanon). The British gained the upper hand in Egypt — where France again tried to gain a foothold but failed — and in Palestine. Meanwhile, on the eve of World War I, Germany made inroads into the Ottoman Empire, and Italy managed to obtain control of Libya.

Persia (Iran) was an object of Russian imperialist aims in the nineteenth century, but Great Britain safeguarded its independence:

> Britain's Persian policy was dictated primarily by her concern for India, and Persia was to be an independent buffer state or neutral zone between the Indian and Russian empires. Britain sought unimpeded commercial opportunity in Persia, and to this extent she was interested in exercising moderate influence in the area. She was unwilling, however, to assume direct imperial responsibilities similar to those in India. It was, therefore, in her interest to see Persia relatively strong and capable of withstanding Russian pressure. It was largely due to this British policy that Persia succeeded in maintaining her independence instead of falling under Russian domination.[12]

The Challenges of Modernity

Many conflicts in the Middle East are rooted in religious and ethnic animosity, but the state of war that has characterized the politics of the region since the late 1940s is perpetuated by another equally divisive issue: How should Arabs and Muslims respond to the challenges of modernity? Should they embrace Western ideas of individual rights and democracy? The secularized and bureaucratic state? Modern science and technology?

Based in part on the responses of their leaders and ruling elites, Arab states can be characterized as either moderate and "traditional" or radical and "revolutionary." Thus, for example, Egypt under Nasser (1954–1970) chose the radical course by following the path of Arab nationalism, non-Marxist socialism, and a secularism that denied any special role for Islam in political life. In contrast, the ruling dynasty of Saudi Arabia chose the traditional path of hereditary monarchy, fidelity to Islamic law, and rejection of Western-style modernization.

Contrast and Comparison

BOX 11.2

Theocracy without Democracy: Iran after the Shah

After the fall of the shah, Iran became a theocracy, a government guided by religious leaders and based on a strict interpretation of the Koran. Islamic law became the law of the land. Ultimate authority became vested in a "supreme legal guide," the ayatollah, responsible only to God. Religious leaders served in the Majlis (parliament) and played an active role in the political life of the nation. The Council of Guardians acted as a kind of supreme court, using the Koran, not the constitution, as the ultimate arbiter. Many of Iran's 80,000 clerics became local political agents of the Islamic Republican Party (IRP).

The first years of Ayatollah Khomeini's rule were chaotic. One outrageous incident was the seizure of the U.S. embassy in Tehran in November 1979. Fifty-two Americans were held hostage until January 1981. To many Iranians, the long history of collusion between the United States and the shah justified a jihad against America (the "great Satan"). Nonetheless, it left Iran diplomatically isolated.

Internally, Khomeini launched a reign of terror; thousands of enemies of the Islamic state — intellectuals, former officials, military officers, and political figures — were arrested, tried, and executed. A series of bombings killed some Khomeini confederates, including the newly elected president (Khomeini had dismissed the first president). In retaliation, Khomeini crushed his political opponents.

In the midst of this instability, Iraq had invaded Iran. The bloody war of attrition that followed led to appalling carnage and suffering, drained the economies of both countries, disrupted oil supply lines, and for seven years held the entire region under the threat of a wider war. When the fighting stopped in 1988, there was no winner or loser.

Within a year of the war's end, the ayatollah died, leaving a bitter legacy. He had inspired the nation to shed Western influences, but the price was a pariah state, a perpetrator of terrorism abroad and human rights violations at home.

Iran's success in rebuilding its petroleum industries and armed forces after its prolonged war with Iraq; its refusal to condemn acts of aggression and international terrorism' and its efforts to acquire a nuclear capability all contributed to a renewed sense of alarm in the early 1990s. Tensions eased later in the decade as more moderate elements gained greater influence in Iran's government, but dipomatic and trade relations with the United States remained frozen.

Syria, Iraq, Algeria, and Libya are among the Arab states that followed the Egyptian model. Jordan, Morocco, and the Persian Gulf sheikdoms have chosen the traditional path — all are moderate regimes that respect Islamic law, spurn revolutionary doctrines (including Islamic fundamentalism), and show little enthusiasm for an Arab superstate.

Iran illustrates the fury generated by these alternative responses to the West. Iran's modernizing elite, led by the shah, Muhammad Reza Pahlavi (1941–1979), hastened the pace of change. The shah accepted massive military aid and economic investment from the West (especially America), attempted to remake Iranian society along Western lines, reduced the role of the imams, and vigorously pursued a pro-West foreign policy. Reaction came in 1979, when the exiled Ayatollah Ruhollah Khomeini led an uprising that toppled the shah and forced him to flee Iran, leaving a power vacuum that fanatical followers of the ayatollah hastened to fill. The revolutionary government arrested opponents (many of whom it executed) and imposed a harsh regime based on strict observance of Islamic law. (See Box 11.2.) Iran then became embroiled in a bloody war with Iraq, which raged throughout the 1980s. Perhaps more than any other country in the

Middle East, Iran epitomizes the conflicts that can be provoked by Western intrusion into Islamic societies.

Another way of differentiating the modern, secular societies of the Middle East from the traditional, religious ones is according to customs, lifestyles, and religious observance. Measured by such indicators as industrialization or the state of technological advancement, Iran and Saudi Arabia are just as modern as Iraq, Syria, and Egypt — perhaps even ahead of them. Oddly enough, some of the most vigorous resistance to modernity can be found in Israel, the most modern society in the Middle East. Extreme Jewish religious sects, like many Islamic fundamentalists, take a dim view of the contemporary world, including modern technology.

An Arab Awakening?

No account of modern Middle Eastern history would be complete without reference to what has been called the "Arab awakening."[13] One reaction to foreign subjugation by both Ottomans and Europeans was the articulation of Arab nationalism. The rhetorical basis for Arab unity is rooted in this history, as is reaction to the establishment of Israel (in which, to Arabs, the West was an accomplice); this history has led Arabs to adopt the Palestinian cause as their own.

Because Egypt is prominent in the Middle East today and because its experience as a Western dependent in many ways typifies that of other Arab countries, it might serve to link the legacy of foreign domination with the persistent urge to create a single Arab superstate. Foreign domination of Egypt dates from the Persian conquest in 525 BCE. Then came the Greeks (Alexander the Great), the Romans, the Byzantines, and, in the seventh century, the Arabs, who introduced Islam and the Arabic language. Large numbers of nomadic Arabs settled in the Nile valley under the rule of the caliphs. In the tenth century, a Shiite group split with the Sunnis, and in the desert south of Alexandria, the ancient capital, they established a new capital, al-Qahira ("City of War"—modern Cairo).

The Ottoman Turks annexed Egypt in the sixteenth century. The Ottoman overlords permitted the Mamluks, former slaves or war prisoners who converted to Islam, to administer the area in return for occasional tribute and taxes. The leaders eventually became slaveholders themselves, formed a military aristocracy, and, as powerful warlords, fought for supremacy. Thus, the Ottoman Empire encompassed Egypt but never penetrated its society and culture the way the Arabs had under the caliphate.

Egypt emerged virtually autonomous under a powerful and visionary Albanian officer, Muhammad Ali, who ruled from the Ottoman garrison at Cairo. Appointed governor by the sultan in 1805, Ali eased Egypt into the modern world. His successors, called *khedives* ("viceroys"), were nominally under the Ottoman sultan but ruled as autocrats in their own right.

The Suez Canal was opened in 1869 under Khedive Ismail. The British were keenly interested in the opening of the canal, not least because it provided a shortcut to India. An attempted military coup against the khedive in 1882 precipitated a British intervention and formation of a "protectorate," which interrupted Egypt's movement toward independence.

The British protectorate lasted until 1922, by which time an Egyptian national movement advocating an Islamic revival as a means of resisting the incursions of European imperialism had emerged. During World War I, Great Britain promised Egypt's leaders that it would back independence after the war but subsequently reneged on the grounds that the Egyptians were not ready for self-rule.

A nationalist party, the Wafd, led the fight against British colonialism until Britain formally ended its protectorate. Egypt was given nominal independence under a new king, but London continued to control Egypt's foreign policy, armed forces, and some internal affairs.

As we will see later, Egypt's history after World War II, like the history of the region as a whole, is about the saga of war and the search for peace. There is no one "Middle East conflict" but many; the most enduring, however, has been the conflict between Israel and its Arab neighbors.

The Arab-Israeli Conflict

The so-called Middle East conflict is semantic shorthand for the de facto state of war, or permanent crisis, between the Arab nations and Israel. The conflict involves a long series of contentions rooted in the Palestinian dispute. In essence, the problem is that Palestine is now called Israel. Palestinian Arabs lived there before the 1948 war for Israeli independence. Most of the Jews who make up the majority of Israel's population are "returned Jews" whose ancestors fled Palestine in ancient times and lost physical contact with the place. The concept of the Promised Land thus became a powerful abstraction, kept alive in the Diaspora by religious symbols and sacred texts that through the centuries have connected Jews everywhere in a community of believers that transcends the boundaries of politics and geography.

A Place Called Palestine

For the Arabs who had lived there for at least 3,000 years, Palestine was no abstraction. To the Zionists of Europe, it was a homeland, but for the Palestinians, it was home. They had been born there; it was family, friends, life. Most of all, it was the piece of earth they possessed — had it not always been so? Most Zionist leaders were Europeans; to the Palestinians, they were interlopers, and Zionism was just another form of imperialism.

Jewish determination to make the abstraction of the Promised Land real was steeled in the 1930s and 1940s; the genocide of the Holocaust made a Jewish homeland not merely desirable but imperative. Jews had tolerated persecution in Europe for centuries, but the atrocity of Hitler's "final solution" made it clear that they would be truly secure only in a land of their own.

These brief comments reveal the deep tragedy of the Palestinian dispute: both sides believe they are fighting for their national survival. For both, it is a life-and-death struggle, and "their leaders have been willing to use any means, including terrorism."[14]

American journalist and author David Lamb has aptly called Palestine "the twice-promised land." His book *The Arabs* sums up the issue succinctly:

> In the midst of the Beirut siege, when Israel was pounding the hell out of the Palestinians, Bill Barrel, the Middle East correspondent for the Dallas *Times Herald,* received a telex at the Commodore Hotel from his editor in Texas. The message, which was in effect a request for a story, read: "Who are these Palestinian people, and why don't they just go home?"
>
> Whether intended or not, there was brilliance in that telex. In twelve words, the editor had cut to the marrow. He had boiled the most complex of Middle East issues into the simplest of terms — land. The Palestinians couldn't go home because they had no home. Their land had been promised by the British after World War I to two peoples, the Jews of Europe and the Arabs of the Middle East. When it came time to fulfill that promise, the former got a state, the latter got dispossessed. And neither has known a day of true peace since.[15]

In the following section, we look at who "these Palestinian people" are and why they cannot "just go home."

The Palestinian Arabs

The number of Palestinian Arabs in the Middle East is roughly equivalent to the total population of Israel (including Israeli Palestinians) at the end of the century. Over a million Palestinians are Israeli citizens (about 20 percent of the total population, and another 2.2 million live in the Israeli-controlled West Bank, East Jerusalem, and Gaza Strip. Thus, if Israel were to annex the Occupied Territories outright, it would have an Arab minority of more than 3 million (compared to roughly 5 million Jews). The rest of the Palestinian Arabs live for the most part in neighboring Arab states, including sizable minorities in neighboring Jordan, Lebanon, and Syria. (See Table 11.2.) Some are still in refugee camps dating from the 1948 war.

The Palestinian Arabs are "as a people, the most literate, industrious and best-educated Arabs in the Middle East."[16] Most Palestinian children attend primary school, and more of them go on to higher education than any other Arab group. Furthermore:

> They are middle class and politically conservative . . . secular and less conservative than other Arabs. (About 12 percent of the Palestinians are Christian.) They wear Western-style clothes, have only one wife and speak English. They run newspapers in Jordan, banks in Lebanon, the civil service in Kuwait, construction companies in the United Arab Emirates. Within their ranks are poets in Syria, millionaire traders in Saudi Arabia, insurance brokers in London, importers in Los Angeles and professors at leading universities in the United States and Europe.[17]

Table 11.2 Where the 6 Million Palestinian Arabs Live

Country or Region	Percentage of Total
Jordan	30%
West Bank	19%
Gaza Strip	11%
Israel	12%
Lebanon	6%
Syria	>5%
Kuwait	>2%
Other Gulf states	>5%
United States	<3%
Other Arab states	<2%
Other	>3%

Source: Calculations based on statistics compiled by the Institute for Palestine Studies.

In Israel, Arabs face many obstacles and do not enjoy equal opportunities, despite equal rights in theory. David Shipler, *New York Times* bureau chief in Jerusalem from 1979 to 1984, gives a glimpse of this double standard:

> A drive down a country road between a Jewish and an Arab town is a journey between privilege and neglect. In the Arab villages, there are no public swimming pools, no neat parks, and often no sewage systems. The narrow streets are sometimes unpaved, often surfaced poorly, and pitted with potholes. Schools have little science equipment, much scarred and broken furniture, and so many pupils that some classes have to be held in rented rooms. In many areas, the government has confiscated land in such tight rings around the villages, and has barred the issuance of building permits for new houses, that the communities have no place in which to expand. Arabs frequently build without necessary permission, thereby risking their future if authorities should decide to have the illegal houses demolished.[18]

We will look in greater detail at the fate of the Palestinians in the Occupied Territories after the outbreak of the "intifada" (1987–1991) in the next chapter. For the moment, it will suffice to note that discrimination against Arabs in the West Bank, East Jerusalem, and Gaza, gave way to harsh repression during this period.

As noted at the beginning of this chapter, the strategic importance of the Middle East inevitably drew outside powers into the conflict — none more often or intrusively in the last half century than the United States. (The United States displaced British and French influence in the 1950s for reasons that are explained in the next chapter.) During the Cold War, the Soviet Union actively contested American influence in the region, backing the Arab cause against Israel. The United States stood firmly behind Israel, but this role as Israel's friend and ally conflicted with the other role the United States sought to play, namely that of "honest broker" or "peacemaker" in the region.

The Middle East Chessboard

Although conflict is endemic in the Middle East, outside powers — especially the United States and the former Soviet Union — had a hand in aggravating it during the Cold War. The East-West rivalry had a negative impact in at least three ways.

First, the superpowers viewed the region as an arena in which to pursue competitive goals. U.S. aims were always to maintain access to Middle East oil for itself and its NATO allies (plus Japan) and to protect oil supply lines. Washington sought stability above all and backed Israel (and moderate Arab regimes) to the point of alienating more conservative Arab states. For its part, the Soviet Union had always viewed Iran and Turkey as within its sphere of influence and jealously guarded its position in the Black Sea area. Protecting its access to the Mediterranean through the Straits of Bosporus and the Dardanelles was also a vital Soviet objective. In the mid-1960s, the Soviet navy acquired a global reach and began to challenge the United States in the Persian Gulf and the Indian Ocean. The Kremlin backed Arab states whose intention was to "drive the Israelis into the sea." To Moscow, Israel was a bastion of American power and influence in the Middle East; to Washington, radical Arab leaders such as Libya's Qaddafi and Syria's Assad were troublemaking sponsors of terrorism.

A second effect of superpower rivalry was the introduction of vast sophisticated arsenals into the region. The United States gave or sold billions of dollars' worth of arms to Israel, Saudi Arabia, Jordan, and Iran (under the Shah) and has supplied Egypt with substantial aid since 1979. The Soviet Union provided weapons and aid to Egypt (until 1973), Syria, Libya, and Algeria, among others; it also supplied weapons to Iraq and to both sides in the Persian Gulf War. Other powers have been involved too: France sent arms to Iraq, and the People's Republic of China sold missiles to Iran. Examples of arms trafficking in the region are easy to come by.

A third negative effect was that superpower politics actually impeded peace negotiations. The Soviet Union insisted on an international peace conference, while the United States backed Israel's position that no such conference could be held until the Arab states recognized Israel's right to secure, defensible borders.

With the collapse of the Soviet Union in December 1991, the dynamics of the situation changed. Gone was the superpower jousting that kept regional rivals flush with military and economic aid from Washington and Moscow.

But the Middle East remained a chessboard on which the major players in the game of international politics sought to gain (or preserve) an advantage — sometimes by promoting peace, sometimes by waging war, as Operation Desert Storm in 1990–1991 demonstrated. (See Box 11.3.) This brief historical overview necessarily omits a great deal, but it sets the stage for a closer look at the recent history of two key Middle Eastern countries: Israel and Egypt.

What If?

BOX 11.3

Saddam Had Not Weathered the "Storm" in 1991

Historically known as *Mesopotamia* ("the land between the rivers"), Iraq is situated in the Tigris-Euphrates valley. Rich in oil reserves but lacking easy access to strategic waterways, it is an almost entirely landlocked country larger than California. The population of around 22 million is largely Muslim. Shiite Muslims comprise a slight majority, but the ruling Baath Party, under the iron-fisted control of former President Saddam Hussein from 1979 to 2003, was Sunni-dominated. (The Shiites predominate in neighboring Iran.)

Saddam Hussein assumed dictatorial powers in 1979. Thereafter, Saddam waged war against all real and imagined internal opposition, including communists, Kurds, and Shiites. Iraq invaded Iran's Khuzistan province in 1980, repudiating a "reconciliation" treaty signed in 1975 and igniting a vicious war that lasted for eight years.

In August 1990, Saddam Hussein ordered his army into Kuwait, catching Iraq's neighbors and the rest of the world by surprise. Tactically, the invasion was brilliant: in mere hours, Iraq seized control of the country and forced the emir to flee. In one fell swoop, Saddam grabbed an extremely valuable parcel of the Middle East, enlarging the considerable oil reserves already under his control and serving notice that Iraq had arrived as a great power in the region.

The forced annexation of Kuwait was a shock, but the greater danger was that Saddam's real aim was to take the Saudi oil fields. To deter such a move, the United States sent a massive force to the Persian Gulf. Dubbed "Operation Desert Storm," it was the largest U.S. military deployment since the Vietnam War. But the United States was not alone in condemning Iraq. Voting for a total embargo against Iraq, the UN Security Council expressed the consensus of the international community that Baghdad's aggression against Kuwait could not go unpunished. Despite the involvement of the international community, it was above all the military might of the United States that confronted Iraq. In no small measure, the future of the Middle East — the regional balance of power — hinged on the outcome of this confrontation. Saddam survived in power for another 12 years, inflicting untold injury and suffering on his own people, especially Iraq's Kurds and Shiites. His capture in December 2003 opened a new chapter, but not necessarily a happy one.

When Saddam refused to withdraw his forces by January 15, 1991, the deadline set by the Security Council, a U.S.-led international coalition launched a fierce air offensive followed by a land invasion deep into Iraq. By the end of February, Kuwait City had been liberated, and Iraq's much-feared armed forces had been vanquished. What is more, Iraq's economy had been demolished: airports, military installations, laboratories, warehouses, power plants, communication systems, bridges, roads, and virtually everything related to Iraq's war-making capacity was destroyed or badly damaged. Critics said President George H. W. Bush missed a chance to get rid of the dictator Saddam. What if the United States had marched all the way to Baghdad? Do you think the Middle East (or the United States) would be better off today?

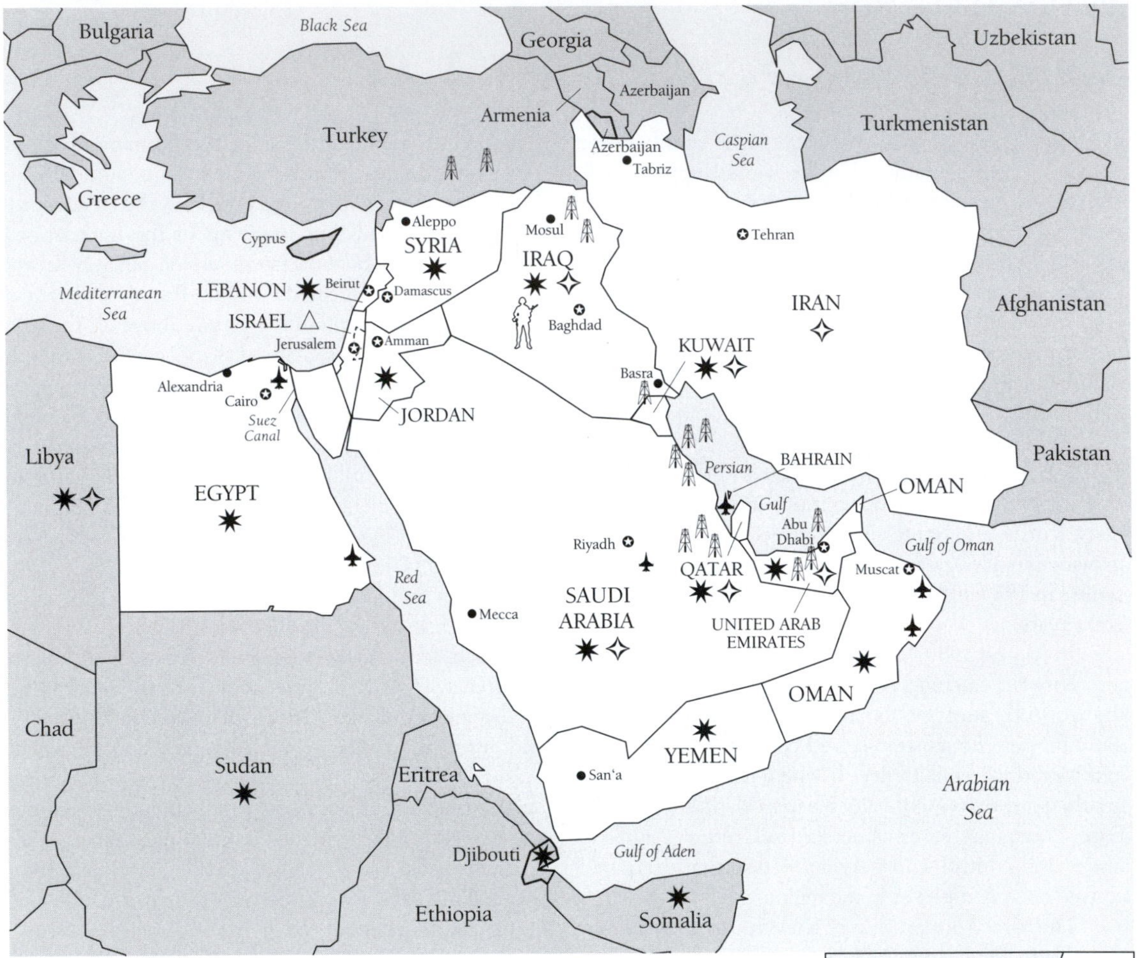

✷ **League of Arab States Member Nations**
Middle East Members:

Bahrain	Kuwait	Saudi Arabia
Egypt	Lebanon	Syria
Iraq	Oman	United Arab Emirates
Jordan	Qatar	Yemen

✧ **Organization of Petroleum Exporting Countries (OPEC) Nations**
Middle East Members:

Iran	Kuwait	Saudi Arabia
Iraq	Qatar	United Arab Emirates

△ **Middle East Nation Thought to Possess Nuclear Weapons: Israel**

U.S. Military Base Access

Major Oil Field Areas

Capital

U.S. occupied

‡ **Arab League States in North Africa (off map): Algeria, Chad, Libya, Morocco, Sudan, and Tunisia**

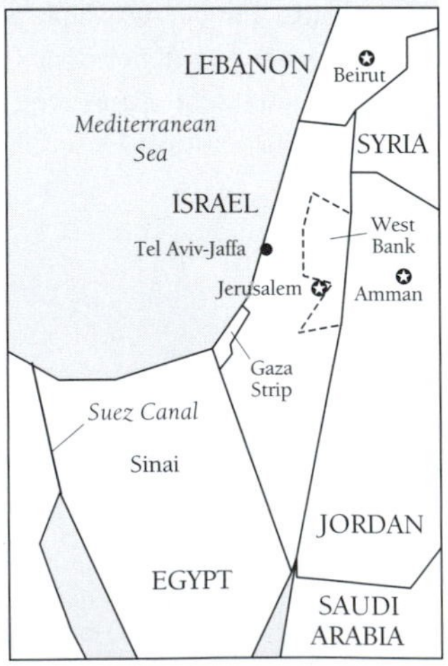

Case Studies: Israel and Egypt

Westerners, especially Americans, often entertain negative images of Arabs. Ignorance and prejudice are to blame:

> Once Jews, blacks and other minorities were subjected to similar degradation; today only Arabs and homosexuals are still fair game for media bashing. The Arabs, I think, are singled out primarily because, unlike most other peoples of the developing world, they have resisted assimilating Western ways or capitulating to Western values. Thus they are seen as a threat and, armed with oil and the ability to make war or peace with Israel, are thought to be in a position to translate that threat into actions that affect the industrialized world.[19]

Whatever its basis, prejudice against Arabs often evokes images of sheiks and harems and nomadic Bedouins with towels on their heads roaming the scorched desert, riding camels, living in tents, and so on. It is a short step to portraying Arabs as barbaric and cruel, treacherous and warlike, fanatical and feudalistic (particularly in their attitudes toward women). Although most Americans are aware that the Middle East has nurtured many advanced civilizations (Egyptian, Sumerian, Babylonian, Assyrian), many remain ignorant of Arabic culture and are indifferent or unsympathetic to Arab concerns.

Western prejudice against Middle Easterners includes a long history of anti-Semitism as well. Hatred of Jews reached a fever pitch in Nazi Germany, of course, but anti-Semitism has also been a recurring element in American life. Extremist groups like the Ku Klux Klan and the American Nazi Party have embraced virulently anti-Semitic doctrines.

Besides breeding suspicion and hostility, prejudiced stereotypes can affect policy. Some critics contend that U.S. policy makers have shown a systematic bias against the Arabs in the Arab-Israeli conflicts of the post–World War II period, while others maintain that State Department career officials have for decades been consistently pro-Arab. Without expecting or even trying to resolve this question, let us examine the politics of the region as impartially and objectively as possible.

Israel

Israel was founded in 1948 under extreme duress. On that date, the British mandate over the territory of Palestine, established after World War I under the auspices of the League of Nations, formally expired.

At its inception, Israel was a small country, approximately the size of New Jersey, surrounded by hostile Arab neighbors — Lebanon to the north, Syria and Jordan to the east, and Egypt to the west. Only the Mediterranean Sea prevented Israel from being completely encircled by enemies. The fact that many charter members of the new Zionist state, including some of its leaders, were survivors of the Holocaust reinforced the fierce determination that marked the Jewish struggle for Palestine.

Nothing has made a deeper imprint on the Israeli psyche than the nation's precarious geography. As a consequence of its exposure to attack on all sides, and given the sizable Palestinian population within its borders, Israel's political life has been permeated by security considerations. Before the 1967 Six-Day War, Israel shared a jagged 50-mile border with Lebanon, a 48-mile border with Syria, and a meandering 335-mile border with Jordan. Israel's frontier with Egypt in the blistering Sinai desert provided a buffer, but even that did not prevent the two nations from fighting three wars in seventeen years (1956, 1967, and 1973). From north to south, Israel was 280 miles long; east to west, it measured nowhere more than 70 miles — its narrow waist, just north of Tel Aviv, was a spare 12 miles wide, and in the south, a mere 9 miles separated Israel's port of Eilat and Jordan's port of Aqaba.

The close proximity of Israel to its Arab neighbors is especially threatening in the age of air power. Flying time from Cairo, Amman, or Damascus to Tel Aviv or Jerusalem is measured in minutes, scant warning time in an attack. Israel's neighbors, for their part, feel vulnerable to Israeli attack and, since 1967, fear Israeli expansionism. In the Six-Day War, Israel trebled its territory, adding about 20,000 square miles by occupying the Sinai (returned to Egypt under the 1979 peace treaty); the Gaza Strip (taken from Egypt); the West Bank, including East Jerusalem (from Jordan); and the Golan Heights (from Syria).

The new Middle East map seemed to make Israel secure at last. But mainly Arabs inhabited the **Occupied Territories,** meaning that Israel now had a major "internal" Arab problem. Besides Israel's own Palestinian population, there are 2.4 million Palestinians living in East Jerusalem and the West Bank today, and another 1.2 million in the tiny piece of real estate known as the Gaza Strip. The seizure of Arab lands — whether justified or not — made future conflict virtually inevitable. To appreciate the situation, it is necessary to consider Israel's origins.

The Idea of Israel Israel was established as a Jewish state following a bitter and bloody struggle with the native Arab population, the Palestinians. The state of Israel was the culmination of **Zionism,** a Jewish national movement dating from the late nineteenth century.[20] Jews had dreamed of being reunited in the Promised Land since their flight from Palestine, known as the **Diaspora,** after a failed rebellion against Roman rule in 70 CE. The fact that Jews had been isolated and persecuted in their adopted lands no doubt helped sustain the dream. For example, although Jews in Eastern Europe and Russia were legally emancipated by the late nineteenth century, they continued to be subjected to anti-Semitism, pogroms (massacres), and cultural isolation. Between 1882 and 1914, several million European Jews emigrated to the United States and tens of thousands went to Palestine, which was still part of the Ottoman Empire.

In 1896, a young Viennese journalist named Theodor Herzl published a pamphlet titled *Der Judenstaat* ("The Jewish State"), advocating the creation of a self-governing community for the Jews. The next year, he convened the First World Zionist Congress in Basel, Switzerland. The delegates declared that the goal of Zionism was to create a "home for the Jewish People in Palestine to be secured by public law" and created the World Zionist Organization to pursue this aim.

Herzl died in 1904, the same year in which Chaim Weizmann, a Zionist and a brilliant chemist, emigrated from Russia to Great Britain. Weizmann's scientific discoveries contributed to the Allied war effort and gave him access to British political elites. He used these connections to persuade the British government to back the cause of a Jewish homeland in Palestine. On November 2, 1917, Lord Balfour, the British foreign secretary, declared that Great Britain favored "the establishment in Palestine of a national home for the Jewish people" and pledged to "facilitate the achievement of this object, it being clearly understood that nothing shall be done which may prejudice the civil and religious rights of the existing non-Jewish communities in Palestine or the rights and political status enjoyed by Jews in any other country."[21]

When the British replaced the Ottoman Turks in Palestine after World War I (Palestine became a British mandate in 1923 under the League of Nations), they were in a position to make good on this promise. The mandate expressly provided for a Jewish home in Palestine, incorporating the **Balfour Declaration** into its text almost verbatim. It also authorized Jewish immigration into Palestine and began to lay the groundwork for a future Jewish state. It divided Palestine, designating the territory east of the Jordan River the "Transjordan." In the truncated Palestine that remained, the British had intended to set up the promised Jewish homeland. But the native Palestinian Arabs had other ideas. Thus began a protracted struggle between the Jews who arrived from abroad and the Palestinian Arabs who resented and resisted the influx of uninvited guests. Of course, Jews did not consider themselves guests in the land of their forefathers. Only time would tell how costly and intractable this struggle — the crux of the Middle East conflict down to the present time — would be.

Between the two world wars, Jews immigrated to Palestine in great numbers. Some were in search of the Promised Land; others, especially from the Soviet Union and Central Europe, were fleeing oppression and persecution. On the eve of World War II, the exodus from Europe turned into a flood as Jews sought refuge from the intolerable conditions created by the Nazis.

In Palestine, a different tempest was stirring. The native Arabs rioted and revolted against the British, culminating in the Arab Rebellion of 1937. The influx of Jews alarmed and dismayed the Arabs, who attacked both mandate authorities and immigrants. The enmities formed in this crucible have fanned the flames of violence in the Middle East to the present day.

The War for Palestine The Palestinian Arabs' attacks on Jews in the 1930s were answered in the 1940s with Jewish terrorist acts by such groups as Irgun and the Stern Gang. Jewish militants of this period included at least two future prime ministers, Menachem Begin and Yitzhak Shamir. The British could not find a solution that was acceptable to both sides, and their vacillation pushed the level of frustration ever higher. The British were committed to the idea of a Jewish state but seemed to envision a federation in which Jews and Palestinian Arabs would participate equally.

World War II gave a new impetus to Zionism. Yet just when so many displaced persons wanted to go, the British government halted Jewish immigration into Palestine. This resulted in highly publicized scenes of refugees on ships being turned away and stories about illegal landings of immigrants. Critics maintain that the ban on immigration was the chief reason Zionist leaders pushed so hard for a Jewish state at that time.

And of course, the Nazis' genocidal intentions for the Jews further steeled the resolve of Zionist leaders to win the struggle for Palestine. The Palestinian Arabs, however, were equally determined to resist.

The British finally brought the issue before the United Nations, which approved a plan to partition Palestine into an Arab state and a Jewish state. It also stipulated that Jerusalem was to become an international city. The Arab states rejected this plan and warned that "any attempt by the Jews or any other power or group of powers to establish a Jewish state in Arab territory is an act of oppression which will be resisted in self-defense by force."[22] The Zionists, however, accepted the plan. The proclamation of the state of Israel cited the UN resolution as its authority. Thus, paradoxically, Palestinian Arabs had been offered a much larger state than they may someday obtain on the West Bank, but they turned the offer down. Had the Arab side accepted the UN resolution, Israel might still be a small enclave in an Arabic Palestine.

Ironically, the UN's attempt to resolve the Palestinian problem peacefully precipitated the first Arab-Israeli war, which did not reach full intensity until after the British had left and the Jewish state was proclaimed. The war lasted about eight months. When the smoke cleared, tiny Israel had prevailed over the armies of Egypt, Transjordan, Syria, Lebanon, and Iraq; it now occupied 30 percent more territory than the United Nations had contemplated. But it left a bitter legacy:

> The war drove nearly one million Arabs out of their homes. This flight was partly due to the fear of Jewish reprisals and partly to the urgings of Arab political leaders to evacuate probable battle areas. The refugees fled to the surrounding Arab countries or to the Arab-occupied parts of Palestine. In the spring of 1949 the number of Arab displaced persons eligible for relief was officially estimated at 940,000. At the beginning of the war there were 1,320,000 Arabs and 640,000 Jews in Palestine. The establishment of Israel resulted in the displacement of nearly 70 percent of the Arab population, which the Israeli government refused to readmit.[23]

Victory and Insecurity, 1949–1973 David Ben-Gurion led Israel through the crucial early years, serving as both prime minister and defense minister. (Weizmann was the nation's first president.) In the 1950s, the Israeli government was made up of coalitions dominated by Ben-Gurion's socialist Mapai Party. Under the Declaration of Independence and the Law of Return, Israel welcomed Jewish immigrants with open arms. The population of Israel, around 900,000 in 1948, nearly doubled by 1955. Jews came from all parts of Europe and the Middle East, an influx that created serious tensions within the new state. For example, the **Sephardic,** or Oriental, Jews — of Spanish, Portuguese, and Middle Eastern background — had a completely different culture from that of **Ashkenazic,** or European, Jews from Central and Eastern Europe. By the mid-1950s, more than half of Israel's population consisted of Sephardim, but Ashkenazim continued to dominate politics and business.

The war for Palestine led to a reshuffling of the population of the Middle East. Palestinian Arabs fled to surrounding Arab states, while Oriental Jews flocked to Israel. The 300,000 or so Palestinian Arabs who remained in Israel became second-class citizens. They were deprived of much of their land, denied freedom of movement and economic opportunities, and shut out of the government.

The treatment of Arabs in Israel was only one grievance of the Arab states. After the war, Israel refused to relinquish the territories in Palestine occupied by its army, arguing that the Arab states had invalidated the UN resolution on Palestine by invading Israel on May 15, 1948. Israel also spurned the UN stipulation that "the refugees wishing to return to their homes and live at peace with their neighbors should be permitted to do so at the earliest practicable date, and that compensation should be paid for the property of those choosing not to return."[24] Though Israel's stand may appear harsh, remember that the new nation was greatly outnumbered and faced constant threats from the Arab states, all of which refused to recognize Israel's right to exist.

During the period leading up to the 1956 Suez Crisis (which was really the second Arab-Israeli war), both sides perpetrated terrorist acts. Ben-Gurion advocated a policy of retaliation; his trusted lieutenant, Moshe Sharett, who served as prime minister during Ben-Gurion's brief retirement from politics (1953–1955), advocated a policy of accommodation. Sharett spoke Arabic and understood Arab culture, which may explain why he believed peace possible. Ben-Gurion's school of thought has prevailed in Israeli politics for most of the years since 1955; Golda Meir, Moshe Dayan, Menachem Begin, and Yitzhak Shamir were all devoted advocates. But the Sharett school has not died; hard-liners and moderates continue to debate how best to deal with Arab discontent.

As Israel's position hardened, so did that of the Arabs, especially in Egypt. In 1956, Egyptian President Nasser nationalized the British-operated Suez Canal. Viewing this as one more in a series of provocations, Israel attacked, with British and French backing. America, however, condemned Israel's action (ironically placing the United States on the same side as the Soviet Union). Although the Israelis won on the battlefield, the superpowers in effect came to Egypt's rescue by creating the United Nations Emergency Force to act as a buffer.

The UN peacekeepers did their job, but from the Arab standpoint the Suez Crisis had added insult to injury. Egypt felt humiliated. Between 1956 and 1967, when the next war was fought, an arms race occurred in the Middle East, with the United States supplying Israel and the Soviet Union supplying Egypt. When Egypt attacked in 1967, Israel was ready. Indeed, it took the Israelis less than a week to score one of the most impressive military victories of modern times. Having defeated both Egypt and Syria in this Six-Day War, Israel seized and occupied territory from both those countries and from Jordan: Sinai, the West Bank, Gaza, East Jerusalem, and the Golan Heights. Of these spoils of war, none would prove to be more fateful — or insoluble at the negotiating table — than control of Jerusalem, which prior to 1967 was an international city under UN administration.

There would be other wars: the Yom Kippur War in 1973, the 1983 war in Lebanon, the first Palestinian intifada ("uprising") of 1989–1991, and the second (or Al Aqsa) intifada in 2000.

Egypt

Egypt is located in the northeastern corner of Africa. The Sinai Peninsula, an uninhabitable wasteland, links it to the Near East. Fully 96 percent of Egypt is desert. Most of Egypt's population (estimated at 68 million in 2003) lives in a crowded, narrow strip along the Nile River, virtually the only area in the country conducive to farming and settlement. Rapid population growth has spurred urbanization, and today almost half of Egypt's population lives in increasingly crowded urban areas. Cairo, the capital, with 13 million people, is one of the most overcrowded cities in the world. Egypt is the only Arab country in which the population explosion has become a pressing problem.

Egypt is a Muslim nation — 94 percent of its people are Sunni Muslims (the remaining 6 percent are Coptic Christians). Egypt has played a key leadership role in the Arab world since the mid-1950s, particularly under President Nasser (1954–1970). The nation's sparse natural resources are offset by a treasure trove of human resources — teachers, doctors, nurses, engineers, and agronomists. Indeed, Egypt supplies much of the Arab world with professionals, specialists, and skilled workers of all kinds.

The Nile River is Egypt's greatest natural resource. Its waters sustain the dense urban population as well as the vital agricultural sector. Without irrigation, Egypt would be forced to import most of its food; instead, the rural economy employs over 40 percent of the labor force and produces crops for export (especially cotton), even though only 4 percent of the land is fit for cultivation.

In its modern form, Egypt is a young country, having gained full independence only after World War II. But it has had a glorious history as a distinctive civilization since ancient times; indeed, its golden age preceded Rome's by thousands of years.

As noted earlier, Egypt has been coveted and dominated by various foreign powers at different times. The isthmus of Suez — and later the canal built through it — was long an essential link between Europe and Asia, and control of it gave Egypt strategic importance. This was underscored during the war in North Africa from 1941 to 1943 when the Axis powers (Germany and Italy) tried to take Egypt but failed.

The Egyptian Revolution The Egyptian national movement, a reaction to Ottoman rule and subsequent European colonialism, was energized and agitated by developments in Palestine. In 1952, popular unrest precipitated a military coup, planned by a secret organization calling itself the Society of Free Officers. The Free Officers persuaded King Farouk to abdicate and create a military junta at first led by Major General Mohammed Naguib.

But the power behind the scenes was a young lieutenant colonel named Gamal Abdel Nasser, who soon emerged as the junta's leader. In 1954, he deposed Naguib and became president and prime minister. Nasser ruled as a popular autocrat (he was "elected" president overwhelmingly in 1956) and created a cult of personality. During the Nasser era, Egypt became a leader not only in the Middle East but also in the Third World. Along with Nehru of India and Tito of Yugoslavia, Nasser was one of the founders of the so-called **nonaligned movement.**

The Egyptian revolution had three major aspects. It was first and foremost a nationalist affair. Egyptians wanted to be free of foreign interference for the first time in thousands of years. Second, it was a socialist revolution: Nasser was anticommunist (he outlawed and persecuted the Egyptian Communist Party), but he was also anticapitalist and anti-imperialist. He railed against everything associated with European (particularly British) domination. This posturing against the West was immensely popular in Egypt at the time. Third, the revolution embraced the goal of Arab unity, or **pan-Arabism.** Nasser recognized that so long as the Arab world was fragmented, Arabs could not win the struggle against imperialism and Zionism.

The Suez Crisis Though committed to Egypt's modernization and economic development, Nasser's preoccupation was foreign affairs, and above all, Israel. In 1956, the Suez Crisis was triggered by Nasser's decision to nationalize the canal. Only U.S. diplomatic intervention saved Egypt from humiliation at the hands of Israel. Despite its claim of a moral victory, Egypt suffered a crushing defeat. Although Suez is no longer as vital as it once was, Egypt is still in a pivotal position, given its proximity to Israel.

To develop Egypt's economy, Nasser sought whatever assistance he could find. When the United States refused to help finance the Aswan Dam project, he turned to the Soviet Union. Moscow not only helped build the dam but also supplied military equipment and advisers to train the Egyptian army. After Egypt signed a historic peace treaty with Israel in 1979, the United States became Egypt's primary source of economic and military assistance.

Nasser's Last Stand: The Six-Day War The Six-Day War in 1967 was the low point of Nasser's political life. Israel invaded Egypt in a preemptive attack after Nasser asked the UN Emergency Force to withdraw; Egypt's defenses were demolished in a matter of days. For the next few years, hostilities continued to smolder, and Nasser once again had to turn to the Soviet Union to rebuild his shattered military.

Nasser died in 1970, before he could redeem himself. Though he had made an indelible mark on Egypt and the Middle East, he also left a legacy of defeat. In internal politics, he had never trusted political parties and had outlawed even the venerable Wafd, which had been so instrumental in resisting the British after World War I. He created instead the Arab Socialist Union (ASU), his own political organization that became a one-party monopoly.

The Ghost of Nasser: A "Civilitary" Legacy The Egyptian revolution became a model for many other developing countries, especially in the Middle East and Africa. By creating a "personality cult" (for example, by constantly putting his idealized image before the public using huge billboards, statues, posters, and the like), Nasser set a precedent for future Arab dictators.

The "civilitary" strongman model is perhaps Nasser's most enduring legacy in the Middle East. Though a dictator, Nasser staged periodic elections to demonstrate his popularity (and thus his legitimacy). An army colonel when he led the coup against the king, Nasser chose the civilian title of president, but retained his military rank and appeared in uniform on ceremonial occasions.

His example was followed in Algeria, Libya, Syria, and Iraq. In Libya, for instance, Colonel Muammar al-Qaddafi, also led a coup that ousted the king, and then established an authoritarian regime based on a mixture of socialism and personal charisma. Like Nasser, Qaddafi also had visions of a pan-Arab superstate and tried to unite Libya with neighboring Tunisia and Algeria. He also emulated Nasser in forging close ties with the Soviet Union and launching vitriolic propaganda campaigns against Israel and the United States. Finally, like Nasser, he remained "Colonel" Qaddafi — a symbol of his closeness to the people.

Sadat: Want Peace? Make War Anwar al-Sadat succeeded Nasser and quickly made his own mark. In 1972, he surprised the world by ordering 15,000 Soviet advisers to leave Egypt because he believed that dependency on a single outside power raised the specter of a new form of colonialism. On October 6, 1973, Sadat, in another surprise, launched an attack against Israel on Yom Kippur, the holiest day on the Jewish calendar. The Egyptian army crossed the Suez Canal and broke through Israel's forward defenses in the occupied Sinai, but Israel quickly recovered and counterattacked, retaking all of the territory it had lost and more. As in 1956 and 1967, only outside intervention stopped the Israelis from marching all the way to Cairo. Nonetheless, Sadat claimed a moral victory. The Egyptian army had proved, he said, that Arabs could fight with modern arms and that Israel was not invincible.

The Camp David Accords In 1977, Sadat caused a sensation when he addressed the Israeli parliament (the Knesset), breaking not only precedent but also the logjam in Egyptian-Israeli relations. There followed a meeting at Camp David, Maryland, where U.S. President Jimmy Carter brokered an agreement embodied in the 1979 peace treaty. In the so-called **Camp David Accords,** Israel agreed to give the Sinai back to Egypt in return for Egypt's recognizing Israel's right to exist. Israel may appear to have given away more than it got, but it was in truth Sadat who went out on a limb. Egypt thus became the first Arab state to recognize Israel. Throughout the Arab world, Sadat was denounced as a traitor to the Arab cause.

Before President Sadat's decision to sign a separate peace with Israel, Egypt was the leader of the Arab world. After the treaty, as Egypt's stance changed from confrontation to mediation (see Chapter 12), its stature as standard-bearer for the Arab cause slipped.

Sadat's actions also rankled Arab nationalists and Islamic fundamentalists in his own country. The fact that he was awarded the Nobel Peace Prize (jointly with Menachem Begin) meant little to his compatriots; to many Egyptians, the peace treaty was a sellout, and Sadat had betrayed a sacred trust. On October 6, 1981 — eight years to the day after his fateful Yom Kippur invasion — Egyptian Islamists assassinated Sadat. Vice President Hosni Mubarak, another strongman with a military background, succeeded him and has ruled Egypt uneventfully ever since.

Sadat versus Nasser: Who's Greater? Like Nasser, Sadat left an ambiguous legacy. On the one hand, having once made war on Israel (and lost), he took a bold and historic step toward peace in the Middle East. On the other hand, he alienated the Egyptian people and made his country a pariah in the Arab world. In internal politics, he continued in Nasser's footsteps, ruling with personal flair and a firm hand. Though attentive to the trappings of democracy, Sadat was no less authoritarian than Nasser. He often displayed an imperious contempt for public opinion, as when he pursued the extremely unpopular economic policy of *infitah* ("opening"); designed to attract foreign investment and spur an economic miracle, the policy succeeded only in making a few Egyptians very rich, including members of Sadat's family.

In the eyes of the West, Sadat is the most admired Arab leader of the postwar period. But to Egyptians and most other Arabs, Nasser is the greatest. Of course, the political culture of the West is very different from that of the Middle East, and Arab and Western perceptions and values are rarely identical. By Western measures, Nasser was a failure: Egypt lost two wars to Israel during his tenure, and the Egyptian economy stalled and stagnated. But Nasser understood the intangible elements of success in the Egyptian context — the yearning for independence, the desire to recapture past glory, the resentment of outside interference, the need to fight the "enemy" (almost as an end in itself).

Ironically, modern Egypt's most durable leader is a figure with less charisma than either Nasser or Sadat, but more political acumen than both. We will take up that part of the story in the next chapter.

SUMMARY

More than in any other region of the world, the history of the Middle East has been dominated by religion. Judaism, Christianity, and Islam all have their roots there, and the cultures of the region are strongly influenced by the aesthetics and ethics associated with these religions. In the past century, religious differences have been exacerbated by rising nationalism. Today, conflicts that appear to be religious are more often the result of rival nationalisms. Political systems in this area are authoritarian and in many cases repressive. The foreign policies of several powerful players in the region at times reflect militancy and an uncompromising spirit often associated with religious zealotry. Chapter 12 will look more closely at the forms of government found in the Middle East today.

KEY TERMS

Middle East
Maghreb
Near East
Northern Belt
North Africa
Fertile Crescent
Arabian Peninsula
nomadic
Islam
Judaism
Talmud
rabbi
Christianity
Jesus Christ
Koran
Muhammad
Allah
theocracy
Sunni
Shiite
imam
mullah
jihad
Muslim Botherhood
Islamism
Occupied Territories
Zionism
Diaspora
Balfour Declaration
Sephardic
Ashkenazic
nonaligned movement
pan-Arabism
Camp David Accords

STUDY QUESTIONS

1. What are the major religions of the Middle East, and in what ways has religion shaped the region's history and culture?
2. Why do Muslims, Christians, and Jews all view Jerusalem as the Holy City? Has this common element in all three religious traditions contributed to greater mutual understanding or has it done the opposite?
3. What inspired the Iranian Revolution? In what sense (if any) was the revolution the cause of the Iran-Iraq War?
4. What role did colonialism and foreign intrusion play in setting the stage for Middle East conflict? When and how did colonialism end in the region?
5. How have international relationships in the Middle East evolved since World War II? How many instances of war and revolution can you cite? How many successful efforts at peacekeeping and conflict resolution?

SUGGESTED READINGS

Benvenisti, Meron. *City of Stone: The Hidden History of Jerusalem.* Berkeley: University of California Press, 1996.

Blackman, Aylward M. *Gods, Priests, and Men: Studies in the Religion of Pharaonic Egypt.* New York: Columbia University Press, 1996.

Farah, Tawfic E. *Pan-Arabism and Arab Nationalism: The Continuing Debate.* Boulder, Colo.: Westview, 1987.

Garfinkle, TK. *Israel: Myth and Reality.* Belmont, Calif: Wadsworth, 1997.

Gershoni, Israel. *Egypt, Islam and the Arabs: The Search for Egyptian Nationhood, 1900–1930.* New York: Oxford University Press, 1987.

Gershoni, Israel, and Jankowski, James P. *Redefining the Egyptian Nation, 1930–1945.* New York: Cambridge University Press, 1995.

Hare, William. *The Struggle for the Holy Land: Arabs, Jews, and the Emergence of Israel.* Lanham, Md.: Madison, 1996.

Inhorn, Marcia C. *Infertility and Patriarchy: The Cultural Politics of Gender and Family Life in Egypt.* Philadelphia: University of Pennsylvania Press, 1996.

Kimmerling, Baruch, and Migdal, Joel S. *The Palestinian People: A History.* Cambridge, Mass.: Harvard University Press, 2003.

Lamb, David. *The Arabs: Journeys beyond the Mirage.* New York: Random House, 1988.

Mackey, Sandra. *The Reckoning: Iraq and the Legacy of Saddam Hussein.* New York: Norton, 2002.

Madawi, Al-Rasheed. *A History of Saudi Arabia.* New York: Cambridge University Press, 2002.

McLoughlin, Leslie. *Ibn Saud: Founder of a Kingdom.* New York: Saint Martin's, 1993.

Meeks, Dimitri. *Daily Life of the Egyptian Gods.* Ithaca, N.Y.: Cornell University Press, 1996.

Merrill, Eugene H. *Kingdom of Priests: A History of Old Testament Israel.* Ada, Mich.: Baker, 1997.

Molavi, Afshin. *Persian Pilgrimages: Journeys across Iran.* New York: Norton, 2002.

Peters, F. E. Mecca: *A Literary History of the Muslim Holy Land.* Princeton, N.J.: Princeton University Press, 1994.

Reich, Bernard, ed. *The Arab-Israeli Conflict and Conciliation: A Documentary History.* Westport, Conn.: Greenwood, 1995.

Reid, Donald Malcolm. *Whose Pharaohs? Archeology, Museums, and Egyptian National Identity from Napoleon to World War I.* Berkeley: University of California Press, 2002.

Rotem, Judith. *Distant Sisters: The Women I Left Behind.* Philadelphia, Pa.: Jewish Publication Society, 1996.

St. John, Robert Bruce. *Libya and the United States: Two Centuries of Strife.* Philadelphia: University of Pennsylvania Press, 2002.

Viorst, Milton. *Sands of Sorrow: Israel's Journey from Independence.* New York: Harper, 1987.

Watterson, Barbara. *The Egyptians.* Cambridge, Mass.: Blackwell, 1996.

Wheatcroft, Geoffrey. *The Controversy of Zion: Jewish Nationalism, the Jewish State, and the Unresolved Jewish Dilemma.* Reading, Mass.: Addison Wesley Longman, 1996.

SUGGESTED WEB SITES

http://www.arab.net/
http://www.palestinehistory.com
http://www.mideastweb.org
http://www.usd.edu/erp/Palestine/history.htm
http://www.arab.net/palestine
http://history.evansville.net/egypt
http://www.opec.org

NOTES

1. James A. Bill and Robert Springborg, *Politics in the Middle East* (New York: Addison Wesley Longman, 2000), p. 32.
2. Ibid.
3. George Lenczowski, *The Middle East in World Affairs* (Ithaca, N.Y.: Cornell University Press, 1980), p. 694.
4. Ibid.
5. Ibid.
6. David Lamb, *The Arabs: Journeys beyond the Mirage* (New York: Random House, 1988), p. 7.
7. Ibid., p. 15.
8. Bernard Lewis, *The Arabs in History* (New York: Harper, 1966), pp. 131–143.
9. Lenczowski, *Middle East in World Affairs,* p. 27.
10. Ibid.
11. Ibid., p. 35.
12. Ibid., p. 46.
13. See George Antonius, *The Arab Awakening* (New York: Putnam, 1965).
14. Lamb, *The Arabs,* p. 200.
15. Ibid., p. 199.
16. Ibid., p. 201.
17. Ibid.
18. David Shipler, *Arab and Jew: Wounded Spirits in a Promised Land* (New York: Viking Penguin, 1987), pp. 443–444.

19. Lamb, *The Arabs,* p. 15.
20. For a concise discussion of the origins and evolution of Zionism, see "Zionism Now," *The Economist,* July 11, 1992, p. 21.
21. Go to http://www.yale.edu/lawweb/avalon/balfour.htm to read the full text of the Balfour Declaration.
22. Arab Higher Committee of Palestine, Feb. 6, 1948; quoted in Lenczowski, *Middle East in World Affairs,* p. 405.
23. Lenczowksi, *Middle East in World Affairs,* p. 410.
24. Go to http://www.pna.net/facts/un_oak_resolutions.htm to read the full text of Resolution 194, cited in this passage.

CHAPTER 12

Monarchies, Dictatorships, and a Garrison State

Political institutions in the Middle East vary, but authoritarian patterns are the rule. Authoritarianism is deeply etched into the templates of Arab history and political culture — witness the survival of traditional monarchies in Arabia and more modern versions in Jordan and Morocco. (Half a century ago, most Arab nations were monarchies.)

Political traditions in the Arab world are also characterized by a tendency toward religious and political intolerance. Islam is not only an Arab religion but also a way of life that does not mix easily with other religions or cultures — even different branches of Islam itself. This intolerance has at various times and places taken a violent turn, as the spectacular September 11, 2001, terrorist attacks on America perpetrated by members of an international Islamist group led by a rich Saudi expatriate named Osama bin Laden and based in Afghanistan demonstrated.

Significantly, bin Laden's hatred for America stems from the first Persian Gulf War when the United States obtained permission from the Saudi monarchy to establish American military bases in Saudi Arabia. After the 1991 war, however, American troops did not leave. In the eyes of bin Laden and his compatriots, this American "occupation" of Islam's holy land — the home of Mecca and Medina and the very ground on which the prophet Muhammad once walked — was deeply humiliating. Worse still, it was a desecration by infidels and Christian "crusaders" who introduced immoral Western ways. The history of colonial rule by the British and French, and the West's unquenchable thirst for Arab oil, lent credence to bin Laden's extreme views in the eyes of even moderate Arabs, who in most cases did not condone his methods.

The zeal often associated with the region's politics is thus rooted in religion-based cultures — which is not to say that Islam advocates terrorism or glorifies war. Although it strictly forbids violence against all noncombatants (not only women and children, but also unarmed men), Islam has a history of conflict, conquest, and conversion going back some thirteen centuries. The concept of **jihad,** or holy war, captures this combative element in Arab culture.

Such turbulent spirits and combative energies are not always directed against outsiders, as the Iraqi invasion of Kuwait in August 1990 attested. Xenophobia is no greater among Arabs than among other groups. Like other peoples, Arabs are intensely nationalistic, and sometimes, like the nations of Europe, they have fought among themselves over religious or other differences. This history of internecine warfare is captured in the following passage:

> The very first anecdote usually told to students of the Middle East is the story of the scorpion and the frog that one day find themselves on a riverbank. The scorpion asks the frog to carry him across to the other shore.
>
> "Don't be ridiculous," answers the frog. "If I let you on my back, you'll sting me."
>
> But the scorpion points out that he cannot swim and if he were to sting the frog in midriver, "we both would drown."
>
> So the frog, persuaded by the logic of the argument, allows the scorpion to climb on his back, and they set out into the river. When they reach the middle, however, the scorpion stings the frog, and the paralyzed amphibian starts to sink beneath the water. "Why did you do that?" he croaks. "Now we'll both die."
>
> "Oh, well"—the scorpion sighs, shrugging his carapace—"after all, this is the Middle East."[1]

A pronounced tendency toward political turmoil has been evident throughout the region as well. This may explain why fallen strongmen or "popular tyrants" have typically replaced monarchs. Barry Rubin, a political scientist who specializes in the Middle East, describes the Arab world as "a stronghold of modern dictators" and uses strong terms — "energy, cleverness, and ruthlessness" — to describe these rulers. They have, in his words,

> constructed populist, repressive regimes able to tame some of the world's most turbulent and violent political systems. To stay atop the tiger, they must have an ideology acceptable to their cultures, a party and mass organizations furnishing a wide base of supporters, and an energetic secret policy to break up antigovernment conspiracies.[2]

Rubin notes that Middle East dictators "must also dominate the economy and control the army" and asserts that they "claim to have discovered a proper ethical and political system for the entire region or even the whole world."[3] Many Middle East experts do not share his extremely dark and disparaging view of Arab politics, but Rubin does raise interesting questions about the nature and origins of modern Arab regimes, which we examine in more depth in the following sections.

Modern Arab Regimes

The new military regimes of the 1950s and 1960s stressed nationalism, pan-Arabism, and socialism. They denounced imperialism, capitalism, and, above all, Zionism. Egypt, Algeria, Syria, Iraq, and the **Palestine Liberation Organization (PLO)** all looked to the Soviet Union for economic and military aid. After 1969, Libya and South Yemen did too (the latter became a Soviet client state in the 1970s). The reason these regimes all embraced the Soviet Union had little to do with ideology (indeed, they typically persecuted their own communists) and much to do with **realpolitik** (political strategy). The

United States supported the old order and Israel, while the Soviet Union backed modern dictatorships and was cool toward Israel.

Once in power, the strongmen combined Arab traditions with modern authoritarian techniques. Nasser set the standard for using symbols, propaganda, and charisma to manipulate the masses. Dictators who have imitated Nasser include the late Hafiz al-Assad (Syria), Saddam Hussein (Iraq), Muammar al-Qaddafi (Libya), and others. But Arab rulers have given autocratic tactics and methods a new wrinkle. For example, the leader's inner circle is typically reinforced with friends, relatives, and others who have special ties to the leader. In Syria, the ruling clique consists mainly of members of Assad's Alawite Muslim minority. Assad groomed his son Bashar to succeed him, much as Saddam Hussein groomed his sons Uday and Qusay to take over one day. (Both were hunted down and killed after U.S. forces ousted Saddam's regime in the spring of 2003.) In Iraq, most of the ruling elite under the brutal Saddam regime came from the Sunni Muslim minority, especially from the town of Tikrit. Similarly, the Libyan dictator Qaddafi relies on loyal confederates from his own clan and home territory.

As military officers who themselves plotted against previous rulers, the new populist dictators know well the danger of coups and have figured out how to prevent them. Typically, they purge any officers who have ties to the old regime or to competing parties, factions, interests, or ideologies. They also tightly control military promotions and rotate or transfer officers so that no one can count on the loyalty of a given unit. Trusted officers are placed in key positions, thus giving the military a stake in the success of the regime and shared responsibility for any failures. Finally, multiple intelligence networks are created, not only to stamp out dissent but also to have each keep an eye on the others.

In modern Arab dictatorships, a single party is at the center of a web of mass organizations (for workers, youths, students, teachers, women, peasants, and so on). The party is an extension of the leader, who uses it to control the society and reward the faithful, in part through patronage appointments in the bureaucracy, schools, mass organizations, industry, and the armed forces. Examples are the Baath Party in Syria and Iraq, the Islamic Republican Party in Iran, and the people's committees in Libya.

The Paradoxes of Arab Politics

The Middle East is a region of paradoxes. Its sun-baked deserts and withering heat disguise the richest oil reserves in the world. Arab nations share a religion, a language, and a cause (Palestine), yet unity has evaded them. Arab culture is permeated by the strict moral codes of Islam, yet the region's history has been one of conflicts, crusades, and cruelties. Modern Arab nationalism is a reaction against Western capitalism and imperialism, yet Marxism has made few inroads, and communist parties are outlawed nearly everywhere.

There is a large gender gap in the Arab world, which is perpetuated by the social conventions of Islam. Women do not enjoy equal rights with men, as a glance at the far-right column in Table 12.1 clearly reveals. A woman's role is to bear many children, keep house, and obey her husband. This subservient role is reflected in demographic patterns of Arab society, which differ quite strikingly from those of the West.

In the 1990s, the population of the Middle East was set to double in twenty to twenty-five years, thanks to high fertility rates (a result of low literacy and poor employment prospects for women) and a sharp drop in the death rate (reflecting better sanitation and more widely available health care). An important characteristic of the rapidly growing Arab population is its youth: four out of ten people are under age fifteen. Urban overcrowding is also a potential problem: three-quarters of the region's population already live in cities. Cairo and Tehran are examples of the modern-day "megalopolis" — congested, clamoring, and polluted — found in many developing countries (China, India, Indonesia, Mexico, Nigeria, Peru, and others).

Despite its huge oil endowment, the region has not experienced the economic awakening that has occurred in such newly industrialized countries as South Korea and Taiwan. (See Tables 12.2 and 12.3.) Economic growth in most Arab countries continues

Table 12.1 A Woman's Place . . .

Country	Population, 1998 (thousands)	Annual Growth Rates, 1990–1998 (percent)	Fertility Rate, 1993* (births per woman)	Female Labor Force (% of total)
Algeria	29,922	2.6	4.3	26
Egypt	68,000	2.3	3.8	30
Iran	61,947	1.9	5.5	26
Israel	6,700	3.5	2.7	41
Saudi Arabia	20,739	3.9	6.4	15
Syria	15,277	3.3	6.1	26
Turkey	63,451	1.8	3.4	37

*The data in this column are taken from *The World Bank Atlas,* 1995.

Source: International Bank for Reconstruction and Development, *The World Bank Atlas* (Washington, D.C.: Author, 2000).

Table 12.2 Economic Profile: Comparison of Selected Middle Eastern States and South Korea

Country	1998 GNP, (billions of U.S. dollars)	Average Yearly Inflation, 1990–1998	Per Capita GNP, 1998 (PPP,* dollars)	Per Capita GNP Growth Rate, 1990–1998 (percent)
Algeria	46.3	21.1	4,595	–1.0
Egypt	79.2	9.7	3,146	2.7
Iran	102.2	28.3	5,121	1.8
Israel	96.5	11.0	16,861	2.2
Saudi Arabia	143.3	–2.4	10,498	–2.4
Syria	15.1	8.9	2,702	1.3
Turkey	200.5	79.4	6,594	2.9
South Korea	399.0	4.9	13,286	4.9

*Purchasing power parity — is what a given number of dollars would actually allow you to buy in the local economy (not in the United States).

Source: International Bank for Reconstruction and Development, *The World Bank Atlas* (Washington, D.C.: Author, 2000).

Table 12.3 Economic Dynamism: Comparison of Selected Arab States and South Korea, 1998

Country	Agriculture (% of GNP)	Trade in Goods* (% of PPP GNP)	Investment (% of GNP)	Personal Computers (per 1,000)
Algeria	12	16.4	27	4.2
Egypt	17	10.2	22	9.1
Iran	25	8.4	16	31.9
Israel	**<6**	**47.7**	**20**	**217.2**
Saudi Arabia	7	31.9	21	49.6
Syria	30†	14.6	29	1.7
Turkey	18	18.8	25	23.2
South Korea	**7**	**35.6**	**34**	**156.8**

*Foreign trade in goods (not services) as a percentage of GNP converted into the purchasing power of dollars in the local economy (not in the United States).

†Estimate.

Source: International Bank for Reconstruction and Development, *The World Bank Atlas* (Washington, D.C.: Author, 1995).

to be slow. More important, per capita growth rates have actually been negative in many Arab countries, meaning that the population is increasing faster than the economy's ability to support it.

The Logic of Arab Politics

There is a notion in the West, reinforced by the behavior of such leaders as Qaddafi, Khomeini, and Saddam Hussein, that Arabs are irrational and that chaos is their natural condition. On the contrary, most Arab rulers are rational—"they act in accordance with domestic and regional needs, rather than behave as the West might think proper." At the same time, however, these rulers "face very exacting demands from Islam and Arab nationalism and are simultaneously manipulators and prisoners of the power symbols of these politics."[4] For example, anti-Zionism is a powerful unifier, but it also locks governments into positions that make seeking peace with Israel untenable. (That is why Arab leaders accused President Sadat of betrayal when Egypt signed its peace treaty with Israel in 1979.)

In the 1930s, Arab nationalism began to eclipse Islam as a force shaping Arabs' identities and aspirations. Two external forces fueled this movement: European imperialism and Zionism. Before World War I, the main motive for unity was anti-imperialism; as Jews flowed into Palestine between the wars, that sentiment merged with anti-Zionism; and after the Palestine War of 1948–1949, the primary motive was hatred of Israel.

But Arab unity is like the weather: easy to talk about but impossible to control. Many attempts have been made to merge Arab nations — Nasser always tried, and

Qaddafi has tried as well. All efforts have failed. One reason why Israel has survived as an independent state despite being isolated and outnumbered is that the Arab states have so often been preoccupied by quarrels among themselves. Even the Palestinians, with a passionate cause to unite them, have at times fought each other, and groups have broken away from the PLO, thus splintering and weakening the Palestinian movement.

Moreover, the bickering sometimes bursts into open hostilities. Iraq's forcible seizure of Kuwait is a case in point; the Lebanese civil war is another. Tense situations have also arisen between Iraq and Syria, Syria and Jordan, Egypt and Libya, Libya and Tunisia, Libya and Chad, and the PLO and Syria. In the Iran-Iraq War, Algeria and Syria backed Persian Iran against Arab Iraq (Saudi Arabia and Jordan, among others, supported Iraq). And in the Persian Gulf War of 1991, most Arab states, including Syria, sided with the anti-Iraq coalition led by the United States.

Sadat's decision to make peace with Israel led to Egypt's expulsion from the Arab League. This illustrates one major verity of Middle Eastern politics: Arab states all agree that Israel is the enemy, but they have never been able to agree on strategy. Some are radical, "rejectionist" states (Iraq, Libya, Syria); others are more moderate (Egypt, Jordan, Saudi Arabia). Even the moderates, however, distrust and detest Israel.

The Arithmetic of Instability

The turbulence that plagued Arab politics in the 1950s and 1960s, when the nationalist regimes were struggling to consolidate their newfound power, can be demonstrated with a few statistics. During the three decades following the Egyptian revolution, no fewer than fifty-five unscheduled transfers of power occurred in Arab nations, including coups, revolutions, and assassinations. (See Figure 12.1.) Arab states outside the Persian Gulf experienced twenty-four coups during the 1950s and 1960s. Syria averaged one coup about every two years. Iraq had coups in 1958, 1963, and 1968. A coup in Libya in 1969 brought Qaddafi to power. The number of such events declined in the 1970s and 1980s, suggesting that Arab leaders had learned techniques for staying in power, and the internal politics of most Arab nations stabilized considerably.

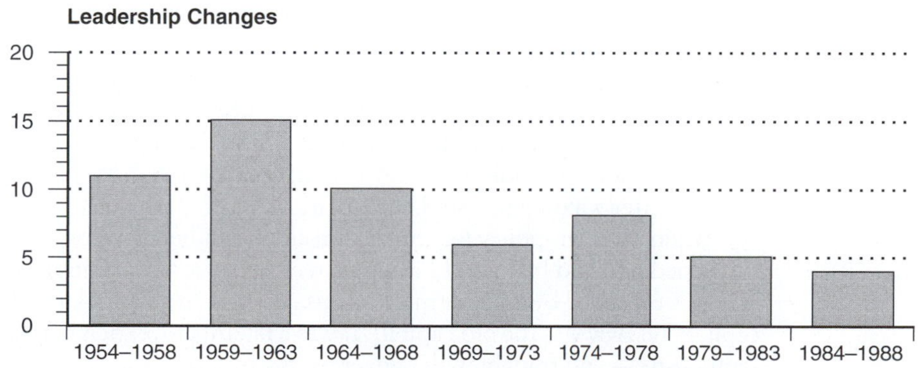

Figure 12.1 Unscheduled Leadership Changes in the Middle East, 1954–1988

Coups and rumors of coups dominated Middle East politics in the 1950s and 1960s. The military took charge in one Arab country after another. Where the military did not take charge, an anachronistic form of authoritarianism — hereditary monarchy — remained in force. Jordan, Morocco, Saudi Arabia, and the oil-rich Persian Gulf sheikdoms of Bahrain, Kuwait, Qatar, Oman, and the United Arab Emirates are cases in point. Western-style democracy made inroads only in Israel, where it does not fully extend to the Arab population.

As noted in the previous chapter, Egypt's President Gamel Abdel Nasser created the prototype for the civilitary dictatorships that replaced the preexisting monarchies in much of the Arab world. Ironically, Egypt made a separate peace with Israel under Anwar al-Sadat, Nasser's successor. It was "separate" in the sense that it excluded Syria, Jordan, and Lebanon, and it was universally denounced in the Arab world. We look next at the bittersweet consequences of the Israeli-Egyptian peace treaty.

Peace and War, 1977–1982

Israel has never lost a war. Nonetheless, Israel's biggest victory came not on the battlefield, but at the negotiating table. The 1979 peace treaty between Egypt and Israel (see Chapter 11) was hailed as a major step toward lasting peace in the Middle East. In accordance with the treaty, Egypt recognized Israel, Israel returned the Sinai to Egypt, and the two nations exchanged ambassadors. The United States underwrote the agreement, making generous new commitments of military and economic aid to both sides. Relations between these former foes have remained cool but correct ever since.

A Separate Peace . . .

Ironically, it was the victory of the hawks led by Menachim Begin (an unabashed Zionist) that made the stunning peace treaty with Egypt possible in 1977–1979. In Israel, as in the United States, a conservative leader is often able to act more boldly in foreign policy than a liberal one, whose patriotism might be more easily questioned. (Hence it was Richard Nixon, the crusading Cold Warrior, who initiated rapprochement with the People's Republic of China and signed the first SALT treaty with the Soviet Union.)

Unfortunately, peace with Egypt was not peace with Arabs, especially Palestinian Arabs. Nor was it peace with Lebanon or Syria. Among the unresolved issues, none would be more incendiary in the coming years than East Jerusalem, which Israel annexed after winning the Six-Day War in 1967.

Begin's foreign-policy feat made him an instant hero in Israel. The national euphoria helped him and his Likud Party win reelection in 1981. Significantly, the Likud victory was preceded by another momentous event — Israel proclaimed Jerusalem its new capital (Tel Aviv was the old capital). It was a fateful move, rich in religious and political symbolism — and fraught with danger for the future.

. . . And Another War

Celebration soon gave way to anguish when Israel invaded Lebanon the following year. (See Box 12.1.) The Likud-led coalition was starting to unravel in 1981. After the invasion, during which Lebanese Christians committed atrocities against civilians in Palestinian refugee camps while Israeli military guards apparently turned a blind eye, Begin survived a no-confidence motion in the Knesset by a single vote. The invasion caused a furor in Israel and elsewhere because it appeared to violate Israel's own precept that the only justification for war is self-defense. Though initially provoked by PLO cross-border raids from Palestinian bases in southern Lebanon, the Israeli army pressed northward. In June 1982, it encircled Beirut and then called in the Israeli air force. The strategy was to drive the PLO out of Lebanon. Massive bombing achieved that goal — at an enormous political cost.

Thus, Israel won the battle but not the war. Prime Minister Begin found himself in the middle of a political maelstrom. Depressed by the turn of events in Lebanon and the death of his wife, Begin retired in 1983. There was still peace with Egypt, but now Israel itself was deeply divided. Even the military was split: some high-ranking officers resigned

Contrast and Comparison

BOX 12.1

Shattered Lebanon

Lebanon is a beautiful land with a religiously and culturally diverse population of only slightly more than 4 million (smaller than Israel). Not long ago, Lebanon's capital, Beirut, was a thriving center of commerce and finance — a vital link between Europe and the Arab world.

Many Palestinian war refugees had fled to Lebanon after 1948 and were absorbed into Lebanese society, working in such fields as business, banking, journalism, and higher education. But a second wave of Palestinians, arriving after the 1967 war, ended up in refugee camps. They were stateless, without a homeland; lacking passports, they could not go anywhere else.

When the PLO was expelled from Jordan in the early 1970s, it moved its headquarters to Beirut, and the refugee camps in Lebanon became PLO strongholds. The PLO launched raids against Israel from southern Lebanon. Eventually, Israel retaliated.

Lebanon's tranquillity was totally shattered in 1975, when a ferocious civil war broke out — sparked, ironically, by the presence of a non-Lebanese group, the Palestinians. Lebanon's civil war soon turned into a free-for-all involving a direct confrontation between Syria and Israel, and indirect conflict with Iraq and Iran. It also entangled other Arab nations (especially Jordan), the superpowers, and ultimately UN peacekeepers.

By 1982, the continuing turmoil had become intolerable, and Israel decided to force the issue. In June, the Israeli army invaded Lebanon, surrounded Beirut, and drove the PLO guerrillas out of Lebanon, but not for good. In April 1983, an explosion at the U.S. embassy in Beirut killed fifty people. In September 1983, the Phalange (a militant Maronite Christian militia) entered two refugee camps in West Beirut and massacred hundreds of people, mostly women and children, in cold blood. The incident outraged public opinion and sent shock waves through Israel's government, whose apparent complicity stunned the world. On October 23rd of that year, 241 American military personnel and fifty-four French soldiers were killed in separate incidents. Amid all this turmoil and depressed by the death of his wife, Prime Minister Begin resigned. But the Israeli army remained in Lebanon until 2000 — twenty-two years later.

their commissions, and many soldiers refused to fight. Meanwhile, the high cost of the war strained the economy and added to growing domestic unrest. Finally, the Arabs had a new cause célèbre and opinion turned sharply against Israel, even in the West.

The economic and political repercussions of the Lebanon invasion made it necessary for Israel to seek a new popular mandate. But the 1984 elections were ambiguous: the Labour Party won the most votes but failed to win a majority of the seats in the Knesset. Both Labour and Likud scrambled to form a coalition government, but neither succeeded. These two odd bedfellows then worked out a so-called government of national unity — the first in Israeli history. The two parties agreed to alternate power, with the leader of the Labour Party serving as prime minister for two years and then handing over the government to the Likud leader. Under this arrangement, Labour's Shimon Peres became prime minister in September 1984 and was succeeded by Likud's Yitzhak Shamir in October 1986.

The Missing Peace, 1983–1993

The **Palestinian question** and the apparent breakthrough in Israeli-Palestinian relations in the fall of 1993 receive special attention in this chapter because the future of the Middle East hinges on its solution. The 1979 Israeli-Egyptian peace treaty was truly historic, but it contained a fatal flaw: it deferred resolution of the nettlesome Palestinian issue to a later time. That time has never come.

Full Autonomy or Empty Promises?

As provided in the treaty, Egypt and Israel began talks in May 1979 aimed at bringing "full autonomy" to the West Bank and Gaza. The intent was to complete arrangements for free elections in the Occupied Territories and to define the powers of a Palestinian "self-governing authority" within a year. But the talks foundered on such issues as security, land, water, Jewish settlements, and Jerusalem. The issue of Jerusalem was (and is) the most emotionally charged. The Palestinians accuse Israel of using endless negotiations to buy time while Jewish settlers move into the West Bank and East Jerusalem, thus "creating facts" in Menachem Begin's memorable words. The Israelis insisted that PLO leader Yasir Arafat did not do enough to stop Palestinian terrorism. Attacks on school buses and public places where women and children are often among the victims, for example, lend credence — or at least moral weight — to this charge.

The Roots of Rebellion

As already noted, Israel seized the West Bank and Gaza Strip, as well as East Jerusalem, after the Six-Day War in 1967. This action created a new category of Palestinian Arabs: those living in Israeli-occupied Arab territory. Unlike Arabs within Israel's pre-1967 boundaries, these Palestinians have no legal rights. No consensus has ever been reached within Israel on what to do with the Occupied Territories. The "hawks" insist that Israel must retain control of the West Bank and Gaza for security reasons; the "doves" contend that the lands will ultimately have to be given up as part of a larger Middle East peace plan. The Rabin government that came to power in the summer of 1992 adopted a position midway between the hawks and the doves — make territorial concessions for peace but protect the West Bank settlements, keep control of East Jerusalem, and do not grant Palestinians (refugees) a broad right of return (to Israel). A significant shift toward peace in Israeli public opinion following the Persian Gulf war made this position politically possible.

One of the most controversial issues involves the Israeli policy of establishing settlements in the Occupied Territories. Since the early 1990s, the controversy has divided Jews in (and outside of) Israel, as well as Israelis and Palestinians. But the roots of the problem go back to the Six-Day War.

In 1967, the Labour government established the first Jewish settlements in the West Bank to defend Israel's new eastern border with Jordan. Between 1976 and 1977, without official approval, the ultraright **Gush Emunim** ("Bloc of the Faithful") set up a number of settlements. The Begin government (1977–1983) shared Gush Emunim's enthusiasm for "the integrity of the whole Land of Israel," and Ariel Sharon, in charge of the policy, called the settlements "the strongest answer to the establishment of a second Palestinian state." (The first, according to Israel's hawks, being Jordan, with more than one-third of all Palestinian refugees.) Begin said that Israel was "creating facts"—meaning that settlements in the Occupied Territories would in effect colonize them. In this way, Israel laid claim to more than half of the West Bank by the mid-1980s, and the number of Jewish settlers had quadrupled. By 1988, the Israeli government had confiscated over half of all land on the West Bank and established 135 settlements there. By 1992, following the influx of Soviet Jews, the number of settlements rose to 212, making settlers a potent special-interest group in Israeli politics. (See Figures 12.2 and 12.3.) The settlers tend to be vehemently opposed to any return of the Occupied Territories, and some even threaten armed resistance should the Israeli army withdraw under a future peace pact.

The basic strategy behind Israel's policy toward the Palestinians after 1967 was contained in the so-called Allon Plan, named after its author, General Yigal Allon. The idea was to create a kind of defensive perimeter around Israel by building secure Jewish settlements on the Arab side of the Green Line (the boundary between Jewish and Arab Palestine established by the United Nations in 1947) — in other words, in the Occupied Territories. The territory open to Jewish settlements kept expanding, thereby contributing to a rising sense of anger and frustration among the native Palestinians. This tension, in turn, led to harshly repressive measures. There were also widespread allegations of torture carried out by Israeli police interrogators (especially members of Shin Beth, the General Security Guard). In 1987, these charges were investigated and confirmed by a special Israeli judicial commission headed by a former supreme court president, Moshe Landau. However, rather than flatly condemning torture, the Landau Commission recommended the use of "psychological pressure and light violence" against individuals suspected of terrorist acts.

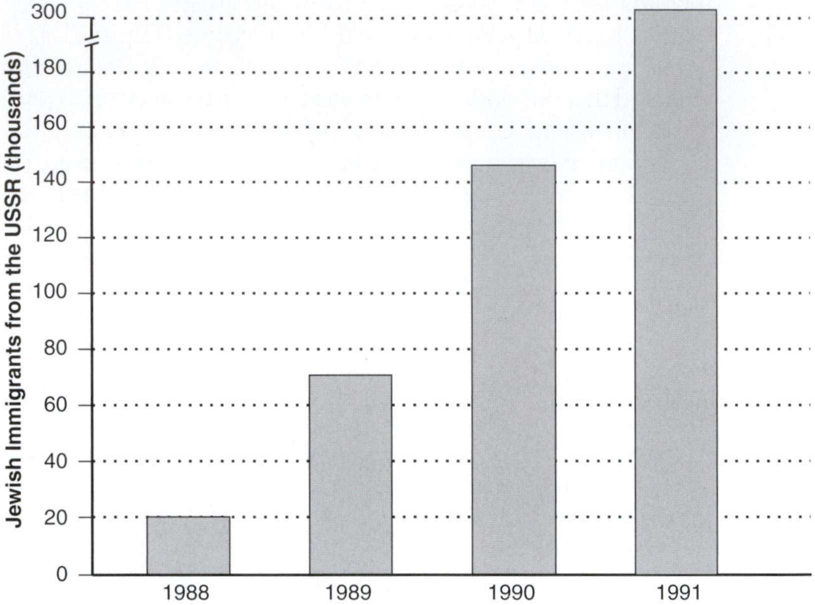

Figure 12.2 Soviet Jewish Emigration to Israel, 1988–1991

Source: Adapted from data presented in Benjamin Cohen, "Israel's Expansion through Emigration," *Middle East Policy,* 1, no 2 (1992): pp. 120–135.

Against this backdrop of rising tempers, terrorism in the West Bank became a daily fact of life. Both Arabs and Jews were victims as well as perpetrators. Palestinian youth became experts at rock throwing. Extremists victimized Israeli civilians using any means at hand — from car bombings to stabbings and shootings. The Israeli "national security state" responded resolutely, deporting Arab suspects and often dynamiting or bulldozing the homes of suspected terrorists — in effect, punishing whole families in a ruthless manner (which Israeli authorities, however, justified as a necessary deterrent). Palestinian Arabs accused of terrorist acts could be detained indefinitely and were tried by military courts without counsel or the right of appeal. Jewish suspects were not prosecuted or were given light sentences.

Little progress was possible on any aspect of the Palestinian question throughout the 1980s. Frustrations built on all sides. One sticking point was the status of the Palestine Liberation Organization (PLO). Israel refused to engage in talks with any Palestinian delegation that included PLO representation, while most Palestinian Arabs continued to look to the PLO for leadership. The Occupied Territories gradually became tinderboxes ready to ignite.

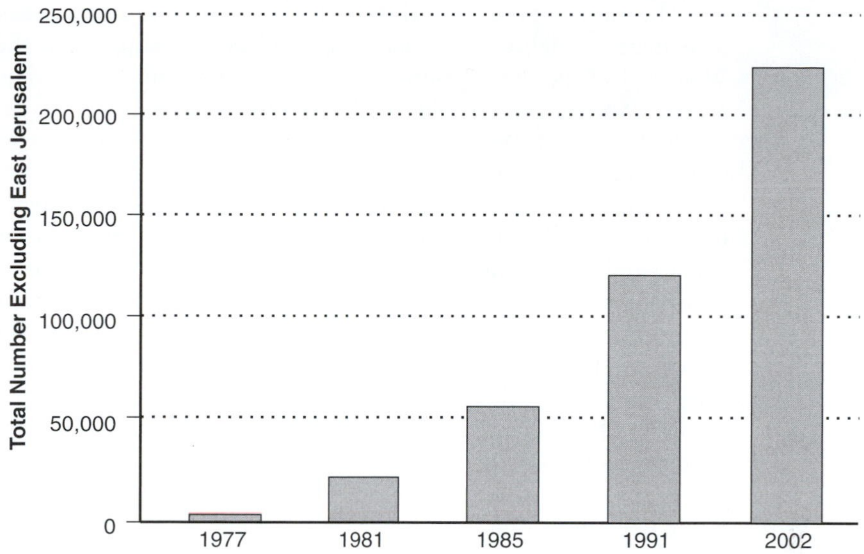

Figure 12.3 Jewish Settlers in the West Bank, 1977–2002

Source: Adapted from data presented in Benjamin Cohen, "Israel's Expansion through Emigration," *Middle East Policy,* 1, no. 2 (1992): pp. 120–135; and Ian Deitch, "Number of Jewish Settlers in West Bank Grew by 12,000," Associated Press, February 3, 2003, accessed at http://www.newsobserver.com.

A Rebellion in Bloom: The Intifada

Censorship was imposed on Arab newspapers in the West Bank, and Arab universities, originally set up under the Israeli occupation, were periodically shut down for disseminating "hostile" or "nationalist" ideas. The situation continued to deteriorate until in December 1987 it erupted in the **intifada,** the Palestinian uprising, first in Gaza and then in the West Bank. Frequent clashes occurred between Israeli security forces and Palestinian youths, armed with little more than sticks and stones:

> For the first time, the Palestinians showed both a willingness to die for their cause and a significant degree of self-restraint. . . . [Israeli] soldiers were ordered to avoid fatalities and instead to resort to a tactic of ferocious beatings. When this policy led to a worldwide uproar it was abandoned, and the world press was soon barred from access to the territories. The Israeli emphasis then shifted to a combination of curfews, searches, spot raids, covert penetration of Palestinian groups and unidentified sabotage, economic pressures, [and] the exile and (reportedly) assassination of political leaders by undercover elite troops.[5]

The intifada posed a dual threat to Israel. First, it might have sparked another war with Israel's neighbors. Second, it eroded Israel's support in the United States and Western Europe, where public opinion was becoming increasingly critical of Prime Minister Shamir and his Likud-led government.

In December 1988, the PLO, led by Yasir Arafat, made what purported to be a peace initiative of its own; it renounced terrorism and implicitly recognized Israel's right to exist. In return, the United States established low-level contacts with the PLO. The Israeli government then announced a plan for elections in the Occupied Territories, but Prime Minister Shamir's hard-line pledges about the peace process put the election plan in doubt. Shamir continued to place obstacles in the path of peace talks — Israel would talk only with non-PLO Palestinian leaders, the Arabs in Jerusalem could not take part in proposed West Bank elections, the intifada would have to stop before talks could start, and so on. Palestinian leaders were also unyielding: they would accept nothing short of an Israeli withdrawal from the Occupied Territories and a return to the pre-1967 borders (permitting the West Bank and the Gaza Strip to form a new Palestinian state).

In the early 1990s, the Labour Party was back in power, led by Yitzhak Rabin. The Rabin government made overtures in the summer of 1992, promising to stop subsidizing "political" settlements (but not "security" settlements) in the West Bank and Gaza. This Israeli olive branch opened a new chapter in the story of war and peace in the Middle East.

The Search for Peace, 1993–2004

In January 1993, Prime Minister Rabin formally lifted the ban on contacts with the PLO. In September, Rabin and PLO Chairman Arafat stunned the world by signing a historic agreement aimed at resolving the decades-long conflict between Jews and Arabs over the rightful ownership of Palestine. Although Norway had acted as the intermediary for the two sides, the ceremony was held on the lawn of the White House in Washington, D.C. With President Bill Clinton looking on, Rabin and Arafat shook hands after signing the agreement: perhaps the most important handshake — and undoubtedly the most famous — in recent history.

Widely hailed as historic, the accord provided for mutual recognition and limited Palestinian autonomy in the Gaza Strip and the city of Jericho in the West Bank (part of Jordan before the Six-Day War in 1967). Most important, it set a timetable for the two sides to negotiate the details of a plan that would transfer governmental power to Palestinians in Gaza and the West Bank in stages over a five-year period.

Nettlesome questions dampened the mood of the signing ceremony from the start. Would Arafat be able to guarantee a stop to terrorist acts against Israel? According to Thomas Friedman, a Pulitzer Prize–winning journalist and expert on the Middle East, "only after the PLO proves it can live with Israelis might it be allowed to live entirely without them."[6]

From 1967 to 1993, Israel controlled all aspects of public life in the occupied territories, "and not simply in military terms, but also in functional ones: from education textbooks, to the number of oranges that a Gaza farmer can export, to taxation, tourism, and even permission to dig for archeological artifacts."[7] Meron Benvenisti, an Israeli historian, explained the apprehensions of many Israelis:

> For us to finally recognize Arafat from the outside is one thing. . . . I can say hello to him on the street. But that is not all. Now he is coming into my house. We are going to share some of the rooms. And he needs space, and that is going to be the difficulty at all levels. Because we are not just talking about physical space. We are talking about everything. It is much more complicated than the peace treaty with Egypt. There, space was being divided. Here it is being shared.[8]

Not surprisingly, the accord was greeted with rejoicing in some quarters and bitter denunciations in others. Opponents on both sides vowed to block progress toward a final Israeli-Palestinian settlement. On the Palestinian side there were public threats to assassinate Arafat. Hamas (a radical Islamic group that rivals the PLO for popular support in the Occupied Territories) vowed to intensify its struggle for Palestinian national rights. This struggle had taken a heavy death toll by the fall of 1993 — more than 1,900 Palestinians and 146 Israelis. It was clear that unless the intifada could be abruptly halted, the Israeli-PLO accord would have little chance of succeeding. Even among moderate Palestinians, there was a fear that Arafat's gambit might open the door for other Arab governments to normalize relations with Israel and leave the Palestinians empty-handed.

On the Israeli side, the leader of the conservative Likud faction, Benjamin Netanyahu, declared that the PLO did not want peace and promised that a Likud government would revoke the treaty. Thus, formidable obstacles to a lasting peace in the Middle East remained.

But these obstacles did not stand in the way — at least not initially. As noted earlier, the accord negotiated at Oslo, Norway, provided for mutual recognition and partial Palestinian autonomy in the West Bank and Gaza. It also provided for the phased withdrawal of Israeli security forces from part of the Occupied Territories. Under the Oslo Accord, a Palestine National Authority was created to govern in the Gaza Strip and Jericho (West Bank) on an "interim" basis. In May 1995, Rabin and Arafat gave the peace process another boost when they signed a permanent pact on Palestinian self-rule. The following September, agreement was reached on the second phase of the 1993 accord involving the transfer of control over most West Bank cities to the Palestinians (Hebron was a notable exception); the new pact provided for elections to an eighty-eight-member Palestinian National Council to hold power initially for three years. PLO leader Arafat was elected its first president in early 1996.

The Palestinians' vote of confidence for Arafat's leadership was widely interpreted as a good sign for a more durable peace; unfortunately, the untimely death of Rabin at the hands of a Jewish extremist the previous November had already thrown a wrench into the machinery of reconciliation. In March, several suicide bombings apparently carried out by Hamas cast a pall over Palestine. The Israelis demanded that Arafat stop these acts of terrorism; Arafat responded by arresting more than nine hundred Palestinians, raiding thirty institutions suspected of having links with Hamas, and taking over sixty mosques in Gaza. These measures alienated radical Palestinians without fully

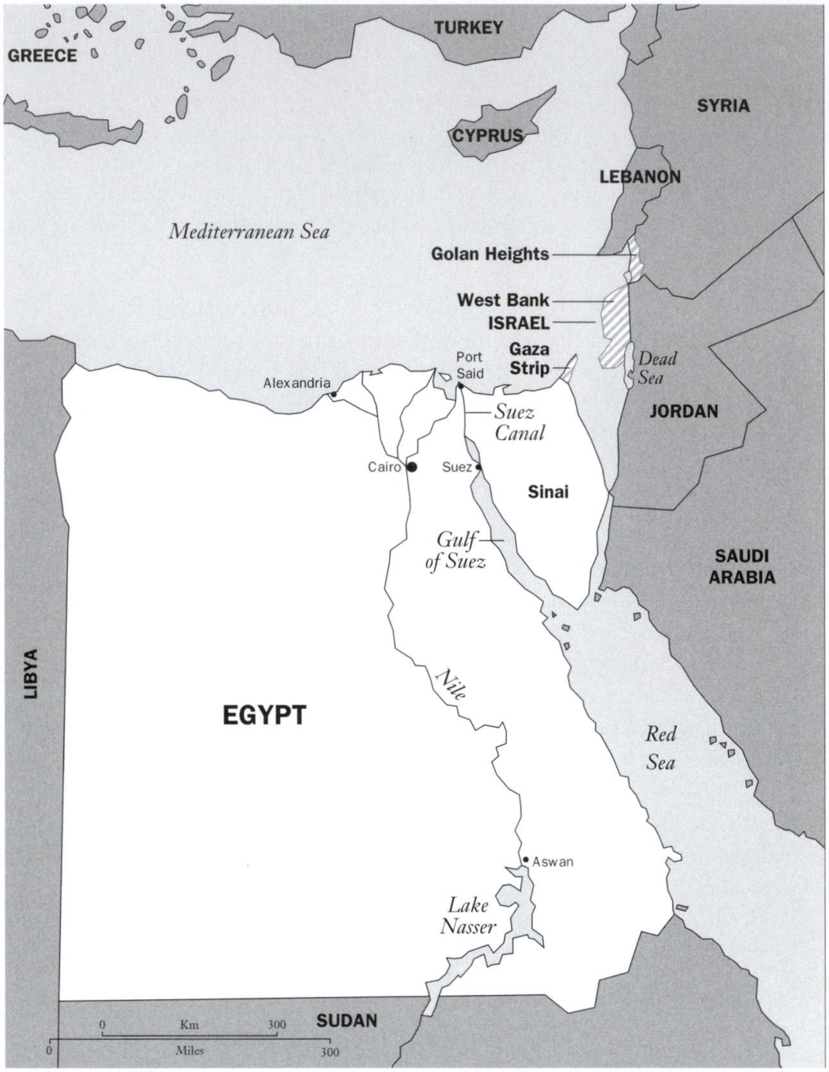

Egypt and Israel

placating Israelis. Arafat now became the number-one acrobat of the Arab world, walking a more precarious tightrope than ever.[9]

Continuing violence in the spring of 1996 contributed to rising tensions on both sides and helped boost the Likud Party, led by the hawkish — and sometimes strident — Benjamin Netanyahu, to an electoral victory on May 29. Attention focused on Hebron, the last West Bank city under full Israeli occupation. Under a previous agreement, partial control of Hebron was scheduled to transfer to the Palestinians before the May elections in Israel. The failure to meet that deadline, combined with the accession of the hard-line Netanyahu to the post of prime minister, once again gave rise to a potentially explosive situation.

The situation did not explode during Netanyahu's truncated tenure. When it did, it rocked the Israeli political system to its foundations and blew the peace process out of the water.

Case Studies: Israel and Egypt

For several decades, Israel and Egypt were at the center of the Middle East. These two countries fought three major wars — in 1956, 1967, and 1973. In fact, Egypt's claim to leadership of the Arab world was based mainly on its belligerency toward Israel. That situation changed in 1979 when Israel and Egypt signed a peace treaty. Many Arab countries were openly outraged at Egypt for making peace with Israel. Saudi Arabia's reaction, however, was subdued and restrained.

What accounts for the extraordinary political behavior of these two states? To answer this question we will look at the political systems and the policy dilemmas facing each. Israel is the only true multiparty democracy in the Middle East. Egypt, an authoritarian state with one dominant party and a few minor parties, is more typical of modern quasi-democratic Arab regimes. We begin with Israel.

Israel: A Garrison State

In the garrison state of Israel, the peace treaty was a major event, but it was offset by the rise of the Ayatollah Khomeini's Islamic fundamentalism, which posed a new threat to the stability of the region. An outpouring of extremism in the Middle East was directed against the United States and, of course, Israel. But despite the pervasive siege mentality in Israel, the state has functioned as a parliamentary democracy since its stormy beginnings in 1948. The inhabitants of the Occupied Territories, however, have not enjoyed the same civil liberties as people who live within the official boundaries of Israel. The Israeli **Law of Return** is unique. It provides that any Jew has the right to immigrate to Israel and become an Israeli citizen at any time. In effect, Jews living in other countries have dual citizenship. In this sense, Israel is a true Jewish homeland.

A Parliamentary System

Israel's pluralistic political system is unique in the Middle East. Perhaps owing to the nation's endemic insecurity, Israel has no written constitution — such a document might complicate matters when, for example, martial-law measures are deemed necessary. Statutory laws define basic rights, election procedures, voting qualifications, military service obligations, and the like.

The government of Israel resembles the British parliamentary system. The **Knesset** (parliament) consists of 120 members elected to four-year terms by proportional representation. The party with the most seats in the Knesset (or the one that can form a majority coalition) chooses a prime minister and a cabinet to run the government. The prime minister is accountable to the Knesset and can be forced to resign by a vote of no confidence. Instead of a British-style figurehead monarch, Israel has a ceremonial president.

Political Parties

Israel is a multiparty democracy. Israeli governments are typically fashioned from coalitions that rely heavily on the support of minor parties. The two major political parties are the center-left Israeli **Labour Party** and the center-right **Likud** (which means "consolidation" in Hebrew, reflecting the fact that Likud is itself a coalition of parties). In addition, there is the dovish Meretz Party (also a "party bloc" comprised of several like-minded smaller political groups), the hawkish Tzomet Party, as well as a host of others on the far-right end of the political spectrum. In Israel, the "others" are more important than in most democracies. They include Zionist and Orthodox parties, which are small but highly motivated (and uncompromising).

There is also an Arab Democratic Party, which represents the roughly 1 million Israeli Arabs in the parliament. In the 1999 elections, for example, the Arab Democratic Party won ten seats in the Knesset — a small but not insignificant number. In fact, the new Labour government of Ehud Barak depended on the support of the Arab Democratic Party to reach a majority in the parliament.

On the "Right" Track? . . . The terms *left* and *right* do not mean the same thing in Israel as they do in many other democracies. Israel is a special case because of the circumstances surrounding its creation (see Chapter 11) and because it is the only state in the world that is politically and militarily isolated within its own region. In Israel, a given party's position on the political spectrum (how far right or left of center it is thought to be) depends more on its foreign-policy stance than on the domestic policies it advocates.

The fact that Israel exists in a permanently hostile environment means that even Labour — sometimes called the "peace party" — embraces a strong national defense and a foreign policy of eternal vigilance. Indeed, it is almost certain that any Israeli leader who appeared too soft in negotiations with Israel's Arab adversaries would quickly fall. There is virtually no "peace at any price" or pacifist sentiment in Israel. For the same reason, the right side of the political spectrum is uncommonly crowded. The "right" includes an assortment of nationalist, Zionist, and Orthodox Jewish parties and runs the gamut from the center-right Likud to the right-wing Eretz Israel, which pushes for continued Jewish settlement of the Occupied Territories (regarded as provocative and expansionist by Palestinian Arabs).

Also, it is often forgotten that Israel is officially a secular state. Religious parties in the Knesset seek state support for Jewish institutions, especially schools. They also seek changes in the law to provide for strict observance of the Jewish faith in daily life. Of course, such measures are vigorously opposed by Israel's Arab (mainly Muslim) population, which as a percentage of the whole constitutes a minority larger than the African American minority in the United States or the Muslim minority in India.

. . . Or the Left? For the first thirty years, David Ben-Gurion's Mapai (Labour) Party dominated Israeli politics. But the Labour Party rarely had a clear majority (the proportional representation system has encouraged party proliferation), so unstable coalition governments have been the rule.

After the Yom Kippur War in 1973, the Labour Party was challenged by opposition hard-liners including the Likud Party, who charged that Israel had suffered heavy casualties because the Labour government of Prime Minister Golda Meir had been caught with its guard down. Labour's economic policies were also called into question after runaway inflation forced the government to adopt an unpopular austerity program. In 1977, the right-wing Likud won more seats than Labour, and Menachem Begin, a veteran of the struggle for Israeli statehood, became prime minister. But because Likud lacked a clear majority, Begin had to make concessions to smaller parties in order to form a governing coalition.

In the 1980s, Likud's popularity faded, but Labour nonetheless failed (twice) to get a solid majority in the Knesset or a clear mandate from the electorate. The result was an attempt to form governments of national unity. These governments were a thin disguise for the growing disunity in Israeli society and threatened to leave the nation adrift in perilous waters with little policy direction.

Backlash: The Extreme "Center" In the 1988 election, both Labour on the left and Likud on the right lost votes to religious parties in the "center"; these single-issue parties were willing to make a deal with either side in exchange for certain concessions on religious issues. Orthodox parties and leaders sought legislation imposing religious restrictions on Jews, funding for religious schools, and draft exemption for rabbinical students.

The trend toward polarization and fragmentation was clear in 1988. Labour again won the largest number of votes, "but only a nationalist bloc could act as an effective pivot of a viable coalition."[10] The upshot was that Likud's Shamir "was able to form a viable government on the basis of another national unity coalition with Labour; his alternative, partnership with the religious and the non-religious right, was abandoned because of the preconditions of the religious right."[11]

As the 1980s drew to a close, consensus seemed more remote than ever. Professor Avner Yaniv of Haifa University summed up the situation as follows:

> More than anything else, the country needed a clear electoral decision that would facilitate a strong government. But the number of parties and the lists [slates of candidates] in the campaign indicated that this was not to be. Almost 30 lists obtained enough signatories to qualify. The total number of eligible voters was 2,840,000. The necessary minimum for a Knesset seat was thus little more than 23,000 valid votes. Half the lists that obtained enough signatures to qualify therefore stood a reasonable chance of winning enough votes to claim a seat in the next Knesset.

> Thus, in addition to Labour and Likud, the two broadly based contenders for national leadership, there were more than 20 single-issue lists standing for anything from the expulsion of the Arab population of the West Bank and Gaza to the drastic reduction of the income tax, the establishment of Orthodox Judaism as the law of the land, the rights of senior citizens, and Israel's recognition of the PLO.[12]

The Israeli Economy 1973–1985 After twenty-five years of impressive achievements, Israel's economy began to sputter during the **OPEC oil embargo** in 1973. Israel's small size and limited natural resources make it vulnerable to economic pressures and reprisals. After the embargo, which led to worldwide recession and inflation, Israeli GNP growth rates dropped to zero. (Between 1950 and 1976, Israel's economic growth was comparable to rates in Japan, South Korea, and Taiwan.) Inflation and trade deficits plagued Israel in the 1980s, reflecting an increased dependency on foreign oil after returning the Sinai wells to Egypt, rising defense spending, and deregulation of the economy after 1977.

Between 1980 and 1984, inflation in Israel ran over 100 percent annually. In 1985, it skyrocketed to 800 percent and forced the national unity government, then headed by Shimon Peres, to declare a three-month state of emergency. Peres ordered a major devaluation of the shekel, a temporary wage-price freeze, a cut in subsidies, and increased income taxes (already the highest in the world). Thousands of government workers were cut from the public payroll (previous Labour governments had created a huge bureaucracy that employed two out of three Israelis). Those who were kept on the job took a pay cut.

Inflation forced the government to keep the shekel artificially high (to dampen down consumer demand), and exports suffered (because the price of a country's goods on the world market reflects the price of that country's currency, its "exchange rate." Belt-tightening continued through the late 1980s, and everyday life was a struggle for most Israelis. It was difficult to make ends meet, there was little time for relaxation, and the nation was sullen and polarized. People sensed that economic prosperity was slipping away, maybe forever. With this new pessimism came a "brain drain" as talented young people left Israel for opportunities abroad. And if young people were leaving, would Jews from other nations want to come to Israel? Or would they, like so many Soviet Jews, choose to go to the United States instead?

The 1990s: So Close (to Peace) and Yet So Far

In the summer of 1992, Yitzhak Rabin's Labour Party won control of the Knesset but failed to win a majority of seats. Forced to seek coalition partners to form a government, Rabin's strategy was to strike a balance between left and right. He thus brought into the coalition the Meretz Party (left) and the Tzomet Party (right). At the top of Rabin's agenda was the issue of settlements and settlers. As noted earlier, Rabin said he would favor only "security" settlements in the future, not "political" ones. But the distinction was unclear. According to one estimate, over half of the West Bank and Gaza, as well as all of Arab East Jerusalem would fall within Rabin's definition of "security."

Several other major issues were connected with the security question. One such issue involved a nonnegotiable demand for defensible borders. Rabin declared that "Tel Aviv must be defended from the Jordan Valley and not from Emmanuel," a West Bank settlement. Another issue was the Palestinians. Reconciliation between Jews and Arabs hinged in large part on the disposition of the Occupied Territories, but Rabin was constrained both by the opposition Likud Party and by the right-wing faction in his own coalition.

Rabin Rolls the Dice The 1992 elections brought a stunning victory for the Labour Party led by Yitzhak Rabin, but it was not enough to allow Labour clear sailing in the Knesset. With forty-four seats (seventeen short of a majority), Rabin was forced to seek coalition partners among the smaller parties. The results of the election confirmed that most Israelis wanted peace and prosperity, but no longer believed that either could be achieved as long as Israel remained in a state of war with the Arabs (including Palestinians). The Rabin government's decision in 1993 to make peace with the PLO must be seen against this backdrop.

Despite the absence of a solid "peace" majority in the Knesset, Rabin moved quickly to reconcile Jews and Palestinian Arabs. The end of the Cold War gave a new urgency to finding a peaceful way out of the impasse over the Palestinian question. It also coincided with a shift in Israeli public opinion. Although external threats remained, internal economic and social problems moved to the forefront.

During the next two years, Rabin and his Palestinian counterpart, PLO leader Arafat, made progress toward a permanent settlement, but they also stirred great enmities within their own populations. There were sporadic attempts to sabotage the peace process by extremists on both sides. Acts of terrorism claimed the lives of innocent Jews and Palestinians alike. Tragically, a young Jewish zealot, alarmed at the prospect of a future Palestinian state, assassinated Rabin in November 1995.

Netanyahu Stacks the Deck Shimon Peres, Rabin's foreign minister, stepped up to the plate, vowing to stay the course. But in elections held the following year the hard-line Likud defeated Peres and the Labour Party.

Likud's victory in 1996 was far from a landslide, however. Indeed, Labour actually won two more seats in the Knesset than the Likud did (thirty-four to thirty-two). The remaining fifty-four seats were divided among nine other parties. Not surprisingly, such fragmentation can easily create a circus. To build a cohesive coalition, Benyamin Netanyahu, leader of Likud, traded away many key cabinet posts and committee chairs. In the end, his coalition consisted of no fewer than six parties. (See Table 12.4.)

The return to power of Likud left the future of the peace process in grave doubt. Netanyahu talked tough both before and after the election, but his policies were milder and less confrontational than many had expected. He placed a lower priority on getting an early agreement with the Palestinians than his center-left predecessor (Rabin) had and engaged in a good deal of foot-dragging, according to his critics. Unsurprisingly, his negotiating tactics were politically motivated and quite transparent — to demand concessions without giving any more than the hard-liners in

Table 12.4 Israel's 1996 Parliamentary Elections*

Government Coalition	(68 seats)	Opposition	(52 seats)
Likud-Tzomet-Gesher	32	Labor	34
Shas	10	Meretz	9
National Religious Party	9	Hadash	5
Yisrael Ba-Aliya	7	United Arab List	4
Third Way	4		
United Torah Judaism	4		
Molodet	2†		

*The total number of seats in the Knesset is 120.
†Not part of a coalition, but supported the government.

his own right-wing coalition would accept. While there was no progress toward peace, neither was there a slide into war.

Netanyahu's abrasive personal style and the pungent smell of corruption led to his early downfall. In the spring of 1999, the voters returned the center-left Labour Party to power. The new prime minister, Ehud Barak, appeared to have a mandate to make peace with PLO leader Arafat — in other words, to take new steps toward a final settlement of the Palestinian issue. In any event, that is how Prime Minister Barak interpreted the election results.

Barak Deals When Barak's Labour Party swept Netanyahu's Likud Party from power, it appeared to be a positive development for peace — it was, after all, a previous Labour prime minister, Yitzhak Rabin, who had signed the first (and only) accord with the PLO in 1993. Labour's solid electoral win set the stage for Barak's attempt to make a breakthrough in the interminable and stalled peace talks with the PLO. In July 2000, President Bill Clinton invited Barak and Arafat to Camp David for negotiations that he hoped would reprise the success of the U.S.-brokered Israeli-Egyptian summit at Camp David in 1977.

In the eyes of many Israelis, Barak was going out on a limb for peace. First, when hopes of achieving a comprehensive peace agreement with Lebanon and Syria collapsed in the spring of 2000, Israel hastily withdrew its military forces from southern Lebanon (after a twenty-two-year occupation). Second, Barak was apparently prepared to concede the issue of a Palestinian state and to return all but between 5 and 8 percent of the West Bank and Gaza to Palestinian Arab control (only the Israeli settlements in the Occupied Territories would be kept out of the deal). Third, Israel would recognize a suburban zone outside of East Jerusalem as the new Palestinian capital and grant the Palestinians sovereignty over the Muslim holy places in the Old City. The final status of East Jerusalem would be left for the future.

But it was not enough to satisfy Arafat at Camp David. The sticking point there was East Jerusalem. Arafat would not sign an agreement that left Israel in control of East Jerusalem. The Camp David talks dragged on for many days — so many, in fact, that President Clinton had to leave while they were still in progress. The negotiations finally broke off after fifteen days — with no agreement. Having gone to the brink of peace, the parties now stared into the abyss of war.

The question in the Middle East conflict has always been easy to frame: Will the incentives for peace prove to be greater than the obstacles to peace? At Camp David in 2000 (unlike 1978) that question was answered in the negative. Disappointment over the failure of the talks once again created a tinderbox in the Occupied Territories. All that was needed was for someone to strike a match. Someone did.

Problems and Prospects

In Israeli politics, there are two problems: the Palestinian question and everything else. The latter includes the state of the economy as well as other key questions (for example, the extent to which the Jewish religion will be favored by the state). But a preoccupation with national security trumps these other questions. Economic prosperity takes a back seat to foreign policy and military preparedness.

The Al Aqsa Incident: Intifada, Part II Tensions ran very high in the weeks and months after the collapse of the Camp David summit. The term *tinderbox* is perhaps overused in reference to the Middle East, but in this case it is no exaggeration. Only the slightest provocation was needed to ignite another Palestinian uprising. The provocation came on September 28, 2000 — and it was not slight. Ariel Sharon, the hawkish leader of Israel's Likud opposition, paid a visit to **Al Aqsa mosque** — the holiest of all Muslim holy sites — in the **Old City of Jerusalem.** As the point man in the campaign to protect Israel's interests in the negotiations, Sharon's high-profile visit was clear in its intent. It was a political show of force, a demonstration of Israel's continued control of East Jerusalem and the Old City. It touched off the bloodiest clashes between Israel and its Palestinian Arab minority in half a century — the worst since Israel's inception in 1948. (See Box 12.2.)

Barak's Political Bombshell In the outbreak of violence that ensued many Israelis were killed and injured, as were many more Palestinians. Each side blamed the other. The Palestinian Arabs in the Occupied Territories were no match for the heavily armed and superbly trained Israeli security forces. But terrorist acts against Israeli civilians posed a clear and present danger to Israel. Once again, the old rancor between Arabs and Jews was renewed and the festering issue of Palestine was sent back to square one. A new wave of violence broke out in late September.

Into the maelstrom of rocks and bullets Prime Minister Barak lobbed a political bombshell of his own. On the Sabbath (the Jewish day of worship), he announced he would resign and ask the president to call a special election in two months' time. The election Barak had in mind was "special" because it would not involve choosing a new parliament. Before the 1996 election, the Knesset had rewritten Israel's election law in a novel way. The new law set up two separate but simultaneous elections — one for parliament and the other for prime minister. As a result, Israel's prime minister is now chosen by direct election rather than by a majority vote in the Knesset. Barak's call

What If?

BOX 12.2

Jerusalem: Holy Battleground

During the 1948 war, the Jews asked that Jerusalem be declared an open city in which there would be no combat. The Jordanians disregarded that request; they surrounded a Jewish quarter of the city, inhabited primarily by old people, and cut off all food and water. The United Nations made no protest, despite the fact that it had already decided to internationalize the city. The Jordanians expelled all Jews from the Old City in East Jerusalem, destroyed Hadassah Hospital, and shut down Hebrew University. Jordanian soldiers destroyed synagogues and used Jewish cemeteries as latrines. Jewish worshippers were forbidden to approach the Western Wall, their holiest site, for prayer. Thus, the emotionally charged nature of the issue of Jerusalem goes far beyond its historical significance.

After 1967, Israel seized control of Jerusalem, turning the tables. Now it was the Arabs' turn to be shut out and outraged. The Old City is home to Temple Hill, where two of Islam's holiest places — the Dome of the Rock and the Al Aqsa mosque — are located.

In 1980, the Knesset declared Jerusalem to be Israel's eternal and undivided capital, even though the Arabs and the United Nations both consider East Jerusalem occupied Arab territory. In the summer of 2000, renewed efforts to settle the dispute over Jerusalem as part of a comprehensive Israeli-Palestinian peace agreement failed, touching off a new cycle of violence.

What if Arabs (Jordanians, in particular) initially had been more sympathetic to Jews, who had only recently been the target of unspeakable evil — the Holocaust? Perhaps Jerusalem — a holy city for three of the world's great religions — would be a source of peace today rather than a cause of war.

for a "snap" election was not an act of surrender; in fact, it was just the opposite. The prime minister was throwing down the gauntlet, hoping to outmaneuver the right-wing opposition led by the Likud Party.

Ariel Sharon had become Likud's leader in the Knesset after Netanyahu's defeat in 1999. Under the new rules, only current members of the Knesset could run for prime minister. That meant that Sharon could run against Barak but Netanyahu could not. Polls showed that Netanyahu's popularity was rising as Barak's (and Sharon's) was falling.

There were immediate cries of foul and calls for a new general election (to choose a new parliament as well as prime minister). Clearly, Barak preferred to run against Sharon rather than Netanyahu, but there was more to it than mere "politics." Barak had put new pressure on the Palestinian leadership. In effect, he was putting this question to Yasir Arafat: Would you rather stop fighting and deal with me — now — or keep fighting and deal with Ariel Sharon later? That's the sort of political maneuver that can work in a rational and reasonable political environment — but in never-ending war for Palestine rationality and reason are largely irrelevant.

An Eye for an Eye: Sharon Takes Charge Sharon won the February 2001 election and proceeded to forge a national unity government with Peres as foreign minister — a first step in launching yet another Israeli war on terrorism. Sharon made no bones about it: Israel would fight fire with fire. Every act of terrorism against Israelis would be met with direct retaliation against Palestinians. If civilians were targeted, Palestinian civilians could expect the same. It would be the justice of the Old Testament: an eye for an eye and a tooth for a tooth. Indeed, Sharon's antiterrorism strategy seemed to take the righteous vengeance of Holy Scripture one step farther: kill two or three Palestinians for every Israeli killed.

Predictably, the violence intensified. Suicide bombers attacked civilian targets in the summer of 2001; the Israeli army retaliated, destroying Palestinian homes and neighborhoods thought to harbor terrorists and assassinating dozens of suspected terrorists. Then came 9/11 and America's own "war on terrorism," which suddenly put the United States and Israel on the same page, so to speak, if not quite in the same boat. A sickening cycle of violence in Israel and the Occupied Territories degenerated to new depths in 2002–2003, as the horrors (and death toll) mounted. Hardly a day passed without more blood being spilled.

Israel launched a major army offensive in the West Bank in late March 2002, two days after a suicide bomber massacred twenty-six Israeli Jews at a Passover celebration. The Israeli army withdrew, only to reoccupy the West Bank in June after another series of suicide bombings. Sharon ordered Arafat's headquarters in Ramallah leveled in September — with Arafat inside. Arafat survived but he was now a captive in the ruins of the Palestinian "capital." In the meantime, Sharon ordered the building of a massive, meandering fence between the West Bank and Israel, a fence that in some cases made it impossible for Palestinians to go back and forth between the village where they lived and the land they farmed, and in other cases placed Israeli settlements in the West Bank *outside* the fence — in effect, annexing Palestinian territory. In fairness, Israel had been provoked into taking extreme measures by terrorist tactics that it could not stop in any other way — namely the use of suicide bombers crossing the "border" from the Occupied Territories into Israel.

However, building a fence was probably not the answer. Sadly, between September 2000 and December 2002, more than 600 Israelis and 1,600 Palestinians died — most of the dead on both sides were civilians. The number of victims is much larger, of course. Many more Israelis and Palestinians were wounded or left homeless or lost jobs and loved ones. Nobody on either side escaped the consequences of this conflict, and nobody on either side had any idea how to stop it.

Sharon's national unity government ended in 2002 when the Labor Party left the coalition. Sharon was undeterred. Gaining the support of smaller right-wing parties, he managed to hang on and remained popular with the embattled Israeli electorate.

The Arab Boycott and Other Burdens A widespread Arab boycott of companies that do business with Israel has also hurt the Israeli economy. It has led large multinational corporations wishing to trade with the oil-rich Arab states to avoid Israel. In recent years, the boycott has weakened, but it still constrains Israeli economic progress.

The largest budgetary drains on Israel are defense, immigration costs, the bureaucracy, and, until recently, financing settlements in the Occupied Territories. In the early 1990s, Israel's economic growth rate was higher than that of the United States, but unemployment remained high because of the great influx of immigrants. For the decade as a whole, Israel's economy grew at a rate (above 2 percent) comparable to that of the United States and Great Britain, somewhat faster than France's, and considerably faster than Germany's.

As a welfare state (social programs equal one-third of the GNP each year) with high defense outlays (about one-fourth of the budget), Israel operates on a deficit. This is alleviated by four sources of funds: donations from abroad (especially Jews in the United States), reparations from Germany for World War II, foreign aid (mainly from the United States), and borrowing from foreign banks. Israel's foreign debt was equal to its GNP by the mid-1980s. Interest on this debt totals billions of dollars yearly.

In the perspective of the Middle East, however, Israel's economy looks like a little miracle. Israel's per capita GNP is fifteen times larger than Egypt's and nearly five times larger than Lebanon's. Amazingly, by this measure Israel's economy is nearly twice as successful as Saudi Arabia's even though Saudi Arabia has the world's largest oil reserves. If Israel were in Europe, it would not be the poorest member of the European Union even prior to EU expansion in 2004 — it would be ahead of both Greece and Portugal in per capita terms. One sign that the renewed violence was taking a toll on the economy: the Israeli shekel depreciated about 12 percent in 2002.

Sources of Vitality In the bigger Middle East picture, Israel is economically more advanced than most Arab states that have greater natural resources. In agriculture, Israel has "made the desert bloom" through sophisticated technology and by diverting water from the Jordan River. More than half its farmland is irrigated, and the nation has nearly achieved food self-sufficiency. Israeli *kibbutzim* (communes) also deserve some credit for this impressive agricultural record. But agriculture represents less than 6 percent of GNP and cannot ensure prosperity by itself. Israel's manufacturing sector is mostly small-scale, except for its aircraft industry.

In the eyes of some observers, Israeli society showed clear signs of dramatic and far-reaching changes in the early 1990s. First, despite its myriad problems, Israel was undergoing a transformation from "a Spartan, socialist, isolated and highly militarized country into a modern consumer society suffused by Western secular culture."[13] Israelis are now more affluent, more consumer-conscious, more individualistic, and less willing to make personal sacrifices in the name of national security or the general good. Israel has thus come of age as a consumer society.

Second, the end of the Cold War brought a diplomatic windfall, even before the 1993 agreement with the PLO, and gave Israel a new place in the world. In a period of four years, thirty-five countries, including Russia and China, recognized Israel. In the last half of the 1980s, its foreign trade nearly doubled, and travel abroad by Israelis rose sharply.

Third, the lines of communication with the outside world suddenly opened for "once-insular communal Israel." According to journalist Jackson Diehl, "In 1967, there was no television in the country."[14] Today, almost all Israeli homes have television sets and most have access to CNN and other satellite-cable offerings from Europe and the United States, as well as the Middle East.

Fourth, hundred of thousands of immigrants from the former Soviet Union settled in Israel in the 1990s. These new arrivals account for about 10 percent of Israel's population and reinforce the larger society's tendencies toward secularization, economic modernization, and individual values. In the 1990s, polls consistently found that most

Israelis wanted the peace process to go forward and favored major reforms in the fragmented political system and state-dominated economy.

Finally, Israeli citizens enjoyed a far higher standard of living at the end of the 1990s than did people in most of the Arab world. Although Israel's per capita GNP is well below that of the United States, Japan, and most of Western Europe, it was actually higher than Spain's.

In Sum . . . Israel has come a long way since 1948. It not only has survived among hostile neighbors but also has won several wars and, as a result, now has more secure, more defensible borders. The peace treaty with Egypt greatly reduced the threat of a two-front war, and it seems unlikely that other Arab states would attack without Egypt's involvement. Thus, Israel has accomplished its original aims of providing a homeland and a safe haven for all Jews. It has built a strong state capable of defending itself against its enemies (Arabs) who greatly outnumber its own Jewish population.

Israel has also built a modern economy and given its people a decent standard of living — one that can only be envied by its Arab neighbors. It has done all this in spite of these neighbors' hostility. The political system has functioned as a parliamentary democracy despite the constant threat of terrorist attacks and frequent national emergencies. Elections are held regularly and all adults (including Israeli Arabs) have the right to vote. Opposition and dissent are protected under the law, though Palestinians deemed to pose a threat to Israeli society are arrested and imprisoned. Israel has had intelligent, courageous, and strong-willed leaders.

In the 1980s, Israeli public opinion polls in Israel consistently demonstrated that Israeli Jews overwhelmingly opposed creation of a Palestinian state or any land-for-peace policy. But in the 1990s, after the crisis touched off by Iraq's invasion of Kuwait, Israeli opinion changed. By 1992, a solid majority of Israelis endorsed a land-for-peace trade and all but a fraction favored negotiation rather than confrontation. These numbers did not change significantly between 1992 and 2000. A 1997 Gallup poll found that "60 percent of Israelis would accept a demilitarized Palestinian state and even some sharing of Jerusalem in order to achieve peace" and another Gallup poll taken the following year concluded that nearly seven Israelis in ten believed that in the future an independent Palestinian state would exist alongside Israel.[15]

But that was *before* the Al Aqsa incident and events of September 11 one year later. Most Israelis no longer believe that peaceful coexistence with Palestinians is possible. The renewed struggle between Israelis and Palestinians has been especially intense and bloody. Israel's strained relations with its neighbors (particularly the Palestinians) remain the major stumbling block on the path to a peaceful and prosperous future.

Whether Israel's leaders have always been wise or prudent is open to debate. What is not debatable is that Israel has yet to find the key to living at peace with the Arabs in its midst. By the same token, most Arab states have refused to recognize Israel's right to exist. Egypt is a notable exception. We look at Egypt's political institutions, policies, and prospects next.

Egypt: The Mask of Democracy

Israel's fragmented electorate and patchwork parliament are problems that have not been allowed to surface in Egypt, where one party continues to dominate the political scene. Nor has Egypt changed leaders very often since the overthrow of the monarchy in 1953.

Nasser's Egocentric "Civilitary" State

Modern Egypt's founding father, Gamal Abdel Nasser, created a one-party state in the 1950s. Nasser outlawed the Wafd Party, despite its heroic role in the struggle for Egyptian independence. Having survived an assassination attempt by the Muslim Brotherhood in the mid-1950s, he retaliated by breaking up that organization, ignoring its popular appeal (membership was estimated at around 2 million). He also outlawed the Egyptian Communist Party, despite his close ties with the Soviet Union. The **Arab Socialist Union (ASU)** was an extension of Nasser's personality and became the sole embodiment of his will — all opposition was outlawed, disbanded, or driven underground. He relied heavily on the loyalty and efficiency of Egypt's security forces, especially the army. Although he ruled as a popularly elected "civilian" president, he never gave up his military rank (colonel) nor officially retired from military service. On patriotic occasions, he often appeared in military dress. A populist dictator par excellence, Nasser's subliminal message to the masses was always, "He who is not with me is against you."

Sadat's Soft(er) Dictatorship

After Nasser's death in 1970, his personalistic one-party dictatorship was continued under President Anwar al-Sadat, with certain cosmetic changes. For example, Sadat abolished the ASU and allowed several new parties to organize. In the meantime, the power elite of the defunct ASU formed the National Democratic Front, headed by Sadat. Many observers found Sadat even more autocratic than Nasser.

In fairness, Sadat took a number of significant steps to broaden human rights in Egypt. According to Middle East expert George Lenczowski:

> Sadat . . . launched a thorough policy of "de-Nasserization" in virtually every field of public policy. In the domestic political process Sadat inaugurated an era of liberalism that contrasted with the police methods used in the last years of Nasser's presidency. Egyptians found travel abroad easier than it had been. Citizens began to move and to express their opinions with much greater freedom. Censorship over the Egyptian press was formally removed, and editorials espousing various points of view began to appear . . . . On his part, President Sadat did not cease to castigate what he called the old centers of power, composed of influential dignitaries in the intelligence and ASU organizations, who, according to him, exercised arbitrary power and were guilty of many abuses.[16]

Despite movement toward pluralism within the ruling party, the Egyptian National Assembly was little more than a debating society and a mere rubber stamp — Sadat's lip service and outward show of respect notwithstanding. This hypocrisy galled many Egyptians, especially the educated. Nasser, they reasoned, made no bones about his authoritarian style, but Sadat pretended to be a democrat. The extensiveness of this cynical view became apparent in October 1981, when Sadat's assassination seemed to cause greater consternation in the West than in Egypt.

Mubarak's Egypt: A Paper Democracy

In theory, Egypt is a constitutional democracy patterned after France's Fifth Republic (see Chapter 4). The president is elected for a six-year term. There is no constitutional limit on the number of consecutive terms a president may serve. The constitution stipulates that the vice president takes over if the president dies in office. Both Nasser and Sadat had vice presidents (Sadat was Nasser's and Mubarak was Sadat's). By contrast, the wily Mubarak has never named a vice president — to do so would be to risk creating a rival and setting the stage for another assassination (Sadat's fate) or a coup (Nasser's path to power).

The president appoints the prime minister and cabinet (Council of Ministers), who are theoretically responsible to the People's Assembly (parliament). Members of the People's Assembly, which is the lower house, are elected for five-year terms, but the parliament can be dissolved at will by the president. The upper house, called the Consultative Assembly, is also a popularly elected body. Oddly enough, its sole official function is to supervise the press.

On paper, the Egyptian system appears to be a constitutional democracy (see Figure 12.4), but in practice powers are not separated, fused, or mixed as they are in the various models of democracy discussed in Chapter 2. Instead, they are concentrated, as in dictatorships. The way this concentration has been achieved within the framework of a "paper democracy" — that is, a government operating under the rules established by a written constitution — is amazingly simple. When President Sadat was assassinated in 1981, then Vice President Mubarak declared a state of emergency. This measure was quite proper under the constitution and quite reasonable under the circumstances. Muburak, however, has never called off the emergency, which means that he has exercised extraordinary powers now for two decades — all the while preserving the fiction of democratic rule.

The litany of presidential powers is familiar to anyone who has glimpsed the face of constitutional dictatorship anywhere. The president can issue decrees and put important matters directly before the electorate via public referendums, thereby circumventing parliament. He can veto legislation and even decide when (or whether) the **People's Assembly** will convene. The president also heads the **National Democratic Party (NDP),** which perennially controls the parliament. Finally, elections are relatively free but they are not fair. The government (in effect, Mubarak's personal political-administrative organization) controls the mass media, the state security apparatus, the bureaucracy, the public treasury, and, to a large extent, the judiciary.

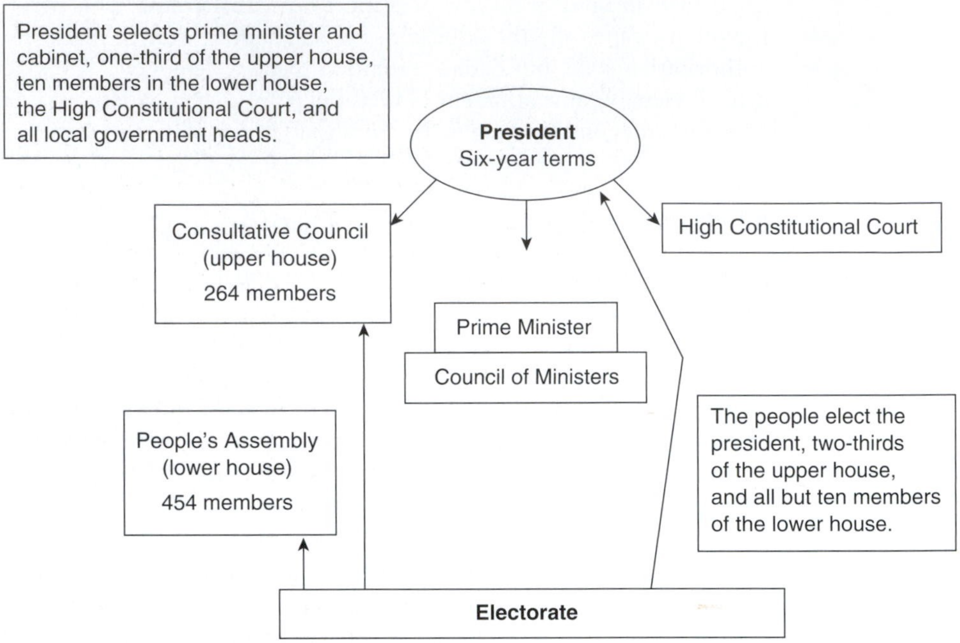

Figure 12.4 Egypt's Presidential "Democracy"

Parties and Elections

Sadat appointed Mubarak leader of the NDP in 1980, when Mubarak was his vice president. It was a stroke of luck for Mubarak because it smoothed his transition into the presidency after Sadat's assassination the following year.

Under Mubarak, several other political parties have been legalized. In 1984, the first multiparty elections since 1952 were held, with no surprises: Mubarak, running unopposed, was reelected to a full six-year term as president, and the ruling NDP won nearly three-fourths of the seats in the National Assembly. The elections appeared to be free and open, but the rule requiring that a party receive at least 8 percent of the popular vote to be awarded any seats in the legislature made it difficult for new parties to make their mark. Only the New Wafd Party was able to qualify.

In 1987, four opposition parties contested the National Assembly elections. The NDP won by the usual landslide, but there was a sizable protest vote for a coalition consisting of two socialist parties and members of the Muslim Brotherhood (running as independents). The New Wafd Party gained ground as well. A prominent newspaper editor in Cairo exuberantly proclaimed, "The one-man system is over."[17]

Mubarak's party swept the assembly elections in 1990, taking 348 of the 444 seats, but the outcome was deceptive. The NDP won largely by default after the main opposition parties abstained. Islamic extremists threatened the stability of the country after 1992. But the embattled president received a strong vote of confidence at the end of 1995 when the ruling NDP won a clear majority of seats in the parliament.

The Challenge of Islamic Fundamentalism

The rise of **Islamic fundamentalism** challenged Egypt's single-party system for two reasons. First, Nasser had led a secular and nationalist revolution; bent on modernization, he was contemptuous of Islamic law and tradition.[18] Sadat was no less confrontational in dealing with Islamic fanaticism. Thus, Egypt was a natural target for groups ranging from the Muslim Brotherhood, which Nasser had crushed, to followers of the Ayatollah Khomeini, who viewed Sadat as a traitor.

Second, Sadat had made peace with the enemy, Israel. This move was risky because it offended both Arab nationalists and Islamic zealots. The group that assassinated Sadat fit both descriptions. Mubarak's strategy for dealing with Islamic tumult has been subtle:

> By gradually shifting its posture toward the religious opposition from indiscriminate confrontation to selective accommodation, the Mubarak government has . . . isolated and discredited the extremist fringes of the Islamic movement, allowing the state security forces to hunt down and crush remaining pockets of armed resistance. It has [also] allowed the . . . moderate mainstream of the Islamic movement to compete more openly in the political system and in the economy. Several groups that Sadat claimed were trying to tear the country apart have already developed a strong interest in expanding Egypt's multiparty capitalism.[19]

In sum, Mubarak has made concessions both to democracy and to Islam. Although his democratic reforms have been largely symbolic, they uphold the principle of pluralism as embodied in competing parties and free elections with meaningful choices. He continues to fit the model of a quasi-civilian strongman (like Nasser and Sadat, he earned his spurs as a high-ranking military officer). Egypt remains a highly centralized, one-party authoritarian state with a populist president who claims to personify the spirit of the nation. In Nasser's case, the claim was arguably justified; in Sadat's case, it was not. Mubarak probably falls somewhere between the two. He commands respect and has restored a measure of trust in the government, but he has not achieved exalted status and his tenure in office ultimately rests on the coercive power of the state, which he controls.

The Egyptian government has weathered four turbulent decades nearly intact. Changes that have been made are more in the nature of fine-tuning than fundamental restructuring. We turn now to Egypt's prospects in the light of this deferred transition.

Problems and Prospects

Egypt's economy remains precarious. Agriculture is the most important sector, accounting for 30 percent of national income, but arable land is limited and population growth tends to cancel out any gains. Cotton and sugar cane are the main crops. Increases in output in the 1980s were accomplished through better irrigation — thanks to the High Aswan Dam, expansion of land devoted to cash crops, and improved planting methods. Unfortunately, the dam has not boosted the economy as much as Egyptians had hoped. The goal was to offset population growth and achieve a measure of food self-sufficiency by reclaiming vast tracts of desert with the abundant waters of the Nile. However, costs have been much higher than expected, and periodic droughts continue to cast doubt as to the security of Egypt's water supply.

Trade, Aid, and Investment Egypt has sizable reserves of oil and natural gas, and new oil discoveries have been made in the Western Desert and the Gulf of Suez. The nation also earns foreign currency from Suez Canal tolls and user fees, tourism, and remittances from roughly 4 million Egyptians working abroad (especially in Saudi Arabia and other Persian Gulf states). U.S. foreign aid — no less than $2 billion annually for more than two decades — has helped a great deal.

President Mubarak's government has sought to reduce dependency on imported goods by encouraging expansion of manufacturing, especially of consumer goods. Incentives include tax exemptions and refunds of customs duties on imported machinery. Foreign investors have shown interest in setting up assembly plants in Egypt to take advantage of the abundant labor supply.

The 1979 peace treaty with Israel has been a mixed blessing for Egypt. Other Arab nations ostracized Cairo for a decade, and the treaty caused political tremors inside Egypt as well, culminating in the assassination of President Sadat. From an economic standpoint, however, the treaty has paid off. It has brought billions in U.S. aid and has created cordial relations with the West, which encourages tourism. (The pyramids are among the world's most famous tourist attractions.) Finally, the treaty has diminished the risk for foreign investors, who fear political instability.

Subsidies and Social Stability Public subsidies are a way of life in Egypt. For example, the government pays high prices to producers of food staples and keeps consumer prices low. That makes both groups happy, but it diverts resources into consumption rather than investment. Similarly, Egypt built a massive bureaucracy under Nasser and Sadat to create jobs for educated youths who otherwise had few career opportunities. The government pursues such policies for at least two reasons. First, as previously noted, Nasserism was and is a socialist philosophy that blends populism and nationalism. Second, subsidies and jobs mollify the people despite lagging economic development. They are a kind of bribe to encourage each side to overlook the other's shortcomings.

President Mubarak is making an effort to get the economy moving, to wean Egyptians from their addiction to subsidies, and to create real jobs by starting new industries. In November 1986, he fired his entire cabinet and assembled a new team of highly qualified technocrats. Egyptian business leaders and foreign investors had confidence in the new cabinet. At the end of the century, Egypt's outlook was neither bright nor bleak. There were signs of progress and reasons for optimism. In 1999–2000, the Egyptian economy grew at a respectable rate of 6.5 percent and inflation was below 3 percent in the summer of 2000, when the economy went into a slump. The downturn was another reminder that rapid and sustained growth of the sort that has occurred in some of Asia's fast-developing countries is unlikely to be achieved in Egypt unless (or until) fundamental economic reforms are given the priority they deserve. It also underscored Egypt's dependency on the United States for billions of dollars in foreign aid — the biggest "subsidy" of all.

Mubarak's Narrow Escape In 1992, mass violence broke out between Muslims and Christians, and the following year Islamic extremists launched a campaign to overthrow Mubarak. Attacks on politicians and other prominent public figures created an atmosphere charged with fear, and foreigners were warned to leave. In the midst of this domestic turmoil, Mubarak was reelected for a third term. In 1994, he ordered a crackdown on Islamic militants. In so doing, Mubarak, like Arafat, found that he had a tiger by the tail, a tiger with the zeal of a true believer and the heart of a terrorist. He was the target of an assassination attempt in June 1995. Although the attempt failed, it sent a powerful tremor through the Middle East — one felt in Europe and as far away as the United States.

In the final analysis, however, it will possibly be judges not assassins who pose the most serious "threat" to Mubarak's personal rule. As noted earlier, Egypt's elections are free, but not very fair. In recent years, the highest court in the land has taken bold steps toward a remedy — one that will either democratize Egypt or expose Mubarak's "democracy" for the farce it really is.

Courting Democracy In July 2000, Egypt's High (supreme) Constitutional Court ruled that judges would have to oversee future elections. There was no mistaking the implied verdict: Egypt's parliament was illegitimate.[20] The same court that had earlier nullified the general elections of 1984 and 1987 on the grounds that the voting procedures used were unconstitutional, now ruled that the elections of 1990 and 1995 were equally unlawful. The high court earlier sentenced four members of Mubarak's ruling party to long prison terms for corruption. Before that, the court overturned a 1999 law restricting nongovernmental organizations and set aside a law that placed the Egyptian Bar Association under state supervision. By acting to protect the integrity of elections and lawyers, as well as the right of citizens to associate without state interference, the court led the fight for democratization.

But the transition process in Egypt is not likely to be smooth. President Mubarak is not likely to bow out gracefully. It is entirely possible that the government will resort to political repression if it is backed into a corner. In fact, persecution of Mubarak's critics was stepped up in the summer of 2000 when police arrested and jailed a leading advocate of "cleaner democracy," holding him without charge under the nineteen-year-old state of emergency.[21]

Egypt, the Arab World, and the Second Gulf War America's war on terror and continuing support for Israel created a no-win situation for Mubarak and highlighted Egypt's dilemma. The famous postulate "the whole is greater than the sum of its parts" finds resonance in many disciplines, including physics, biology, economics, and politics. The Arab world is *less* than the sum of its parts both politically and economically. In a real sense, it exists only in the imagination because the Arab states lack at least two essential ingredients to form a distinct "world": unity and leadership. Egypt is the logical (and only possible) leader of the twenty-two-member Arab League. Indeed, Egypt under Nasser attempted to play this very role, but failed. The only noteworthy instance of Arabs making common cause in modern times was the 1973 OPEC oil embargo. If this situation ever changes, Egypt will be in the forefront, but Egypt cannot play that role unless it can energize its economy and pursue an independent course in foreign policy.

The events of 9/11 put Mubarak (and other Arab leaders) in a very precarious position. On the one hand, there is a powerful undertow of popular support for Islamic fundamentalist causes in Egypt and throughout the region. Mubarak cannot afford to ignore the sentiment of millions of Egyptians who sympathize with militant Islamist groups and see Osama bin Laden as a hero for striking a blow at America. On the other hand, Egypt is dependent on America. Mubarak publicly denounced the 9/11 terrorist attacks on America and pledged Egypt's cooperation in the Bush administration's war on terrorism. Mubarak's actual policy boiled down to this: He would refrain from public criticism of the United States, continue to hunt down terrorists in Egypt, and keep the lid on anti-U.S. demonstrations — in essence, he would do what he had been doing all along. However, for Mubarak, doing more of the same was riskier than ever in the emotionally charged post-9/11 atmosphere.

Not surprisingly, Muburak opposed the U.S. decision to invade Iraq in 2003. He expressed his displeasure very openly and was humiliated when President Bush aggressively pressed the case against Saddam and demanded "regime change" (translation: democracy) in Iraq. Bush's penchant for linking legitimacy and democracy in the Middle East probably angered Mubarak as much as the American president's romance with "preemptive" war. (See Box 12.3.) Relations between Cairo and Washington plunged to the lowest level in Mubarak's twenty-one-year presidency in 2002–2003. The fact that the Bush administration paid no heed to his views — or the predicament that the White House's Middle East policies put him in — made Mubarak appear impotent. That is a dangerous situation for any dictator, even one who pretends to preside in a democracy.

In Sum . . . Egypt's government is a personal dictatorship masked as a multiparty democracy. Since the late 1970s, the Egyptian economy has been generously subsidized by the United States under the terms of the peace treaty negotiated at Camp David. But subsidies from abroad are a poor substitute for the basic reforms needed to fuel sustained growth. Egypt's stability has been achieved at the expense of liberty and prosperity. At the same time, Egyptian society remains politically divided and tends at the extremes to be violence-prone (not unlike many other Arab societies). Mubarak has stayed in power by using police-state tactics against Islamic extremists and keeping Egypt's relations with the United States uppermost. But America's 2003 war against Iraq and the continuing war between Israelis and Palestinians have made Mubarak's position increasingly untenable both in Egypt and in the Arab world as a whole.

Postscript: Is the Arab World "Self-Doomed"?

The heading for this section is borrowed from a 2002 special report in *The Economist* entitled "Self-Doomed to Failure."[22] The article pointed out that a recent in-depth UN study of "Arab Human Development" found that the Arab Middle East lags behind most other regions of the world and asked why.[23] It noted that this region encompasses a population almost exactly equal to that of the United States (280 million), but that it has "the largest proportion of young people in the world — 38 percent of Arabs are under

Post-Saddam Iraq and Middle East Politics BOX 12.3

In March 2003, the United States, impatient with the reluctance of the UN Security Council to authorize military action, invaded Iraq. The immediate justification for the invasion was to prevent Iraq from threatening its neighbors with "weapons of mass destruction." The Bush administration's avowed aim was to remove Saddam Hussein from power and install a democratic government friendly to the United States and its Western allies. The invaders met with little direct resistance in overrunning the country and ousting the dictator.

The U.S. occupation, however, did not go so smoothly. American forces (numbering 130,000–146,000) were charged with maintaining law and order while trying to locate the alleged weapons of mass destruction. As this book went to press, no such weapons were found. Guerrilla-style attacks on American troops and terrorist bombings became daily occurrences.

Toward the end of 2003, as the American public grew increasingly disaffected with the course (and cost) of the war and its aftermath in Iraq, the following scenario was emerging: (1) Saddam's loyalists were determined to fight on indefinitely; (2) the United States would have little choice but to dig in; (3) the future Iraqi government envisaged by the Bush administration would require an American military presence to keep it in power; and (4) the long-term presence of a large American army in Iraq would have profound (but unpredictable) consequences for the regional balance of power in the Middle East. The capture of Saddam in December 2003 was played up as a major success by the Bush administration, but the violence continued unabated.

President Bush expressed a desire to see democracy flourish not only in Iraq, but also throughout the Arab world. However, this vision posed a challenge to existing Arab regimes, including such pro-Western states as Saudi Arabia, Jordan, Egypt, and Morocco. For anti-Western states — especially Iran and Syria — the new Bush doctrine of preemption was a clear threat. Meanwhile, the U.S. invasion and occupation of Iraq inflamed anti-American feelings among rank-and-file Arabs, thus undermining political stability in a notoriously volatile part of the world. With the 2004 presidential election looming, there was no "light at the end of the tunnel" as costs and casualties in Iraq mounted daily.

fourteen — and it is calculated that the population will top 400 [million] in 20 years' time." Arabs on average can expect to live fifteen years longer today than thirty years ago and Arab babies are much less likely to die before the age of five. Arab per capita income is higher than in most developing areas due to a single factor: oil. Of course, oil wealth is not evenly spread among the Middle East kings or sheiks ruling sparsely populated states in the Persian Gulf that control most of it. Surprisingly, however, the Arab states' total output of goods and services taken together is smaller than Spain's.

Many Arabs at the bottom of the income ladder continue to be mired in poverty — one in five exist on less than two dollars a day. Moreover, things are not getting any better: growth in per capita income in the Arab Middle East over the past two decades was lower (0.5 percent) than any other region's except sub-Saharan Africa. Unemployment for the region as a whole runs at around 15 percent, a figure that would be totally unacceptable anywhere in the developed world. That figure translates into 12 million jobless adults — an idle population larger than Belgium or the Czech Republic. Indeed, demographics (a combination of youthfulness and joblessness) combined with political repression largely accounts for the rage that turn young boys into suicide bombers.

Significantly, the UN study concluded that the absence of freedom (the flip side of repression) is also one of the causes of lagging economic development in the Arab

Democracy in America

BOX 12.4

Gender and Equal Rights

When the amendment guaranteeing "equal rights under the law shall not be denied or abridged by the United States or any State on account of sex" failed to gain approval by the necessary three-fourths of the State in the late 1970s, its backers were disappointed, but it did not mean that women would have no legal protection. The Civil Rights Act of 1964 prohibits sex discrimination in hiring, firing, and pay. The 1972 Civil Rights Act bans sex discrimination in local schools receiving federal funds. These laws apply to private as well as government action. The U.S. Supreme Court has ruled in many "sex discrimination" cases over the years. The net result is the following set of "rules":

Illegal Discrimination:

- States cannot set different "legal adult" ages for men and women
- States cannot set different ages at which men and women can buy beer
- Employers cannot bar women from jobs by arbitrary height and weight requirements
- Employers cannot force women to take pregnancy tests
- Girls cannot be barred from Little League baseball teams
- Service clubs (such as Kiwanis or Rotary) cannot exclude women from membership
- Employers must pay men and women the same monthly retirement benefits
- High schools must pay coaches of girls' and boys' sports the same

Court-Approved Differences Based on Gender

- A law that punishes males but not females for statutory rape
- All-boy and all-girl public schools provided enrollment is voluntary and quality is equal
- A law that gives widows a property-tax exemption not given to widowers
- A navy policy letting women remain officers longer than men without being promoted

Now, look over the list and try to find one or two rules that would *not* cause a riot in Riyadh.

Middle East. Freedom was one of three "deficits" the authors of the study identified. The other two were knowledge and womanpower. *The Economist* writes:

> The area is rich in all the outward trappings of democracy. Elections are held and human-rights conventions are signed. But the great wave of democratisation that has opened up so much of the world over the past 15 years seems to have left the Arabs untouched.[24]

The knowledge deficit is perhaps the most puzzling in light of the strong emphasis on education found in Arab-Islamic cultures. Arab governments spend more on education than any other developing region but the quality of education and the "fit" between the teaching methods and subject matter on the one hand, and needs of modern technologically advanced economies on the other, is not good. As elsewhere, adult illiteracy has declined, but an estimated 65 million Arabs, two-thirds of them women, cannot read or write. Moreover, despite the fact that Arabs led the world in science in centuries past, investment in research and development is only a small fraction of the world average, only about 6 persons per 1,000 use the Internet, and only 12 per 1,000 have a computer.

The Arab world's self-imposed intellectual isolationism is also striking. According to the UN report, Spain alone translates as many foreign books in one year as the Arabs have translated in the last thousand years.

Finally, it is generally known that in Arab societies the life possibilities for most women are extremely limited, that women face high barriers to university education or participation in the professions, and that women are generally barred from leadership positions in government and business. (See Box 12.4.) What is worse, however, is that fully half of all Arab women cannot read or write. The fact that women are not allowed to drive a car in Saudi Arabia, for example, is appalling to Westerners, but trite in the context of the political and social repression so common in the Arab world and the mountains Arab women must climb in order to gain basic (to say nothing of equal) rights.

The mention of "basic rights" brings us full circle, because any lasting solution to the problems of economic development involves the expansion of human freedom as a first step. Clearly, so long as Arab societies continue to exclude half the population from the full participation in the economy while excluding nearly all of it from participation in the political system, the region will continue to stagnate.

SUMMARY

The political systems of the Middle East are authoritarian and range from personalistic military or civilian dictatorships to hereditary monarchies. Most of the monarchies are found on the Arabian Peninsula and are blessed with large oil reserves. Israel is the only parliamentary democracy in the Middle East, but a two-tiered system has evolved: Jewish citizens enjoy broad civil and political rights that are denied to Palestinian Arabs in the Occupied Territories. Egypt now has the trappings of a Western-style multiparty democracy but retains many of the elements of a civilian dictatorship. This chapter explored the problems and prospects for the region in general and for Israel and Egypt in particular. It also considered several "hot spots" that cloud the prospects for peace and stability in the Middle East.

KEY TERMS

jihad
Palestine Liberation Organization (PLO)
realpolitik
Palestinian queston
Gush Emunim
intifada
Law of Return
Knesset
Labour Party
Likud
OPEC oil embargo
Al Aqsa mosque
Old City of Jerusalem
Arab Socialist Union (ASU)
People's Assembly
National Democratic Party
Islamic fundamentalism

STUDY QUESTIONS

1. What forms of government are most prevalent in the Middle East? How have governments typically changed in the past?
2. How is Egypt ruled? Has the Egyptian political system changed much since the overthrow of the monarchy? Since the death of Nasser? If so, what are the significant changes?
3. How is Israel ruled? Is it a theocracy? A democracy? Police state? What are the salient characteristics of Israeli politics? What issues dominate the political scene? Which party or parties control the Knesset and the government? Why?
4. How is Iran ruled? What accounted for the enormous power of the Ayatollah Khomeini during the Iranian Revolution and in the theocratic state that emerged from it? How did Khomeini's ideas about Islamic law and ethics shape Iranian politics, and with what consequences? Is Iran changing again now?
5. Why has the Arab world lagged behind other regions in the areas of social modernization and economic development in modern times?

SUGGESTED READINGS

Ajami, Fouad et al. "Middle East Countdown." Special issue, *Foreign Affairs,* January/February 2003. (The lead article by Ajami is entitled "Iraq and the Arabs' Future.")

Aruri, Nasur, ed. *Palestinian Refugees: The Right of Return.* London: Pluto Press, 2002.

Azzam, Henry T. *The Arab World Facing the Challenge of the New Millennium.* London: Tauris, 2002.

Bakhash, Shaul. *The Reign of the Ayatollahs: Iran and the Islamic Revolution.* Rev. ed. San Bernardino, Calif.: Borgo Press, 1991.

Barnett, Michael N., ed. *Israel in Comparative Perspective: Challenging the Conventional Wisdom.* Albany: State University of New York Press, 1996.

Cordesman, Anthony H. *Saudi Arabia Enters the Twenty-First Century: The Political, Foreign Policy, Economic, and Energy Dimensions.* London: Praeger, 2003.

Bill, James A., and Springborg, Robert. *Politics in the Middle East,* 5th ed. New York: Addison Wesley Longman, 2000.

Esposito, John L. *The Islamic Threat: Myth or Reality?* 3rd ed. New York: Oxford University Press, 1999.

Felder, David W. *Palestinians and Israel.* Tallahassee, Fla.: Wellington, 1996.

Henry, Clement M., and Springborg, Robert. *Globalization and the Politics of Development in the Middle East.* New York: Cambridge University Press, 2001.

Rubin, Barry. *The Tragedy of the Middle East.* Cambridge: Cambridge University Press, 2003.

Ryan, Curtis. *Jordan in Transition: From Hussein to Abdullah.* Boulder, Colo.: Lynne Rienner, 2002.

Shamir, Shimon, ed. *Egypt from Monarchy to Republic: A Reassessment of Revolution and Change.* Boulder, Colo.: Westview, 1995.

Shehadeh, Raja. *Strangers in the House: Coming of Age in Occupied Palestine.* South Royalton, Vt.: Steerforth, 2002.

Siddig, Mohammed H. *Why the Boom Went Bust: An Analysis of the Saudi Government.* Kearney, Neb.: Morris, 1995.

Springborg, Robert. *Mubarak's Egypt: Fragmentation of the Political Order.* Boulder, Colo.: Westview Press, 1989.

Telhami, Shibley. *The Stakes: America and the Middle East.* Boulder, Colo.: Westview, 2002.

al-Yassini, Ayman. *Religion and State in the Kingdom of Saudi Arabia.* Boulder, Colo.: Westview, 1985.

SUGGESTED WEB SITES

http://www.state.gov/www/regions/nea/isspeech.html
http://www.arab.net/
http://www.arabworldnews.com
http://inic.utexas.edu/menic/
http://www.keele.ac.uk/debts/por/mebase.htm
http://www.israel-mfa.gov.il/peace/
http://www.pirsonet.co.il/IPCRI/
http://www.mcgill.ca/icames
http://eecilmarie.web.prw.net/arabworld/
http://www.aaiusa.org/arab_world.htm

NOTES

1. Barry Rubin, *Modern Dictators: Third World Coup Makers, Strongmen, and Populist Tyrants* (New York: NAL-Dutton, 1988), p. 201.
2. Ibid., p. 200.
3. Ibid.
4. Ibid., p. 202.
5. Avner Yaniv, "Israel Comes of Age," *Current History,* February 1989, p. 101.
6. Thomas L. Friedman, "Dividing a Homeland," *New York Times,* September 15, 1993, p. 1.
7. Ibid.
8. Quoted in ibid.
9. See "Arafat Acrobatics," *The Economist,* July 6, 1996, p. 39.
10. Yaniv, "Israel Comes of Age," p. 102.
11. Ibid.
12. Ibid.
13. Jackson Diehl, "New Mall in Israel Gives Better Clues than Old Politics," *International Herald Tribune,* June 9, 1992, p. 1.
14. Ibid.
15. James A. Bill and Robert Springborg, *Politics in the Middle East,* 5th ed. (New York: Addison Wesley Longman, 2000), p. 244.
16. George Lenczowski, *The Middle East in World Affairs* (Ithaca, N.Y.: Cornell University Press, 1980), p. 562.
17. Jane Friedman, "Egyptian Elections Marred by Opposition's Allegations of Fraud," *Christian Science Monitor,* April 7, 1987, p. 13.
18. See Robert Bianchi, "Islam and Democracy in Egypt," *Current History,* February 1989.

19. Ibid., p. 94.
20. "The Law vs. the State," *The Economist,* July 22, 2000, pp. 42–43.
21. Ibid., p. 42.
22. "Self-Doomed to Failure," special report, *The Economist,* July 6, 2002, pp. 24–26.
23. See, "Arab Human Development 2002," United Nations Development Programme (UNDP), on the World Wide Web at http://www.undp.org/rbas/ahdr/.
24. "Self-Doomed to Failure," p. 25.

PART VII
Sub-Saharan Africa

Nigeria

Area: 356,667 square miles

Population: 136.5 million

Density per square mile: 350

Languages: English (official), Hausa, Yoruba, Igbo (Ibo)

Female school enrollment: not available

Major religion(s): Islam (50%) in north, Christian (40%) in south, indigenous (10%)

Monetary unit: naira

GNP (2003): $45 billion (est.); 1998 = $36.3 billion

Recent GNP growth rate: 4.3% (2003 est.)

GNP per capita (2003): $360 (est.); 1998 = $300 (PPP = $740)

Per capita GNP growth rate, 1990–1998: 0.4%

Inflation rate, 1990–1998: 38.7% (yearly average)

Recent inflation rate: 12–15% (2003 est.)

Female labor force (1998): 36% of total

Personal computers per 1000 people: 5.7

South Africa

Area: 472,359 sqare miles

Population: 46.4 million

Density per square mile: 95–100

Languages: English, Afrikaans (Dutch derivative), Xhosa, Zulu, other local tongues

Female school enrollment (1998): 100%

Major religions: Christianity (majority), Islam, Hindu

Monetary unit: rand

GNP (2003): $100–105 billion (est.); 1998 = $136.8 billion

Recent GNP growth rate: 1.5% (2003)

GNP per capita (2003): $2,200 (est.); (1998): $3,310 (PPP = $8,296)

Per capita GNP growth rate, 1990–1998: –0.1%

Inflation rate, 1990–1998: 10.6% (year-on-year average)

Recent inflation rate: 6.7% (June 2003)

Female labor force (1998): 38% of total

Personal computers per 1,000 people: 47.4

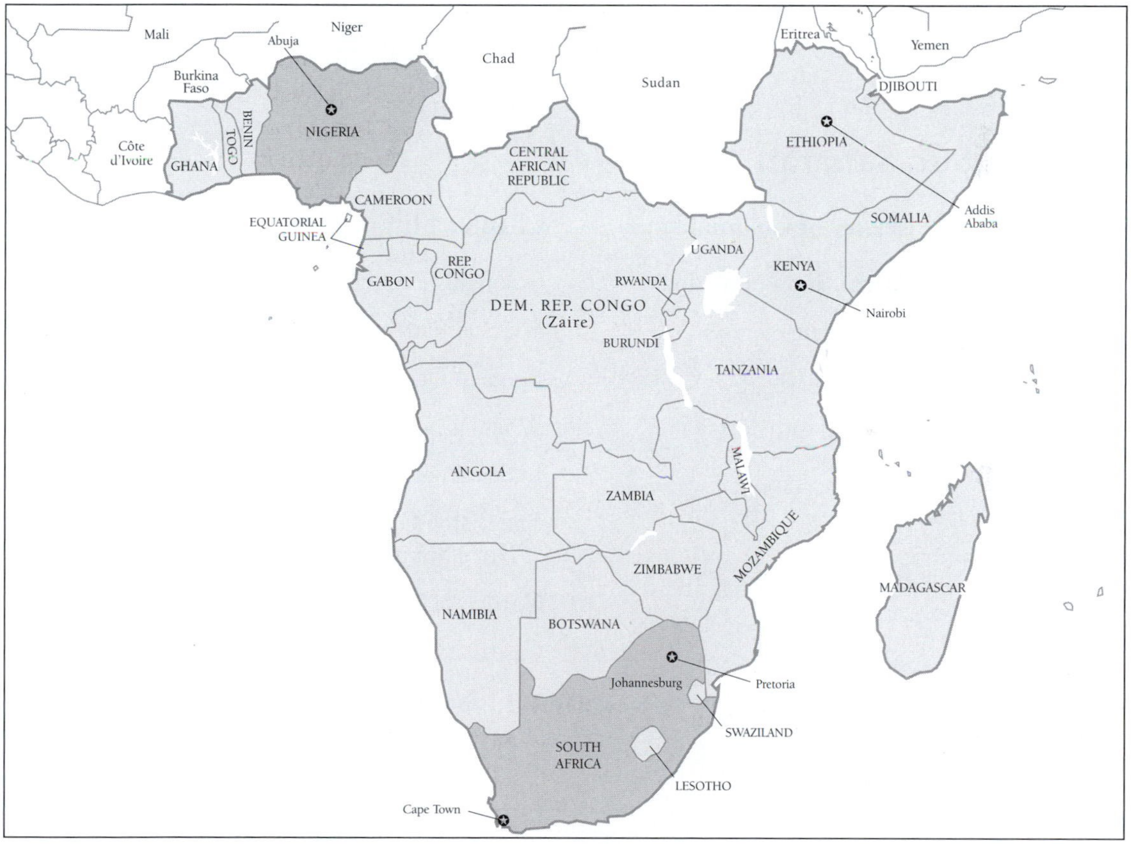
Mali
Niger
Abuja
Chad
Eritrea
Yemen
Burkina Faso
Sudan
DJIBOUTI
BENIN
TOGO
NIGERIA
ETHIOPIA
Côte d'Ivoire
GHANA
CENTRAL AFRICAN REPUBLIC
CAMEROON
SOMALIA
Addis Ababa
EQUATORIAL GUINEA
UGANDA
REP. CONGO
KENYA
GABON
RWANDA
DEM. REP. CONGO (Zaire)
Nairobi
BURUNDI
TANZANIA
MALAWI
ANGOLA
ZAMBIA
MOZAMBIQUE
ZIMBABWE
MADAGASCAR
NAMIBIA
BOTSWANA
Johannesburg
Pretoria
SWAZILAND
SOUTH AFRICA
LESOTHO
Cape Town

Part VII: Sub-Saharan Africa

CHAPTER 13

The Legacy of Colonialism

The nations of **sub-Saharan Africa** share a continent with a number of predominantly Arab countries, including Algeria, Egypt, Libya, Morocco, Tunisia, and Sudan, also known as North Africa. The rest of the continent can be divided into East Africa, West Africa, and Southern Africa. Sudan is the only true "pan-African" country — ethnically, two-fifths of the population (northern) is Arabic and one-half the population (southern) is black. The religion of northern and central Sudan is Islamic; that of southern Sudan is indigenous (highly localized and based on age-old beliefs, ceremonies, and rituals).

Sub-Saharan Africa hosts a great diversity of cultures and environments that have shaped its traditions and institutions. The region comprises 80 percent of Africa's landmass and more than 70 percent of the continent's population

In all, Africa is home to fifty-five independent states. Of these, forty-nine are located in the region south of the Sahara (sub-Saharan Africa accounts for roughly one-fourth of the votes in the UN General Assembly). Most are artificial creations, a legacy of colonialism. The borders — drawn by the great powers of Europe for their own convenience — in some cases arbitrarily divide ethnic groups between two or more states; in other cases, they combine several ethnic groups into a single state.

The very idea of the nation-state clashes with Africa's cultural geography and political history. Westerners can easily be misled by a concept of "country" that is appropriate enough in the context of European civilization but does not, in fact, have universal validity. In Africa, a country is not necessarily an aggregation of people whose primary allegiance is to a single state. Rather, it is a state or government recognized by other states or governments as having a legitimate claim to rule a certain territory and population, even though its native inhabitants may reject that claim or view it with indifference.

Land, Climate, Resources, and Population

Africa is a continent of extremes. Whether the topic is climate, geography, natural beauty, population, poverty, or politics, it is difficult to avoid the word *extreme* in describing Africa.

There are three distinct geographical areas on the continent — the Northern Plateau, the Central and Southern Plateau, and the Eastern Highlands. The first of these areas is dominated by the Sahara, the world's largest desert, which spans one-quarter of Africa's landmass. It divides Arab North Africa from Black Africa. Several millions of square miles in area and 3,000 miles long, the Sahara stretches from the east coast to the west coast of the continent, creating a formidable natural barrier between the Arab world to the north and Black Africa to the south. The desert is extremely hot and arid — the highest temperature ever recorded (136 degrees Fahrenheit) was in the Sahara. In some places, there is not a living thing to be found — no plants or animals, not even an insect. The parched Sahel region — the transitional zone between the Sahara and the tropical rain forests and savannas to the south — typically receives a mere four to eight inches of rain in a year. For a stretch of time between the late 1960s and the early 1980s, it rained even less, leading to the worst drought there in 150 years.

Beyond the Sahel a higher plateau stretches across the central and southern parts of Africa — the second area mentioned previously. Several major depressions, including the Congo Basin and the crimson Kalahari Desert, give this area its unique character. This is the part of Africa many outsiders "know" best, where the fictional Tarzan ("King of the Apes") swings in the trees. Western films often give moviegoers false impressions of Africa, but the part about the trees is true enough. There are lush tropical forests (jungles), as well as great savannas, in this area. (Many of the exotic animals of Africa are actually creatures of the savanna rather than the jungle.) The area is also rich in diamonds, gold, uranium, and petroleum, among other valuable natural resources — a fact that contrasts sharply with the popular image of Africa as a place where poverty and suffering are decreed by fate. There is also rich farmland along the southern coastal plain, where fruits and plantation crops flourish. Africa's people *are* poor, but Africa is a land of amazing treasures — including plants and animals most Westerners see only in botanical gardens and zoological parks.

The third area is the Eastern Highlands, bordered on the north by the Red Sea and on the south by the Zambezi River. It is where the famed Mt. Kilimanjaro (altitude: 19,341 feet) is found, as well as the Great Rift Valley (in Kenya), created by a massive geological fault system, and the spectacular Victoria Falls of the Zambezi River (on the frontier between Zambia and Zimbabwe), which plunge some 360 feet.

Sub-Saharan Africa boasts five great rivers: the Nile, the Congo, the Niger, the Zambezi, and the Orange. These rivers are not hundreds but thousands of miles long. (The Nile is the longest river in the world.) That fact, plus the rivers' abrupt descents, has led to estimates that Africa has perhaps 40 percent of the world's hydroelectric potential. These mighty rivers played a significant role in Africa's political, economic, and cultural development before the colonial era, for centuries serving both as natural boundaries and as barriers against foreign intrusion. Ironically, during the nineteenth century, the same waterways were important conduits for Africa's colonization by European powers.

The ancient Greeks, who claimed the first European contact with this part of the world, called the region Ethiopia ("land of the burned faces"). During the eighteenth century, European explorers and geographers dubbed sub-Saharan Africa the "Dark Continent," revealing an astonishing ignorance of the cultures and geography of the region. (It is ironic that the term *dark* was ever applied to such a sun-drenched part of

What If? BOX 13.1

Out of Africa

Human life probably started in Africa between 5 to 8 million years ago. It is significant that one of the world's earliest civilizations flourished in Egypt perhaps 7,000 years ago, although very little is known about the origins of the ancient Egyptian empire. Where did these people come from? How long had scattered, localized human cultures existed on a small scale before the first great civilization emerged? The last five hundred years have brought upheaval and decline to the continent, including the slave trade, colonization, famine, epidemics, and an endless succession of bloody and brutal wars in which millions of innocents have been caught in the crossfire. The fate of Africa's children has been especially tragic. What if *we* were the children of Africa? In a sense, we are.

the world.) This ignorance of Africa is all the more surprising in light of archaeological evidence that sub-Saharan Africa is the birthplace of *Homo sapiens* and, in a real sense, the source of world civilization.[1] (See Box 13.1.)

One of sub-Saharan Africa's most intractable problems is the population explosion. The rate of population growth for the region as a whole is about 3 percent, the highest in the world. Due to this high natural rate of increase, sub-Saharan Africa, which had a population of about 385 million in 1985, surpassed the 600 million mark by the year 2000.[2] One way to understand the effect of population growth is to look at the doubling time — how long it will take for the population to double at current growth rates. Demographers simply divide 70 by the growth rate to calculate this figure. The result is alarming — a growth rate of 2 percent, for example, yields a doubling time of only thirty-five years. To repeat, in sub-Saharan Africa, the rate is about 3 percent.

The region will thus be squeezed in a deadly vise as the population gets younger and the carrying capacity of the economy fails to keep pace. Estimates put 80 percent of Ethiopia's population under age forty, and more than half of all Kenyans at (or under) age thirty, in 2000.[3] In east Africa as a whole, perhaps 45 percent of the population is under age fifteen. Thus, in the coming years there will be a bulge in the female population of childbearing age. This demographic time bomb means the political systems of sub-Saharan Africa, many of them already unstable, will come under even greater stress as the needs of growing populations outstrip the pace of overall development.

Ethnicity, Culture, and History

In the culture and history of African politics, nothing has been more significant than European imperialism. What explains the origins and patterns of colonial rule in Africa? Why were Europeans able to conquer this vast region in so short a time? Geography and ethnic rivalries were two key factors. So was the state of the various civilizations at the time. It is important to remember that African history did not begin with the arrival of the Europeans.

As prominent Africanist Ali Mazrui has pointed out, most of Africa has a **triple heritage**—African, Islamic, and Western.[4] These overlapping traditions are manifested most clearly in the prevalence of externally derived religions and languages in Africa. Most educated Africans, like Mazrui, are likely to speak three languages — an ethnic language, a national language, and Arabic or a European language.

Africa's Ethnic and Cultural Kaleidoscope

In an infomercial seen all over the world on CNN International in 2000, the government of South Africa told viewers, "we speak eleven different languages." Perhaps the world was impressed, but most Africans were probably shrugging and saying, so what? Multilingual societies are the rule, not the exception, in Africa.

Sub-Saharan Africa is a mosaic of ethnic groups and cultures — most experts set the total number at more than 1,000. Ethnic composition ranges from essentially homogeneous countries (such as Botswana, Lesotho, Seychelles, and Swaziland) to extremely heterogeneous ones (Cameroon and Chad each have 200 groups, Tanzania has 130, and Zaire has 80). Most sub-Saharan countries have two to five ethnic groups, and this diversity is matched by a great diversity of religions and languages. The resulting sociocultural fragmentation is compounded by the presence of non-African religions (Islam and Christianity) and languages (English, French, Spanish, Portuguese, and Afrikaans, derived from Dutch).

The countries of sub-Saharan Africa vary tremendously in size. They range from tiny Seychelles (small islands in the Indian Ocean) to Sudan, nearly four times the size of Texas. The smallest five countries take up only about 2,000 square miles of real estate, while the largest five countries encompass nearly 3 million.

Territorial size, however, in Africa as elsewhere, does not necessarily reflect population size. Nigeria, for example, with less than 4 percent of the region's land, holds nearly 25 percent of its population. Sudan, three times the size of Nigeria, has less than 4 percent of the region's population. Nigeria's population density is about ten times Sudan's.

Geography has had an influence on national development in sub-Saharan Africa. Some countries are landlocked, whereas others have long seacoasts. Proximity to oceans (or distance from them) often determined exposure to foreign intruders. The countries blessed with nearness to the oceans were at the same time cursed by being the first to be colonized. They were also often the last to gain their independence, in part because their harbors and ports made them strategically valuable.

The countries of West Africa along the Atlantic coast are generally richer in mineral wealth than the highlands of the interior, where agriculture and livestock form the basis of local economies. Location, size, population, topography, and natural resources have shaped relations among the states in the region. For example, Mali, Mauritania, Nigeria, and other nations of West Africa called for economic and military solidarity against South Africa during the heyday of apartheid, while Malawi, Mozambique, and Botswana, aware of the costs of antagonizing their powerful neighbor, were more cautious and conciliatory. By the same token, South Africa has long enjoyed generally good relations with the West, for it offers major seaports, vast mineral wealth, and access to some of the world's most important maritime and naval routes.

The Language of Politics

The linguistic legacy of colonialism in African political culture is no less striking than the impact of imported religions. Non-African languages have both united and divided the societies of Black Africa. Thus, if the classification of a country as Anglophone (English-speaking), Francophone (French-speaking), or Lusophone (Portuguese-speaking) has provided a sense of group identity, it also points to one of the nation's most intransigent problems: deciding which language should be the official one. Some Africanists ascribe the failure of efforts to launch a pan-African movement to the absence of a common indigenous language region.

English or French is used in business or official matters in most sub-Saharan countries. Portuguese is spoken officially in five countries; Spanish, Italian, German, and Dutch (Afrikaans) is spoken in others. Despite the spread of Islam, which is the religion of about 250 million Africans, Arabic is not widely spoken anywhere in sub-Saharan Africa; it is a minority tongue in Somalia, Ethiopia, Eritrea, Djibouti, and Sudan.

To capture the kaleidoscopic character of African societies, some scholars talk about Africanity:

> Those with a superficial knowledge of black Africa see it as a monolithic culture in which everyone lives, feels and thinks alike . . . [but] those who know it really well detect beneath the diversity a large cultural unity. . . . The cultural unity of the diverse African people — the sum of all the component parts that give the various societies of traditional Africa their common characteristics — is known as "Africanity."[5]

This diversity gives rise to some contradictions. In a number of sub-Saharan countries, conflict born in cultural pluralism and social rifts has led to bloody rebellions and massacres. In some countries (Senegal, Tanzania, Zambia), statesmanship has contained ethnolinguistic tensions. But where group affinity is stronger than national identity (as in Angola, Burundi, Ethiopia, Nigeria, Sudan, Somalia, and Uganda), ethnic and religious tensions have erupted in full-scale civil wars.

Where imported or imposed cultural differences have generated conflict, indigenous religions and languages have sometimes ameliorated civil strife. In fact, African leaders who recognize the unifying force of indigenous culture may politicize local traditions to gain legitimacy or to galvanize popular support for particular policies.

Religion and Politics

Islam is the majority religion in fourteen sub-Saharan countries and virtually the only religion in Mali, Somalia, Mauritania, and Djibouti. Large Muslim communities can be found in many others, including Nigeria and Ethiopia. Christianity is the main religion in eighteen sub-Saharan countries.

In recent years, the Islamic nations have exhibited greater religious activism than the predominantly Christian ones. No doubt this phenomenon is related to Arab militancy regarding the Palestinian question and to other turbulent events in the Middle East, including the Iranian Revolution, which replaced the secular Western-oriented regime of the Shah with a fundamentalist Islamic theocracy. This event provoked a sharp increase in Islamic religious fervor not only in the Arab world but also in certain African countries. For example, more Nigerians (which is 50 percent Muslim) are likely to make pilgrimages to Mecca in any given year than, say, Egyptians or Iranians.[6] Five of Nigeria's seven heads of state since independence have been Muslims. Moreover, the influence of Islam transcends national politics in Africa: nineteen of the forty-five members of the Islamic Conference are from sub-Saharan Africa.

Some scholars question whether Africans who embrace Christianity are as devout as Muslims.[7] Studies have shown that although European and American missionaries were the most aggressive in evangelizing, they did not teach their religion within the context of local African traditions. **Mission Christianity,** according to African scholar John Mbiti, isolated new members from their roots without grounding itself in their cultures. Moreover, to most converts, the Christian missionaries, as role models, were often indistinguishable from other Europeans whose lifestyle was identical. Then, too, some locals converted to Christianity for opportunistic reasons, such as gaining employment in mission projects or wanting to appear "modern." Indeed, a self-conscious preference for modernity set mission-educated Africans apart from most other Africans, at least until quite recently.

Thus, the mission legacy produced new elites, but some of those elites rejected the philosophy of the missions, which discouraged higher education and secular pursuits in politics or the sciences. Some mission students, including Jomo Kenyatta, the "George Washington of Kenya," even came to resent the missions: "When the Europeans first came to Africa, they told us to shut our eyes and say amen."

Kenyatta was a gifted public speaker, thanks in part to his mission background. As W. H. Taylor noted in a study of Nigeria, the missions succeeded most in teaching such things as interpersonal relations and verbal self-expression.[8] Moreover, even if the missionaries avoided politics, their students often applied religious lessons to political and social analysis and used their verbal skills to persuade and politicize people. This may explain why so many of Africa's most illustrious independence leaders had an early affiliation with mission Christianity.

Traditional religions continue to predominate in some sub-Saharan countries. These religions are sometimes lumped together under the name of **animism.** Unlike Christianity and Islam, which are monotheistic, indigenous African religions espouse a multiplicity of divinities and spirits. Thus, for the Oromos of Ethiopia, Abdari represents a universal deity in whom all spirits and nature are unified and in whose name ancestral gods and natural divinities are called on to perform miracles and fulfill needs. The Yoruba of Nigeria have Ashe, or Arisa, the god of all power who can make all things happen. The Yoruba can also call on 1,700 other divinities and spirits for specific needs and occasions.[9] That traditional religions continue to thrive in many parts of the region must not be ignored by African leaders, who themselves are likely to be Muslim or Christian.

Africa's Neglected Precolonial History

Historian Basil Davidson has written:

> For most of Africa, the effective time-span of history, insofar as it can now be understood, reaches back over about two millennia, and is divided from prehistory — along a line that is always faint and sometimes arbitrary — by the development of iron-working

> and cultivation, as early populations dispersed and spread through the plains, hills and forests south of the Sahara. . . .
>
> It is the Negroes [*sic*], evolving a thousand languages and cultural variants over the past several thousand years, who have been responsible for the peopling of Africa with most of its modern inhabitants. Almost certainly they were dominant among the Late Stone Age pastoralists of the Saharan regions before the area began to become dessicated around 2000 BC; thus they formed or helped to form the early populations of Pharaonic Egypt and other peripheral areas along the Nile.[10]

The long history of Africa's social and political evolution cannot be recounted in detail here; only its contours can be traced. Civilization is always cumulative, a process of accretion spanning many centuries, at once differentiating and ordering human existence. One of the principal aims of society is to enable communities to cope with nature. This interaction of invention and environment, however, is only part of the story. The interaction of self-contained social groups — often with different rituals, languages, and customs — is equally important. As our case studies later in this chapter will illustrate, ethnic particularism and interethnic conflict have often gone hand in hand in Africa.

The Colonial Legacy

The geography of Africa — its size, surface features, climate, resources, and strategic importance — gave rise to a paradox: although physically remote from the principal power centers of Europe, North America, and East Asia, Africa is surrounded by water and thus can be reached easily via the maritime "highways" between the continents.

For centuries, outsiders viewed Africa with curiosity, awe, and greed. Before the modern era, however, foreign intrusions were hindered by geography. The regularity of Africa's coastlines put the perimeter within reach, but the interior was largely impenetrable because of the rugged terrains, tall mountains, hot and rainy seasons, unnavigable rivers, swamps, jungles, tropical rain forests, and the vast and forbidding Sahara. No other continent had such effective natural defenses.

By the second century CE, Arab merchant caravans were moving along the coast of the Sahara and East Africa, and various crusades in the seventh century spread Islam among Africans along the trans-Saharan trade route. The Romans had gained a foothold on the Mediterranean coast of Africa as early as the second century BCE, but further European encounters with Africa were minimal and sporadic for nearly 2,000 years. Thus, while the Africans of the interior were adapting to their environment — cultivating land, herding cattle, inventing implements, building societies and kingdoms — coastal African societies were trading goods and establishing ties with foreign traders, explorers, and missionaries. In this manner, coastal Africans themselves helped Europeans explore and eventually colonize the African interior by befriending the foreigners, serving as their guides and interpreters, protecting them from hostile interior inhabitants, repairing their ships, and giving them food and shelter. In the final analysis, the geography that had deterred foreign intruders could not prevent gradual encroachment by the European powers with the natives as their helpmates.

European explorers began sailing along Africa's coasts around 1450. Portugal, under the stewardship of Prince Henry the Navigator, sponsored many seafaring expeditions. Bartolomeu Dias rounded the Cape of Good Hope (the southern tip of Africa) in 1488, and in 1497–1498, Vasco da Gama became the first European to reach India by this route. The Portuguese successes attracted other European naval powers. Propelled by the new mercantilist ideology, the balance of influence in Africa shifted from Arabs to Europeans, setting the stage for the later arrival of Christian missionaries seeking converts, even in Muslim-dominated areas. A host of other highly destabilizing changes accompanied the European influx.

From 1795 to 1930, European geographers and missionaries took it as their duty to explore the African interior and to map and settle the continent. Europeans flocked to Africa in the second half of the nineteenth century in search of riches and adventure. Missionaries came to fulfill the "Great Commission," Christendom's solemn duty to save African souls (the "white man's burden," in Rudyard Kipling's famous phrase). These activities ultimately led to Europe's colonial domination over African cultures and politics and helped create some of the continent's most intractable problems.

By the mid-nineteenth century, Europeans had established colonies and were vying for hegemony. Their push for overseas territories was propelled in part by the Industrial Revolution and the need for cheap labor, raw materials, and new markets. In 1884, this "scramble for Africa" culminated in the **Conference of Berlin** (1884–1885), at which the European powers divided up Africa. At the end of the century, nearly all of Africa was under European colonial rule.[11] By 1914, only Ethiopia and Liberia remained self-governing. Although the colonial empires gradually broke up after World War II, most of southern Africa remained under white minority rule for decades.

The Aftershocks of Independence

Patterns of government and politics vary throughout sub-Saharan Africa, but there are common threads. For example, upon achieving independence, the nations of the region sought to adapt the forms of government that the colonial powers had established earlier. But the grafting of foreign models onto African cultures and the neglect of African traditions led to neither peace nor stability. Since independence, almost all the states in the region have experienced political violence, including assassinations, massacres, coups and coup attempts, revolts, insurgencies, and civil wars. To many experts, this chronic instability can be ascribed to the artificial boundaries drawn by the European powers. But, there were empires and dynasties in West Africa and South Africa and monarchies in East Africa long before the Europeans arrived. Thus large-scale political organization is not simply a colonial artifact. What colonialism did was wipe out virtually all traces of preexisting political institutions in sub-Saharan Africa, much as the Spanish did in Latin America.

From their earliest contacts with Africa, Europeans typically found nothing cultural that engaged their interest. They did, however, find resources they coveted: ivory, gold, and diamonds; lush and productive land; and people they could exploit. Systematically, they deprived the Africans of their dignity, their land, and their natural riches and denied them the fundamental right to self-determination. On their own soil, Africans were obliged to learn foreign languages, take foreign names, and worship

Contrast and Comparison

BOX 13.2

The "Republic" of Kenya

Kenya became a British crown colony in 1920. The English language and the Anglican church made a lasting imprint on the nation, but Kenya's recent history is also a product of tradition, geography, and other factors.

Swahili is the main indigenous language. Over two-thirds of the population is Christian (38 percent, Protestant; 28 percent, Roman Catholic).

Like other sub-Saharan countries, Kenya is a multiethnic society. With a total population of about 30 million, Kenyan society is composed of some forty ethnic groups, including the Kikuyu (21 percent), Luhya (14 percent), Luo (13 percent), Kelenjin (11 percent), Kamba (11 percent), Kisii (6 percent), and Meru (5 percent), along with Asians, Arabs, and Europeans.

Kenya has the highest population growth rate in the world (4.2 percent per year in the 1990s), and over half the population is fourteen years of age or younger. The economy has barely kept pace. With an annual per capita income of less than $400, Kenya has struggled to meet the many challenges of economic and political development since independence. In the 1990s, Kenya's real per capita growth was nil. It would be bad enough if wealth were evenly distributed, but that is not the case: one-tenth of the population receives nearly half the national income.

Jomo Kenyatta became Kenya's first prime minister upon independence in 1963. The government proclaimed Kenya a republic, with Kenyatta as president, the following year.

After independence, the government made an effort to replace ethnic particularism with Kenyan nationalism. Kenyatta championed Swahili over English. Concluding that a competitive multiparty arrangement would not work, Kenyatta moved to establish a one-party system with a strong executive. Some of Kenyatta's critics considered him a virtual dictator. His successor, Daniel arap Moi, followed in Kenyatta's footsteps, ruling with a firm hand — one more in keeping with a dictatorship than a democracy.

foreign deities. Many suffered a loss of self-esteem and experienced self-doubt. Some resolved their "identity crisis" by fully assimilating foreign norms and values; others, by rejecting foreign ways. During most of the twentieth century, the societies of sub-Saharan Africa were torn by conflicts between **rejectionists,** demanding political independence and national liberation, and **assimilationists,** accepting of foreign domination.[12]

Even the religions that were brought to Africa have contributed to hostilities. In a book titled *Things Fall Apart,* Nigerian novelist Chinua Achebe illustrated how mission Christianity created tension among Africans when the converts denigrated the unconverted as "pagans," and the unconverted maligned the converts as traitors who fraternized with foreign gods. In the same vein, Jomo Kenyatta, in *Facing Mount Kenya,* explained how colonial religions disrupted Kikuyu sociopolitical institutions. During colonization and the later struggle for independence, some Africans fought on the side of the Europeans with whom they shared religion, employment, and social status. To combat the fractionalizing effects of alien religions, many postcolonial leaders persecuted local converts, shut down mission operations, and restricted missionaries to teaching only government-approved subjects. (See Box 13.2.)

Neocolonialism In the **postindependence** period, sub-Saharan Africa has struggled to overcome the lingering effects of economic and political domination, known as **neocolonialism.** The economic legacy of colonialism limited Africa to producing raw materials for Europe and consuming finished products imported from overseas, often with borrowed capital or foreign aid. For all its long association with Europe, sub-Saharan Africa's average per capita gross domestic product was a paltry $450 at the end of the 1980s. All of Africa accounts for only 1 percent of world industrial output, yet the continent still supplies significant amounts of raw materials to the industrialized world. To describe this relative deprivation another way, the sub-Saharan countries, which account for about one-third of UN membership, together cannot afford to contribute even 1 percent of the UN budget.

Militarization Despite widespread poverty, sub-Saharan countries spend huge sums of money importing military hardware from former colonial powers. Such arms purchases not only divert foreign-exchange earnings and domestic revenues from indigenous economic development but also nurture militarism among national groups.[13] Blaming this particular distortion of priorities on imperialism, however, is a cop-out. African leaders have all too often sold out the interests of their own people for the sake of personal power and glory.

Nonetheless, the legacies of colonialism have provoked and prolonged conflicts among sub-Saharan countries. The long duration of wars for independence — nearly two decades in Angola, Mozambique, and Zimbabwe — is attributable in part to foreign influences. When Angola finally won independence from Portugal in 1974, the Soviet-backed Popular Movement for the Liberation of Angola (MPLA) seized power in most of the country, touching off a civil war. The Soviets used Cuban troops as a proxy army to defend the Marxist regime, while the United States and South Africa backed Joseph Savimbi's guerrilla forces (known as UNITA — the National Front for the Total Liberation of Angola).[14] South Africa sent troops across the southern Angola-Namibia border in June 1981, killing three hundred people and occupying several towns. South African forces withdrew the following September, but the war raged on until the late 1980s. Following a peace agreement and free elections, fighting again broke out in 1993.

Civil Wars The independence struggle has given way to civil war in other places as well. In Mozambique, an insurgency during the 1980s took many lives and left a wake of economic devastation. Struggles for majority rule in South Africa and for independence in Namibia — both against the same white minority regime — continued for more than two generations. As the century drew to a close, there were bloody wars raging in central Africa (Congo), East Africa (between Ethiopia and Eritrea), and West Africa (Sierra Leone). The Congo war involved all six of that country's neighbors and qualified as the world's worst contemporary conflict. (In total area, Congo is roughly the same size as Western Europe.) The war in Sierra Leone saw young boys used as soldiers and sex slaves, and was shockingly brutal. Only in East Africa did peace appear to be dawning — the two belligerents signed a peace treaty on December 12, 2000, with U.S. Secretary of State Madeleine Albright and other foreign dignitaries in attendance.

Poverty and Anarchy Toward the end of the nineteenth century, the European powers engaged in a mad scramble for colonial territories. France had lost a war to

Prussia (Germany) and was not about to lose out in the struggle for overseas possessions. France's great advantage over Germany and others in this race was geostrategic. With direct access to both the Atlantic Ocean and the Mediterranean Sea, France was able to knock together an impressive empire both in North Africa (Algeria and Tunisia) and in West Africa (the present nations of Senegal, Mauritania, Mali, Niger, Chad, Guinea, Côte d'Ivoire, Burkina Faso, Togo, Benin, Cameroon, Gabon, Congo, and the Central African Republic). French West Africa was considered an integral part of France, and its residents were French citizens. In time, an African elite educated in France emerged.

Although France's colonies outnumbered those of Great Britain, the British grabbed most of the prize territories (from a strategic or geopolitical standpoint, at least)—Nigeria in West Africa, South Africa and Rhodesia in the south, and Kenya in East Africa. After World War II, the United States and the Soviet Union emerged as superpowers, with continental rather than overseas empires. The British (but not the Portuguese or the Belgians) let go of its colonies without a struggle. France did, too, with two glaring exceptions — Indochina and Algeria.

In West Africa, France's colonies became independent states through a peaceful process of transition that was completed by 1960. Today, West Africa is one of the poorest and most unstable parts of the world. Unlike Asia, the range between the best and the worst-off is not very wide. With the lone exception of Gabon, countries in West Africa are extremely poor. War-ravaged Sierra Leone, with a paltry per capita GNP of $140, is possibly the poorest of the poor. The demographic picture is also alarming. Population growth rates are extremely high throughout the area (typically around 3 percent), and life expectancy is shockingly low in some countries — 37 years in Sierra Leone (the lowest in the world). Sierra Leone's infant mortality is the highest in the world (one in four children die before the age of five) and nearly 80 percent of the population is illiterate. These numbers are indicative of the extreme poverty and hardship found throughout the area. In the late 1990s, things actually got worse in West Africa when Sierra Leone plunged into civil war and anarchy.

African Unity: The Elusive Ideal

The years since 1960 have received the most attention in the literature of comparative politics in Africa. This exciting new era of self-rule also brought enormous challenges in nation building, including the search for unifying political philosophies and administrative systems and for models of economic development that would foster national integration and regional cooperation. The relics of colonialism have continued to work against African unity and self-reliance.

One of the most persistent problems is that the prevailing model of state administration embodies European approaches to hierarchy and authority that are alien to Africa's tradition of direct access and communication between the people and their leaders.[15] Thus, Africans have had to choose whether to go back to traditional modalities, adopt colonial institutions, or try to combine the two into a unique African blend — a task that is much easier said than done.

The Early Conferences

After independence, African leaders had to walk a tightrope — trying to act independent and negotiate the best terms for self-rule on the one hand, and having to operate within the constraints of continuing economic dependency on the other. Many of these leaders had returned from the battlefront, prison, or exile and suddenly had to master political skills, such as administration and persuasion. They attended conference after conference, seeking answers to common problems; they met in Accra, Addis Ababa, Algiers, Cairo, Casablanca, and Monrovia. They also went to non-African capitals and met with leaders of other developing nations, comparing notes and sharing ideas.

The Bandung Conference in 1955 brought together all thirty-eight of the developing countries at that time. The attendees promised to cooperate by sharing information, especially pertaining to economic and political development. A series of such conferences ensued and were institutionalized in the 1960s and 1970s in such forums as the nonaligned movement and the Group of 77.

Third World leaders launched the nonaligned movement at the Bandung Conference as an alternative to choosing sides in the East-West conflict. It thus helped focus attention on the North-South conflict — the tension resulting from the maldistribution of wealth between the industrial democracies of the Northern Hemisphere and the developing nations, mostly located in the Southern Hemisphere. The **Group of 77,** formed in 1964, is the largest caucus group in the United Nations. Its membership has grown to over 120 developing countries, and it is the primary means by which the South pressures the North to promote a new international economic order. The goal is to bring about greater global equity by redistributing resources (principally in the form of foreign aid and trade concessions) between North and South.

The issue of African unity topped the political agenda at the early regional gatherings. In the realm of economics, African leaders optimistically forged a consensus in favor of self-reliance. Meeting in Accra in 1958, the first Conference of Independent African States declared that, although the political domination of colonialism was over, the economic domination of neocolonialism remained.[16] Kwame Nkrumah, Ghana's prime minister and a participant at the meeting, wrote a book in which he asserted that neocolonialism was incompatible with economic development in the African context.[17]

Nkrumah's Vision

Pan-Africanism emerged when Ghana and Guinea gained their independence in 1957 and 1958, respectively. Nkrumah was a leading advocate of African unity, but his views were not original. They were based on the writings of African descendants like Edward Blyden, George Padmore, Marcus Garvey, and W. E. B. Du Bois, who had lived, traveled, and taught in the United States, Europe, and the West Indies.[18]

As a visitor to Europe and the United States, Nkrumah had become acquainted with the works of these black intellectuals. He was captivated by the idea of promoting a collective African consciousness.[19] What Nkrumah had in mind was not only the political and economic unification of sub-Saharan Africa but also the solidarity of all Africans worldwide.[20] His was a vision of revolutionary black power on a global scale;

he was saying, in effect, "Africans of the world, unite!" In Nkrumah's quasi-Marxist worldview, Africans were the proletariat, and Europeans were the capitalist oppressors.

But Nkrumah's concept of African unity, for all its intellectual and emotional appeal, was too radical or too idealistic for many other leaders, and the unity movement soon broke into factions. The more radical Casablanca group wanted immediate political unity; the more conservative Monrovia group preferred to start with socioeconomic and cultural cooperation. Sensitive to Africa's cultural and political fragmentation, they spurned the idea of pan-African unity at a time when sub-Saharan states were facing basic nation-building tasks, including the inculcation of a sense of national identity.[21]

The Organization of African Unity

Various groups continued to hold unity conferences until a third faction emerged, taking a position midway between the radicals and the conservatives. The setting was a 1963 conference in Addis Ababa at which thirty-two independent states agreed to establish the **Organization of African Unity (OAU).** Patterned after the United Nations, the OAU adheres to the basic UN principles of noninterference in the internal affairs of member states, respect for the territorial integrity of member states, human rights, and peaceful settlement of disputes.[22] Nkrumah proposed that the OAU have a standing army, but the majority of participants opposed this measure. Subsequently, most OAU member states abstained from military intervention in regional conflicts that did not affect them directly. But Libya did send troops into Chad in the 1980s in an effort to influence the outcome of a civil war there (and to seize a strip of land reputed to hold deposits of uranium); Libyan forces also helped Tanzania defeat Idi Amin (who died in exile in the summer of 2003) in the Ugandan civil war.

The ideal of African unity remains a distant hope. The OAU has played a useful role in settling conflicts among its member states, and it acts as a moral restraint on aggression. It has also helped newer members through the critical early stages of independence and has used its influence to pressure South Africa to free Namibia and to end apartheid. But it has made little headway against human rights abuses, hunger, and other forms of deprivation in many parts of the region.

Like people elsewhere, Africans have taken to nationalism much more readily than to regionalism (or pan-Africanism). Julius Nyerere of Tanzania, one of the founders of the OAU, lamented the fact that the idea of Africa has faded since the days of the early conferences: "At that time we saw Africa and we talked about Africa; today we are more Tanzanian than African, and Kenyans are more Kenyan than African."[23]

According to one interpretation, nationalism and the nation-state are legacies of colonialism; Africa's predicament, including fragmentation, is of external origin.[24] Other observers point out that Africa has had time to put its own house in order. These critics maintain that, whatever the causes of Africa's current problems, only Africans can solve them.

In any event, the OAU still holds annual conferences of African political and economic leaders. Yet there have been at least seventy-five coups and military interventions since 1963, and the OAU — founded in the name of African unity — has had to devote most of its energy and resources to mediating conflicts arising from African disunity and civil wars.

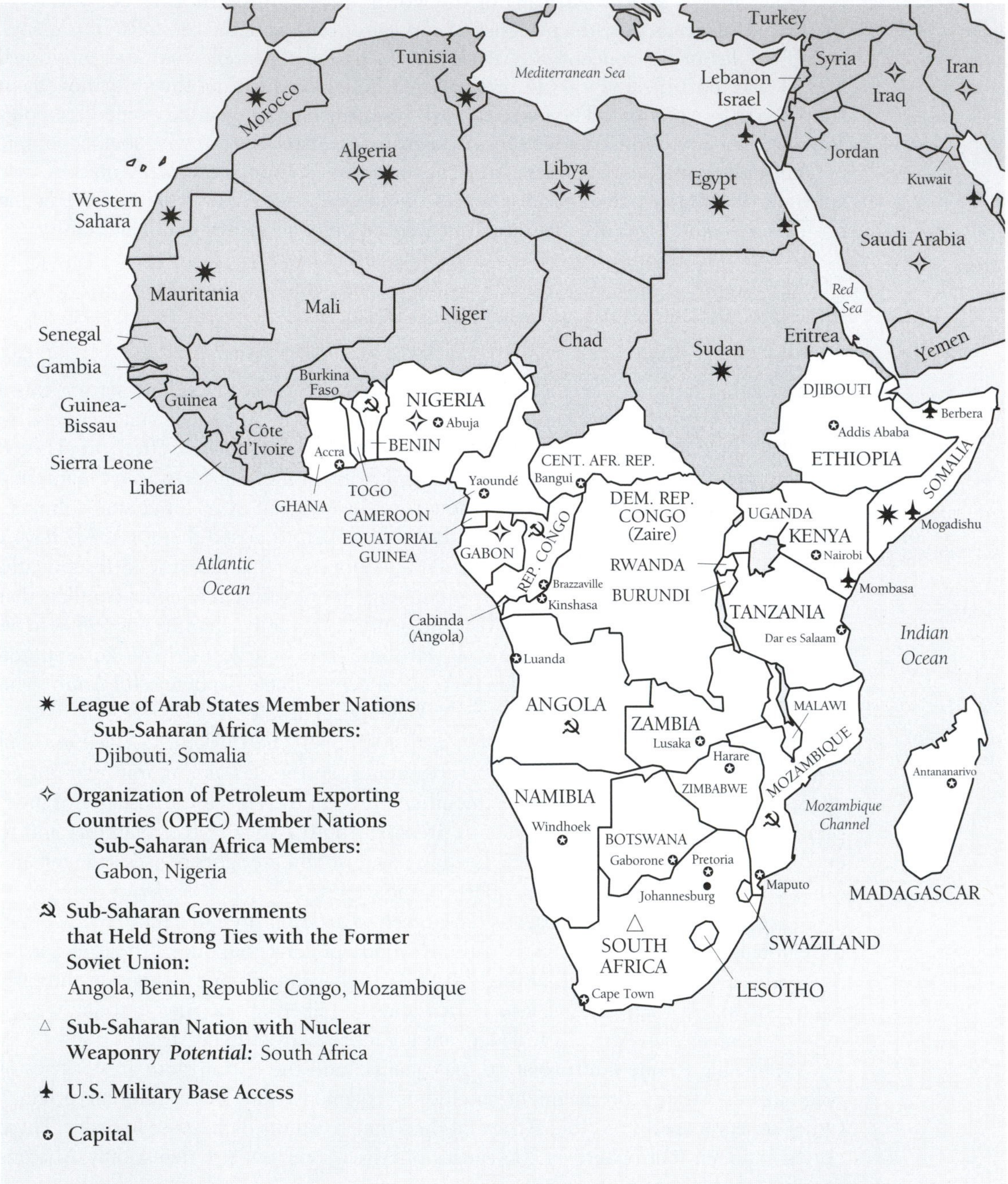
Turkey
Tunisia
Mediterranean Sea
Lebanon
Israel
Syria
Iraq
Iran
Jordan
Kuwait
Morocco
Algeria
Libya
Egypt
Saudi Arabia
Western Sahara
Mauritania
Mali
Niger
Chad
Sudan
Red Sea
Eritrea
Yemen
Senegal
Gambia
Guinea-Bissau
Guinea
Burkina Faso
NIGERIA
Abuja
DJIBOUTI
Berbera
Addis Ababa
ETHIOPIA
Sierra Leone
Liberia
Côte d'Ivoire
Accra
BENIN
GHANA
TOGO
CENT. AFR. REP.
Bangui
Yaoundé
CAMEROON
EQUATORIAL GUINEA
GABON
REP. CONGO
DEM. REP. CONGO (Zaire)
UGANDA
KENYA
Nairobi
SOMALIA
Mogadishu
Mombasa
Atlantic Ocean
RWANDA
BURUNDI
Brazzaville
Kinshasa
Cabinda (Angola)
TANZANIA
Dar es Salaam
Indian Ocean
Luanda
ANGOLA
ZAMBIA
Lusaka
MALAWI
Harare
ZIMBABWE
MOZAMBIQUE
Mozambique Channel
Antananarivo
NAMIBIA
Windhoek
BOTSWANA
Gaborone
Pretoria
Johannesburg
Maputo
MADAGASCAR
SOUTH AFRICA
SWAZILAND
LESOTHO
Cape Town
League of Arab States Member Nations
Sub-Saharan Africa Members:
Djibouti, Somalia
Organization of Petroleum Exporting Countries (OPEC) Member Nations
Sub-Saharan Africa Members:
Gabon, Nigeria
Sub-Saharan Governments that Held Strong Ties with the Former Soviet Union:
Angola, Benin, Republic Congo, Mozambique
Sub-Saharan Nation with Nuclear Weaponry *Potential:* South Africa
U.S. Military Base Access
Capital

Case Studies: Nigeria and South Africa

Nigeria, a former British colony, is potentially a leader in West Africa. South Africa, the most powerful nation south of the Sahara, was ruled until 1994 by a white minority government under an oppressive system of racial discrimination known as apartheid. As such, it was an anachronism, a vestige of European colonialism. First, we look at Nigeria, a nation with great potential and even greater problems.

Nigeria

Nigeria is by far the most populous country in Africa. It holds one-fifth of Africa's total population — about 136.5 million total in 2004 — on only 3 percent of its land. The terrain spreads through two main zones, savanna and rain forest. There is a ten-mile thick belt of mangrove swamps and lagoons along the coast. This swamp bulges inland more than sixty miles in the Niger River delta. Beyond the coastal lowlands the terrain gradually rises to a rocky plateau, then to savanna, and finally to a semi-arid zone in the extreme north.

The Niger River system drains most of Nigeria. Along with its main tributaries, the Niger provides an extensive inland navigation network. In the north is a very wide and shallow body of water, Lake Chad, which Nigeria shares with three other countries.

Nigeria has two distinct climate zones. In the coastal and southern parts the maritime equatorial air mass brings high humidity and heavy rainfall. To the north, the continental tropical air mass brings dry, dusty winds — the *harmattan* — from the Sahara.

Population pressure and years of corrupt military rule have led to severe environmental damage. About 85–90 percent of Nigeria's forests have been destroyed. Desertification caused by excessive irrigation — and too many reservoirs — has ravaged the land in places, as has uncontrolled grazing and livestock migration. Oil extraction and the infrastructure associated with it have also contributed to this problem.

Pressures on the land and resources are likely to grow. Nigeria's population is still growing at nearly 3 percent a year. At this rate, the population will double in less than twenty-five years and will exceed 200 million before 2020.

Well over half of Nigeria's people are classified as rural dwellers. The life expectancy of Nigerians, both men and women, was below age fifty-five at the end of the century. In most developed countries, people live more than 20 years longer on average.

The interplay of geography, history, environment, and economic development in Nigeria can be exemplified by the problem of the tsetse fly, for which science still has no solution. The tsetse fly is the deadly enemy of cattle and horses. This problem has far-reaching implications for agriculture and transportation and hence for the diet and living standards of Nigerians. It also played a surprising role in Africa's colonial history. As one noted Africanist has written:

> . . . the tsetse fly and forest stopped invading cavalry as man could not. These hills and mountains provided refuge; so too did the swamps and creeks far to the south, which must have been as unfathomable to African outsiders as they were to the succession of European explorers trying to solve the great geographical mystery of the Niger.[25]

A Cultural Crucible Nigeria's geographic diversity is matched by ethnic and cultural diversity. The major ethnic groups are the Hausa and Fulani (in the north), the Yoruba (in the southwest), and Igbo (in the southeast). These four ethnolinguistic groups account for over two-thirds of the total population. The final third, however, is an ethnic jigsaw puzzle. In fact, Nigeria is home to several hundred different ethnic groups — so many that estimates vary widely on the exact number.

Many Nigerians are multilingual and many speak some English. English is the official language of Nigeria — a convenient carryover from colonial times. Ironically, university-educated Nigerians speak English, a European language, which is not true of university-educated Czechs, for example, who live in Europe. In fact, educated Africans are no less sophisticated — and often far less provincial — than educated East Europeans.

Half the population of Nigeria is Muslim; the other half is mostly Christian. Only about one in ten Nigerians embrace a traditional belief system exclusively, but many mix animistic with Muslim or Christian beliefs. The north is Muslim and the south is predominantly Christian. Nigeria is not often mentioned in discussions about Islam, but the number of Nigerian Muslims is roughly equal to the total population of France or Italy.

The divisions in Nigerian society often take the form of reinforcing rather than crosscutting cleavages. In other words, geographical location (place), ethnicity, religion, and history tend to amplify Nigeria's many dissonant voices. As we will see, politics in Nigeria has frequently given way to rioting, repression, civil war, and even anarchy.

Over centuries, a variety of political systems evolved, including states, confederations, and empires. Some polities were localized and relatively democratic (though far less institutionalized than modern democracies) and most developed without foreign intrusions until the nineteenth century. Northern traders crossed the Sahara during the tenth century and introduced Islam. European traders did not appear until the sixteenth century and then did not venture beyond the Niger delta for another two hundred years.

In the north, the Fulani conquered the Hausa by the early nineteenth century and built an impressive empire, which lasted until the British arrived on the scene later in the century. In the southwest, the Yoruba established the kingdom of Oyo. The Igbo were dominant in the southeast. Only in the late nineteenth century was the full impact of British expansionism felt.

British Colonial Rule The British drew the boundaries of the country that came to be called Nigeria after 1914. They were latecomers and made the mistake of trying to impose uniform administrative and political structures throughout the territory. But what worked in the north did not work in the south. The decision to divide the country initially into only two parts now seems a major blunder. This north-south division reinforced a psychological split: British-educated southerners who lived in the coastal areas believed themselves more fit to rule than Islamic and supposedly insular northerners, who were widely scorned in the south.

The trauma that the Great Depression of the 1930s wrought on Europe's economies had repercussions in the colonies as well. Nigeria was a source of export revenue for beleaguered Britain, a fact that intensified Nigerians' desire to cast off British rule. Even so, Nigeria did not become independent until 1960.

World War II was the catalyst for decolonization throughout Asia and Africa. Before the British left Nigeria, they divided it into three regions (splitting the south into east and west). A distinct ethnolinguistic group dominated each region: the Hausa in the north, the Yoruba in the west, and the Igbo in the east. In 1967, the government, then under military control, replaced the regions with twelve states.

The Politics of Particularism The three major ethnic groups — Hausa, Yoruba, and Igbo — have dominated Nigerian politics, and the most popular and most charismatic political figures have usually been identified with one of them. Other sizable groups are the Nupe, Edo, Ijaw, Tiv, Fulani, and Kanuri. After independence in 1960, the Igbo, Yoruba, and Hausa each advanced a political party, resulting in a three-party system.

During the 1950s, when independence was being negotiated, there were two main sources of domestic tensions: the north-south split and the resentment of minority groups against the majority in each of Nigeria's administrative subdivisions. Violence erupted at times and smoldered even in periods of apparent tranquility.

In Nigeria, as elsewhere, the British did not foresee the issues of ethnic politics that they had helped create and consequently did little to resolve them. As a result, within a few years after the British left, Nigeria was convulsed by one of the bloodiest civil wars in modern African history, precipitated when the Igbo declared an independent republic, Biafra, and attempted to secede. One vital political lesson to be drawn from Nigeria's turbulent past is that a multiparty system in an ethnically fragmented society — particularly when that society faces enormous economic challenges — is likely to be unworkable.

Nigeria's political experience since independence will be detailed in Chapter 14. Briefly, at its inception, the British and other outsiders hailed Nigeria as a "model of democracy." But that was not to last. The first government after independence, elected in the first nationwide elections, was a coalition whose stability was threatened from the start. After a succession of political crises, in January 1966 the military staged a coup — the first in a series — and assumed power. Ever since, democracy has vied with dictatorship; the latter has prevailed most of the time.

South Africa

Nowhere was the colonial legacy more tenacious and invidious than in South Africa. **Afrikaners**—the dominant white minority of Dutch descent — claim that, when their ancestors arrived in the seventeenth century, the southern tip of Africa was largely uninhabited. They claim to have been the first to settle it. In time, they moved into the interior. What they eventually discovered was a gold mine — and much more.

An African El Dorado Most of South Africa is a great plateau. Its highest elevation (about 11,000 feet) is found at the southeast escarpment that runs along the coast of the Indian Ocean. The terrain varies from undulating to hilly to mountainous, and the climate in most of South Africa is mild, influenced by moist trade winds blowing from the Indian Ocean. South Africa has an abundance of natural resources, national parks (home to many species of exotic animals), and rich farmland. South Africa ranks number one in the world in the production of gold and platinum-group minerals (PGM), number two in manganese, and number four in gem-quality diamonds. It is also a major producer of antimony, chromium, uranium, vanadium, and other valuable minerals. South Africa is a rich country but most South Africans have not benefited from that wealth.

Who Are South Africans? This simple question puts a crucial issue in the spotlight. When the Dutch arrived on the scene in the seventeenth century, they were thousands of years behind the area's earliest inhabitants. Africans, by definition, originate in Africa, not Europe. Today, three-quarters of South Africa's population are black Africans — the true aborigines. The legendary Zulu constitute the largest of these groups. The other main groups are the Chosa, North Sotho, South Sotho, Tswana, Tsonga, South Ndebele, and Venda, each with its own distinct culture and language.

Prior to recent migrations that created a mixing bowl effect, these groups lived in distinct areas. Thus, although there were no maps or legally recognized boundary lines, members of each group claimed a certain territory. Those who ventured beyond that territory did so at their own risk. To murder a solitary stranger ("foreigner") was normal and war was often the first resort, not the last. To understand contemporary politics in South Africa, it helps to keep these tribal political traditions in mind. Although southern Africa has changed greatly since the European intrusions, the peoples of modern South Africa have long premodern histories, as well as languages and customs, which (naturally) continue to influence the way they look at the world.

Whites constitute a large minority. The white population of South Africa is about the same proportion of the total as the black population in the United States (12–14 percent). So-called Coloureds (people of mixed race) constitute another 8–9 percent. Indians (immigrants from India) make up the remainder (about 2 percent).

As mentioned earlier, South Africa has eleven official languages. Afrikaans (a Dutch offshoot) is the language of the majority of whites and most Coloureds. English is the language of most other whites (the British element) and Indians. Most blacks speak indigenous languages but relatively few whites do (although more whites are making an effort now that apartheid has ended). Many native Africans also speak Afrikaans or English (or both), one positive legacy of white rule in a world where English is the language of diplomacy and international business.

The decade of the 1990s was a watershed in South Africa's history. Today, South Africa is a multiethnic society in transition. The shape of the future is not clear, but it bears the imprint of the past no matter what happens. Any mention of South Africa's past calls up a single word — *apartheid.* In Afrikaans, **apartheid** simply means "separateness"; it refers to the legally required separation of the racial communities in the Republic of South Africa.

The Roots of Apartheid In truth, when the Dutch East India Company set out to establish a way station at the Cape of Good Hope in 1652, the expeditionary force of two hundred men encountered an indigenous group, the Khoikhoi, whom they enslaved. The Khoikhoi (called Hottentots by whites) were eventually wiped out by smallpox, and the Dutch colonialists then imported slaves from the East Indies and Madagascar. The resulting racial mixture of Khoikhoi, Dutch, Malay, and others produced the group now known as the Cape Coloured, who in time were classified by the Afrikaners as a distinct inferior group. ("Coloureds" are not to be confused with "blacks"; the majority blacks ranked below Coloureds in the apartheid system.)

The **Boers,** Dutch farmers who immigrated to what is now South Africa, pushed outward from the Cape Colony. Many Boers settled only long enough to exhaust the soil and then moved on. As they penetrated into the interior, they encountered another indigenous group, the San. The Boers wiped out the San, whom they called Bushmen and disdainfully regarded as savages and thieves.

The Kaffir Wars The Boers met no serious challenge from the indigenous Africans until the late eighteenth century. As Dutch settlers moved northward along the Indian Ocean coast, Africans were moving south to escape population pressure, tribal wars, and British slave raids. In the ensuing **Kaffir Wars,** which lasted over a century, the Boers subdued the Africans, with great loss of life on both sides.

Reverberations from the Napoleonic Wars in Europe were felt as far away as South Africa. When France occupied the Netherlands in 1795, the Dutch asked the British to take over the Cape and keep the French out. The British obliged but then decided to stay; in 1814, the Netherlands ceded South Africa to Great Britain, thereby legitimizing what was plainly a fait accompli (an established fact).

The Great Trek The Dutch in the Netherlands could adjust to the loss of South Africa more easily than the Boers could. The British takeover turned the tables: now it was the Afrikaners who were forced to live under rules made by "foreigners." For example, the British insisted that everyone be equal before the law, regardless of color or creed, and in 1834, to the dismay of many Boers, slavery was abolished. (See Box 13.3.) Two years later, the Boers, convinced that the British were out to destroy their way of life, began the **Great Trek.** Between 1836 and 1838, about 12,000 Dutch farmers and their families headed out in search of new frontiers. Afrikaners venerate these stouthearted forebears much as Americans honor the pioneers. As on the American frontier, these ***voortrekkers*** set out in caravans, endured tremendous hardships, and occasionally fought battles with natives, drawing their wagons into a circle called a *laager.* One ill-fated group vanished without a trace. When Zulus massacred 570 Boer settlers in 1838, the Boers retaliated by killing 3,000 Zulus. In general, the *voortrekkers* dealt with Africans just as the pioneers dealt with Native Americans: they used persuasion, force, and fraud to push the native inhabitants off the land. The very idea of owning land was alien to Africans, as it was to most Native Americans.

The *voortrekkers'* destination was the fertile Natal region, on the Indian Ocean coast. But in 1843, the British annexed Natal, outraging the Boers and prompting them to undertake yet another great trek. This time they moved inland and established two small republics, the Transvaal and the Orange Free State. Again ensconced in their own enclaves, the Boers coexisted with the British, uneasily but peacefully, until 1867, when diamonds were discovered in the Transvaal.

The Boer War The discovery of diamonds drew the British into the Transvaal; the flow became a flood when gold was discovered there in 1886. So many British *uitlanders* (settlers) rushed into the Transvaal that they soon outnumbered Afrikaners two

Democracy in America

BOX 13.3

The Other Face of Apartheid

In 1954, the U.S. Supreme Court paved the way for a social transformation in its landmark decision in *Brown vs. Board of Education.* In this famous case, it overturned the "separate but equal" doctrine on the grounds that "separate educational facilities are inherently unequal" in the context of U.S. social history.

There are historical parallels between the United States and South Africa in the nineteenth century, especially involving the treatment of nonwhites. In the United States, slavery was not abolished until the time of the Civil War in 1861–1865. Only Africans were enslaved in the United States (and South Africa). At the same time, Native Americans (often called "Indians" in the United States) were demonized ("savages"), dehumanized ("Redskins"), brutalized, forced onto reservations, and given only land that whites did not want. Similarly, South Africa created reservations (called *Bantustans*) for the indigenous peoples whose lands the Afrikaners coveted.

If whites treated Native Americans unjustly, the way they treated black slaves was even worse. Slaves had no rights. They were considered chattel under the laws of the slave states in the South, which meant that they had the same status as domestic animals and other "movable property." Slaveowners could buy and sell blacks (including small children) at will. Whites could also beat, rape, and murder blacks with impunity.

This shocking system ended in the United States in the 1860s, but blatant forms of racial discrimination — including a form of apartheid (segregation) — continued to exist especially, but not exclusively, in the South. It was not until a century after the Civil War that the first major piece of civil rights legislation was passed in the U.S. Congress. The 1964 Civil Rights Act barred racial discrimination in voting, public accommodations, schools, employment, and any activity receiving federal funding.

The laws changed in the United States more than a quarter of a century before they did in South Africa. But in South Africa, the coming of majority rule in the 1990s put blacks in control of the government. In the United States, progress toward social justice (and racial equality) depends on the white majority — and a political tradition which places respect for the Constitution above class interests, race, religion, or gender. It is one thing to change laws, and quite another to change facts. The most important "facts" in politics often boil down to values, attitudes, and opinions. These facts are often the hardest — and slowest — to change.

to one. The Transvaal government, headed by Paul Kruger, attempted to undercut the British by denying them the right to vote — this practice of disenfranchising the British was a favorite Boer tactic.

The British in the Cape Colony cast a covetous eye at the Transvaal and the Orange Free State. Sir Cecil Rhodes, founder of Rhodesia (and of Oxford's Rhodes scholarships), conspired with the British high commissioner, Alfred Milner, to provoke Kruger into declaring war; their goal was to annex the Boer republics.

The ensuing **Boer War** (1899–1902) was bitter and bloody. The Boers fought valiantly; the British resorted to drastic measures, including what today would be considered human rights abuses (such as putting Boer women and children in concentration camps, where an estimated 26,000 of them died of typhus). When the Boers finally sued for peace in 1902, the British had won the war but lost the territory: guilt-ridden and dispirited, London extended full political rights to the defeated Boers, who eventually converted their numerical advantage over the British into full control of the republics.

Ascent of the Afrikaners The British allowed the Afrikaners (Boers) of the Transvaal and the Orange Free State to govern themselves, which ushered in a brief era of goodwill. In 1910, the Boer-run colonies were yoked to Natal and Cape Province in a new nation-state, the Union of South Africa. World War I produced new strains on British-Afrikaner relations: although South Africa's foreign policy was dictated by Great Britain, many Afrikaners were sympathetic to the Germans, and the German colony of South-West Africa (now Namibia) was right next door. When the British pressured the South African government to join an invasion of South-West Africa, many Afrikaners were opposed; Pretoria participated anyway. Many Afrikaners similarly opposed South Africa's entry into World War II.

Anti-British sentiment also had economic causes. The British dominated South African industry and commerce, whereas the Afrikaners were primarily farmers. When the Great Depression disrupted world trade and precipitated a collapse in farm prices, many Afrikaners, now desperate, streamed to the cities in search of jobs. Against this backdrop, they became mobilized and radicalized. They set about creating the infrastructure of a new Afrikaner state and society — cultural associations, schools and universities, insurance companies, and political parties.

The **National Party** was founded in 1914 as the vehicle of Afrikaner self-assertion. At first, the party was moderate and conciliatory toward the British, but in the1930s, under the leadership of Daniel Malan, it became a militant instrument of Afrikaner nationalism. The doctrine of white supremacy — the cornerstone of apartheid — was solidified in the worldwide depression between the wars. Thus, the South African system originated in the same turbulent era as Nazi Germany, Fascist Italy, and other extreme right-wing regimes and movements founded on notions of racial superiority.

The Nationalists did not simply build a party; they launched a movement. With patience and persistence, they spread their ideology of white supremacy, using the emotionally charged image of wagons huddled in the *laager:* anyone who resisted indoctrination into the movement was breaking the circle and aiding the enemy. In 1948, the National Party won the general election — what Afrikaners had lost by the bullet they now recaptured by the ballot. Spurred by their tragic history, the Afrikaners dug in, building a fortress state prepared to meet all challenges with force.

The Apartheid System To the outside world, South Africa has long been synonymous with apartheid. One way to understand the apartheid system is to look at the legal structure that supported it. In all, some 350 laws were passed to implement the system. Here are a few of the most important ones:

- Land Act (1913): Prohibited Africans from acquiring land outside their native reserves
- Mines and Works Amendment Act (1926), also known as the "Color Bar" Act: Prohibited Africans from skilled work in the mines
- Group Areas Act (1950): Outlawed racially mixed residential areas; specified which races live where
- Native Building Workers' Act (1951): Extended the earlier mining color bar to skilled construction trades

- Native Act (1952): Required all Africans over age sixteen to carry a passbook specifying where they may live and work
- Native Laws Amendment Act (1952): Prohibited most Africans from remaining in urban areas for more than seventy-two hours
- Separate Amenities Act (1953): Segregated virtually all public transportation, facilities, and accommodations, including beaches (led to WHITES ONLY signs, which have now disappeared)
- Riotous Assemblies Act (1956): Outlawed protest gatherings
- Separate Universities Act (1959): Prohibited nonwhites from most universities except by special permission
- General Law Amendment Act (1963): Let police hold anyone considered suspicious for renewable ninety-day periods (later reduced to renewable fourteen-day periods) without trial or legal recourse
- Bantu Homelands Citizenship Act (1970): Made all Africans citizens of "tribal homelands" (Bantustans) and deprived them of South African citizenship (the low point of apartheid)

As the list suggests, apartheid evolved through a steady accretion of laws and amendments. The cumulative effect was to create a comprehensive and deeply entrenched system of racial discrimination.

A Half-and-Half System The popularity of apartheid and its elevation to an ideology among Afrikaners dates back to the election of 1948, when the present Nationalist Party came to power. The main agenda in that early political campaign was to find a workable solution for the ethnic and racial issues that had bedeviled South Africa since the founding of the union in 1910. Having won the election, the Nationalist Party sought to fulfill its campaign pledge to keep the races separated. To this end, the new government designed a set of social policies based on the permanent separation of the whites, blacks, Coloureds, and Indians. The ***Bantustans*** (homelands)—areas reserved for various black ethnic groups — were part of this policy, which was designed to mollify blacks and perpetuate exclusion of nonwhites from power.

South Africa had a dual political system, run according to two separate sets of rules. For whites — Afrikaners and British — the system functioned as a democracy. Multiple parties contested free elections (for whites only), and voters cast secret ballots for the candidates of their choice. From 1910 to 1984, the British Westminster model operated: following national elections, the majority party in the all-white House of Assembly chose a prime minister (in practice, the leader of the majority party), who then formed a government.

The 1984 Constitution: Bandage at Best In 1984, South Africa adopted a new constitution, which had been approved by two-thirds of the (white) electorate in a national referendum. The constitution provided for a new three-chamber parliament: the House of Assembly (whites; 178 seats), the House of Representatives (Coloureds; 85 seats), and the House of Delegates (Indians; 45 seats). Thus the legislature came to include Coloured and Indian representatives but continued to exclude the black majority.

The more things changed, the more they stayed the same. The white minority remained firmly in control: the three houses met separately, and the Coloured and Indian chambers could not override the white chamber. Perhaps more significant was the adoption of a presidential model in place of the traditional parliamentary model. An electoral college consisting of the three chambers of the legislature indirectly elected the president. Under that system, the president could dissolve the parliament on any number of grounds. In the event of a parliamentary deadlock — a strong possibility under the new tricameral configuration — he could rule in consultation with the President's Council, a purely advisory body that he appoints. In a crisis, the president could proclaim martial law. So broad were the president's powers that some critics viewed the new system as a potential dictatorship.

The 1984 constitution was a bandage applied to a severed limb. As we shall see, it did not prevent the demise of the political system it was designed to save. Both Nigeria and South Africa were still burdened by governments unresponsive to their majority populations in the 1980s — but there were critical differences between the two countries. In contrast to Nigeria, civilians ruled South Africa. However, South Africa's rulers were members of a privileged white minority who benefited from the oppression of the black majority. South Africa's economy was far superior to that of Nigeria, but whites did not share the wealth with blacks. As a result, life for the vast majority of South Africans was little better than for most Nigerians.

SUMMARY

Politics and government in sub-Saharan Africa are conditioned by such factors as geography, ethnic and cultural diversity, and especially colonialism. This part of Africa is separated from North Africa and the Arab world by a natural barrier (the Sahara Desert) and by language, race, culture, and history. Economically, much of sub-Saharan Africa is extremely poor. But if the image of Africa as a wonderland of exotic jungles, wild animals, and primitive tribes is a Hollywood creation, the other familiar image of poverty, drought, and famine gives the false impression that Africa is a wasteland. Indeed, some countries in the region are scenes of great human misery, but others are not so blighted.

In reality, sub-Saharan Africa is a region where, partly reflecting the legacy of colonialism, good government and political stability have been elusive. As we will see in subsequent chapters, however, the departure of the European powers also removed an important source of stability and order. One of the case studies in Part VII, Nigeria, illustrates this point. The other, South Africa, is a special case because of its long history of white minority rule under the apartheid system. We will take a closer look at patterns of politics in sub-Saharan Africa in the next chapter.

KEY TERMS

sub-Saharan Africa
triple heritage
mission Christianity
animism
Conference of Berlin
rejectionists
assimilationists
postindependence
neocolonialism
Group of 77
Organization of African Unity (OAU)
Afrikaners
apartheid
Boers
Kaffir Wars
Great Trek
voortrekkers
Boer War
National Party
Bantustans

STUDY QUESTIONS

1. What factors influenced the early economic development of African countries? To what extent do these factors remain in force today?
2. Why is one-party polyarchy more common in sub-Saharan Africa than multiparty systems like those in Europe?
3. What was apartheid? Why did it last for so long?
4. Contrast and compare the governments of Nigeria and South Africa. Prior to the 1990s, which country had the worse government?
5. What is the primary cause of Nigeria's poverty? Nature? Politics?
6. What group(s) rule South Africa today? When, how, and why did the "revolution" occur?

SUGGESTED READINGS

Alden, Chris. *Apartheid's Last Stand: The Rise and Fall of the South African Security State, 1978–90.* New York: St. Martin's, 1996.

Crocker, Chester A. *High Noon in Southern Africa: Making Peace in a Rough Neighborhood.* New York: Norton, 1993.

Davidson, Basil. *Africa: History of a Continent.* New York: Macmillan, 1972.

Davidson, Basil. *Africa in History: Themes and Outlines.* Rev. ed. New York: Collier Books and Macmillan, 1991.

Ekwe-Ekwe, Herbert. *The Biafra War: Nigeria and the Aftermath.* Lewistown, N.Y.: Edwin Mellen, 1991.

Emerson, Rupert. *From Empire to Nation: The Rise to Self-Assertion of Asian and African Peoples.* Boston: Beacon Press, 1960.

Johnson, Douglas H. *The Root Causes of Sudan's Civil Wars.* Bloomington: Indiana University Press, 2003.

July, Robert W. *A History of the African People.* 4th ed. Prospect Heights, Ill.: Waveland, 1994.
Kershaw, Greet. *Mau Mau from Below.* Athens: Ohio University Press, 1996.
Kingsolver, Barbara. *The Poisonwood Bible.* New York: HarperCollins, 1998.
Mandela, Nelson. *Long Walk to Freedom.* New York: Warner Books, 1994.
Martin, Meredith. *In the Name of Apartheid: South Africa in the Postwar Period.* New York: Harper, 1988.
Mazrui, Ali A. *The Africans.* Boston: Little, Brown, 1986.
Mbiti, John S. *African Religions and Philosophy.* London: Heinemann, 1990.
Meriwether, James H. *Proudly We Can Be Africans: Black Americans and Africa, 1935–1961.* Chapel Hill: University of North Carolina Press, 2002.
Mokoenak, Kenneth. *South Africa and the United States: The Declassified History.* New York: New Press, 1994.
Newman, James L. *The Peopling of Africa: A Geographical Interpretation.* New Haven, Conn.: Yale University Press, 1995.
Nzongola-Ntalaja, Georges. *The Congo from Leopold to Kabila: A People's History.* New York: Zed Books, 2002.
Shillington, Kevin. *History of Africa.* New York: St. Martin's, 1989.
Sharkey, Heather. *Living with Colonialism: Nationalism and Culture in the Anglo-Egyptian Sudan.* Berkeley: University of California Press, 2003.

SUGGESTED WEB SITES

http://www.scholars.nus.edu.sg/landow/post/nigeria/nigeriahistor.html
http://www.anc.org.za/sanet.html
http://www.hmnet.com/africa/1africa.html
http://www.fordham.edu/halsall/africa/africasbook.html
http://www.ids.ac.uk/eldis/ggov/afri.html
http://www.sas.upen.edu/African_African_Studies/About_African/ww_hist.html
http://www.bbc.co.uk/worldservice/africa/features/storyofafrica/index.shtml
http://www.columbia.edu/cu/lweb/indiv/africa/cuvl/

NOTES

1. See for example, Alan Walker and Mark Teaford, "The Hunt for Proconsul," *Scientific American,* January 1989, pp. 76–82.
2. Robert Pear interview with Jonathan Moore, U.S. coordinator for refugee affairs, "The World's Debt to 12 Million Refugees," *New York Times,* August 21, 1988, p. E3.
3. World Bank, *World Development Report* (New York: Oxford University Press, 1987), p. 17.

4. Ali A. Mazrui, *The Africans* (Boston: Little, Brown, 1986); for an opposing viewpoint, see Hailu Habtu, "The Fallacy of the Triple Heritage Thesis: A Critique," Issue, vol. 13, no. 1 (1984), pp. 26–29.
5. Georges Balandier and Jacques Marguet, eds., *The Dictionary of Black African Civilization* (New York: Amiel, 1974), p. 3; see also Jacques Marquet, *Africanity: The Cultural Union of Black Africa* (New York: Oxford University Press, 1972).
6. Ali A. Mazrui, "The Semitic Impact on Black Africa: Arab and Jewish Cultural Influences," *Issue,* vol. 13, no. 1 (1984), pp. 3–8.
7. See, for example, John S. Mbiti, *African Religions and Philosophy* (London: Heinemann, 1990), pp. 75–91.
8. W. H. Taylor, "Missionary Education Reconsidered: The Nigerian Case," *African Affairs,* vol. 83, no. 331 (1984), pp. 189–205.
9. Mbiti, *African Religions and Philosophy,* pp. 75–91.
10. Basil Davidson, *Africa South of the Sahara,* 17th ed. (Lanham, Md.: Europa Publications, 1988), p. 4.
11. See, Frantz Fanon, *Black Skin, White Mask,* C. Van Markman, trans. (New York: Grove, 1967); T. Walker Walbank, *Contemporary Africa: A Continent in Transition* (New York: Van Nostrand, 1956), pp. 107–110; and Basil Davidson, *Africa: History of a Continent* (New York: Macmillan, 1972), pp. 275–293.
12. Fanon, *Black Skin, White Mask;* and Frantz Fanon, *The Wretched of the Earth,* Constance Farrington, trans. (New York: Grove, 1988).
13. See, for example, John D. Rusk, "Warfare and Human Rights in Angola and Mozambique," *Africa Today,* vol. 34, no. 4 (1987), pp. 33–44.
14. See, for example, John Stockwell, *In Search of Enemies* (New York: Norton, 1978).
15. Jeffrey Sachs, "Growth in Africa: It Can Be Done," *The Economist,* June 29, 1996, p. 19.
16. See, for example, Walter Rodney, *How Europe Underdeveloped Africa* (Washington, D.C.: Howard University Press, 1974); and Samir Amin, *Imperialism and Unequal Development* (New York: Monthly Review Press, 1977).
17. *UN Chronicle,* vol. 22, no. 2 (1985), p. 7.
18. See, for example, Chinua Achebe, *Arrow of God* (London: Heinemann, 1958); Chinua Achebe, *Things Fall Apart* (London: Heinemann, 1958); T. M. Aluko, *The Gab Boys* (London: Fontana Books, 1969); Ola Rotimi, *The Gods Are Not to Blame* (London: Oxford University Press, 1971); and Ayi Kwei Armah, *The Beautiful Ones Are Not Yet Born* (Boston: Houghton Mifflin, 1968).
19. Talcott Parson, *The Social System* (New York: Free Press, 1951); see also Talcott Parson, "Evolutionary Universals in Society," in *Socialization Theory and Modern Society,* Talcott Parson, ed. (New York: Free Press, 1967).
20. See, for example, Seymour Martin Lipset, "Some Social Prerequisites of Democracy, Economic Development, and Political Legitimacy," *American Political Science Review,* vol. 53, no. 3 (March 1969).
21. Theotonio Dos Santos, "The Structure of Dependence," *American Economic Review,* vol. 60, no. 5 (May 1970), p. 231.
22. Lois Eugenio Di Marco, ed., *International Economics and Development: Essay in Honor of Raul Prebisch* (Philadelphia: Academic Press, 1972), pp. 1–34.

23. See, for example, James A. Caporaso, "Introduction," *International Organization,* vol. 32, no. 1 (Winter 1978), p. 6; James A. Caporaso, "Dependence, Dependency, and Power in the Global System: A Structural and Behavioral Analysis," *International Organization,* vol. 32, no. 1 (Winter 1978), pp. 13–43, 121–125; Patrick J. McGowan and Dale L. Smith, "Economic Dependency in Black Africa: An Analysis of Competing Theories," *International Organization,* vol. 32, no. 1 (Winter 1978), pp. 179–235; and R. Dan Walleri, "Trade Dependence and Underdevelopment: A Causal Chain Analysis," *Comparative Political Studies,* vol. 11, no. 1 (April 1978), pp. 94–121.
24. Dos Santos, "Structure of Dependence," p. 231.
25. Jean Herskovitz, *Power and Democracy in Africa,* Headline Series No. 257 (Washington, D.C.: Foreign Policy Association, 1982), p. 8.

CHAPTER 14

An Epidemic of Anarchy?

In the eighteenth century, a Swedish civil servant named C. B. Wadstrom became fascinated with Africa as a result of reading and hearing about it from Europeans who had been there. His curiosity got the best of him: in 1787, at a time when Hamilton, Madison, and the other Founders were meeting in Philadelphia to forge a constitution and launch a new nation in North America, Wadstrom set sail for Africa. His odyssey serves as a reminder that America was not the only "new world" two centuries ago. Wadstrom spent a year in Africa, making observations on what he called the "character and disposition" of the inhabitants (much as Alexis de Tocqueville would do in America a half century later).[1]

What Wadstrom learned about Africans contrasted sharply with the stereotypes he had gleaned from the writings of his European contemporaries. Rather than primitives and savages, he discovered that Africans possessed many civil and cultural virtues.

Anyone who picks up a daily newspaper today will get a very different picture. Africa is a continent beset by all sorts of horrors from the AIDS epidemic and famine to failed states and political chaos that threatens the lives of millions and does not spare even small children. The degenerate state of government and society in parts of Africa in the 1990s led one close American observer to suggest that a "coming anarchy" threatens to spread from sub-Saharan Africa to other regions.[2] Turmoil approaching anarchy has plagued the Horn of Africa, West Africa, and the Congo region in recent times. The worst human suffering is found in places like Somalia, Ethiopia, Rwanda, Congo, and Liberia, but to mention these countries runs the risk of misleading the reader because misery can be found nearly everywhere. In most cases, the causes can be traced to bad government — *bad* in this case means not simply incompetent, but corrupt and brutal dictators. It is not a pretty picture.

As we examine the political structures, processes, and problems of sub-Saharan Africa, remember that the multiethnic states of this region are almost all newcomers, having gained independence only since World War II. The Why? question is irrepressible: Why is Africa tearing itself apart? We begin with a look at key patterns and themes.

Democracy in America

BOX 14.1

Liberia: An Unsuccessful Transplant

In 1816, white people concerned about the fate of freed slaves got together and formed the American Colonization Society. This organization was created with a specific (and rather ambitious) purpose: to find a new home for ex-slaves — back in Africa. On its face, sending blacks back to Africa was a decent enough thing to do. But there was another, less charitable motive, as well: finding a solution to the "problem" of having to integrate blacks into a society from which they had always been excluded.

In 1822, native African rulers granted U.S. representatives a tract of land on Cape Mesurado (later named Monrovia in honor of President James Monroe) in West Africa, and the first African Americans began a settlement there. As more freed slaves arrived, new settlements were established. In 1847, representatives met in Monrovia and established the republic of Liberia (the name comes from the word *liberty*).

Most Americans know nothing about the origins of Liberia. The flag of Liberia, however, is a replica of the American Stars and Stripes (but with just one star). The official language of Liberia is English. Liberia's monetary unit is the Liberian dollar. Under the 1986 constitution, Liberia's president is elected by universal suffrage to a six-year term. Like the United States, Liberia has a bicameral legislature consisting of a Senate and a House of Representatives. But as an experiment in transplanting democracy, Liberia is a failure.

Located between Sierra Leone and Côte d'Ivoire (Ivory Coast), Liberia is an extremely poor country about the size of Virginia with a population of roughly 2.8 million people. According to the U.S. Census Bureau's International Population Center, Liberia's growth rate in the late 1990s was an astonishing 5–6 percent — the highest in the world. Most Liberians are indigenous peoples; only about 5 percent of Liberians are repatriated descendants of American slaves, and only about 20 percent speak English. More than half the population is illiterate (only about a quarter of all females can read and write). Liberia has a war-ravaged economy for which no figures are available.

Liberia has been the scene of political turmoil since 1980 when a junior army officer, Master Sargeant Samuel Doe, led a successful coup following the assassination of President William Tolbert. Between 1989 and 1996, Liberia was engulfed in a bloody civil war in which tens of thousands of Liberians were killed and hundreds of thousands fled to neighboring countries. Finally, in 1996, the warring parties signed a peace agreement and Charles Taylor, who had launched the rebellion in 1989, was elected president. Under Taylor's corrupt rule, Liberia plunged ever deeper into anarchy, civil war raged, and the economy remained in ruins. People were starving, yet the government spent its scant resources (mostly obtained from diamond-smuggling) on illegal arms imports (in violation of a UN ban). In the summer of 2003, the international community, backed by the United States, forced Taylor to resign and go into political exile, but Liberia's future appeared bleak unless the international community came to its rescue and stayed long enough to bring real social, economic, and political change.

Colonialism and Decolonization

As noted in Chapter 13, the political systems of contemporary sub-Saharan Africa were formed in the crucible of colonialism and, later, in the process of decolonization. For more than seventy years after the Conference of Berlin that parceled out Africa among the European powers, all of sub-Saharan Africa, with the exception of Ethiopia and Liberia, was under colonial rule. In most cases, this meant either direct foreign rule or **trusteeship**, somewhere between sovereignty and subjugation. (See Box 14.1.)

Divide and Rule: The Conquest of Africa

In some countries, nationalist guerrillas attempted to resist European colonizers, but such efforts proved futile. The balance of power favored the Europeans, who had professional armies and superior weapons and were adept at using a divide-and-conquer strategy, playing off rival ethnic groups against each other and hiring African mercenaries to fight rebellious African nationalists.

Origins of Tribal Trouble? Long-standing ethnic rivalries in Africa made it relatively easy for the colonial powers to pit African against African. In addition, the rich European intruders had the wherewithal to entice segments of the native population into alliances. Human frailties are not confined to any one culture; the complicity of Africans in their own subjugation testifies to this. The interethnic conflicts and violence associated with European colonialism in Africa set the stage for the internal instability so prevalent in the region today.

World War II ushered in a new epoch in the history of sub-Saharan Africa. The international system collapsed, and the nations of the world realigned. The Cold War (and anticommunism) was now the West's obsession. World opinion turned against colonialism: what had been a status symbol at the turn of the century became an anachronism. The UN Charter enshrined the principles of self-determination and noninterference, and this gave the African struggle a new moral impetus.

The Imprint of Colonialism Colonialism left an indelible mark on the face of Africa. First, it engendered values and imposed structures associated with the European nation-state system on a region that had no preexisting concept of nations or states. Second, it partitioned Africa into colonies, which later became the framework for independent states. Third, across sub-Saharan Africa, it incorporated many "nations" (ethnic groups) into one state. Fourth, it destroyed familiar, permanent systems of authority and replaced them with the alien, temporary rule of colonial administrators. Finally, the end of colonialism left political vacuums all over Africa and enormous potential for social and ethnic conflict. Into this vacuum rushed leaders who had little experience but great ambition. Often these figures turned out to be ruthless, as well. An authoritarian model known as *Bula Matari* ("he who breaks all rocks") sprang up all over the continent.[3]

End of the Colonial Era

The cracks in the edifice of colonialism became increasingly apparent. Among the new factors in world politics was the spontaneous blossoming of **national liberation movements** throughout the colonized world, later called the **Third World.** The economic and political costs of maintaining overseas empires for war-torn European nations preoccupied with their own recovery and reconstruction were now prohibitive. The three former Great Powers of Europe — Great Britain, France, and Germany — were replaced by two superpowers, the United States and the Soviet Union. A global balance wherein the Western European nations, once colonial overlords, were no longer even autonomous or self-reliant replaced the Eurocentric balance of power.

In this new world, Africans found ready allies among emerging socialist revolutionary states such as Cuba, China, and the Soviet Union. The radical anticapitalist and anti-imperialist ideology of these states struck a responsive chord among Africans, for whom capitalism and imperialism had meant exploitation. When Europeans conscripted Africans to fight in World War II, they did not realize that they were also preparing colonial peoples for armed resistance against their oppressors.[4] Meanwhile, the United Nations provided a new forum for all nations seeking liberation, and Articles 1 and 2 of its charter obligated member states to support the cause of self-determination everywhere.

Sudan became the first sub-Saharan country to obtain independence (1956), followed by Ghana (1957) and Guinea (1958). In 1960, seventeen new sub-Saharan nations gained independence, bringing the total to twenty-two; by the end of 1965, the number had climbed to thirty. African nationalists deserve some of the credit for pushing the pace of **decolonization**, but larger historical forces also played a crucial supporting role.

The momentum of decolonization, which seemed so irresistible in the beginning, was thwarted south of the equator. The Portuguese clung tenaciously to Angola and Mozambique; protracted civil wars had to be fought there and in Namibia (formerly ruled by South Africa) before these nations won independence.

Elsewhere, however, the colonial powers bowed out gracefully, even too quickly. The relatively benign process of independence in French and British colonial Africa did not necessitate armed resistance. Ironically, the fact that political separation was not marked by a sharp break in existing relations tended to perpetuate a colonial mentality in Black Africa even after independence. Given the hasty, improvised nature of this whole process, and the poor preparation of the ethnically diverse indigenous peoples for self-rule, it is little wonder that weak governments and internal fragmentation afflict so many countries in the region today.

Colonialism as Scapegoat

Foreign intrusions cannot be blamed for all the socioeconomic problems of sub-Saharan Africa. Africa's leaders have often raised expectations, but too seldom delivered on promises.[5] National unity and economic development have been hindered by political instability, frequent coups, border conflicts, bloated and inefficient bureaucracies, official corruption on all levels (including the police), and widespread abuses of human rights.

In many ways and most countries, the situation has gone from bad to worse. During the 1960s, sub-Saharan Africa enjoyed a modest but steady economic growth rate. That gradually ascending curve flattened in the 1970s and turned negative in the 1980s.[6] Natural calamities (droughts, floods, epidemics) and political ones (wars, insurrections, and anarchy) have both contributed. To blame colonialism makes less and less sense as time goes by. Many Africans do not use the past as an excuse for the present — unfortunately, those who do are often in power.

Political Patterns in Sub-Saharan Africa

Geography, history, culture, and the physical environment impinge on politics and government everywhere, and Africa is certainly no exception. Since independence in the 1950s and 1960s, the people of sub-Saharan Africa have endured a variety of governmental forms, but there have been few examples of democracy — tyranny and a tendency toward anarchy have been far more common.

Scholar Christian Potholm developed a useful classification of African political systems that identifies two basic regime types: polyarchic and authoritarian. He subdivided the **polyarchies** (representative democracies) of Africa into single-party and multiparty forms, and the authoritarian regimes into civilian oligarchies and military praetorian forms.[7] Potholm distinguished one form from another by looking at such characteristics as the extent to which there is electoral competition, the level of demonstrable support for law, and governmental protection of civil liberties.

Not all polyarchic systems are all equally liberal nor are all authoritarian systems equally repressive. Potholm recognized that significant differences exist within his classifications; hence he did not talk about a single type of system in each category but rather about a polyarchic and authoritarian spectrum.

Although military-bureaucratic states came to be most prominent in sub-Saharan Africa, the military was not a prominent force in African politics at the time of independence. Instead, single-party systems — often headed by an authoritarian chief executive — were the rule. Hence, we look at this regime type (or model) first.

Single-Party States

Single-party systems were established in many newly independent states in sub-Saharan Africa. Often the founding of these states and monopoly parties was linked to a charismatic leader — for example, in Tanzania to Julius Nyerere and in Kenya to Jomo Kenyatta. The idea behind a single-party state was to downplay ethnic differences and to emphasize the ideal of unity. The element of "polyarchy" existed (if at all) within the framework — or under the umbrella — of one all-encompassing party. Interests were expressed, compromises reached, and conflicts resolved in a consensual manner. There was supposedly no need for a messy multiparty system based on the divisive "zero-sum" principle of majority rule.

In this type of system, the ruling party typically nominates only one candidate for president, and the nominee must receive a majority of the votes in the party's central committee, whose members may vote "yes" or "no." In Kenya before 1992, for example, the National Assembly indirectly elected the president. Party approval and confirmation are typically required for the presidential candidate but are not always needed for candidates in legislative contests. In Tanzania's general election in 1985, President Ali Hassan Mwinyi received a 92-percent "yes" vote — a suspiciously large share. But in 1992, Tanzania's constitution was amended to allow opposition parties to participate in elections.

To Western eyes, one-party systems do not appear to be very democratic, however Zambia's United National Independence Party nominated hundreds of candidates to contest seats in various general elections. Voter turnout was low, but voters who did go to the polls unseated nearly half the incumbents each time.[8] The combination of low turnout and substantial voting against incumbents generally suggests dissatisfaction with the system. Significantly, in 1991 Zambian voters were given a chance to turn President Kaunda out of office, and did so.

In most cases, however, leaders of single-party states have not given voters a real opportunity to replace them. Instead, they have gravitated toward highly authoritarian practices — sometimes even degenerating into brutal despotism. In addition to banning rival political parties, leaders of single-party states typically adopted the following measures to ensure against sedition or secession:

- Appointing members of their own clan or ethnic group to key positions in the bureaucracy, party, military, and police
- Rejecting proposals for "federalism," which would grant political autonomy to groups or regions based on ethnic, linguistic, or religious distinctions
- Turning parliaments and judiciaries into rubber-stamp institutions or abolishing them
- Imprisoning political opponents, dissidents, and critics from civil society, including labor unions, student organizations, and religious organizations [9]

Lawmaking and Legislatures In single-party states, the legislatures have several similarities. First, most sub-Saharan political systems, including authoritarian regimes, have a formal legislative body — a parliament, constituent assembly, or national assembly.

Election to the legislature often brings prestige to members as well as the families and friends of members. One reason may be that African legislators typically do not have to compete with lobbyists for the government's attention. In the absence of organized interest groups, so prevalent in the West, legislators in Africa often carry a greater share of responsibility not only for lawmaking but also for focusing on special-interest issues, articulating them, and incorporating the various demands into coherent public policy. One theory argues that the prevalence of single-party polyarchies or authoritarian regimes partly reflects distaste for interest-group politics, which many Africans view as unseemly and divisive. In African legislatures, issues tend to be debated on their merits, and relatively little attention is paid to special interests.

Legislatures in sub-Saharan Africa tend to be unicameral (Zimbabwe's is an exception). Routes to the legislature vary, but the main avenue continues to be direct appointment by the chief executive. Sometimes members can appoint additional members to represent professional organizations, tribal groups, and trade associations. Such legislators have earned recognition in their chosen fields or have demonstrated support for the ruling party. Some legislatures (Botswana, Sierra Leone, Zambia) include consultative chiefs as ex officio members.

As elaborate as legislative debates often are, the independence of the legislature is diminished by constitutional advantages given to the chief executive, who can veto legislation, dissolve the parliament, and appoint legislative members who thereafter owe a debt of loyalty. In Zaire, former President Mobutu routinely bypassed the legislative assembly altogether, making laws by personal fiat or in consultation with his ministerial council.

The Extremely "Chief" Executive In the executive branch, these political systems reveal one of the ambivalences of the triple heritage discussed earlier: the head of state is adorned with traditional powers but holds a title borrowed from the West — usually president, but without presidential constraints. Presidents in sub-Saharan Africa often have powers more typical of an emperor or a king.

Generally speaking, the chief executive is both head of state and head of government, with powers and duties that are broadly and often vaguely defined. The ambiguities are deliberate, used to stretch presidential prerogatives as far as necessary. The president is always male and is expected to be fatherly, personable, and charismatic. When these expectations are met, the national leader commands popular respect and even adulation; often he will be given lofty titles bespeaking awe and deference. For example, Premier Nkrumah of Ghana was called *Osagyefu* ("savior"), President Kenyatta of Kenya was addressed as *Mzee* ("wise man"), and President Nyerere of Tanzania was revered as *Mwalimu* ("teacher"). Such titles engender both intimacy and legitimacy; at the same time, the constitution gives leaders like these nearly absolute power.

African premiers and presidents are not constrained by checks and balances or a separation of powers. Not only do many African chief executives have the power to appoint members of the legislature (an unthinkable breach of the separation of powers in the United States), but they can also dissolve the parliament without risk of impeachment or electoral defeat.

Chief executives in sub-Saharan Africa have been selected in various ways. In Botswana and Zimbabwe, the president is elected by the legislature. In Senegal and Gambia, the people elect the president by secret ballot from a slate of candidates nominated by competing parties. In some one-party systems, a single candidate is nominated by the party congress, and the people simply cast a yes or no vote. Another method is military intervention, followed by the establishment of a provisional or caretaker government (which, as we have seen, tends to become permanent). The leader of the coup usually becomes the acting president.

The term of office is typically five years in sub-Saharan countries; the president of Zimbabwe serves a six-year term, and the presidents of Gabon, Sierra Leone, and Zaire serve seven years (though the new rulers of Zaire will most likely write a new constitution). No country has a constitutional limitation on the number of consecutive terms that the president or legislators may serve.

In Africa's single-party states, the president heads the party, and self-succession is virtually guaranteed. This system obviously makes a changing of the guard problematic. Jomo Kenyatta of Kenya died in office at the age of 88 in 1978, as did Houphouët-Boigny of Côte d'Ivoire, at the same age, in 1993. A geriatric President Senghor of Senegal resigned in 1980 for reasons of advanced age and failing health. Julius Nyerere of Tanzania is a rare case of a one-party president who departed from office with grace and style: in 1985, he stepped down because it was time, he said, to inject new dynamism into the political system. (Nonetheless, he retained the powerful position of party chairman.)

The Road to Hell . . . Why was single-party polyarchy more popular in sub-Saharan Africa than the multiparty democracy prevalent in Western Europe? First, mindful of the colonial past, Africans sought to avoid imitating European political institutions, preferring instead to develop their own models and methods of governing. Second, the fragmented condition of many African states that resulted from the drawing of political boundaries by European colonial powers made it necessary to devise ways and means of mitigating conflict and unifying the nation. Obviously, this task is complicated by the existence of competing parties, which tend to perpetuate and institutionalize social divisions. Third, a single umbrella party that encompasses a variety of interests was perhaps more appropriate for the level of development in many sub-Saharan states; a multiparty system places a premium on compromises and coalition building — a luxury that many developing countries can ill afford.

Unfortunately, even an impressive list of "good" reasons for single-party systems in Africa did not guarantee success. The evidence speaks for itself. The story it tells is one of false promises, lost opportunities, failing economies, and untold human misery.[10]

. . . Runs through West Africa Single-party democracy (polyarchy) has not worked in sub-Saharan Africa. Even where it looked like it was working, it has failed — in some cases, miserably. Nowhere has it failed more miserably than in West Africa, especially Sierra Leone, Liberia, and Côte d'Ivoire.

When legislative elections were held in Sierra Leone in 1986, the aptly named All Peoples Party approved 335 candidates to contest 105 elective seats. The party typically offered at least three contestants for each seat, a common practice among one-party states in sub-Saharan Africa. So voters in Sierra Leone actually had more choices — relative to personalities at least — than voters do in most U.S. legislative races.

Nonetheless, Sierra Leone began a steady descent into anarchy in the 1990s. This was the political house of horrors that inspired Robert Kaplan's book, *The Coming Anarchy.* Between 1996 and 1998, the government changed hands four times. Then all hell broke loose, and rebels (members of the so-called Revolutionary United Front) began chopping hands off right and left. They chopped off heads, too. They recruited (kidnapped) small boys and turned them into sex slaves and killers.

How could such a thing happen in the modern world? Neither the civil institutions nor the political culture necessary to support and sustain democracy ever developed in Sierra Leone. For several decades, the appearance of democracy masked the reality of a society capable of erupting into volcanic civil violence at any moment. When it did finally erupt it was part of a larger upheaval that forced hundreds of thousands of impoverished and panic-stricken West Africans to flee, even though they had nowhere to go. (See Box 14.2.)

Sierra Leone: The Fate of Civilization BOX 14.2

In February 1994, Robert Kaplan's article, "The Coming Anarchy," appeared in the *Atlantic Monthly*. The article appeared as the first chapter in a book of the same name in 2000. Kaplan's analysis is insightful and prescient. The following excerpt, penned in 1994, is a sample of political journalism at its best:

[C]riminal anarchy emerges as the real "strategic" danger. Disease, overpopulation, unprovoked crime, scarcity of resources, refugee migrations, the increasing erosion of nation-state and international borders, and the empowerment of private armies, security firms, and international drug cartels are now most tellingly demonstrated through a West African prism. West Africa provides an appropriate introduction to the issues, often extremely unpleasant to discuss, that will soon confront our civilization . . .

There is no other place on the planet where political maps are so deceptive — where, in fact, they tell such lies — as in West Africa. Start with Sierra Leone. . . . In the government's territory the national army is an unruly rabble threatening drivers and passengers at most checkpoints. In the other part of the country units of two separate armies from the war in Liberia have taken up residence, as has an army of Sierra Leonian rebels. The government force fighting the rebels is full of renegade commanders who have aligned themselves with disaffected village chiefs. . . .

As a consequence, roughly 400,000 Sierra Leonians are displaced, 280,000 more have fled to neighboring Guinea, and another 100,000 have fled to Liberia, even as 400,000 Liberians have fled to Sierra Leone. The third largest city in Sierra Leone, Gondama, is a displaced-persons camp. With an additional 600,000 Liberians in Guinea and 250,000 in the Ivory Coast, the borders dividing these four countries have become largely meaningless. . . .

[In West Africa] . . . most of the primary rain forest and the secondary bush is being destroyed at an alarming rate. I saw convoys of trucks bearing majestic hardwood trunks to coastal ports. When Sierra Leone achieved its independence, in 1961, as much as 60 percent of the country was primary rain forest. Now 6 percent is. In the Ivory Coast the proportion has fallen from 38 percent to 8 percent. The deforestation has led to soil erosion, which has led to more flooding and more mosquitoes. Virtually everyone in the West African interior has some form of malaria.

Sierra Leone is a microcosm of what is occurring, albeit in a more tempered and gradual manner, throughout West Africa and much of the underdeveloped world: the withering away of central governments, the rise of tribal and regional domains, the unchecked spread of disease, and the growing pervasiveness of war.

Source: Robert D. Kaplan, *The Coming Anarchy: Shattering the Dreams of the Post Cold War* (New York: Vintage, 2000), pp. 7–9.

The Authoritarian Spectrum

Authoritarian regimes may be military or civilian, and they may be autocratic (ruled by one) or oligarchic (ruled by a few). In sub-Saharan Africa, the most common forms of authoritarianism are civilian oligarchies and military praetorian regimes, to use Potholm's terminology.

First, note that it is often difficult to distinguish between a single-party polyarchy and an authoritarian regime. For example, authoritarian regimes may have political parties and may hold elections. The key is not whether parties and elections are present but whether they are politically meaningful. If parties are merely symbolic and elections are nothing more than rituals, then the political system that sponsors them is most likely authoritarian.

Second, not all authoritarian regimes are brutal and repressive, although many certainly are both. Political scientist J. Gus Liebenow identifies five empirical models ranging from the most democratic (civilian supremacy) to the most authoritarian (social transformation) as a convenient way to think about the spectrum of regimes in sub-Saharan Africa. (See Figure 14.1.) Monarchs can be good or bad, according to Aristotle, but the history of the world since Aristotle's time suggests that power seldom falls into the hands of saints. As Lord Acton astutely observed, "Power corrupts; absolute power corrupts absolutely." Africa's recent history offers little to contradict this assertion.

Third, in the African context, it is important to note that some authoritarian regimes claim to be transitional, while others are well entrenched and more or less permanent. The former, often called **provisional governments**, are likely to follow a military coup.

Politics in Coup-Coup Land Regime change has occurred in many African countries primarily through a sudden power seizure or **coup d'etat**. These "surprises" make for unsteady and unstable politics by fostering suspicion and mistrust and undermining the rule of law. Many African countries gained independence in the late 1950s or early 1960s. Between 1958 and 1965, coups resulted in the overthrow of five civilian governments. In 1966, military coups toppled eight more governments — easily a world

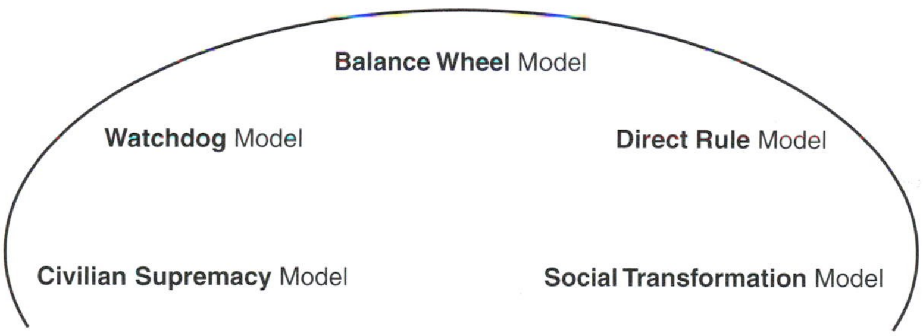

Civilian Supremacy—The military is firmly under the control of civilian leaders (Botswana).

Watchdog—The military backs and protects the civilian government, but sees itself as the guarantor of stability and will seize power to restore order (Mali, 1991).

Balance Wheel—The military proclaims itself the legitimate source of authority but leaves the actual running of the government to civilians (Liberia, 1980–1986).

Direct Rule—The military not only monopolizes power and decision-making authority, but also assumes responsibility for day-to-day functioning of the state bureaucracy (Nigeria, 1966–1999).

Social Transformation—The military not only takes over all the functions of government but also seeks to remake society (Ethiopia, 1974–1991).

Figure 14.1 The Spectrum of Civil-Military Relations in Sub-Saharan Africa

Source: Adapted from J. Gus Liebenow, *African Politics: Crises and Challenges* (Bloomington: Indiana University Press, 1990).

record. Between 1951 and 1985, the region witnessed no fewer than 131 attempted coups — nearly half (60 to be exact) succeeded. This number does not include military plots that were foiled before an actual attempt was made. Three countries in sub-Saharan Africa have had six successful coups since independence (Benin, Burkina Faso, and Nigeria) and only six countries have no history of military meddling in politics (Botswana, Djibouti, Cape Verde, Eritrea, Namibia, and South Africa).[11]

The existence of weak states with underdeveloped political and civil structures (bureaucracies, political parties, interest groups) invited military intervention in troubled times. The army is typically the source of coup plotting and staging. Senior officers usually carried out the early coups, but in more recent times junior officers seized power in several countries. Even where a given set of military leaders was overthrown (for example, senior officers ousted by junior officers in a "palace coup"), a *military regime* almost always remained in place — only the faces changed.

Entrenched Authoritarian Regimes Zaire (until May 1997), Somalia (until 1991), Malawi, Guinea, and Côte d'Ivoire are examples of authoritarian rule in Africa. With the exception of Somalia, these regimes remained unchanged for a quarter century or longer under the same autocratic ruler. As aging leaders become senile and fall into poor or failing health, autocracy gives way to **gerontocracy** (rule by the old and infirm). The absence of electoral competition, repression of civil liberties, and arbitrary arrest, however, are still used or even intensified — often directed by hangers-on who stand to lose power and privileges when the paramount leader dies.

Authoritarian rulers come to power in various ways: by rising through the ranks a step at a time, by a military coup d'état, or by promotion from the traditional hierarchy. Once in power, they employ age-old techniques of governing; they enforce compliance with accommodation, coercion, and co-optation of critical elites and the masses.

Accommodation may involve government programs to revive indigenous cultures and traditional values, thus neutralizing popular aspirations for liberalization and modernization. Symbols of nationalism are exploited to negate any social or political ideas that might challenge the policies of the rulers. The first president of Zaire, for example, changed the Belgian Congo's name to Zaire and all other European place names to Zairean names; he even Africanized his own name (from Joseph-Désiré Mobutu to Mobutu Sese Seko) and urged his people to do likewise. Recalling the evils of colonialism is a common device used to instill patriotism.

In Côte d'Ivoire, Malawi, Somalia, and Zaire, elections were long manipulated and modified in ways designed to mollify the people without giving them a real voice. When former President Mohammad Siad Barré stood for reelection in Somalia in 1986, he received a 99.9 percent yes vote. Similarly, former President Félix Houphouët-Boigny garnered 100 percent approval in his 1988 reelection in Côte d'Ivoire, and when Mobutu Sese Seko was reelected in 1984, he was approved by 99.6 percent of Zaire's voters. All these men, along with Hastings Kamuzu Banda, were more like monarchs than presidents. Some, like Mobutu, stole massive sums of money, giving rise to a new term, **kleptocracy** — rule by thieves.

Co-optation is entwined with carrot-and-stick methods in a strategy of divide and rule. The cabinet is frequently reshuffled, and various privileges and perquisites are given to the bureaucratic functionaries in the civil service, to the armed forces, and to the business and economic elites such that their long-term interests coincide with the status quo. The political order rests on an intricate network of patron-client relationships. In time, the authoritarian rule of a single strongman and his cronies can become self-legitimizing; in effect, the state becomes the patrimony of an autocratic or oligarchic leadership. One danger is that as the leader ages, the system can become increasingly ossified.

Another danger in personalistic authoritarian regimes arises from the absence of orderly procedures for succession. Who will replace the existing leader, and how? Such questions are especially important in a political system that concentrates power and authority in the hands of a single individual. The political climate can become extraordinarily uncertain, especially if the leader is very old, falls ill, or is the target of an assassination attempt. At such times, the possibility of a succession crisis looms large, and political stability may give way to chaos and confusion.

An illustration or two may help make the point. Sékou Touré ruled Guinea for twenty-six years (1958–1984), and his regime was harshly authoritarian. He died without making any provision for his own succession. (Often personalistic rulers are reluctant to name an heir apparent for fear of creating a rival.) His death left a power vacuum that has since been filled by the military. To cite another example, Emperor Haile Selassie of Ethiopia was dethroned after forty years of authoritarian rule; his ouster was followed by a bloody revolution.

As noted earlier, not all Africa's autocratic rulers have been unpopular, incorrigible, or unwise. For example, Julius Nyerere, who ruled Tanzania for two decades after independence, improved health and education but was less successful in tapping his country's economic potential. In 1985, Nyerere stepped down after handing power over to a democratically elected successor. Similarly, Malawi's president Hastings Kamuzu Banda stepped down in 1994 after he put a new constitution into effect and allowed the voters to choose a new leader in multiparty elections.

But benevolent dictators are rare exceptions in Africa. Somalia's Siad Barré hung on until the bitter end: when Somalia plunged into anarchy in 1991, he fled the country. In Zaire, the notoriously corrupt Mobutu Sese Seko celebrated his thirtieth anniversary in power in November 1995, but was finally overthrown in the spring of 1997 by the rebel forces of Laurent Kabila, another corrupt dictator, who was murdered in January 2001.

Provisional Authoritarian Regimes Provisional regimes are self-consciously transitional and usually look ahead to a time when they will give way to constitutional government. Such regimes are usually run by the military because, typically, that is who has overthrown the old government. In sub-Saharan Africa, the military almost always proclaims its goal to be corrective — to rescue the nation from economic malaise or mismanagement, to stem subversion or national disintegration, or to stamp out graft and corruption. (See Box 14.3.) Even the names these provisional regimes give themselves are instructive: the Committee for National Redemption (Burundi), the Provisional National Defense Council (Ghana), the National Resistance Movement (Uganda), the Provisional Military Administrative Council (Ethiopia).

At first, military juntas almost always claim to be temporary. Some do ultimately return the government to civilian control, but most do not. Military takeovers have

Contrast and Comparison

BOX 14.3

The Logic of Military Rule: A Regional Model

Political scientist J. Gus Liebenow has carefully studied the phenomenon of military-bureaucratic rule in Africa. In his book *African Politics: Crises and Challenges,** Liebenow uncovered some interesting patterns, which help to explain how and why the military seized power in so many places. The inexperience of the leaders after independence is an important element in this model. New leaders underestimate the difficulties of governing. At the same time, they are inclined to showing hubris (personal vanity, arrogance, a sense of invincibility). As a result, they rely on rhetoric and charisma (personal appeal), to the neglect of institutions needed to govern effectively.

Neglect of the military is a common but fateful, mistake. Even though the military lacks adequate education, equipment, training, and strong morale, soldiers are exposed to modernization. Officers in particular are aware of the new technology — as well as the pay and privileges — available to the military in developed countries. In fact, some officers receive training in the United States or elsewhere abroad. They resent being deprived of resources by civilian leaders whom they consider corrupt and incompetent. When these same leaders call on the military to rescue the government in an emergency — by fighting a secessionist movement or suppressing a riot — the resentment reaches the boiling point.

Fearing a coup d'état, civilian leaders react defensively, cutting military budgets and interfering with promotions, thus further antagonizing the military. They also create paramilitary structures for self-protection — hence the term *praetorian* to describe these regimes. As added insurance, they try to bribe the generals, but in so doing they only reveal their own weakness and growing dependency on coercive instruments, while inviting the contempt of senior officers (mingled with jealousy in the ranks of junior officers).

When the military takes over, however, the new leaders are also inexperienced in the art of governing. They overestimate their own legitimacy and quickly learn that they do not have a mandate to rule indefinitely — only to prepare for a new civilian government. Faced with declining popular support, the military digs in, turns to repressive measures, and develops an "us against them" psychology toward society. But it lacks expertise and must seek technical support from outside the military. In addition, it is unsuited to compromise by virtue of its own structure and culture. In the final analysis, it cannot govern society effectively and the attempt to do so only magnifies unresolved internal conflicts within the military (which often reflect rifts and conflicts within society).

Like the civilian leaders it ousted, the military turns increasingly to force and fraud (corruption and bribery) to stay in power. Across sub-Saharan Africa, the result is plain to see: the worst collection of governments found anywhere in the world.

*J. Gus Liebenow, *African Politics: Crises and Challenges* (Bloomington: Indiana University Press, 1990).

occurred repeatedly in Ghana, Nigeria, Sudan, and Uganda. In Ghana, for example, Flight Lieutenant Jerry Rawlings led a successful military coup in 1979. (The fact that a mere lieutenant could overthrow a government suggests that political life in some parts of sub-Saharan Africa is capricious and that political authority is precarious. A ruler with legitimacy and credibility cannot be cast aside so easily.) Rawlings returned the government to civilian rule in 1980, warning that the military would step in again if the politicians failed to govern effectively. Alleging corruption and mismanagement, Rawlings led a second coup and returned the country to military rule in 1981. After ruling as a dictator for more than a decade, Rawlings held multiparty elections in 1992 and put his personal popularity on the line. He won.

Weak or Strong States? Governing involves the formulation, implementation, and adjudication of rules. These functions often fall correspondingly to the legislative, executive, and judicial branches. No modern polity can operate well without such a division of responsibilities. Although the societies of sub-Saharan Africa are still evolving politically, they contain many institutional elements — including structural differentiation and functional specialization — that are associated with modern political systems. One fundamental question is whether recently established states are weak or strong relative to the societies in which they are embedded. Political scientist Joel Migdal developed a theory of politics, which turns on the state-society dichotomy. His thesis that most states in the Third World are weak — often deliberately undercut by leaders who are trying to keep a mélange of groups in balance (and any real or imagined opposition off-balance) — is somewhat surprising but has gained general acceptance among comparativists and specialists on African politics.[12]

Roots of Despair: The Economic Crisis

A year after the UN General Assembly emergency session on the economic crisis in sub-Saharan Africa, then UN Secretary-General Javier Pérez de Cuéllar reported that Africa's economic plight was not improving and that the industrialized nations had not fulfilled their promises to provide additional foreign aid. The proportions of this crisis became alarmingly evident in the 1980s.

The 1980s: Decade of Decline

During the first half of the 1980s, Africa's combined gross national product dropped steadily. Net exports were negative in every year except 1985, when exports barely exceeded imports. The trade deficit for the continent as a whole mounted year by year. Meanwhile, the exploding population helped plunge Africa into a severe debt crisis: by 1986, its external debt equaled its GNP and was still climbing. The legacy of this decade of stagnation is a stark one, indeed: in 1995, the combined GDP of sub-Saharan Africa, not counting South Africa, was less than that of Belgium (population: 10 million), one of western Europe's smallest countries.

To meet this crisis, the African nations were to raise $82.5 billion under the plan adopted by the UN General Assembly in June 1986, and the industrial nations pledged $9 billion annually for five years. In addition, yearly debt service requirements were projected at $14.6 billion, bringing total external financing needs to about $24 billion. Despite good intentions, the net inflow of external funds amounted to $18 billion — a decrease in real terms over the 1985 level.

According to the UN secretary-general's report, "Serious initiatives have yet to be taken by the international community . . . to respond to the increasingly tightly entwined debt, commodity, and resource-flow problem in Africa." The net flow of resources was "grossly inadequate" to compensate for Africa's drastically reduced export revenues and mounting debt service obligations. Moreover, industrialized nations had failed "to deal urgently with commodity issues." On the contrary, the report asserted that there had been almost no effort to stabilize the prices of raw materials (commodities and minerals), Africa's major exports. Indeed, falling commodity prices cost Africa $50 billion in lost export earnings between 1986 and 1990, according to UN statistics.

By contrast, the report noted that no fewer than twenty-eight African nations had adopted at least some of the recommended reforms. For example, more than four-fifths had created price incentives to boost agricultural production and rural development, two-thirds had taken steps to improve internal distribution, and even more had allocated at least 25 percent of total investment to agriculture. Furthermore, there had been movement toward privatization as public-enterprise subsidies were being curtailed in many countries and laws affecting investment and business were being liberalized.

The report also noted the downside of these economic reforms. They had adversely affected immediate social well-being (health, education, and employment) in a region with the lowest quality-of-life indicators in the world. (See Table 14.1.) "Africa's margins of maneuver to implement the program of action are being reduced," the secretary-general inveighed. This sentiment was echoed by many African leaders,

Table 14.1 Development Profile: Selected Countries in Sub-Saharan Africa

Country	Life Expectancy at Birth	Infant Mortality Rate, 1998*	Females in Primary School (% in 1997)	Female Labor Force, 1998 (percent of total)
Angola	47	124	34	38
Botswana	46	62	83	46
Burkina Faso	44	104	25	47
Burundi	42	118	33	49
Congo	51	90	48	43
Côte d'Ivoire	46	88	50	33
Ethiopia	43	107	27	41
Kenya	51	76	67	46
Nigeria	53	76	39	36
Rwanda	41	123	—	49
Senegal	52	69	54	43
Sierre Leone	37	169	—	37
Somalia	48	121	—	43
South Africa	63	51	100	38
Sudan	55	69	—	29
Uganda	42	101	—	48
Zambia	43	114	72	45
Zimbabwe	51	73	92	44

*Per 1,000 live births.

Source: International Bank for Reconstruction and Development, *The World Bank Atlas* (Washington, D.C.: Author, 2000).

including Kenneth Kaunda, then president of Zambia, who warned of the dangers of adopting painful economic reforms.

In the mid-1980s, Zambia was a kind of microcosm of the dilemma that Africa faced. The Zambian government reduced urban food subsidies and raised farm prices in compliance with the 1986 UN blueprint. The idea was to cut deficit spending and to encourage greater agricultural output, which it did. On the one hand, food production jumped 15 percent and manufacturing rose 5 percent. On the other, food prices also rose, sparking urban riots that left at least fifteen people dead and forced Kaunda to rescind the offending measures.[13]

Tanzania encountered another kind of pitfall: it increased cotton production by 75 percent in 1986 but actually earned less from this export than in 1985. There were two reasons, both external: world cotton prices fell sharply in 1986, and Tanzania devalued its currency to comply with the rules of the International Monetary Fund. The Tanzanian case illustrates how dependent many African nations are on world commodity prices. Cotton is Tanzania's major export, and commodity prices on the world market often fluctuate wildly. At the same time, the IMF lends money on easy terms to finance international trade. Many countries in the developing South experience chronic hard-currency shortfalls and depend on IMF loans to facilitate imports, especially manufactures, from the industrial North. As a consequence, they are often at the mercy of external forces — one reason why the rallying cry of neocolonialism is still a factor in sub-Saharan Africa.

The Myth of Overpopulation

Many observers contend that Africa's economic ills are caused primarily by overpopulation. In the West, government officials and scholars alike accept this contention almost unquestioningly, and it does seem plausible, considering that Africa's population growth rate is the highest in the world. (See Table 14.2.) The region has also been hardest hit by food shortages. Thus, a strong case can be made for the view that the population explosion is the root cause of deprivation and decline in Africa.

But is this argument accurate? Djibril Diallo, chief spokesperson for the UN Office for Emergency Operations in Africa, says no:

> Of all the myths about Africa prevailing in the West, none is propagated with more vigor and regularity than the notion that overpopulation is a central cause of African poverty. The recent famine has given propagators of this myth fresh ammunition with which to press home their argument. . . . The overpopulation myth is particularly harmful because it preempts deeper probing into the complex causes of underdevelopment.[14]

Diallo argues that the popularity of this myth in the West actually complicates efforts to launch family-planning programs in Africa: "After centuries of foreign domination, many Africans are deeply suspicious of any campaigns designed to alter the way they live and behave." Diallo gives a clear example of how sensitive the issue of population control can be in the multiethnic context of African society:

Table 14.2 Demographic Facts: Selected Countries in Sub-Saharan Africa

Country	Population 1998 (thousands)	Annual Growth Rates, 1980–1991 (percent)*	Annual Growth Rates, 1990–1998 (percent)	Net Change in Growth Rate (percent)
Angola	12,001	2.6	3.8	+1.2
Botswana	1,562	3.3	2.9	–0.4
Burkina Faso	10,730	2.6	2.7	+0.1
Burundi	6,548	2.9†	2.6	–0.3
Côte d'Ivoire	14,492	3.8	3.1	–0.7
Ethiopia	61,266	3.1	2.6	–0.5
Kenya	29,295	3.8	3.1	–0.7
Nigeria	120,817	3.1	3.3	+0.2
Rwanda	8,105	2.9†	2.2	–0.7
Senegal	9,093	3.8	3.0	–0.8
Sierre Leone	4,855	2.4	2.8	+0.4
Somalia	9,076	3.1	2.2	–0.9
South Africa	41,402	2.4	2.3	–0.1
Sudan	28,347	2.7	2.3	–0.4
Uganda	20,897	2.5	3.5	+1.0
Zaire (Congo)	48,216	3.2	3.6	+0.4
Zambia	9,666	3.1†	3.1†	0
Zimbabwe	11,689	3.4	2.6	–0.8

*Numbers in this column are taken from *The World Bank Atlas.* December 1992.

†1985–1993.

Source: International Bank for Reconstruction and Development, *The World Bank Atlas* (Washington, D.C.: Author, 2000).

> Just as the Kenyan government was concluding careful negotiations with the United States Agency for International Development to launch a major marketing drive for contraceptives in the rural areas, children in the central highlands areas suddenly stopped taking their free milk drinks at school. The reason became clear a few days later when a man appeared in court charged with spreading the rumor that the milk had been treated with contraceptive chemicals. The implication behind the rumor was that the authorities wished to reduce the population increase of the ethnic groups living in the region.[15]

Diallo plausibly argues that experts who stress the link between food supply and population size often apply a double standard. Japan, Switzerland, and the Netherlands are not self-sufficient in food and have relatively little available farmland, yet they are not charged with being overpopulated. By contrast, "Africa has more arable land per capita than any other developing region." Under the right conditions, Chad alone could feed the whole Sahel (the area from Chad westward to the Atlantic Ocean just south of the Sahara). Second, Africa's average population density is only 16 people per square kilometer, much lower than China's (100) and India's (225). Nonetheless, India and China have both made impressive strides toward food self-sufficiency.

According to Diallo, "In their quest for appropriate solutions to their own food predicaments, more and more Africans are making their way to India to study break-throughs there."[16] But even Africans who criticize the critics do not argue that family planning is unnecessary in many sub-Saharan countries, only that it is not a cure-all.

What (Who) Is to Blame?

Sub-Saharan Africa is the poorest, least developed region in the world. Many of its nations have a tiny GNP — less than even the poorest countries in Latin America. (See Tables 14.3 and 14.4.) Although Black Africa achieved a composite growth rate of

Table 14.3 Falling behind Botswana?

Country	1998 GNP (millions of dollars)	GNP Growth Rate (%), 1980–1991	Per Capita GNP, 1998 (dollars)	Per Capita GNP, 1998 (PPP)*	Per Capita Growth Rate, 1990–1998
Angola	4,578	n.a.	380	999	−8.2
Botswana	4,795	9.3	3,070	5,796	0.9
Burkina Faso	2,575	4.0	240	866	1.1
Burundi	911	—	140	561	−5.5
Côte d'Ivoire	10,196	0.3	700	1,484	1.4
Ethiopia	6,169	1.5	100	566	2.6
Kenya	10,201	4.1	350	964	nil
Nigeria	36,373	1.4	300	740	0.4
Rwanda	1,864	—	230	n.a.	−4.3
Senegal	4,863	2.9	520	1,297	−1.7
Sierra Leone	703	1.1	140	445	−6.0
Somalia	n.a.	n.a.	n.a.	n.a.	n.a.
South Africa	136,568	3.3	3,310	8,296	−1.5
Sudan	8,224	0.3	290	1,240	3.6
Uganda	6,566	5.9	310	1,072	4.3
Zaire (Congo)	5,433	1.6	110	733	−8.5
Zambia	3,234	—	330	678	−0.9
Zimbabwe	7,214	3.6	620	2,489	−0.2

*Purchasing power parity; denotes how much purchasing power the same number of dollars would give a hypothetical consumer in the relevant country.

Source: International Bank for Reconstruction and Development, *The World Bank Atlas* (Washington, D.C.: Author, 2000). The numbers in the column showing the various GNP growth rates in the 1980–1991 time period are from *The World Bank Atlas*, 1992.

Table 14.4 Behind China and Losing Ground?

Country	Share of Agriculture in GDP (percent)	Trade Balance (percent of GDP)	Share of Investment in GDP (percent)
Angola	12	–23.8	20
Botswana	4	3.5	21
Burkina Faso	19	–8.7	29
Burundi	54	–11.7	18
Côte d'Ivoire	26	–1.9	9
Ethiopia	50	–8.0	18
Kenya	26	–3.1	14
Nigeria	32	–10.3	20
Rwanda	47	–7.1	16
Senegal	17	–1.7	20
Sierre Leone	44	—	8
Somalia	65*	—	—
South Africa	4	–1.5	16
Sudan	39	–19.3	—
Uganda	45	–10.4	15
Zaire (Congo)	58	–8.4	8
Zambia	17	—	14
Zimbabwe	19	—	17
China	**18**	**3.1**	**38**

*1991, see *The World Bank Atlas,* December 1992.
Source: International Bank for Reconstruction and Development, *The World Bank Atlas* (Washington, D.C.: Author, 2000).

3.8 percent in 1995, according to the World Bank, most of the region's economies have grown at a glacial pace, if at all. What is worse, the per capita growth rate in many nations has been negative, meaning that population growth is outstripping economic development. Output per head fell 0.7 percent between 1978 and 1987, and 0.6 percent during 1987–1994. Even in 1995 the income per person rose by a paltry 1 percent. In most other years, an already low quality of life for millions of people has dropped even lower.

The low level of per capita growth in Black Africa is not endemic to developing countries. According to Jeffrey Sachs, the highly acclaimed director of Harvard's Institute for International Development, "Many low and middle-income nations are averaging per capita growth of more than 5 percent per year."[17] But only three countries in Africa — Botswana, Mauritius, and Uganda (since 1989)—have come close to that average. Uganda achieved an impressive 10 percent growth rate in 1995. On the other hand, oil-dependent Nigeria stagnated; the economies of Congo, Zaire (renamed the Democratic Republic of the Congo), Zambia, and Zimbabwe shrank; Liberia and Rwanda were torn asunder by internal conflict.

Contending Theories

Scholars have debated the causes of Africa's economic and political problems, and a variety of theories have emerged. One view holds that the European colonial powers intentionally impeded economic and political development.[18] Another view stresses the debilitating but unintentional consequences of colonial exploitation. A variation on this theme was offered by Adebayo Adedeji, head of the UN Economic Commission for Africa, who blamed colonialism for changing Africa's agricultural priorities from food production for local consumption to export crops such as cocoa, coffee, and tea, the prices of which depend on demand in foreign markets.[19]

More introspective African writers blame certain African traditions for creating resistance to social change and progress.[20] They also accuse political elites of abusing power and lacking the vision needed to lift Africa out of deprivation.

Western development theorists sometimes draw on social psychology and cultural anthropology to explain why some societies advance more easily than others. This perspective focuses on variations in social rules, behavioral norms, lifestyles, and expectations.[21] Other development theorists, as noted in Chapter 2, draw on political economy — more specifically, on incentives theory, which looks at the presence or absence of formal rules, legal structures, and contractual relations that underpin commercial activity, define rewards and punishments, and reinforce the work ethic.[22]

Some African societies exhibit a kind of family-centered particularism that breeds social attitudes inimical to individual success and economic development. For example, the Oromos and Amharas of Ethiopia are very conscious of how they are perceived by others. In their culture, a person must not become too ambitious because individual achievement can bring social stigma. To ignore this norm is to be ostracized as greedy or overzealous. In principle, the morality of modesty, cooperation, and sharing is good, but in practice, the taboo on individualism both constrains competition and stifles personal aspirations.

Colonialism as the Culprit

Colonialism and certain nonindigenous socioreligious practices were equally detrimental to personal growth and national self-reliance. Colonialism undercut Africans' sense of personal efficacy; at the same time, it introduced individualism into a society that had traditionally stressed collective or community values. The colonial white man was the bwana, the master benefactor, who established new values and behavioral norms. By the same token, non-African religions were often at odds with African belief systems and seemed self-contradictory. For example, missionaries taught the equality of all God's children, yet they themselves often behaved in a condescending manner to their converts.

Furthermore, as colonial administrators and missionaries dispensed food, medicine, and education, they created a socioeconomic environment conducive to low self-esteem and dependency. Ironically, the colonizers cast themselves in the role of givers and the Africans in the role of receivers. This ascription of roles shaped African politics: when a colonial society is judged for generations by foreign standards and its people are forced into the habit of uncritical receiving, economic development is certain to suffer once the colonizers have gone.

The benevolence of colonial administrators and the charity of missionaries were thus a mixed blessing. Religiously motivated altruism encouraged generosity, but it also stifled individual initiative and the desire for worldly possessions. Indeed, in some places, religion was a barrier to economic development. For example, the Ethiopian Orthodox church designated a great many days as religious holidays for one saint or another, and believers were encouraged to roam the streets on these days, asking for charity in the names of saints. By sanctioning such beggary, the church taught peasants who might have spent their time in productive labor instead to abandon material values and to live off the meager bread of others in return for heavenly rewards.

With respect to education, students in church-sponsored schools studied humanities rather than science, engineering, and technology, which churches spurned as too materialistic and worldly. In this way, too, the new religions discouraged attitudes and orientations associated with free enterprise in the West. The Orthodox, Roman Catholic, and Protestant churches also encouraged tithing (giving one-tenth of one's earnings to the church) and the belief that it is more blessed to give than to receive.

Finally, the search for an alternative to the Western capitalist model of development tainted the very idea of entrepreneurship throughout sub-Saharan Africa. Only a new way of thinking that encourages individual initiative is likely to spur an era of progress and rapid economic growth in this region. Such a change in attitude will probably not occur at the grassroots level unless it is fostered by African leaders who themselves set a positive example by fighting corruption, creating jobs, building schools, and the like. In the past, demagogues parading as nationalists and populists have too often rejected Western values while embracing dependency theory uncritically because it is an easy way to explain Africa's ills without putting any of the blame on Africans.

In Search of Africa: Failed Models

A fundamental choice for the newly independent states of sub-Saharan Africa was whether to adopt the Soviet model of central planning and collective farming, the Western free-market model, or a composite African model based on local traditions and methods. A fourth alternative was to design a new model tailored to fit Africa. Meeting the challenge of economic and political development necessitated a series of interconnected policy decisions about strategies, resources, and procedures.

Most African nations chose neither the Soviet model nor Western-style capitalism — both models, though starkly different, were European. Emerging from the experiences of colonialism, war, and the relatively peaceful struggle for independence, they opted for a model based on self-affirmation and self-reliance. They wanted to be masters of their destiny. They stressed cooperative social values and relations in which the members of society work and produce for the good of the whole and the state acts as the agent of society, protecting and promoting the freedom and well-being of the individual. Debates over policy, both domestic and foreign, were almost always undertaken within the context of shared assumptions about the need for socialist self-reliance.

African Socialism

Self-reliance, as discussed here, is part of an ideology known as **African socialism,** which draws on the traditional system of the extended family, the members of which are expected to work for the common good and to share benefits and burdens equally.[23] African socialism has been espoused by such prominent leaders as Kwame Nkrumah and Léopold Senghor in West Africa and Julius Nyerere, Tom Mboya, Oginga Odinga, and Kenneth Kaunda in East Africa. All recognize the imperatives of material progress but place human development above capital accumulation. In short, social well-being takes precedence over industrial growth.

For Nkrumah, the starting point was affirmation of the African personality, enriched by Africa's traditions and its heritage of cultural pluralism, including Islamic and Christian values. He put it this way:

> With true independence regained, however, a new harmony needs to be forged, a harmony that will allow the combined presence of traditional Africa, Islamic Africa and Euro-Christian Africa, so that this presence is in tune with the original humanist principles underlying African society. Our society is not the old society, but a new society enlarged by Islamic and Euro-Christian influences. A new emergent ideology is therefore required, an ideology . . . which will not abandon the original humanist principles of Africa.
>
> Such a philosophical statement . . . will give the theoretical basis for an ideology whose aim shall be to contain the African experience of Islamic and Euro-Christian presence as well as the experience of the traditional African society, and, by gestation, employ them for the harmonious growth and development of that society.[24]

Léopold Senghor of Senegal struck a similar chord in arguing that the African outlook is humanist and that Africa must build on this foundation. He used the concept of what he called **negritude** to encompass the cultural values of blacks everywhere. He expanded the idea of an African personality to include all actions and principles necessary to enhance the cultural development of people who have been deprived of identity and self-esteem by the inhumane experiences of slavery or colonialism.[25]

For Tanzania's first president, Julius Nyerere, the essential ingredient of self-reliance was more social and political than psychological. It was intimately tied to the broadening of human freedom:

> If the purpose of development is the greater freedom and well-being of the people, it cannot result from force. . . . By orders, or even by slavery, you can build pyramids and magnificent roads, you can achieve expanded acreages of cultivation, and increases in

> the quantity of goods produced in your factories. All these things, and many more, can be achieved through the use of force; but none of them results in the development of people.[26]

The method of self-reliant development envisaged by Nyerere is cooperation between society and state, but starting with the smallest unit, the individual: "To maintain our independence and our people's freedom, we ought to be self-reliant in every possible way and avoid depending upon other countries for assistance."[27]

As president of Tanzania, Nyerere devoted himself to thinking, speaking, and writing about self-reliance and socialism in the African context. Like Ghandi and Mao, Nyerere stressed the necessity of a national work ethic and moral character. He asserted that true development comes from indigenous resources — the land and the people (both abundant in Tanzania)—not from capital and technology (both scarce, not only in Tanzania but throughout sub-Saharan Africa). In 1967, Tanzania issued the **Arusha Declaration,** a socialist program of development known as *ujamaa*, or "familyhood."[28]

The expression of African socialism began introspectively in Kenya. Tom Mboya and Oginga Odinga defined what self-reliance and socialism came to mean there. Although they differed on the details, they agreed that Kenya's economic development should be based on indigenous resources and values. Mboya wrote:

> When I talk of "African Socialism," I refer to those proved codes of conduct in the African societies which have, over the ages, conferred dignity on our people and afforded them security regardless of their station in life. I refer to universal charity which characterized our societies and I refer to the African's thought processes and cosmological ideas which regard man, not as a social means, but as an end and entity in the society.[29]

Another advocate of socialist self-reliance for Africa was Kenneth Kaunda, former president of Zambia. Kaunda's humanist approach to economic development contrasted sharply with Western capitalist views, which stress the profit motive, or self-interest. "I have a passionate belief in the worth and possibilities of man," Kaunda once confessed, "and I expect him someday to achieve a perfection."[30]

Kaunda's vision may seem idealistic and naive to Western observers, but it is an authentic expression of African values, which tend to be group-oriented rather than individualistic and are not tied to Western logic and pragmatism. Kaunda is not a utopian dreamer; on the contrary, he emphasizes the work ethic and the need to modernize. The way to prove one's worth, he says, is with "a spade or a sickle."[31]

In the following passage, Kaunda synthesized hard work, humanism, and modernity into a philosophy of African economic development:

> Modern Africa is no place for the uncommitted. Life here demands cool nerves, perpetual optimism and great faith in human possibilities. Those who live with their bags mentally packed are of all men the most miserable. They are like hypochondriacs, taking their temperature and feeling their pulse every hour to see whether they are still fit. They are blind to the positive aspects of independence. They do not notice the

> immense nerve and dedication of our people — their gritted-teeth determination to make Zambia great — because they are utterly preoccupied with the search for cracks in the foundation. They magnify every isolated incident into a full-blown calamity. Every loose stone heralds an avalanche, every gust of wind a tornado. They wish to feast upon the fruits of our prosperity but will slink off at the first sign of adversity.[32]

Neither Communism nor Capitalism

In sum, Africans have embraced a worldview that is neither communist nor capitalist, neither revolutionary nor conservative. Rather, it reflects Africa's cultural diversity and unique historical experience. One scholar noted that Africa has

> one continent, Africa; two permanent [geographic parts], the Arab North and black South; three religious systems, African traditional religions, Christianity and Islam; four dominant international languages, English, French, Arabic and Portuguese; five external hegemonic systems competing for influence or profit within Africa, Western Europe, North America, the Soviet bloc, China and Japan; six political traditions partly fed by those five hegemonic systems and partly in opposition to those systems, liberal capitalism, socialism, nationalism, conservative traditionalism, militarism, and pan-Africanism; [and] seven combat traditions, the warrior tradition, the jihad, passive resistance, guerrilla warfare, revolutionary terrorism, modern conventional warfare, and prospects for a nuclear option first in South Africa and later elsewhere in Africa.[33]

In this mosaic of social, cultural, and historical diversity can be seen the need for an African synthesis. As we have noted, the principal elements of this have been self-reliance, socialism, and pan-Africanism (this last has remained a distant ideal). Self-reliant socialism, in the African context, is predicated on the values of social equality and harmony and has provided a conceptual framework for development strategies and policies. It may seem as though self-reliance and African unity are contradictory aims, but the African notion of self-reliance does not imply autarky at all. On the contrary, most African leaders advocate equitable interdependence. (What they mean by "equitable" will be discussed later in this chapter.)

The Blame Game (Again): A Theory, Not a Solution

Coups, revolutions, secessionist movements, civil wars, and popular disenfranchisement since independence point to the weakness of political institutions in sub-Saharan Africa and support the view that political and economic development are linked. Nowhere in the world is the problem of "failed states" more pervasive. Various theories have been put forward to explain Africa's chronic political and economic instability. One approach that has a wide following, especially among Third World development scholars, is dependency theory.

Diagnosing the Disease

Political scientist Theotonio Dos Santos has defined dependency as "a situation in which the economy of certain countries is conditioned by the development and expansion of another economy to which the former is subjected." He argues that interdependence gives way to dependency "when some countries (the dominant ones) can expand and be self-sustaining, while others (the dependent ones) can do this only as a reflection of that expansion which can have either positive or negative effect on their immediate development."[34]

Dependency theory and the concept of neocolonialism gained currency in the late 1950s and early 1960s, after the UN Economic Commission for Latin America published a study by Raul Prebisch.[35] Originally conceived as an explanation for the consequences of Latin America's economic exploitation by the United States, the dependency perspective eventually came to be seen as especially applicable to Africa and Asia. Its relatively benign interpretation of colonialism has attracted many scholars from the United States and Europe, widening its acceptance and application to the entire Third World.

The concept of dependency transcends economic and political realms; it includes social and psychological attitudes and behaviors of dominant and dependent nations toward one another. Dependency connotes a relationship that is not equal or reciprocal.[36] Although the ties between the developed center and the underdeveloped periphery can be negative or positive, the gains for the periphery are, at best, indirect. According to Dos Santos, multinational companies based in the developed countries enjoy "monopolistic control of the market, which leads to transfer of surplus generated in the dependent countries to the dominant countries." Moreover, he argues, loans and other capital exports flowing in only one direction (from rich to poor countries) cause interest and profits to flow only in the other direction. The result, in this view, is not only to stunt the growth of internal financial markets but also "to limit the development of [the] technical and cultural capacity as well as the moral and physical health" of the people in the dependent countries."[37]

A Capital Offense

James Caporaso stresses the role of transnational ties between foreign and local capitalists, restricted development choices, and distortions in the domestic economy caused by the incorporation of the less developed nations into the world market system:

> Structural asymmetries are the basis for power, i.e., these asymmetries provide the resources to affect others by depriving them of the desired exchange of goods. When one actor supplies another with large amounts of important goods which cannot be easily replaced at tolerable costs, that actor is in a position to influence the dependent actor.[38]

As a consequence, domestic economic structures are distorted, and development policies are responsive to external market conditions rather than internal needs. For Africans, poverty and despair are inherent in this system, Caporaso argues, because the power to improve their plight in life is outside their own societies.

Dependent development exists where a given nation can take only limited initiatives and has limited access to such vital resources as capital and technology, which are externally controlled. According to many dependency theorists, who are often influenced by the turn-of-the-century writings of J. A. Hobson and V. I. Lenin, underdevelopment is perpetuated by the workings of the world capitalist systems.[39]

A. G. Frank advanced this argument:

> Underdevelopment, no less than development itself, is the product but also part of the motive power of capitalism. Capitalist development everywhere has been . . . contradictory . . . [and] based on exploitation . . . [which has resulted in] simultaneous development and underdevelopment. [Furthermore,] the growth and expansion of European mercantilism of the sixteenth century led to the development of a single, integrated capitalist system of worldwide scope. Associated ever since the beginning with the growth of powerful states, the expansion of mercantilism-capitalism led to the development of a metropole and, related to it through ties of commerce and force, of a periphery. . . . Through colonialism, free trade, imperialism, and "neocolonialism," the metropole exploited the periphery in such a way and extent that the metropole became what we today call developed while the periphery became what we now call underdeveloped.[40]

The economies of the underdeveloped countries have not only become "asymmetrically" integrated with those of the industrially developed nations but, in this view, have also become permanently unequal partners in the global system. Not surprisingly, dependency theorists tend to be anticapitalist and usually advocate socialism as the best cure for underdevelopment and the best hope for transforming the international economic order. They reject the existing system of foreign trade, aid, and investment as a capitalist web that ensnares developing nations and holds them in economic bondage, but they offer no solutions that are both theoretically sound and politically possible. In sum, dependency theory raises provocative questions but for answers to Africa's problems we have to look elsewhere.

Are Open Markets the Answer?

In sharp contrast to the dependency theorists, Harvard economist Jeffrey Sachs argues that Africa's "anti-market orientation" is the source of its economic predicament. "After more than a century of colonial depredations," Sachs notes, "African nations understandably if erroneously viewed open trade and foreign capital as a threat to national sovereignty.[41]

The gist of Sachs's thesis is as follows. The fact that Africa's economy has grown at a much slower long-term rate than economies in other developing regions is surprising because Africa started later and had a lower per capita income (hence the chance for catch-up growth). Africa has lagged "because of much higher trade barriers; excessive tax rates; lower saving rate; and adverse structural conditions, including an unusually high incidence of inaccessibility to the sea (fifteen of fifty-three countries are landlocked) plus a high reliance on natural resource exports." In short, Africa's economic woes are largely attributable to a "lack of openness, lack of market incentives, and lack of national saving."

What then must be done? The answer in a nutshell is rapid integration into the world economy through market reforms and trade liberalization. Eighteenth-century British philosopher Adam Smith's assertion that prosperity needs only "peace, easy taxes, and a tolerable administration of justice" is still highly relevant to the African situation. By the mid-1990s, many of Africa's worst conflicts in recent decades were either resolved or receding. What is needed is to cut tax rates from 40 percent or higher to between 20 and 30 percent "as in the outward-oriented East Asian economies." Decent government is also needed, meaning, among other things, a reduced scope for official corruption through market mechanisms such as free trade, currency convertibility, and automatic incorporation of business. African governments must learn to function on public spending of 20 percent of GDP or less. Donor countries can help through debt cancellation that is "deep, phased over time, and conditional on fundamental reforms."[42] The rest is up to Africans themselves.

The Search for a Synthesis

The development debate is far from academic. In Africa more than anywhere else, development policy has remained entangled in an ideological rivalry between socialism and capitalism, between anticolonialism and Western-style liberalism. One close observer of this value conflict suggests that a viable strategy for developing nations may be to pursue "selective socialism" or "selective capitalism," regarding both as means to an end measured by the same yardstick: Does this approach help or hinder the achievement of society's goals? [43]

Garden of Eden in Decay

In a lecture series for the British Broadcasting Corporation, noted African scholar Ali Mazrui took an unusual approach to describing Africa's condition. He used a powerful metaphor that no doubt shocked some of his audience:

> It is as if I were a doctor and Africa came to me and asked for a comprehensive medical examination on the eve of a particular anniversary. The most important century in Africa's relations with Europe is the century from the 1880s to the 1980s. It was in the 1880s that the Conference of Berlin was held to agree on the terms of the European partition of Africa. It was in the 1880s that Egypt was occupied, that the Nile Valley was scrambled for, and that the repercussions for the rest of the continent were released. It was in the 1880s that the map of Africa began to acquire more decisively the different flag colours of the occupation powers of Europe. Let us assume Africa has come to my clinic for varied medical tests on the eve of the hundredth anniversary of Europe's rape of the body and her possessions.[44]

Mazrui proceeded to diagnose Africa's condition in terms of multiple maladies, most of which, he asserted, were caused by European colonialism and economic dependency. Mazrui characterized Africa as "a garden of Eden in decay"—the first habitat of mankind, but the last to be truly habitable.[45]

Too Strong for Hollywood

Human deprivation in sub-Saharan Africa has been a series of horror stories even Hollywood does not dare (or care) to put on the big screen. However, television has brought the grim spectacle of emaciated and starving children in Ethiopia, Sudan, and Somalia into American homes. A killing famine in the Horn of Africa in the early 1980s resulted from the combined effects of continuous warfare and a disastrous drought, ultimately causing 2 to 3 million deaths and placing some 30 million at risk of starvation.[46] Angola and Mozambique in southern Africa suffered too. In the early 1990s, the most critical food shortages occurred in Somalia, where civil war and drought conspired to cause terrible human suffering. In August 1992, the United Nations Children's Fund (UNICEF) triggered a massive international relief effort when it warned that 2 million Somalis faced starvation within six months. Liberia also joined the list of famine-stricken African nations.

The droughts that triggered Africa's worst famines in memory were a grim reminder of the region's fragile economic and political condition. The droughts, in turn, triggered alarm bells in Western capitals. For example, the U.S. Agency for International Development published these stark and startling facts:

- The region's forty-eight nations have 450 million people from a thousand ethnic groups speaking more than eight hundred languages.
- If current demographic trends continue, the population will double in twenty-three years.
- After 1972, per capita food production decreased in every year but one.
- Health and education standards are the worst in the world, and millions of Africans (including newborn babies) are infected with the AIDS virus.
- Of every hundred children born in the region, twenty die before age five, and nearly half the survivors are malnourished.

In October 1993, Rwanda and Burundi erupted in bloody conflict between the Tutsi minority and the far more numerous Hutus. In 1994, a Hutu killing frenzy in Rwanda resulted in at least 800,000 deaths. Tutsi insurgents launched a war to stop the genocide, which sent about 2 million Hutu refugees pouring into neighboring countries. Most of these refugees landed in squalid camps in eastern Zaire.

In the ensuing years, the spillover from Hutu-Tutsi war turned into another African nightmare. In October 1996, two years after the genocide in Rwanda, the government of Zaire attempted to drive out hundreds of thousands of its own Tutsi citizens living in the same region where the Hutu refugee camps are located. The Tutsis, faced with imminent expulsion, launched a wave of armed assaults against the camps, spreading panic among the Hutu refugees and sparking fears of a bloody regional war. In the face of this crisis, Zaire's dictator, Mobutu Sese Seko, lay sick with cancer in a Swiss hospital. Zaire's 50,000-strong regular army was poorly equipped and poorly disciplined. Zaire, a country with a long reputation for human wretchedness, slid into a civil war, which culminated in Mobutu's long-awaited overthrow, but not in civil peace. Zaire became the Democratic Republic of the Congo, but the change in name changed nothing else: in 2000, the Congo was the scene of the worst civil war in the world.

In addition to war, ethnic conflict, drought, and famine, disease is a major killer in sub-Saharan Africa, where doctors, hospitals, clinics, and medicines are frequently unavailable even for the gravely ill. Inadequate health care has always been a major problem in developing countries, but since the 1980s a new specter has stalked Africa: acquired immunodeficiency syndrome (AIDS). AIDS remains Africa's biggest and potentially most catastrophic health problem.

As noted earlier, foreign governments and humanitarian agencies responded to the crisis in sub-Saharan Africa in several ways. Creditors considered various types of debt relief, and celebrities turned their talents to worldwide fund-raising efforts. At the peak of the crisis, in 1985, official emergency aid amounted to several billion dollars, and as many as 1 million lives were saved.[47] But these efforts were short-lived, and the world's attention soon turned to other regions and other problems:

> Africa has seen only a marginal increase in overseas development assistance (ODA), while international export credits and commercial bank loans have all but dried up. . . . Even as aid flows in at a lower rate, domestic resources are flowing out at a higher rate, as capital flight and high debts deplete national savings.[48]

The Enemy Is Us

One upshot of the crisis was to accentuate the failure of African nations to achieve key goals. Julius Nyerere, former president of Tanzania and longtime champion of African socialism and self-reliance, criticized fellow African leaders for reacting to the crisis of the moment but failing to engage in longer-term problem solving:

> Virtually all African governments are now almost entirely occupied with crisis management — that is, with searching for foreign capital even to maintain the very minimum administrative and economic structures, and with keeping the economy running somehow. In the process, we have ourselves begun to believe that all Africa's problems are the result of Africa's mistakes, Africa's incompetence, and its political and economic venality. We are apologetic and demoralized in the face of the rest of the world.[49]

But Nyerere failed to mention the role of African socialism itself in either causing or failing to prevent the region's economic distress. Another omission is the definition of self-reliance. What does it mean? Autarky? Interdependence in some sort of pan-African economic grouping? Neither alternative has been realistic at any time since decolonization. Ironically, heavy borrowing from the West — hardly consistent with self-reliance — has led to sub-Saharan Africa's most pressing economic problem, the mountain of foreign debt.

One of sub-Saharan Africa's most agonizing issues is the refugee problem. Dependency theorists argue that the militarization of African society is one of the consequences of European colonialism. One of the consequences of militarization, in turn, is refugees. Their numbers reached crisis proportions in the 1980s, when war and revolution, drought and famine produced a tidal wave of displaced and destitute souls.

Conflict, Famine, and the Refugee Problem

Africa is a war-torn region. The persistence of armed conflict, both domestic and international, has been a stubborn fact of life for many sub-Saharan nations since the early years of independence in the 1950s. Hardly a country in the region has not been involved in a civil war or a border war. Conflicts have plagued the region and continue to sap its resources while undermining cooperative efforts.

Fight or Flight In both human and economic terms, the toll of border conflicts, civil and ethnic strife, and chronic political instability is enormous. The human cost is counted not only in battle casualties but also in ordinary people fleeing war, persecution, and hunger. Of the estimated 12 million refugees worldwide in the late 1980s, nearly half of them were Africans, and more than three-fourths of those were from four nations: Ethiopia, Mozambique, Angola, and Sudan. At least an equal number of displaced Africans were living in temporary settlements in their own countries. (People who do not cross an international border are not officially considered refugees.) Black South Africans and Angolans accounted for more than 40 percent of this population. All told, there were close to 17 million refugees and displaced persons in sub-Saharan Africa in the late 1980s. Although the numbers declined in the 1990s, the refugee problem did not disappear.

Though impossible to quantify, the economic and human costs of conflict and famine are readily apparent. Refugees suffer severe deprivation, unfathomable indignities, and loss of self-respect. Whatever systems the host governments may have in place for providing education, health care, housing, sanitation, and other human services can be easily overwhelmed but cannot be rapidly expanded. Even food reserves are often insufficient, thus deepening external dependencies.[50] It is easy to see how internal conflicts can spill over, giving rise to border tensions and international strife. Thus conflict begets conflict in a vicious cycle that only serves to perpetuate the militarization of African politics.

Horn of Sorrows The Horn of Africa has been the scene of some of the worst human tragedies in recent times. In 1975, a military coup led by Colonel Mengistu Haile Miriam ousted Ethiopian Emperor Haile Selassie from power. Mengistu established a Marxist-style police state and ruthlessly repressed all opposition. Mengistu's rise to power ushered in a period of bloody turmoil: a war with Somalia over the Ogaden (a region inside Ethiopia inhabited largely by Somalis) and major guerrilla insurgency movements in Eritrea and Tigré provinces.

In the first half of the 1980s, a severe drought caused widespread famine and threatened millions of Ethiopians with starvation. A massive international relief effort was mounted, but military victories by Eritrean rebels in 1988 forced the government to curtail the activities of relief agencies in drought-stricken areas. The corruption, brutality, and incompetence of the Mengistu regime also contributed to the economic and humanitarian crisis. The Eritreans defeated Mengistu's forces in May 1991, and Mengistu fled. In April 1993, Eritrea voted overwhelmingly for independence from Ethiopia. This event was the culmination of a thirty-year war against the Ethiopian army.

Eritrea has a population of only 3.5 million and is one of the poorest countries in the world. Tens of thousands of Eritreans died in the war, and some 750,000 fled its terrors, most of them landing in squalid refugee camps in Sudan. In 2000, Eritrea held national elections and the new president promised to lead the country into a new era of peace and prosperity.

Even without Eritrea, Ethiopia's population is about 61 million (larger than France, Italy, or the United Kingdom). The annual population growth rate in the 1980s was over 3 percent and remains high (although it declined in the 1990s). Ethiopian women have seven or eight babies, on average; the mortality rate is among the highest in the world (still over 100 per 1,000 live births in the late 1990s). The illiteracy rate remains high as well. Ethiopia's GNP in 1998 was roughly $6 billion, less than one-third that of tiny Luxembourg (population: 378,000). The economy grew at a snail's pace between 1980 and 1991, and the per capita growth rate was actually negative. By that measure, the economy began to creep ahead in the 1990s. Ethiopia relies on agriculture for over 50 percent of its gross domestic product.

Next door in Somalia, rebels ousted the dictator Siad Barré in January 1991. Civil war and famine followed, leaving 300,000 people dead and another 2 million at risk of starvation (out of a total population of slightly over 8 million). A near-total breakdown of law and order plunged the country into anarchy and placed women and children at the mercy of armed bandits who disrupted relief efforts by international agencies, stole food intended for starving children, and murdered relief workers. At the end of 1992, outgoing U.S. President George Bush ordered a military intervention (backed by the United Nations) to safeguard relief supplies and workers. This ill-fated operation became the subject of the well-known Hollywood movie *Black Hawk Down,* which depicts hellish conditions and extreme dangers American warriors faced in Mogadishu, the capital. Long after the American-led UN forces departed in March 1995 (having accomplished little and changed nothing), Somalia remained a country without a national government: maps showing what areas were controlled by what factions looked more like a jigsaw puzzle than a political configuration.

Somalia remained one of the poorest countries in Africa, with a per capita GNP of less than $500 and an illiteracy rate of more than 75 percent in the 1990s. Moreover, Somalia was underdeveloped politically as well as economically. The structure of Somali society is based on kinship ties, or clans, and the civil war was in fact a clan war. If a country like Somalia cannot find a formula for political stability, it cannot rebuild its economy. The reverse is also true: stability depends on economic and social progress. The following case studies also illustrate this point, although, unlike Somalia, neither Nigeria nor South Africa has disintegrated — yet.

Case Studies: Nigeria and South Africa

Before 1999, Nigeria was a military dictatorship whose rulers made a periodic pretense of returning to parliamentary democracy. In South Africa, the last surviving white-minority regime operated a dual system — democracy for the white minority, tyranny for the black majority — until the early 1990s, when everything changed. We look at Nigeria first.

Nigeria: A Military Retreat

We begin this section with a comment on the importance of making connections in the study of comparative politics. Often factors that at first glance do not appear to be connected really are. In the case of Nigeria, for example, colonialism, climate, and culture are linked in a politically important way.

When France and Great Britain colonized West Africa they did not understand the mosaic of indigenous languages and cultures nor did they take this mosaic into account during decolonization. They also did not pay attention to differences in climate, which are closely linked to differences in culture. Political scientists, too, often ignore the links between climate-ecology and culture to the detriment of clear analysis. Few places on earth have a climate-culture nexus more apparent than in West Africa in general and Nigeria in particular. Climate and ecological zones in West Africa run from east to west and resemble a layer cake. That is, they are stacked on top of the other. In the north is the Sahara Desert. Below it is the Sahel, below that the savanna, and below the savanna is the equatorial rain forest.

The colonial-political boundaries of West Africa (and Nigeria) ignored this east-west axis of climate and ecology. The thrust of colonial expansion in this area was northward from the Gulf of Guinea, intersecting climate zones and creating political-administrative entities encompassing peoples of sharply contrasting cultures. The rest, as they say, is history. In Nigeria, as elsewhere in sub-Saharan Africa, history has a way of repeating itself, as we are about to see.

Political Patterns in Nigeria

Since gaining independence from Britain in 1960, Nigeria has oscillated between civilian and military rule. Civilians were in charge for a total of ten years (from 1960 to 1966 and from 1979 to 1983). Until 1999, five military regimes ruled the rest of the time.

The civilian regimes came to power by means of ballots; the military regimes, by means of bullets and bullying. The cast of characters has changed frequently and abruptly in Nigeria, but the promises of every government have been remarkably constant: to eliminate official corruption, foster good government, improve the quality of life, and establish a pluralistic political order based on the consent of the governed. These lofty aims long eluded Nigeria.

Elections and Coups: A General Disorder The first Nigerian republic lasted only six years; it was toppled by a 1966 military coup d'état led by General Yakubu Gowon (who was in turn ousted in 1975 for failing to curb corruption and restore civilian rule). No sooner had the military government seized power than a crisis arose that imperiled the very survival of Nigeria as a nation-state: civil war. In 1967, the eastern region known as Biafra seceded. The war pitted the Igbos (the majority population in Biafra) against the politically dominant Yoruba. The Igbos believed that they were being exploited and neglected by the central government. With casualties exceeding 1 million — many Biafrans starved to death despite international relief efforts —

the secessionists capitulated in January 1970. The central government quickly reintegrated the Igbos into national life, but mistrust among the regions persists.

The second republic came into existence in 1979, when General Olusegun Obasanjo, who took charge after the 1975 coup, kept his promise to restore civilian rule. Following national elections, General Obasanjo returned power to the victors — a new president and parliament — in accordance with a highly acclaimed democratic constitution. The election itself was vigorously contested by several national parties, including the Unity Party of Nigeria (UPN), the Peoples' Redemption Party (PRP), the Greater Nigerian Peoples' Party (GNP), and the National Party of Nigeria (NPN).

The NPN candidate, Shehu Shagari, narrowly won the 1979 election to become the first (and last) president of the second republic. At the end of 1983, a newly reelected Shagari, in a now-familiar pattern, was ousted by the military on the grounds that his government was guilty of economic mismanagement and corruption. Many of his cabinet members were put on trial and barred from public life. Nigeria again reverted to military rule.

After another coup in August 1985, the Supreme Military Council and the Federal Executive Council were reconstituted as the Armed Forces Ruling Council (AFRC) and the Council of Ministers, respectively. In 1987, the ruling AFRC oligarchy announced that Nigeria would be returned to civilian government in five years and created a Constitutional Review Committee. The following year, the Constituent Assembly was set up to finish this work and give it a democratic veneer. The most controversial issue the Constituent Assembly addressed was whether to enshrine Islamic law, a move opposed both by the Muslim head of state, General Ibrahim Babangida, and by Nigeria's Christian population. In the end, the general and his ruling council decided to put the issue on the back burner. Other than incorporating new anticorruption measures and extending the presidential term to six years, the draft constitution of the "third republic" closely resembled the 1979 basic law.

Generals and Degenerates In Nigeria, the armed forces claimed to intervene for the sake of restoring public confidence in government, eradicate corruption and mismanagement, and improve living standards.[51] The military also pledged to return the country to civilian rule. As a step in this direction, General Babangida created two political parties — the National Republican Convention (NRC) and the Social Democratic Party (SDP)—by presidential decree in October 1989. Both are mainstream parties by design, with one "a little bit to the right" and the other "a little bit to the left."

When local elections were held in December 1990, only 10 percent of the electorate actually voted. Still, the balloting was orderly, and the new two-party system functioned as intended. The SDP won assembly elections held in 1992, but Babangida postponed the opening of the assembly until after a new president could be elected. That poll actually did take place as planned in 1993. What was widely hailed as Nigeria's first free presidential election, however, turned out to be a hoax.

Moshood Abiola won the 1993 election, but Babangida nullified the results and promised fresh elections. Instead, he persuaded the two political parties to enter talks aimed at establishing an interim government. But in August he postponed the talks and stepped down, naming Ernest Shonekan, a civilian, as his successor. Shonekan headed an interim government until November, when General Sani Abacha replaced him. In June 1994, Abacha arrested Abiola and charged him with treason, triggering antigovernment protests. The military rulers, in turn, dealt harshly with leaders of the growing democratic movement. Nigeria became an international pariah in 1995 after the political execution of Ken Saro-Wiwa and eight other human rights activists.

In 1983, Nigerian novelist Chinhua Achebe in a book significantly entitled *The Trouble with Nigeria* wrote:

> The trouble with Nigeria is simply and squarely a failure of leadership. There is nothing basically wrong with the Nigerian character. There is nothing wrong with the Nigerian land or climate or water or air or anything else. The Nigerian problem is the unwillingness or inability of its leaders to rise to the responsibility, to the challenge of personal example which are the hallmarks of true leadership.[52]

Like many successful novelists, Achebe is a keen observer and critic of the contemporary scene in his own country. Not until 1999 would Nigeria's military leaders finally step aside.

Sudden Death In May 1998 General Abacha, Nigeria's paramount ruler, died of a heart attack. Abacha was the last of a long line of military dictators who had run Nigeria into the ground. Between 1966 and 1999, under military rule during all but six years, Nigeria

> suffered one civil war, six violent changes of government, and the continual theft and squandering of public funds by its leader. Blessed with fertile soil, floods of oil, and a huge, energetic, talented population, Nigeria should be Africa's giant. That it is instead one of the poorest countries in the world is largely the fault of a succession of awful military dictators. But the sudden death of the most recent and perhaps worst of them, Sani Abacha, has given Nigeria a chance to recover.[53]

. . . And New Life Nigeria's next military dictator, General Abdulsalam Abubakar, like his predecessors, promised to hold elections, but in a step-by-step progression from local to state to national levels of government. Unlike his predecessors, Abubakar kept his word. In the spring of 1999, Olusegun Obasanjo became Nigeria's first democratically elected president since 1983. The last time the military had handed the reins of government back to civilians, it was Obasanjo who did it. Ironically, Obasanjo's elected (civilian) successor, Shehu Shagari, turned out to be utterly corrupt (unlike Obasanjo, who was honest and honorable, a rarity in the Nigerian high command).

The election of Obasanjo was appropriate and a good omen, but Obasanjo had his work cut out for him. After decades of mismanagement and plundering by venal rulers, Nigeria's economy is among the worst in the world. The visible ravages are readily apparent in society and in the environment. Perhaps worse is the invisible damage to the moral fabric of a country where, "For as long as most Nigerians can remember, the rewards for honesty and industry have been miserable, whereas corruption has paid magnificently."[54]

Can Nigeria rehabilitate itself? Is national self-redemption on the scale required possible? In the next section, we examine the challenges facing Nigeria and consider whether the resources available are adequate to the task of meeting those challenges.

Instituting Democracy: Parliamentary or Presidential? That Nigeria lacks well-established constitutional principles and structures ought to be clear by now. Decades of military rule precluded any sort of continuity in the country's democratic development. Nigerians have even vacillated over what type of democracy — parliamentary or presidential — is best for Nigeria. For the first two decades after, a British-style parliamentary was theoretically in effect (as we have seen, the military actually ruled most of the time). After 1979, when democracy was temporarily restored, the Constitution of the Second Republic, established a presidential system. That system was basically preserved when another constitution was promulgated a decade later. Just the fact that Nigerians have seen their constitution rewritten three times in sixteen years (the 1995 constitution was never promulgated) is indicative of the weakness of Nigerian political institutions. Is it also the reason why the present discussion of Nigerian politics devotes relatively little attention to formal political structures, which are still in the formative stages as these lines are being written.

About all that can be said with certainty in this area is that Nigeria has a federal structure and will probably continue to be federal rather than unitary. This federal structure reflects the size and diversity of the country, but this structure, too, has been in continual flux. The number of states has ranged from as few as twelve (after the outbreak of the war in Biafra in 1967) to thirty-six in 1996. In addition, Nigeria's federal system is three-tiered rather than two-tiered as most federal systems are. It incorporates local governments as integral parts of the federal structure. Here, too, there has been restructuring and confusion. When the civilians returned to power in 1979, for example, they created hundreds of new local governments, which the military promptly abolished four years later. Nonetheless, the fact that the Nigerian constitution creates a uniform structure and set of functions for local government and places local government within the federal system rather than under the control of the states is noteworthy. It is an interesting example of political engineering — an attempt to adapt political structures to circumstances of extreme social diversity.

Problems and Prospects

Nigeria is one of the poorest countries in the world (only twelve nations rank below it). Even compared to other large and populous developing countries with histories of corrupt military rule — Indonesia or Brazil, for example — Nigeria is a failure. Its population growth rate at around 3 percent a year is one of the highest in the world, outpacing both food production and new job opportunities.

By almost any reckoning, Nigeria before 1999 was one of the worst governed states in the world, plagued not only by the centrifugal forces resulting from extreme ethnic diversity (250 separate ethnic and language groups) but also by a no less extreme brand of official corruption. Nigeria's uncommonly venal rulers have systematically plundered the public treasury, which depends on oil exports for over 95 percent of its revenues.

Africa's Prodigal Son Nigeria and Indonesia, an island republic in Southeast Asia, have many common characteristics. Both are large and populous developing countries. Both are also ethnically diverse, both have a history of rule by corrupt military dictatorships, and large oil reserves. And both were miserably poor at independence. Finally, when the oil boom hit in 1973–1974, both (like all the oil-exporting states) benefited from windfall profits.

Indonesia is no model of good government, but has nonetheless fared far better than Nigeria. In Nigeria's case, the windfall was wasted, and then some. The military rulers also borrowed billions and squandered or simply stole that, as well. Nigerians are poorer today than they were in 1974. Per capita income in 1998 stood at less than $350, far below where it was twenty years earlier.

According to the UN Development Project (UNDP), Nigerians are far more likely than Indonesians to be illiterate or die before the age of forty. The comparison in the area of access to basic health care is still worse. A World Bank study concluded: "Indonesia turned oil income into productive investment, whereas Nigerian oil income was either siphoned abroad or used for prestige projects."[55]

The "prestige projects" include idle steel mills built at a cost of many billions of dollars, at least one of which has never produced a single piece of steel. There was also a public housing project in the early 1980s that turned into a fiasco but not before corrupt officials made huge fortunes selling cement import licenses. Yet the greatest and most extravagant folly of all was the building of a new capital, Abuja, in the center of the country — perhaps in imitation of Brazil. (Recall that Brazil also built a new inland capital, Brasília). There was a day-and-night difference between Brazil's economy, however, and Nigeria's — and between Brazil's military rulers and Nigeria's.

Brazil had its fair share of corruption in high places during these years, but this is one area in which Nigeria had few peers. In fact, Transparency International, a Berlin-based think tank that studies honesty in government, consistently rated Nigeria (prior to 1999) as one of the most corrupt regimes in the world.

Brazilians and Indonesians have not enjoyed the blessings of good government for the most part. But things could be worse. Just ask a Nigerian.

Turning a Windfall into a Wasteland A member of the Organization of Oil Exporting Countries (OPEC), Nigeria is one of only two major oil producers in sub-Saharan Africa (Gabon is the other OPEC member; Angola and the Congo also have oil reserves). Skyrocketing prices following the 1973 OPEC oil embargo enabled Nigeria to launch a major economic development program. But this effort foundered, partly because of political instability and official corruption and partly because of plummeting oil prices in the early 1980s. Between 1981–1985 average per capita income in the OPEC nations dropped 23 percent. Nigeria's extreme dependency on oil — the source of roughly 95 percent of its exports — made it particularly vulnerable. During the last two decades of the century, Nigeria's per capita income plunged until 1987, remained in the doldrums for the next six years, improved slightly in 1993, fell again in 1995, and stagnated thereafter.

The combination of oil wealth and mass poverty is rare in the world: Nigeria shares this dubious distinction with only one other nation, Indonesia (which, as noted earlier, is still doing better than Nigeria). The mushrooming populations of these two countries set them apart from the oil-rich Arab states of the Persian Gulf. The contrast in per capita GNP between densely populated Nigeria ($300 in 1998) and the sparsely populated United Arab Emirates (nearly $18,000) is striking — both are members of OPEC, but that is where the similarity ends. The average per capita income of all major oil-exporting countries in 1988 — a decade earlier — was around $5,000. Gabon, the only other OPEC member state in sub-Saharan Africa, had a per capita income in 1991 more than thirteen times that of Nigeria. Indonesia, with a population of more than 200 million, 80 percent larger than Nigeria's, has a per capita income more than twice that of Nigeria. So from every angle Nigeria stacks up poorly against other oil-producing nations (not to mention most others).

Poverty and degradation are the dry tinder of ethnic violence in Nigeria (as elsewhere in the region). Ethnic hatred, always seething beneath the surface of Nigerian society, once again erupted in violent clashes in 1992. In this charged atmosphere General Babangida, postponed scheduled elections, using reports of unfair campaign practices by leading candidates as a pretext.

When the presidential poll was finally held in June 1993 after it had been postponed three times, it was greeted with voter apathy. Turnout was correspondingly low. A candidate from southern Nigeria, Chief Moshood Abiola, won the election. The military oligarchy saw Abiola's victory as a threat to northern dominance, so Babangida simply nullified the election. Babangida's cynical about-face was widely criticized in the Western press, but public opinion in Nigeria was not greatly aroused.

In the meantime, Nigeria's economic ills went untreated. Costly fuel subsidies remained in force despite the government's earlier acceptance of an IMF-structured adjustment program that called for an end to such subsidies. Inflation was climbing at an annual rate of 40 to 50 percent, and the local currency (the naira) was falling even faster. Nigeria needed a changing of the guard. New ideas and fresh faces were clearly necessary to rejuvenate the country.

The "face" Nigeria chose in 1999 — Olusegun Obasanjo — was not really fresh, but he had a reputation for personal integrity and a commitment to democratic rebuilding rare in Nigerian politics. His job is daunting. Consider the list of urgent tasks:

- Cure (or at least curb) corruption
- Eradicate waste and inefficiency
- Restructure and revitalize the moribund economy
- Heal the social wounds inflicted by decades of ethnic and regional strife
- Provide for basic human needs (health, education, nutrition)
- Pay off Nigeria's foreign debt
- Restore the country's tarnished international reputaton

No single leader can do all these things, nor can they be done overnight. But a new beginning is long overdue in Nigeria — overdue, but possible.

In Sum . . . In this section, we have compared Nigeria and Indonesia, both of which have large populations and a host of economic, social, and political problems. We close with another arresting comparison, again between Nigeria and a populous developing country. Bangladesh, formerly East Pakistan, has a population only slightly larger than Nigeria's. Unlike Nigeria, however, Bangladesh has no oil to export. In fact, Bangladesh has almost no natural resources whatsoever. Instead of oil, Bangladesh exports jute — a far less lucrative commodity, to say the least. And yet even Bangladesh had a per capita income higher than Nigeria's in the late 1990s — twice as high when measured in purchasing power parity. Clearly, Nigeria can do better.

With the advent of democracy in Nigeria, there is a chance that the future will brighten. However, if there is any truth in the saying that "the past is prologue," it would be foolhardy to expect an immediate end to political corruption or a serious start to the kind of fundamental economic reforms that are needed to turn Nigeria around.

South Africa is our last country study in this book, an appropriate way to end — on a note of cautious optimism. The reasons for both caution and optimism are elucidated below.

South Africa: After Mandela, What?

Despite the appearance of change, white minority power remained largely intact in South Africa during the 1980s. However, intense domestic and foreign pressures were brought to bear on the government of President Pieter W. Botha. In response, the Botha government made important, though limited, concessions. Between 1979 and 1986, blacks won the right to belong to trade unions, to own their own homes, and to move freely around the country. In 1985, the government repealed the Mixed Marriages Act and the part of the Immorality Act that prohibited interracial sex. These and other concessions only fanned the flames of political protest. In July 1985, Botha declared a state of emergency in thirty-six black districts and townships where the rioting was the worst. To die-hard white supremacists, any olive branch was an invitation to anarchy; to black leaders and moderate whites, the government's peace offerings were too little, too late. For his part, Botha vacillated between compromise and intransigence. Nonetheless, it was a sign of the times that an opinion poll taken in South Africa in 1986 showed that nearly three-fourths of the whites and a solid majority of the blacks believed that apartheid would be gone within ten years.[56] The last laws reserving certain jobs for whites were repealed in 1987.

When Botha appeared to turn away from further reforms, warning the world not to push South Africa too far, the international reaction was swift and damaging. A spate of economic sanctions and diplomatic protests left Pretoria, South Africa's capital, isolated and ostracized from the international community. Foreign banks called in loans early, multinational firms quit South Africa, and the value of the rand plummeted. These external pressures precipitated the deep economic recession into which the country sank in the second half of the decade.

Intensified political pressures both at home and abroad accompanied South Africa's mounting economic troubles. Botha was ultimately defeated by a wide array of opposition forces. His successor, F. W. de Klerk, could read the handwriting on the wall: negotiate with the black majority (and protect white interests as far as possible), or risk a convulsive end to white rule (in which case Afrikaners might lose everything). In February 1990, de Klerk not only released Nelson Mandela from prison (where he had languished since 1961) but also legalized the **African National Congress (ANC)** and invited thousands of ANC exiles to return to South Africa and take part in seeking accommodation between blacks and whites.

Direct talks between Mandela, as the ANC leader, and de Klerk, beginning in the spring of 1990, brought a further dismantling of the apartheid system. The ANC laid down two conditions before the talks: an end to the four-year-old state of emergency and amnesty for all political prisoners and exiles. During the next year, with negotiations in progress, de Klerk abolished the Reservation of Separate Amenities Act establishing "petty apartheid"; the Group Areas Act designating racially segregated residential zones; the Lands Acts of 1913 and 1936 setting aside 87 percent of the land for the white minority; and the Population Registration Act classifying South Africans by race were all abolished. In early 1991, the government and the ANC agreed to convene an all-party (hence multiracial) constitutional convention.

More radical black parties and leaders, including the Pan-Africanist Congress and the South African Communist Party, did not support the relatively conciliatory stance toward the government adopted by Mandela and the ANC. The politically moderate Zulu-based **Inkatha Freedom Party** of Chief Mangosuthu Buthelezi distrusted the ANC as well. Mandela and Buthelezi met for the first time in thirty years on January 29, 1991, but they failed to defuse the fierce rivalry that had already caused 4,000 deaths and divided the antiapartheid movement.

Despite the difficulties, events moved at a dizzying pace in the 1990s. Against a backdrop of social turmoil and sporadic township violence, de Klerk and Mandela negotiated the dismantling of the apartheid system. In February 1993, they agreed to form a government of national unity following free, color-blind elections in 1994. Chief Buthelezi, leader of the Zulu tribe, as well as many right-wing Afrikaners and the leaders of the black homelands of Ciskei and Bophuthatswana (the so-called Freedom Alliance), vigorously opposed the idea of a single democratic state. Undaunted, de Klerk and Mandela hammered out the terms of an interim constitution.

The new constitution provided for free elections based on universal suffrage in April 1994, created a four hundred–member National Assembly, and envisaged a South Africa without "homelands" (these were to become nine new provinces). It also made Xhosa and eight other native languages, as well as English and Afrikaans, official.

The rapid progress toward ending apartheid was accompanied by continued turbulence. The Freedom Alliance fell apart, but Chief Buthelezi remained intransigent (in early 1994 violence broke out in KwaZulu-Natal after Inkatha demonstrations in Johannesburg, and a temporary state of emergency was imposed there).

None of the political disturbances derailed the transition process. In April 1994, the first open national elections in South Africa's history were held. The ANC won the elections handily. Mandela was inaugurated as president, with Thabo Mbeki as first deputy president and de Klerk as second deputy president. It was a remarkable turn of events, hardly less dramatic than the fall of the Berlin Wall or the collapse of communism.

The 1999 and 2004 National Elections

Postapartheid South Africa crossed a major hurdle in 1999. The second majority election — and the first without Nelson Mandela as a presidential candidate — took place

What If? BOX 14.4

What If the Black Majority Ruled in South Africa?

That was the question Afrikaners asked during the era of apartheid. Now we know the answer: the African National Congress (ANC) easily wins general elections, but the political rights of the white minority are respected. Here are the results of the first two elections since the adoption of majority rule in South Africa:

	Seats	
Political Party	**1994**	**1999**
African National Congress	252	266
Democratic Party	7	38
Inkatha Freedom Party	43	34
New National Party (formerly National Party)	82	28
United Democratic Movement	—	14
Freedom Front	9	3

Note: In 2004, the ANC won more than two-thirds of the votes in the country's third election since the end of apartheid.
Source: South Africa Independent Electoral Commission.

in June without violent eruptions. The voters returned the ruling ANC, with Mbeki as its new head, by an even larger majority than in 1994. But the ANC fell short of a two-thirds majority in parliament by one vote — important because some ANC figures in the election run-up had talked about changing some parts of the constitution. That would have probably led to pitched battles among parties and groups, but the election outcome averted any such crisis.

In all, there are more than a dozen parties represented in South Africa's parliament. (See Box 14.4.) In 1999, the former ruling party gained only twenty-eight seats, a net loss of nearly two-thirds (fifty-four seats). In April 2004, President Mbeki was re-elected in a landslide and the ANC garnered more than two-thirds of the popular vote. The good news is that the right to vote is guaranteed to all South Africans now, that some 16 million people turned out to vote in 1999, and that opposition parties are free to criticize the government — and contest elections — without fear of retaliation. The bad news is that the economy shrank slightly during the 1990s. South Africa's struggling economy is the main focus of the next (and concluding) section of this book.

Problems and Prospects

South Africa represents one of the most remarkable "transition" success stories in modern history. In a decade that has witnessed many ambitious efforts at economic and political transition in Slavic Europe and elsewhere, South Africa stands out as proof of the axiom that politics is the art of the possible and as a reminder that in politics anything is possible. Today, South Africa is ruled by a black-majority government functioning under a liberal constitution, with basic civil and economic rights guaranteed to all South Africans regardless of race, gender, creed, or color. That alone is a monumental achievement in a country, which at the beginning of the decade was still ruled by an entrenched white minority that monopolized South Africa's wealth and power.

New Houses, New Hopes There is still much to be done, however, before the budding new South Africa flowers into a steady society with a broad-based middle class that fairly reflects the country's racial composition. To that end, Nelson Mandela made a campaign promise in 1994 to create a "reconstruction and development program," popularly known as the RDP, which involved a massive home building project and bringing piped water and electricity to millions of poor black South Africans. As South Africa's new president, Mandela made a good-faith effort to deliver on this promise. Over half a million houses or shacks did get electricity in the next two years. Water taps were installed in at least hundreds of thousands of houses during this same period. But by the end of 1995, only a fraction of the planned RDP houses had been built. In March 1996, Mandela announced that he was closing the RDP office, giving the money back to the treasury and moving the minister.[57] The reasons: bureaucratic red tape and mind-numbing problems of intergovernmental relations between the center and South Africa's nine new provinces.

The problems arising from the uneasy coexistence of a rich white minority and a poor black majority did not disappear with the passing of apartheid. Many whites continue to live in the posh, well-protected suburbs of Johannesburg and other cities, while most blacks remain mired in poverty. In the former white-ruled South Africa, blacks were allowed to own land in only 13 percent of the country allocated to the black "homelands." Between 1960 and 1980, the white government forcibly removed 3.5 million blacks and dumped them in these reservations (much as the U.S. government did to Native Americans a century earlier). Naturally, blacks want their land back, and the whites who now own and farm it want to keep it. The ANC promised land reform affecting no less than 30 percent of South Africa's farmland in five years — both the restitution of land to blacks from whom it was confiscated and the redistribution of land to those who have none. At the same time, the bill of rights in the constitution protects private ownership of land and guarantees "just and equitable compensation" to any owner whose land is expropriated. Meanwhile, the possibility that disgruntled blacks will take matters into their own hands — seizing land or squatting on it — is a potential source of conflict.

The Zulus: A "Chief" Problem? The rivalry between Zulu Chief Buthelezi's Inkatha Party and Mandela's ANC could also destabilize South Africa's fledgling democracy. Inkatha controls the province of KwaZulu-Natal, but its support is strongest in the rural areas; in black townships, the ANC (and Mandela personally) enjoys a wide following. After the 1994 general election, political violence subsided throughout South Africa. But in 1995, a new spate of politically motivated murders occurred in KwaZulu-Natal. The violence came against the backdrop of continued tension between Buthelezi and Mandela over the division of powers between the center and the provinces: Buthelezi and Inkatha wanted more than Mandela and the ANC were willing to concede. The power struggle between Mandela and Buthelezi escalated in 1995, as Buthelezi demanded real financial independence and Mandela sought to undercut Buthelezi by courting the local chiefs (traditional pillars of Inkatha's political power in the KwaZulu-Natal hinterlands). Perhaps shamed by the Zulu-on-Zulu killing, the provincial leaders of Inkatha and the ANC began working together in 1996 to curb the violence.

Race and Crime South Africa's whites are another important piece in the political puzzle. The white minority constitutes a privileged economic elite facing an uncertain political future in the new South Africa. If the white population were a separate country, South Africa would rank 24th in the world, according to the UN Human Development Index; black South Africa, by contrast, would rank 123rd. On average, white South Africans are nine times richer than blacks. The wealthiest 10 percent of the population rakes in half the country's income. However, the whites now constitute only about 12 percent of the population. Demographic trends will lower this figure to less than 10 percent by 2010. (South Africa's black population is growing rapidly.) Perhaps the most arresting (and revealing) statistic, however, is life expectancy: seventy-three for whites and fifty-seven for blacks in the mid-1990s. Obviously, such a severe maldistribution of wealth favoring whites over blacks in a free society where blacks outnumber whites by a nine-to-one margin cannot be sustained indefinitely.

Crime is also rising rapidly in black-ruled South Africa, a malady that has afflicted most other transitional societies, too. Violent crimes such as rape and murder are especially common in the black township of Soweto. The annual murder rate in the mid-1990s was among the highest in the world (five or six times that of the United States). The same is true of car thefts and burglaries. South Africans own millions of guns, licensed and unlicensed.

Crime hits blacks and whites alike. Not surprisingly, property crimes hit whites hardest: of the thousands of carjackings in Johannesburg in 1995, for example, around one in seven happened in Soweto. Nearly everybody in South Africa, blacks and whites alike, is alarmed at the deterioration in public safety.

Violence involving blacks skyrocketed in the early 1990s. In 1992, black South Africans were reported to be "dying daily in an undeclared war apparently fueled by right-wing elements with links to the security forces."[58] Unfortunately, it was a continuation of a trend going back to the bad old days of apartheid: between 1984 and 1992, more than twelve thousand people, most of them black, perished in a vicious circle of civil strife.

To a great extent, the future of every society depends on economic factors, and South Africa is certainly no exception. It is said that a rising tide lifts all boats, but in South Africa's case, the tide must lift the vast majority of South Africans who have never had a boat while keeping the yachts of the wealthy Afrikaners from heading out to sea.

Jump-Starting a Stalled Economy South Africa's economy in 2004 was larger than any other country in Africa south of the Sahara (but smaller than Norway's). Mining is still the major industry, bringing in over 70 percent of South Africa's export revenues; but slightly more than half of the country's GNP per capita now comes from services, and nearly a quarter comes from manufacturing. Judging from GNP per capita, South Africans are definitely better off than their neighbors. But where South

Africa is concerned, all such statistics are misleading due to apartheid and its legacy of racial inequality.

In the first half-century following independence in 1911, during a period of rapid population growth, South Africa's real GNP per capita more than doubled. In the 1960s, South Africa rivaled Japan in economic vitality. The 1970s, however, saw the beginning of a long, slow economic slide induced by a combination of political problems, international sanctions, and weak world prices for gold and commodities. In the decade preceding 1993, per capita GNP actually declined. This trend continued in the 1990s, as South Africa endured the longest recession in its history. Unemployment reached epidemic proportions. For example, tens of thousands of jobs were wiped out in mining alone (over a fourth of the total). Despite the creation of 2 million jobs between 1996 and 2002, the official unemployment rate in 2004 still stood at 31 percent, and the real rate was 40–50 percent. The high jobless rate no doubt helps to explain the soaring crime rates in contemporary South Africa. Unemployment is the biggest single problem facing the country, according to opinion polls, ahead of both AIDS and crime.

Despite the downturn associated with the death throes of apartheid, South Africa's economy has great potential and has shown signs of recovery in recent years. The economy started expanding again in the mid-1990s, and inflation dropped to the lowest levels in twenty-two years. And South Africa's foreign debt relative to GNP was modest, but its public-sector debt climbed to 55 percent of GNP. The savings rate in South Africa was well below that of many emerging-market economies (for example, the Czech Republic and Thailand). If South Africa is once again to enjoy the surging growth rates of the 1960s, the government has to find a remedy for the deadly combination of big deficits and low savings rates.

Labor costs are lower in South Africa than in Mexico, South Korea, or Taiwan, all of which participate vigorously in international trade. Wages are only one side of the equation, however: in 1989, workers in South Africa produced less than half as much as their counterparts in South Korea or Taiwan and less than a quarter as much as Mexican workers.

Protectionism, another obstacle to rapid growth, is also a hangover from the past when the country's white rulers sought to insulate South Africa from outside pressures. Oligopolies went unchecked or were even encouraged during the era of apartheid. At the same time, high tariff walls were erected around a fortress economy. The result was creeping complacency on the part of industry managers and unexposed inefficiency in production processes. South African goods were often priced higher at home than in foreign markets. For example, there has long been a high tariff on imported cars, and South Africans pay 30 to 40 percent more than Americans for the same make of car. The new South Africa will now have to learn to compete in the global economy against other relatively recent entrants who nonetheless have a running head start.

If South Africa is to harness its human potential and give all its people a real chance in life, it must find a way to motivate and educate black children whose parents are, in many instances, illiterate. Under the old system of racial segregation, the curriculum of black schools was quite consciously designed to keep blacks subservient to whites by stifling ambition and discouraging initiative. One result of these invidious policies and inferior schools is that adult illiteracy for blacks was 45–50 percent, compared with 1 percent for whites. In the mid-1990s, the pass rate for blacks in school-leaving exams was still only half that for whites, and lower than in 1970. The problem will not be easy to tackle without placing an even heavier burden of deficit spending on the government.

A Democratic Africa?

At the beginning of the 1990s, there were signs that the trends toward democracy and respect for human rights in Latin America and Eastern Europe were also having an impact in sub-Saharan Africa. In Niger, Côte d'Ivoire, Benin, Gabon, Cameroon, Kenya, and Zaire, opponents of authoritarian government pressed for democratization.[59] In Benin, for example, President Mathieu Kérékou renounced Marxism in late 1989 and called for talks with the democratic opposition. In March 1990, he resigned and transferred power to a noncommunist prime minister. Meanwhile in Niger, government security forces responded to demands by professionals and government workers for better pay by shooting demonstrators. Following this outrage, President Ali Saibou fired his cabinet ministers and promised to introduce democracy. In Côte d'Ivoire, doctors and teachers went on strike against a government austerity program. President Houphouët-Boigny responded by closing the schools for the year. Angry students then clamored for multiparty elections, and the government gave in.

Toying with Democracy

The sort of ferment that led to free elections in Côte d'Ivoire became almost a commonplace in Africa as the 1990s wore on, as we noted in the previous chapter. All told, the region witnessed more than thirty elections between 1991 and 1996. Voters in no fewer than eighteen countries were set to go to the polls in 1996, and in eight more countries in 1997.

But another phenomenon was no less prominent in the early 1990s: sudden leadership changes in countries such as Ethiopia, Somalia, Liberia, and Chad threw governments into a transitional state, leaving the affected societies with no clear direction or destination. In several instances, military rulers permitted free elections and were rewarded with a popular mandate to stay in power.

These developments were only straws in the wind, and it is doubtful that they portend far-reaching changes of the kind that occurred in Eastern Europe in 1989. Obviously, authoritarian rule is deeply rooted in Africa. In one sense, a discussion of whether multiparty democracy will prevail there begs the question, As they are presently constituted, is political pluralism a viable model in these multiethnic societies? Given the instability that has become a hallmark of African politics, a sudden lurch toward democracy raises the possibility of a slide into civil strife and social chaos that could end tragically, as it did in Nigeria in the late 1960s. Otherwise put, democracy is not a panacea for Africa's ills; in some cases, it might even exacerbate existing problems.

New Game, Old Tricks

In the mid-1990s, democratic elections were not uncommon in sub-Saharan Africa. Democracies could be found in varying guises in Benin, Botswana, Burundi, Cameroon, the Central African Republic (CAR), the Congo (Republic), Côte d'Ivoire, Djibouti, Equatorial Guinea, Gabon, Guinea, Kenya, Mauritania, Mozambique, Namibia, Tanzania, Senegal, South Africa, Zambia, and Zimbabwe. But the wide spectrum of African polyarchies included only a few cases (Benin, Botswana, Malawi, Mali, Mozambique, Namibia, Senegal, and South Africa) where free elections led to a functioning multiparty system. In all the others, Africa's new democracies were in trouble. In CAR, Congo (Republic), Côte d'Ivoire, Guinea, and Sierra Leone they were at risk from coups or mutinies.

There were noteworthy changes in many countries. For example, in 1991, Zambia's venerable President Kenneth Kaunda, the country's founder and autocratic leader for twenty-seven years, lost a free election (by a large margin) and relinquished power. One journalist observed, "Frederick Chiluba's victory in Zambia's first multi-party elections in nearly 20 years stands as a new high-water mark in an extraordinary process of democratization in Africa that began in earnest in Zambia and other nations several years ago."[60] On the other hand, a junior army officer named Yahya Jammeh overthrew Gambia's nearly thirty-year-old democracy in 1994.

The initial wave of democracy in Africa was nothing like the tidal wave that hit Eastern Europe after 1989. Rather, there was a series of democratic stirrings. In tiny Cape Verde, for example, the Marxist president, Aristides Pereira, handed over power to Antonio Monteiro, a free-market liberal, after a peaceful election in February 1991. Then Mathieu Kérékou, Benin's longtime military ruler stepped down after losing an election to Nicéphore Soglo, a former World Bank governor. But elections in Côte d'Ivoire and Gabon in the same year left autocratic presidents in power. (Critics charged that the elections had been rigged.)

Pressure for political change mounted throughout the region. Leaders in Somalia, Ethiopia, Liberia, and Mali were ousted by civil war or military coups in 1990 or 1991, but in only one of the four, Mali, was the system transformed into a working democracy.

In 1992, Jerry Rawlings, who had long ruled Ghana as a military dictator, became the legitimate president by winning an election. Soldiers were also elected in Benin, Burkina Faso, Chad, Ghana, Guinea, Sudan, and Togo. If these countries are any indication, elections are no guarantee that most governments in the region will now be run by civilians. Moreover, civilian rule is no guarantee of progress toward democracy, peace, and prosperity, as Zimbabwe under the autocratic rule of Robert Mugabe clearly demonstrates. His disastrous economic mismanagement, manipulation of elections, and divide-and-rule tactics brought the country to the brink of economic and political chaos at the end of the decade.[61]

In Cote d'Ivoire, after the elected president was ousted by a military coup in 1999 the coup leader called a new election. When he lost he tried to claim victory anyway but mass protests broke out and he fled, only to be killed in Abidjan (the unofficial capital) in 2002. In Liberia, Charles Taylor was elected president in 1997, but the UN imposed sanctions in 2001 to punish Liberia for aiding the Revolutionary United Front (RUF) insurgency in Sierra Leone. (Recall that in 2003 Taylor was forced into exile.) In Sierra Leone, a coup paved the way for election in 1996 and a brief lull in the civil war. A coup in 1997, however, ousted the elected president. Emboldened by an outraged world community, Nigeria intervened militarily and restored the president to power in 1998. But RUF guerrillas launched a vicious counteroffensive killing and mutilating thousands of civilians, leading the government to sign a power-sharing agreement in July 1999. The accord was short-lived, as the RUF took some 500 UN peacekeepers hostage. The hostage crisis ended only after the rebel leader was captured in Freetown (the capital). Thereafter, the level of violence subsided under the auspices of a UN disarmament program. In early 2002 the government and RUF leaders officially declared the war at an end. Finally, with the ouster of Charles Taylor in August 2003 there was a glimmer of hope that anarchy in West Africa was going rather than coming (to recall the title of Robert Kaplan's book).

Meanwhile, the civil war in Congo claimed not thousands but millions of lives between 1998 and 2002; estimates of casualties, mostly civilians, ranged in the neighborhood of 3 million — and counting. "Some were shot or hacked to death; many more succumbed to starvation or disease as nine national armies and a shifting throng of rebel groups pillaged their country."[62] According to the World Bank and Oxfam, there was 1 doctor for every 24,319 Congolese, only 1 in 1,000 had a telephone, nearly half the population did not have access to safe water, and two-thirds were undernourished. The eastern Congo was a war zone occupied by neighboring Rwanda but controlled by no one. Unspeakable atrocities occurred day and night. Rape and murder were routine. No place was safe or off-limits, not even a hospital. On the other side of the country, in Kinshasa (the capital), the government was on autopilot, headed by a drunken and incompetent despot named Laurent Kabila. Only after Kabila was assassinated (by one of his own bodyguards) in January 2001 and Rwanda, under pressure from South Africa and the United Nations, finally withdrew its 20,000-strong army in October 2002, was there any prospect of peace in the eastern Congo.

These examples underscore the fact that anarchy continues to stalk sub-Saharan Africa, a place where this book on comparative politics in the modern world will end. Recall that we began by looking at Western Europe, a collection of wealthy and democratic states where violent crime is punished, poverty is rare, and starvation is nonexistent. The world West Europeans (and North Americans) inhabit is very different from the one West Africans or Congolese live and die in. At the very least, we are obliged as human beings to think about such things and to recognize that the absence of political order is an open invitation to unspeakable evil.

When and if real democracy does come to sub-Saharan Africa, it will most certainly bear a "made in Africa" imprint. For example, Ethiopia held multiparty elections in 1995, but Ethiopia's new president, Meles Zenawi, insisted that parties could only represent ethnic groups. In Uganda, President Yoweri Museveni allows political parties to exist but does not allow partisan elections. In other words, parties cannot sponsor candidates, but individuals are free to run for office. In Kenya, Daniel arap Moi won an American-style, first past the post multiparty election in 1992, but then curbed freedom of speech and association and denounced political parties for fostering tribalism. In 1996, no fewer than eighteen African countries scheduled national elections, and eight more were planning elections for 1997. Some thirty countries in the region had held elections of one kind or another. Only four had military dictators, but several — including Burkina Faso (Captain Blaise Campaore), Ghana (Flight-Lieutenant Jerry Rawlings), Guinea (Colonel Lansana Conté), and Niger (Colonel Mainassara)—were ruled by military figures who simply changed clothes and ran for election.

Some countries that pretend to be democratic clearly are not. Sudan, for example, has nearly thirty political parties but has not put in place a system of competitive parties and elections; changes of government have been wrought by military coups, and Sudan's authoritarian rulers have never felt constrained by party leaders or democratically elected legislatures. Nonetheless, Sudan's military rulers, like their counterparts in Gambia and Sierra Leone, scheduled elections in 1996. Brigadier Umar al-Bashir stood for an "election" of sorts but did not bother to exchange his uniform for civilian attire.

Here we end our journey around the world. We began with Western Europe, a region where democratic traditions are the strongest and ended with sub-Saharan Africa, the region where they are the weakest. On the way, we "toured" Eastern Europe, Asia, the Middle East, and Latin America. In three of these regions — all except the Middle East — democracy has made major gains in recent years. Only in the Arab Middle East, where tradition-bound cultures are reinforced by a change-resistant religion (Islam), are authoritarian political structures, including monarchies, unashamedly embraced by ruling elites and unquestioningly accepted by the people.

SUMMARY

Authoritarian rule has been common throughout sub-Saharan Africa, but not all governments of the region are equally repressive or corrupt. In Nigeria, promises of democracy by the military rulers have not been fulfilled. South Africa has been ruled by a white minority government but is now going through a critical transition to a power-sharing system in which the black majority will be included for the first time. Throughout the region, there has been a trend toward liberalization and democratization.

As the colonial era fades, the governments of sub-Saharan Africa will no longer be able to attribute policy failures manifested in unrelieved poverty, oppression, and stagnation solely to colonialism and neocolonialism. A trend toward democratization is evident throughout much of the region, but democracy is not likely to take root unless nurtured by economic development. Africa south of the Sahara remains the poorest region in the world, and the most unfortunate. Since independence, millions of Africans have endured natural disasters and corrupt, repressive governments — the worst of these (such as Zaire under Mobutu) have often abused power, stolen from the public treasury, and squandered resources on foolish projects.

KEY TERMS

trusteeship
national liberation movement
Third World
decolonization
polyarchies
provisional government
coup d'état
gerontocracy
kleptocracy
African socialism
negritude
Arusha Declaration
African National Congress (ANC)
Inkatha Freedom Party

STUDY QUESTIONS

1. What factors influenced the early economic development of African countries? To what extent do these factors remain in force today?
2. Why is one-party polyarchy more common in sub-Saharan Africa than multiparty systems like those in Europe?
3. What was apartheid? Why did it last for so long?
4. Contrast and compare the governments of Kenya and Nigeria. Which country has the worse government?
5. Who rules South Africa today? Why did the white minority government finally relinquish power?
6. What problems does the new South Africa face?
7. In what sense is Africa a "garden of Eden in decay"?
8. To what extent are the problems faced by Kenya, Nigeria, and South Africa part of a larger pattern found throughout the region?
9. How do scholars explain Africa's social, economic, and political problems? Which theory makes the most sense to you, and why?
10. Compare Kenya and Nigeria in terms of social diversity, political stability, and economic development. Which country has the better future prospects?
11. What are the major problems facing South Africa today, and what obstacles stand in the way of solving them? Is democracy the answer?

SUGGESTED READINGS

Achebe, Chinua. *The Trouble with Nigeria.* Enugu: Fourth Dimension Press, 1983.

Barnett, Michael N. *Eyewitness to a Genocide: The United Nations and Rwanda.* Ithaca, N.Y.: Cornell University Press, 2002.

Falola, Toyin. *Development Planning and Decolonization in Nigeria.* Gainsville: University Press of Florida, 1996.

Gordon, April A., and Gordon, Donald L. *Understanding Contemporary Africa.* Boulder, Colo.: Rienner, 1997.

Howe, Herbert M. *Ambiguous Order: Military Forces in African States.* Boulder, Colo.: Rienner, 2001.

Robert Guest, "Nigeria: Under New Management," (A Survey), *The Economist,* January 15, 2000. (Published as an insert and paginated separately, pp. 1–16)

Keller, Edmond J., ed. *Africa in the New International Order: Rethinking State Sovereignty and Regional Security.* Boulder, Colo.: Rienner, 1996.

Mazrui, Ali A. *The African Condition: A Political Diagnosis.* Cambridge: Cambridge University Press, 1980.

Nnoli, Okwudiba. *Ethnicity and Development in Nigeria.* Brookfield, Vt.: Ashgate, 1995.

O'Meara, Dan. *Forty Lost Years: The Apartheid State and the Politics of the National Party 1948–1994.* Athens: Ohio University Press, 1997.

Ottaway, David B. *Chained Together: Mandela, de Klerk, and the Struggle to Remake South Africa.* New York: Random House, 1993.

Potholm, Christian. *The Theory and Practice of African Politics.* Lanham, Md.: University Press, 1985.

Power, Samantha. *"A Problem from Hell": America and the Age of Genocide.* New York: Basic Books, 2002.

Publius: The Journal of Federalism 21, No. 4 (Fall 1991). [Special issue on Nigeria]

Reynolds, Andrew. *Election 1994 South Africa: The Campaigns, Results and Future.* New York: St. Martin's, 1995.

Rosenblum, Mort, and Williamson, Doug. *Squandering Eden: Africa at the Edge.* San Diego: Harcourt, 1987.

Schraeder, Peter J. *African Politics and Society: A Mosaic in Transformation.* New York: Bedford/St. Martin's, 2000.

Soyinka, Wole. *The Open Sore of a Continent: A Personal Narrative of the Nigerian Crisis.* New York: Oxford University Press, 1996.

Suberu, Rotimi T. *Federalism and Ethnic Conflict in Nigeria.* Washington, D.C.: U.S. Institute of Peace Press, 2001.

Umoren, Joseph A. *Democracy and Ethnic Diversity in Nigeria.* Lanham, Md.: University Press of America, 1996.

Van De Walle, Nicolas. *African Economies and the Politics of Permanent Crisis, 1979–1990.* New York: Cambridge University Press, 2001.

SUGGESTED WEB SITES

http://www.africa2000.com/
http://www.sas.upenn.edu/African_Studies/Home_Page/Country.html
http://nigeriaworld.com/

http://odili.net/nigeria.html
http://minotaur.marques.co.za/
http://www.southafrica.co.za/
http://www.southafrica.co.za/govt/constitution.html

NOTES

1. C. B. Wadstrom, *An Essay on Colonialization* (London: Darton & Harvey, 1794), p. 9.
2. Robert D. Kaplan, *The Coming Anarchy: Shattering the Dreams of the Post Cold War* (New York: Vintage Books, 2000.
3. See Peter J. Schraeder, *African Politics and Society: A Mosaic in Transformation* (New York: Bedford/St.Martin's, 2000), pp. 98–105.
4. Ali A. Mazrui and Michael Tidy, *Nationalism and New States in Africa* (London: Heinemann, 1984), pp. 13–15.
5. Peter Robbs, "Privatization in Africa," *Development International,* March–April 1987, pp. 27–30.
6. International Bank for Reconstruction and Development, *World Development Report, 1987* (New York: Oxford University Press, 1987), p. 171.
7. Christian Potholm, *The Theory and Practice of African Politics* (Lanham, Md.: University Press, 1985), chaps. 5 and 6.
8. C. Chikulo Bornwell, "The Impact of Elections in Zambia," *Africa Today,* vol. 35, no. 2 (1988), pp. 37–41.
9. Schraeder, *African Politics and Society,* p. 269.
10. See, for example, Peter Anyang' Nyong'o, "Africa: The Failure of One-Party Rule," *Journal of Democracy* 3, No. 1, 1992, pp. 90–96; and Samuel Decalo "The Process, Prospects, and Constraints of Democratization in Africa," African Affairs 91, 1992, pp. 7–35.
11. Pat McGowan and Thomas Johnson, "African Military *Coups d'Etat* and Underdevelopment: A Quantitative Analysis," *Journal of Modern African Studies,* vol. 22, no. 4, 1984, pp. 634–635; and "Sixty *Coups* in Thirty Years," *Journal of Modern African Studies,* vol. 24, no. 3, 1986, pp. 539–546.
12. See Joel Migdal, *Strong Societies and Weak States: State -Society Relations and State Capabilities in the Third World.* Princeton, N.J.: Princeton University Press, 1988.
13. Ted Morello, "UN's Africa Recovery Program Fails to Make Dent in Crisis," *Christian Science Monitor,* November 6, 1987, p. 14.
14. Djibril Diallo, "Overpopulation and Other Myths about Africa," *Christian Science Monitor,* April 22, 1986, p. 15.
15. Ibid.
16. Ibid.

17. Jeffrey Sachs, "Growth in Africa: It Can Be Done," *The Economist,* June 29, 1996, p. 19.
18. See Walter Rodney, How Europe Underdeveloped Africa (Washington, D.C.: Howard University Press, 1974); see also Samir Amin, *Imperialism and Unequal Development* (New York: Monthly Review Press, 1977).
19. *UN Chronicle,* vol. 22, no. 2 (1985), p. 7.
20. See Chinua Achebe, *Arrow of God* (London: Heinemann, 1958); Chinua Achebe, *Things Fall Apart* (London: Heinemann, 1958); T. M. Aluko, *The Gab Boys* (London: Fontana Books, 1969); Ola Rotimi, *The Gods Are Not to Blame* (London: Oxford University Press, 1971); and Ayi Kwei Armah, *The Beautiful Ones Are Not Yet Born* (Boston: Houghton Mifflin, 1968).
21. Talcott Parsons, The Social System (New York: Free Press, 1951); see also Talcott Parsons, "Evolutionary Universals in Society," in *Socialization Theory and Modern Society,* Talcott Parsons, ed. (New York: Free Press, 1967).
22. See, for example, Seymour Martin Lipset, "Some Social Prerequisites of Democracy, Economic Development, and Political Legitimacy," *American Political Science Review,* vol. 53, no. 3 (March 1969).
23. See William Friedland and Carl G. Rosenberg, Jr., eds., *African Socialism* (Stanford, Calif.: Stanford University Press, 1964), pp. 250–258; and Tom Mboya, *Freedom and After* (Boston: Little, Brown, 1963), pp. 164–178.
24. Kwame Nkhrumah, *Consciencism* (London: Heinemann, 1966), p. 70.
25. Wilford Curtey and Martin Kilson, eds., *Independent Africa: A Reader* (New York: Random House, 1970), pp. 179–192.
26. Clyde R. Ingle, *From Village to State in Tanzania: The Politics of Rural Development* (Ithaca, N.Y.: Cornell University Press, 1972), p. 99.
27. Julius K. Nyerere and Uhuru Na Moja: *Freedom and Unity* (New York: Oxford University Press, 1973), p. 247.
28. Ibid., p. 232.
29. Quoted in Friedland and Rosenberg, *African Socialism,* p. 251.
30. Quoted in Colin Morris, *A Humanist in Africa: Letters to Colin Morris from Kenneth Kaunda* (Nashville, Tenn.: Abingdon Press, 1966), p. 19.
31. Colin Legum, ed., *Independence and Beyond: A Collection of Speeches by Kenneth Kaunda* (London: Nelson, 1966), pp. 18–19.
32. Quoted in Morris, *Humanist in Africa,* p. 63.
33. Ali A. Mazrui, *The African Condition: A Political Diagnosis* (Cambridge, UK: Cambridge University Press, 1980), p. 92.
34. Theotonio Dos Santos, "The Structure of Dependence," *American Economic Review,* vol. 60, no. 5 (May 1970), p. 231.
35. Lois Eugenio Di Marco, ed., *International Economics and Development: Essay in Honor of Raul Prebisch* (Philadelphia: Academic Press, 1972), pp. 1–34.
36. See James A. Caporaso, "Introduction," *International Organization,* vol. 32, no. 1 (Winter 1978), p. 6; James A. Caporaso, "Dependence, Dependency, and Power in the Global System: A Structural and Behavioral Analysis," *International Organiza-*

tion, vol. 32, no. 1 (Winter 1978), pp. 13–43, 121–125; Patrick J. McGowan and Dale L. Smith, "Economic Dependency in Black Africa: An Analysis of Competing Theories," *International Organization,* vol. 32, no. 1 (Winter 1978), pp. 179–235; and R. Dan Walleri, "Trade Dependence and Underdevelopment: A Causal Chain Analysis," *Comparative Political Studies,* vol. 11, no. 1 (April 1978), pp. 94–121.

37. Dos Santos, "Structure of Dependence," p. 231.
38. Caporaso, "Dependence, Dependency, and Power," p. 28.
39. See Immanuel Wallerstein, *The Modern World System* (San Diego: Academic Press, 1974), pp. 67, 301; Immanuel Wallerstein, ed., *World Inequality: Origin of and Perspectives on the World System* (Montreal: Black Rose Books, 1975), p. 16; Celso Furtado, "Development and Stagnation in Latin America: A Structuralist Approach," *Studies in Comparative Development,* vol. 1, no. 11 (1965).
40. André Gunder Frank, *Capitalist Underdevelopment* (New York: Oxford University Press, 1976), pp. 94–95.
41. Sachs, "Growth in Africa," p. 20.
42. Ibid.
43. Peter Berger, *Pyramids of Sacrifice: Political Ethics and Social Change* (Garden City, N.Y.: Anchor/Doubleday, 1976), chaps. 5 and 6.
44. Mazrui, *The African Condition* (Cambridge, UK: Cambridge University Press, 1980), pp. 1–2.
45. Ibid., pp. 6–9.
46. "The President's Initiative to End Hunger in Africa," *USAID Highlights,* vol. 4, no. 3 (Summer 1987); and George D. Moffett III, "Africa Teeters on Famine's Edge," *Christian Science Monitor,* June 25, 1991.
47. *UN Chronicle,* vol. 24, no. 1 (February 1987), p. 47.
48. Amy Kaslow and George D. Moffett III, "UN Renewing Effort to Rescue Sliding African Economies," *Christian Science Monitor,* p. 1.
49. Julius K. Nyerere, *Africa Recovery,* vol. 2, no. 2 (June 1988), p. 9.
50. See, for example, Sheila Rule, "Refugees Tax Already Desperate Malawi," *New York Times,* July 18, 1988, p. 1A.
51. Toyin Falola and Julius Ihonvbere, *The Rise and Fall of Nigeria's Second Republic, 1979–1984* (London: Zed Press, 1985), pp. 248–256.
52. Quoted in Robert Guest, "Nigeria: Under New Management," (A Survey), *The Economist,* January 15, 2000, p. 1 [of special insert].
53. Ibid.
54. Ibid.
55. David L. Bevan, Paul Collier and Jan Willem Gunning, *Nigeria and Indonesia: The Political Economy of Poverty, Equity, and Growth* (New York: Oxford University Press, 1999).
56. Adam Chimes, "Poll in South Africa Shows a Rise in Whites' Distaste for Apartheid," *New York Times,* August 3, 1986, p. 1.
57. "Reconstructed," *The Economist,* April 6, 1996, p. 43.

58. John Battersby, "Violence Clouds S. African Hopes," *Christian Science Monitor,* March 23, 1992, p. 2.
59. See, for example, Robert M. Press, "Africans Join Protests for Multiparty Rule," *Christian Science Monitor,* April 11, 1990, p. 1.
60. Neil Henry, "Kaunda Graciously Bows to 'Verdict,'" *Washington Post,* November 3, 1991, p. A2.
61. "Zimbabwe: The Mess One Man Makes," *The Economist,* April 22, 2000, pp. 17–19; in the same issue, see also, "At Risk in Africa," pp. 11–12.
62. "Africa's Great War," *The Economist,* July 6, 2002, pp. 43–45; see also, "A Long Step Towards Peace," *The Economist,* October 12, 2002, pp. 43–44.

GLOSSARY

This glossary identifies and defines the key terms that are listed at the end of each chapter. At the end of each definition, the number of the chapter (or chapters) in which the term is identified as a key term is given in parenthesis.

***Aberatura* (opening)** the name for Brazil's movement toward democracy in the early 1980s. **(10)**

Absolute monarchy a monarchy in which an omnipotent king (or queen) exercises power arbitrarily, deals with enemies ruthlessly, taxes the population heavily, and lives in extravagant splendor; also called "absolutism." **(2)**

African National Congress the political party of former President Nelson Mandela, South Africa's popular leader; contemporary South Africa's ruling party. **(17, 14)**

African socialism a uniquely African form of socialism that draws on the central importance of the extended family in traditional African society; according to this tradition, family members are expected to work for the common good and to share benefits and burdens equally. **(14)**

Afrikaners in South Africa before the 1990s, the white minority of Dutch descent who invented the defunct apartheid system to keep the black majority powerless. **(13)**

Age of Imperialism the name given to the new wave of European colonial expansion in the second half of the nineteenth century. **(3)**

Al Aqsa mosque the holiest of all Muslim holy sites; located in the Old City in Jerusalem (12)

Alienation in Marxism, a feeling of profound discontent that inevitably arises when workers (producers) are not the owners of their own labor and when they are deprived of the fruits of that labor (products). **(5)**

Allah the Arab and Islamic word for God. **(11)**

Alliance for Progress in the early 1960s, President John Kennedy launched this program, which was aimed at fostering economic cooperation and development in Latin America. **(9)**

Andean Pact a free-trade area in South America; members include Ecuador, Colombia, Peru, Bolivia, Chile, and Venezuela. See also *Mercosur.* **(10)**

Animism the catchall name for indigenous African religious beliefs, practices, and traditions. **(13)**

Antidefection bill In India, a law passed in 1985 that disqualifies members of parliament (and state legislatures) who switch party allegiance. **(8)**

Anti-*yanquismo* a term, literally meaning "against Yankees," that refers to the widespread hostility in Latin America toward the United States and North Americans. **(9)**

Apartheid a term meaning "separateness" in Afrikaans (the language of Dutch South Africans), it was the label for an elaborate system of racial segregation and discrimination in South Africa imposed on blacks by the dominant white minority. **(13)**

Appeasement making concessions for the sake of avoiding conflict; in political science the term is most often associated with British and French acceptance of Adolf Hitler's demand for a part of Czechoslovakia known as the Sudetenland at Munich in 1938. **(5)**

Arabian peninsula a vast, arid, and thinly populated part of the Middle East containing the world's richest oil reserves, and which is almost synonymous with Saudi Arabia. **(11)**

Arab Socialist Union (ASU) in Egypt, Nasser's political party, which became the sole embodiment of his will; the opposition was outlawed, disbanded, or driven underground. **(12)**

Article 9 in the Japanese constitution, renounces the right to establish military forces. **(8)**

Arusha Declaration in 1967, Tanzania unveiled a socialist program of development known as *ujamaa,* or "familyhood," with this initiative. **(14)**

Ashkenazic European Jews, from Central and Eastern Europe; the Ashkenazim dominate politics and business in Israel. See also *Sephardic.* **(11)**

Asian tigers Hong Kong, Singapore, South Korea, and Taiwan, also called the "four little dragons"; these titles reflect the world's admiration for the economic success achieved by these countries in the past decades. **(7)**

Assimilationists in the context of modern African politics, those who favored acceptance of foreign (Western) domination. See also *Rejectionists.* **(13)**

August coup the name given to the 1991 crisis, in which Soviet leader Mikhail Gorbachev was kidnapped by his political opponents as part of an abortive attempt to seize power and turn back the clock. **(6)**

Autarky a strategy of going it alone in the world; protecting domestic industry against foreign competition, declining to participate in international trade, spurning outside economic aid and investment, and so on. **(5)**

Authoritarian regimes a form of government characterized by a concentration of political power in the hands of one or a few, arbitrary action by the ruler(s), limited and unprotected civil liberties, and often a heavy reliance on internal security forces (the police and the military) to maintain public order. **(2)**

Authoritarian rule government or rule by one (for example, a king or a dictator) or by the few (a supreme council or military junta), often in an arbitrary manner and without the protection of a bill of rights or other legal guarantees; authoritarianism is the opposite of constitutionalism or liberal democracy. **(2)**

Aztecs one of the most advanced native cultures in the Americas, they appeared in Mexico in the thirteenth century and, by dint of war and conquest, built an empire with its center at what is today Mexico City; they flourished until the arrival of the Spanish conquistadors in the sixteenth century. See also *Incas* and *Mayas.* **(9)**

Balance of payments the bottom-line measure of a given country's financial balance sheet including all trade in goods and services plus loans, remissions, and any other sources of hard currency from abroad. **(3)**

Balance of power in Europe before the twentieth century, the international system that was thought to be instrumental in preserving order and preventing the hegemony of any one state over the others. **(3)**

Balance of trade ratio of goods and services exported to goods and services imported during a specific time period, usually monthly or yearly. **(3)**

Balfour Declaration the démarche by which the British government expressed support for the "establishment in Palestine of a national home for the Jewish people." **(11)**

Bantustans meaning "homelands," areas reserved for various black ethnic groups under the apartheid system; the main purpose for creation of the *Bantustans* was to exclude nonwhites from positions of power and privilege in South Africa. **(13)**

Basic Law the "temporary" constitution adopted by the Federal Republic of Germany under the supervision of the United States after World War II. **(4)**

Behavioralism an approach to the study of politics that emphasizes scientific methodology and human behavior. **(1)**

Bharatiya Janata Party (BJP) in India, a Hindu-based nationalist party that has become the main rival of the Congress Party in recent years. **(8)**

Big-stick diplomacy the name given to the historical role of the United States in Latin America, which has often been to use military intervention as the preferred method of dealing with Latin American governments that offend the United States in some way. **(9)**

Blat a generic term for the pervasive corruption, cheating, and dishonesty that permeated everyday life in the USSR. **(5)**

Boers Dutch farmers who immigrated to what is now South Africa in the seventeenth century and became colonists; sometimes compared with pioneers and settlers on the American frontier. **(13)**

Boer War fought between the British colonial administration and the Boers (whites of Dutch descent) in South Africa in 1899–1902; the British won the war but later ceded the colony to the Boers. **(13)**

Bolsheviks the name Lenin gave to his faction (loyal followers) within the Russian Social Democratic Party; literally it means "those in the majority" (in truth, Lenin was outnumbered by Mensheviks within the party, but he disingenuously chose this label anyway for tactical political reasons). **(5)**

Bosnian Muslims the largest ethnic group in Bosnia-Hercegovina (formerly part of Yugoslavia) also inhabited by large Serbian and Croat minorities. **(6)**

Bosnian War a major ethnic conflict in the 1990s involving three indigenous groups (Serbs, Croats, and Muslims), the governments of Yugoslavia (Serbia) and Croatia, and eventually leading to NATO military intervention. **(6)**

Boxer Rebellion a xenophobic (antiforeign) uprising against Western intrusion in China in 1900, it was crushed by the joint intervention of British, French, German, American, Russian, and Japanese troops; China's humiliation at the hands of the West was complete. **(7)**

Brady Plan named after its author, Nicholas Brady, a former U.S. secretary of the treasury, it spearheaded debt relief in the Third World. **(10)**

Brezhnev Doctrine enunciated in 1968 by Soviet leader Leonid Brezhnev, it asserted that the socialist states (led by Moscow) have an obligation to aid any member of the socialist commonwealth beset by counterrevolution. **(6)**

British East India Company the royal-chartered British agency that colonized India in the eighteenth century. **(7)**

Buddhism a major Asian religion based on the ideas of the Buddha (563–483 BCE), a legendary and deified religious teacher; it originated in India and spread to China and Korea; in the sixth century, it caught fire in Japan (Zen Buddhism), where its influence can still be seen today. **(7)**

Bundesrat the upper house of the German legislature. **(4)**

Bundestag the lower house of the German legislature. **(4)**

Cabinet rule an integral part of the British constitutional system in which the leaders of the majority party in Parliament act like a board of directors (officially called "the Government") to set policy, make key decisions, and manage the bureaucracy. **(3)**

Cacique the pejorative name given to corrupt local political bosses in Hispanic Latin America. See also *Caciquismo.* **(9)**

Caciquismo a local variant of caudillismo. See also *Cacique.* **(9)**

Camp David Accords a 1979 agreement by which Israel gave the Sinai back to Egypt in return for Egypt's recognition of Israel's right to exist. **(11)**

Capitalism an economic system in which the private sector (mainly business and consumers) rather than government controls the economy and makes most of the key decisions about production, employment, savings, investment, and the like; this system is the opposite of a centrally planned economy such as existed in the Soviet Union under Stalin and Stalin's successors. **(2)**

Caribbean Basin Initiative in the 1980s, President Ronald Reagan sponsored this program designed to promote prosperity, trade, and free enterprise in the Caribbean. **(9)**

Caste system abolished by law, it is the basis for traditional Indian society, in which there were (are) four castes, or classes: Brahman (priests and scholars), Kshatriya (warriors and rulers), Vaisya (artisans, shopkeepers, farmers), and Sudra (farm laborers and menial workers); in addition, a wretched underclass of outcastes are the Panchamas, or "untouchables." **(7)**

Caudillismo in the Latin American political tradition, the phenomenon associated with the romantic (and sometimes popular) figure of the man on horseback who gains power by force and fraud. See also *Caudillo.* **(9)**

Caudillo in Latin America, the name given to a strong political boss or a military dictator, widely feared and sometimes admired for his prowess in gathering wealth and power by foul means or force. See also *Caudillismo.* **(9)**

Central America comprises seven independent entities: Belize, Costa Rica, El Salvador, Guatemala, Honduras, Nicaragua, and Panama; Mexico, though often considered part of Central America, is historically and geographically apart from it. See also *Latin America* and *South America.* **(9)**

Central Committee in the USSR, the Communist Party's "legislative" body — a rubber stamp for the Politburo. In China, an organ of the Communist Party consisting of roughly 350 members (only 60 percent of whom can vote), which is elected by the National Party Congress and, in turn, elects the Politburo. **(8)**

Central planning the basis for a Soviet-type command economy in which fundamental economic decisions are made by a state planning agency (called Gosplan in the Soviet Union) rather than by individuals free to act as rational consumers, producers, and investors. **(6)**

Chancellor the head of government in Germany; the same as the prime minister in Great Britain and other parliamentary democracies. **(4)**

Christianity a monotheistic religion with origins in Judaism but predicated on belief in Jesus Christ as the Son of God who came to save humankind from sin; the principal source of dogma in Christianity is the Bible (both the Old and New Testaments). **(11)**

Civil disobedience in India, a strategy of nationwide passive resistance (*satyagraha*) to British rule led by Mahatma Gandhi, using the National Congress as the vehicle, after World War I. **(8)**

Cohabitation in France, a government based on a divided dual executive (a president and prime minister who belong to opposing parties). **(4)**

Cold War the name given to the long period of ideological and military rivalry between the United States and the Soviet Union after World War II; the Cold War ended in 1991 with the collapse of Soviet communism. **(2)**

Collective ministerial responsibility in the British system, a principle dictating that government ministers (who compose the executive, or cabinet) are expected to support all policies, actions, and decisions of the government in public, although they may (and no doubt do) debate issues and express dissenting opinions among themselves. **(4)**

Collectivization in the Soviet Union under Stalin, seizing the land from private owners and forcing peasants into farming enterprises called *kolkhozi* (collective farms), which were controlled by the party and the state. **(5)**

Colonialism another word for Western imperialism in Latin America, Africa, and Asia, where the major powers of Europe established colonies and seized control of the local populations and resources in what amounted to a global land rush beginning in earnest in the fifteenth century. **(7)**

Comecon the framework created by the Soviet Union for facilitating (and controlling) trade among the communist states it dominated in Eastern Europe. **(6)**

Command economy an economy based on central planning and state control and thus run from the top down. See also *Market economy.* **(2)**

Common law in the Anglo-Saxon tradition, judge-made law, as opposed to laws adopted by the parliament. **(4)**

Common Market see *European Union.* **(3)**

Communism an extreme form of socialism that advocates violent revolution, most closely associated with the writings and rule of Vladimir Lenin, Joseph Stalin, and Mao Zedong, among others; also associated with the totalitarian form of government that existed in the Soviet Union (1917–1991) and its allies, and still exists in China, Cuba, and a few other countries. **(3)**

Comparative politics in political science, a method of inquiry that seeks to explain government and politics by examining multiple cases taken from several different political systems or different time periods; for example, voting behavior in France, West Germany, and the United Kingdom between 1945 and 1958 (from the end of World War II to the signing of the Rome Treaty, which launched the Common Market). **(1)**

Compradors the disparaging name given by dependency theorists to the indigenous elites in former colonies, whom they consider to be part of a class created by foreign imperialists and capitalists who needed the help of local elements. **(9)**

Concurrent List the part of the Indian constitution that spells out the powers to be shared by central governments and provincial governments. See also *State List* and *Union List.* **(8)**

Conference of Berlin the meeting in 1884 at which the European imperialist powers divided up Africa, deciding which country would have the right to colonize which parts. **(13)**

Confucianism in Imperial China, an ethical system based on the teachings of Confucius, who emphasized filial piety (obedient children) and respect for authority. **(7)**

Congress Party also known as simply the Congress, it was the dominant political party in India after independence; the party of Mahatma Gandhi and Jawaharlal Nehru. **(8)**

Congress of People's Deputies the successor to the Supreme Soviet (or legislature) in the period immediately preceding the Soviet Union's demise. **(6)**

Consensual decision making a procedure for arriving at decisions by seeking consensus; used in Japan and some other Asian countries instead of Western-style majority rule. **(8)**

Conservatism a political philosophy, often associated with Edmund Burke (1729–1797), which generally seeks to preserve traditional values and protect the old, established order. **(3)**

Constitutional democracy a republic in which the basic institutions and procedures of government, and often the rights and liberties of citizens as well, are defined in a supreme law (higher than normal statutory law) that can only be changed by an extraordinary and deliberately cumbersome process. **(2)**

Constitutional monarchy a political system in which the monarch reigns but does not rule; the king or queen is the ceremonial head of state, but an elected parliament makes the laws and chooses the prime minister. **(4)**

Co-prosperity sphere the euphemistic name Japan gave to its short-lived colonial empire in Asia before and during World War II. **(7)**

Coronels in Brazil, a pejorative name for unpopular political bosses, implying a panoply of corrupt practices. **(9)**

Corporatist model a system characterized by an alliance of government, labor, and business forged in order to shape public policy more effectively; also known as *corporatism.* **(4)**

Council of Ministers the chief decision-making body of the European Union. **(4)**

Council of Ministers (USSR) headed by the premier (same as prime minister), it was the Soviet equivalent of the "government" in a parliamentary system, although in the Soviet Union it was always subordinate to the Communist Party's Politburo. **(6)**

Coup d'état a French term meaning literally to "strike a blow against the state"; used whenever there is a sudden and illegal seizure of power by an individual or clique. **(2, 14)**

Creoles in the context of Latin America's colonial history, Spanish descendants born in the New World. See also *Peninsulares.* **(9)**

***Cruzado* plan** part of the Brazilian government's effort to deal with the nation's economic problems in 1986, it created a new unit of currency, the cruzado; it also froze wages and prices and abolished indexation (pay hikes pegged to inflation). See also *Real plan.* **(10)**

Current account deficit equal to the amount of hard currency (dollars, for example) a government has to borrow in order to cover the gap between the value of exports and the value of imports in a given time period. **(10)**

Custom and convention in the British legal tradition, long-standing practices not based on statutory law (legislation) or common law (judicial rulings). **(4)**

Daimyo in feudal Japan, powerful warlords. **(13)**

Dalits another term for "untouchables," or outcastes; there are an estimated 160 million Dalits in India. See *Untouchables.* **(7)**

Dayton Peace Accord the UN-brokered agreement that ended the war in Bosnia in November 1995. **(6)**

Debt crisis in Latin America and other developing regions many countries fell deeply into debt to foreign creditors in the 1980s, causing economic upheaval and financial upheaval in many Third World countries. **(10)**

Decolonization the often disorderly and tumultuous dismantling of Europe's colonial empires after World War II. **(14)**

Deductive approach the use of logic and abstract reasoning to arrive at the truth. See also *Inductive approach.* **(1)**

Democratic regime a form of government in which power and wealth are widely distributed (and, in the modern welfare state, redistributed). **(2)**

Democratic centralism a key Leninist principle governing the organization and operation of the Communist Party; in theory, everything would be discussed before anything would be decided, but when an order was issued or a decision made, all party members were expected to obey without hesitation and to ask no questions. **(5)**

Democratic Opposition of Serbia (DOS) a coalition of eighteen parties that swept the elections in Yugoslavia following the overthrow of the dictator Slobodan Milovsevic and gave Serbia a popularly elected president, parliament, and prime minister for the first time since World War II. **(6)**

Demokratizatsiia in the Soviet Union before 1991, the aspect of Mikhail Gorbachev's reforms aimed at bringing out a measure of political pluralism. **(6)**

De-Stalinization in the Soviet Union after 1956, the easing of Stalin-type repression. **(5)**

Détente a French term meaning "relaxation of tension"; the term used to describe a warming of relations between the United States and the Soviet Union in the early 1970s. **(5)**

Developing countries Term used loosely to denote any country that has not achieved levels of economic prosperity and political stability found in North America, Western Europe, Australia, New Zealand, and parts of Asia (particularly Japan, South Korea, Taiwan, and Singapore); developing countries (also known collectively as the Third World during the Cold War) are found mainly in Africa, Asia, the Middle East, and Latin America and are characterized by high levels of unemployment, widespread poverty and malnutrition, highly restricted access to education and medical care, official corruption, and social inequality. **(2)**

Development in political science, the name given to the process by which societies move from a traditional mode of existence to a modern mode characterized by rising literacy rates, falling fertility and infant mortality rates, a growing number of women in the workforce, and so on. **(2)**

Diaspora literally meaning "the dispersion," it was the result of the flight of the Jews from Palestine after a failed rebellion against Roman rule in CE 70; the scattering of the Jewish people nearly two millennia ago became a major factor in Middle Eastern and world politics after World War II. **(11)**

Dictatorship rule by a dominant figure also known as a tyrant or strongman; tyranny. **(2)**

Dictatorship of the proletariat in Marxist theory, a temporary phase after the revolutionary takeover of power, designed to forestall counterrevolution, during which a dictatorship by the victorious workers is necessary. **(5)**

Diet the Japanese parliament. **(8)**

Dirty war the name given to the anti-insurgency campaign carried out in Argentina after 1976; for two years, the military regime cracked down on subversion — people were arbitrarily arrested, imprisoned, tortured, and murdered by the security forces, who were given carte blanche to do whatever was necessary to crush the insurgency. **(10)**

Divided (dual) executive in France, characterized by a president and a prime minister who belong to opposing parties, have different agendas and look to different constituencies. **(4)**

Divine right a doctrine claiming that God has ordained a certain ruler or ruling family to rule; often used by absolute monarchs, notably in Europe before the twentieth century, to justify the exercise of state power. **(2)**

Dual economy Japan's two-tier economy in which half is highly efficient and competitive in global markets and the other half is not. **(8)**

Dual rule in Communist China, a principle adopted in 1956 under which state organs are responsible both to the next higher level of state administration and to the party organization on the same level. **(8)**

Dynastic authoritarianism characterized by the concentration of power in a single potentate (monarch) who claims to rule by divine authority. **(7)**

Dynastic rule another term for hereditary monarchy; a system of government in which the rulers are chosen from the royal family; when the king or queen dies, power passes to the eldest male heir. **(2)**

Eastern Europe the predominantly Slavic-speaking region of Europe, most of which was largely untouched by the Renaissance and Reformation in the West. See also *Slavic Europe.* **(5)**

École Nationale d'Administration **(ENA)** elite French graduate school for professionals in the civil service. **(4)**

Emerging democracies Countries formerly in the grip of authoritarian or totalitarian regimes now undergoing a democratic transition, often applied to East European states. **(2)**

Emerging markets term for those economies in Eastern Europe and Asia that are making the transition from state planning or extensive protectionism to market principles. **(6)**

Empire building a tendency present in the history of most great societies characterized by territorial expansion, political domination, economic exploitation, and the imposition of an alien culture, religion, and language on subjugated peoples. **(7)**

Encomienda **system** when the Spanish needed laborers to build their cathedrals and cities in Latin America, and to work on their plantations, they conscripted the Indians; this system, which organized the Indians by village, was designed to compel them to do what was supposedly in their own best interest: to work for (meager) pay while learning the Christian religion. See also *Encomiendero.* **(9)**

Encomiendero in Latin America under Spanish rule, one who supervised the work, religious instruction, and welfare of Indians; granted virtually unlimited authority over his wards, this colonial boss also collected all fruits of the land and labor he managed. See also *Encomienda system.* **(9)**

Enlightenment a philosophic movement of the eighteenth century, characterized by a lively questioning of authority, prolific theorizing in the realm of politics, emphasis on critical thought and inquiry, skepticism (expressed as a demand for empirical evidence), and the scientific method. **(3)**

Estado Novo meaning "new state" in Portuguese, this term comes from the presidency of Getúlio Vargas of Brazil; Vargas, elected president in 1933, ruled as a relatively benevolent dictator until 1945, banning political parties, censoring the press, and creating a corporatist state, in which the interests of business, labor, landowners, and bureaucrats were fused. **(9)**

Ethical hedonism the doctrine that sees ordinary human desires as natural and good, not things to be denied or ashamed of. **(3)**

Ethnic cleansing the genocidal policy of removing an unwelcome ethnic group from territory desired by another ethnic group through whatever means possible, including mass murder, torture, terror, and forcible expulsion; there is much evidence that Bosnian Serbs, in particular, engaged in ethnic cleansing against Bosnian Muslims during the war in Bosnia, but there were atrocities committed on all sides (including Croatians). **(6)**

Ethnocentrism placing a very high value on ethnicity or ethnic origins often to the exclusion of neighboring ethnic groups; the prejudices associated with this tendency have often contributed to confrontation and conflict in various regions of the world, most notably in Eastern Europe and sub-Saharan Africa in recent decades. **(1)**

Euro the single currency now in use in most of the European Union. **(4)**

Euro zone the twelve members of the European Union who have agreed to use the euro as legal tender (currency), including France, Germany, Italy, Spain, the Netherlands, Belgium, Austria, Luxembourg, Ireland, Portugal, Finland, and Greece. **(4)**

European Monetary Union (EMU) the plan to create a common European currency within the EU, adopted at the Maastricht summit meeting in 1991. **(4)**

European Parliament the popularly elected legislature of the European Union; this body shares the power of the purse with the Council of Ministers and has the right to reject the budget. **(4)**

European Union (EU) the successor to the original European Economic Community (EEC) created by the Rome Treaty in 1958, popularly known as the Common Market; from six members at its inception the EU has expanded to fifteen (France, Germany, Italy, Belgium, the Netherlands, and Luxembourg were later joined by Denmark, Greece, Ireland, Portugal, Spain, the United Kingdom, Austria, Finland, and Sweden). **(3, 4, 6)**

Factions formed by politicians from the same political party or coalition who win seats in parliament. **(8)**

Fascism an extreme right-wing ideology that first appeared in Italy but soon caught on in Germany (the Nazi movement) and other European countries between World War I and World War II; any extremely nationalistic ideology that glorifies war, seeks to crush its domestic opponents, uses hate campaigns to stir up the masses, and regards terrorism as an appropriate means to its totalitarian ends. **(3)**

February Revolution the first of two revolutionary uprisings in Russia in 1917; often seen as a dress rehearsal for the October Revolution, which toppled the monarchy of Czar Nicholas II. **(5)**

Federal Parliament in India, the national legislature, or parliament. **(8)**

Fertile Crescent the geographical area that includes Iraq, Syria, Lebanon, Israel, Jordan, and Egypt. **(11)**

Fertility rate the average number of live births per year for all women of childbearing age. **(1)**

Feudal system during medieval times in Europe, a system of land ownership in which powerful barons or feudal lords owned vast tracts of land worked by serfs (also known as vassals, who were poor indentured servants, meaning that they were legally bound to the lord by vows of homage and fealty in return for protection). **(3)**

Fifth Republic in France, the name given to the constitutional democracy created in 1958 under the leadership of General Charles de Gaulle. **(4)**

First past the post principle basis of the electoral system long used in Great Britain (and the United States) in which each party in a single-member district fields one candidate, and whoever gets the most votes (a plurality) wins; this method of election leads to a two-party system, in contrast with the proportional method used in many countries. **(4)**

First vote in Germany, the part of each national election in which candidates for the Bundestag are chosen by plurality vote in single-member districts. **(4)**

Fiscal policy Pertaining to the public budget, including revenues (taxation), spending, and borrowing. **(2)**

Four Modernizations the name given by China's supreme leader Deng Xiaoping to his market-oriented economic reform program in the late 1970s. **(8)**

Fraktionen factions organized along party lines in the German parliament (Bundestag). **(5)**

Free-enterprise system also called "private enterprise"; another name for profit-seeking business and commerce carried out within the private sector. **(2)**

French Revolution social and political upheaval in France in 1789, which brought down the monarchy of King Louis XVI under the slogan "liberty, equality, and fraternity"; often seen as a turning point in French and European history, when absolute monarchy began to give way to constitutional democracy. **(3)**

Fusion of powers in British-style democracy, the practice of creating the executive (prime minister and cabinet) from the legislature (Parliament), thus melding the legislative and executive powers rather than separating them. **(2, 4)**

Gang of Four the name given to four zealots in Mao Zedong's inner circle — including Mao's wife, Jiang Qing, and the PLA leader, Lin Biao — who masterminded the Great Proletarian Cultural Revolution. **(8)**

Gaullist parties center-right political parties in France named after former President Charles de Gaulle who stressed French national independence and asserted France's right to a strong leadership role in Europe — one at least equal to that of Germany. **(4)**

General secretary the head of the Chinese Secretariat and, as such, the highest-ranking party official (but not necessarily the supreme leader). **(8)**

Gerontocracy rule by the aged (or, to be politically correct, senior citizens). **(14)**

Glasnost a Russian word meaning "openness" or "transparency"; the label former Soviet leader Mikhail Gorbachev gave to his policy of removing many long-standing taboos in the realm of journalism, scholarship, culture, and the arts between 1985 and 1991. **(6)**

Globalization the process by which values, attitudes, and preferences associated with the most technologically advanced democracies are being spread via mass communications (including satellite telecommunications and the Internet) around the globe. **(1)**

Good life in normative political theory, a concept denoting the elements of a properly ordered life or the nature of true happiness (for example, having access to security, prosperity, and fulfilling work; enjoying liberty, equality, and justice; and being free from poverty, ignorance, and oppression). **(1)**

Good Neighbor Policy in the history of U.S.–Latin American relations, the opposite of big-stick diplomacy; a policy of using the carrot (diplomacy and economic aid) rather than the stick (military might) in international affairs within what is often called the Western Hemisphere. **(9)**

Gosplan the name of the organization that developed economic blueprints (called five-year plans) in the Soviet Union. **(6)**

Great Leap Forward a mass campaign launched in 1958 by Chairman Mao Zedong aimed at transforming China into a model communist society. **(8)**

Great Proletarian Cultural Revolution a mass campaign launched in 1966 by Chairman Mao Zedong to rekindle the spirit of revolution in China, which he thought was running out of steam; Mao urged the youth (especially students) to go on a rampage to "rev up" the revolution, and they did. **(8)**

Great Trek in the 1830s, after the British had acquired the colony of South Africa from the Netherlands in the early part of the nineteenth century, thousands of Dutch colonial farmers (Boers), dismayed at British policies, set out in wagon trains in search of new frontiers, much as the American pioneers did in North America later in the century. **(13)**

Group of 77 a loose-knit organization of developing countries, formed in 1964, that seeks to promote the common interests of former colonies (the South) against the Western powers (the North); membership has grown from the original 77 to 120. **(13)**

Guerrilla administration Communist China's approach to administration, which is a legacy of the long civil war, when necessity required that the functions of party, state, and army be fused into an efficient instrument of mass mobilization **(8)**

Gush Emunim in Israel, an ultraright group (translated, the name means "bloc of the faithful") that set up a number of settlements in the West Bank in 1976 and 1977, when Menachem Begin was prime minister, without official approval. **(12)**

Heir apparent a highly placed individual who is expected to succeed the one who is in power when she or he dies or steps down. **(2)**

Hinduism the religion of India's great majority and the moral foundation of Indian society. **(7)**

Hiroshima and Nagasaki two Japanese cities best known in history for being the targets of U.S. atomic bombs at the end of World War II. **(7)**

House of Commons the popularly elected lower house of the British Parliament, which is the primary lawmaking body. **(2, 4)**

House of Lords the upper house of the British Parliament; the members are mainly hereditary peers (bearing aristocratic titles) or distinguished citizens appointed by the monarch (known as life peers). **(2, 4)**

Hundred Flowers movement in China, the 1957 invitation by Chairman Mao Zedong, then the supreme leader, to professionals and intellectuals to criticize the political system; it caused a furor. **(8)**

Ideology a political belief system; in the context of the old Soviet Union or of China at the present time, it is the official set of political beliefs that everyone is expected to embrace. **(5)**

Imam for Shiite Muslims, one of the twelve descendants of Muhammad. **(11)**

Imperialist powers such European countries as Great Britain, France, Spain, and the Netherlands, which amassed far-flung territories known as colonies over hundreds of years prior to the twentieth century; these colonial empires disintegrated after World War II (1939–1945). **(1)**

Incas a lost civilization in South America once centered in what is now southern Peru near the city of Cuzco; one of the most advanced native cultures in the Americas. See also *Aztecs* and *Mayas.* **(9)**

Indian National Congress founded in about 1885, when Indian nationalists began to hold annual conferences called by the same name; these meetings were the seed from which the Indian independence movement sprang. **(8)**

Indicative planning in Yugoslavia (and France for a time after World War II), the practice of setting overall targets for the economy but treating them as guidelines rather than as obligatory goals (in contrast to rigid, Soviet-type central planning). **(5)**

Inductive approach the use of observation and the reliance on empirical evidence to arrive at the truth. See also *Deductive approach.* **(1)**

Industrial Revolution the rapid development of a robust factory system in England, Western Europe, and North America in the eighteenth and nineteenth centuries, along with the rise of a commercial middle class, a downtrodden working class, and a new awareness of the relationship between science-based technology and business. **(3)**

Infant industries new industries often incapable of competing with older established foreign firms and, arguably, in need of at least temporary governmental protection in the form of tariffs and other barriers to imports. **(3)**

Infant mortality rate the number of infant deaths relative to the number of live births in a given year. **(1)**

Institutional Revolutionary Party (PRI) in Mexico, the party that dominated the political scene since its inception in 1946. **(9)**

Inkatha Freedom Party in South Africa, a political party and popular movement led by Zulu chief Mangosuthu Buthelezi. **(14)**

Intifada in the Middle East, the name given to the Palestinian uprising against Israeli rule in Gaza and the West Bank in 1987 and 2000. **(12)**

Iron rice bowl in Communist China, name given to the state's guarantee of employment and basic social benefits to all. **(8)**

Islam one of the world's major monotheistic creeds, it is the basis for not only religion but also culture and law in the Arab Middle East; Islam has a mass following in South and Southeast Asia, as well. **(11)**

Islamic fundamentalism characterized by a fanatical allegiance to a particularly militant brand of Islam and widely associated, rightly or wrongly, with political terrorism. **(12)**

Islamism an extremist political ideology associated with hatred for Western values, anti-Zionism (jihad against Israel and Israel's supporters), and anti-Americanism; Islamists seek to reestablish "pure" Islamic society under *sharia* (religious) law and they are willing to use violent means, including terrorist acts, to achieve this goal. Islamism as an ideology differs radically from Islam as a religion although the concept of jihad and opposition to secularism, among other things, link the two. **(11)**

Jacobins in the French Revolution, a radical party led by Maximilian Robespierre, who set out to create a "republic of virtue" and ended up establishing a tryanny run by ideological zealots with a vision of a utopian society. **(3)**

Jainism one of several important religions indigenous to India. **(7)**

Janata Party in India, a loose-knit coalition of opposition parties forged by Morarji Desai to defeat Indira Gandhi in 1977; the Janata Party won that election, but it lacked either consensus or a coherent program and fell apart two years later. **(8)**

Japanese economic miracle refers to Japan's unprecedented economic growth in the post–World War II era prior to the 1990s. **(8)**

Jesuits a Roman Catholic religious order founded in 1534 that played a leading role in the colonial phase of the Spanish inquisition; they were expelled from Spain and the colonies in 1767 by Charles III at the beginning of what turned into a long struggle between church and state in Latin America. **(9)**

Jesus Christ a historical figure who proclaimed himself to be the Son of God, was crucified by the

Romans for heresy, and is now worshipped by Christians as their Lord and Savior. **(11)**

Jihad an Arab word that means "holy war"; a key concept in the Islamic faith, especially for Shiites. **(11, 12)**

Judaism the Jewish faith, which traces its origins to Abraham, his son Isaac, and Isaac's son Jacob; the religion of the Hebrews based on the teachings found in the Torah (the first five books of the Old Testament) and in the Talmud (rabbinical commentaries on religious and civil law). **(11)**

Junta originally a ruling group of army generals who monopolize power in Latin America, but now the term is also used in other contexts. **(2)**

Justice a political condition in which society's members are rewarded in proportion to their individual merit; incompatible with popular rule, according to Aristotle. **(2)**

Kaffir Wars in late eighteenth century, as Dutch settlers (Boers) moved northward along the Indian Ocean coast, Africans were moving south to escape population pressure, tribal wars, and British slave raids; the resulting encounters, often taking the form of violent clashes, lasted over a century, by which time the Boers had subdued the Africans, with great loss of life on both sides. **(13)**

Keiretsu cartel-like arrangements in Japan linking manufacturers, wholesalers, and retailers; these structures make it difficult for foreign companies to compete with Japanese producers. **(8)**

Keynesian economic theory named after its creator, British economist John Maynard Keynes, this theory describes the natural business cycle in market economies as an alternation between boom and bust periods, and it prescribes governmental policies designed to keep the economy on an even keel; Keynes believed that economies left unregulated by monetary policy would experience inflation in boom periods and recession in bust periods. **(4)**

Kleptocracy a government characterized by extreme corruption on the part of the ruler(s); a system in which the few use the government to exploit the many. **(14)**

KGB *Komityet Gosudarstvennyi Bezopostnostyi,* or Committee for State Security; the euphemistic name for the old Soviet secret police. **(5)**

Knesset the Israeli parliament. **(12)**

Koenkai personal support groups of prominent politicians in Japan, which are sources of money and influence required by faction leaders in parliament to "feed" (give rewards to) loyal faction members. **(8)**

Koran in the Islamic faith, the principal source of doctrinal authority (dogma); it covers politics, law, and social behavior and even sets forth procedures for divorce, loans, and wills. **(11)**

Kosovo a province of Yugoslavia (Serbia) inhabited mainly by ethnic Albanians, where a violent conflict occurred in the late 1990s after the Serbian (Yugoslavan) Army intervened to crush a secession movement led by the Kosovo Liberation Army (KLA). **(6)**

Kosovo Liberation Army (KLA) the name of the guerrilla organization that fought for independence against Serbia (Yugoslavia) in the late 1990s. **(6)**

Kulaki in Russia, rich peasants whose property was seized by Stalin during the drive to collectivize Soviet agriculture in the early 1930s. **(5)**

Kuomintang in twentieth-century, pre-Communist China, the Nationalist Party founded by Sun Yat-sen and propelled to power before World War I by Chiang Kai-shek, who became the bitter rival of the communist leader, Mao Zedong. **(7)**

Labour Party in Israel, a left-of-center party long committed to a negotiated peace with Israel's neighbors and a peaceful settlement of the nettlesome Palestinian question. **(12)**

Ladino in Latin America, anyone who has been latinized; the word means different things in different places (in Guatemala, it is synonymous with mestizo, a person of mixed blood; elsewhere in Central America, it refers to an Indian who has adopted European ways). **(9)**

Laissez-faire a French term meaning "to let alone" or "hands off"; it usually refers to a policy of noninterference by the state in economic matters, allowing business and industry to make decisions about production, investment, hiring and firing, and so on, based on the profit motive. **(2)**

Länder the main territorial administrative subdivisions in the Federal Republic of Germany; equivalent to states in the United States. **(4)**

Latin America a global region that encompasses Mexico, Central America, the Caribbean, and South America and includes thirty-four sovereign states ranging in size from Brazil, which is larger than the contiguous United States, to the tiny Caribbean island-states such as Barbados. See also *Central America* and *South America.* **(9)**

Law of capitalist accumulation in Marxist theory, the inexorable process of monopolization; competition squeezes out little producers and creates opportunities for big ones to get bigger (leading to "monopoly capitalism"). **(5)**

Law of pauperization a Marxist contention that the workings of capitalism dictate that the rich will get richer and the poor will get poorer (become paupers) over time. **(5)**

Law of Return provides that any Jew has the right to immigrate to Israel and become an Israeli citizen at any time. **(12)**

Les grands corps the basic components of the French civil service. **(4)**

Les grandes écoles in France, the prestigious public-policy and engineering schools. **(4)**

Less developed countries (LDCs) mostly found in Africa, Asia, and Latin America, they are also called "underdeveloped" or "developing countries"; the countries falling into this category are characterized by mass poverty, illiteracy, and unemployment as well as high birthrates and high infant mortality rates. **(2)**

Liberal Democratic Party (LDP) in Japan, the leading political party, which occupies the center-right on the political spectrum. **(8)**

Liberalism a philosophy with origins in the late eighteenth and nineteenth centuries that represented a middle way between the extreme egalitarianism of the Jacobins and the inherited wealth, power, and privilege of the old aristocratic order. **(3)**

Liberman reforms an ill-fated attempt in the 1960s to introduce some market-type mechanisms into the Soviet economy (for example, a more rational system of cost calculation and pricing, as well as interest charges on loans and use of profit as a measure of performance); named after Soviet economist Evsei Liberman, who wrote scholarly articles advocating such changes. **(6)**

Likud party in Israel, a right-wing coalition party that favors a policy of swift retribution against terrorists and, despite serious (and sometimes fruitful) efforts by Likud leaders to negotiate peace agreements with the Arabs, has not discouraged Jews from building settlements in the Occupied Territories. **(12)**

Localismo in Latin America, a strong identity with, or attachment to, a particular geographic area; the name for the traditional fragmentation found in many Latin American societies where powerful local dictators long held sway. **(9)**

Lok Sabha in India, the lower house of the Federal Parliament; the House of the People. **(8)**

Long March in China, to escape repeated Nationalist (see *Kuomingtang*) attacks, the communists led by Mao Zedong embarked on this arduous march during 1934 and 1935, trekking from Jiangxi Province in the south to Shaanxi Province in the north, where they set up headquarters at Yenan. **(7)**

Maghreb the part of the Middle East located in North Africa — including the countries of Morocco, Algeria, Tunisia, Libya, Sudan, and Egypt. **(11)**

Maoism the ideas associated with the Chinese leader Mao Zedong; especially, the notions that human will can overcome all material obstacles and that leadership is more important than economics as the driving force in society. **(8)**

Mao Zedong thought Mao Zedong's ideas about revolution, which were put in little red books for everyone to study and carry around for inspiration. **(8)**

Market economy also known as a "mixed economy"; stresses free enterprise and minimal state interference in commerce, finance, industry, and agriculture. See also *Command economy.* **(2)**

Marshall Plan officially the European Recovery Program, it was initiated by the United States after World War II to help America's allies in Europe rebuild their war-shattered economies. **(4, 5)**

Marxism-Leninism the hybrid ideology embraced by Soviet-style communists and based on the ideas of Karl Marx and Vladimir Lenin (who borrowed heavily from Marx but gave Marxism a more violence-prone, action-oriented spin than Marx intended). **(2, 5)**

Mass mobilization inducing the population to do whatever the ruler(s) demand by use of propaganda and police terror. **(2)**

Maurya Empire established by Chandragupta in northern India and expanded by his successor, Asoka (273–232 BCE), who unified all of India. **(7)**

Mayas a lost civilization in Central America on the Yucatán peninsula; one of the most advanced native cultures in the Americas. See also *Aztecs* and *Incas.* **(9)**

Meiji Restoration in Japan, samurai from several southern clans forced the Tokugawa shogun to abdicate and restored the emperor, Meiji, to power in 1868, sparking a modernization drive that brought

Japan to a position of preeminence in Asia by the end of the nineteenth century. **(7)**

Member of Parliament (MP) in the British system, the official name given to an elected lawmaker in the House of Commons. **(4)**

Mensheviks the label Lenin gave to the faction within the Russian Social Democratic Party that opposed his revolutionary ideas; literally it means "those in the minority" (although, in reality, the *mensheviki* constituted a majority). **(5)**

Mercantilism a system of political economy that developed in Europe following the decay of feudalism; characterized by policies aimed at securing a favorable balance of trade, developing a merchant marine, opening up foreign markets, and establishing foreign trade monopolies while aggressively promoting the growth of a new manufacturing sector. **(3)**

Mercosur a free-trade area in South America; members include Argentina, Brazil, Paraguay, and Uruguay. See also *Andean Pact.* **(10)**

Mestizo in Latin America, the name given to people of mixed (Spanish and Indian) blood. See also *Mulatto* and *Zambo.* **(9)**

Middle East a region spanning Northern Africa and Southwest Asia that encompasses all the Arabic-speaking countries from Morocco to Iran; the only non-Arab nations in the region are Turkey, Iran, and Israel (Palestinian Arabs make up roughly 18 percent of Israel's population, however). **(11)**

Ministry of International Trade and Industry (MITI) in Japan, the ministry charged with stimulating export-oriented industrial development and promoting Japanese products abroad. **(8)**

Mission Christianity in colonial Africa, missionaries proselytized among the Africans, winning some converts in the process but failing to relate Christianity to African culture; to most converts, mission Christians, as role models, were often indistinguishable from other Europeans whose lifestyle was identical. **(13)**

Mobilization systems political systems characterized by such a high degree of power concentration that the leadership can bend the whole society to its will; totalitarian states such as Hitler's Germany, Stalin's Russia, or Mao's China are among the most spectacular examples. **(2)**

Modernization the process of becoming modern or internalizing new ideas, discoveries, and technologies. **(2)**

Moguls the Muslim rulers of India; the greatest of the Moghul sultans (kings) ruled over a vast empire in India during the sixteenth and seventeenth centuries. **(7)**

Monarchy rule by a benevolent dictator; the direct opposite of tyranny, monarchy was Aristotle's choice for the best form of government possible, although he recognized that it was rare in the real world. **(2)**

Monetary policy Pertaining to the money or currency, including interest and exchange rates. **(2)**

Monroe Doctrine enunciated by President James Monroe in 1821, it declared the Western Hemisphere off limits to the great powers of Europe. **(9)**

Muhammad the Prophet in the Islamic (or Moslem) religion; the founder of Islam. **(11)**

Mulatto in Latin America, a person of mixed Spanish and African blood. See also *Mestizo* and *Zambo.* **(9)**

Mullah Islamic religious leader. **(11)**

Muslim Brotherhood in the Middle East, a militant Sunni secret society that seeks to establish a single universal Islamic state. **(11)**

National Assembly in France, the name given to the legislature, or the parliament. **(4)**

National Action Party (PAN) in Mexico, a center-right party whose candidate, Vincente Fox, won the presidential election in 2000; now the major rival of the long-ruling Institutional Revolutionary Party (PRI). **(10)**

National Democratic Alliance in India, a broad coalition of political parties led by the Bharatiya Janata Party (BJP), which won the national elections in 1999. **(8)**

National Democratic Party the ruling party in Egypt under Mubarak. **(12)**

National Front in France, an extreme right-wing political party headed by Jean Le Pen; opposes liberal immigration policies. **(4)**

National Front (NF) in India, an electoral coalition of political parties, which opposed the Congress (I) in the late 1980s and managed to form a short-lived government. **(8)**

National liberation movements the popular name for independence movements after World War II, especially in Africa, Asia, and Latin America. **(14)**

National Party founded in 1914, it quickly became the main vehicle of self-assertion for Afrikaaners in South Africa. **(13)**

National Party Congress in theory, the highest-level policy-making body in Communist China, it normally convenes every five years to elect the Central Committee. **(8)**

National People's Congress (NPC) the legislature in Communist China (not to be confused with the National Party Congress). **(8)**

National Revolutionary Party (PNR) in Mexico, a party founded by former President Plutarco Elías Calles in the late 1920s, which was instrumental in institutionalizing civilian rule and demilitarizing the political system; the precursor to the ruling Institutional Revolutionary Party (PRI). **(9)**

National Socialism (Nazism) the totalitarian political ideology and system created by Adolf Hitler and his followers in Germany in the 1930s, characterized by racism, militarism, and the ruthless use of police terror — along with a vicious hate campaign directed against the Jewish people — to achieve its goals. **(3)**

Near East a geographic area that includes Iraq, Israel, Jordan, Lebanon, Yemen, the Persian Gulf ministates, Saudi Arabia, and Syria. **(11)**

Negritude a term coined by Léopold Senghor, the former president of Senegal, who used it to encompass the cultural values of blacks everywhere; it was Senghor's way of expanding the idea of an African personality to include all actions and principles necessary to enhance the cultural development of people who have been deprived of self-esteem and identity by slavery, subjugation, and colonialism. **(14)**

Neocolonialism in Asia and Africa, the lingering effects (dependency, poverty, underdevelopment) of prolonged Western economic and political domination. In general, the term refers to the economic domination and alleged exploitation of former colonies by industrially developed nations such as the United States, France, and Great Britain. **(7, 14)**

Neo-Stalinism in reference to Leonid Brezhnev's tenure in Russia, a period characterized by repressive policies reminiscent of Joseph Stalin. **(5)**

New Congress Party (Congress I) in India, the successor to the Congress Party, so named by its onetime leader, Indira Gandhi (the I in Congress I stood for "Indira"), who twice served as prime minister (1966–1977 and 1980–1984). **(8)**

New Democratic Party the new name given to Mubarak's National Democratic Party before the National Assembly elections in 1987. **(11)**

New Economic Policy (NEP) In the early 1920s, Lenin's plan to allow a temporary letup in the campaign to take over all economic enterprises and to collectivize all agriculture in the Soviet Union. **(5)**

New Frontier Party (NFP) called *Shinshinto* in Japanese, this is a short-lived splinter party that was formed as a new opposition group following a serious rupture in the Liberal Democratic Party (LDP) in 1993. **(8)**

New legality China's somewhat greater emphasis on the role of law in Chinese society after 1978. **(8)**

New Labour the label given to Tony Blair's market-friendly economic policies aimed at stimulating faster growth by encouraging business optimism and consumer confidence; Blair patterned his formula for job creation and budget balancing after former President Bill Clinton. **(4)**

Nomadic moving about constantly in search of food, pasture, and so forth; the opposite of a settled or sedentary lifestyle. **(11)**

Nonaligned movement a loose-knit association of Third World countries founded in the mid-1950s by the leaders of India (Nehru), Yugoslavia (Tito), and Egypt (Nasser), with the aim of protecting the interests of the less-developed countries (LDCs) and resisting pressure from the two superpowers to choose sides in the Cold War. **(11)**

Nontariff barriers (NTBs) regulations, restrictions, and standards applied to imports that make it difficult for foreign producers to compete in domestic markets. **(8)**

Normative political theory an approach to the study of politics that emphasizes logic and ethics. **(1)**

North Africa a part of the Middle East located on the African continent but inhabited by Arab-speaking peoples and separated from the rest of Africa by the Sahara Desert. **(11)**

North American Free Trade Agreement (NAFTA) signed by Canada, Mexico, and the United States in 1992, it seeks to eliminate customs duties on tens of thousands of items involved in cross-border trade in North America. **(10)**

North Atlantic Treaty Organization (NATO) established in 1949, it is the framework for a peacetime military alliance through which the United States made a long-term commitment to the security and freedom of Western Europe in the face of a perceived threat from the Soviet Union. **(4, 5, 10)**

Northern Belt sometimes called the Northern Tier, a geographic area that includes Turkey and Iran (along with Afghanistan); the northernmost, non-Arab parts of the Middle East. **(11)**

Occupied Territories in the Middle East, Arab lands taken over by Israel following the Six-Day War, including the Sinai (returned to Egypt under the 1979 peace treaty); the Gaza Strip (Egypt); the West Bank and East Jerusalem (Jordan); and the Golan Heights (Syria). **(11)**

October Revolution the name for the fateful uprising led by Lenin in November 1917, during which he seized power from a weak and inept autocrat (Czar Nicholas II); called the October Revolution because Russia used a different calendar from the one used in the West at that time. **(5)**

Old City of Jerusalem an ancient precinct in East Jerusalem, which holds the greatest historical and religious meaning for both Muslims and Jews; the focus of intense negotiations in the 1990s between Israel and the Palestinian Liberation Organization (PLO). **(12)**

Oligarchy in Aristotle's typology, self-interested rule by the few. **(2)**

OPEC oil embargo the action of the Organization of Petroleum Exporting Countries (OPEC) in 1973 following the Yom Kippur War in which the Arab oil-producing states withheld oil from the world market to punish the West for supporting Israel in the war; the embargo led to worldwide recession and inflation and caused a strain in relations between the United States and its hard-hit NATO allies. **(12)**

Open-door policy forced on Japan by the United States in the midnineteeth century, it signaled the end of Japan's historic self-isolation. **(7)**

Opium War British demands for more trade and Chinese anger over illegal opium imports from British-controlled India led to this war in 1839, which China lost. See also *Treaty of Nanjing.* **(7)**

Opposition Agreement in the Czech Republic, a 1998 pact between the two largest parties, the center-left Social Democrats (CSSD) and the center-right ODS, according to which the Social Democrats would form a minority government and ODS would limit its opposition role in parliament to make governance possible. **(6)**

Organization of African Unity (OAU) the name is self-explanatory; OAU's charter adheres to the basic UN principles of noninterference in the internal affairs of member states and respect for territorial integrity, human rights, and peaceful settlement of disputes. **(13)**

Organization of American States (OAS) spearheaded by the United States after World War II, its purpose is to provide a multilateral framework for collaboration between North and South America (within the Western Hemisphere). **(9)**

Organization for European Economic Cooperation (OEEC) the apparatus created to administer Marshall Plan aid to Western Europe beginning in the late 1940s. **(4)**

Oriental despotism most often associated with Imperial China, the model is that of political orders in Asia (the "orient") ruled by hereditary autocrats who governed through centralized administrative systems embedded in hierarchical societies in which the common people were virtual slaves. **(7)**

Output quotas in the Soviet Union, quantitative targets set by Gosplan (the planning agency) used as the basis for macro-management of the Soviet economy. **(6)**

Overdevelopment a condition that arises in rich, industrially advanced societies, characterized by urban sprawl, noise and air pollution, traffic jams, exorbitantly expensive housing, and the like; in Asia, Japan is a prime example. **(7)**

Package vote in France, a rule that allows the government to bundle unrelated legislative proposals together and thus force the National Assembly to approve all or none of the proposals with a single vote. **(4)**

Palestine Liberation Organization (PLO) a militant political party representing displaced Palestinians and long led by Yasir Arafat; the PLO is committed to the creation of a Palestinian homeland. **(12)**

Palestinian question Where, when, and how to create a homeland for displaced Palestinians in the Middle East. **(12)**

Pan-Arabism a vague ideology characterized by the desire for Arab unity. **(11)**

Parliament originally, a representative council in old England, on which townspeople were allowed to sit; later, the name given to Great Britain's bicameral lawmaking body (called the "mother of parliaments"), which consists of a popularly elected lower house (the House of Commons) and a mainly hereditary upper house (the House of Lords). **(3)**

Parliamentary democracy a republic in which the parliament (or legislature) chooses the head of government (variously called a prime minister, premier, or chancellor) who shares executive functions with the head of state, who may be a monarch or an indirectly elected president; based on the fusion of powers (a melding of the legislative and executive powers). **(4)**

Parliamentary sovereignty the doctrine, evolved in England over many centuries, that Parliament is superior to the monarch; in Great Britain, where no written constitution has ever existed, Parliament has supreme power to make or unmake any law. **(4)**

Parliamentary systems governments based on fusion of powers (for example, the United Kingdom) rather than the separation of power found in the United States. **(2)**

Patron-client relations an Asian tradition, characterized by informal, affective social and political ties (in other words, ties based on friendship or familiarity); in such societies, ties are personal and particularistic (excluding all but kinfolk or members of some in-group) rather than formal, cognitive, and universalistic (as in Western societies). **(7)**

Pax Sovietica a term for Soviet domination in Eastern Europe during the Cold War (1945–1991). **(5)**

Pearl Harbor the American naval base in Hawaii bombed by the Japanese in 1941; this surprise attack outraged public opinion and triggered a declaration of war against Japan, paving the way for America's entry into World War II. **(7)**

Peninsulares in Latin American colonial history, immigrants from Spain. See also *Creoles.* **(9)**

People's Assembly The Egyptian parliament. **(12)**

People's Liberation Army (PLA) the name of Mao Zedong's guerrilla army and later of the PRC's army; the PLA played a key role in running China after the devastation wrought by the Cultural Revolution. **(8)**

Per capita gross national product (GNP) GNP is the total value of all goods and services produced by a given country's economy in a single year; per capita GNP is the total value divided by the total number of people living in that country. **(1)**

Perestroika a Russian word meaning "restructuring"; the name given to Mikhail Gorbachev's promised economic reforms before the collapse of Soviet communism in 1991. **(6)**

Permanent agriculture in ancient China, nature was assisted in the growing of crops by vast irrigation works (dams and dikes) built with slave labor, as well as by the disciplined use of organic fertilizers (including human waste). **(7)**

Philosophes name given to skeptical thinkers in France during the Enlightenment. **(3)**

Plebiscite a direct vote of the people about an important issue or question of policy. **(4)**

Policy Affairs Research Council (PARC) in Japan, the permanent policy-formulating machinery of the dominant Liberal Democratic Party (LDP). **(8)**

Politburo shorthand for "political bureau," in the Soviet Union this comprised about a dozen of the most powerful bosses and was the supreme decision-making body in the Soviet system. In China, the Politburo is an elite policy-making body comprising about twenty top party leaders; unlike its former Soviet counterpart, the Chinese Politburo is not the most powerful decision-making body. See also *Standing Committee.* **(6, 8)**

Polyarchy a fancy name for representative democracy used by political scientist Christian Potholm in creating a typology of African governments. **(14)**

Porfiriato the name given to the rule of Mexican dictator Porfirio Díaz, which represented the triumph of pragmatism over ideology and ushered in a period of accelerated economic development; the longest career of period personal dictatorial rule in Mexican history (1876–1911). **(9)**

Postindependence when decolonization occurred after World War II and the former colonies became self-governing. **(13)**

Post-totalitarian state countries that existed under a Soviet-style one-party dictatorship prior to 1989–1991 but have since converted to liberal-democratic government and a market economy; most post-totalitarian states are found in Eastern Europe. **(2)**

Praetorian states characterized by military rule or frequent military intervention in politics; common in Latin America prior to the 1980s and still common in sub-Saharan Africa; also found, but to a lesser extent, in the Middle East and Asia. **(2)**

Prague Spring the term for the 1968 movement to liberalize communist rule in Czechoslovakia, ultimately suppressed by the Soviet Union. **(6)**

Prefects in the French political tradition, these were powerful administrative officials appointed by Paris. **(4)**

Presidential democracy a republic in which the chief executive is popularly elected, serves as both head of government and head of state, and is neither a member of the legislative body nor dependent on it for continued tenure in office; based on the tripartite separation of powers (clearly delineated roles for the executive, legislative, and judicial branches). **(2)**

Presidential rule in India, when the federal (central) government takes over direct rule of a state until order and stability are fully restored. **(8)**

Private sector The part of the economy not controlled — or owned and operated — by the state; in the United States it includes nearly all business enterprises, as well as most land, natural resources, and other assets. **(2)**

Privatization in communist (and former communist) countries, the process of converting from a command economy to a market economy by deemphasizing or getting rid of central planning and by encouraging free enterprise. **(2)**

Proletariat a term for the supposedly exploited working class, in Marxist jargon. **(5)**

Provisional Irish Republican Army (IRA) the military wing of the Irish Republican Movement that claims to represent Catholics in Northern Ireland and opposes British rule there; the IRA has often used terrorism as a means of achieving its main political aim — union with Ireland. **(4)**

Provisional government a government that is (or claims to be) a temporary expedient, ruling only until a follow-on government can be properly constituted. **(14)**

Qualified majority voting a step toward majority voting within the Council of Ministers which sets policy for the European Union; member states retain a veto over certain key issue areas (taxation, foreign policy, and environment), however. **(4)**

Quechua the language of the Incas, still spoken today by the rural natives of southern Peru. **(9)**

Rabbi in Judaism, a master of Talmudic law; a Jewish wise man, teacher, or scholar. **(11)**

Rajya Sabha in India, the upper house of the Federal Parliament; Council of the States. **(8)**

***Real* plan** in Brazil, the centerpiece in an inflation-fighting campaign in 1994 masterminded by then finance minister Fernando Henrique Cardoso (who used his resulting popularity to become president); named after Brazil's then-new currency, which was a key part of the plan. See also *Cruzado plan.* **(10)**

Realpolitik term meaning "power politics" and actions based on self-interest rather than ideals or altruism. **(12)**

Reconciliation systems political systems that value social harmony, personal liberty, and political compromise at least as much as rapid economic development; characterized by governments that try to accommodate rather than repress competing interests. **(2)**

Red Guards in China's Great Proletarian Cultural Revolution (1966–1969), these were high school and university students who, waving little red books containing the "thoughts of Chairman Mao," pillaged and plundered at will and staged frequent attacks on adult authority figures (teachers, bureaucrats, and party officials) — all in the name of revolution. **(8)**

Reformation name given to the religious movement in western Christendom beginning in the sixteenth century, from which Protestant churches were formed. **(3)**

Refuseniks Jewish dissidents in the Soviet Union who applied for permission to emigrate to the United States or Israel and were turned down (refused) by the Soviet government. **(5)**

Rejectionists in the context of modern African politics, those who advocated political independence and national liberation. See also *Assimilationists.* **(13)**

Renaissance a French term meaning "new birth" or "revival," it here refers to the transitional movement in Europe between the medieval and the modern, which occurred between the fourteenth and sixteenth centuries (starting in Italy) and was marked especially by a new interest in the classical art and architecture of ancient Greece and Rome. **(3)**

Reverse development characterized by outmigration from cities to suburbs, leaving slums and deteriorating schools, services, and tax bases. **(4)**

Rossianiye a Russian term for citizens of Russia who are not ethnic Russians. See also *Russkye.* **(6)**

Rule of law in the English tradition, the ideas that nobody can be punished except for a clear violation of preexisting laws established before ordinary courts and that nobody, not even the king or queen, is above the law. **(4)**

Russian Federation the name of the successor state to the Soviet Union, commonly known as Russia. **(6)**

Russification the policy of imposing the Russian language and Russian culture on non-Russian peoples living within the Russian (later, the Soviet) empire. **(5)**

Russkye in the Russian language, this word means "ethnic Russians" as opposed to citizens of Russia who have some other ethnic background. See also *Rossianiye.* **(6)**

Samurai in feudal Japan, members of the professional warrior class. **(7)**

Scientific method an approach to the accumulation of knowledge that stresses careful observation and analysis. **(1, 3)**

Scientific Revolution the sixteenth- and seventeenth-century movement in Europe that placed science rather than theology or philosophy at the forefront of intellectual endeavor, and that viewed science as the pathway to human progress. **(3)**

Second vote in Germany, the part of each national election in which candidates are chosen by proportional representation. **(4)**

Secretariat depending on context, the chief administrative organ of the Communist Party in the Soviet Union; or the main administrative apparatus of the Chinese Communist Party. **(6, 8)**

Secret Speech also known as the "crimes of Stalin" speech, this was delivered by Nikita Khrushchev in 1956 at the Twentieth Party Congress of the Soviet Communist Party; it was the beginning of a long, slow process of easing Stalinist controls. (See *de-Stalinization*). **(5)**

Secular humanism a modern philosophy that stresses the potential of humankind, using scientific as well as political means, to solve social and economic problems. **(3)**

Self-defense forces the euphemistic name of Japan's modest military capabilities. **(8)**

Senate the upper house of the national legislature in France (and elsewhere). **(4)**

Sendero Luminoso the Peruvian insurgency movement that started in the early 1980s and used terrorist methods to threaten and embarrass the Peruvian government. **(10)**

Separation of powers The system of dividing the powers of a government into three branches — the legislative, executive, and judiciary — and giving each branch a unique role to play while making all three interdependent. **(2)**

Sephardic Oriental Jews, of Spanish, Portuguese, and Middle Eastern background. See also *Ashkenazic.* **(11)**

Sepoy Mutiny a revolt against the British presence by the Indian army (1857–1858); it prompted the British crown to abolish the powers of the East India Company and assume direct control over India in 1858. **(7)**

Shiite an adherent of the Shiite branch of Islam; the Shiite sect is predominant in Iran. **(11)**

Shinto the native religion of Japan based on worship of natural spirits, it developed under the influence of Chinese Confucianism and eventually grew into an instrument of Japanese nationalism. **(7)**

Shock therapy in economics, the strategy of converting rapidly from a command economy to a market economy; the harsh effects on society (including plant closings, job losses, curtailment of social services and states subsidies, and inflation) make it a kind of "shock treatment" for the majority, who are typically called on to sacrifice before they experience any real benefits; the term used to describe the radical market reforms put into effect very quickly in some East European countries (notably Poland) after the collapse of Soviet-style communism in 1989. **(6)**

Shogun in feudal Japan, the supreme warlord who wielded actual political power. See also *Shogunate.* **(7)**

Shogunate in Japan, a feudal form of government based on hereditary land ownership, vassalage, and military prowess that prevailed for seven hundred years; the emperor remained as a figurehead, but political power was monopolized by the dominant military clan whose leader was the shogun. **(7)**

Sikhism a monotheistic Hindu sect founded in the fifteenth century, it is the dominant religion in Punjab; originally an effort to reconcile Muslim and Hindu doctrine, Sikhism evolved into a militant sect that violently opposes Islam. **(7)**

Single European Act approved in 1986, it set the stage for the creation of the European Union in 1992. **(4)**

Slavic Europe includes the European parts of the old Russian empire (Russia, Belarus, and Ukraine); East Central Europe (Poland, the Czech Republic, Slovakia, and Ruthenia); and the Balkans (Bulgaria, Serbia, Croatia, Montenegro, and Slovenia). See also *Eastern Europe.* **(5)**

Solidarity in Poland, the trade union that turned into a political movement (*Solidarnost*) led by Lech Walesa in the 1980s, that ultimately was instrumental in overthrowing Polish communism. **(6)**

Socialism an ideology, most often associated with the ideas of Karl Marx, that views capitalism and private ownership of the means of production as the root of all evil in society, generally deplores the profit motive, and advocates equality in the distribution of material goods. **(2, 3)**

Some get rich first a policy associated with the economic reforms in China instituted by Deng Xaioping after 1978 that justifies inequalities arising from the emergence of a new class of rich entrepreneurs. **(8)**

South America with a land area of nearly 6.9 million square miles, it is the world's fourth-largest continent; it includes two populous states with relatively advanced economies, Argentina and Brazil, and two smaller but relatively prosperous states, Chile and Uruguay, as well as poor states such as Bolivia, Ecuador, Paraguay, and Peru (Colombia and Venezuela fall somewhere in between the rich and the poor). See also *Central America* and *Latin America.* **(9)**

Soviets a Russian word meaning "councils"; the Soviets were in theory the source of state power in the Soviet Union after the October Revolution, but in fact were mere window dressing. **(5)**

Spanish Inquisition the power of the Catholic Church in Latin America reached its zenith during this sixteenth-century crusade against infidels and heretics; the Spanish crown established tribunals in Lima in 1570 and in Mexico City in 1571 to punish heretics and other religious offenders with property loss, imprisonment, exile, or even death, sometimes by burning. **(9)**

Special economic zones (SEZs) introduced in China in the late 1970s as one of Deng Xiaoping's most controversial and most innovative economic reforms, SEZs were intended not only to attract foreign capital but also to stimulate exports and improve access to modern technologies and management methods. **(8)**

Special regimes in France, arrangements that give public-sector employees generous pension terms compared with private-sector employees. **(4)**

Special relationship a term used to describe the close ties between the United States and the United Kingdom during and after World War II. **(4)**

Stagflation a paradoxical economic condition characterized by stagnating growth (recession) and high inflation. **(4)**

Stalinism shorthand for the policies associated with Soviet dictator Joseph Stalin, including the brutal repression of all opposition and complete takeover of the economy by the state (in the guise of the Communist Party) from about 1925 until Stalin's death in 1953. **(5)**

Standing Committee the highest decision-making body in Communist China, it consists of six or seven top leaders who set economic priorities, formulate defense and foreign policies, and direct the pursuit of these priorities and policies. **(8)**

State a self-conscious and self-governing political community; a territorially based unit of civil government. **(2)**

State Council in China, the chief executive organ of the state, headed by the premier, who is theoretically appointed by the president with the approval of the National People's Congress (NPC), or legislature. **(8)**

State List the part of the Indian constitution in which the powers reserved to the provincial governments are enumerated. See also *Concurrent List* and *Union List.* **(8)**

Statutory law law based on a code of written statutes. **(4)**

Subordinate system a concept defining regions as "two or more proximate and interacting states that have some common ethnic, linguistic, cultural, social, and historic bonds, and whose sense of identity is sometimes increased by the actions and attitudes of states external to the system" (note 9, Chapter 1). **(1)**

Sub-Saharan Africa the common name given to Africa south of the Sahara Desert; also frequently called Black Africa. **(13)**

Sunni an adherent of the Sunni branch of Islam; the predominant form of Islam in the Arab world. **(11)**

Supreme Soviet the bicameral legislature in the Soviet Union, which served as a rubber stamp for the Communist Party. **(6)**

Surplus value a Marxist term for the exploitation of workers that in Marxist theory results from the wide gap between what a worker produces and the wages he or she is actually paid, or between how many hours each day an individual would theoretically have to work in order to provide for his or her family, versus how long he or she actually is forced to work under an exploitative wage-labor system **(5)**

Taiping Rebellion in Chinese history, a bloody and prolonged revolt that occurred in the middle of the nineteenth century; aimed at overthrowing Manchu rule, it reduced southern China to ruins. **(7)**

Talmud in Judaism, the collected decisions of the rabbis (scholars) concerning civil and religious law. See also *Rabbi.* **(11)**

Technocrats professionals in the French civil service, often being well-grounded in technical fields requiring advanced training in applied science and engineering. **(4)**

Theocracy a political order (state) predicated on religious law and run by priests, or imams (holy men). **(11)**

Third World the name given to the former colonial regions of Latin America, Africa, the Middle East, and Asia after World War II; when the colonies gained independence in the 1950s and 1960s, they emerged as a new group of actors — the so-called less-developed countries (LDCs) — in the international arena. **(2, 14)**

Tiananmen Square massacre in Beijing, China, 100,000 students and workers staged a march in May 1989 to demand democratic reforms; as the ranks of the protesters swelled to 1 million, troops entered Beijing with tanks and armored personnel carriers, brutally crushing the revolt; thousands of demonstrators in Tiananmen Square were killed, injured, or arrested. **(8)**

Tokugawa shogunate named for Ieyasu Tokugawa, a great military clan leader who was appointed shogun in 1603; his rule saw the consolidation of Tokugawa power, closed Japan to the outside world, and ushered in a "golden age" of stability and cultural vitality; the Tokugawa dynasty ruled Japan for the next 250 years (until the Meiji Restoration in 1868). **(7)**

Totalitarian a form of government characterized by the total concentration of power, often in the hands of one individual (for example, Hitler or Stalin), the propagation of an official ideology that all members of society must embrace, and the use of state terror carried out by the secret police with the purpose of motivating and intimidating the population; the polar opposite of anarchy. **(2)**

Totalitarian dictatorship a form of government characterized by the total concentration of power, often in the hands of one individual (for example, Hitler or Stalin), the propagation of an official ideology that all members of society must embrace, and the use of state terror carried out by the secret police with the purpose of motivating and intimidating the population. **(2)**

Transnational transcending national borders and boundaries. **(1)**

Treaty of Guadalupe Hidalgo foisted on Mexico by the United States following a war between the two countries in 1848, it made Texas, New Mexico, Arizona, Nevada, Utah, and California part of the United States. **(9)**

Treaty of Nanjing signed at the end of the Opium War (1839–1842), it forced China to open five major seaports and to cede Hong Kong to Great Britain. **(7)**

Trilateral Commission a private foreign-policy interest group founded by David Rockefeller in 1973, consisting of representatives from the United States, the European Community, and Japan. **(7)**

Triple heritage characteristic of Africa, in which the influence of indigenous African culture mingles with the influence of the West and of the Arab world (particularly Islam). **(13)**

Trusteeship under the United Nations Charter, member states can be authorized to supervise the administration of territories that may lack the prerequisites for self-government through an agreement approved by the General Assembly or, in certain cases, the Security Council. **(14)**

Tupac Amaru Revolutionary Movement (MRTA) a small terrorist group in Peru that seized the Japanese Embassy in 1996, taking many high-level political and diplomatic hostages and demanding immediate release of imprisoned MRTA members. **(10)**

Tutelage system in France, based on the traditional role of prefects as powerful intermediaries between the central government in Paris and the local governments in the provinces; eclipsed in recent times by reforms, which give more power both to local and to regional levels of government. **(4)**

Two-ballot system used in France, this voting system is based on the rule that winning the presidency necessitates an absolute majority vote; if no candidate wins such a majority in the first round of voting, a runoff election is held. **(4)**

Two-party system a democracy characterized by the perennial presence of two major political parties that alternate in power and always serve as either the governing party or the main opposition party. **(4)**

Tyranny rule by one in his or her own interests; the worst form of government possible, according to Aristotle. **(2)**

Ulster the six counties of Northern Ireland that remained within the United Kingdom when the rest of Ireland broke away to form a separate state in 1921. **(4)**

Underdeveloped countries a term often applied to the poor countries of Latin America, Africa, and Asia in the past that lag behind the rich and technologically advanced Western societies; the term *underdeveloped* is synonymous with "less developed," as in less developed countries (LDCs). See *Developing countries.* **(3)**

Underemployment the absence of steady work (for example, part-time or seasonal employment) or appropriate work (for example, a university-educated ditch digger); a common problem in developing countries where there are not enough jobs to go around and job creation cannot keep pace with population growth. **(8)**

Unfair trade practices in general, protectionist measures (for example, high tariffs) designed to help domestic industries by limiting foreign competition; a complaint often made against Japan by its trading partners, especially the United States. **(8)**

Unification in the context of recent European history, a term denoting the 1990 merger of the two German states (West Germany and East Germany) into a single Germany. **(4)**

Union List the part of the Indian constitution that enumerates the powers of the central government. See also *Concurrent List* and *State List.* **(8)**

Unitary system a centralized democratic republic; the opposite of a federal system. **(4)**

Untouchables term for members of the lowest social stratum in traditional India; they are outside the caste system because their ancestors were scavengers and "night soil" collectors, among other "unclean" occupations. See *Dalits.* **(7)**

Vanguard of the proletariat Lenin's name for the Communist Party (which he headed); Lenin self-servingly asserted that revolution would occur only if the workers had leaders with a finely refined revolutionary consciousness. **(5)**

Velvet Revolution the popular movement that spearheaded the peaceful overthrow of communism in Czechoslovakia in 1989. **(6)**

Viceroy an official ruling a province, colony, or occupied territory as the deputy of a sovereign; a proconsul in the Roman Empire; in Spanish-ruled Latin America, the all-powerful governors appointed by the Spanish crown; they were responsible for enforcing laws, collecting taxes, running the government, spreading Christianity, and commanding the Spanish army within their jurisdiction. **(9)**

Virgin lands campaign an ill-fated attempt by Khruschev in the late 1950s to boost Soviet agricultural production by plowing up vast, arid regions east of the Urals. **(5)**

Voortrekkers the Dutch farmers (Boers) of the Great Trek, who settled the South African frontier beginning in the 1830s; Afrikaners venerate these stouthearted forebears, who endured tremendous hardships and occasionally fought battles with natives, as much as Americans honor the pioneers; to native Africans, however, the Boers were alien intruders. **(13)**

War communism the period in Soviet Russian history immediately following the October Revolution, when the fate of communism hung in the balance and Lenin's regime was assaulted from within and without by forces opposed to his rule. **(5)**

Warsaw Pact officially called the Warsaw Treaty Organization (WTO), it was a military alliance created by the Soviet Union in Eastern Europe as an answer to the perceived threat posed by U.S.–sponsored North Atlantic Treaty Organization (NATO). **(5)**

West Indies the early generic name given to the islands of the Caribbean. **(9)**

Westminster model the British parliamentary system based on a fusion of powers and a unitary rather than a federal structure; this model of democracy is often contrasted with the American model. **(2)**

Weighted voting a system of voting used in some international organizations (including the European Union), which bases voting power on the size of a given member state's population. **(4)**

Workers' self-management in Yugoslavia under Tito, a much-touted (but not very successful) attempt to give the workers control over the management enterprises. **(5)**

Works of authority tracts esteemed for the quality of reasoning they exhibit and the reputation of the scholars who penned them. **(4)**

Writ of amparo a writ of protection, this served as the major restraint on arbitrary presidential acts in Mexico by empowering federal judges to protect citizens from violations of their constitutional rights by stopping a government agency from taking any action until the supreme court has ruled on appeal. **(10)**

Zambo in Latin America, a person of mixed African and Indian blood. See also *Mestizo* and *Mulatto.* **(9)**

Zapatista National Liberation Army (ZNLA) a Mexican insurgency group in the southwestern state of Chiapas; the ZNLA led an armed rebellion in the mid-1990s. **(10)**

Zaibatsu Japan's prewar industrial conglomerates, which have long been protected and given various anticompetitive advantages by the government. **(7)**

Zionism a Jewish national movement calling for creation of a Jewish state; dating from the late nineteenth century, Zionism and the long dream of a Jewish homeland inspired the founding of Israel after the nightmare of the Holocaust in World War II. **(11)**

INDEX